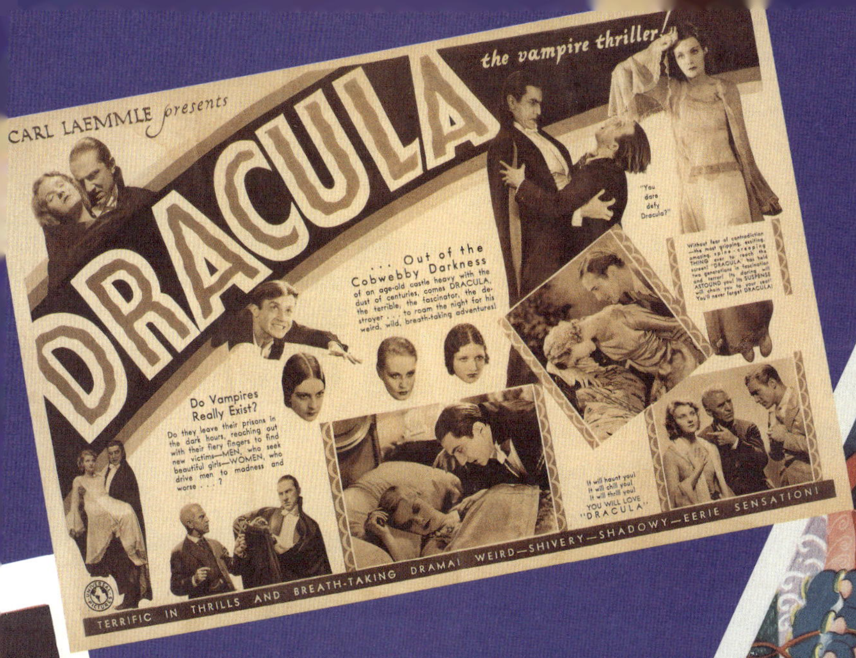
CARL LAEMMLE presents
DRACULA
the vampire thriller!
Do Vampires Really Exist?
TERRIFIC IN THRILLS AND BREATH-TAKING DRAMA! WEIRD—SHIVERY—SHADOWY—EERIE SENSATION!

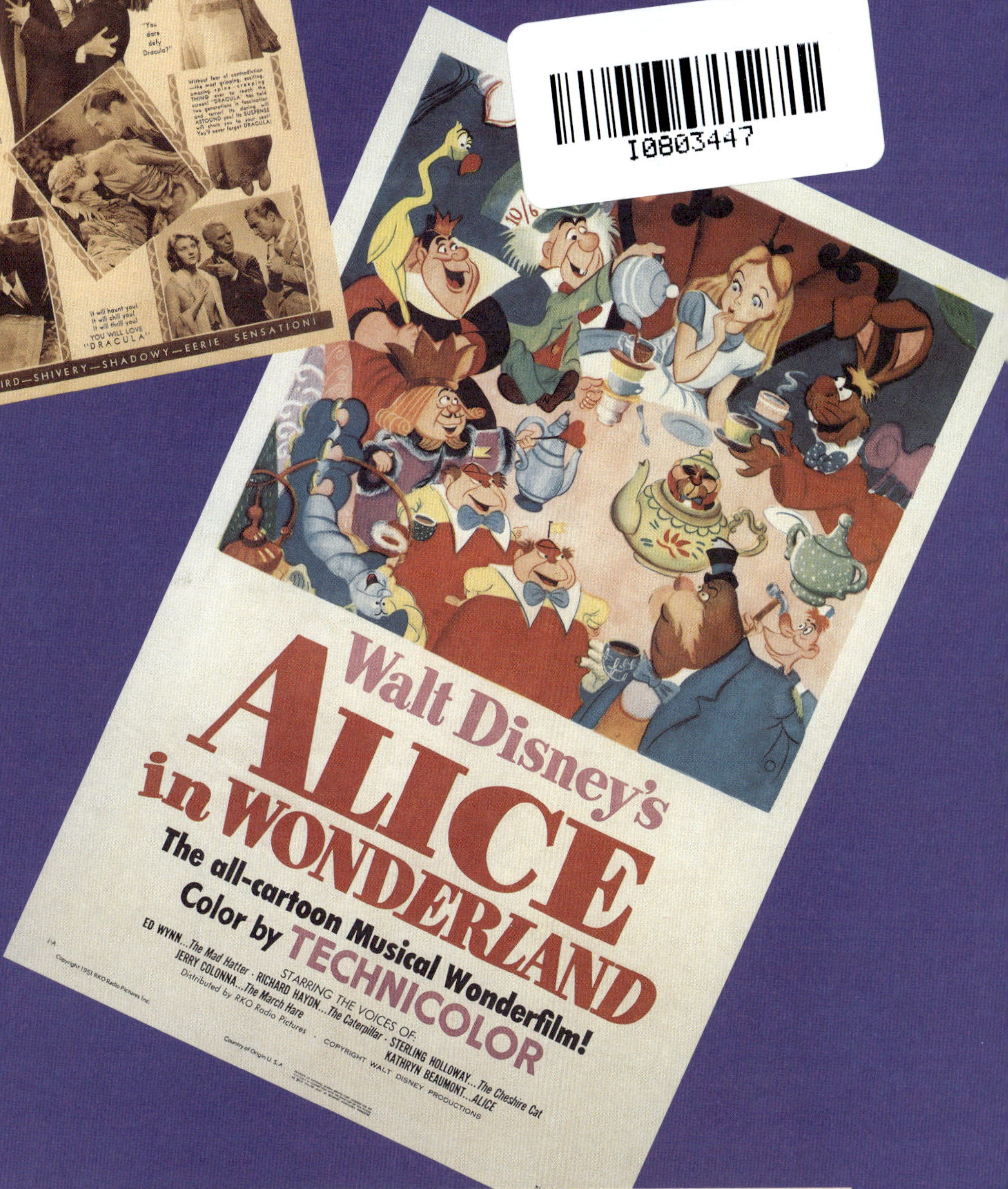
Walt Disney's
ALICE
in WONDERLAND
The all-cartoon Musical Wonderfilm!
Color by TECHNICOLOR

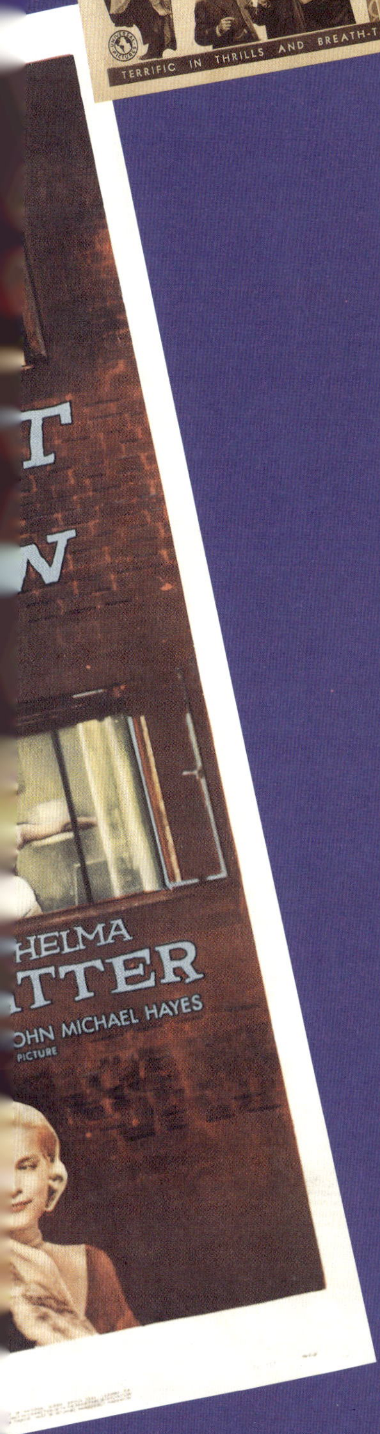
HELMA
TTER
OHN MICHAEL HAYES

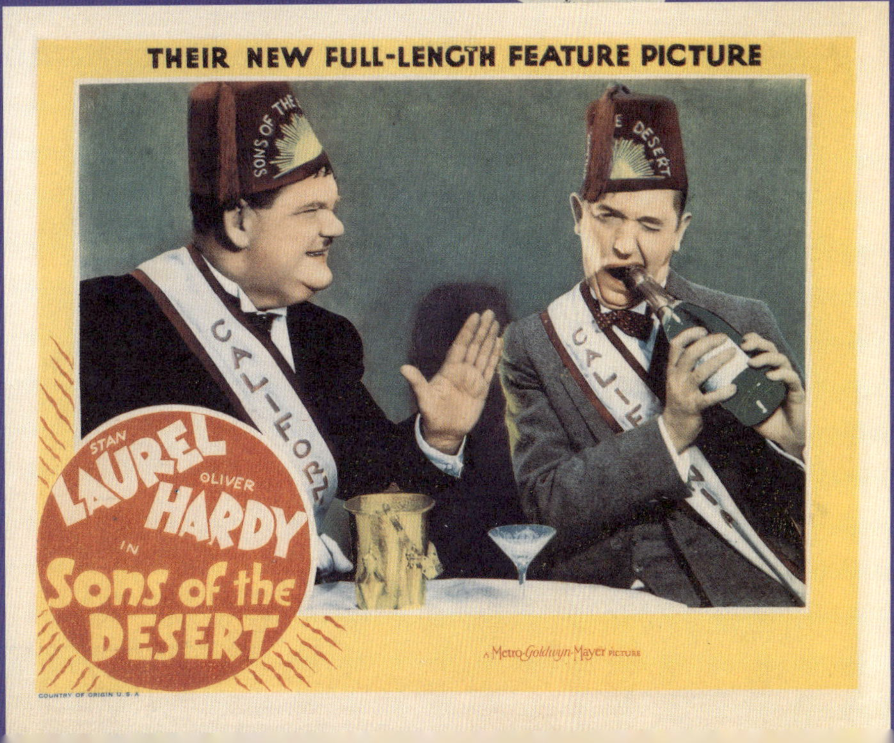
THEIR NEW FULL-LENGTH FEATURE PICTURE
STAN LAUREL
OLIVER HARDY
IN
Sons of the DESERT
A Metro-Goldwyn-Mayer PICTURE

Hollywood Movie Posters

1914-1990

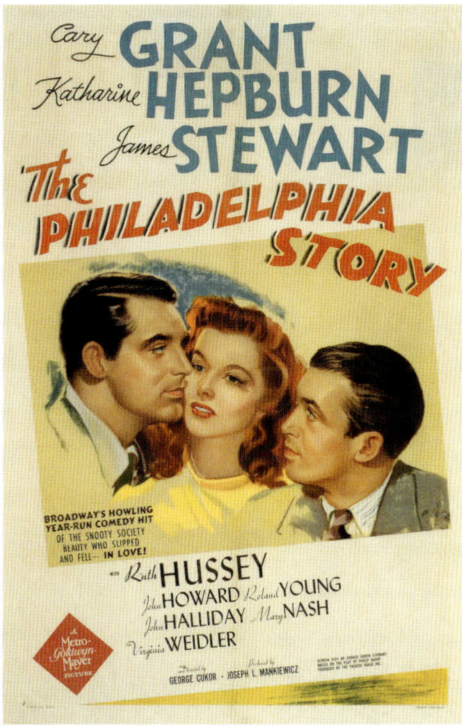

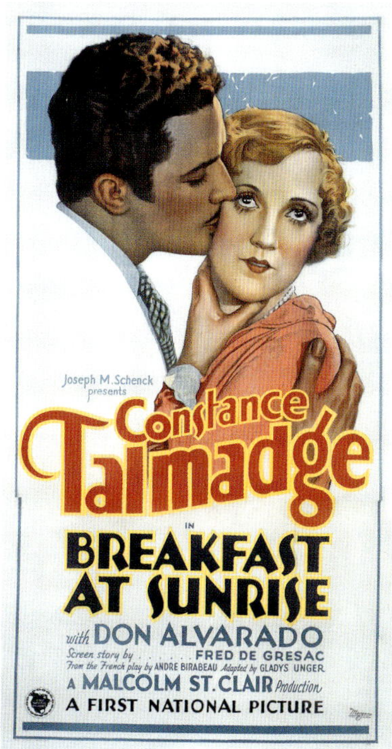

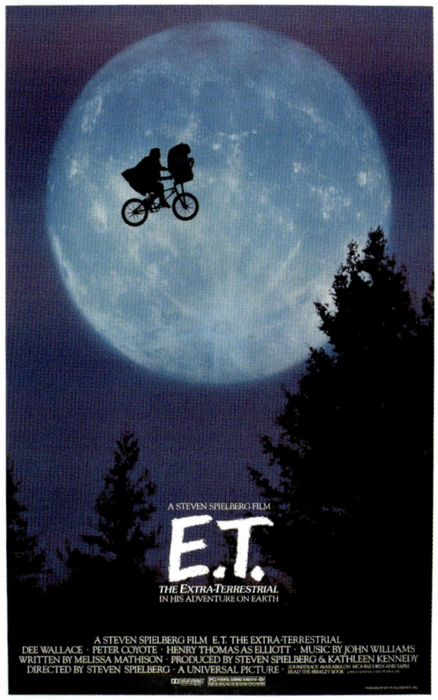

Miles D. Barton

Schiffer Publishing Ltd®
4880 Lower Valley Road, Atglen, PA 19310 USA

Dedication

To my parents for their love
and support through the years

Acknowledgments

Invaluable help has been forthcoming from the following without whom this book would not have been possible: Sotheby's Inc., Dana Hawkes, Vanessa Peters for picture research, Greg Edwards, James McAlister, Scott Michell, both my parents for their distant memories of old Hollywood and my editor Peter Schiffer.

Disclaimer and acknowledgments of Trademarks

Library of Congress Cataloging-in-Publication Data

Barton, Miles D., 1968-
Hollywood movie posters, 1914-1990 / by Miles D. Barton.
p. cm.
ISBN 0-7643-2010-6 (Hardcover)
1. Film posters, American—catalogs. 2. Film posters, American—Collectors and collecting. 3. Motion pictures—United States—History. I. Title.
PN1995.9.P5 B374 2004
791.43'75'075—dc22
2003023927

Designed by Mark David Bowyer
Type set in Dutch801 Rm BT

ISBN: 0-7643-2010-6
Printed in China
1 2 3 4

Published by Schiffer Publishing Ltd.
4880 Lower Valley Road
Atglen, PA 19310
Phone: (610) 593-1777; Fax: (610) 593-2002
E-mail: Schifferbk@aol.com

For the largest selection of fine reference books on this and related subjects, please visit our web site at
www.schifferbooks.com
We are always looking for people to write books on new and related subjects. If you have an idea for a book please contact us at the above address.

This book may be purchased from the publisher.
Include $3.95 for shipping.
Please try your bookstore first.
You may write for a free catalog.

In Europe, Schiffer books are distributed by
Bushwood Books
6 Marksbury Ave.
Kew Gardens
Surrey TW9 4JF England
Phone: 44 (0) 20 8392-8585; Fax: 44 (0) 20 8392-9876
E-mail: info@bushwoodbooks.co.uk
Free postage in the U.K., Europe; air mail at cost.

Contents

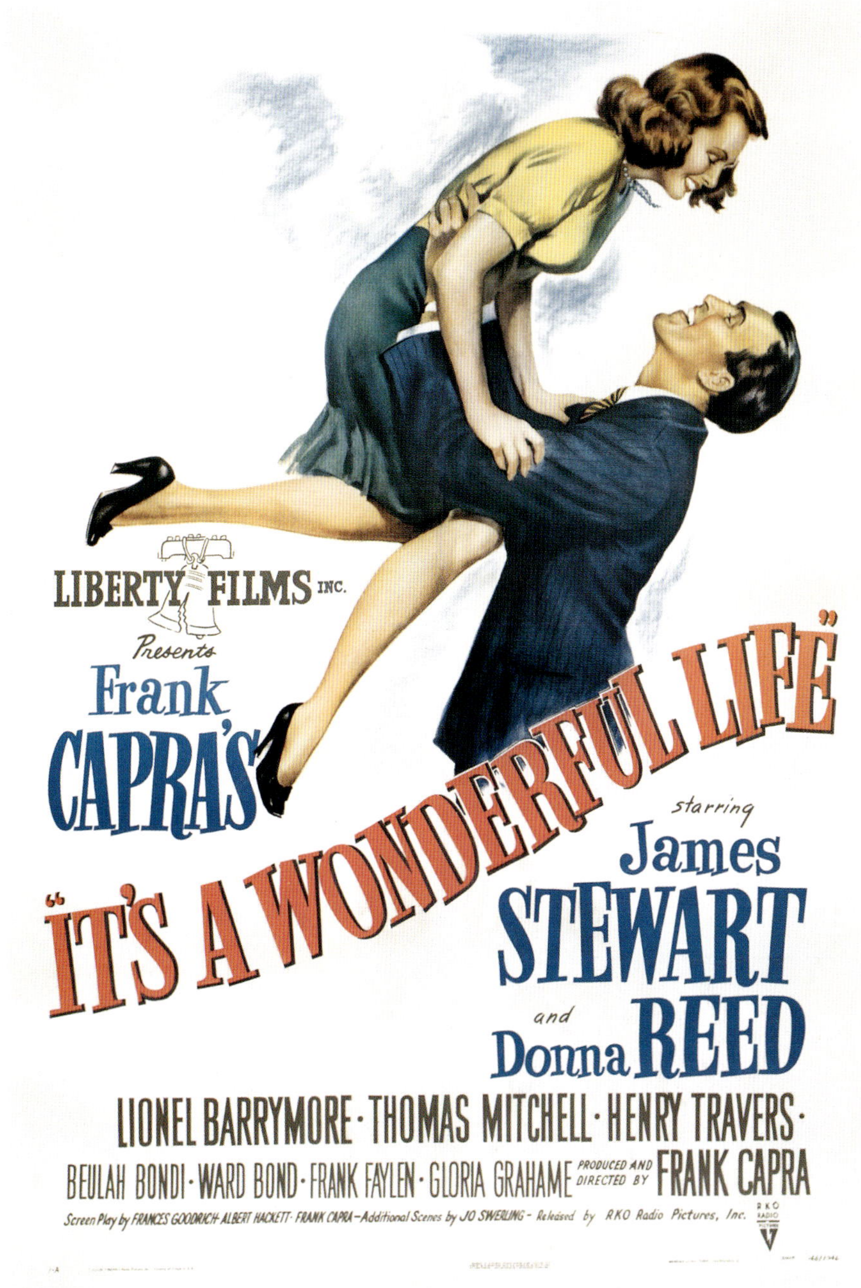

LIBERTY FILMS INC.
Presents
Frank CAPRA'S
"IT'S A WONDERFUL LIFE"
starring
James STEWART
and
Donna REED
LIONEL BARRYMORE · THOMAS MITCHELL · HENRY TRAVERS ·
BEULAH BONDI · WARD BOND · FRANK FAYLEN · GLORIA GRAHAME
PRODUCED AND DIRECTED BY FRANK CAPRA
Screen Play by FRANCES GOODRICH · ALBERT HACKETT · FRANK CAPRA – Additional Scenes by JO SWERLING – Released by RKO Radio Pictures, Inc.

Foreword

by Gregory J. Edwards

My own interest in collecting movie posters came from an involvement in running a local film society in Britain during the early 1970s. Where could one find the original posters used to advertise the movies that we were playing? A search around all the collectors' shops in London initially proved fruitless, but eventually I came across the poster for Stanley Kubrick's *The Killing* and coincidently, what I thought at the time to be, a treasure trove of goodies!

Posters old and new were to be found that not only sowed the seeds for a fine collection but also sent me in a direction I'd never dreamed of. My original graphic design business got sidelined and I threw myself wholeheartedly into dealing in movie posters. Traveling extensively, I also began advertising to buy these posters and was soon swamped with deliveries from all over the country. In 1976 I published my first illustrated film poster catalogs, advertising in movie magazines such as *Photoplay* and *Film Review* . Looking at my prices now for one-sheets it is quite sobering: *You Only Live Twice,* $6; *Strangers On A Train,* $15; *Breakfast At Tiffany's,* $8; *On The Waterfront,* $16; *Rebel Without A Cause,* $20.

Apart from some of the real old time poster hoarders most collectors seemed more interested in film magazines like *Picturegoer, Picture Show* and *Film Pictorial* and film star postcards. Poster collecting was all part of general film memorabilia collecting, where items ended up either in filing cabinets, the bottom of the chest of drawers or even under the bed! In Britain at this time poster restoration was unheard of, so any that were actually displayed at home usually went up folds and all, with gum or drawing pins!

In the mid-1980s I noticed that a few more discerning customers began collecting well-designed or well-drawn posters for their favorite movies. One or two people already had an eye on an investment but it wasn't until more recent years that movie posters started to get serious press coverage and consequently prices started to escalate rapidly.

Looking through this book is a chance, for me at least, to see how things have changed. The glorious images that were preserved and held so dear by just a few are now sought out by a new generation who are just as seduced by the striking designs as I was. The only thing now is that you need much deeper pockets to get your hands on them!

Introduction

Advertising Hollywood

Movie posters offer a clear insight into the history and development of Hollywood as the film capital of the world. The posters, through their design, betray the ideas, attitudes and aspirations of American society throughout the 20th century. Events that altered and shaped the lives of generations were often reflected in the evolution of the Hollywood studios and the movies they produced. The movie posters left to us chart this rocky ride through the twentieth century.

The art of the poster was to seduce the public with the essence of the film. In most cases this was blown out of all proportion, (quite literally, with some posters being 20 feet long). The idea, to get people through the theater doors, was plain and simple enough. The poster was the key promotional item produced by a studio in a broad advertising campaign created to sell tickets. Ephemeral products, they were meant only to have a life as long as the movie they heralded. It is fortuitous indeed that so many have survived, particularly from the early days, and have gained a truly remarkable value.

Many posters could have been included that have not. The exclusion of some, as opposed to others, is no reflection on significance or value; a book can only be so large! Where possible a good variety and selection of posters were considered, not necessarily focusing on retail worth, but more on their design, history, or obscurity.

People collect for all sorts of reasons and this book is not intended to speculate as to why individuals are motivated to do so with movie posters, but rather to introduce some of the posters that, fortunately, have survived the ravages of time. The posters illustrated throughout are all in near mint or mint, or condition A status. Both dealer and auction house markets have been studied and values are quoted on this basis. No book can claim to give the exact value to an unseen object. It is, though, fair to suggest that most examples of a similar standard and type would be available to purchase close to the price region mentioned. Always bear in mind superlative examples of anything command a premium.

The early studios had firm ideas on how to produce their advertising and now decades later we are still enthralled by the poster in the way we were always supposed to be. Let the history of Hollywood unfold through their imagery.

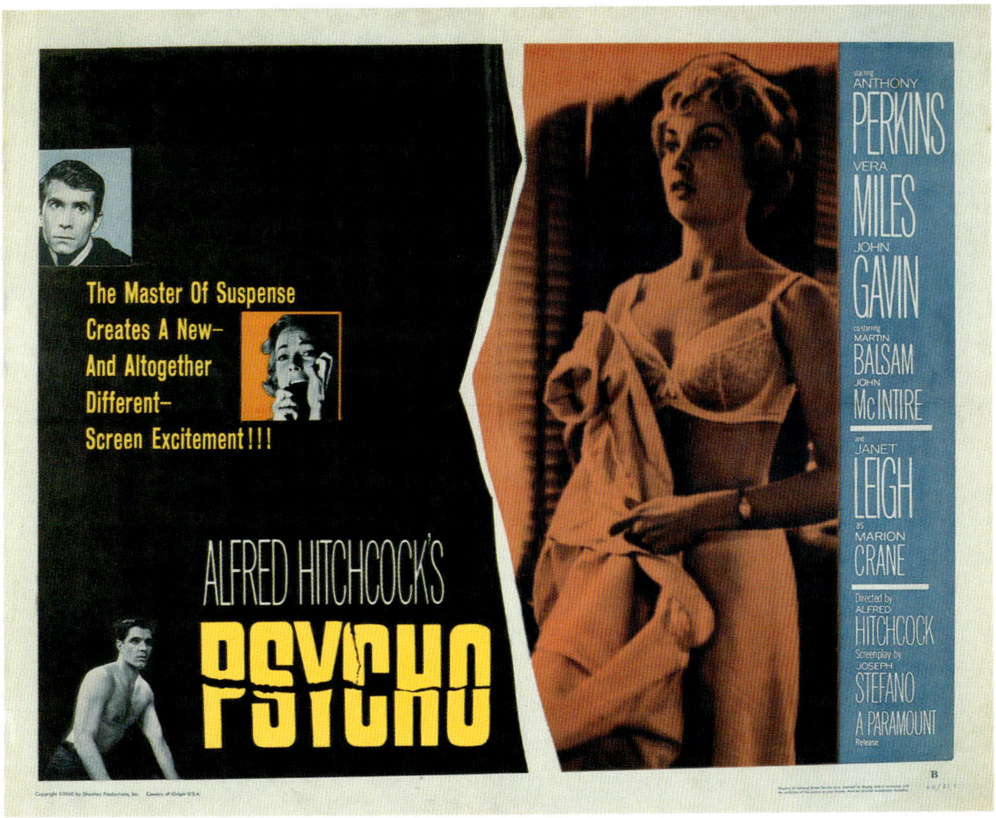

Chapter One

Early Hollywood: The Twenties and Before

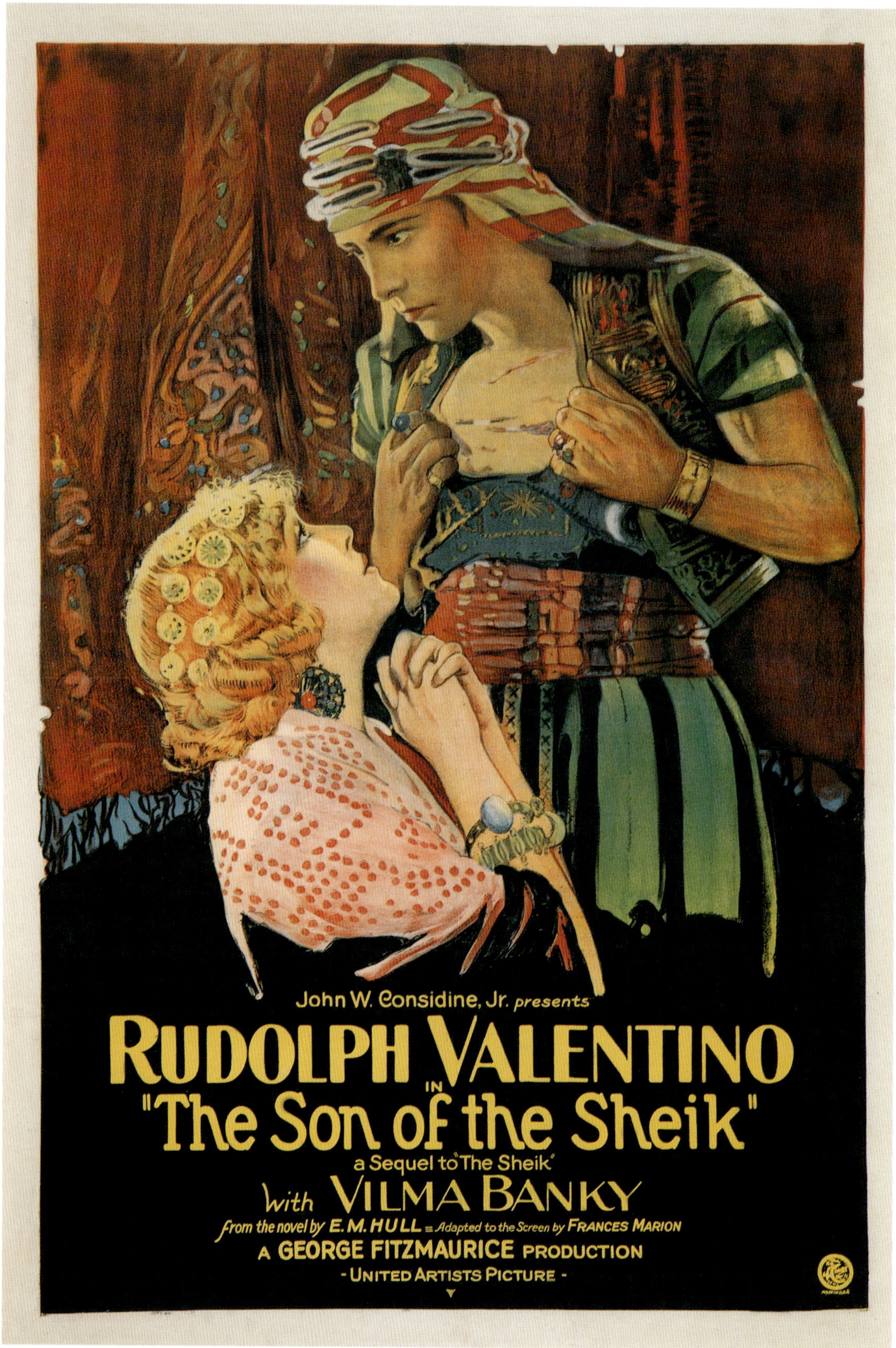

The Son Of The Sheik. 1926. One-sheet. $15,000-20,000

Hollywood became the name synonymous with the movies by a quirk of fate. In the first decade of the 20th century the east coast of America saw the rapid growth of small individual movie production companies selling their product to the eager audiences in the expanding "nickelodeons." These small-time filmmakers were quick to develop and make the most of the opportunities available to them, but in no time at all they found their early cinematic freedoms being challenged. In 1908 a group of larger, more powerful, east coast-based companies formed a partnership to control this flourishing industry in their own image. This newly formed Motion Picture Patents Company imposed fees and generally restricted freedom of creativity and business, principally defending their exclusive rights in patenting motion picture equipment. Not surprisingly, young independent filmmakers, indignant and threatened, started to look way beyond the confines of New York City and the reach of this powerful organization. Soon they had fled the east coast and made for southern California, where low cost real estate, lavish locations, and constant sunshine were plentiful. A sleepy backwater on the outskirts of Los Angeles named Hollywood became the place of choice.

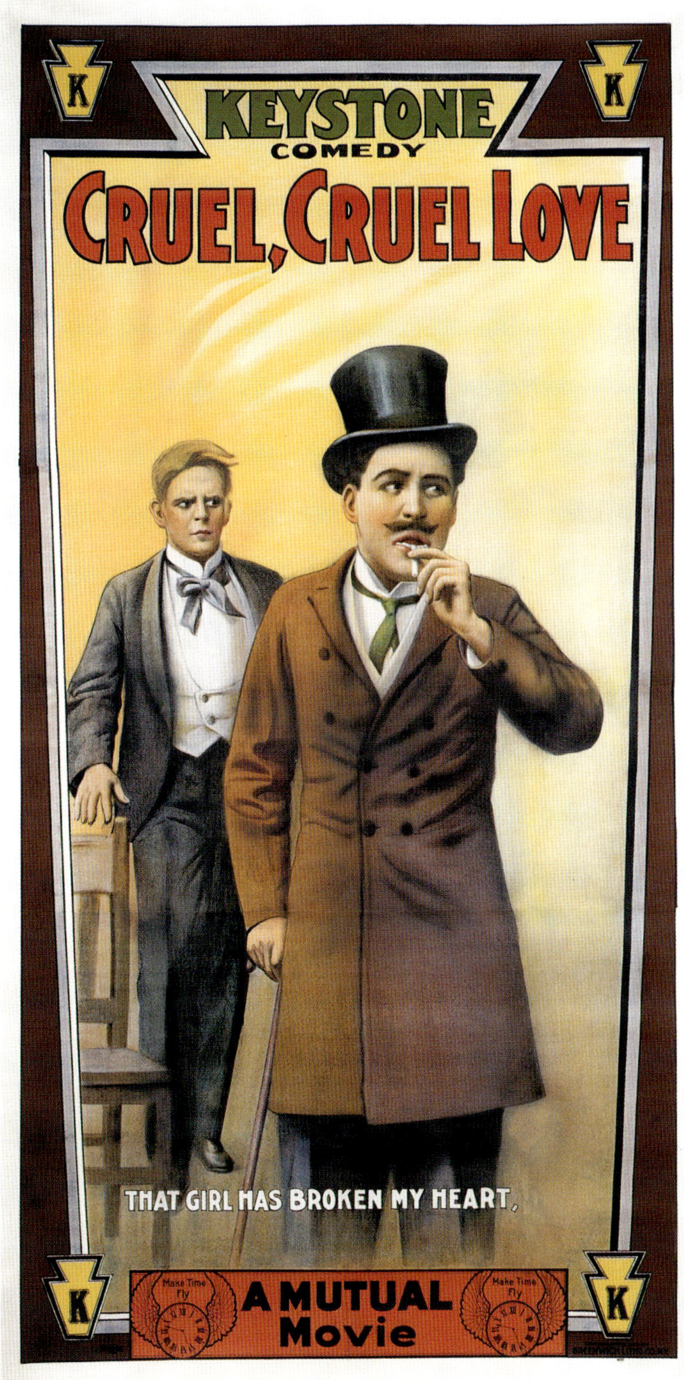

Cruel, Cruel Love. 1914. Three-sheet. $10,000-15,000

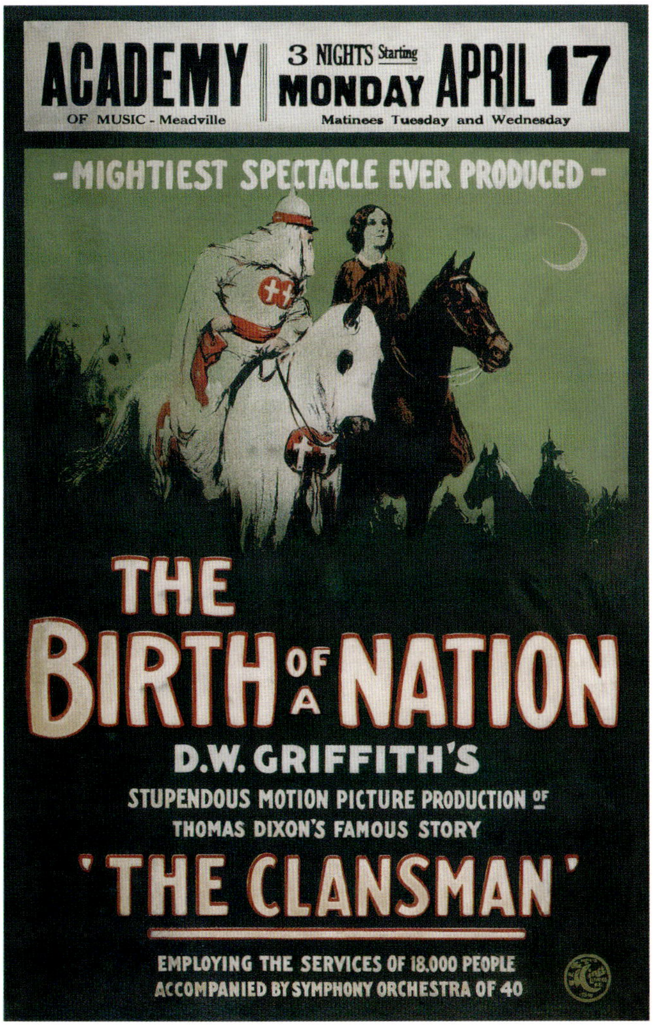

The Birth of a Nation. 1915.
Window card. $6000-8000

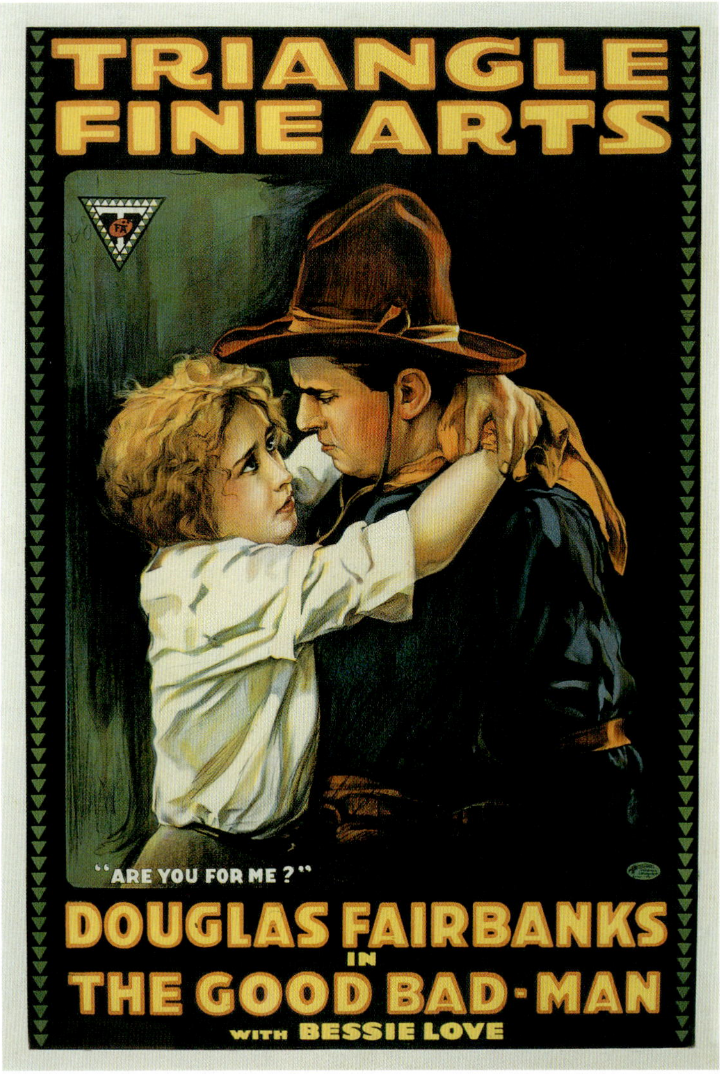

The Good Bad-Man. 1916. One-sheet. $2,000-3,000

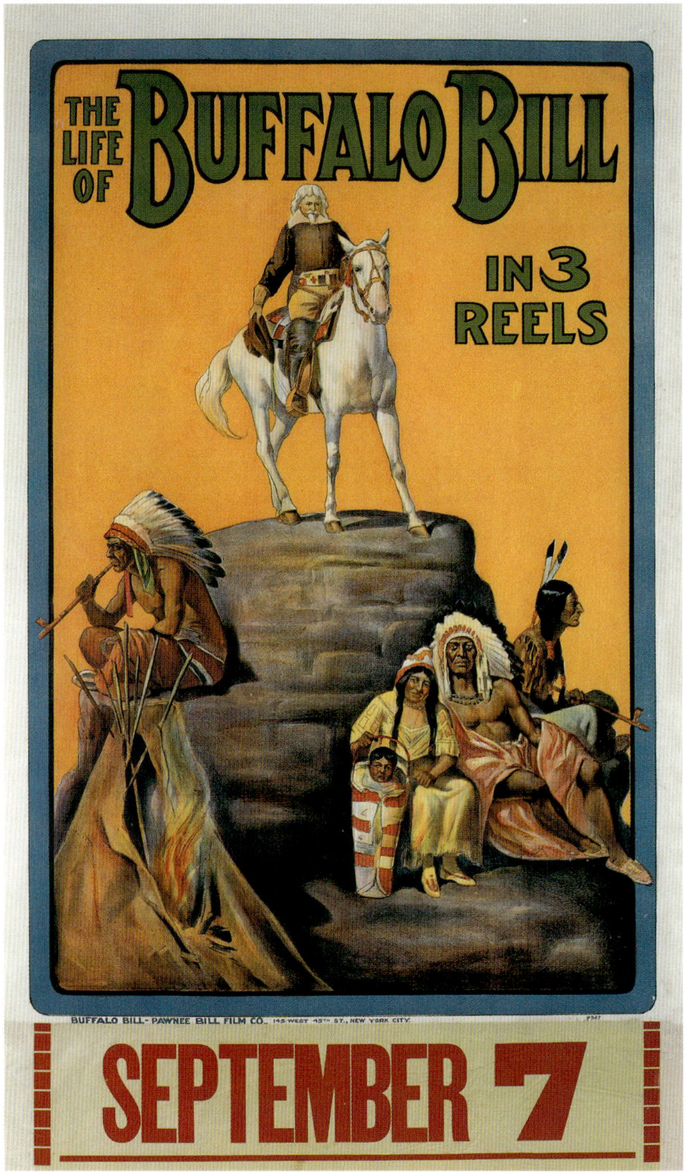

The Life of Buffalo Bill. 1917.
One-sheet. $1,500-2,000

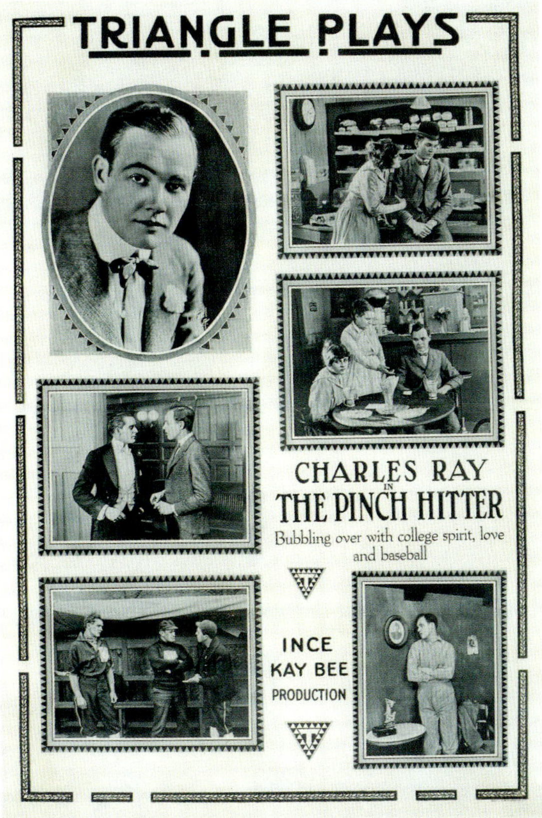

The Pinch Hitter. 1917. One-sheet.
$2,000-3,000

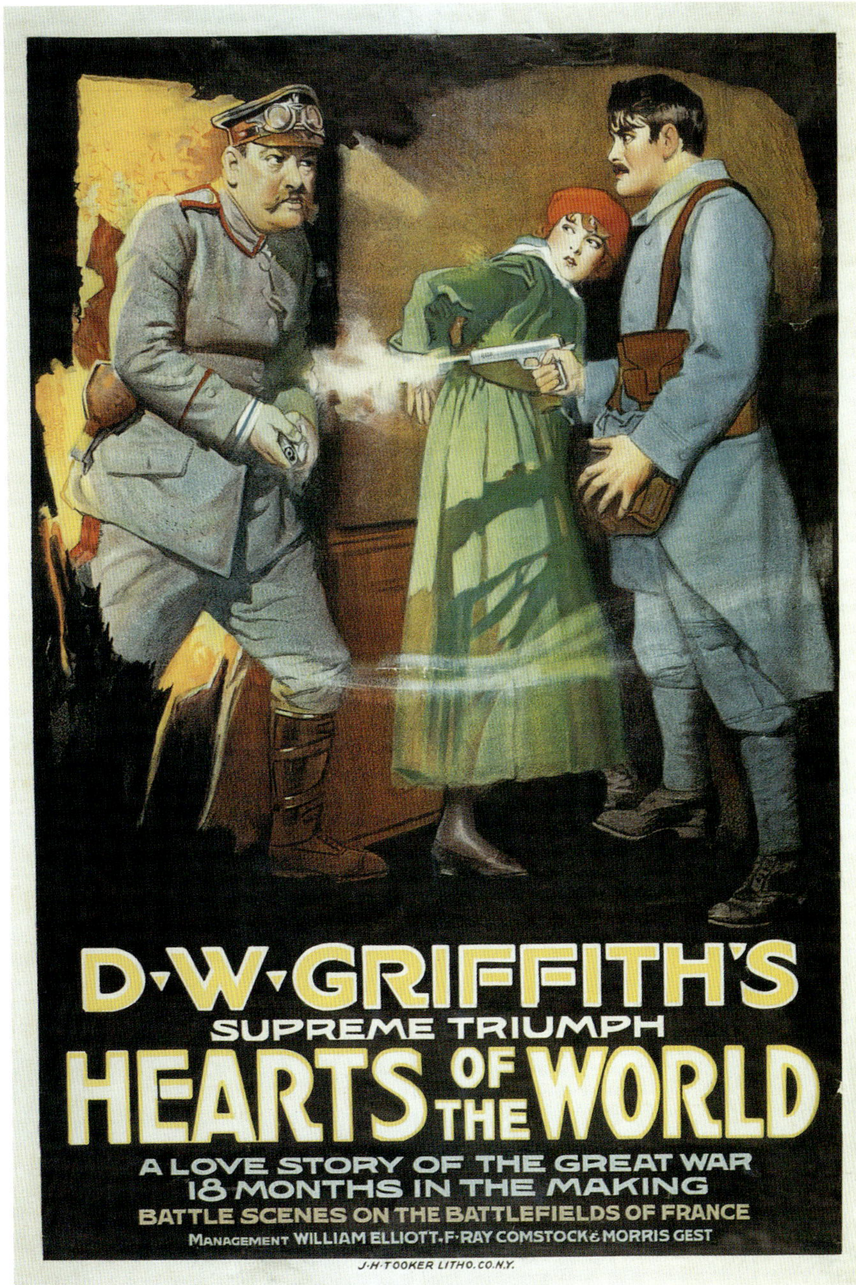

Hearts of the World. 1918.
One-sheet. $3,000-5,000

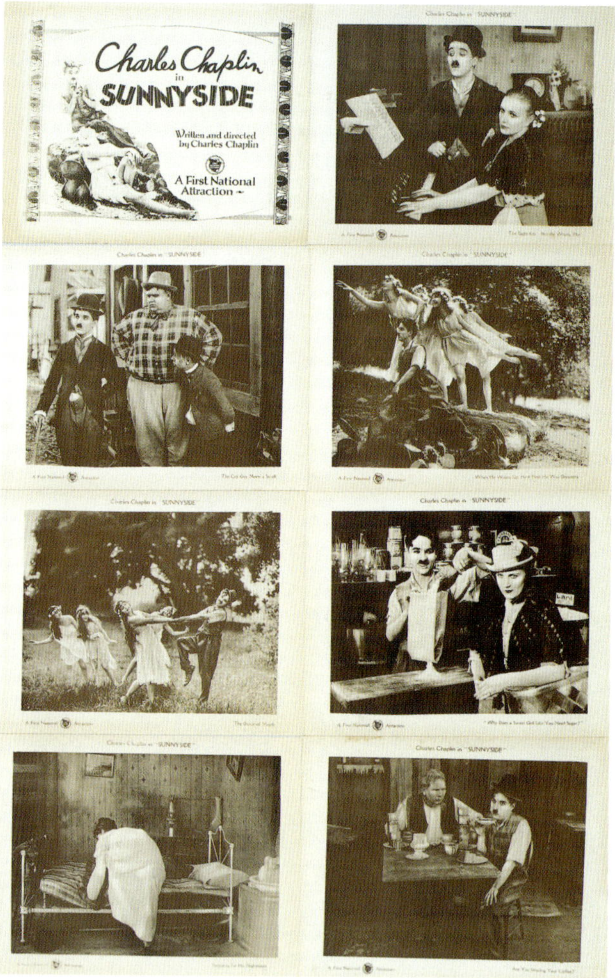

Sunnyside. 1919. Lobby card set. $1,500-2,000

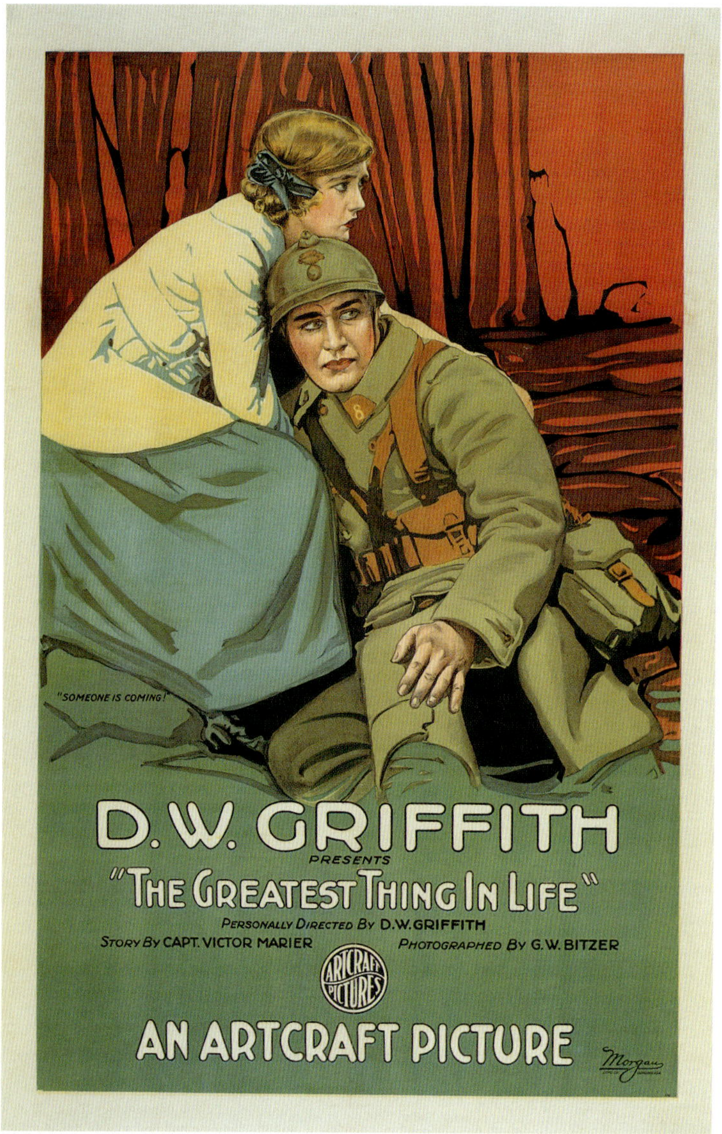

The Greatest Things in Life. 1918. One-sheet. $2,000-2,500

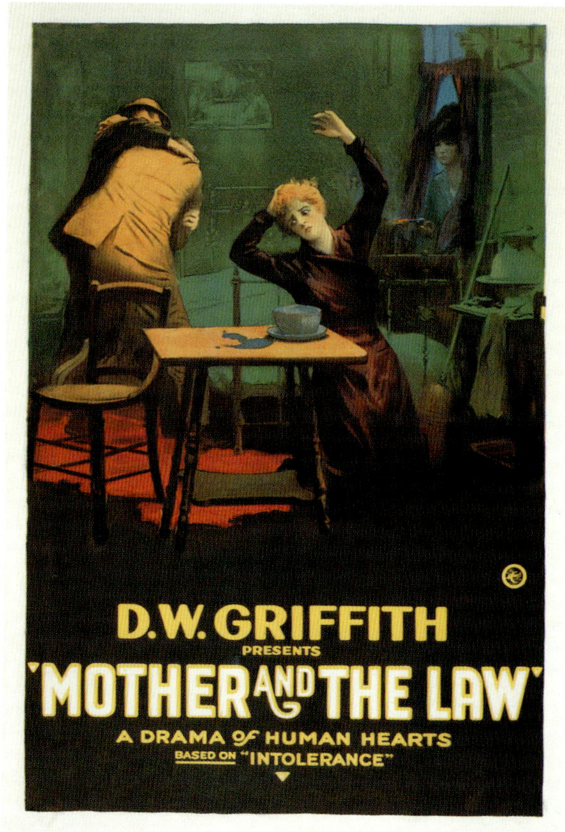

Mother and the Law. 1919.
One-sheet. $2,000-3,000

Development in and around this sun-drenched, orange-growing area was fast and Hollywood evolved quickly as a large town. In 1907, the first movie was made in Los Angeles and by 1911 the Nestor Film Company established the first motion picture studio in Hollywood. As early as 1912, fifteen film companies were operating in the area with production starting to rival seriously the east coast studios. Later the same year a successful anti-trust suit was filed by the US government resulting in the dissolution of the unpopular, monopolistic Motion Picture Patents Company. By 1915 Carl Laemmle, the German immigrant and hugely successful nickelodeon owning businessman, had opened Universal City, then California's largest studio, in the San Fernando Valley. This together with some other studios located in the desert still necessitated the use of a stagecoach by many expeditious visitors!

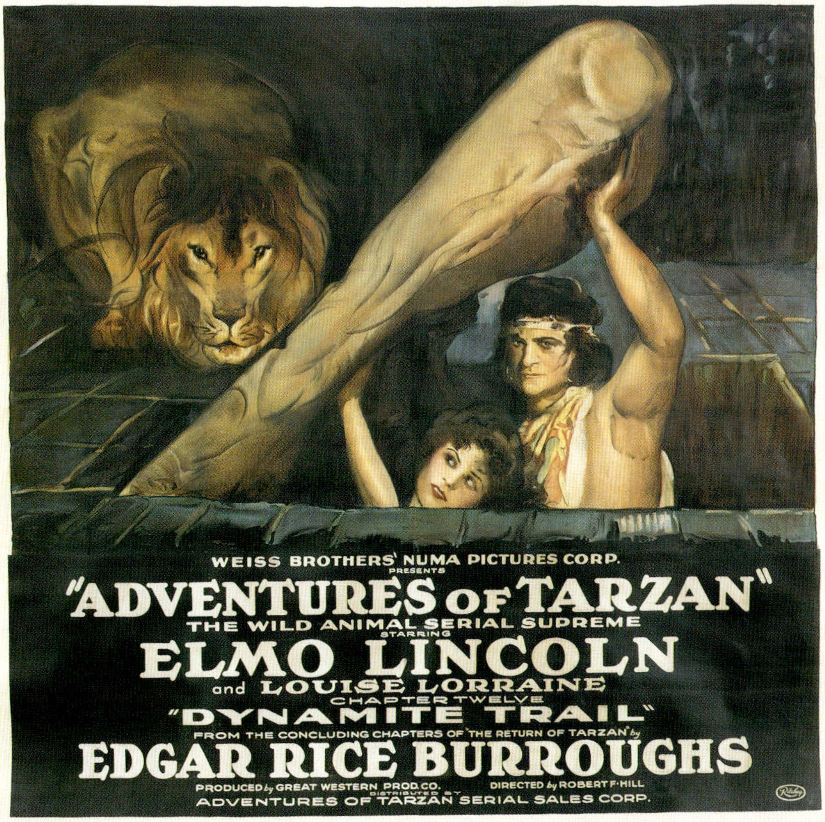

Adventures of Tarzan. 1921. Six-sheet. $5,000-7,000

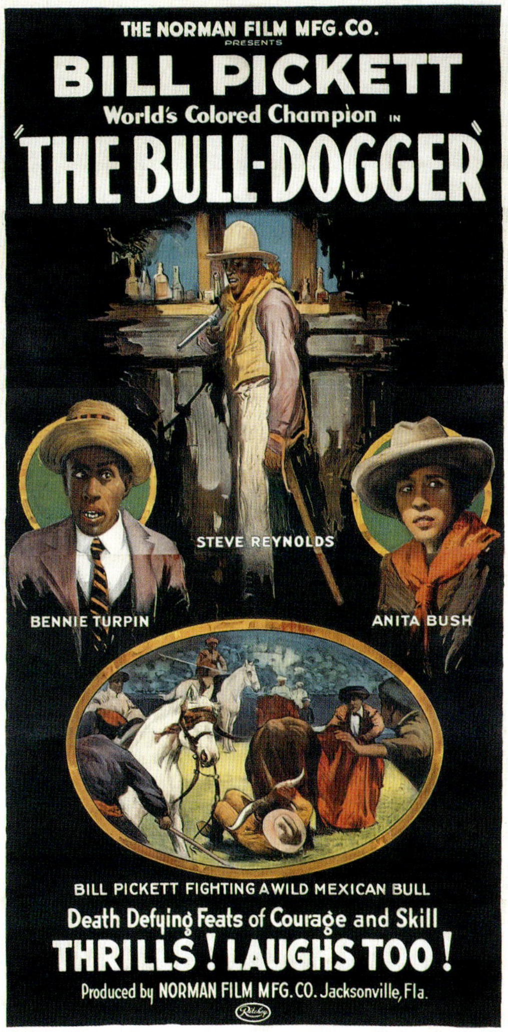

The Bull Dogger. 1923. Three-sheet. $3,000-5,000

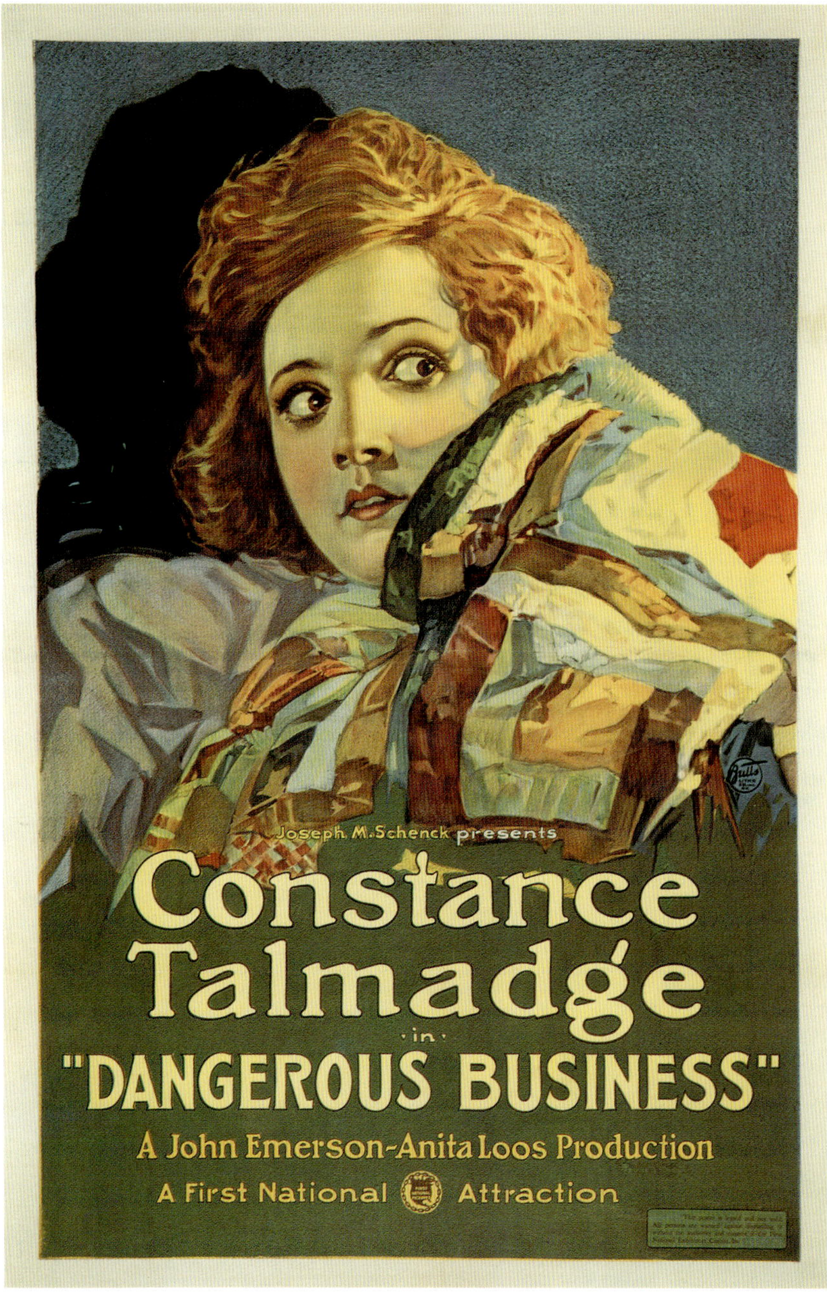

Dangerous Business. 1920. One-sheet. $1,200-1,800

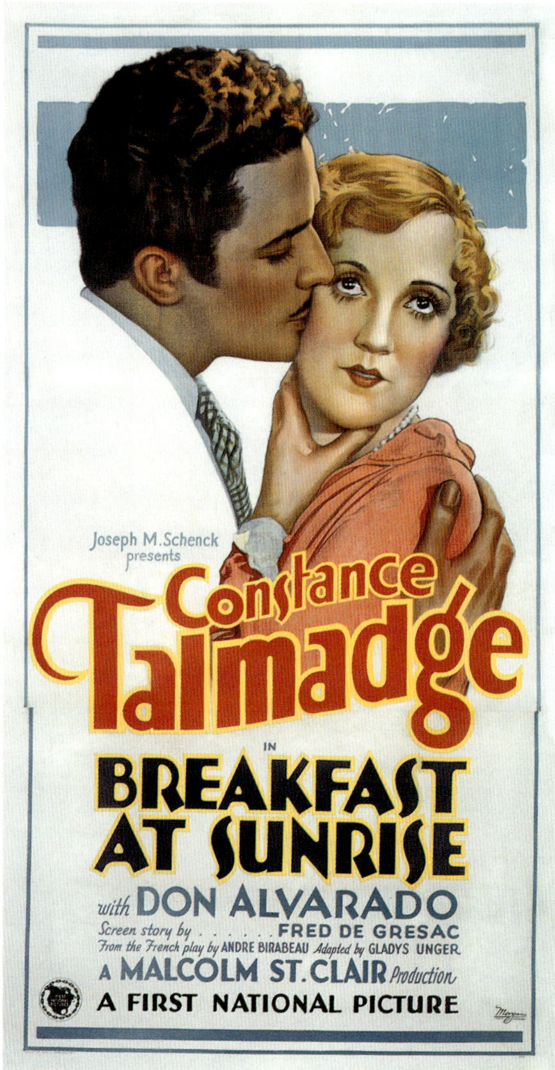

Breakfast at Sunrise. 1927. Three-sheet. $1,000-1,500

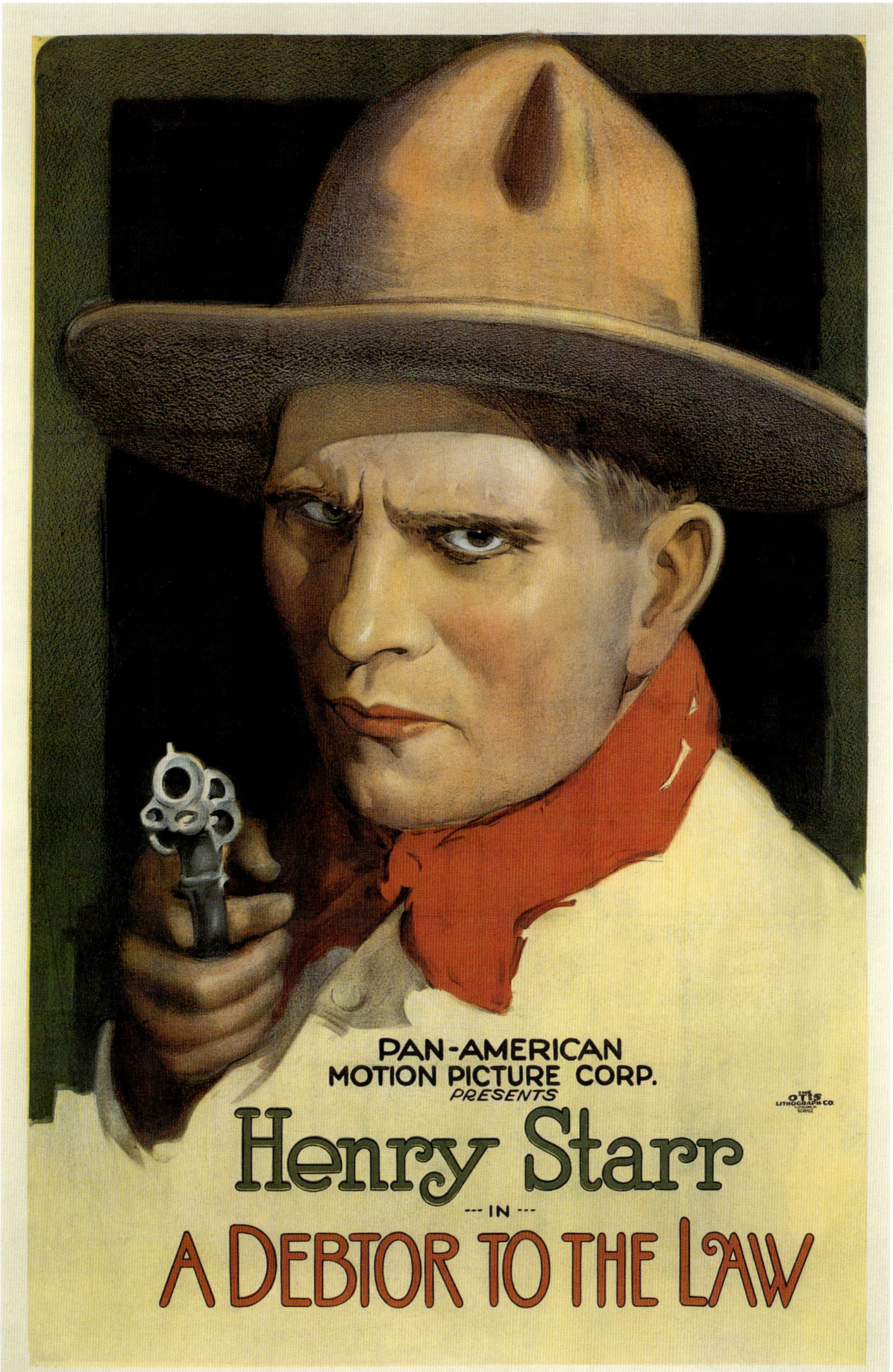

A Debtor to the Law. 1922. One-sheet. After making this movie real outlaw Henry Starr was later killed in a bank robbery. $3,000-5,000

The decade of 1920-1930 saw the end of the First World War and the beginnings of the Depression, heralded by the Stock Market Crash of 1929. On the whole movie theaters and studios managed to weather the storm quite well, and though times were often hard, production really flourished. The names that were to be associated with the industry for decades to come established themselves as powerful studio heads having started life as either proprietors, investors, or distributors in small town "nickelodeons:" Adolph Zukor, Marcus Loew, Jesse Lasky, Sam Goldwyn, the Warner brothers, Carl Laemmle, William Fox, and Louis B. Mayer. Confidence in the industry was maintained by the banks that were willing to loan large sums to get the right stars signed up with these expanding studios. First National was loaned an enormous $250,000 towards the making of *The Kid* (1921) on the strength of Chaplin's name alone. The studio soon found themselves with a hit and were able to pay back the bank within six weeks. The simple business of making movies was evolving in to a fully-fledged industry of high turnover and profits, so much so that even by 1920 it was the fifth-ranked industry in America.

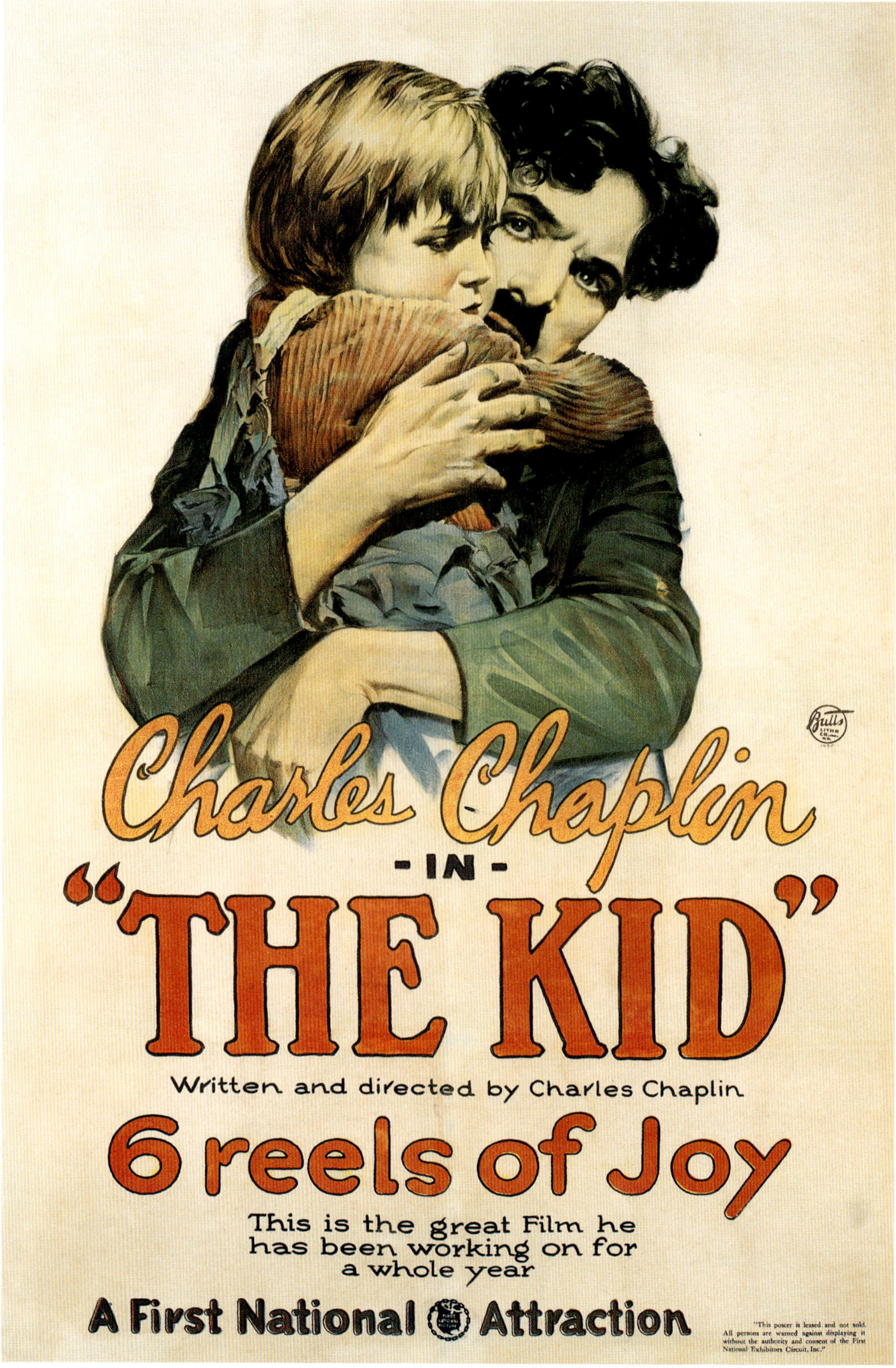

The Kid. 1921. One-sheet. $20,000-30,000

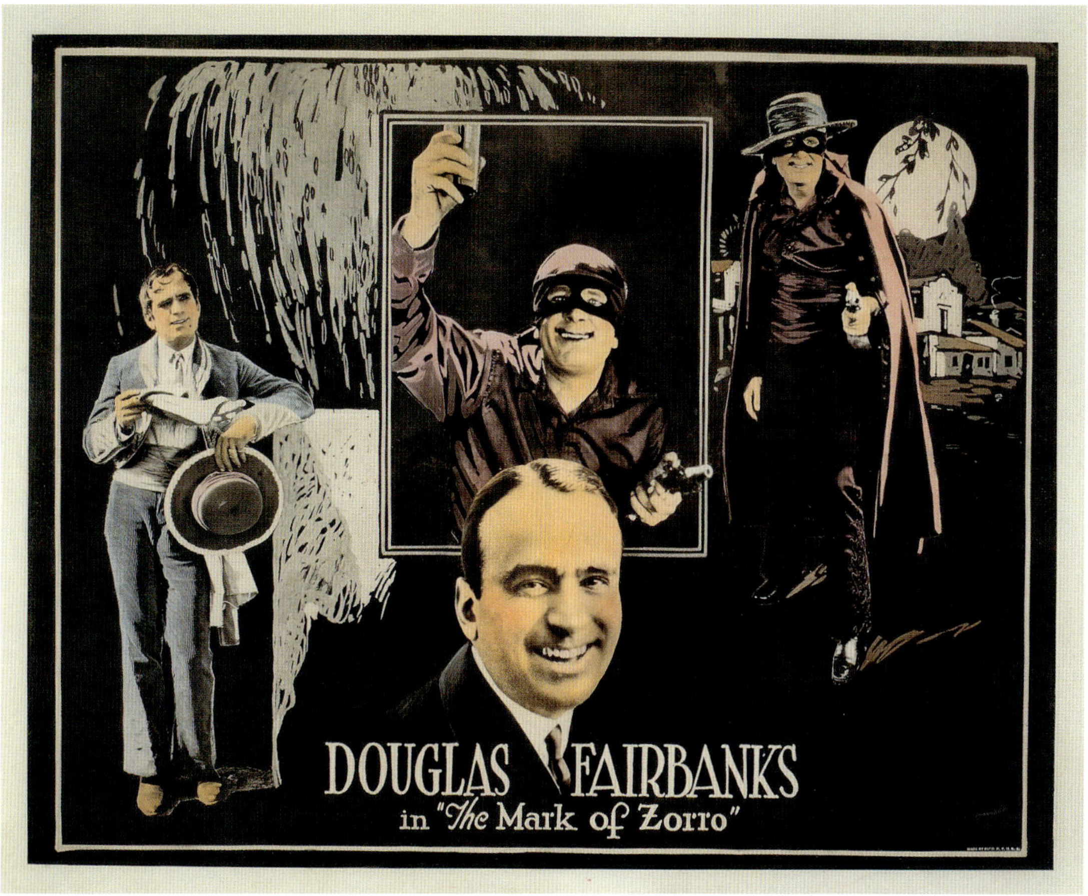

The Mark of Zorro. 1920. Half-sheet. $1,000-1,500

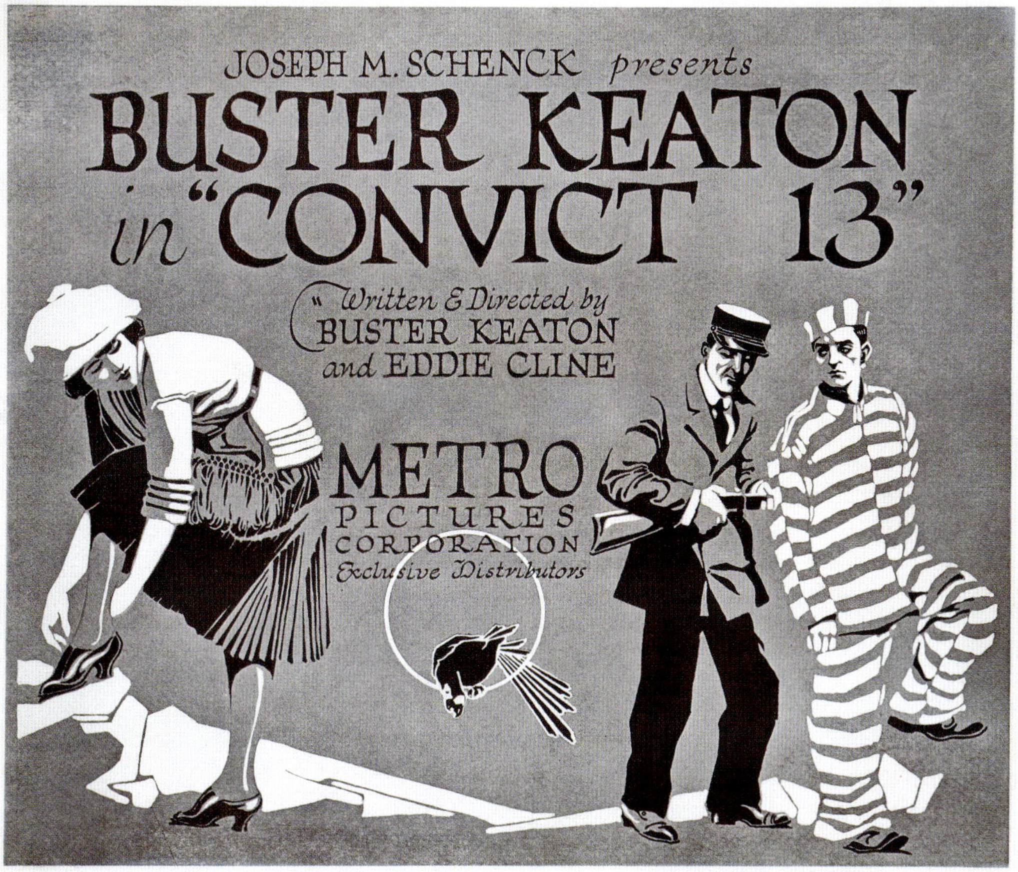

Convict 13. 1920. Title lobby card. $1,000-1,500

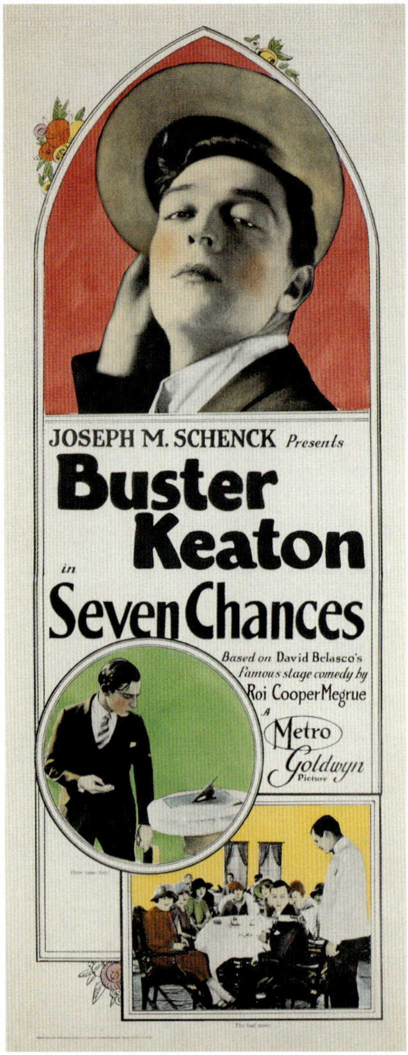

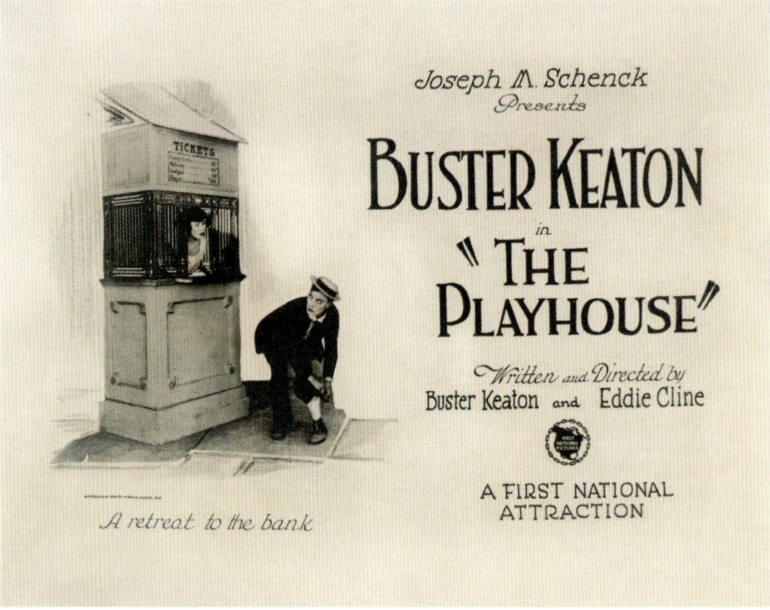

The Playhouse. 1921. Title lobby card. $1,000-1,500

Seven Chances. 1925.
Insert. $2,500-3,500

The Gold Rush. 1925. Half-sheet. $15,000-18,000

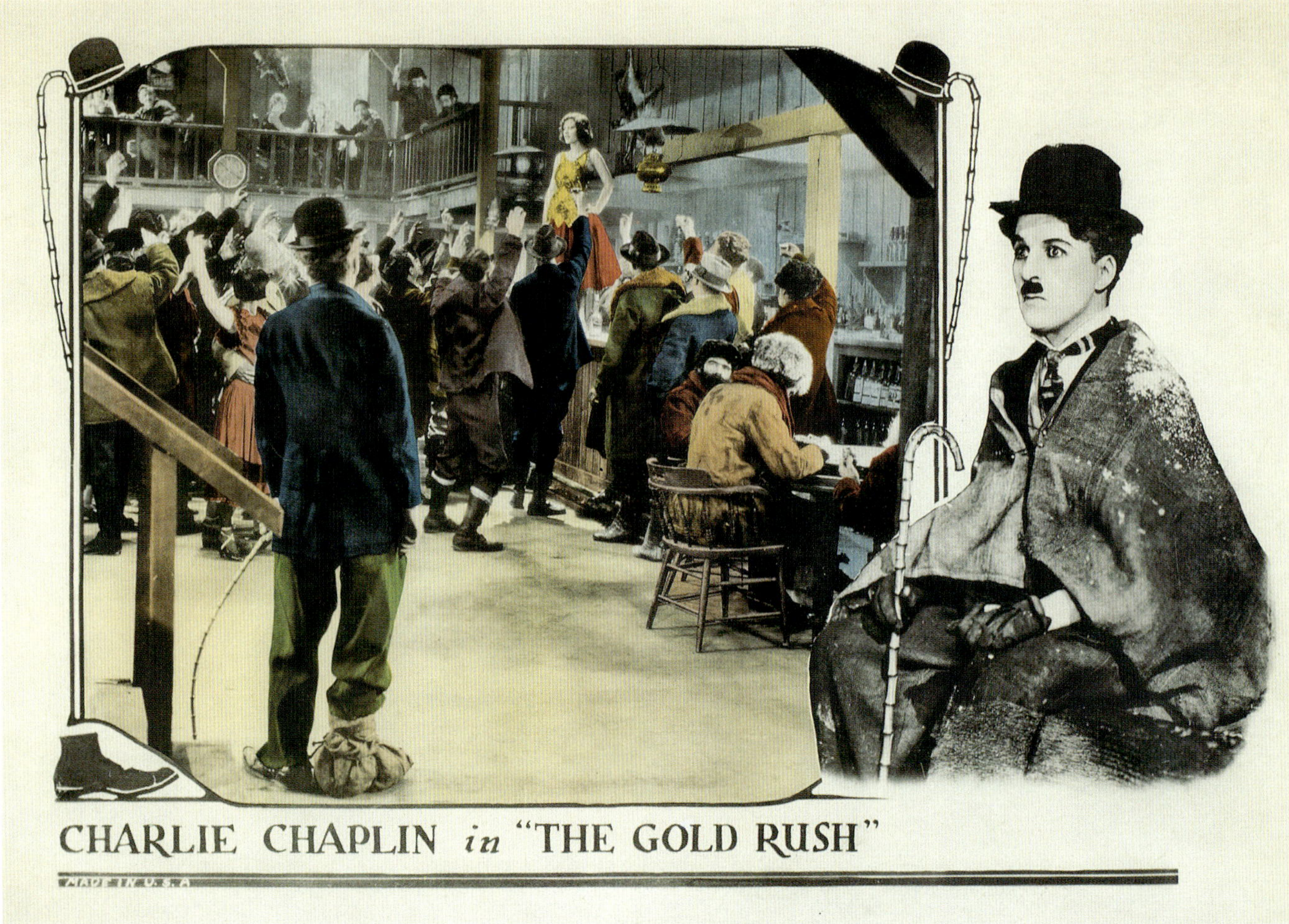

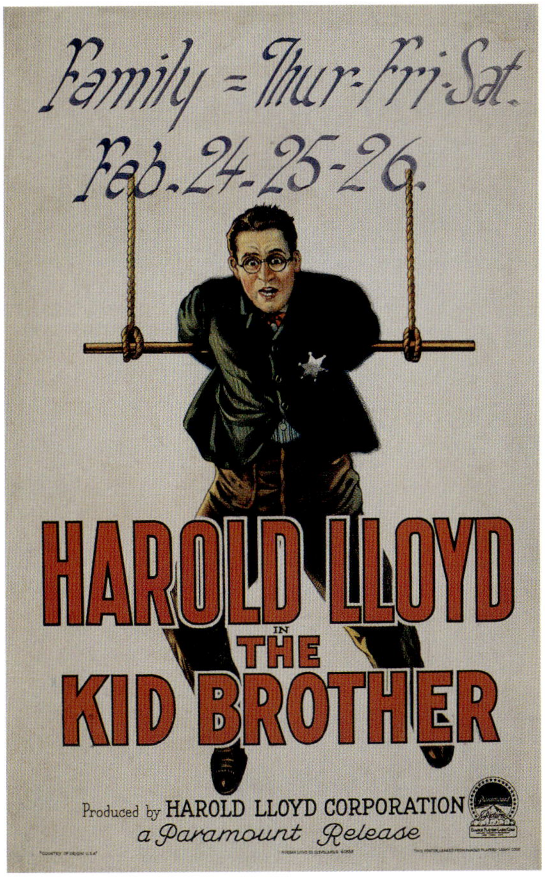

The Kid Brother. 1927.
Window card. $700-1,000

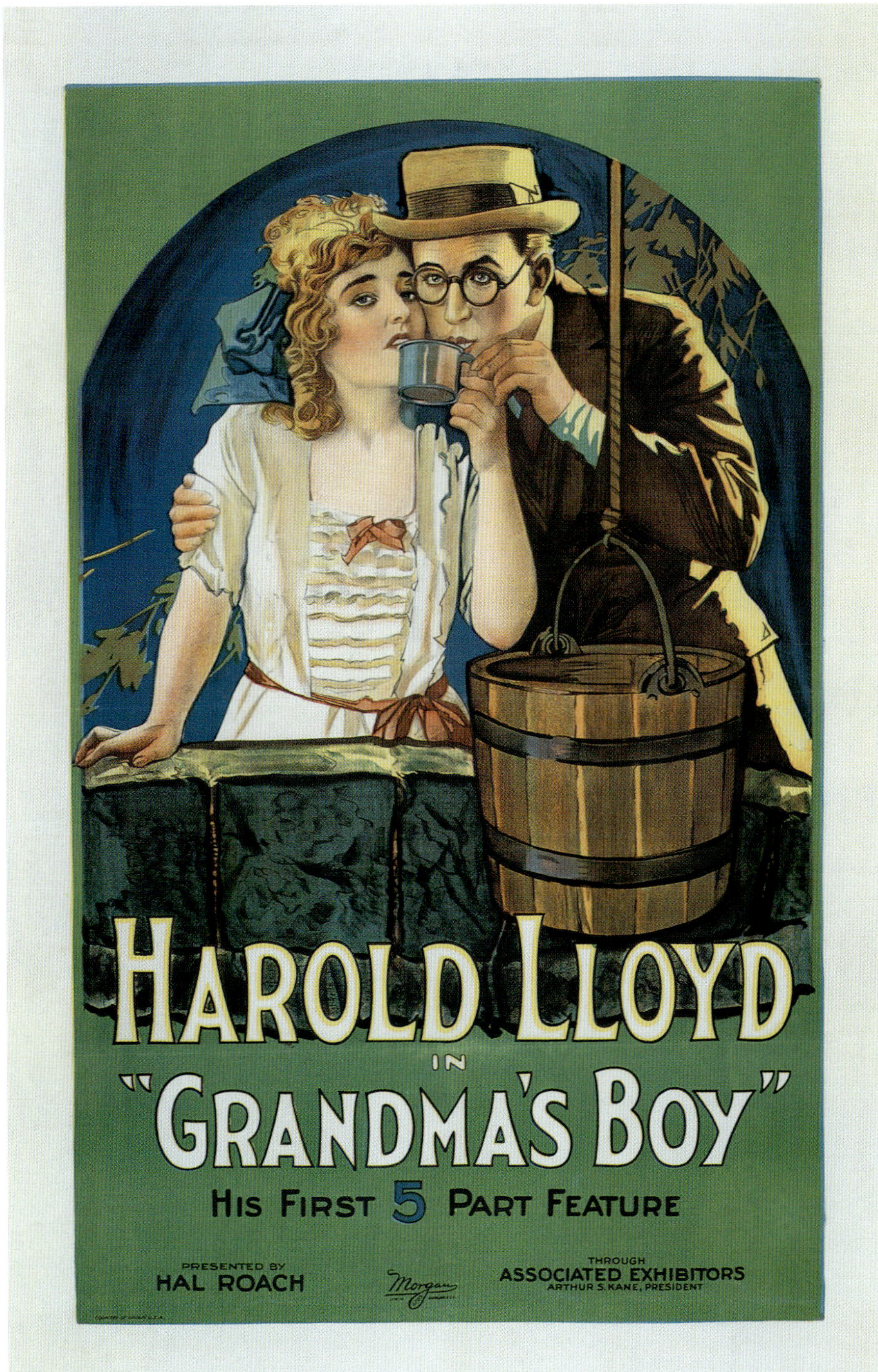

Grandma's Boy. 1922.
One-sheet. $5,000-8,000

The studios made the stars and, in turn, the stars made the studios, a successful relationship that was to serve Hollywood well for the next 25 years. The power in the industry lay with the stars the individual studios could contract to create the movies that would increase the box-office returns. Competition was rife among the individual companies and the importance of the poster in the marketing war can never be under estimated. Top billing stars in the 1920s included Harold Lloyd, Charlie Chaplin, Gloria Swanson, Tom Mix, Norma Talmadge, Rudolph Valentino, Douglas Fairbanks Sr., Colleen Moore, Norma Shearer, John Barrymore, Greta Garbo, Lon Chaney, Clara Bow and Mary Pickford.

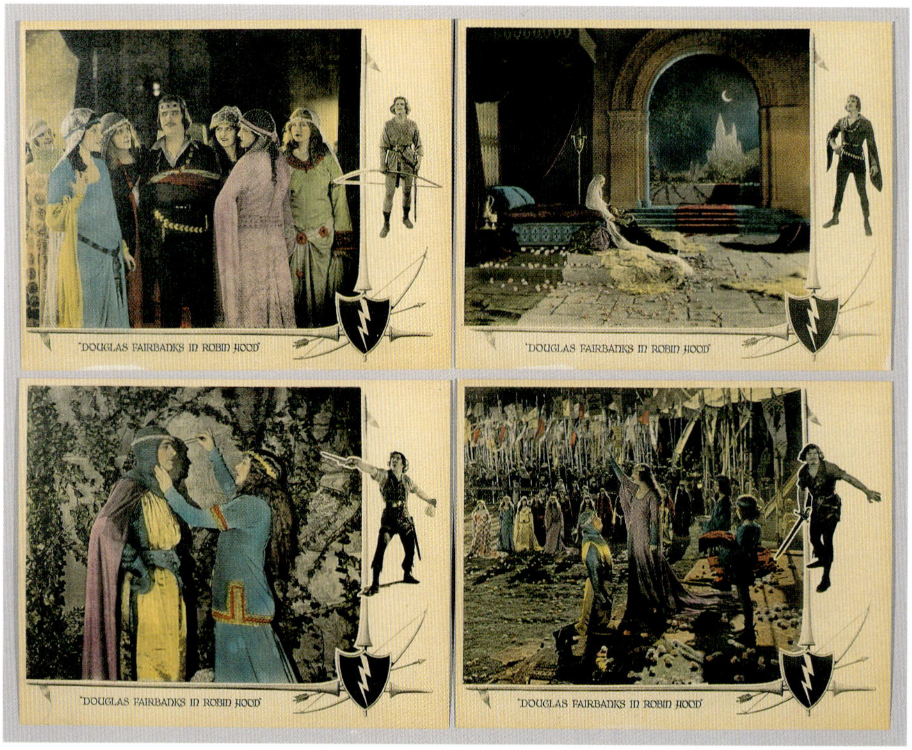

Robin Hood. 1920. Lobby card set. $1,500-2,500

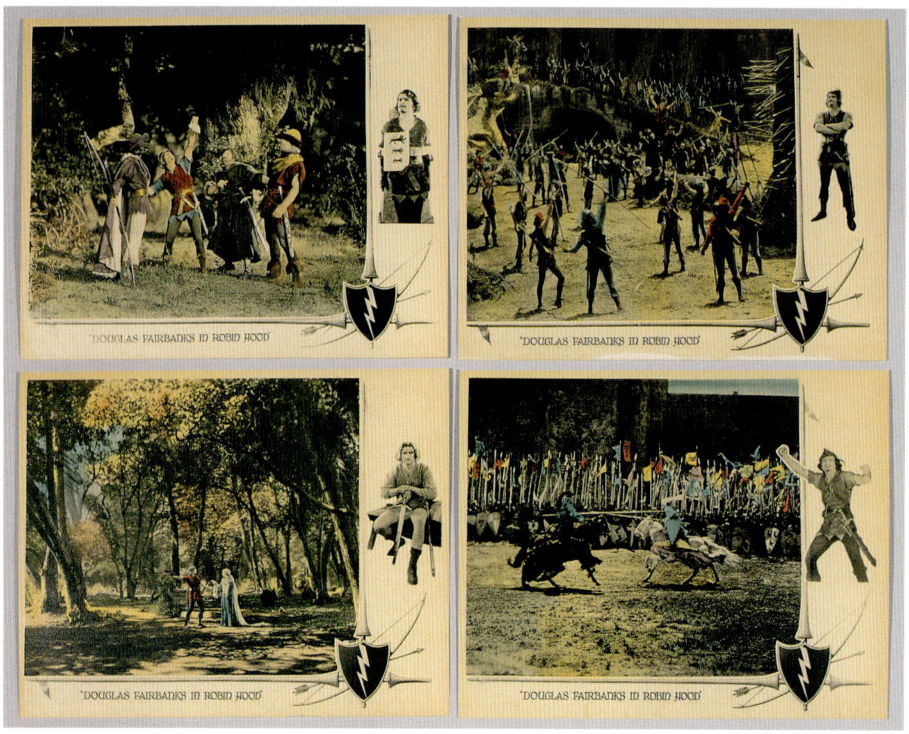

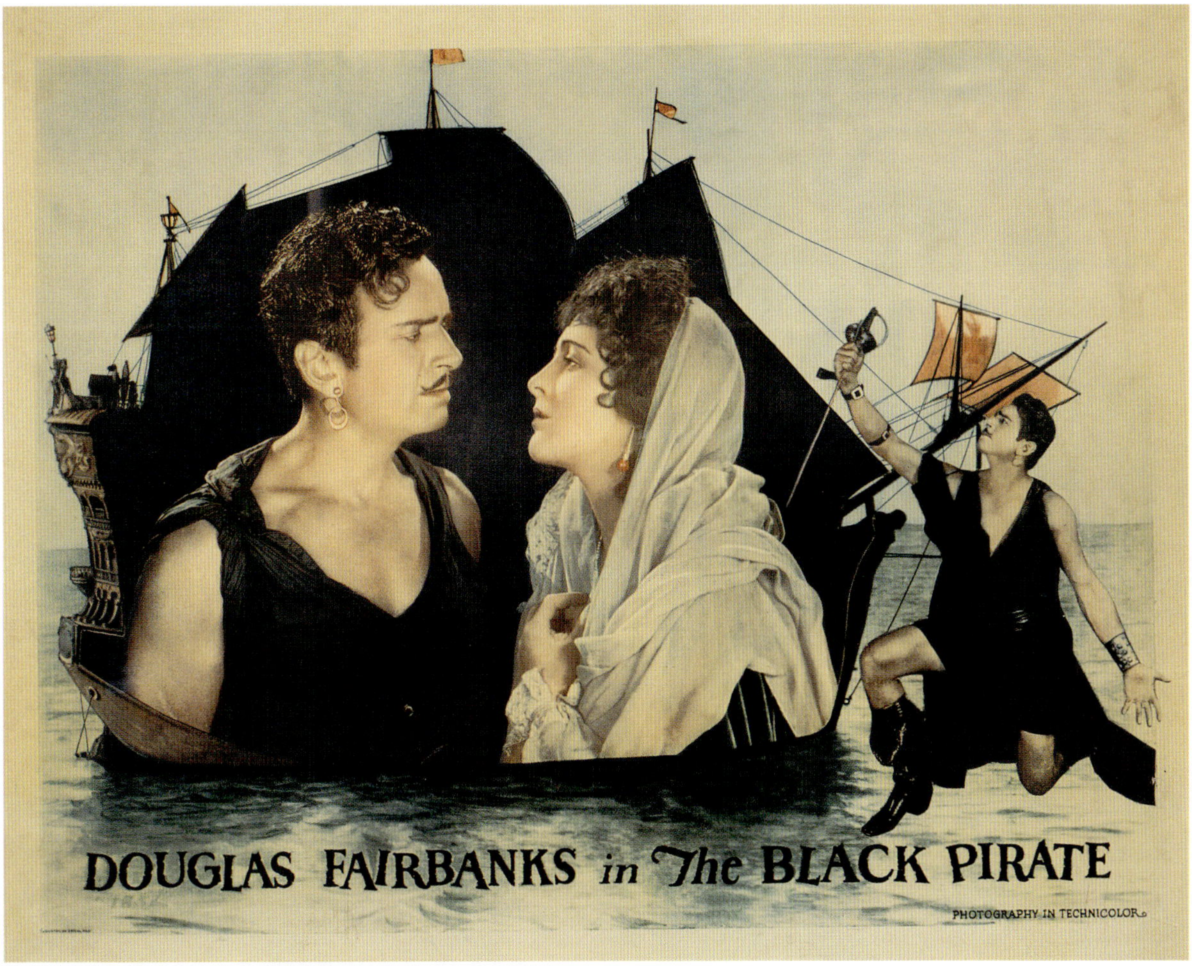

The Black Pirate. 1926. Half-sheet. $1,500-2,000

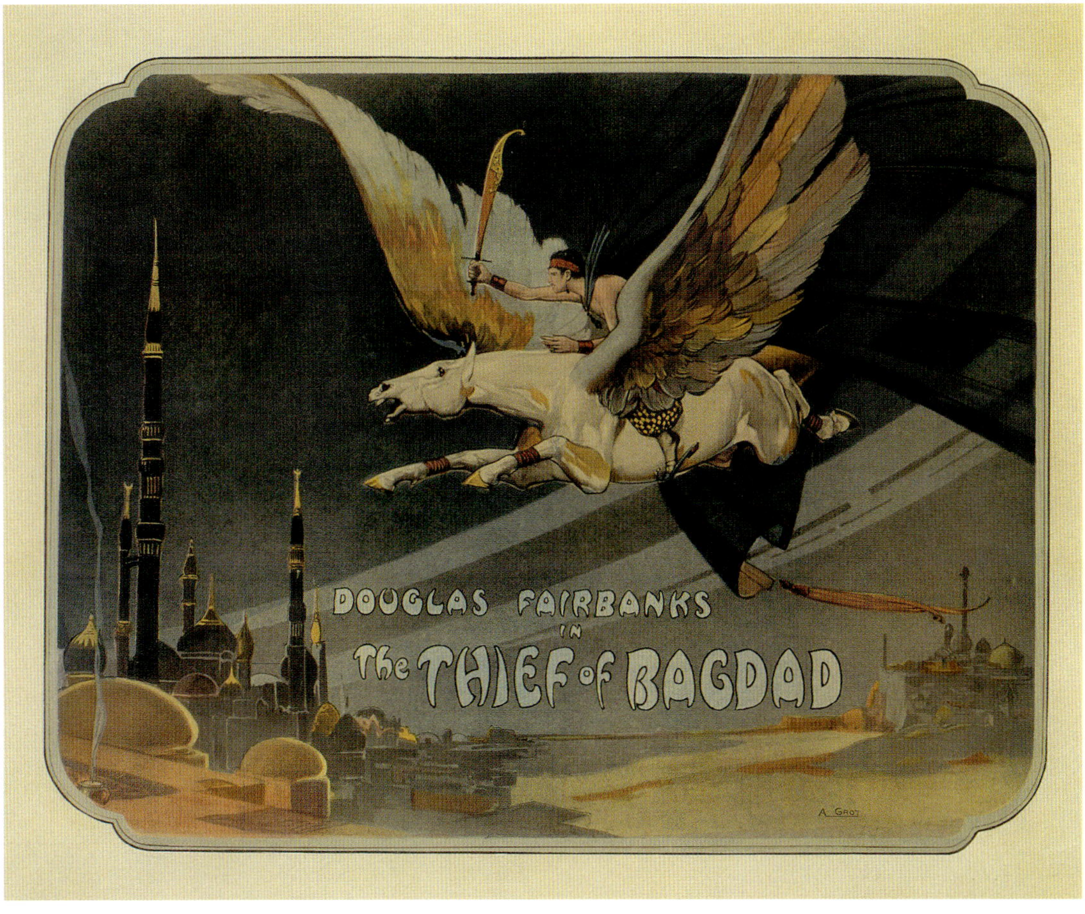

The Thief of Bagdad. 1924.
Half-sheet. $3,000-5,000

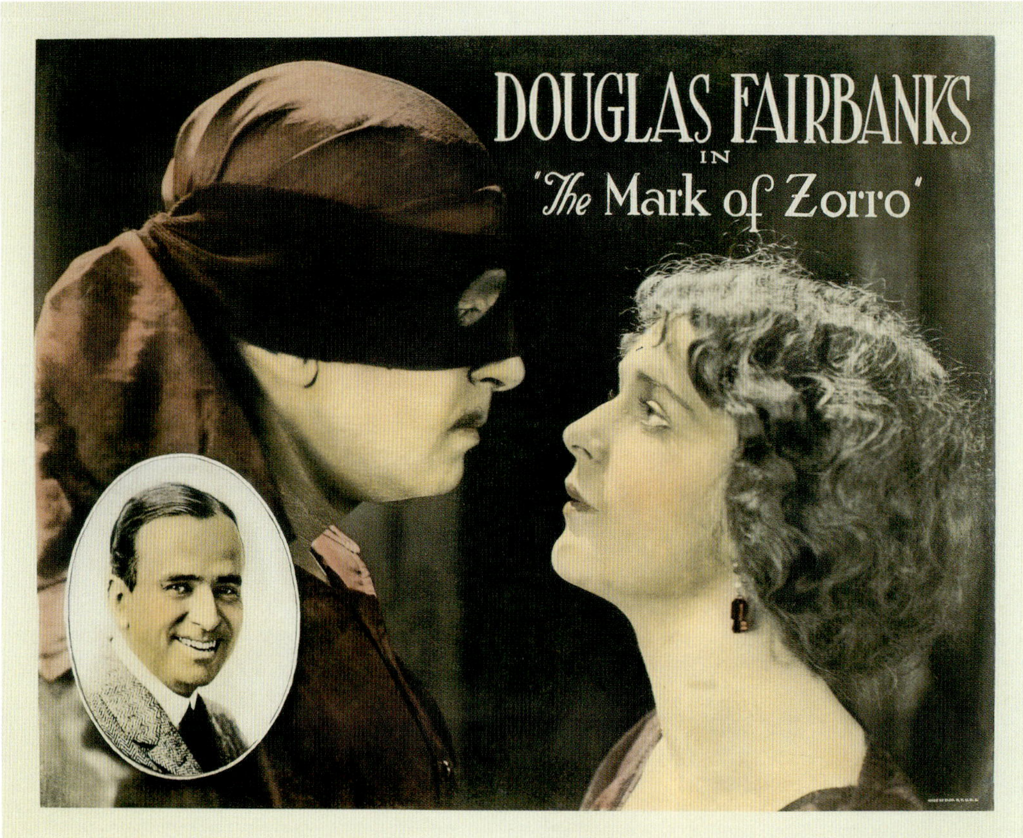

The Mark of Zorro. 1920.
Half-sheet. $1,000-1,500

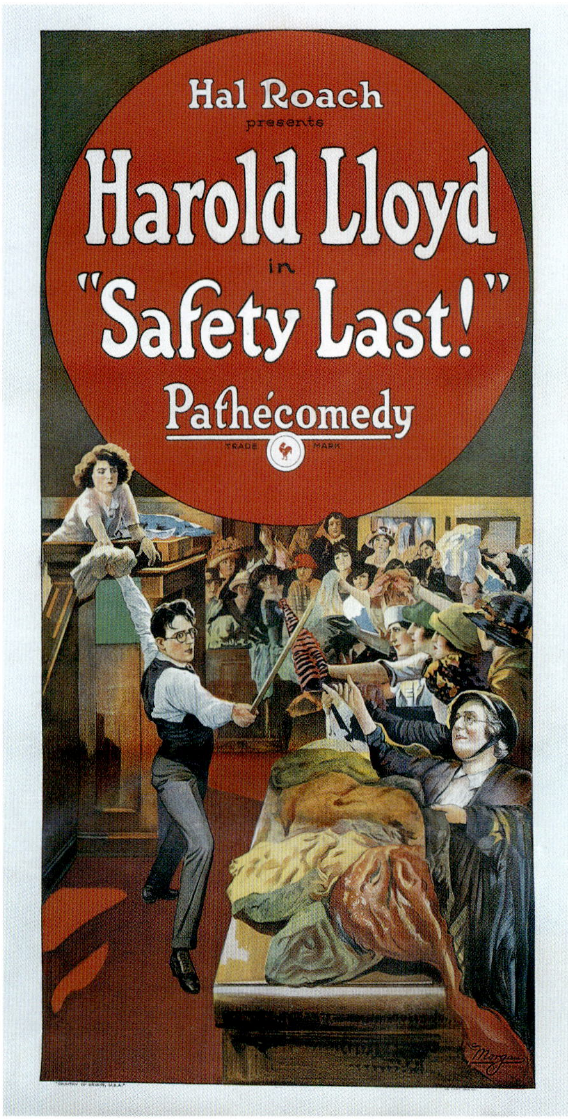

Safety Last. 1923. Three-sheet. $5,000-8,000

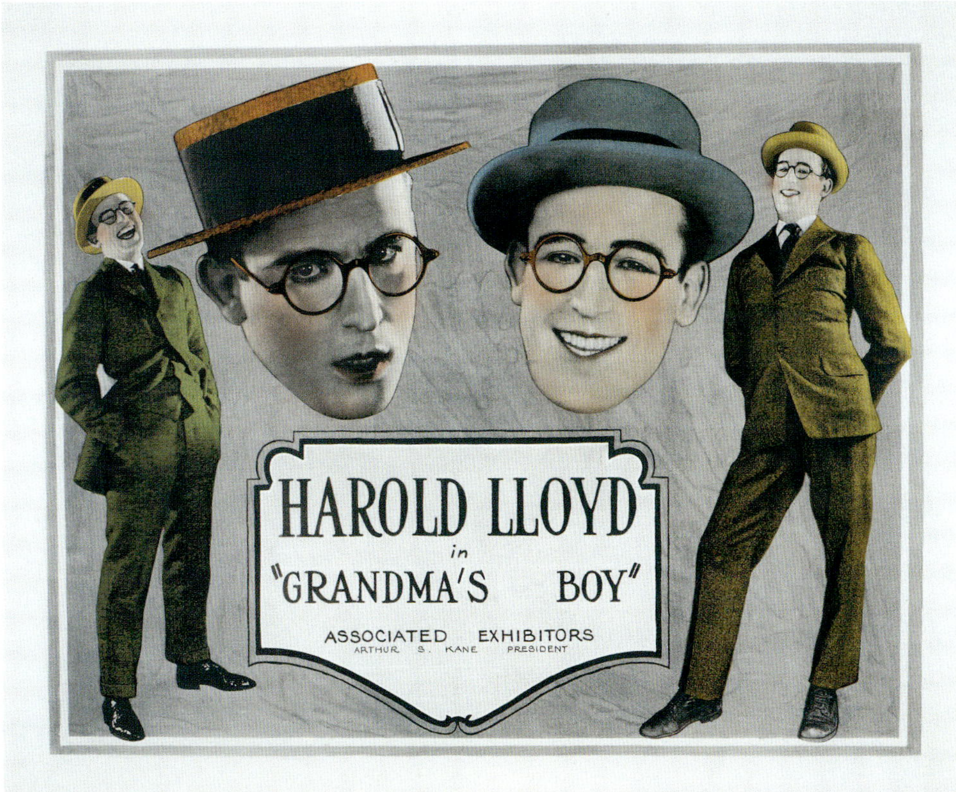

Grandma's Boy. 1922. Half-sheet. $1,000-1,500

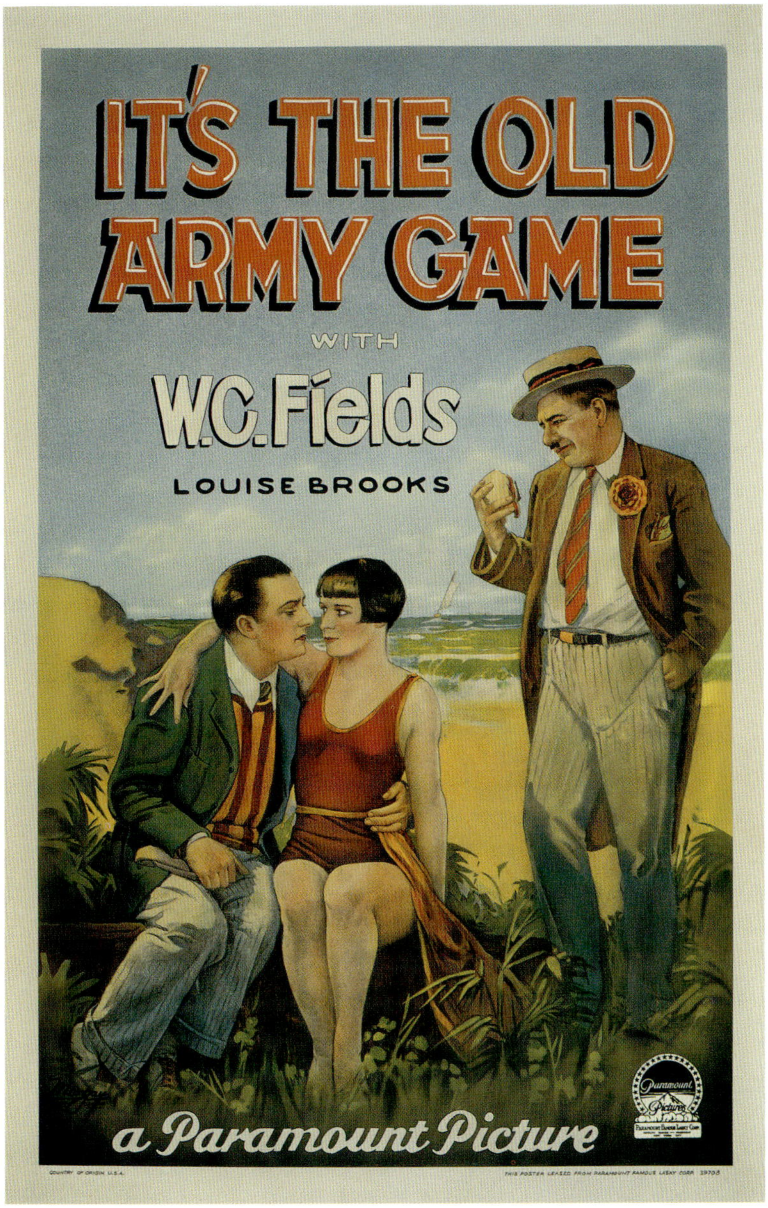

It's the Old Army Game. 1926. One-sheet. $3,000-4,000

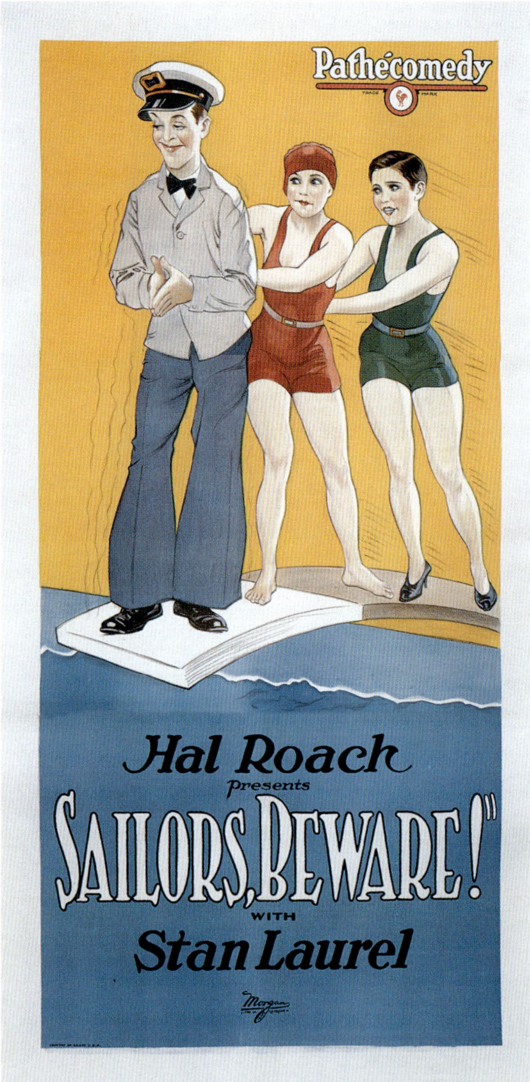

Sailors, Beware! 1927. Three-sheet. $2,500-3,500

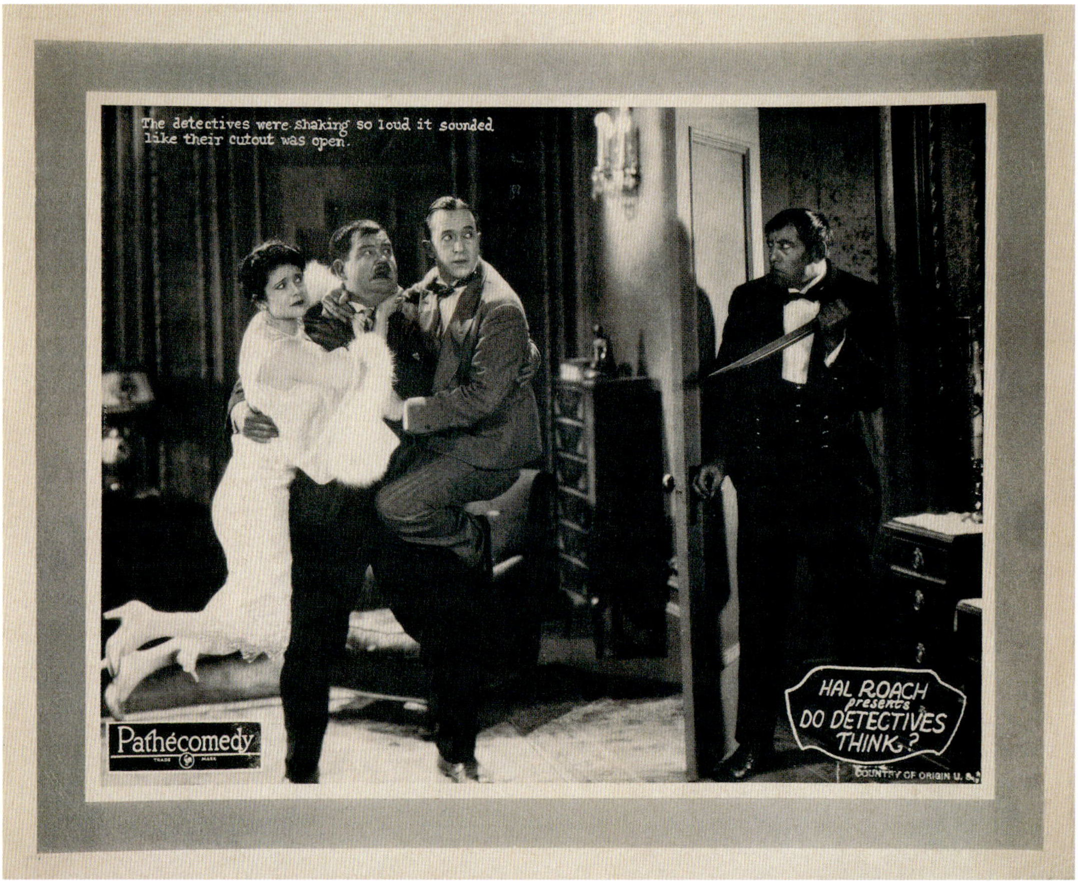

Do Detectives Think? 1927. Lobby card. $1,000-1,500

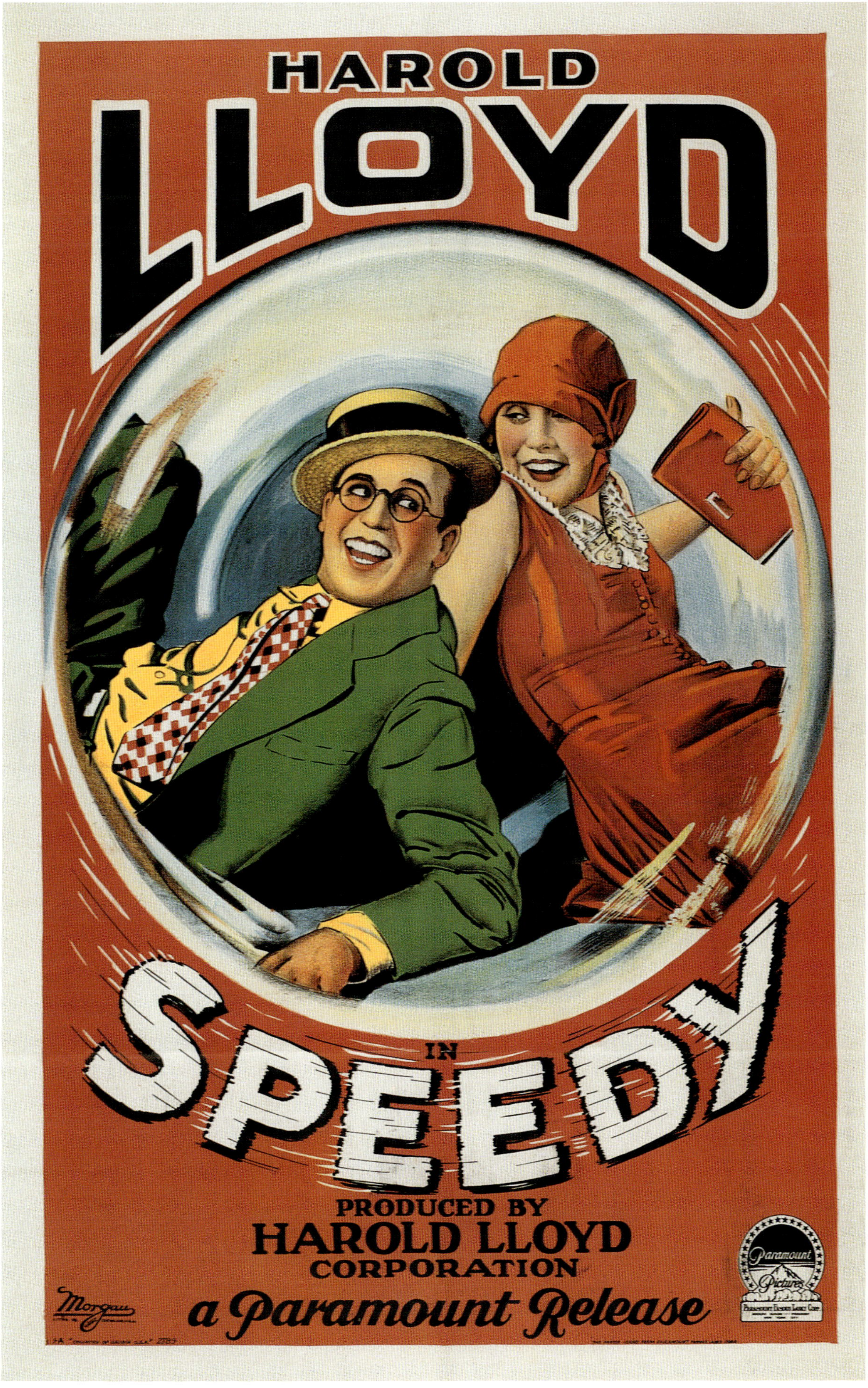

Speedy. 1928. One-sheet, style A. $4,000-6,000

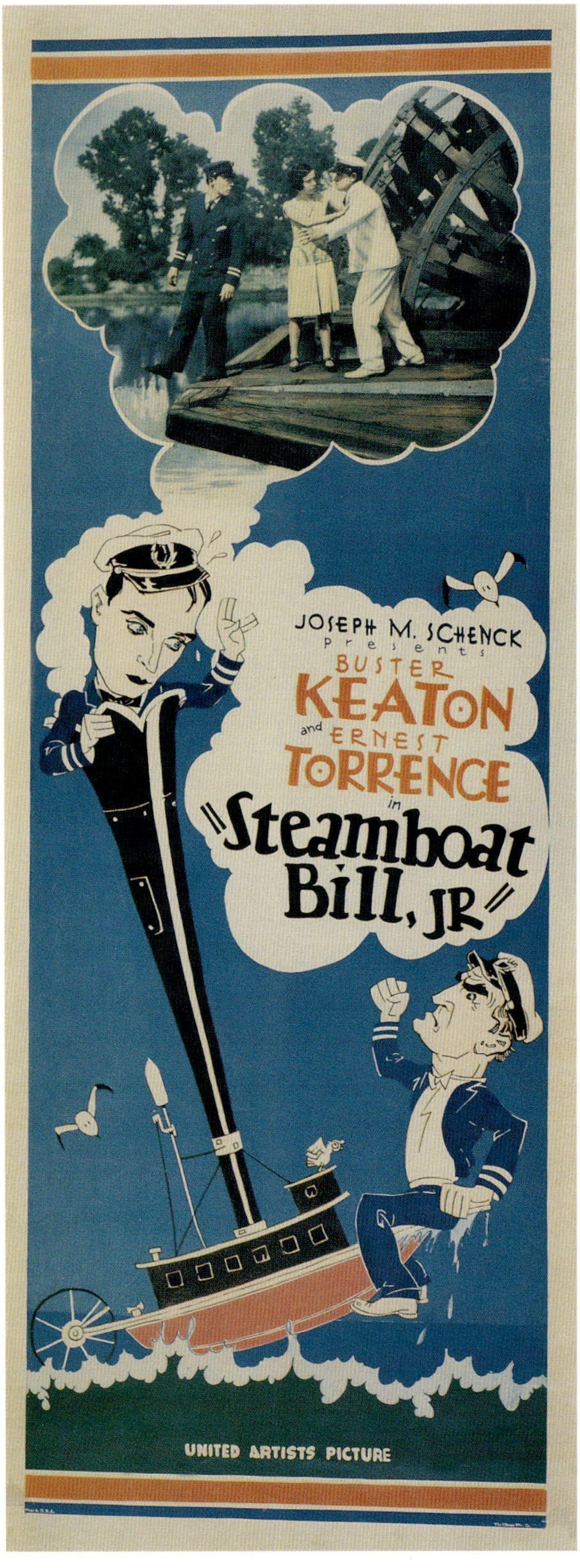

Steamboat Bill, Jr. 1928. Insert. $4,000-6,000

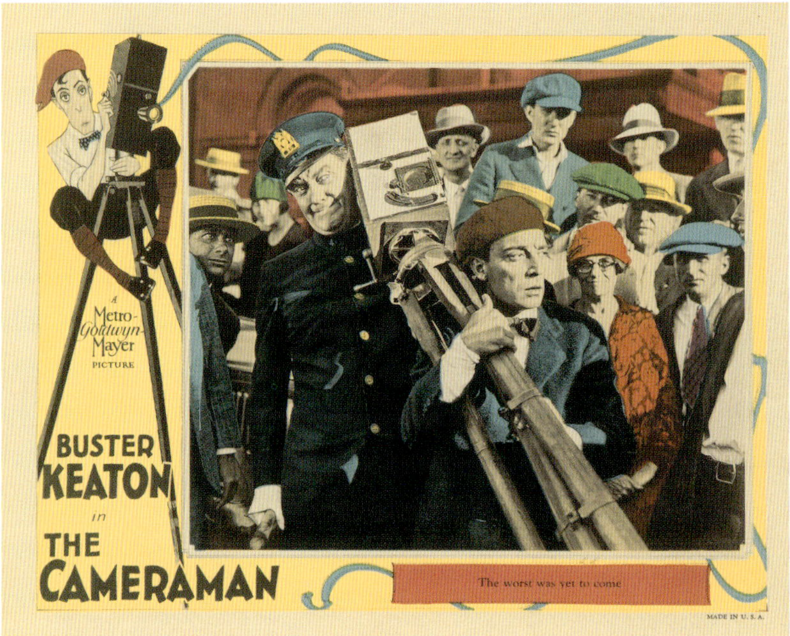

The Cameraman. 1928. Lobby card. $1,000-1,500

Hollywood flourished during these early days largely due to the significant contribution played by an influx of talent from European countries, perhaps most notably Germany. Some were enticed by the financial advantages of working for the big studios and others for political reasons. Either way some of the best were drawn to Hollywood and became hugely bankable stars in the recently established contract "studio system." Greta Garbo, Bela Lugosi, Conrad Veidt, directors Rouben Mamoulian, F. W. Murnau, Ernst Lubitsch, Michael Curtiz, and producer Alexander Korda all established their careers in these early years.

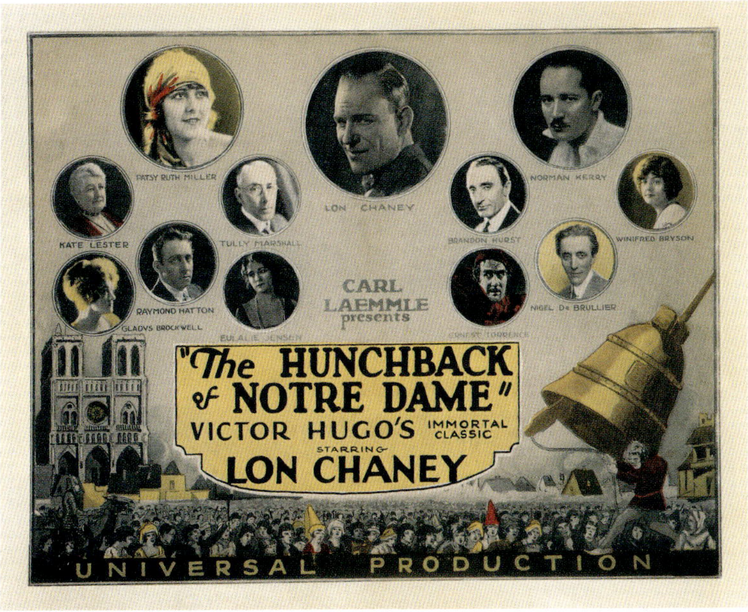

The Hunchback of Notre Dame. 1923. Title lobby card. $1,500-2,500

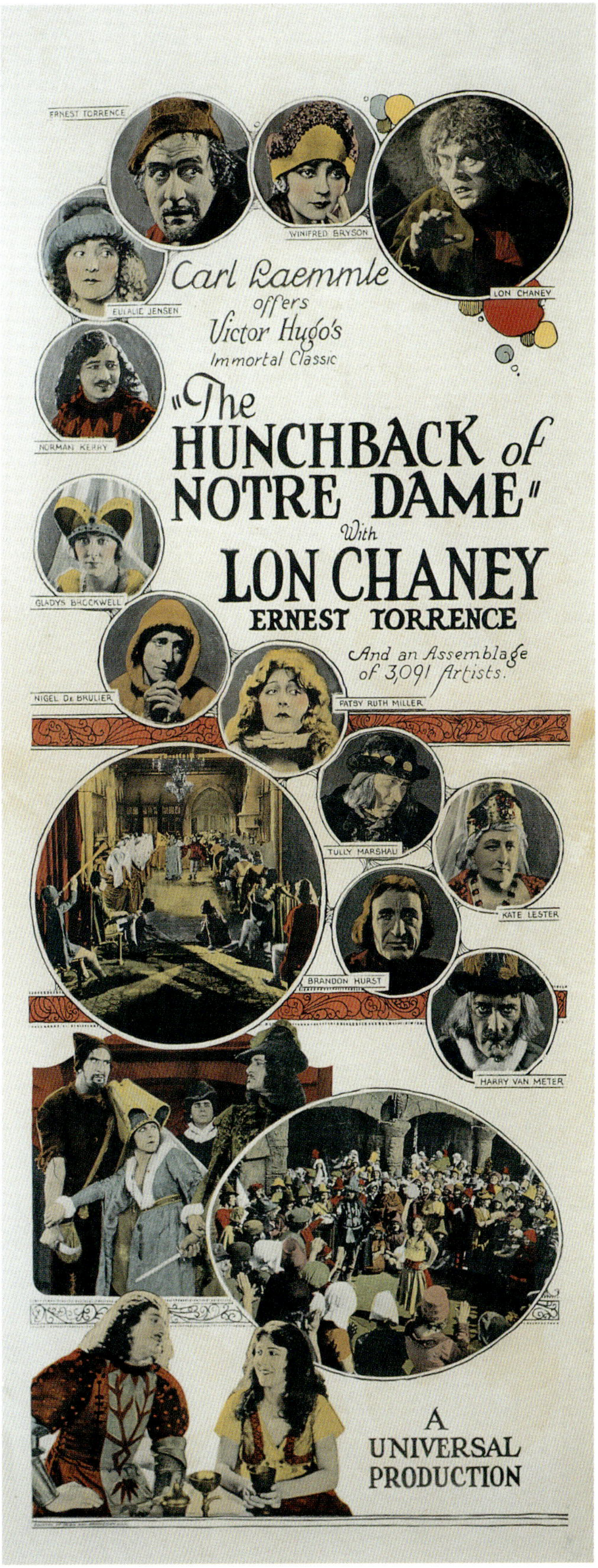

The Hunchback of Notre Dame. 1923. Insert. $8,000-12,000

The style and content of many thought-provoking movies from Europe helped to shape and develop aspects of the creative mind within the early Hollywood studios. The German expressionist horror film *The Cabinet of Dr. Caligari* (1920) and Murnau's classic vampire tale, the first on celluloid, *Nosferatu* (1922), were both stylishly directed and hauntingly lit with severe shadows, sharp camera angles, and much visual story telling rather than the traditional captioned title cards. This influence can also be seen through another German, Fritz Lang, who directed his last major silent film and the first great science-fiction feature *Metropolis* in 1926. His deft use of innovative technique and design sets his work apart from all others of the era. Director Josef von Sternberg, a brilliant addition for Paramount, proved his worth by ushering in the seemingly very American gangster genre with the atmospheric *Underworld* (1927), followed by *The Drag Net* (1928), and *The Docks of New York* (1928). Another notable foreign director was Austrian born Erich von Stroheim. After his initial success in 1918 with *Blind Husbands* he went on to become one of the leading Hollywood directors and helped boost both the prestige and coffers of Universal Studios. The high point of his early directorial career was in 1922 with *Foolish Wives.*

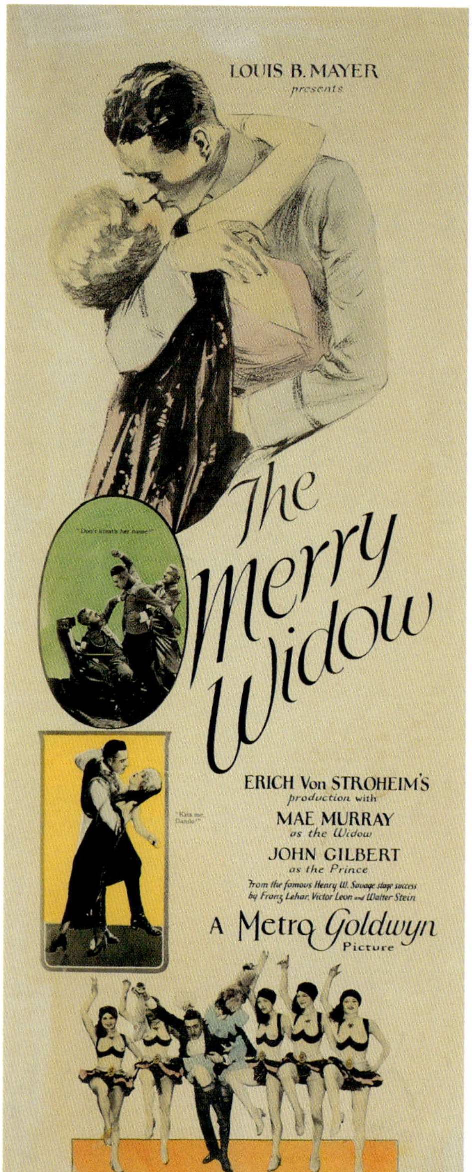

The Merry Widow. 1925. Insert. $1,200-1,800

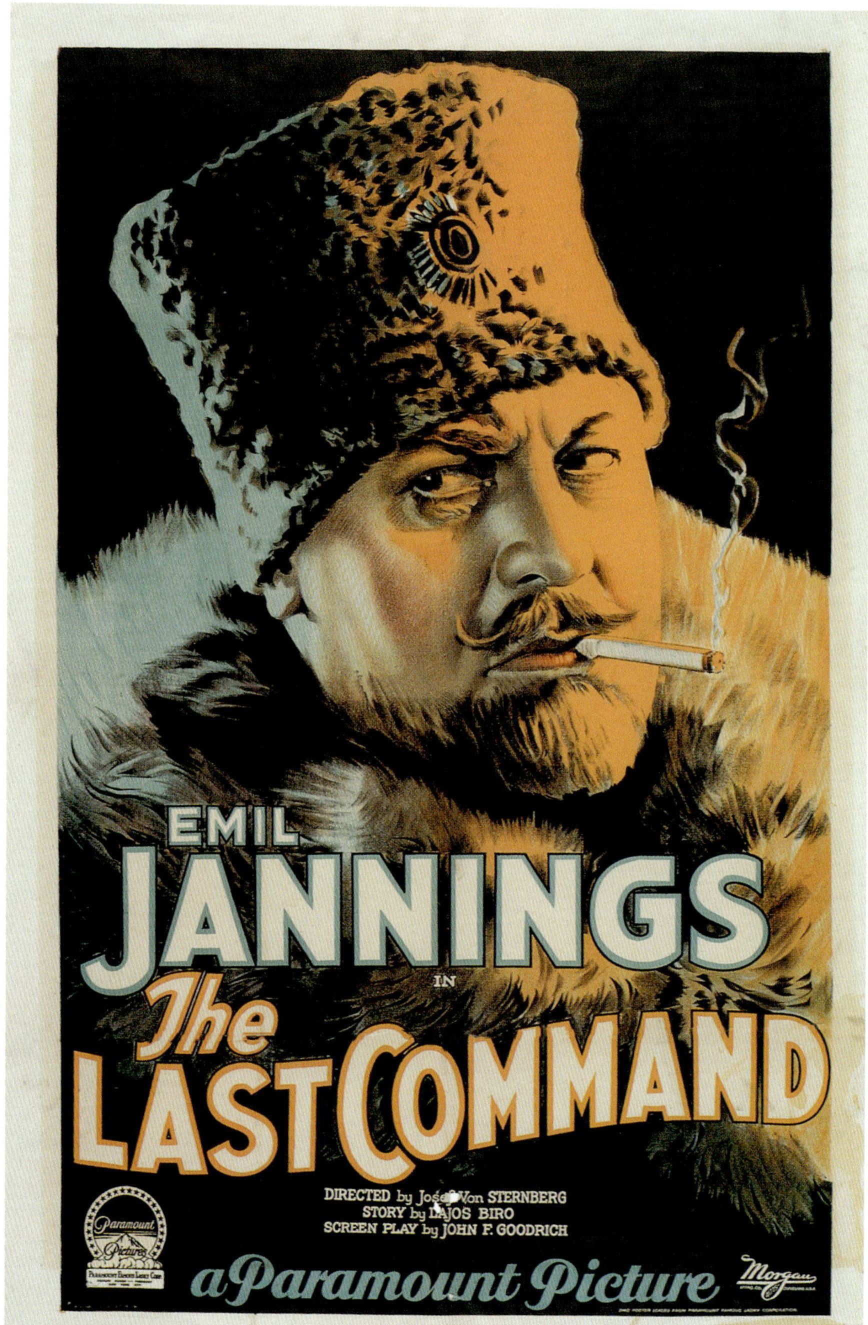

The Last Command. 1928. One-sheet. $2,000-2,500

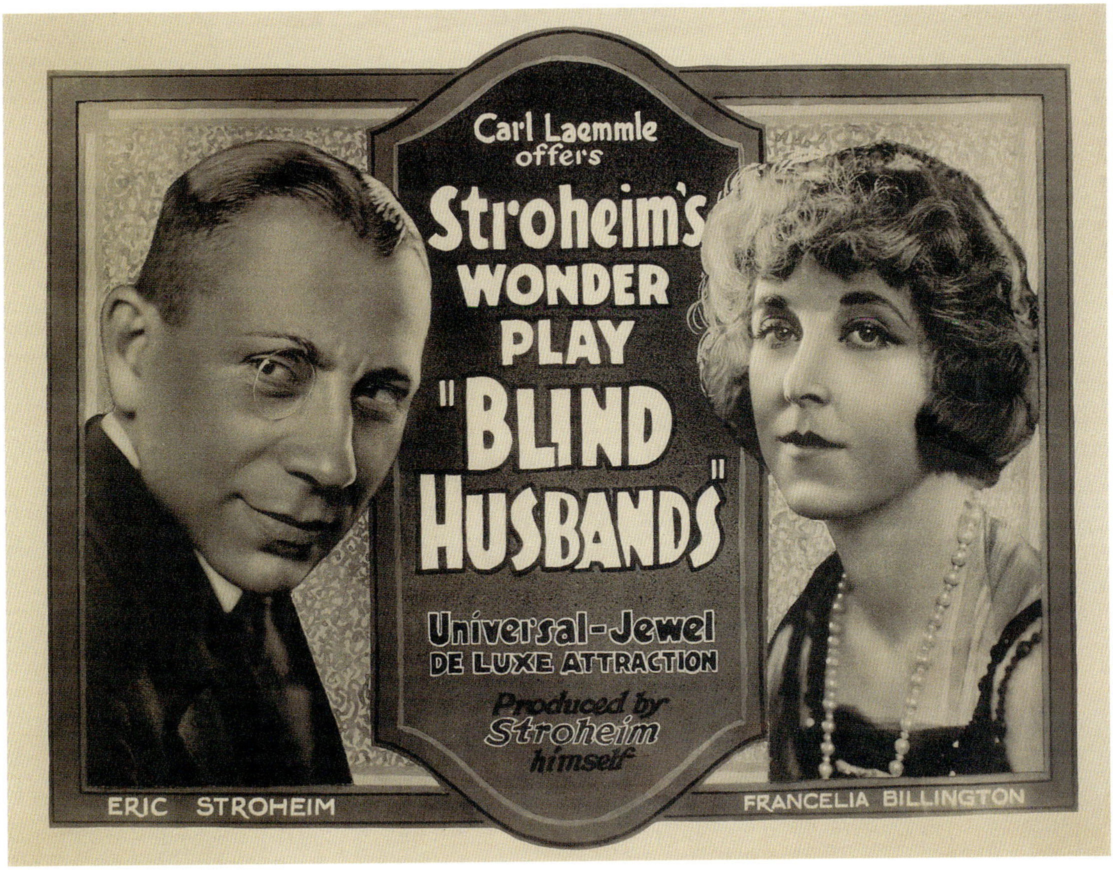

Blind Husbands. 1919.
Half-sheet. $2,000-3,000

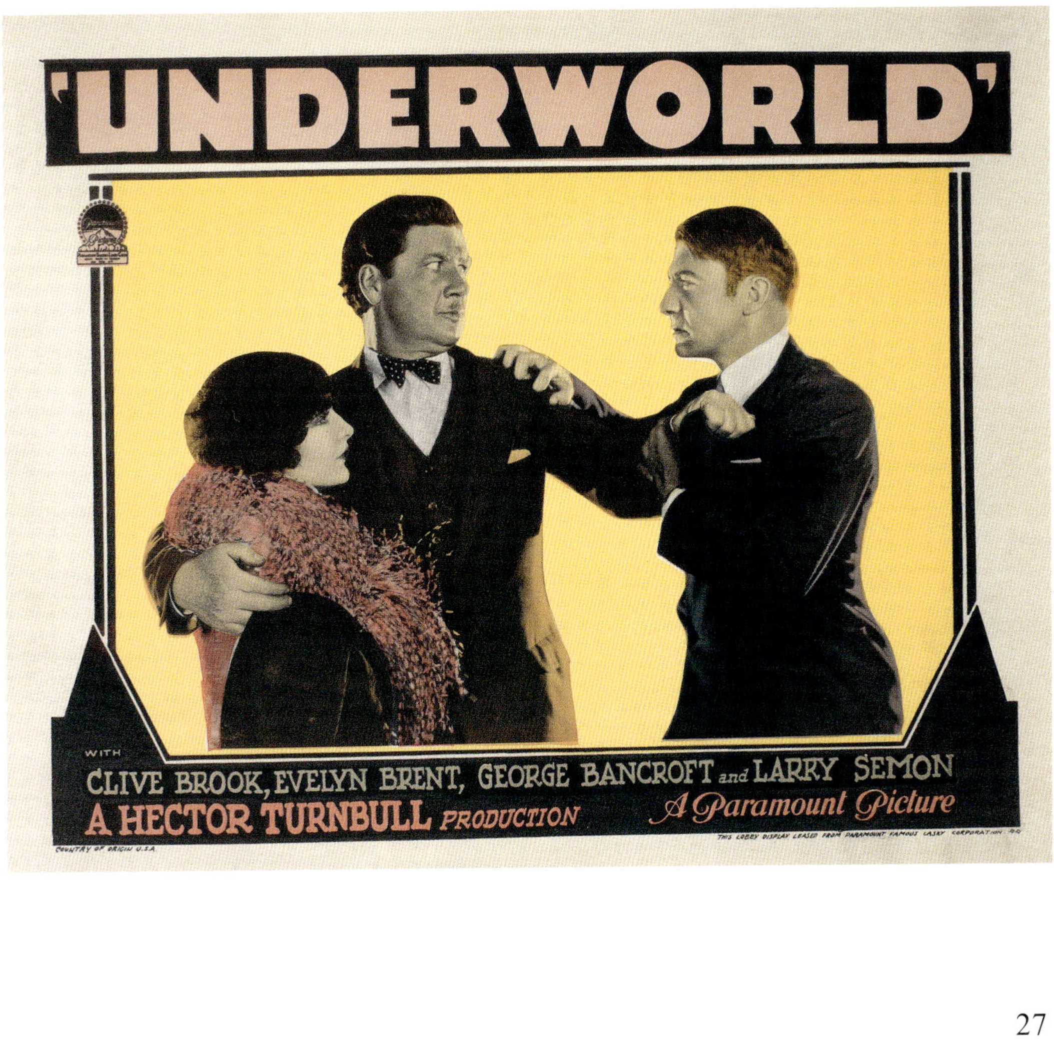

Underworld. 1927. Lobby
card. $600-900

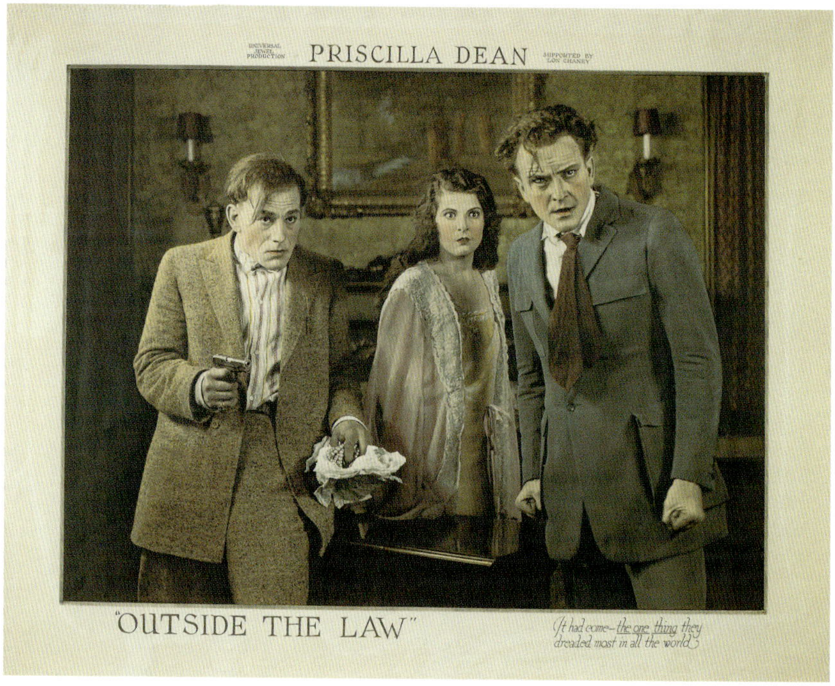

Outside the Law. 1921. Half-sheet. $1,000-1,500

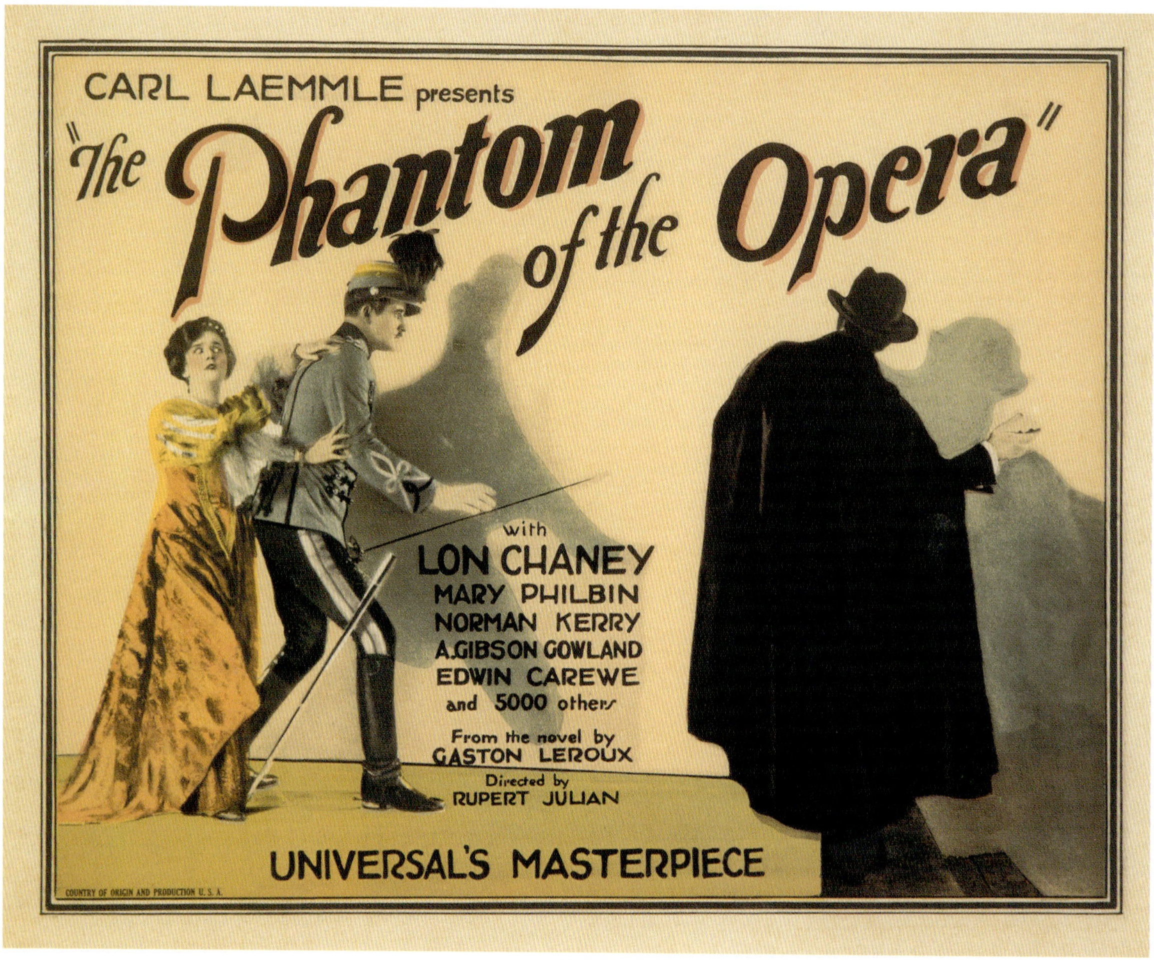

The Phantom of the Opera. 1925. Title lobby card. $1,000-1,500

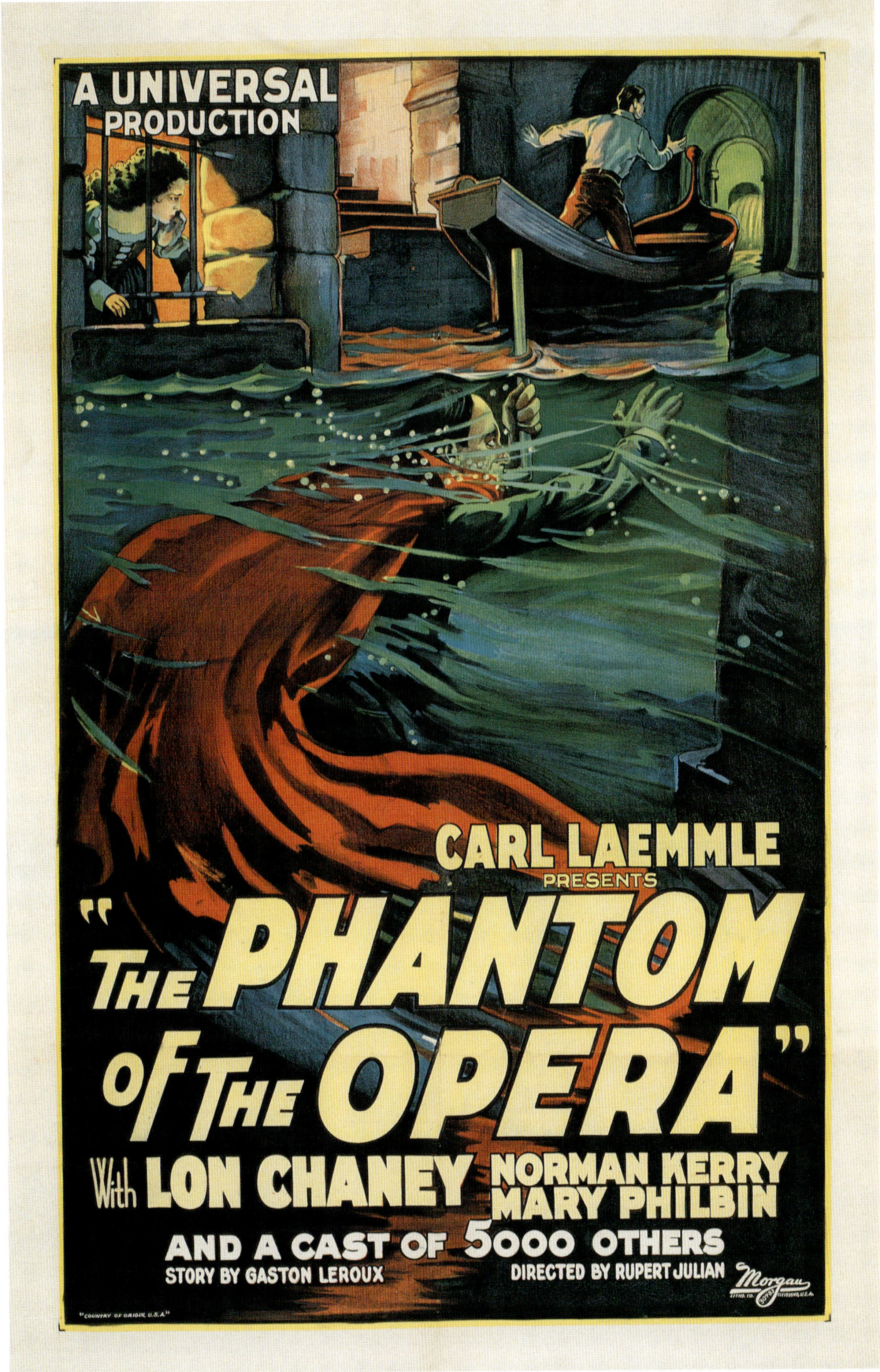

The Phantom of the Opera. 1925. One-sheet. $40,000-60,000

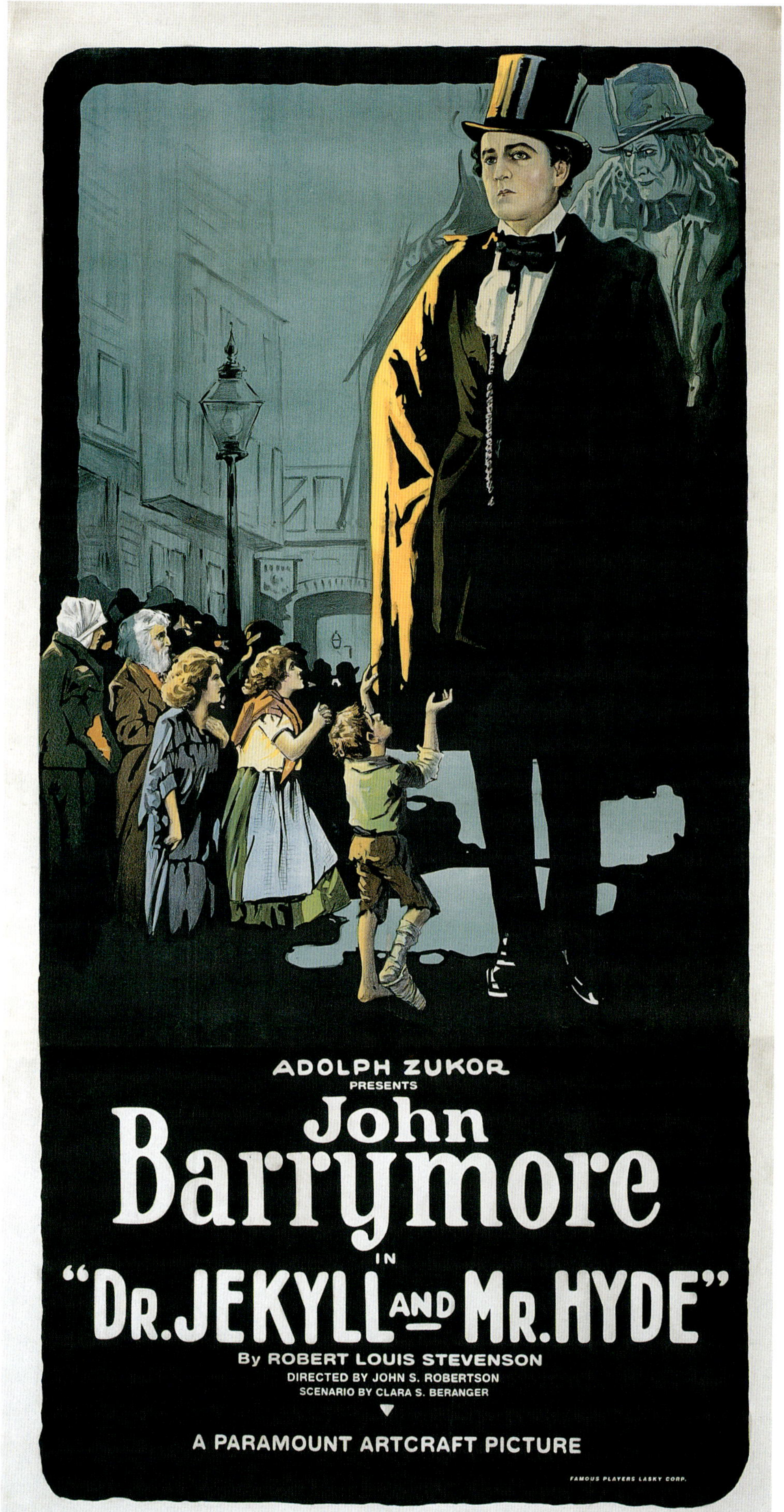

Dr. Jekyll and Mr. Hyde. 1920. Three-sheet. $20,000-30,000

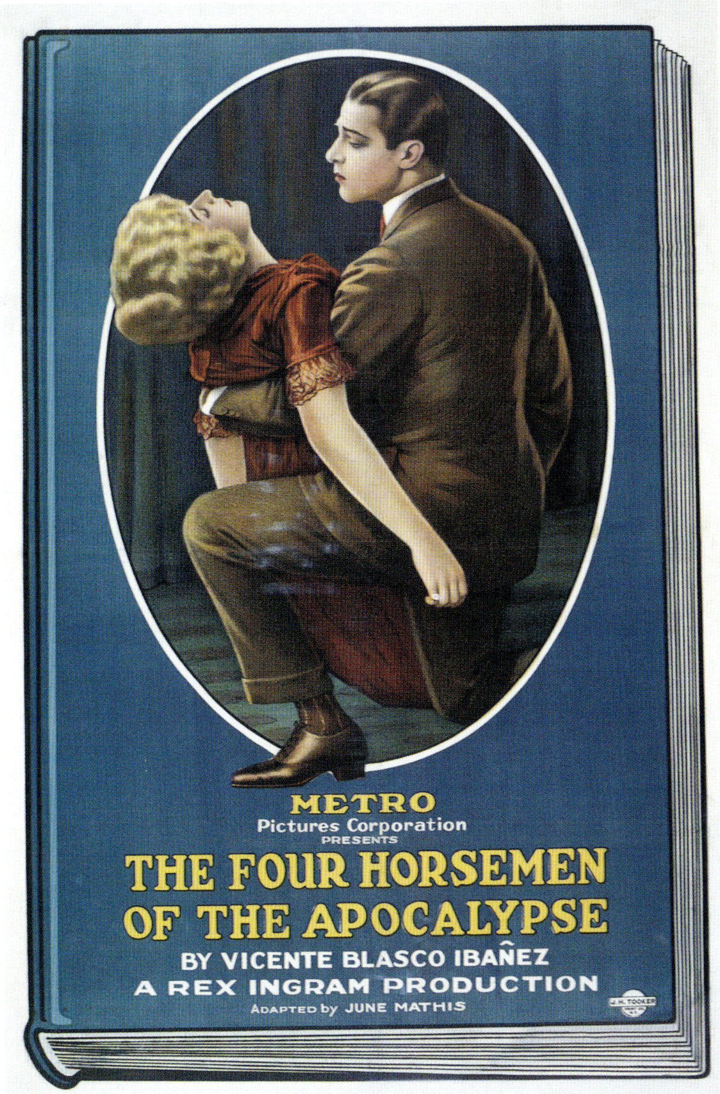

The Four Horsemen of the Apocalypse.
1921. One-sheet. $4,000-6,000

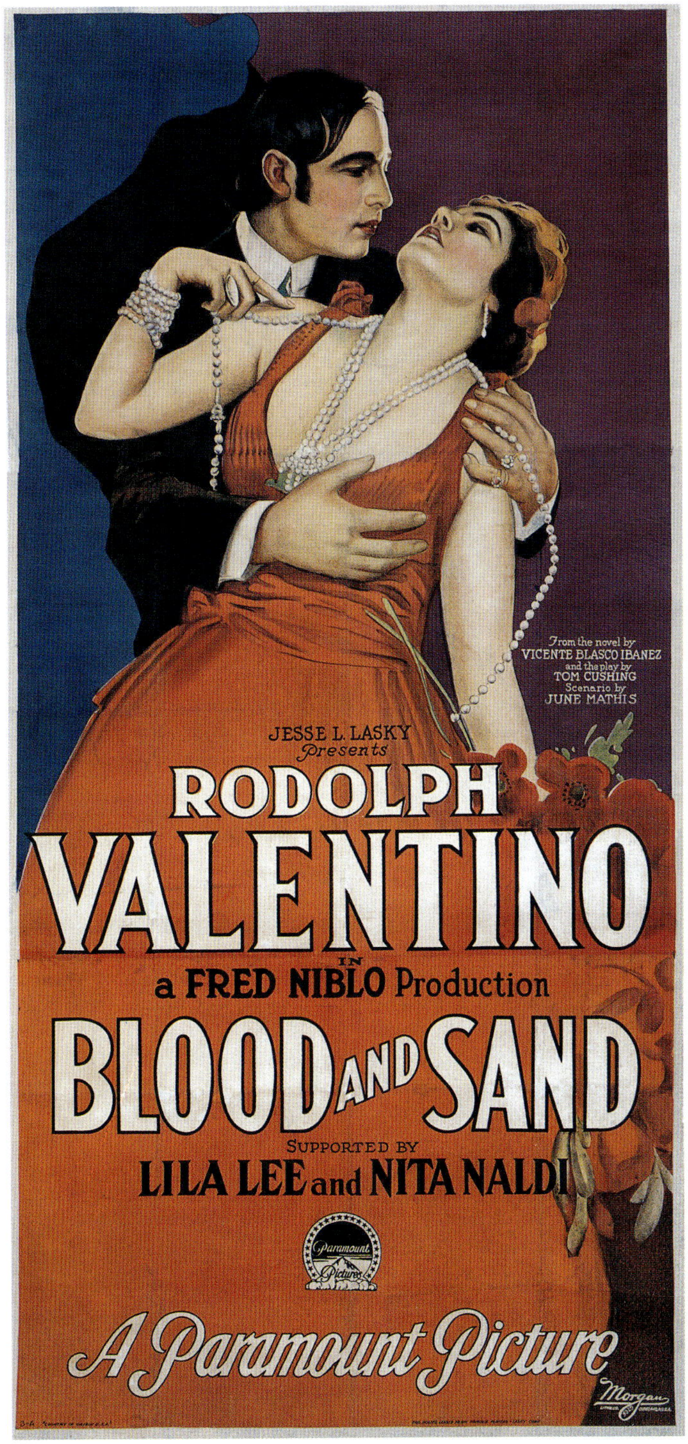

Blood and Sand. 1922. Three-sheet. $4,000-6,000

The studios produced movies on a variety of different genres including romance, history, melodrama and comedy, appealing to the full range of human emotions. They prospered as a result, as did the stars, but old Hollywood had its fair share of problems that it encountered for the first, but not the last, time. The all American movie star, Wallace Reid, succumbed to drug addiction and died tragically young in 1923; the director William Desmond Taylor was murdered in 1922; Roscoe "Fatty" Arbuckle's career was publicly destroyed by an accusation of rape and Rudolph Valentino, the first worldwide celluloid movie star, died suddenly at the height of a glittering career in 1926. Real life in Hollywood was every bit as dramatic as that created for the silver screen.

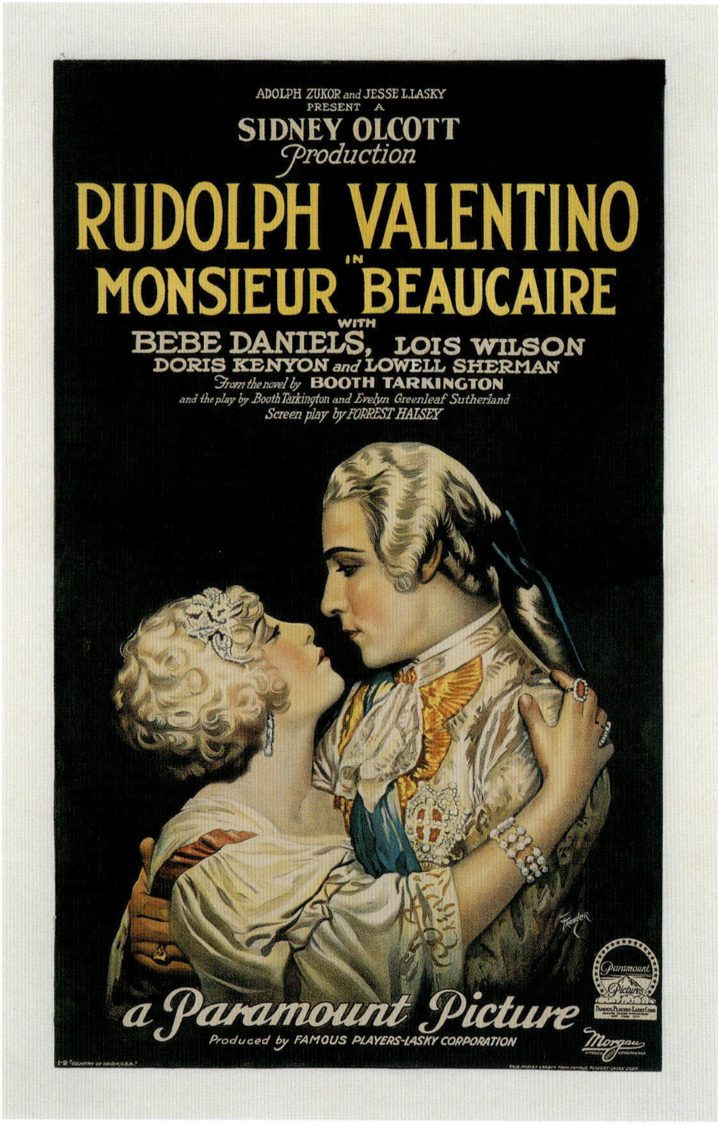

Monsieur Beaucaire. 1924. One-sheet. $4,000-6,000

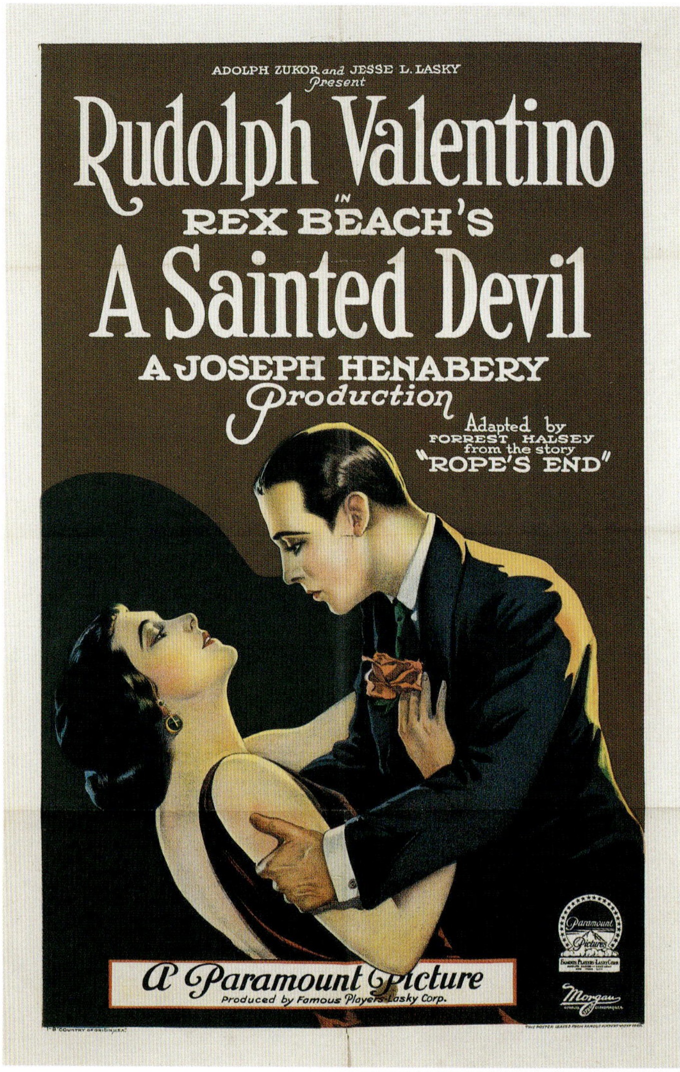

A Sainted Devil. 1924. One-sheet. $6,000-8,000

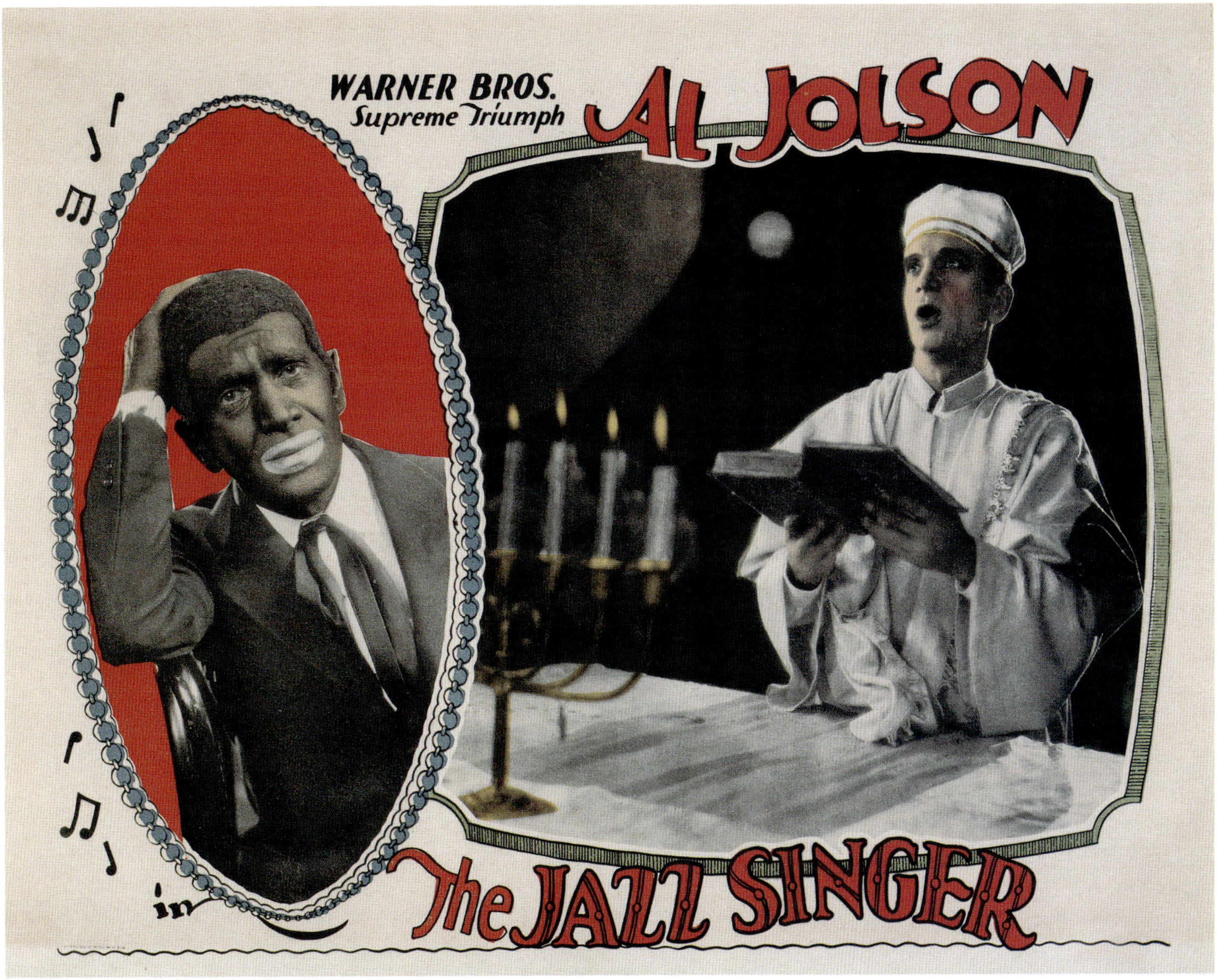

The Jazz Singer. 1927. Lobby card. $3,000-5,000

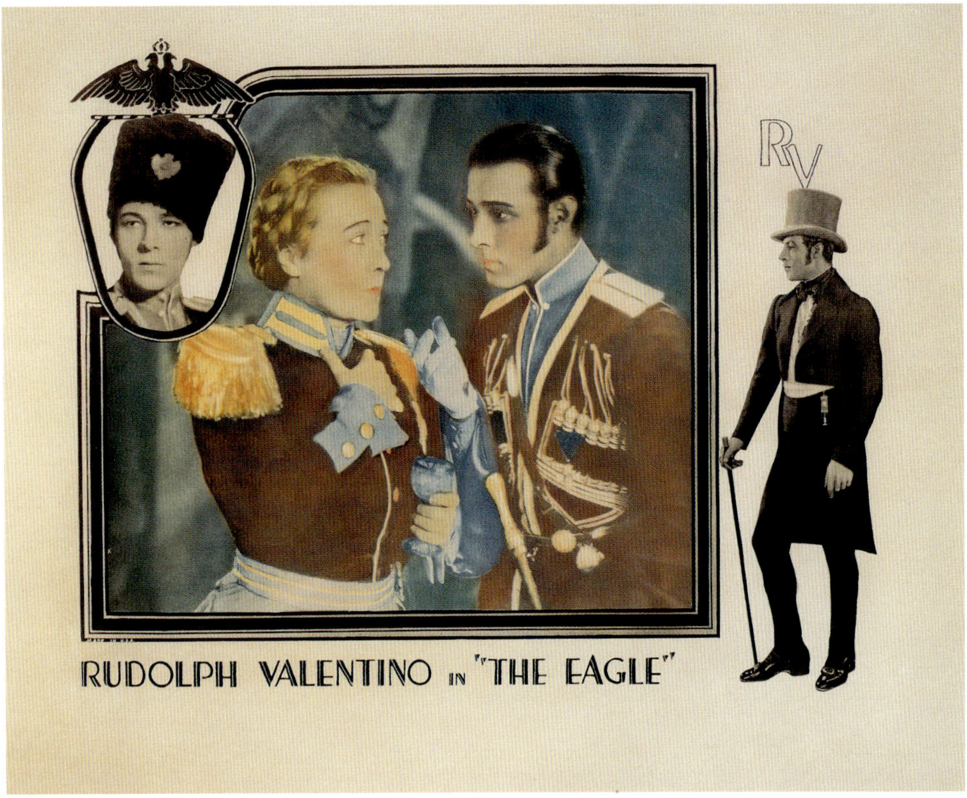

The Eagle. 1925. Half-sheet. $1,000-1,500

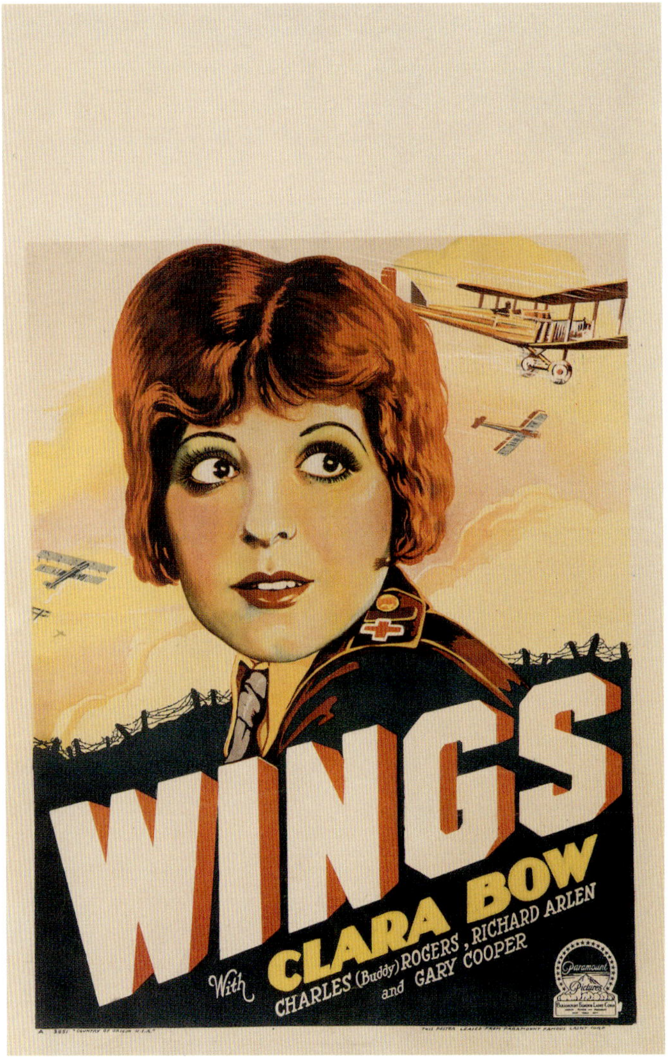

Wings. 1927. Window card. $2,000-2,500

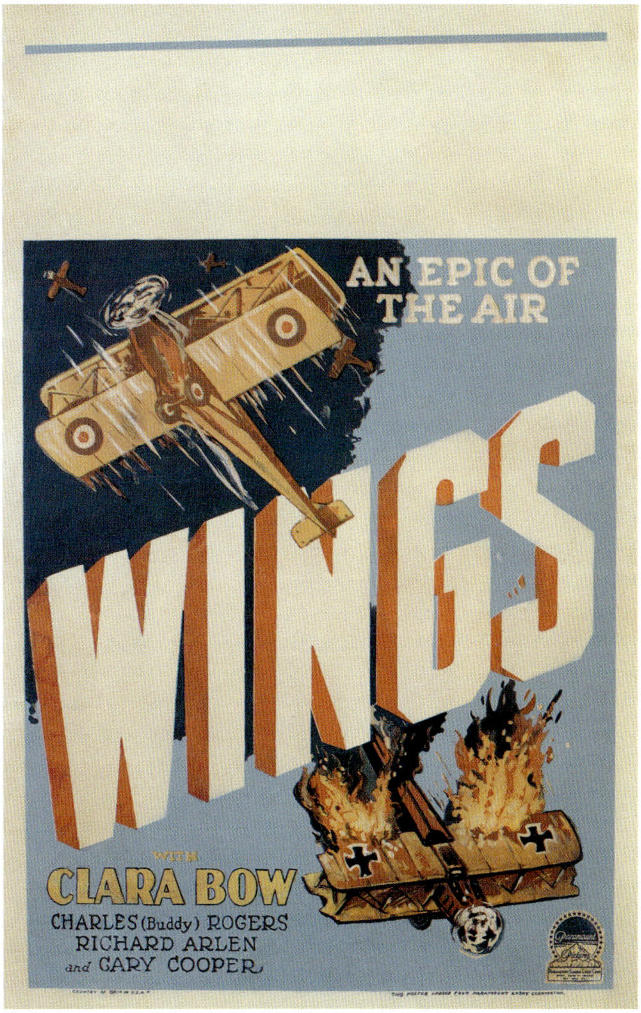

Wings. 1927. Window card. $1,500-2,500

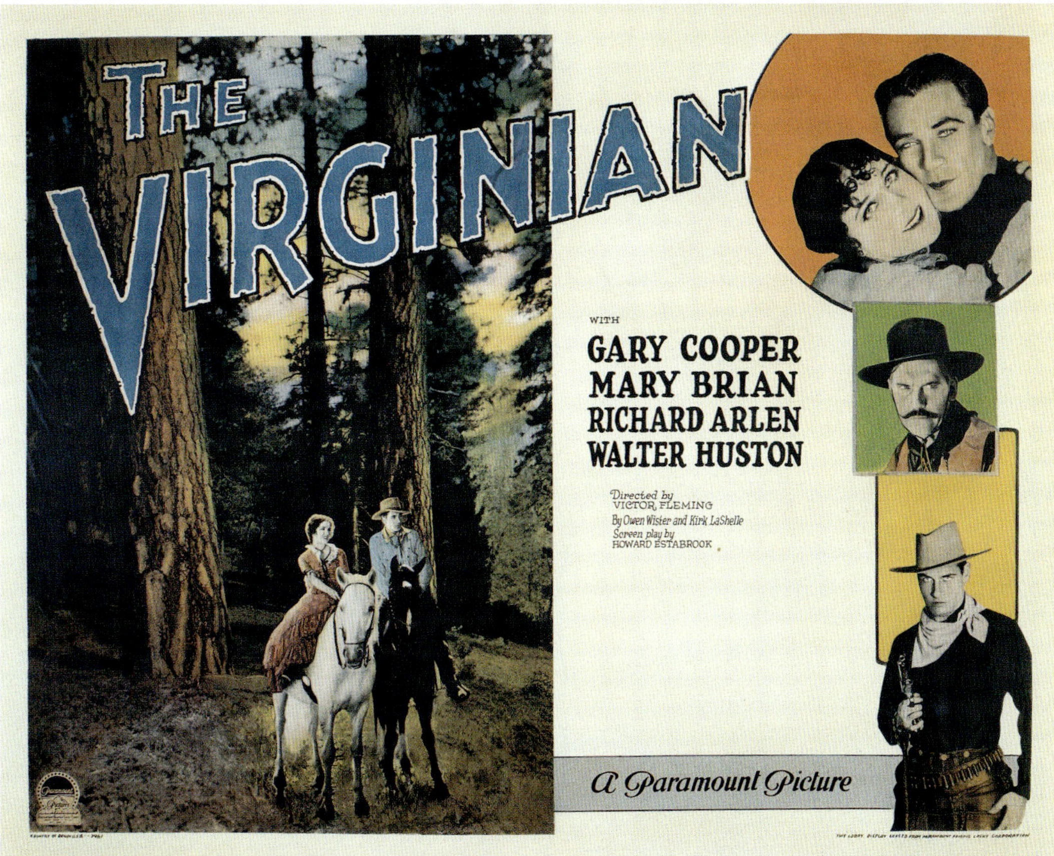

The Virginian. 1929. Half-sheet. $2,000-3,000

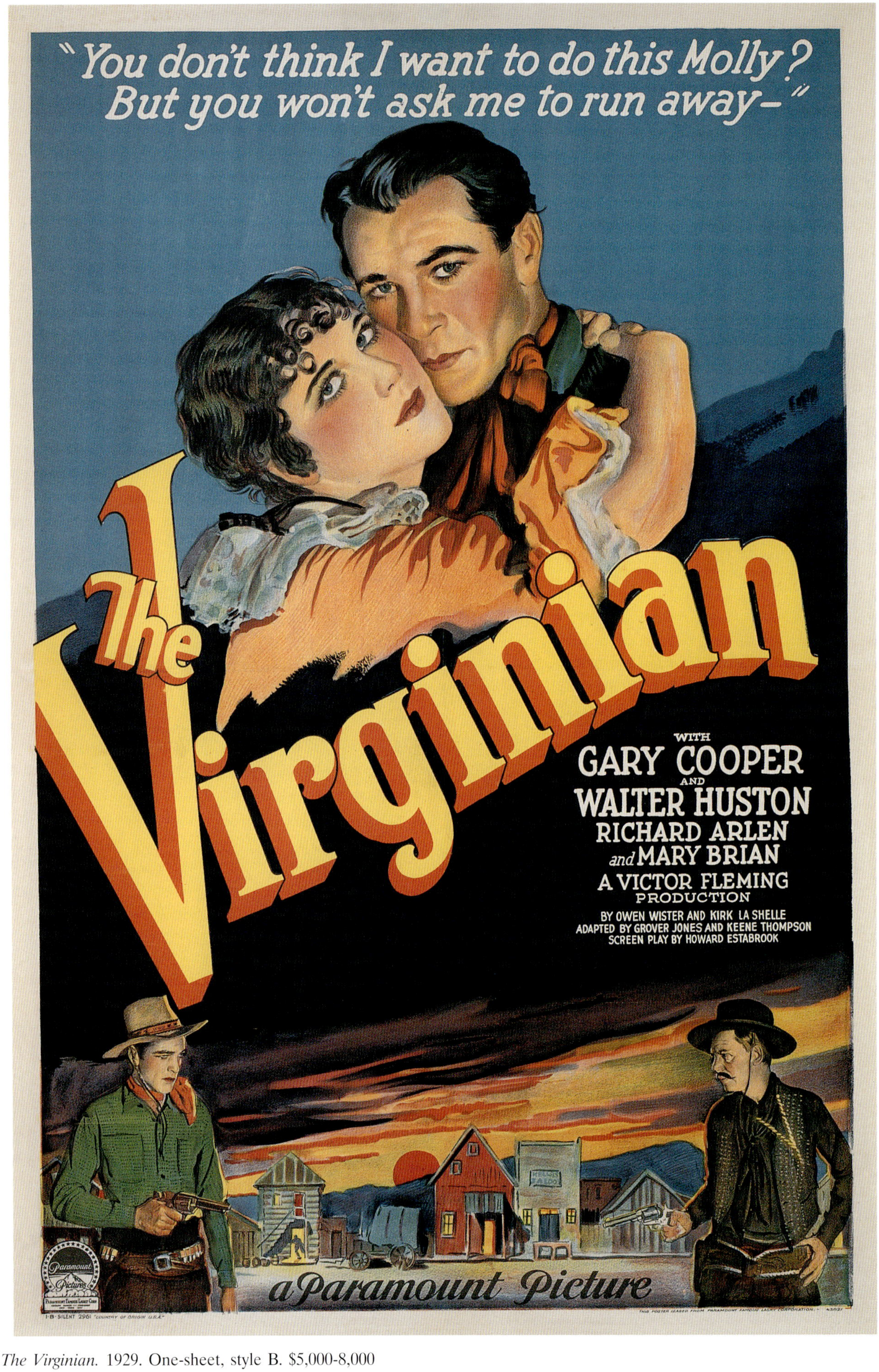

The Virginian. 1929. One-sheet, style B. $5,000-8,000

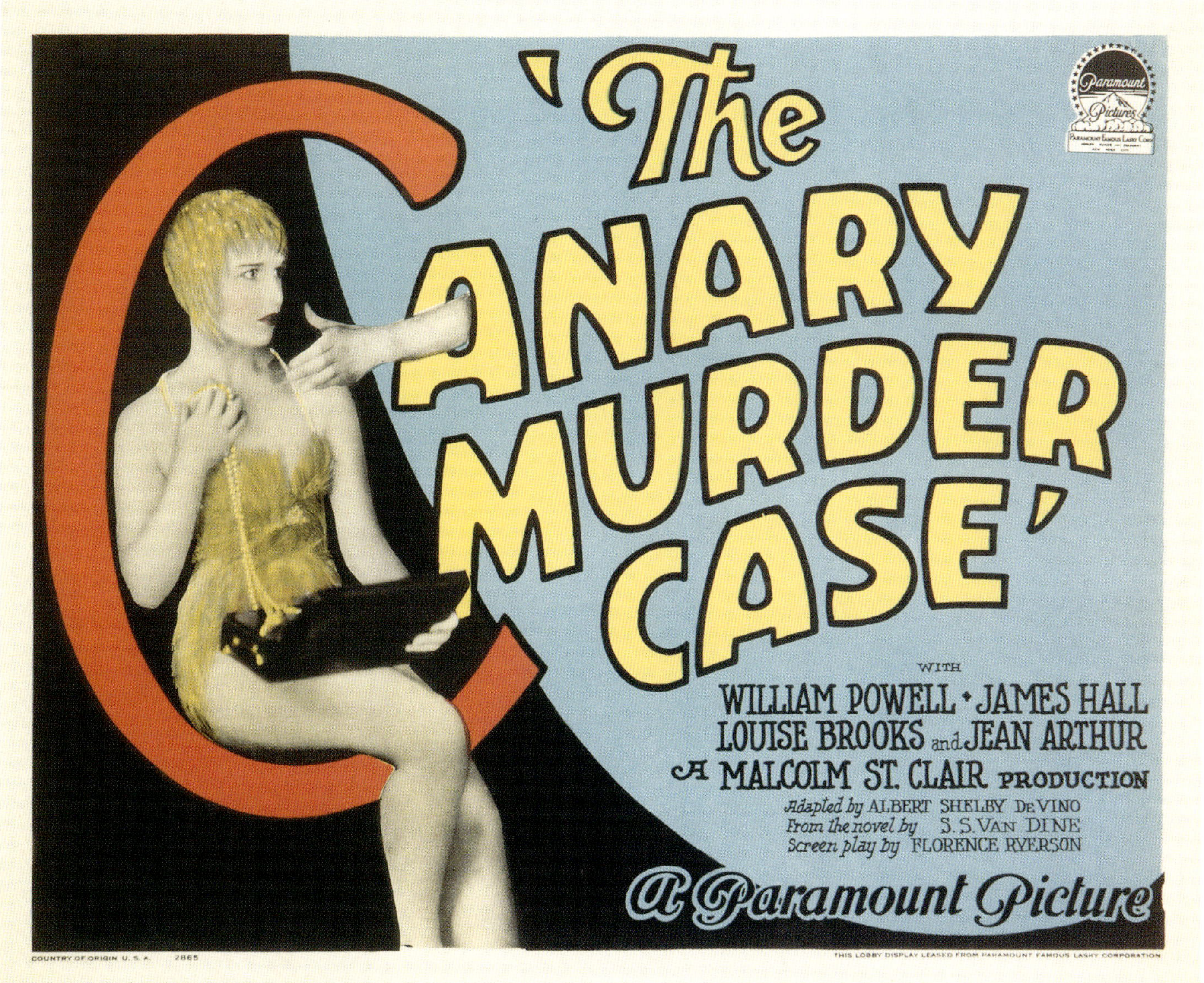

The Canary Murder Case. 1929. Title lobby card. $2,000-3,000.

Chapter Two

Golden Hollywood: The Thirties

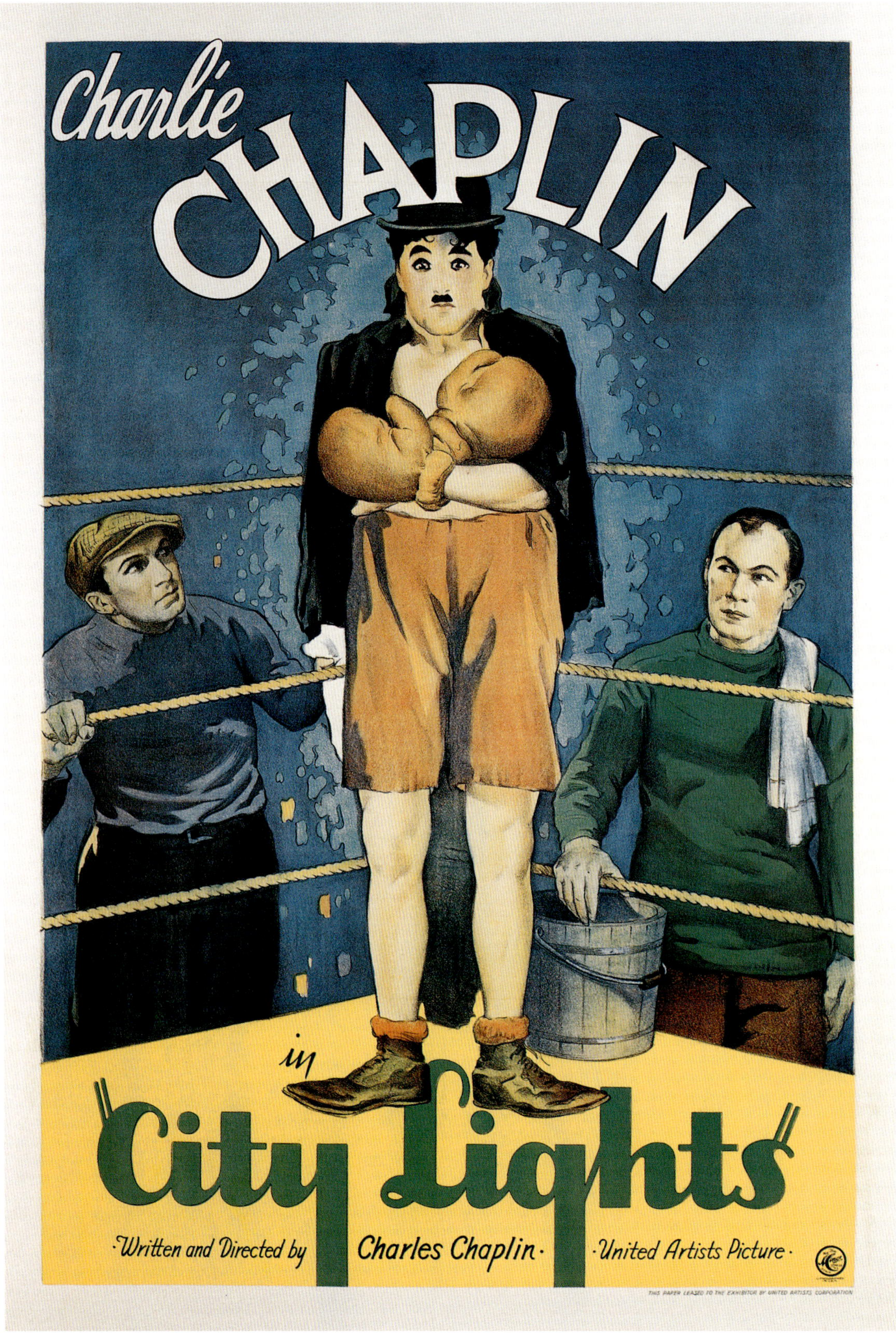

City Lights. 1931. One-sheet. $20,000-30,000.

The 1930s saw the massive expansion of the movie studios in Hollywood and heralded a new era of creativity with the widespread introduction of sound and later color. New major stars were discovered while others found it hard to maintain their status after their voices were heard for the first time. Many were dropped by the big studios, unceremoniously and often unfairly. John Gilbert, the heartthrob of the audiences and Greta Garbo's off-screen lover, was one such star whose fate was sealed by the introduction of sound. With such public humiliation he was soon to turn to drink and sadly met an early death in 1936.

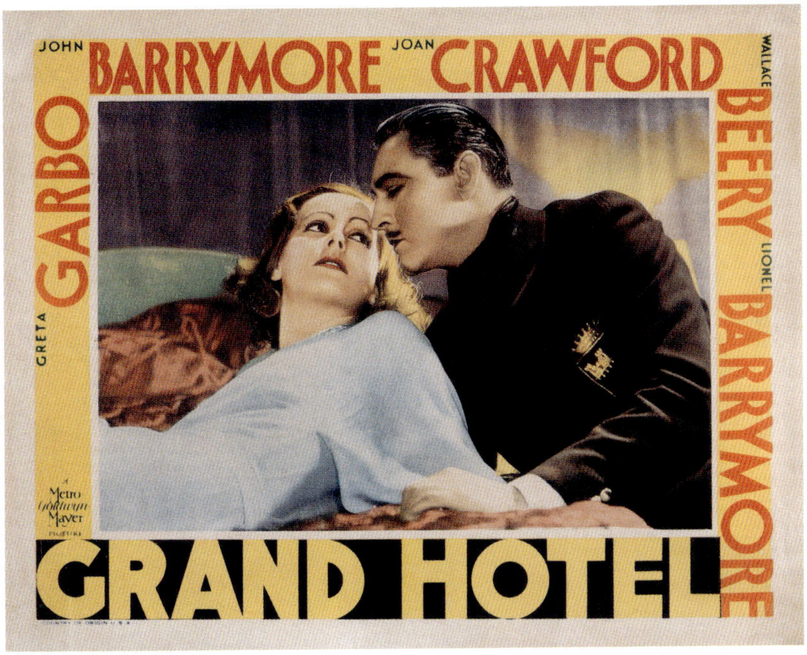

Grand Hotel. 1932. Lobby card. $1,000-1,500.

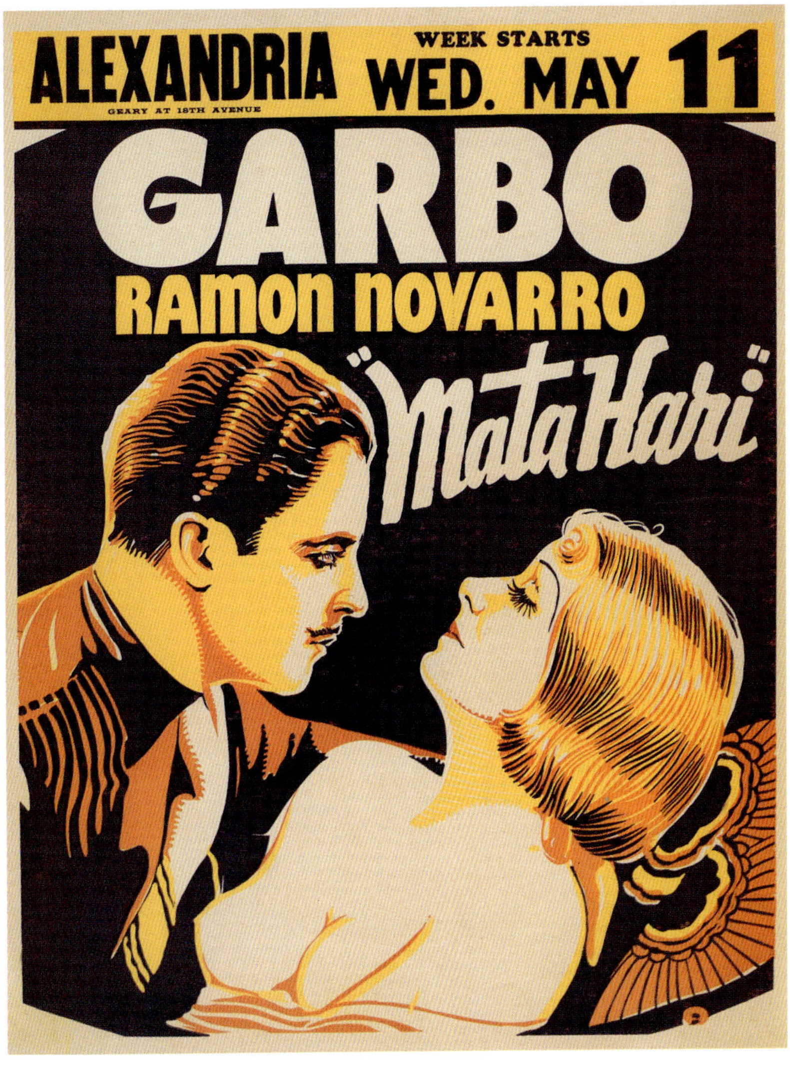

Mata Hari. 1932. Trolley window card. $2,000-2,500.

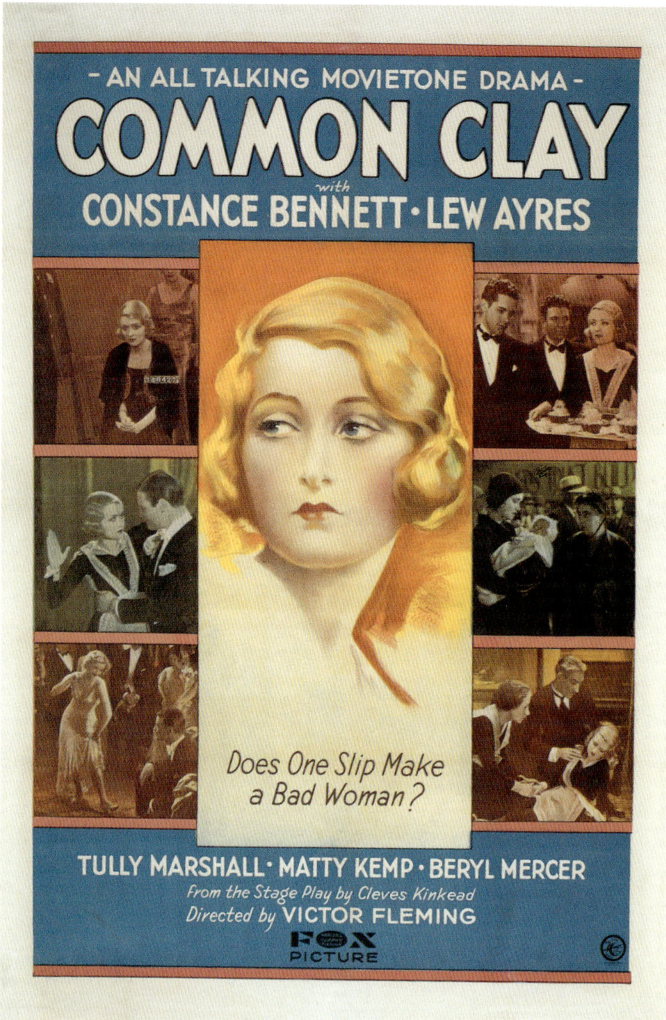

Common Clay. 1930. One-sheet. $1,000-1,500.

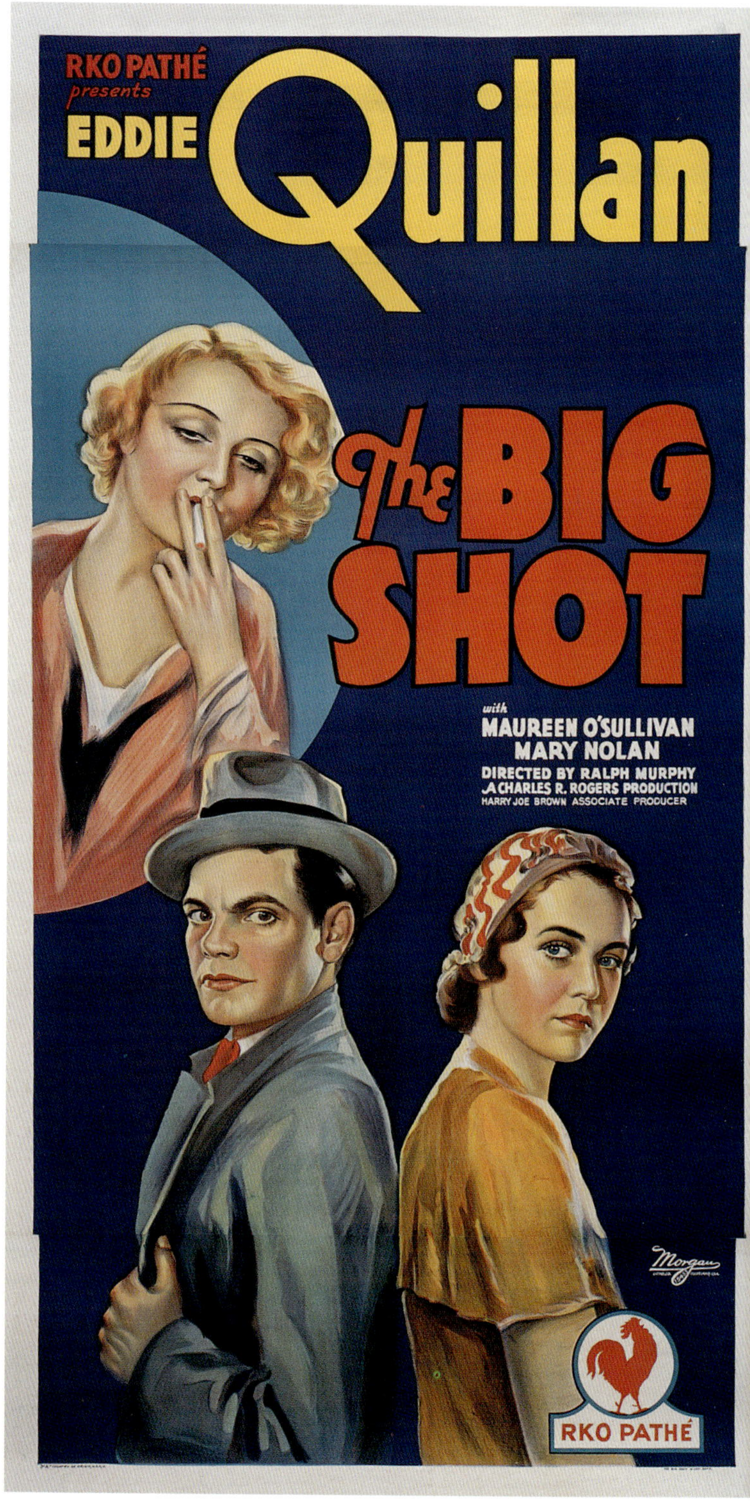

The Big Shot. 1931. Three-sheet. $1,000-1,500.

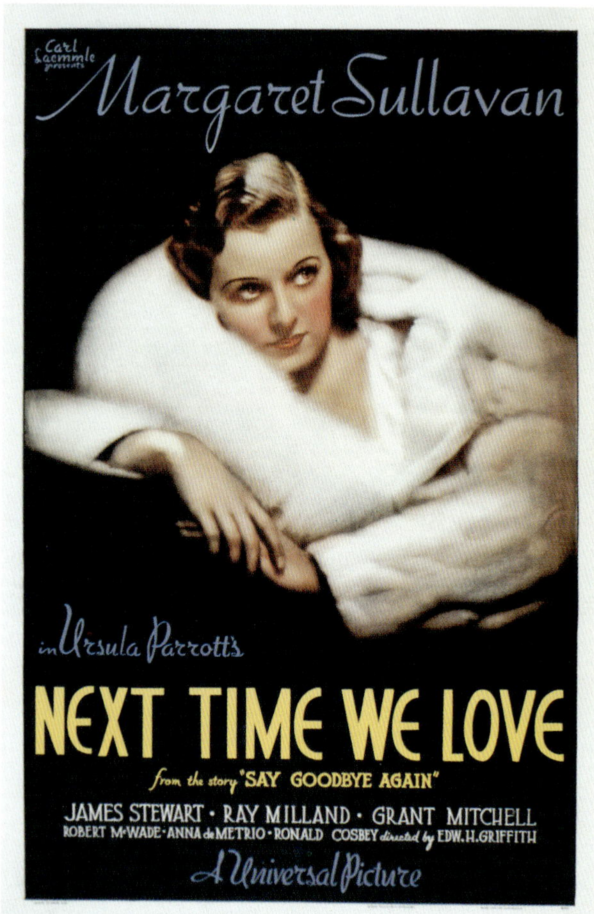

Next Time We Love. 1936.
One-sheet. $1,500-2,000.

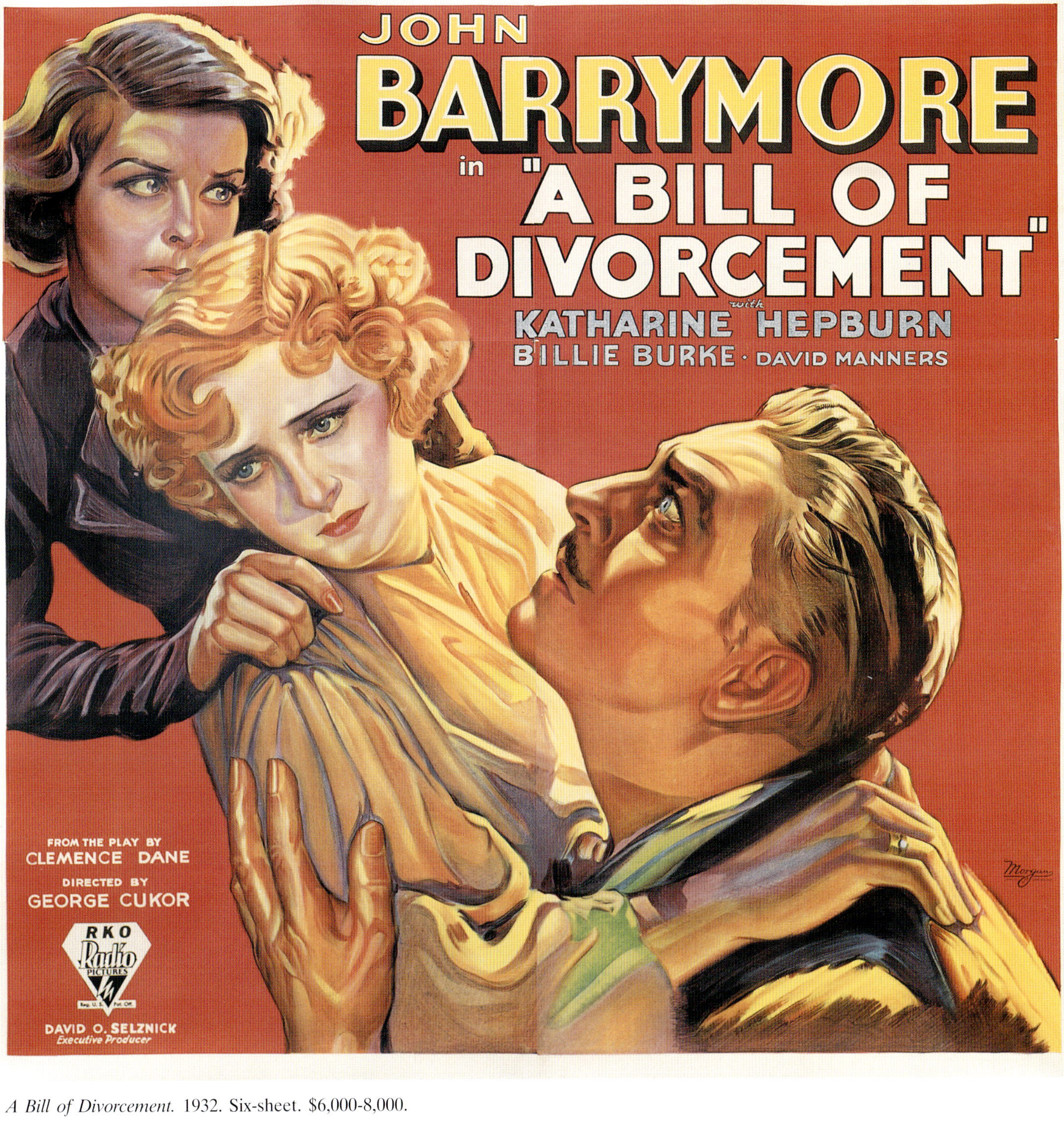

A Bill of Divorcement. 1932. Six-sheet. $6,000-8,000.

The consolidation of the big studios really took place during this decade with Hollywood becoming dominated by seven corporate-style operations that had evolved from various mergers: Columbia, 20th Century-Fox, Metro-Goldwyn-Mayer, Paramount, R.K.O., Universal, and Warner Bros. The notorious absolute control they exerted over actors, directors, writers, and producers seemed just as dictatorial and restrictive as the old Motion Picture Patents Company had been. Yet, having said this, many wonderful films were created within this powerful system and many stars owed their lucrative, glittering, lives to this modern day Mammon.

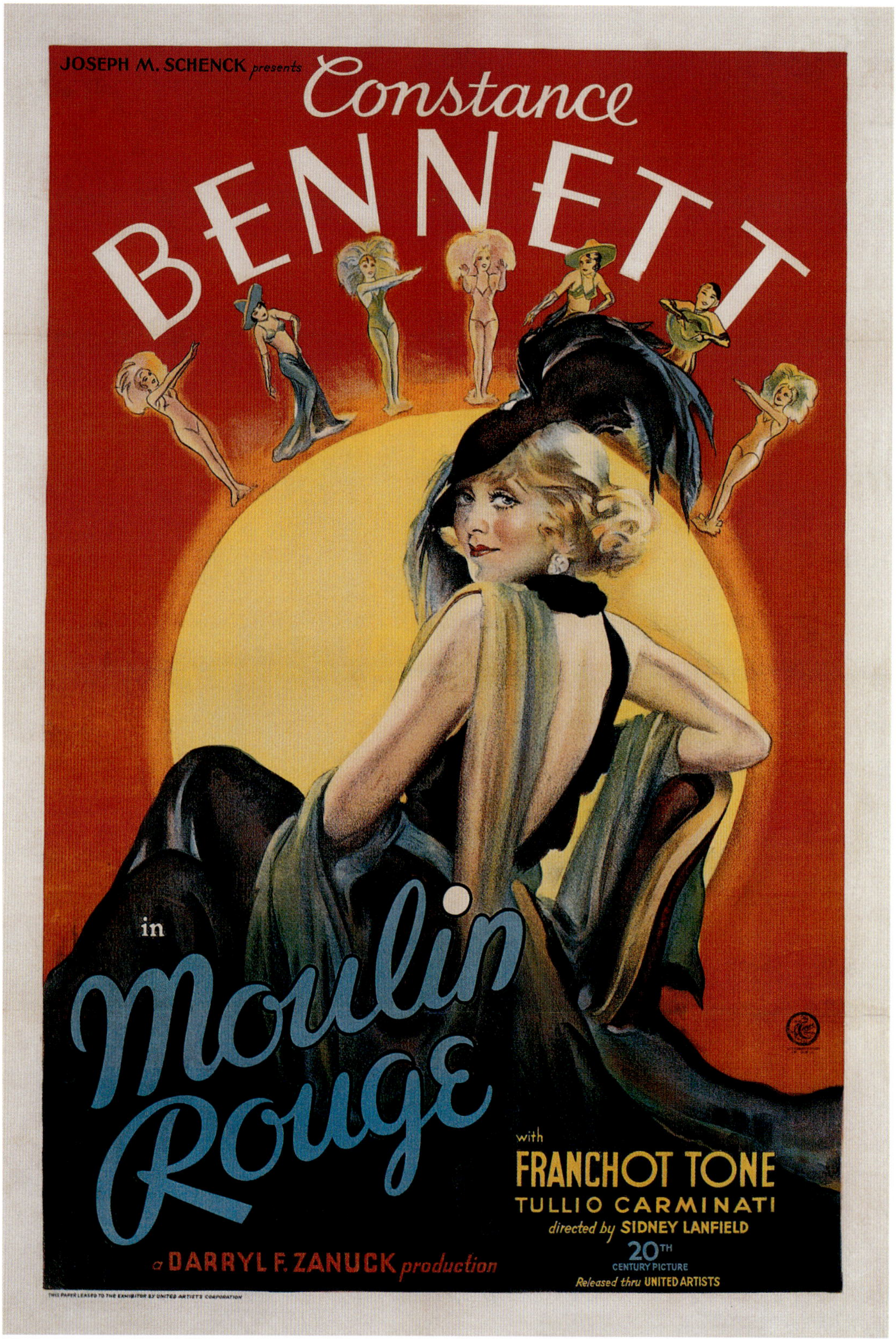

Moulin Rouge. 1934. One-sheet. $3,000-5,000.

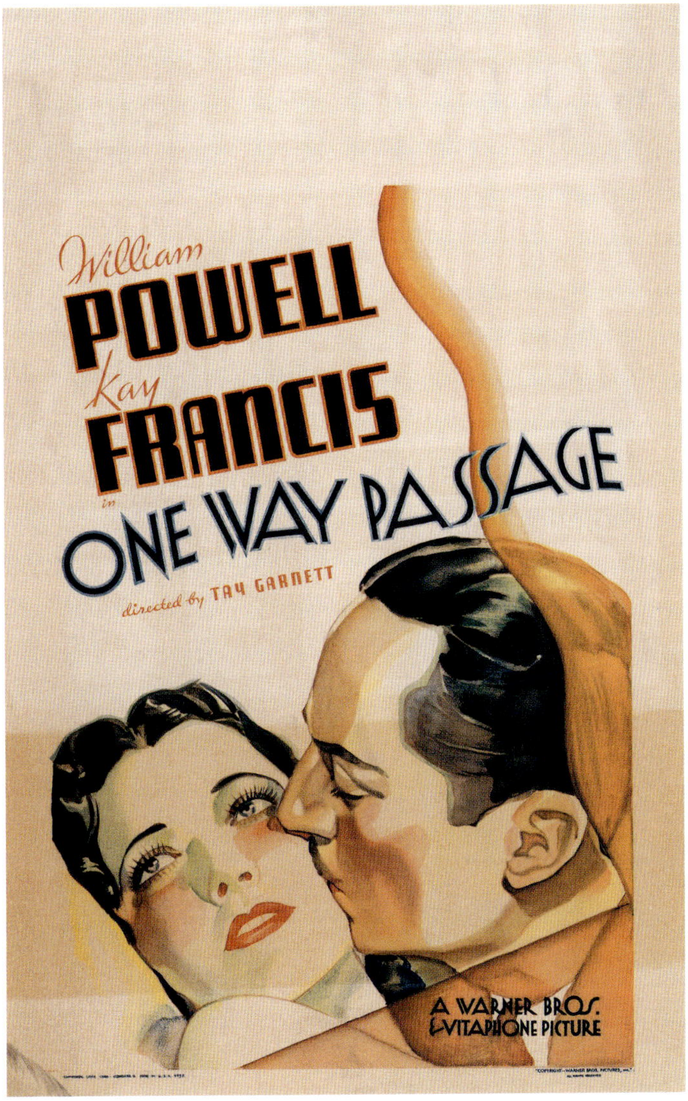

One Way Passage. 1932. Window card. $1,200-1,800.

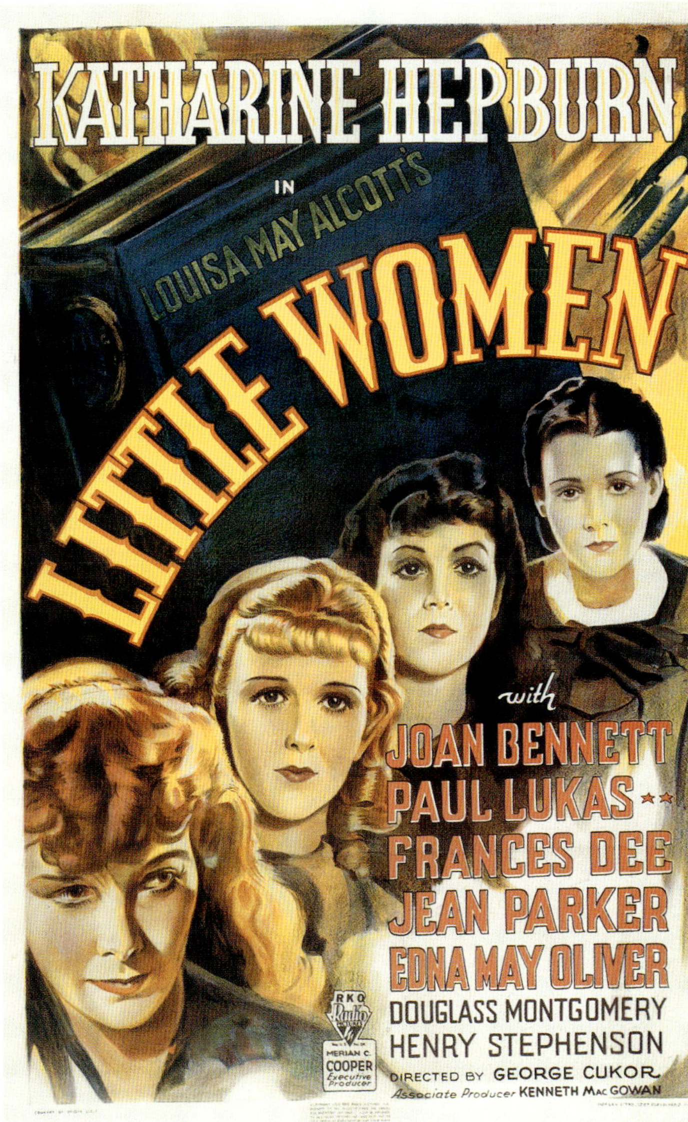

Little Women. 1933. One-sheet. $3,000-4,000

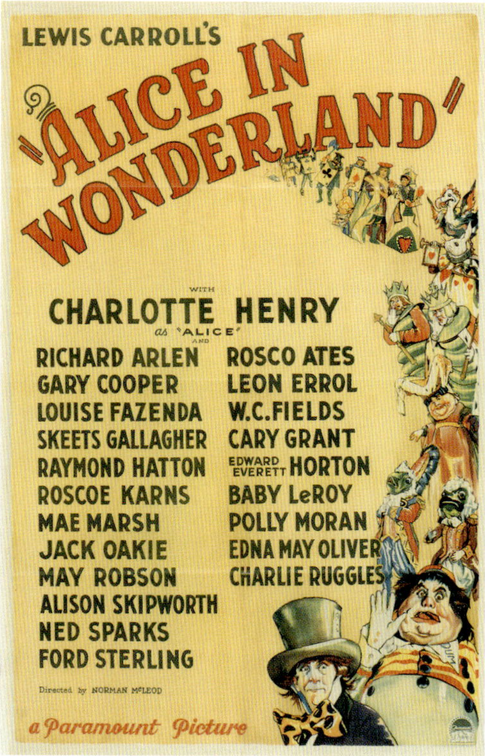

Alice in Wonderland. 1933. One-sheet. $1,000-1,500.

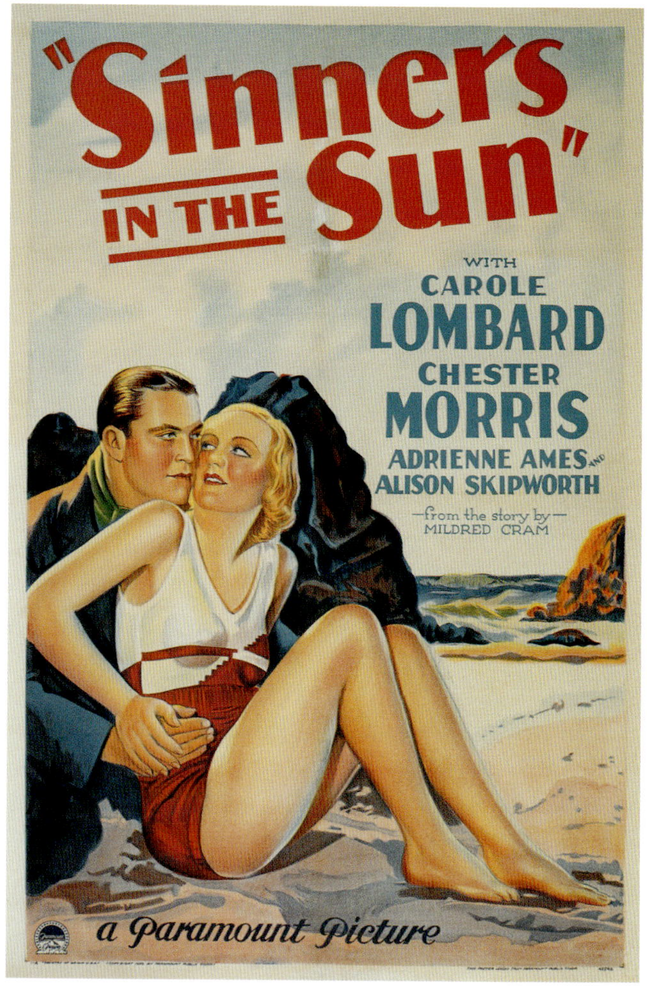

Sinners in the Sun. 1932. One-sheet. $1,500-2,500.

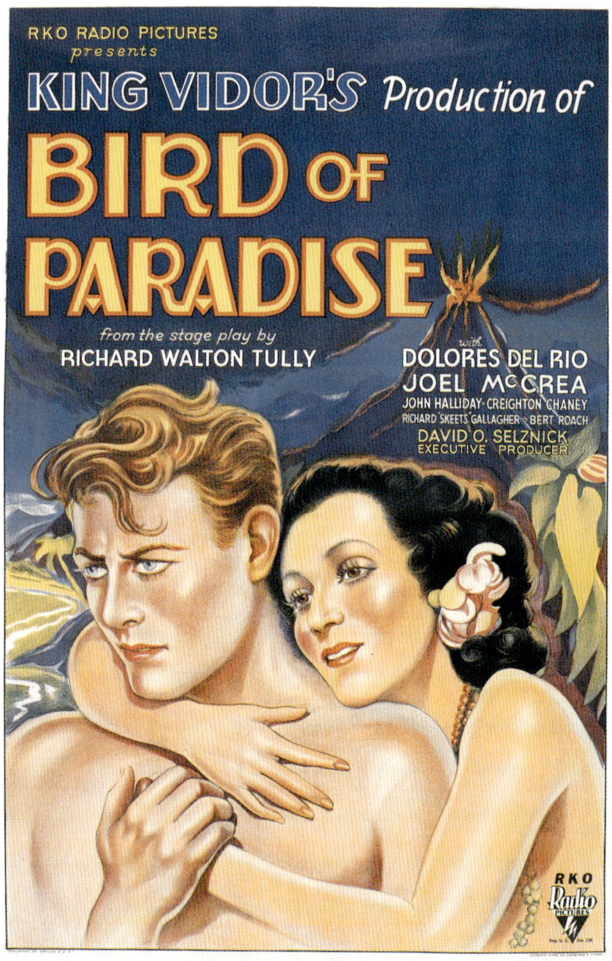

Bird of Paradise. 1932. One-sheet. $1,500 - $2,500.

During this Depression decade, many studios were forced to make dramatic cuts. Audience attendances, however, were not as bad as might be expected and there seemed to be the belief that the movies were one good way to hide from the harsh realities of life. The studios responded to this by producing a vast variety of glamorous escapist pictures that have become recognized as hallmarks of "the golden age of Hollywood."

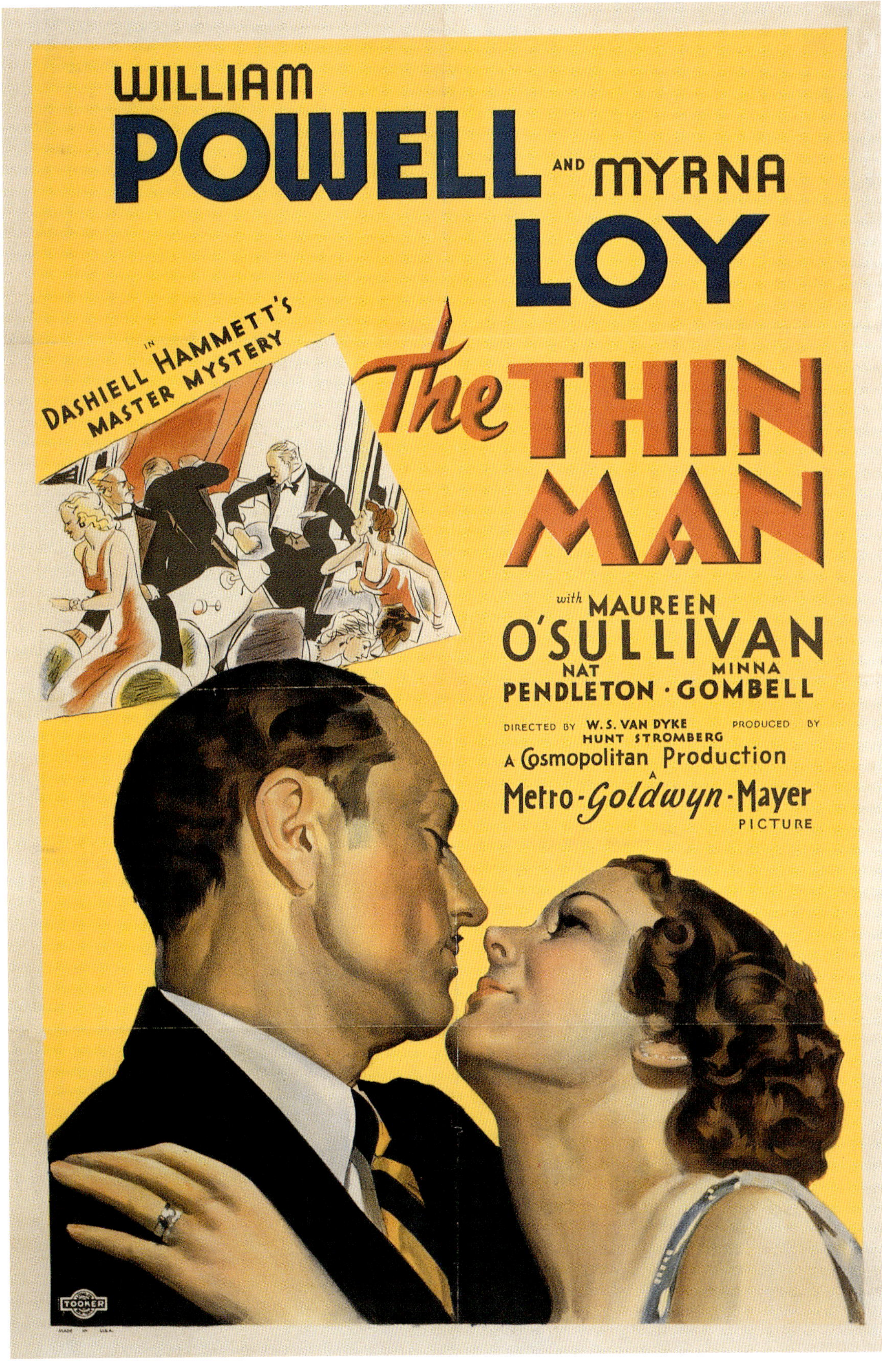

The Thin Man. 1932.
One-sheet, style D.
$10,000-15,000.

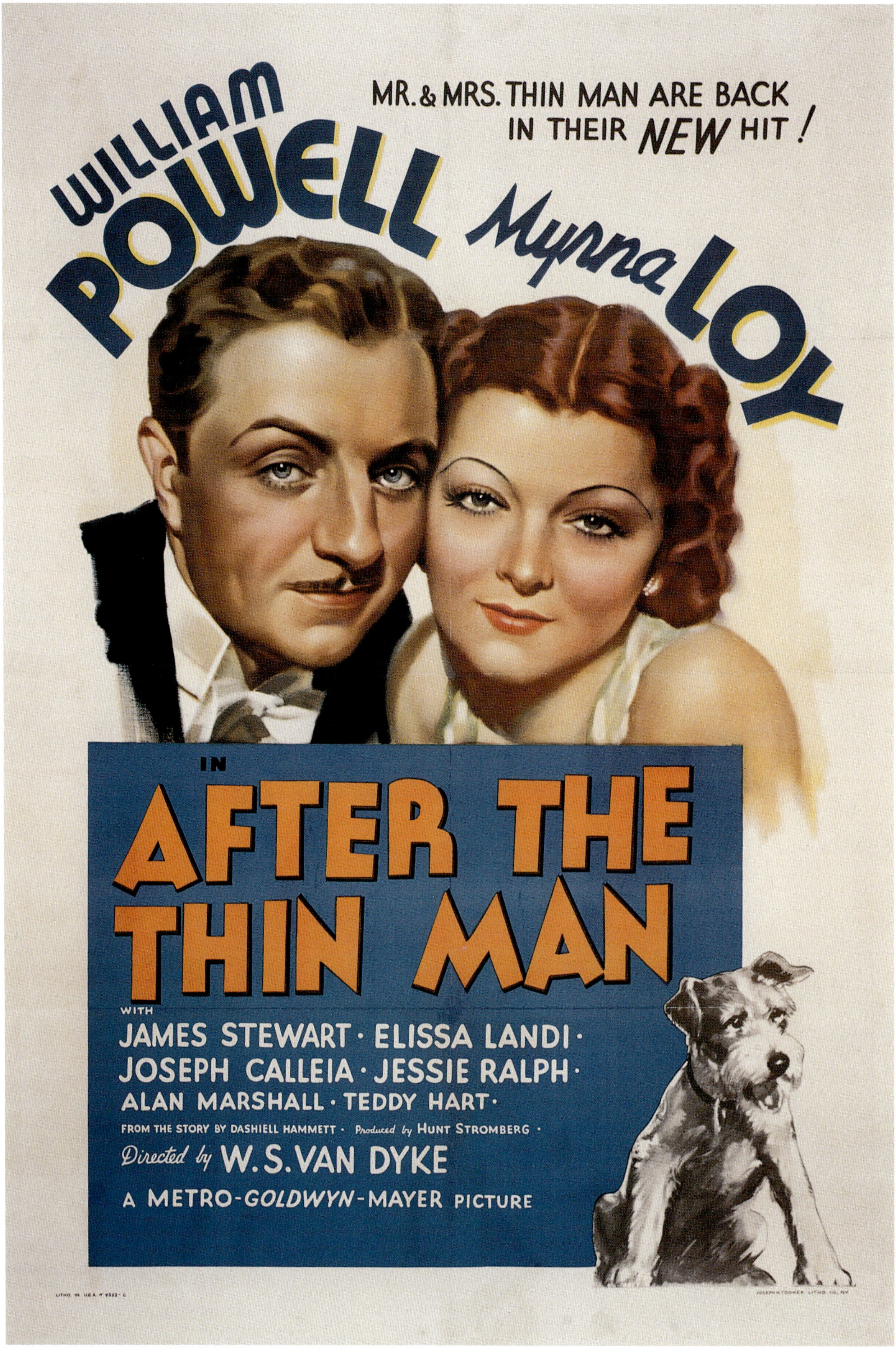

After The Thin Man. 1936. One-sheet, style C. $4,000-6,000

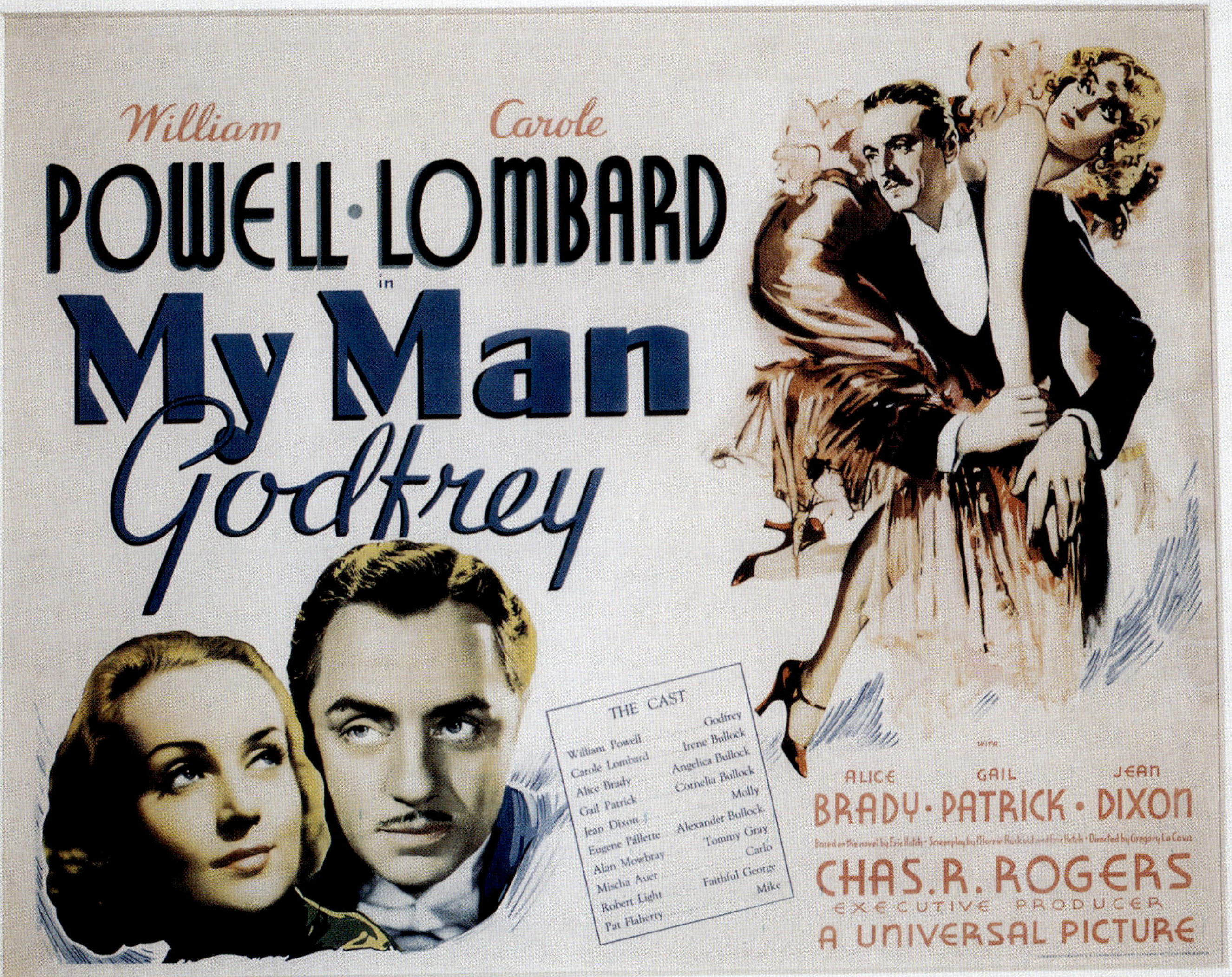

My Man Godfrey. 1936. Half-sheet. $2,000-3,500.

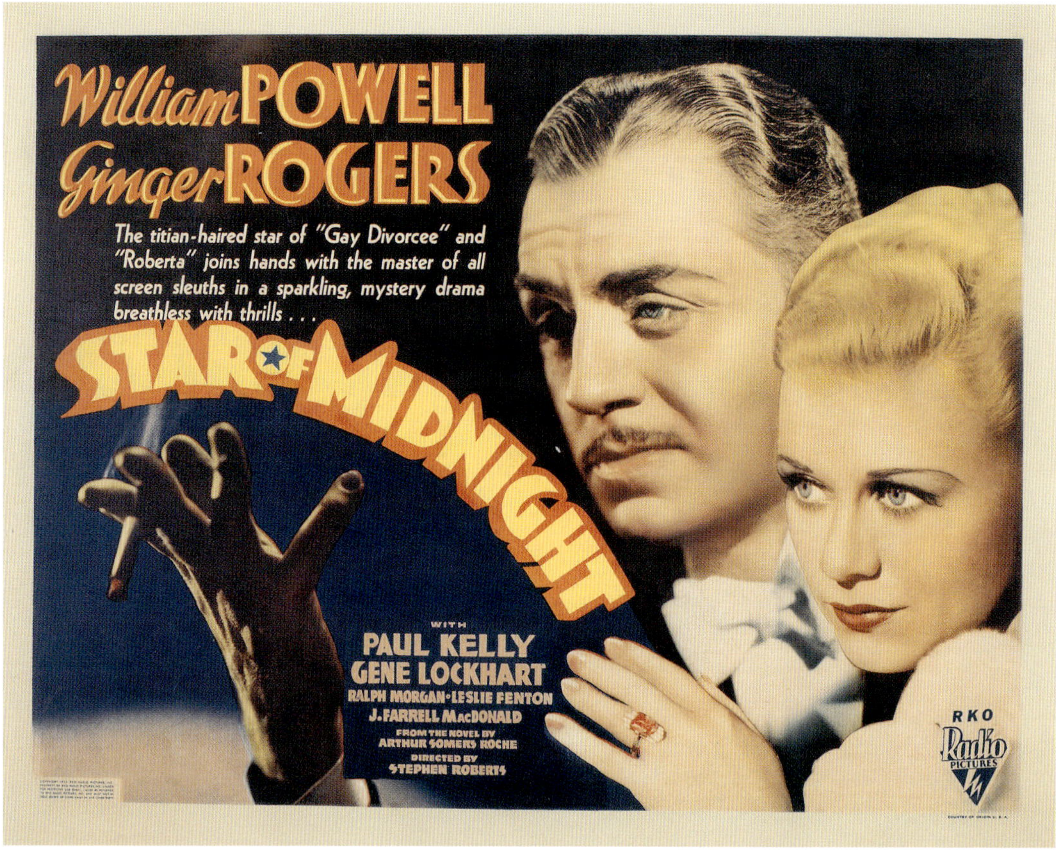

Star of Midnight. 1935. Half-sheet. $1,200-1,800.

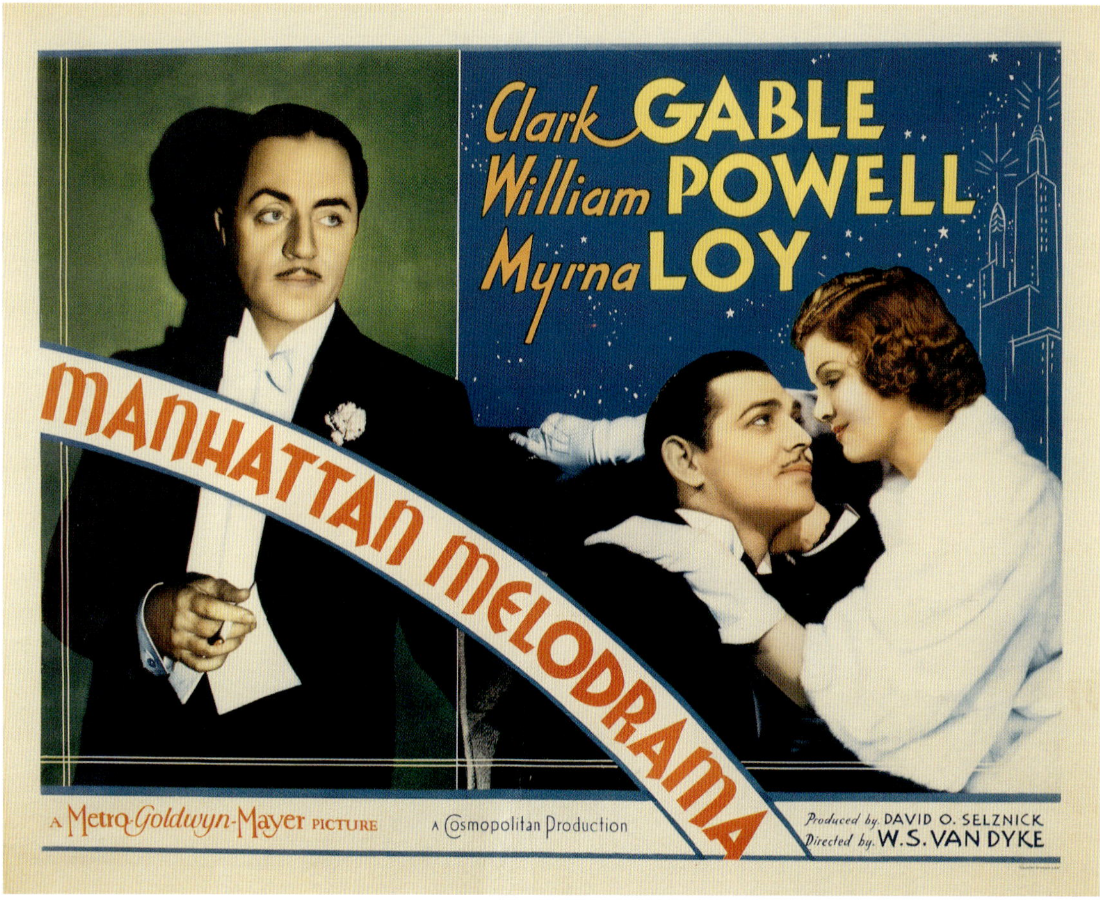

Manhattan Melodrama. 1934. Half-sheet. $2,000-3,000.

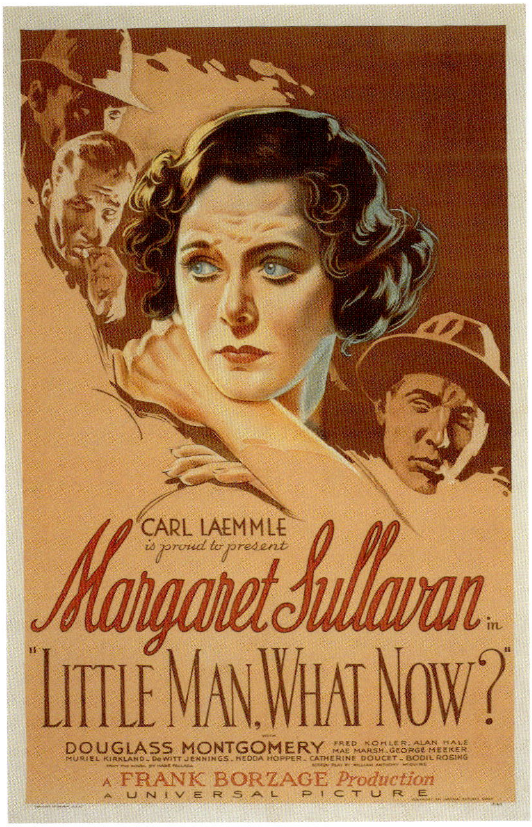

Little Man, What Now? 1934.
One-sheet. $1,500-2,000.

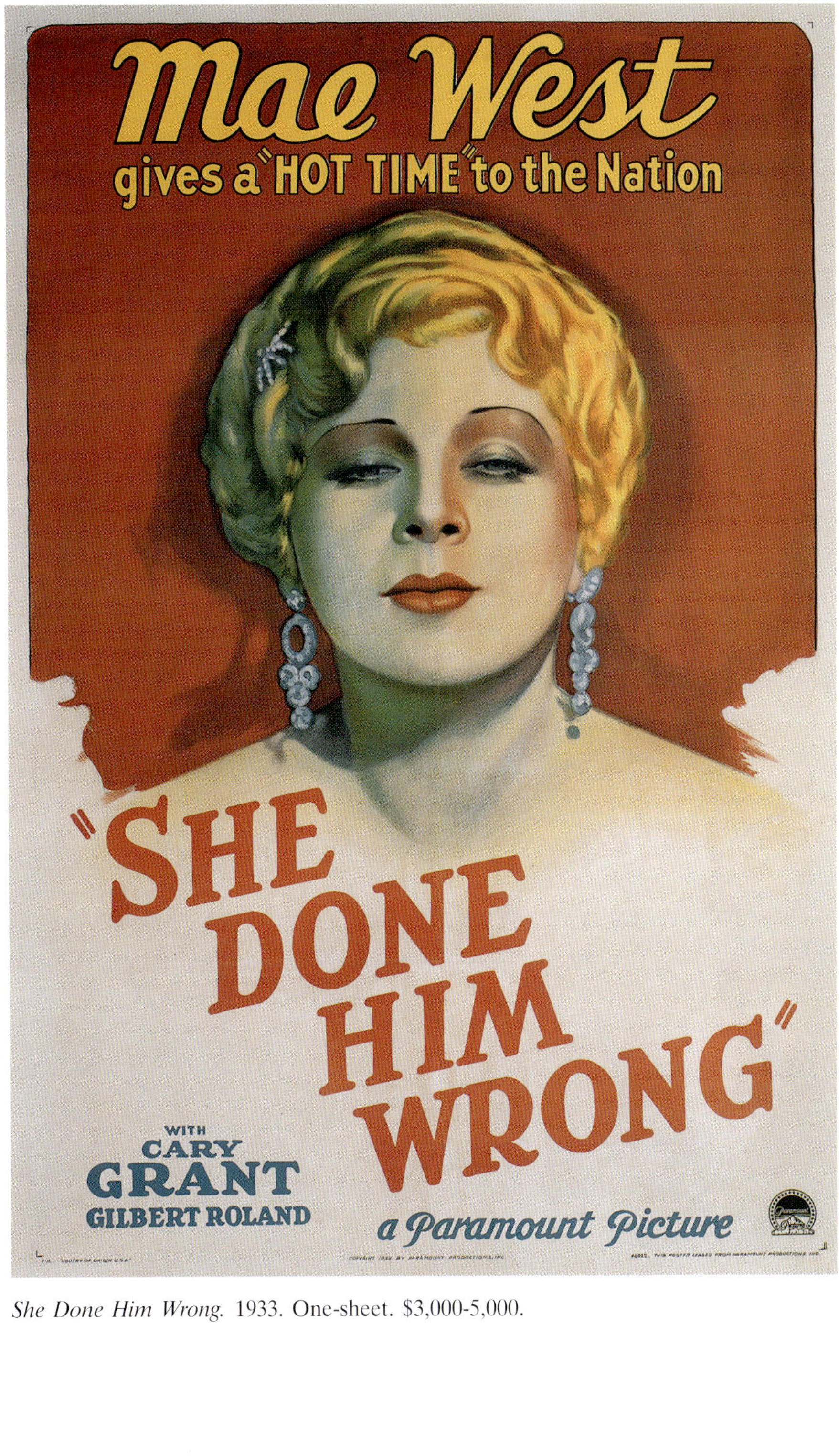

She Done Him Wrong. 1933. One-sheet. $3,000-5,000.

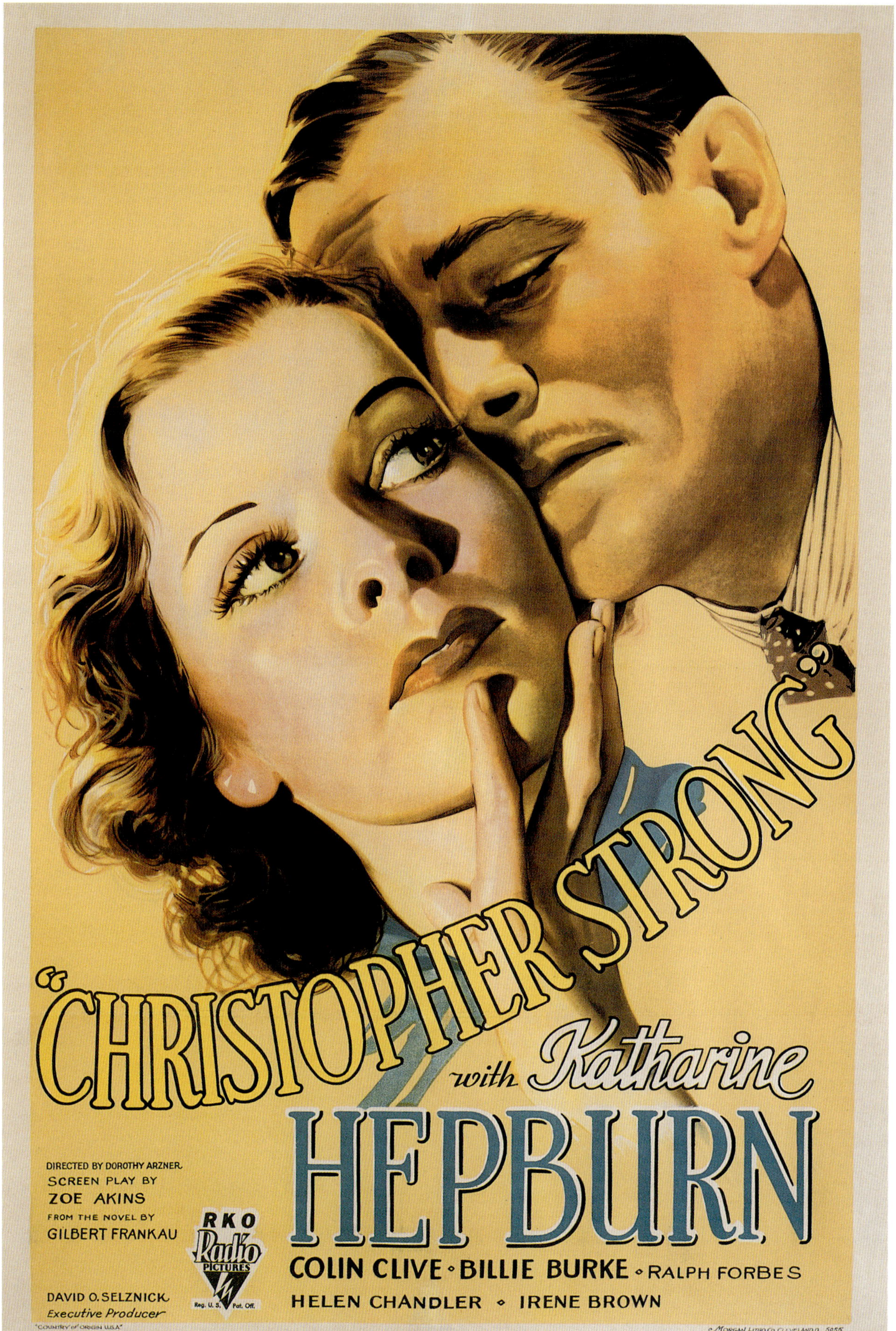

Christopher Strong. 1933. One-sheet. $2,500-3,500.

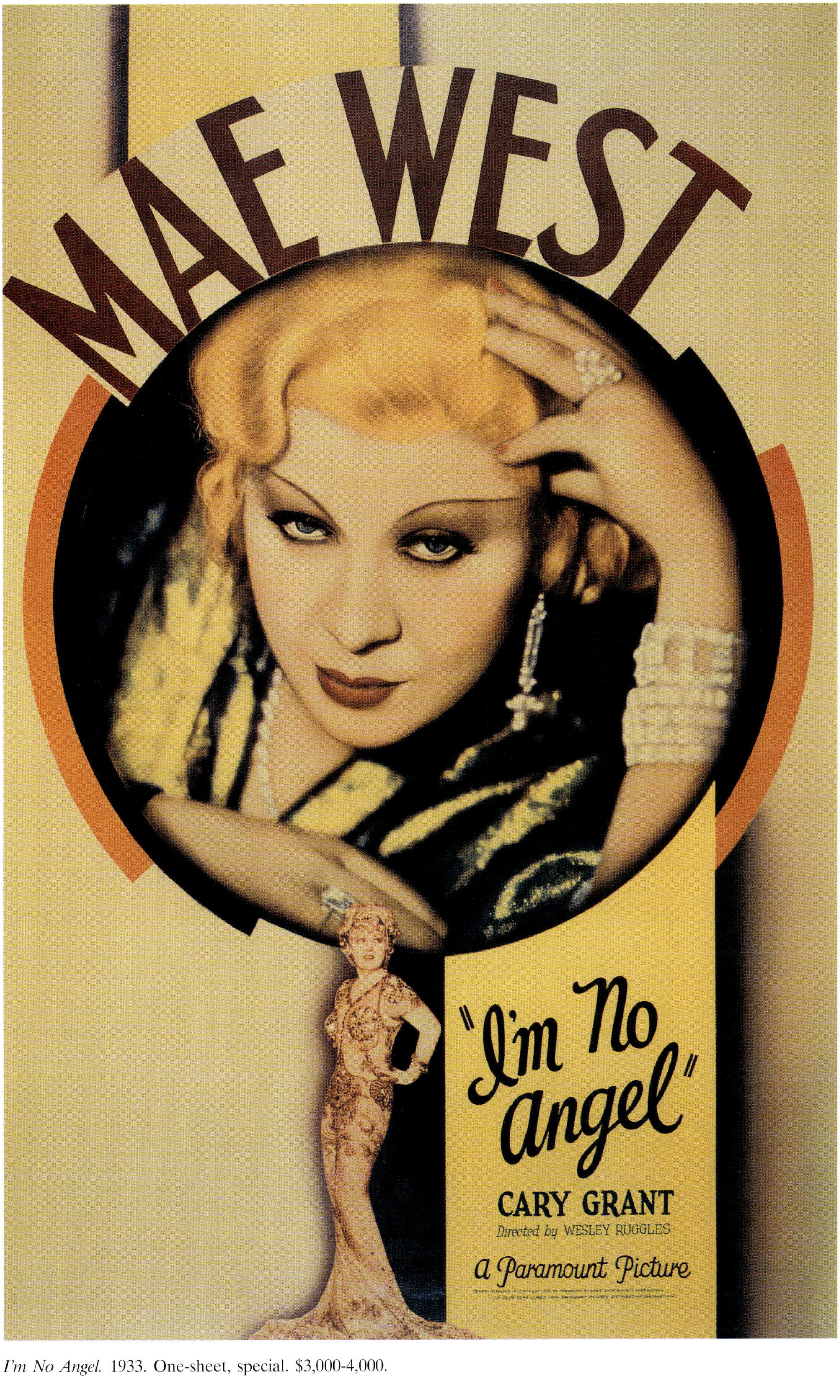

I'm No Angel. 1933. One-sheet, special. $3,000-4,000.

It is no coincidence that during this time Frank Capra at Columbia directed a host of movies that appealed to a broad audience hungry for sentimental fairy-tale stories often asserting the underlying goodness of the common man. Such populist fare included *It Happened One Night* (1934), *Mr. Deeds Goes To Town* (1936), *Lost Horizon* (1937) and *Mr. Smith Goes To Washington* (1939).

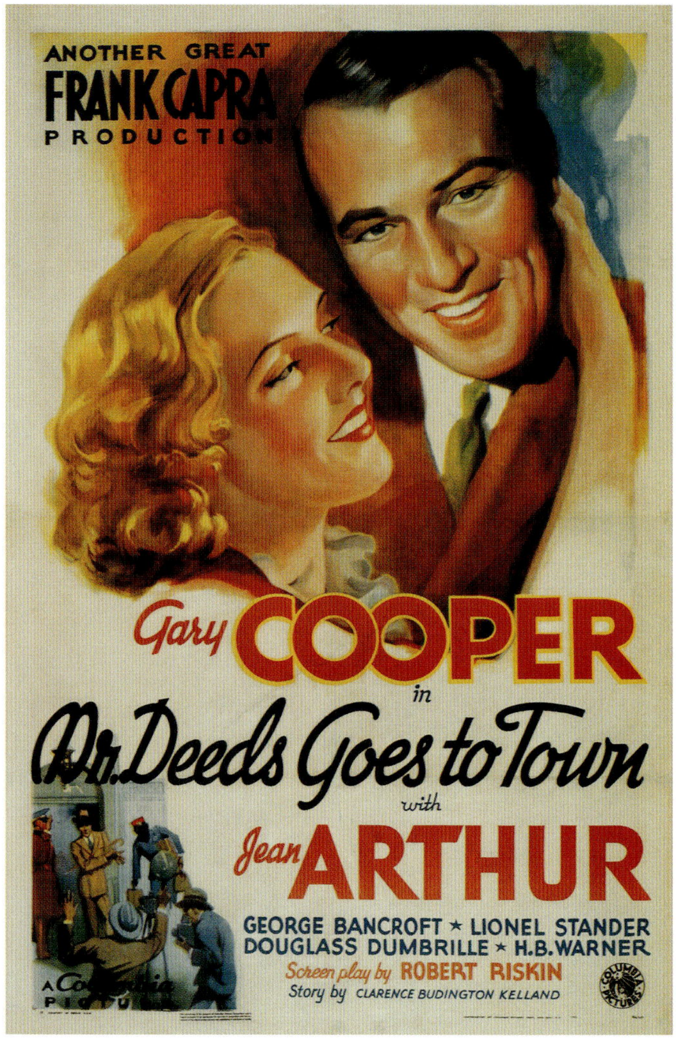

Mr. Deeds Goes to Town. 1936. One-sheet. $4,000-6,000

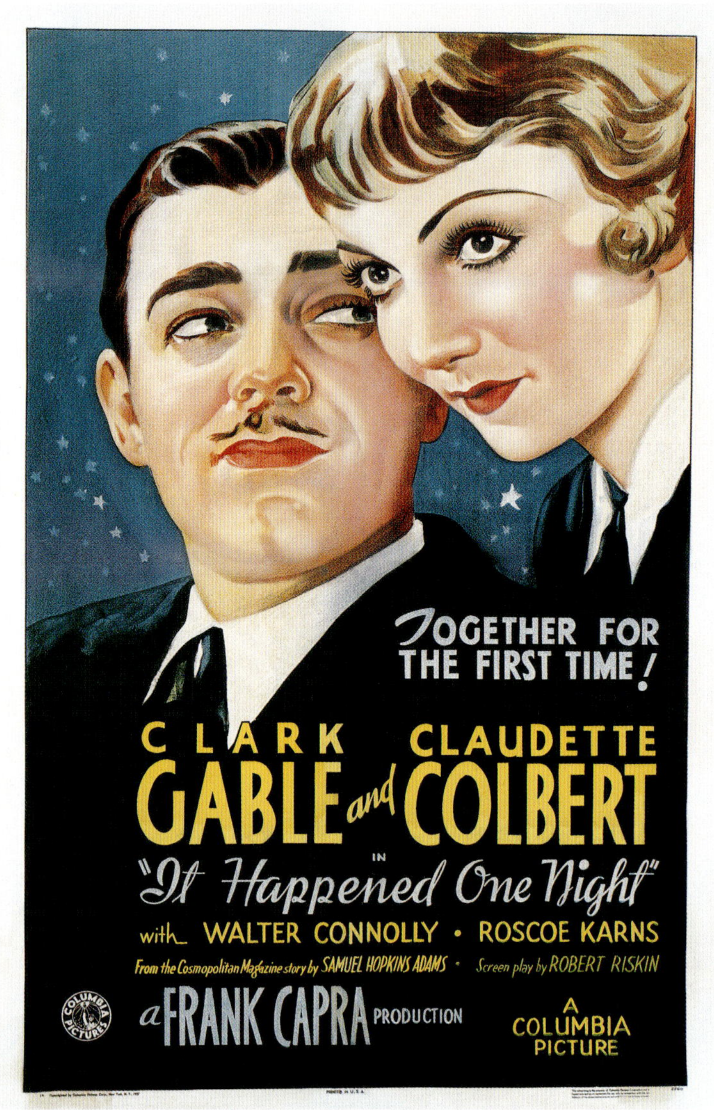

It Happened One Night. 1937. One-sheet, re-release, style B. $1,500-2,500.

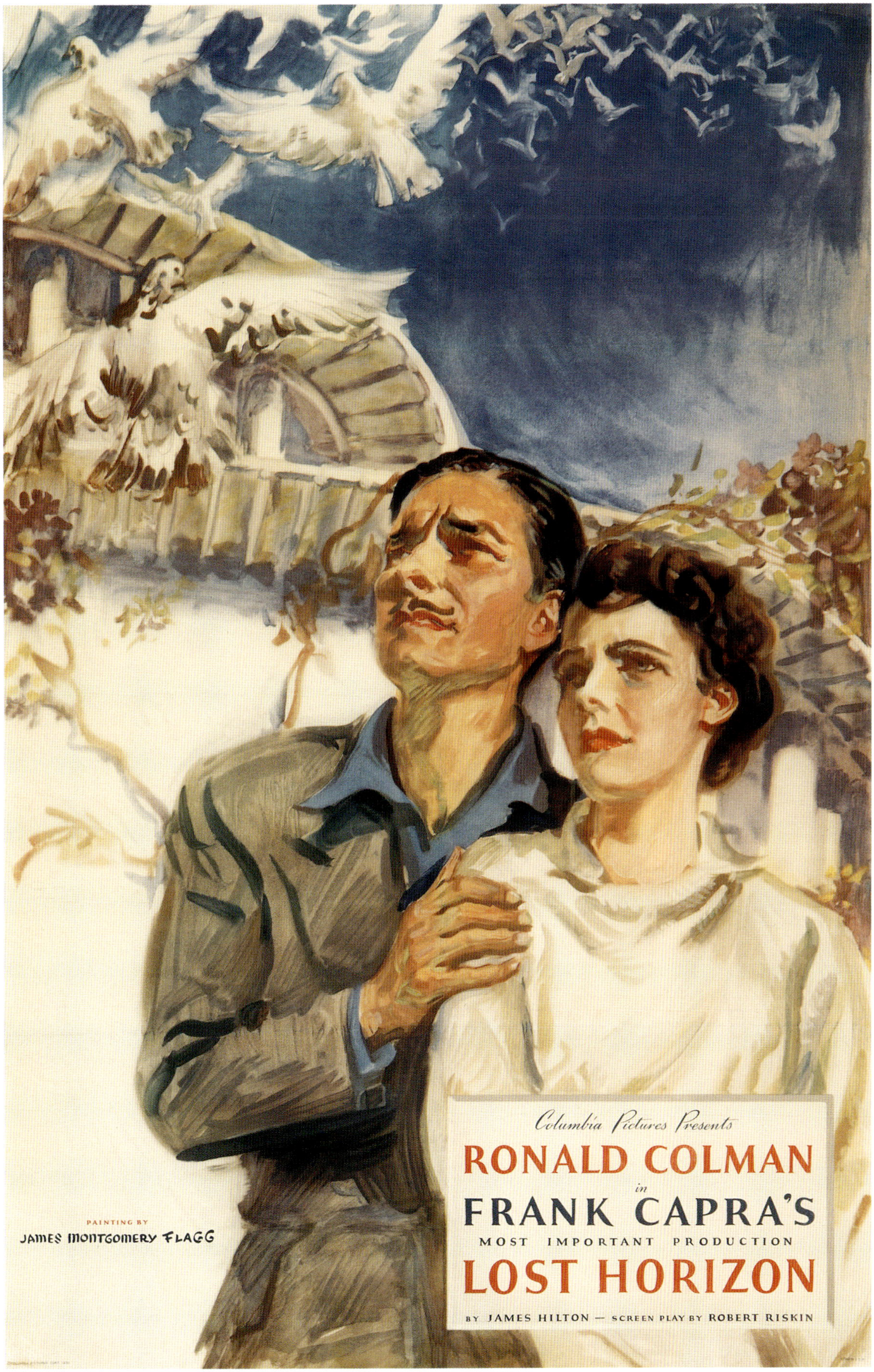

Lost Horizon. 1937. One-sheet, style D, art by James Montgomery-Flagg. $7,000-10,000.

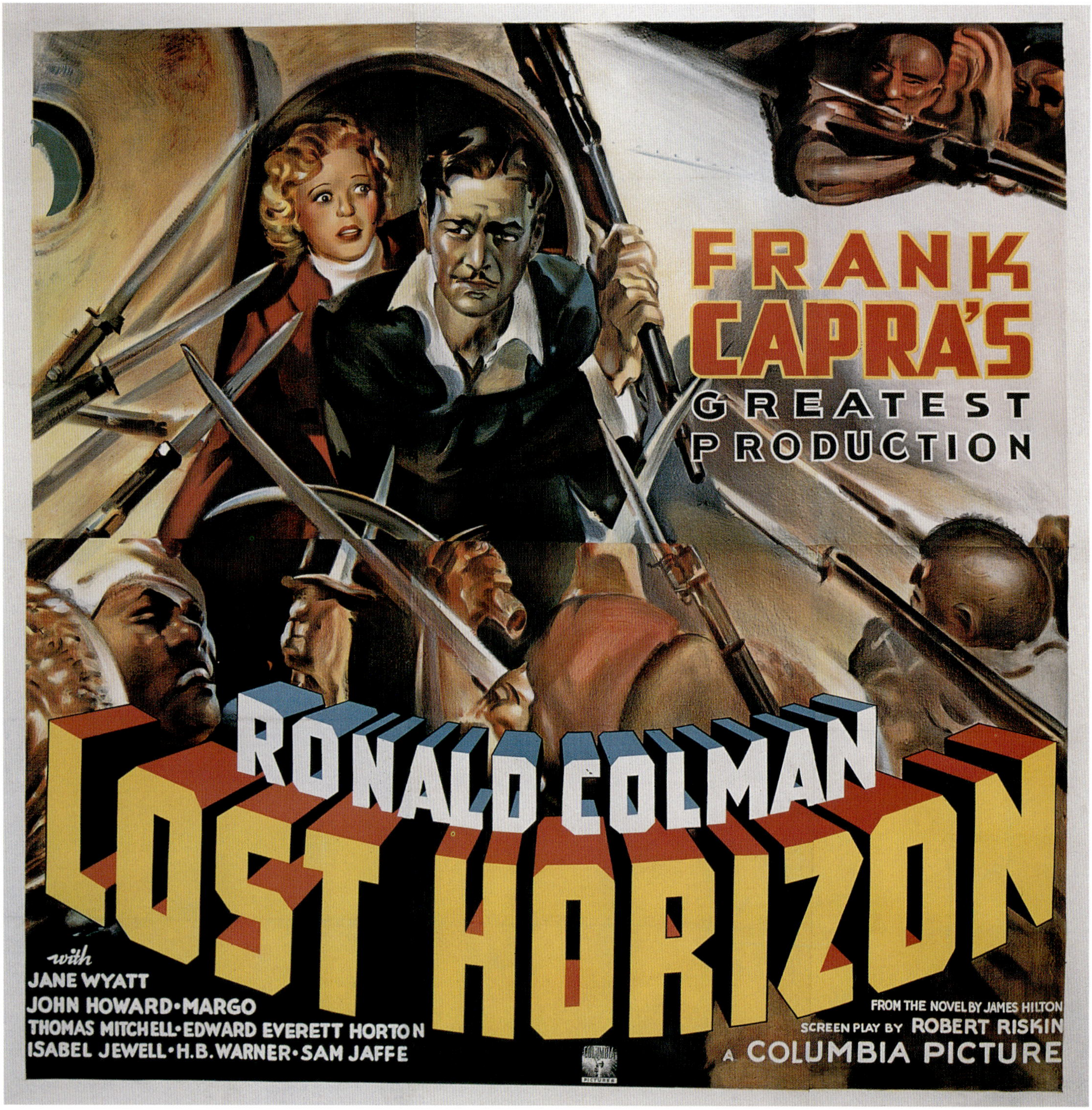

Lost Horizon. 1937. Six-sheet, art by James Montgomery-Flagg. $20,000-30,000.

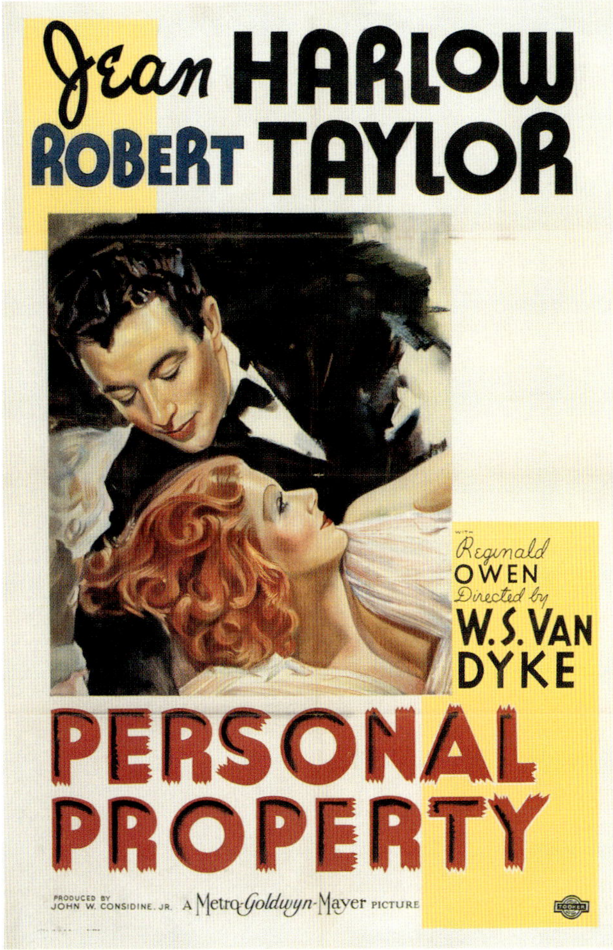

Personal Property. 1937. One-sheet, style C. $1,000-1,500.

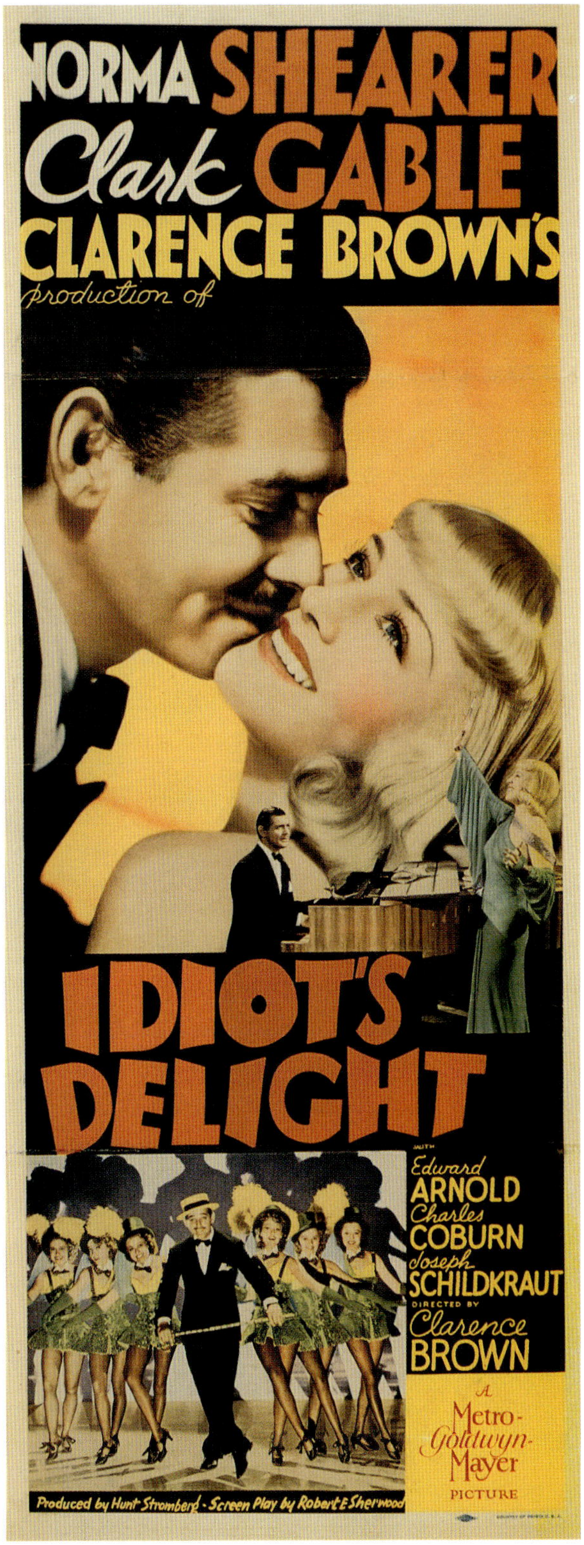

Idiot's Delight. 1939. Insert. $800-1,200

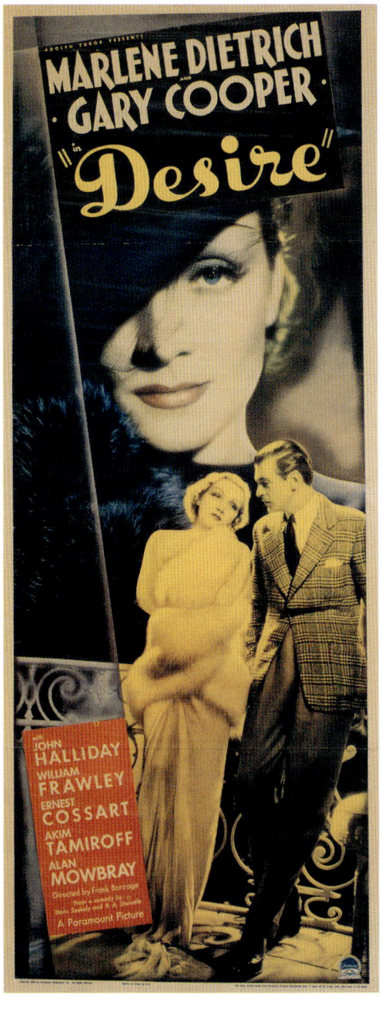

Desire. 1936. Insert. $1,000-1,500.

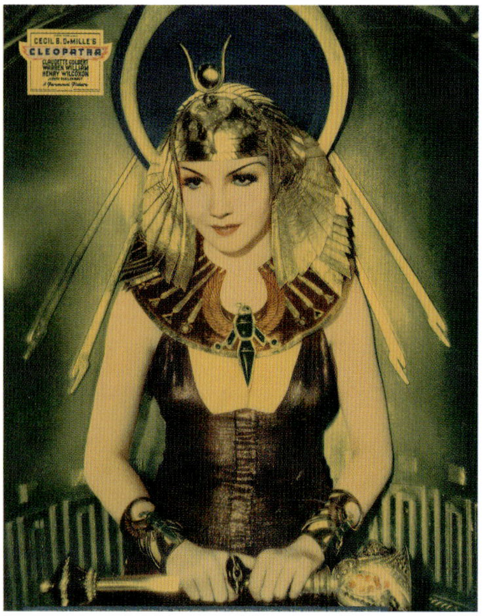

Cleopatra. 1934. Jumbo lobby card. $800-1,200

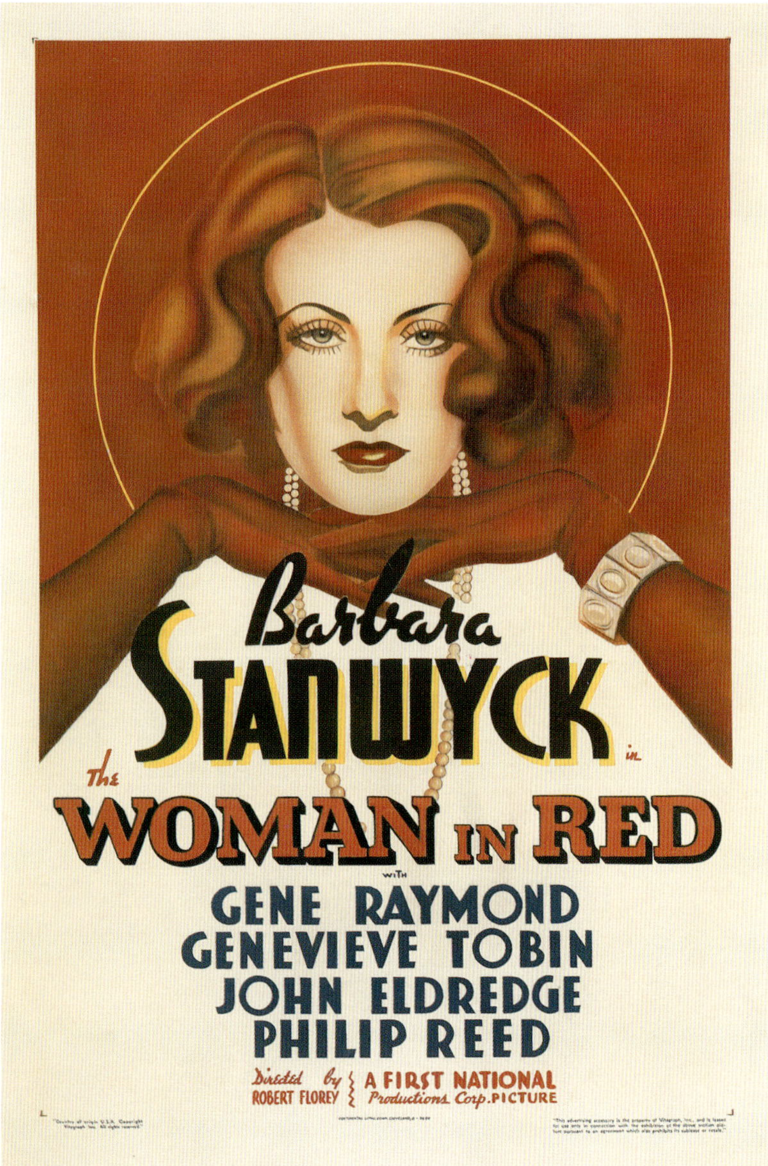

Woman In Red. 1935. One-sheet. $4,000-6,000.

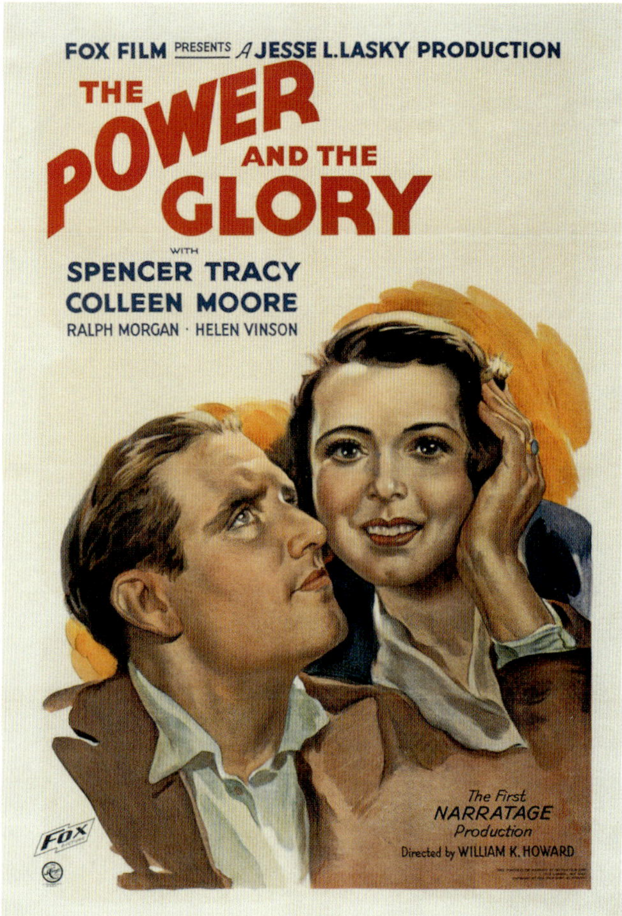

The Power And The Glory. 1934. One-sheet. $2,000-3,000.

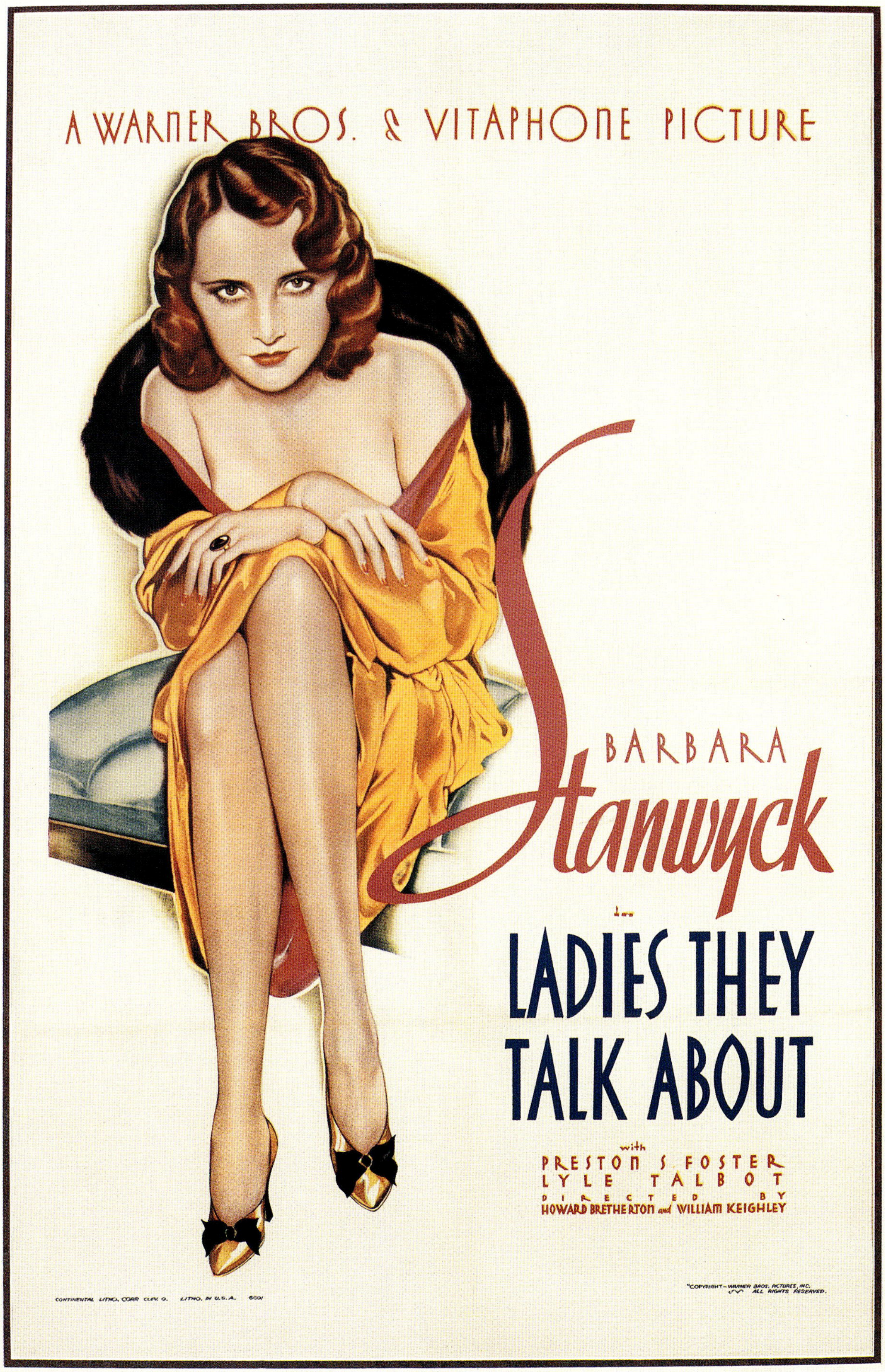

Ladies They Talk About. 1933. One-sheet, art by Alberto Vargas. $8,000-12,000.

The extremely upbeat musicals that came from Warner Bros. and R.K.O. also prove the point that Hollywood was trying to fight the Depression blues. Dancing duo Fred Astaire and Ginger Rodgers first teamed up in *Flying Down to Rio* (1933) and performed together throughout the decade in such classics as *The Gay Divorcee* (1934), *Top Hat* (1935), *Swing Time* (1936), *Follow the Fleet* (1937) and *Shall We Dance?* (1937). Their pictures, a combination of wit, style and sophisticated dance routines, appealed massively to a financially stressed and depressed populous at home as well as abroad.

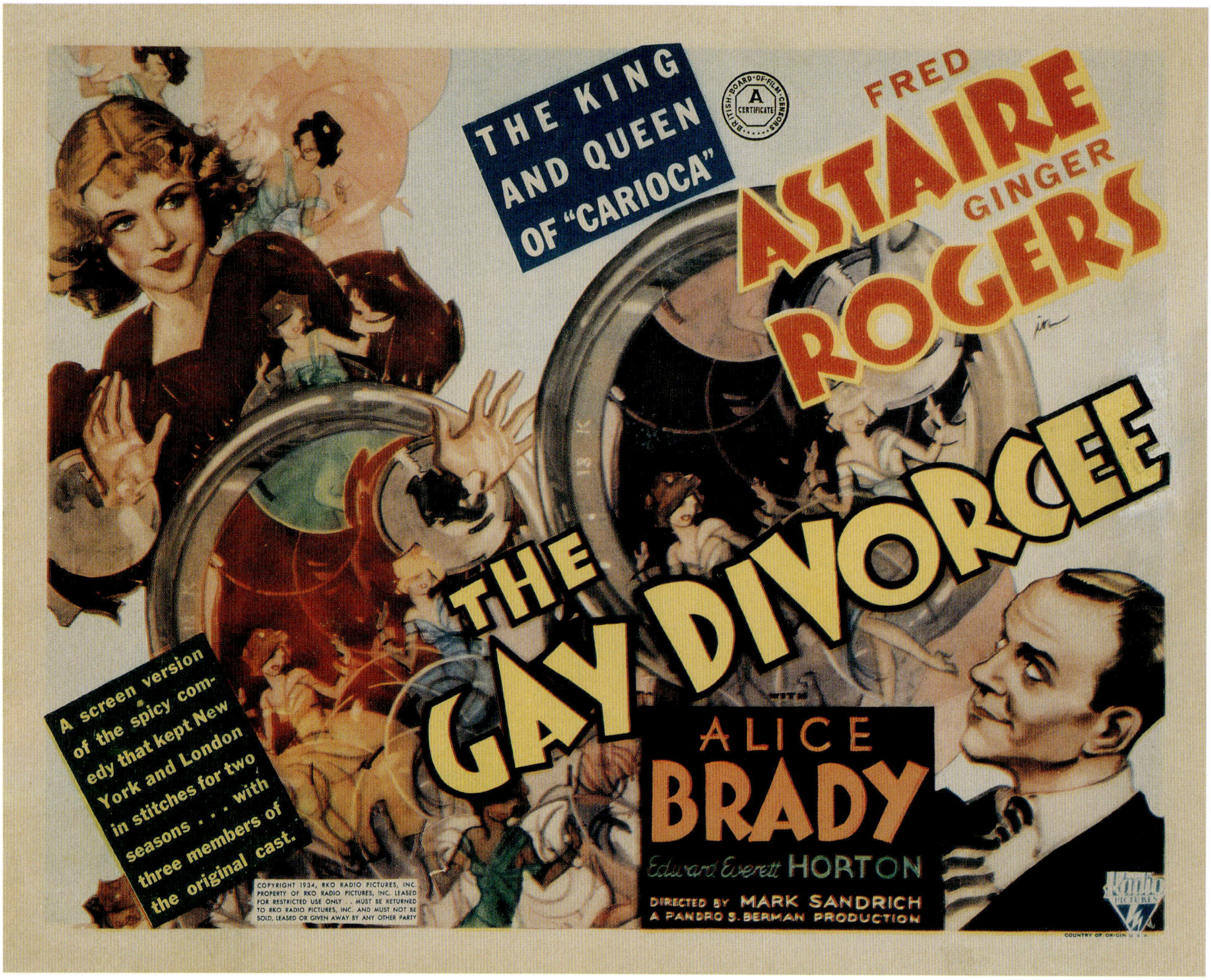

The Gay Divorcee. 1934. Title lobby card. $1,500-2,000.

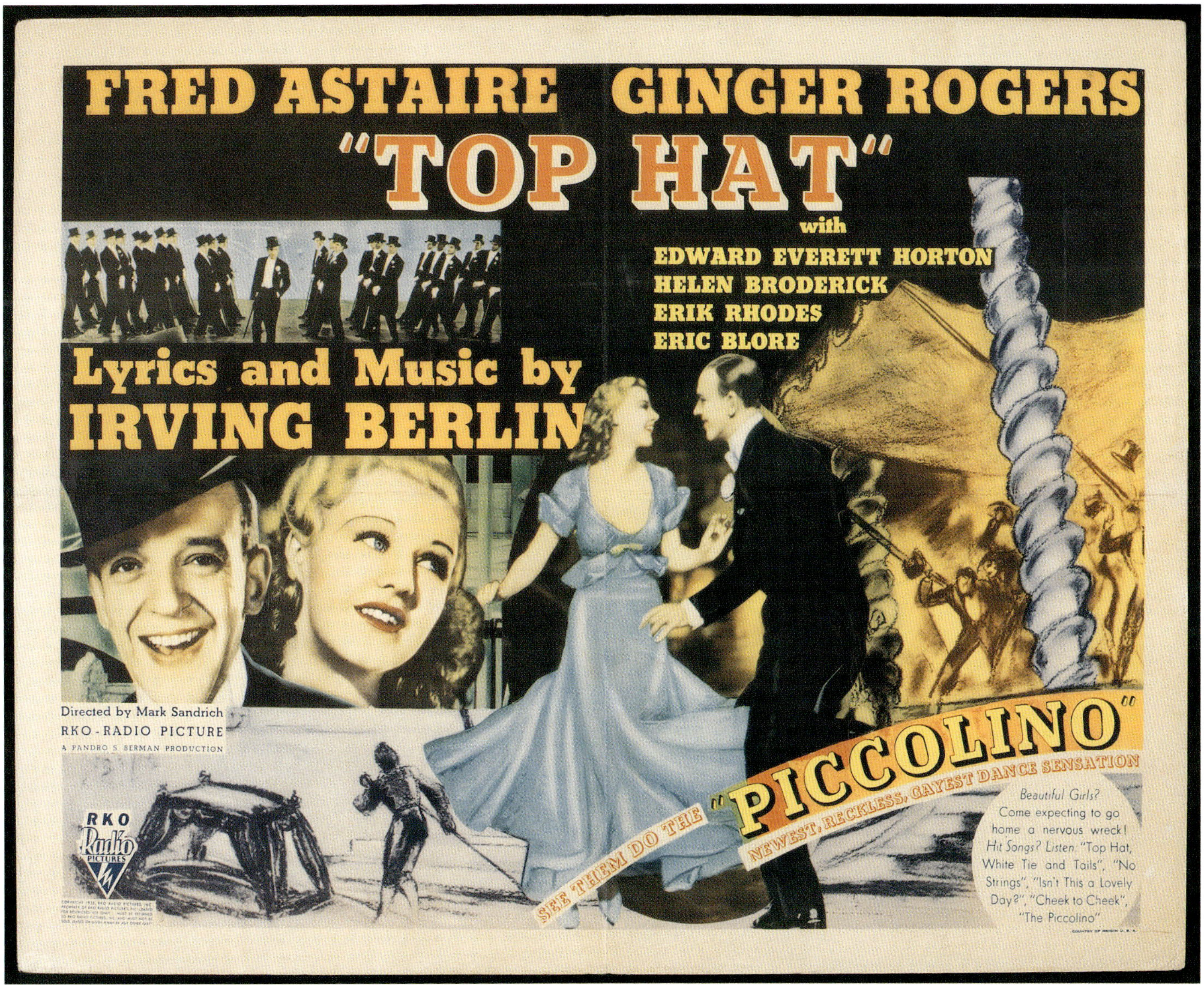

Top Hat. 1935. Half-sheet. $6,000-8,000.

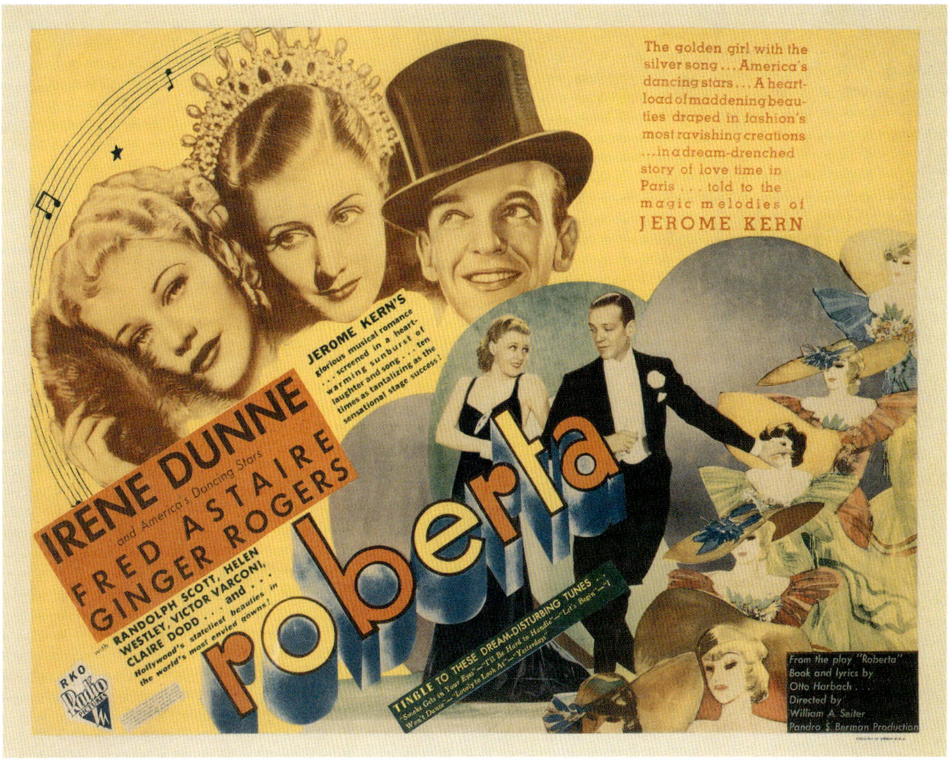

Roberta. 1935. Half-sheet. $2,000-2,500.

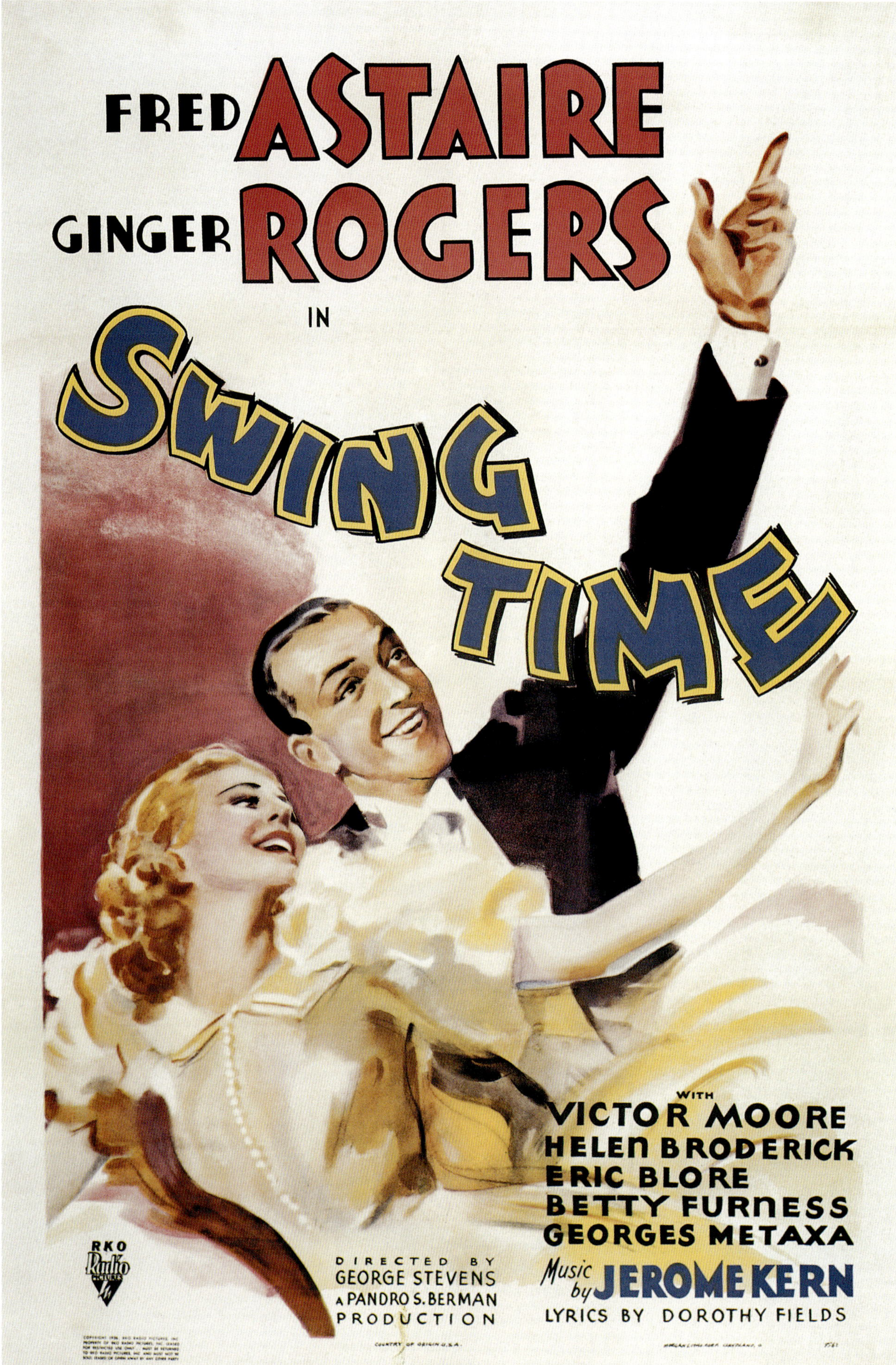

Swing Time. 1936. One-sheet. $3,000-5,000.

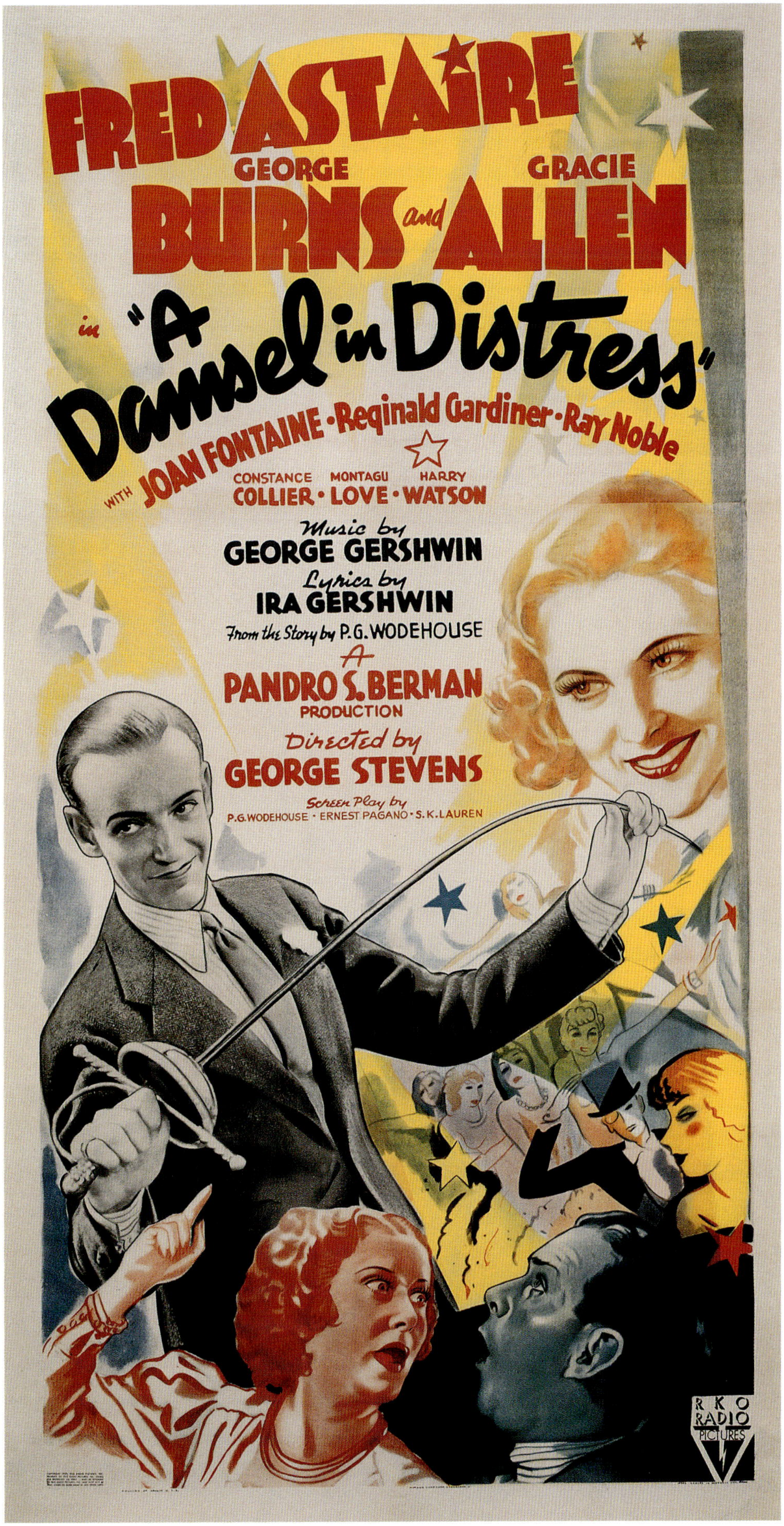

A Damsel in Distress. 1937. Three-sheet. $1,500-2,000.

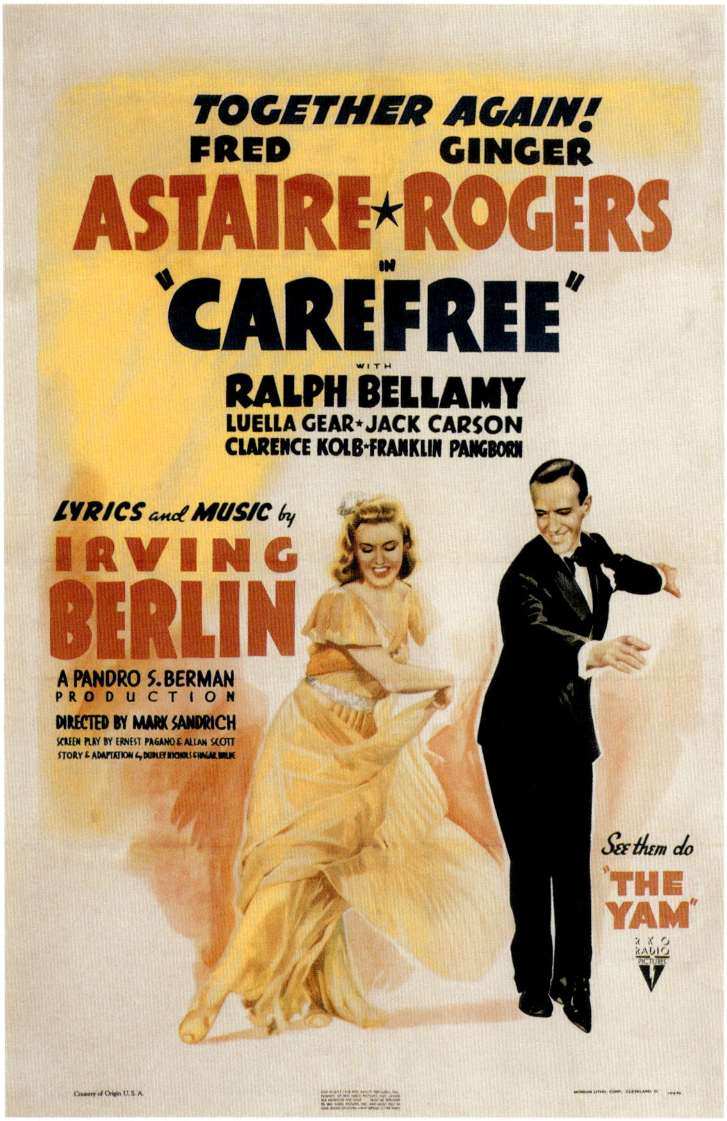

Carefree. 1938. One-sheet. $2,500-3,500.

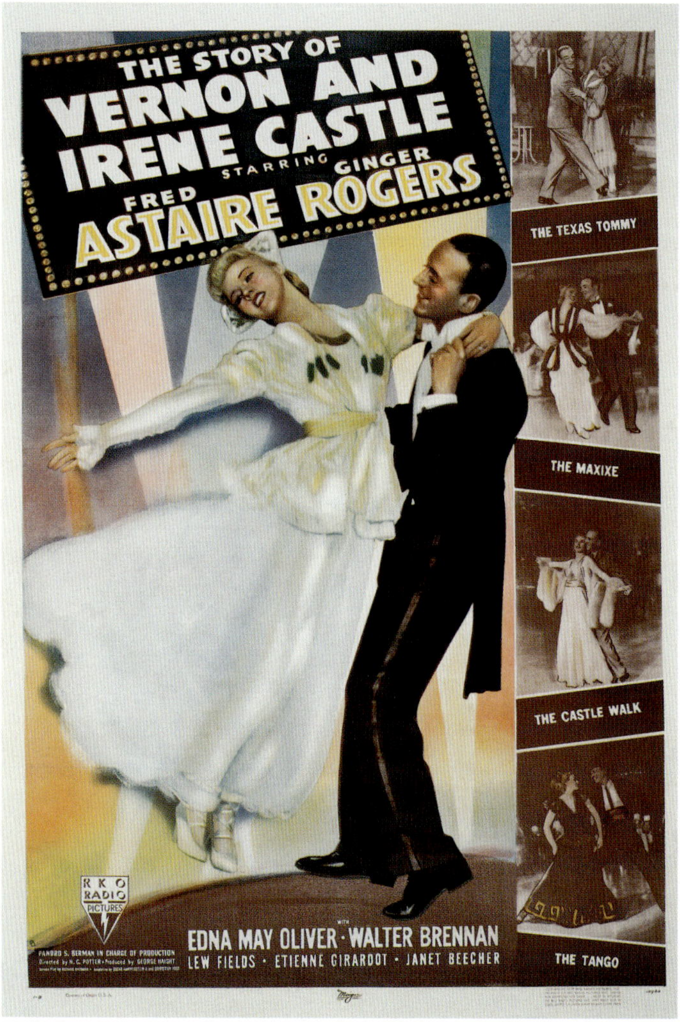

The Story Of Vernon And Irene Castle. 1939. One-sheet, style B. $1,500-2,000.

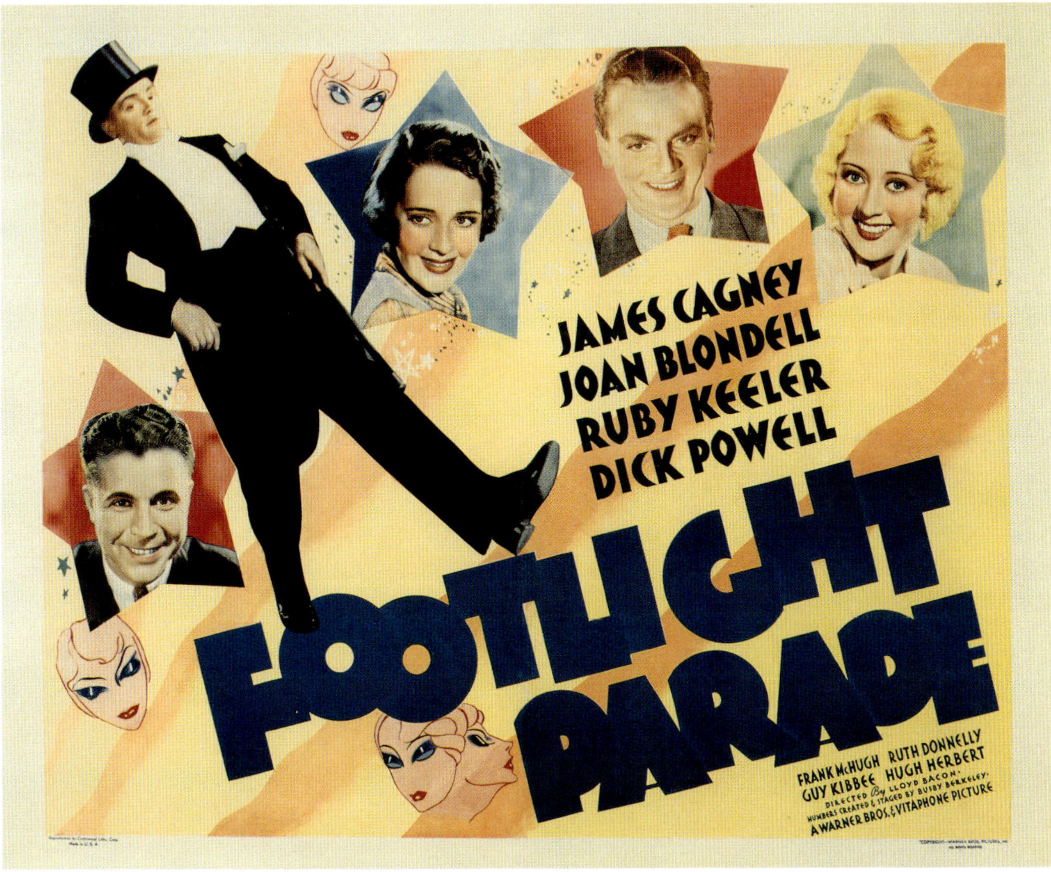

Footlight Parade. 1933. Half-sheet. $2,000-3,000.

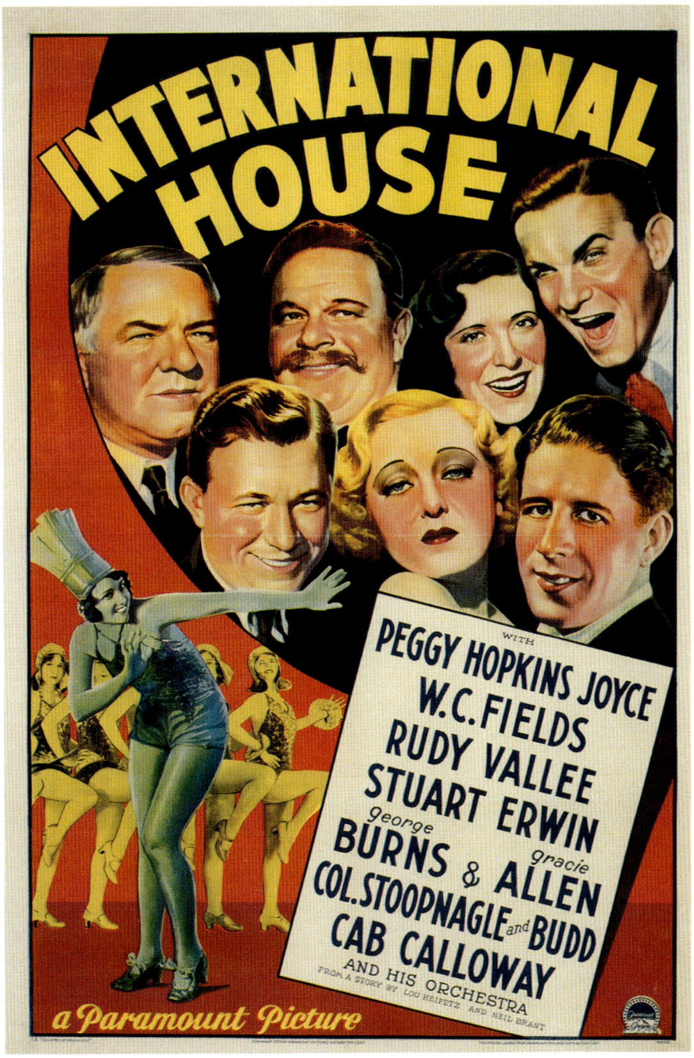

International House. 1933. One-sheet, style A. $2,000-3,000.

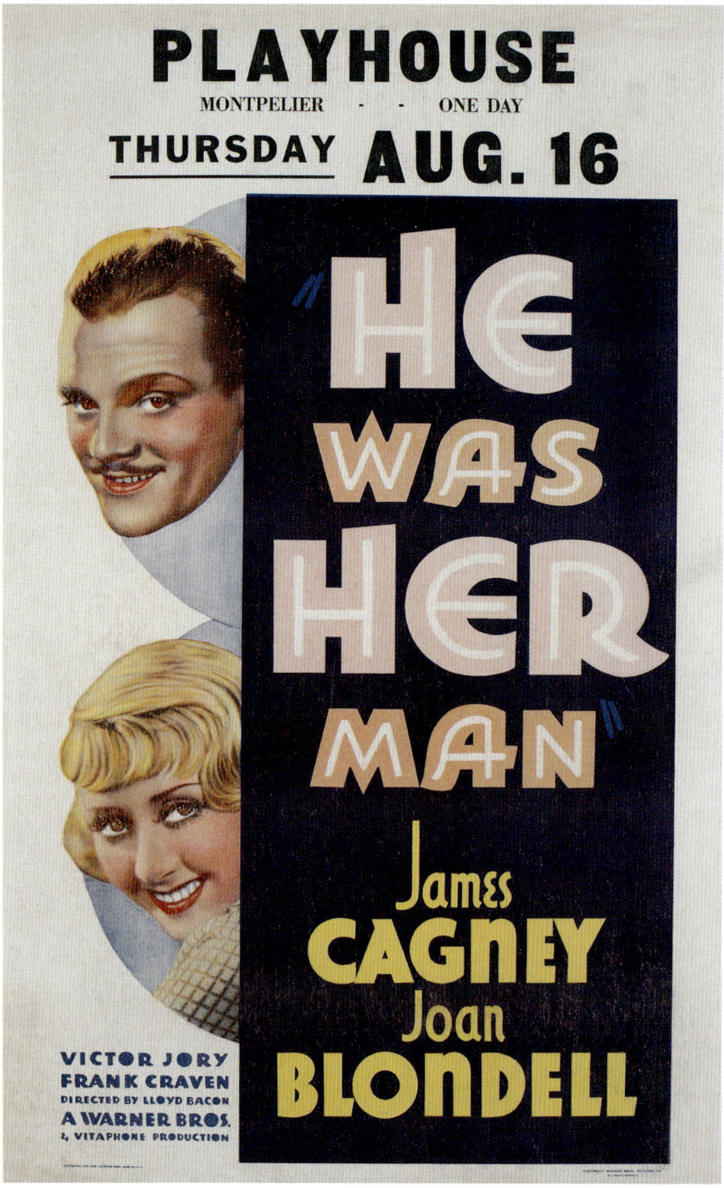

He Was Her Man. 1934. Window card. $1,000-1,500.

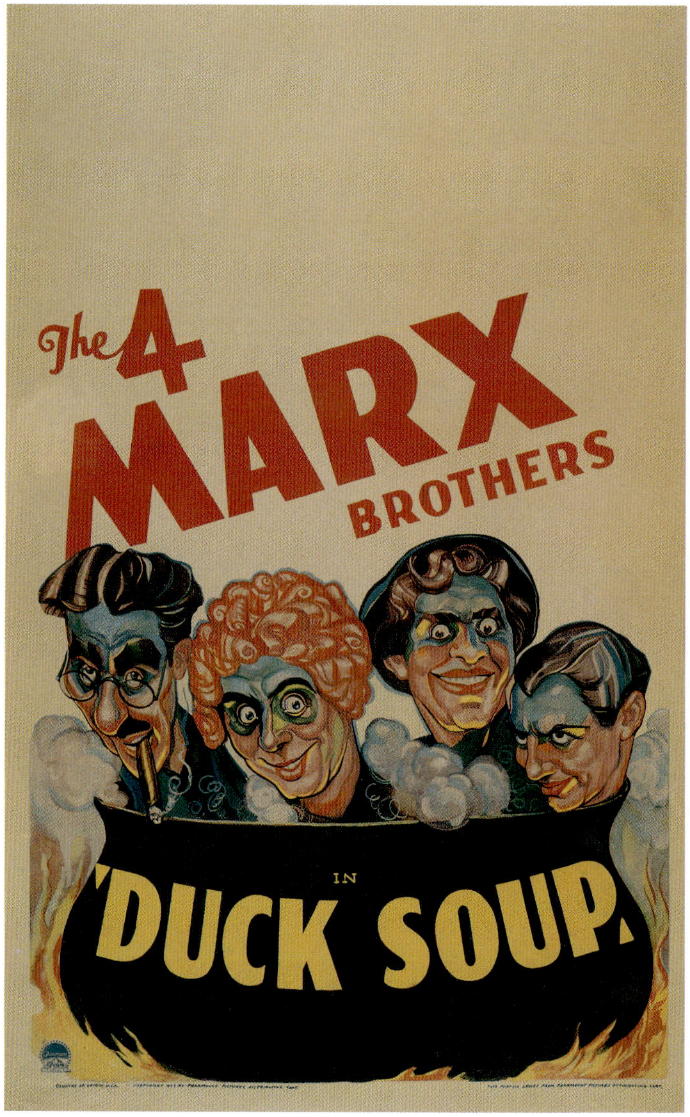

Duck Soup. 1933. Window card. $2,000-3,000.

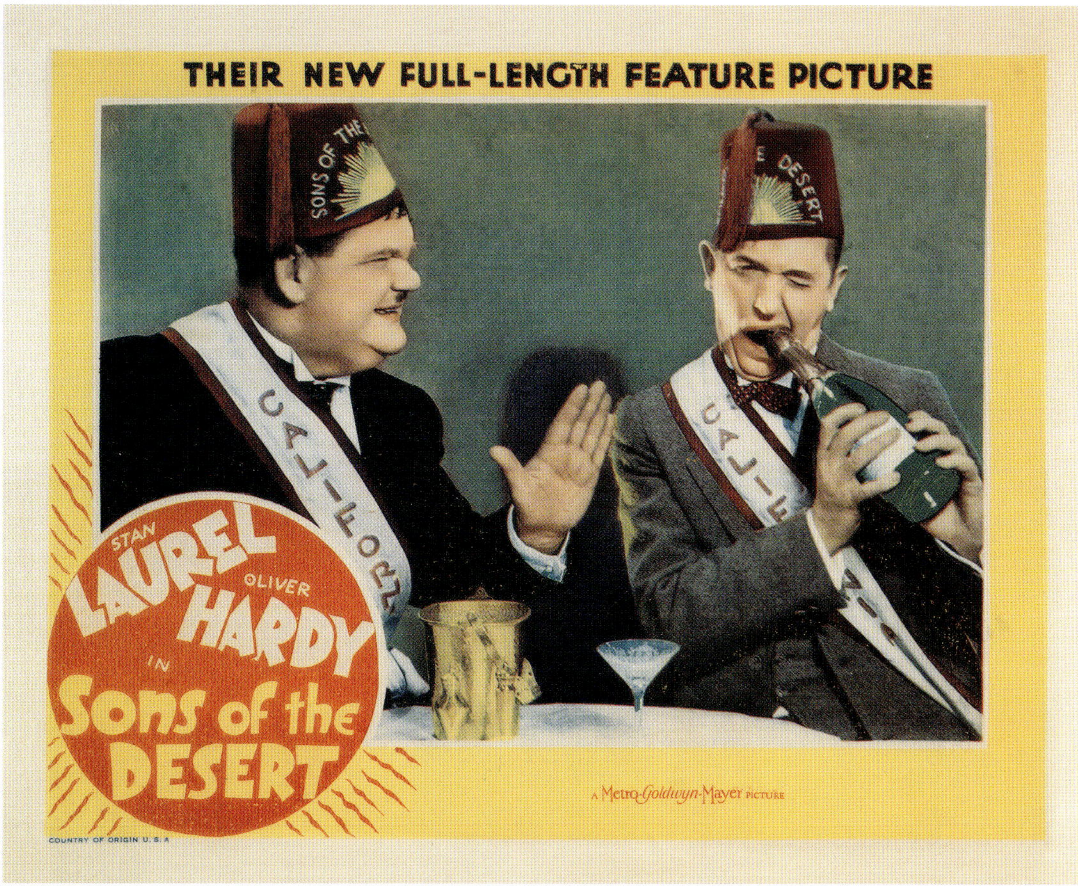

Sons of the Desert. 1933. Lobby card. $800-1,200.

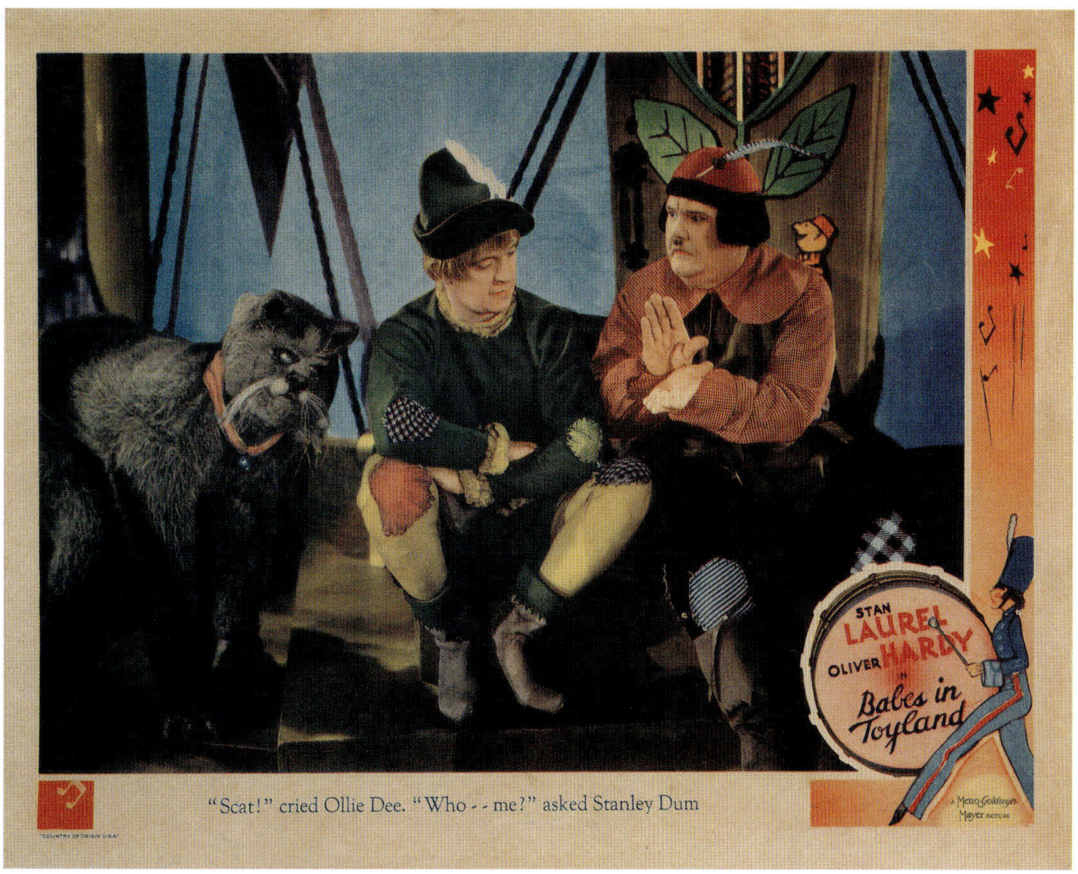

Babes in Toyland. 1934. Lobby card. $800-1,200.

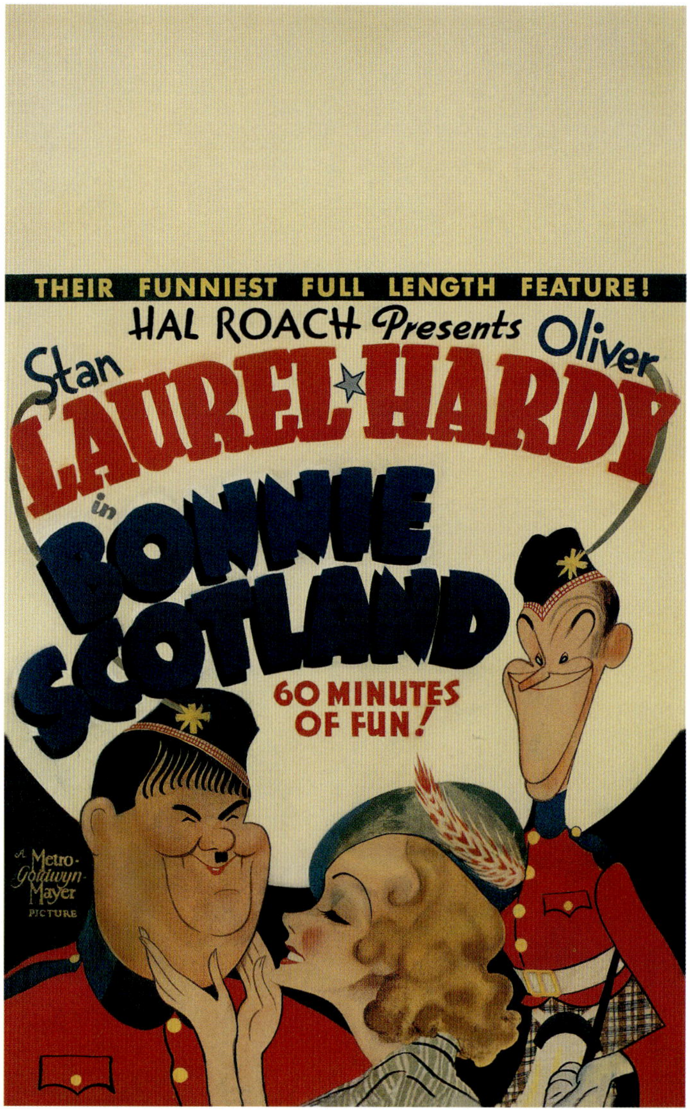

Bonnie Scotland. 1935. Window card. $1,000-1,500.

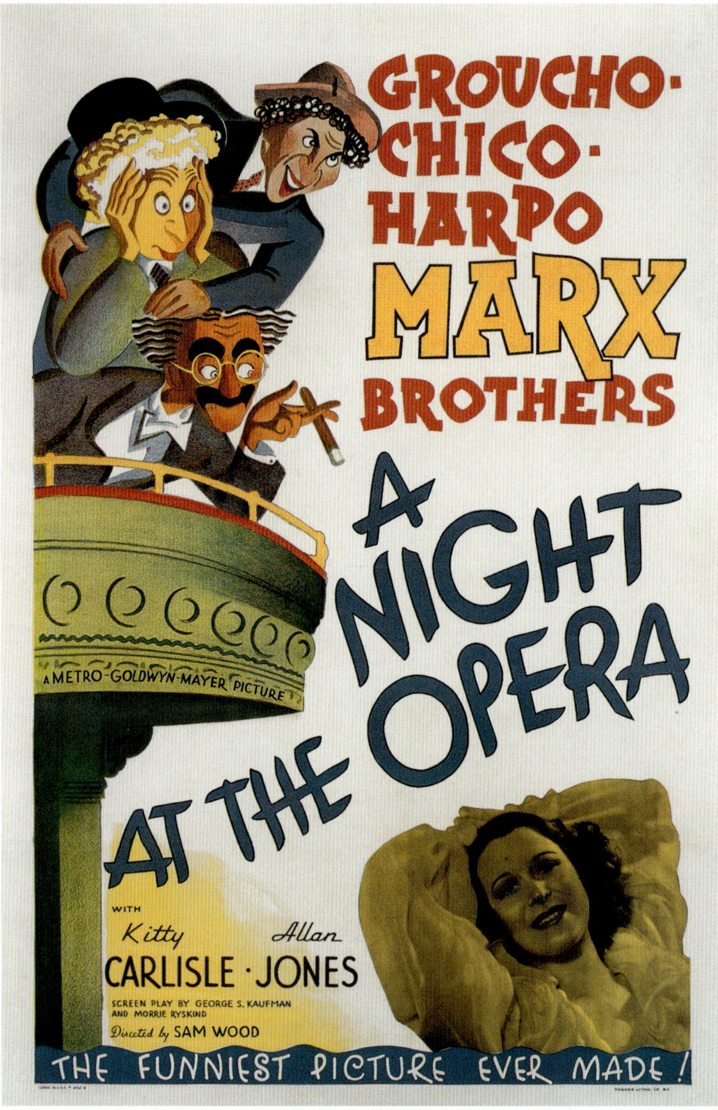

A Night at the Opera. 1935. One-sheet, style D. $3,000-5,000.

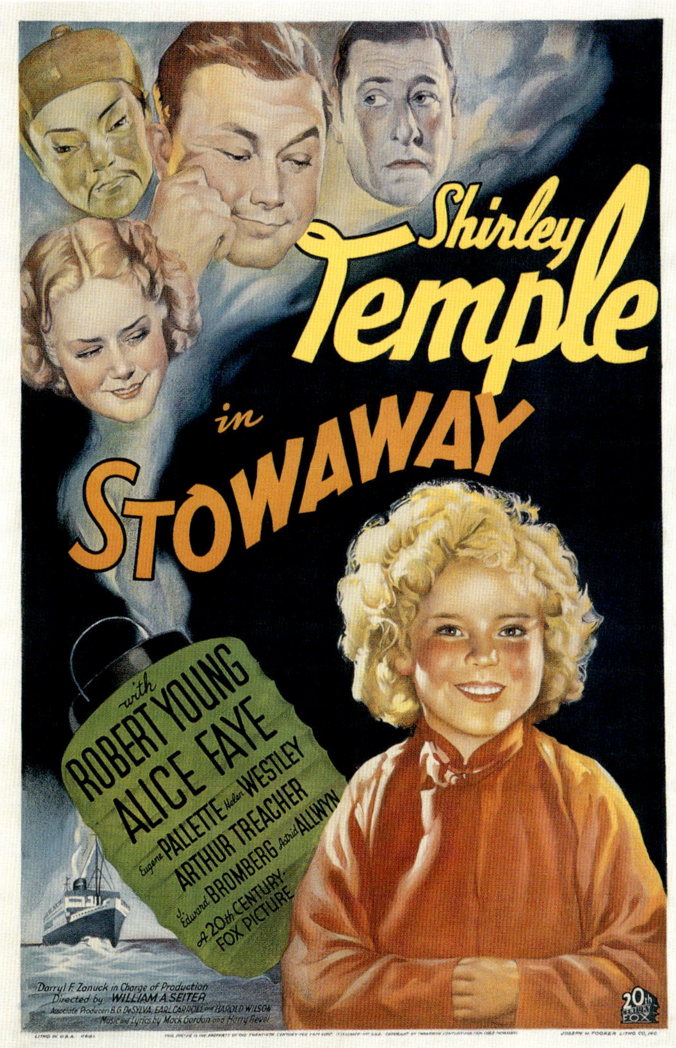

Stowaway. 1936. One-sheet. $1,500-1,800.

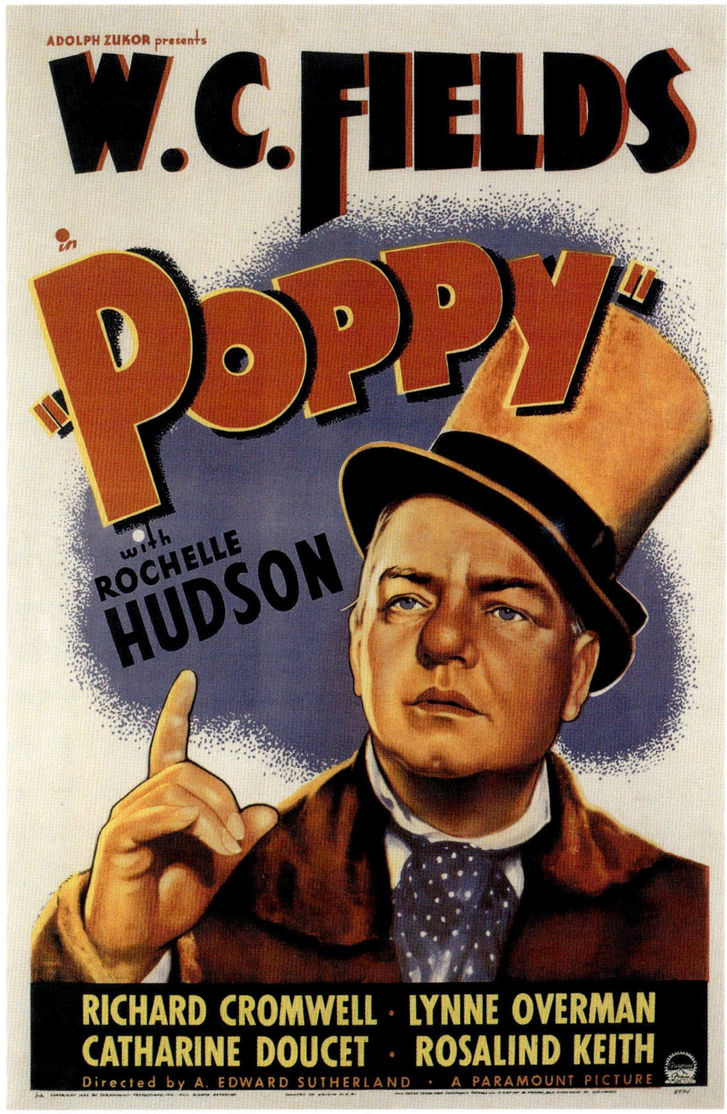

Poppy. 1936. One-sheet. $2,000-3,000.

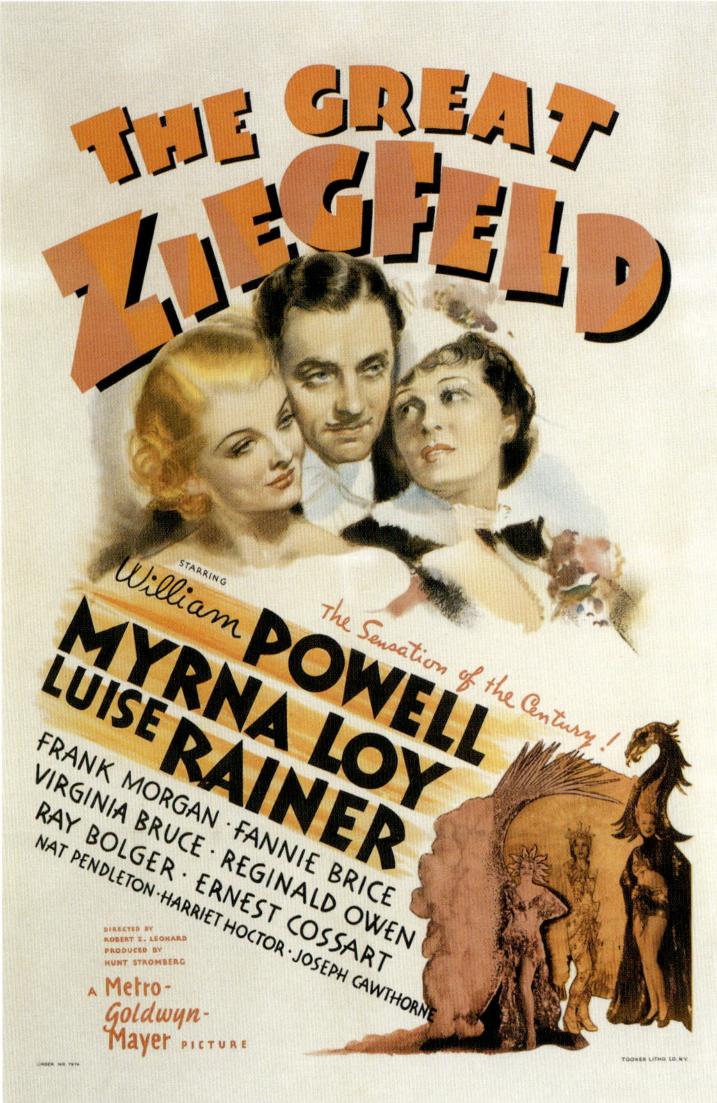

The Great Ziegfeld. 1936. One-sheet, style D. $4,000-6,000.

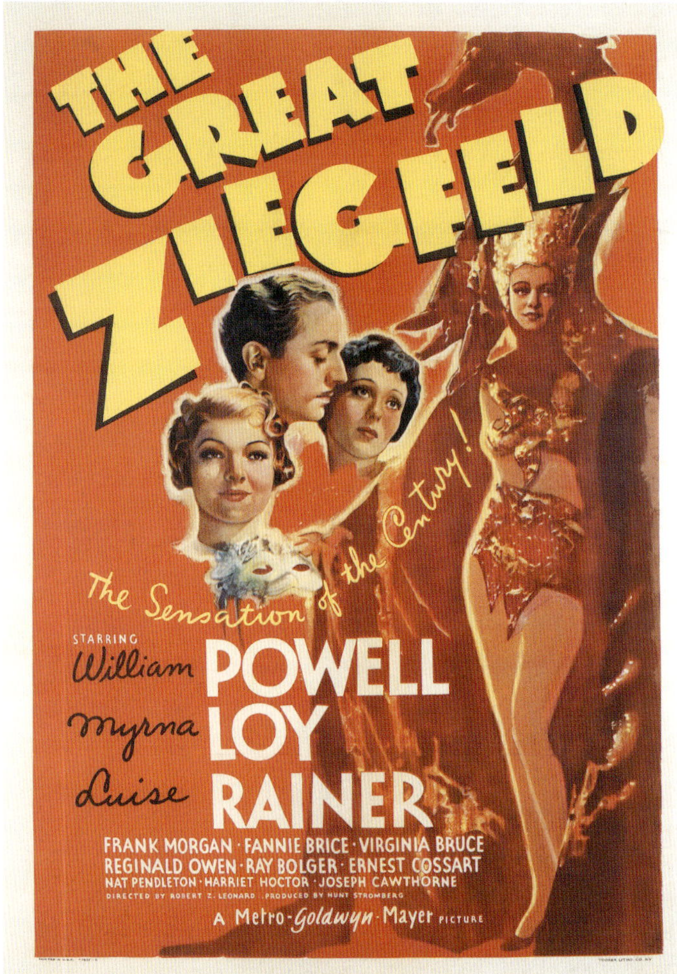

*The Great Ziegfel*d. 1936. One-sheet, style C. $3,000-5,000.

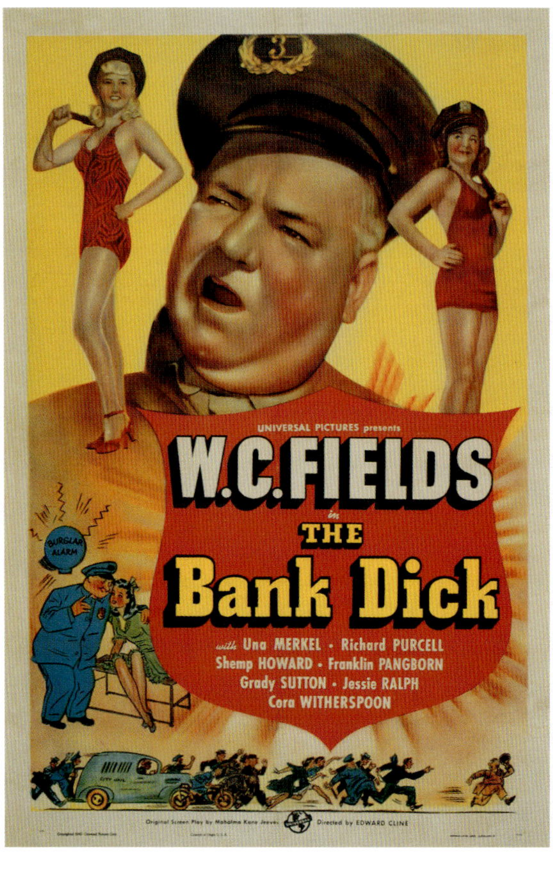

The Bank Dick. 1937. One-sheet, style C. $1,000-1,500.

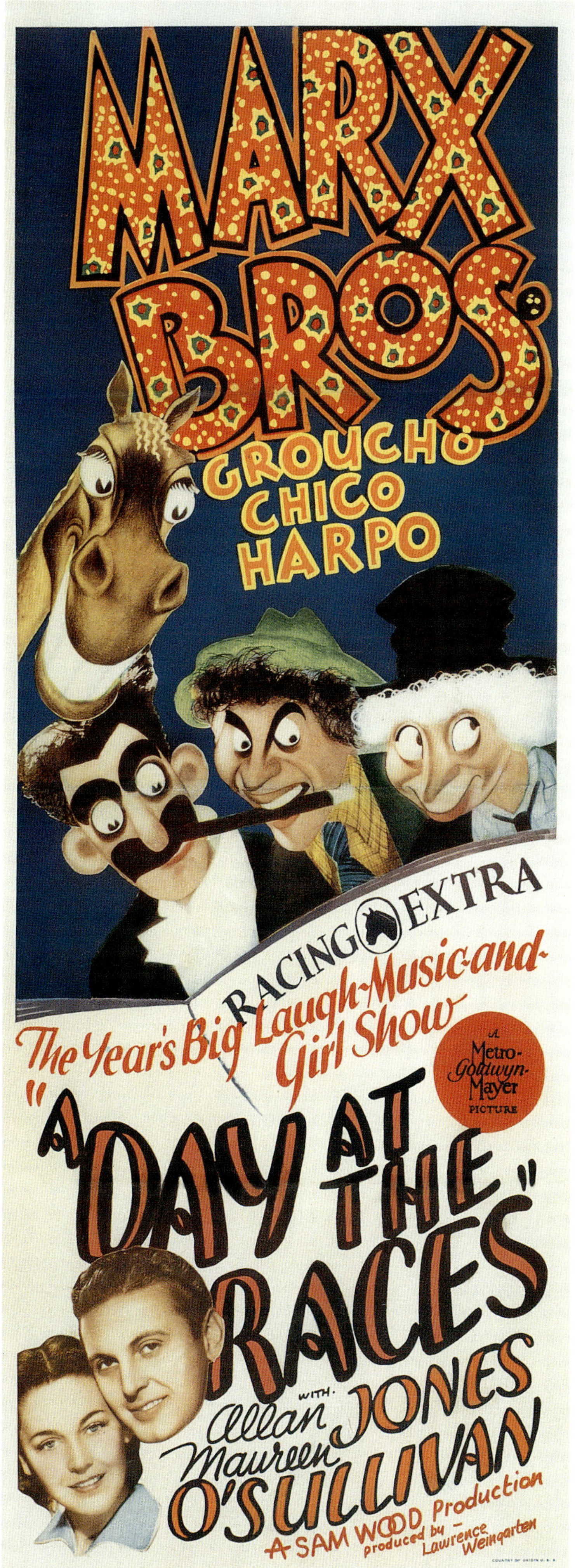

A Day at the Races. 1937.
Insert. $2,000-3,000.

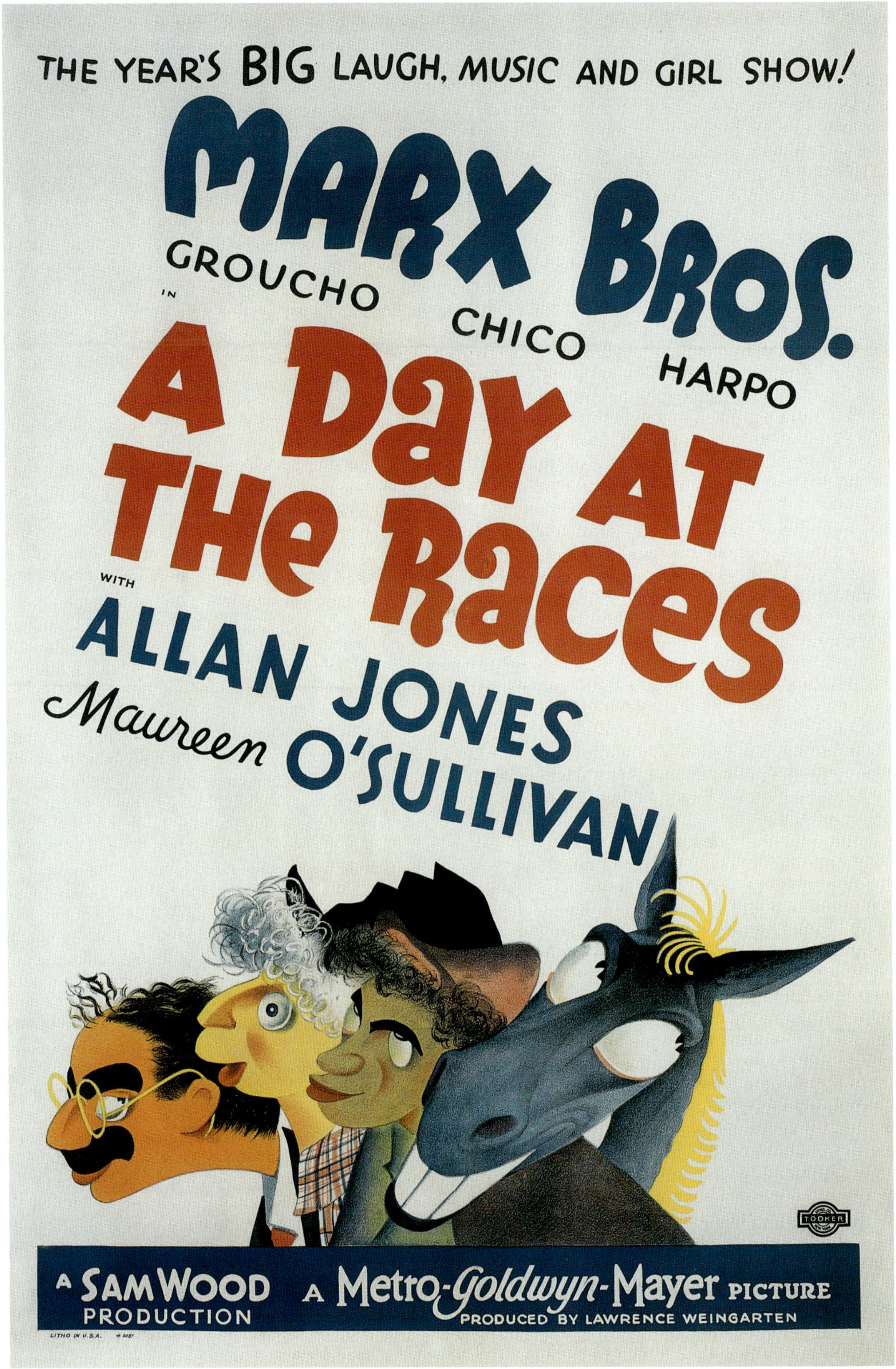

A Day at the Races. 1937. One-sheet, style C. $3,000-5,000.

Fox, meanwhile, was making its name with Westerns, and, with the director John Ford, produced the legendary *Stagecoach* (1939). Tales of the wild frontier between the good, the bad, and vengeful transported audiences back to a time early in their country's history when life also was a struggle and often involved a hero or two. One such hero was John Wayne who starred in the 1930 flop *The Big Trail* and continued with a long line of average westerns throughout the decade until he finally got the big break in Ford's classic.

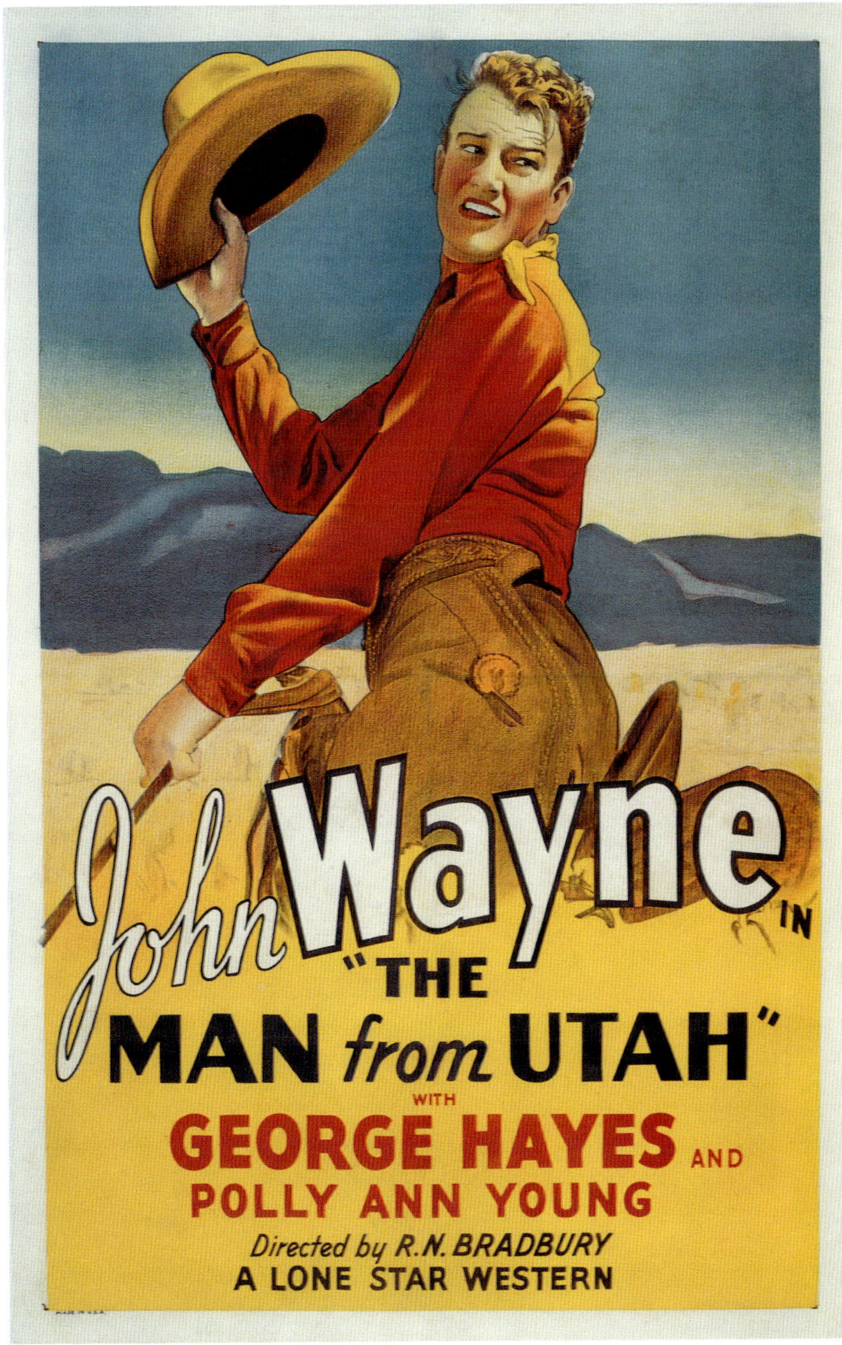

The Man from Utah. 1934. One-sheet. $2,500-3,500.

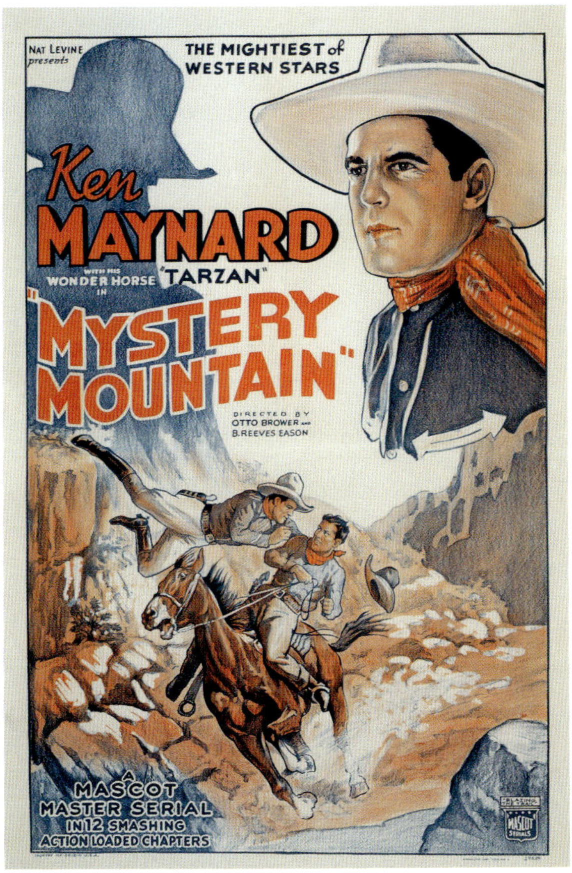

Mystery Man. 1934. One-sheet. $800-1,200.

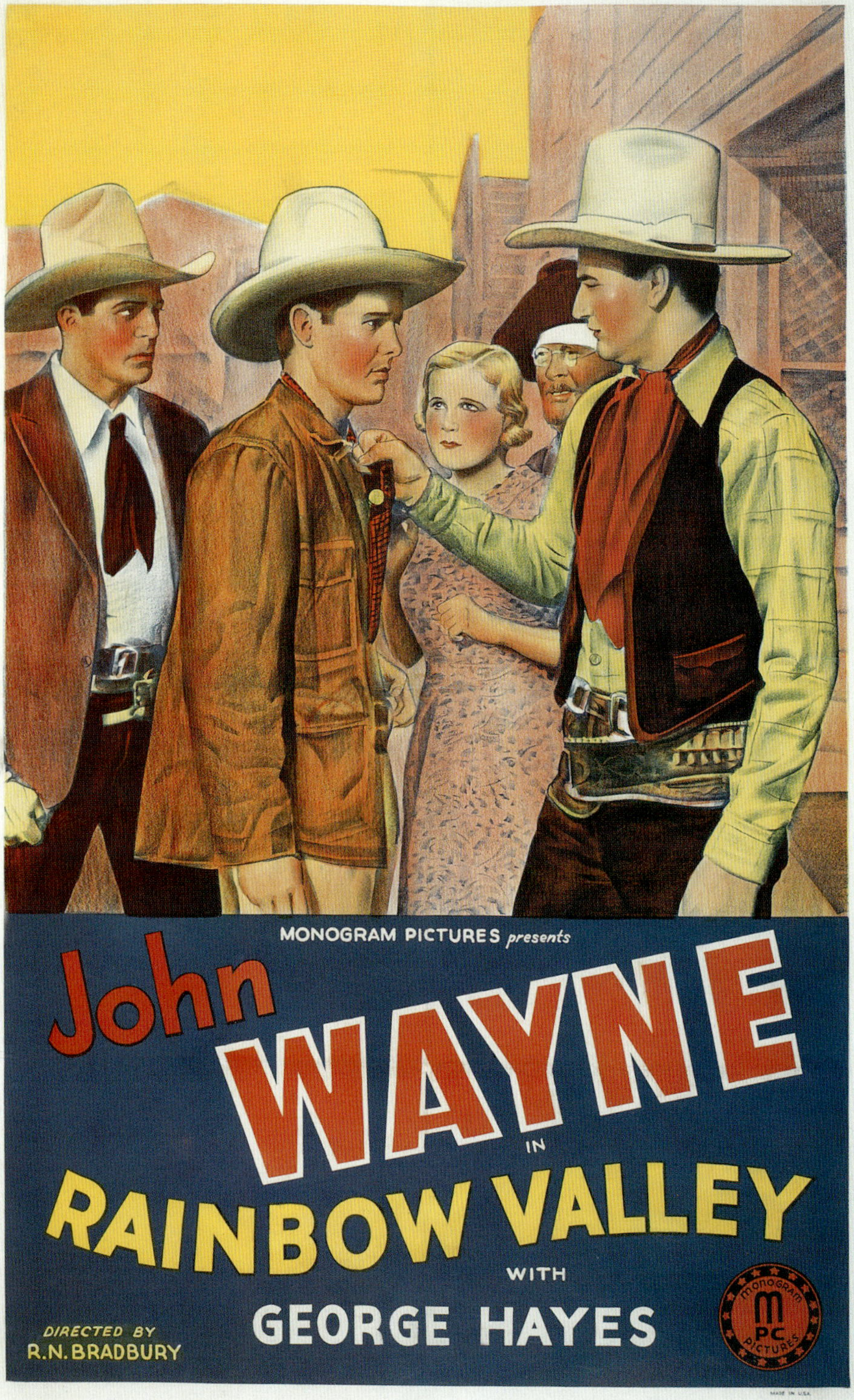

Rainbow Valley. 1935. One-sheet. $2,000-3,000.

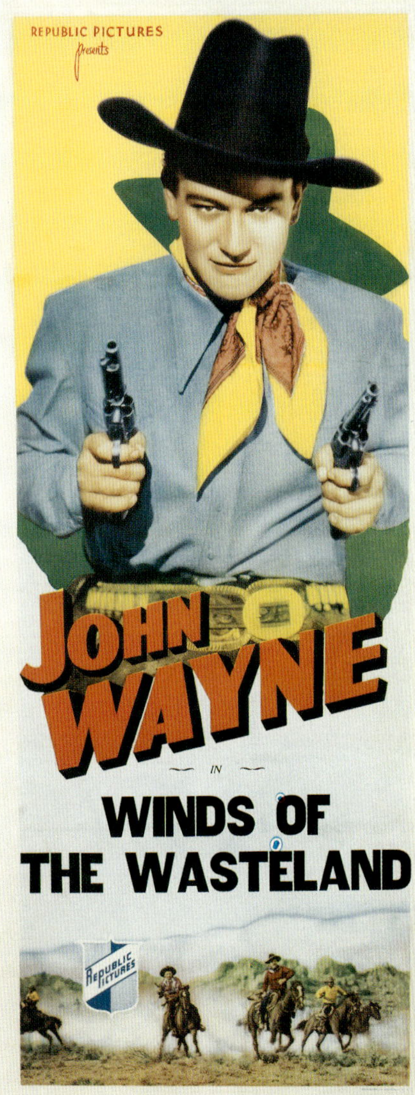

Winds of the Wasteland. 1936.
Insert. $1,200-1,800.

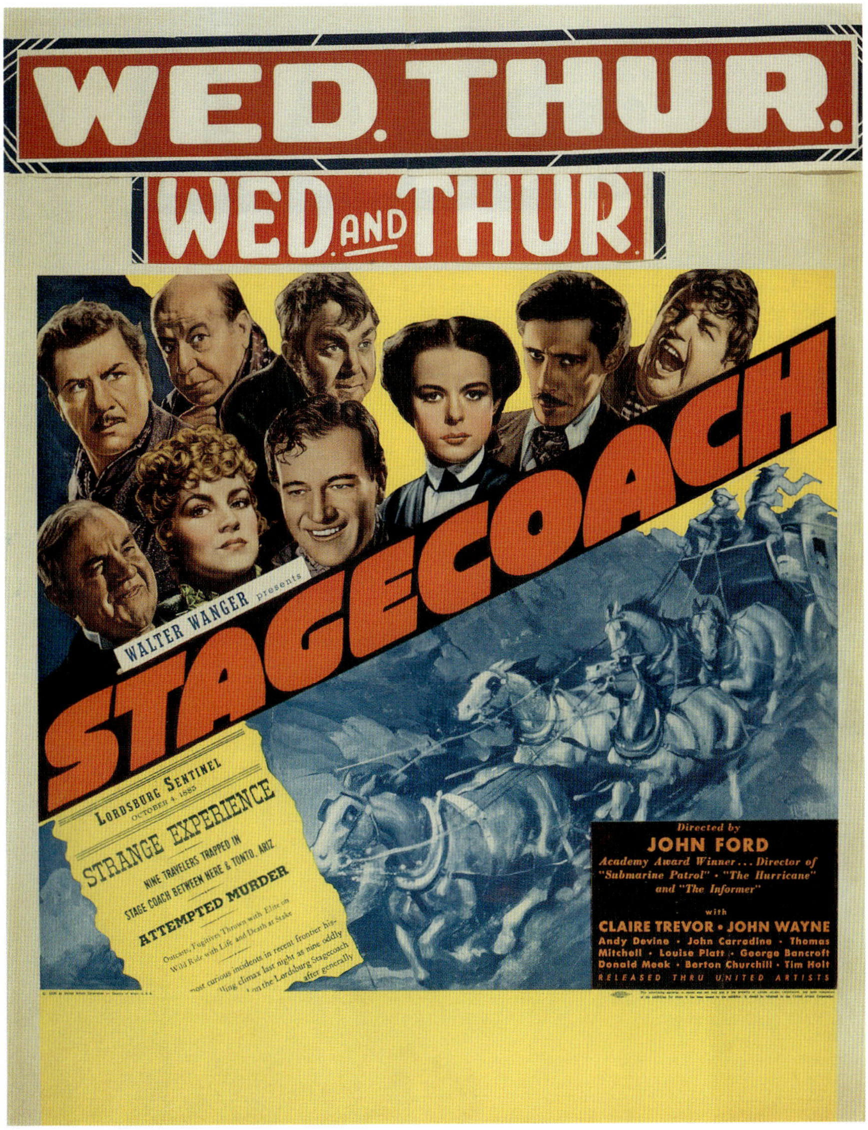

Stagecoach. 1939. Jumbo window card. $3,000-3,500.

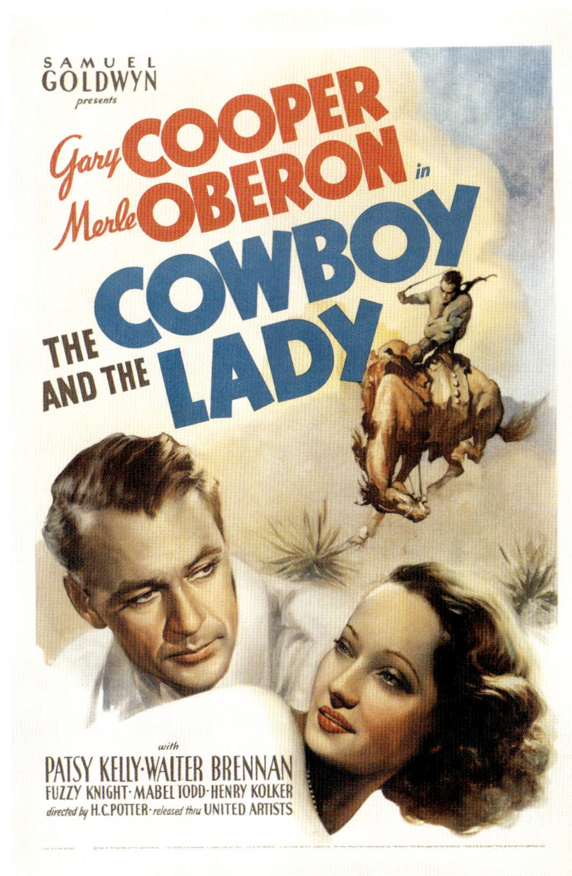

The Cowboy and the Lady. 1938. One-sheet. $2,000-2,500.

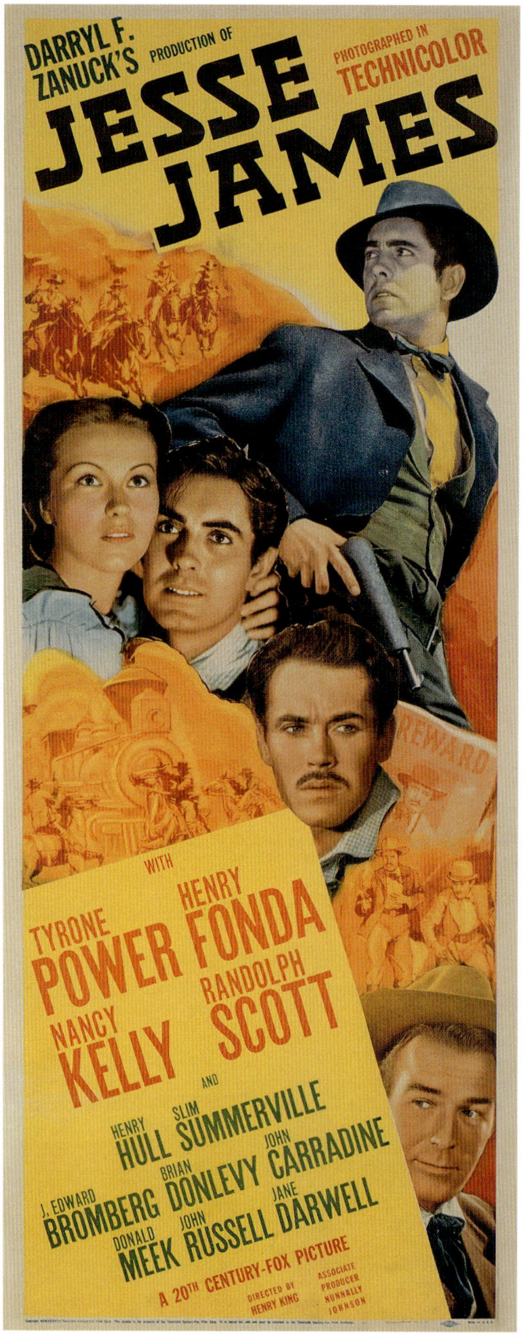

Jesse James. 1939. Insert. $1,200-1,800.

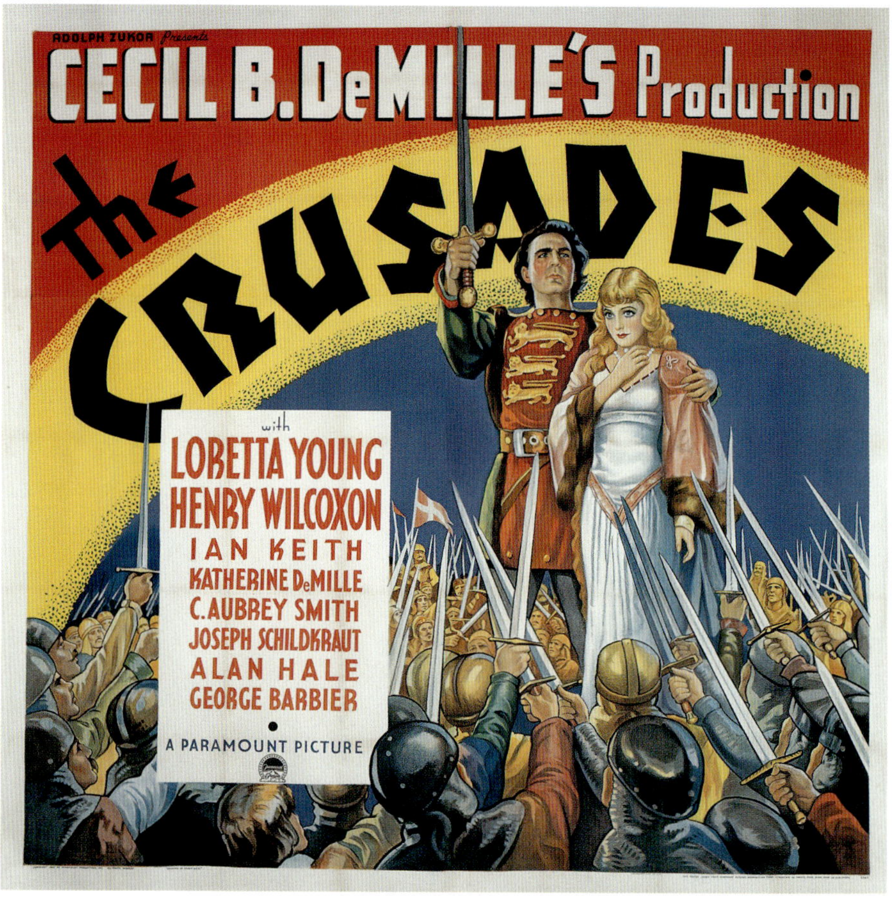

The Crusades. 1935. Six-sheet. $2,500-3,500.

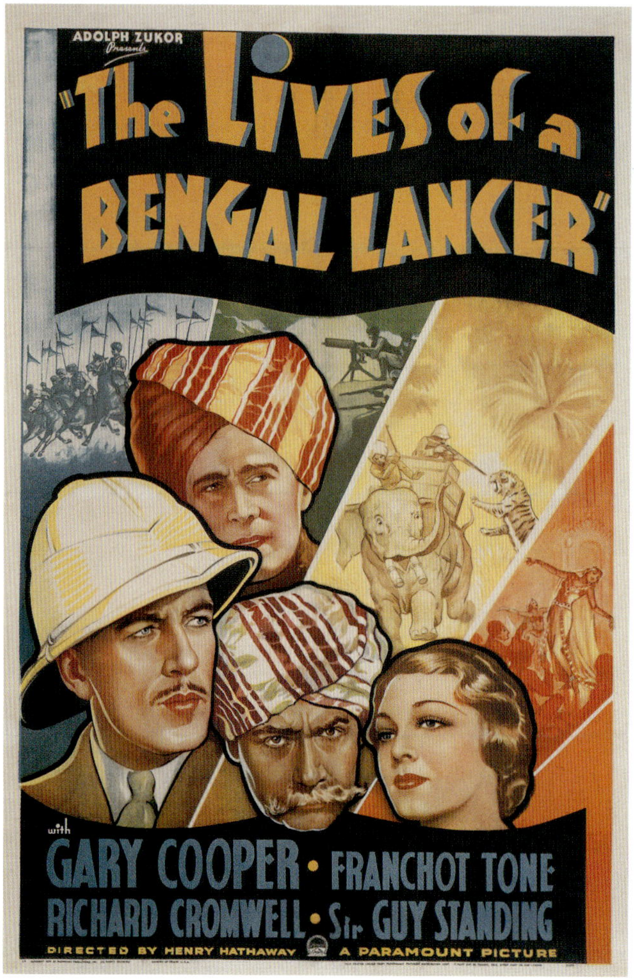

The Lives of a Bengal Lancer. 1934. One-sheet. $3,000-5,000.

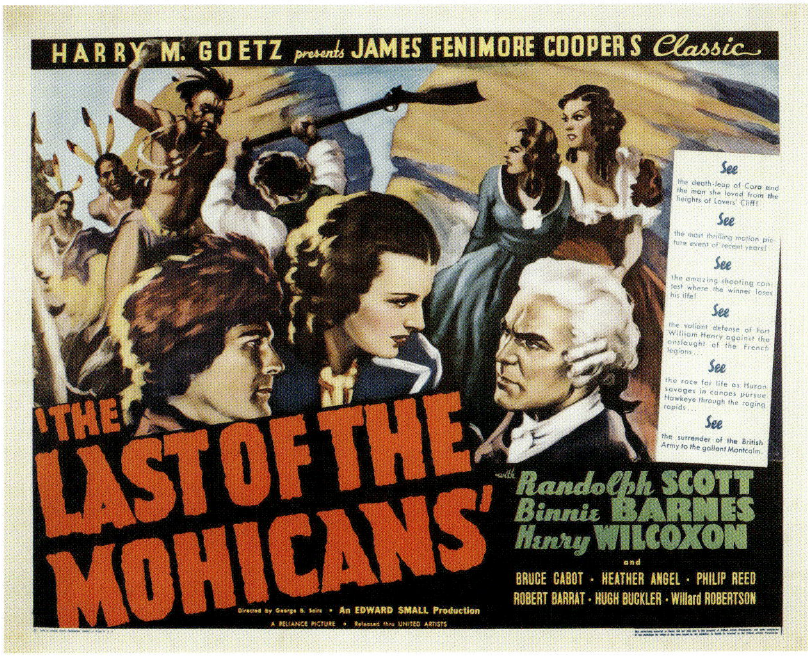

The Last of the Mohicans. 1936. Half-sheet. $700-1,000.

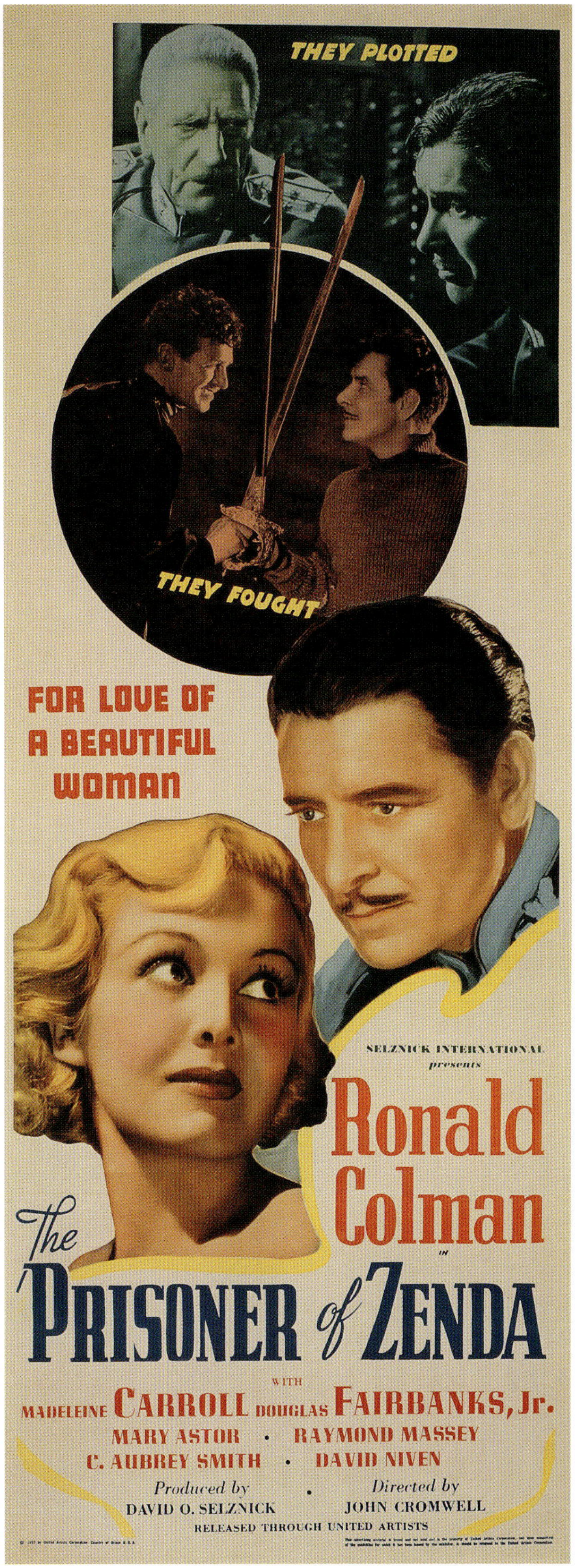

The Prisoner of Zenda. 1937. Insert. $800-1,200.

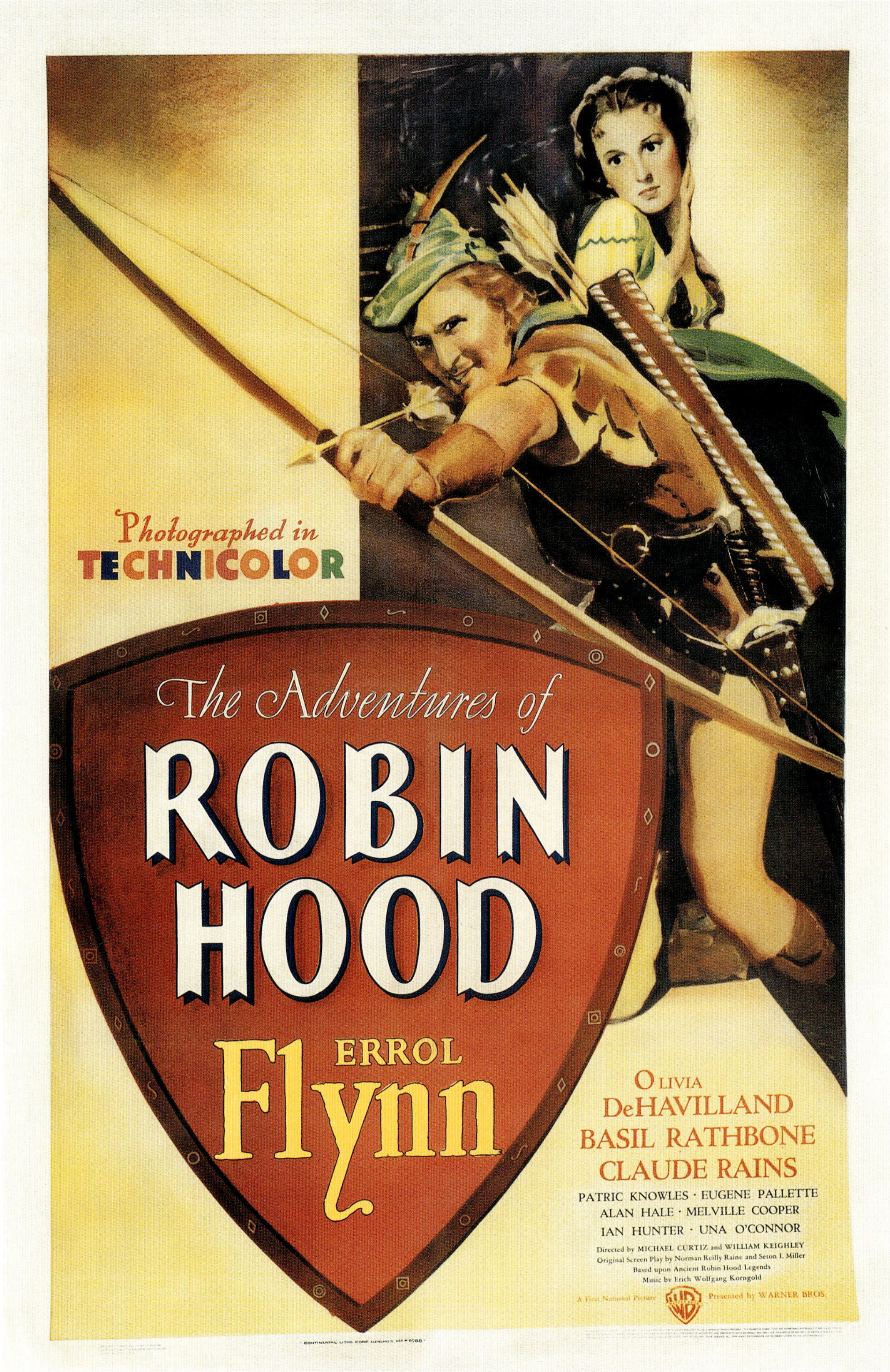

The Adventures of Robin Hood. 1938. One-sheet. $8,000-12,000.

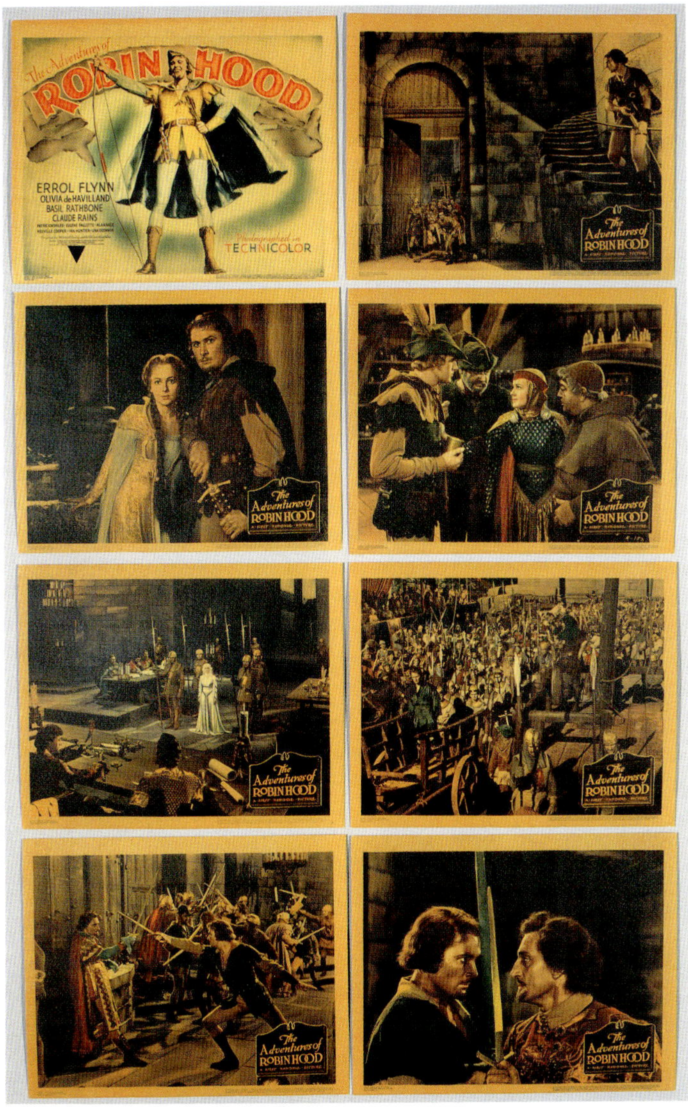

The Adventures of Robin Hood. 1938.
Set of lobby cards. $5,000-7,000.

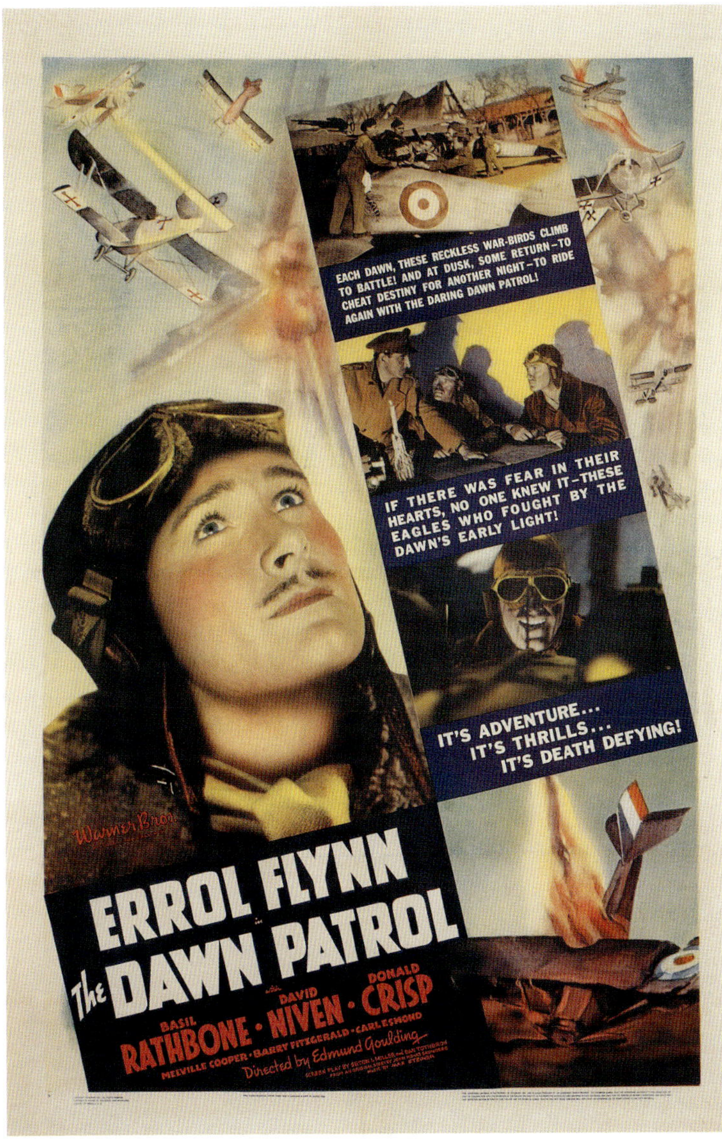

The Dawn Patrol. 1938. One-sheet. $2,000-3,000.

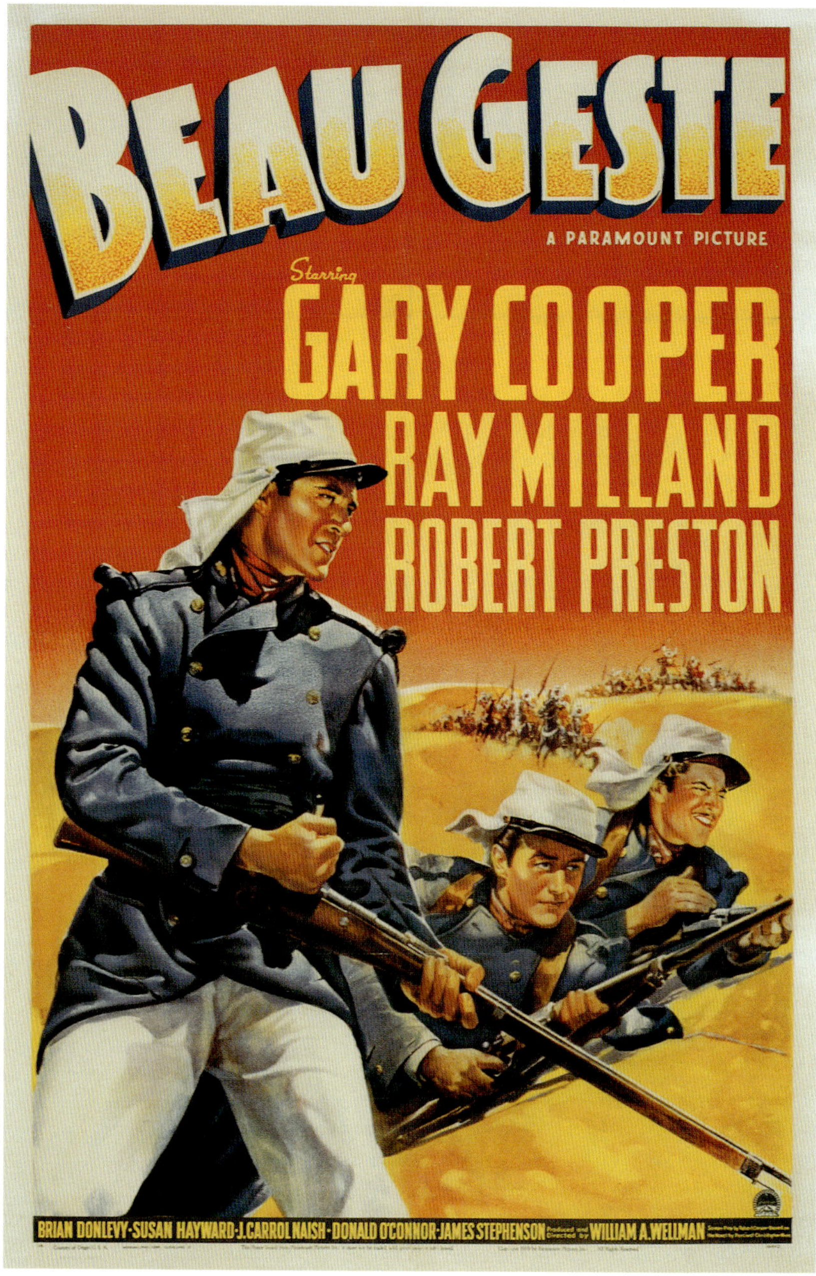

Beau Geste. 1939. One-sheet, style A. $4,000-6,000.

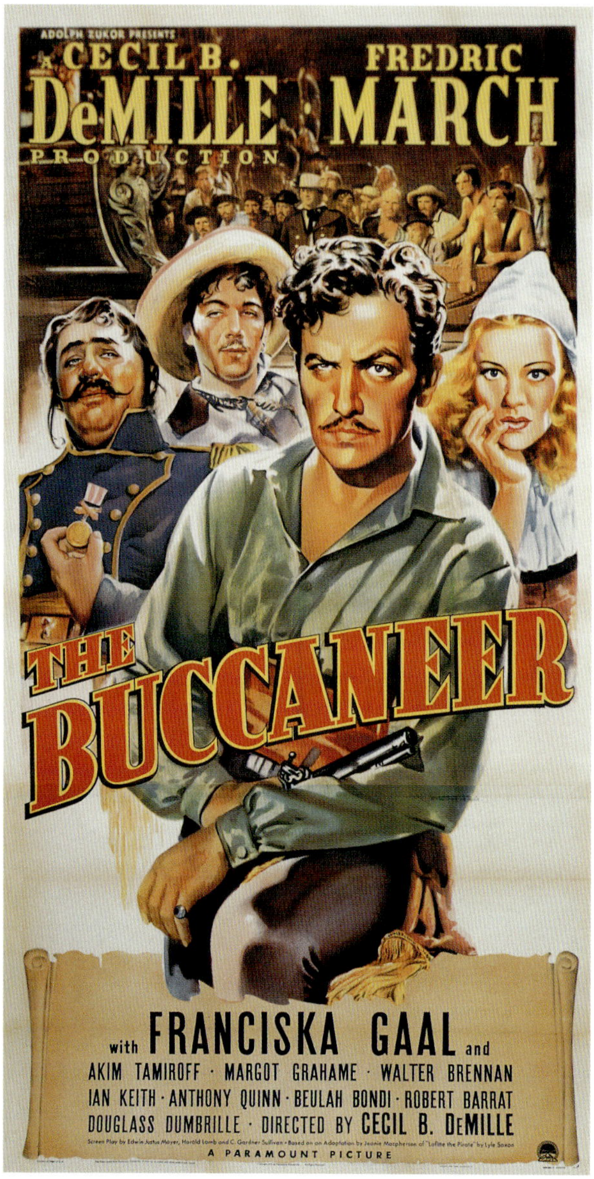

The Buccaneer. 1938. Three-sheet. $1,500-2,000.

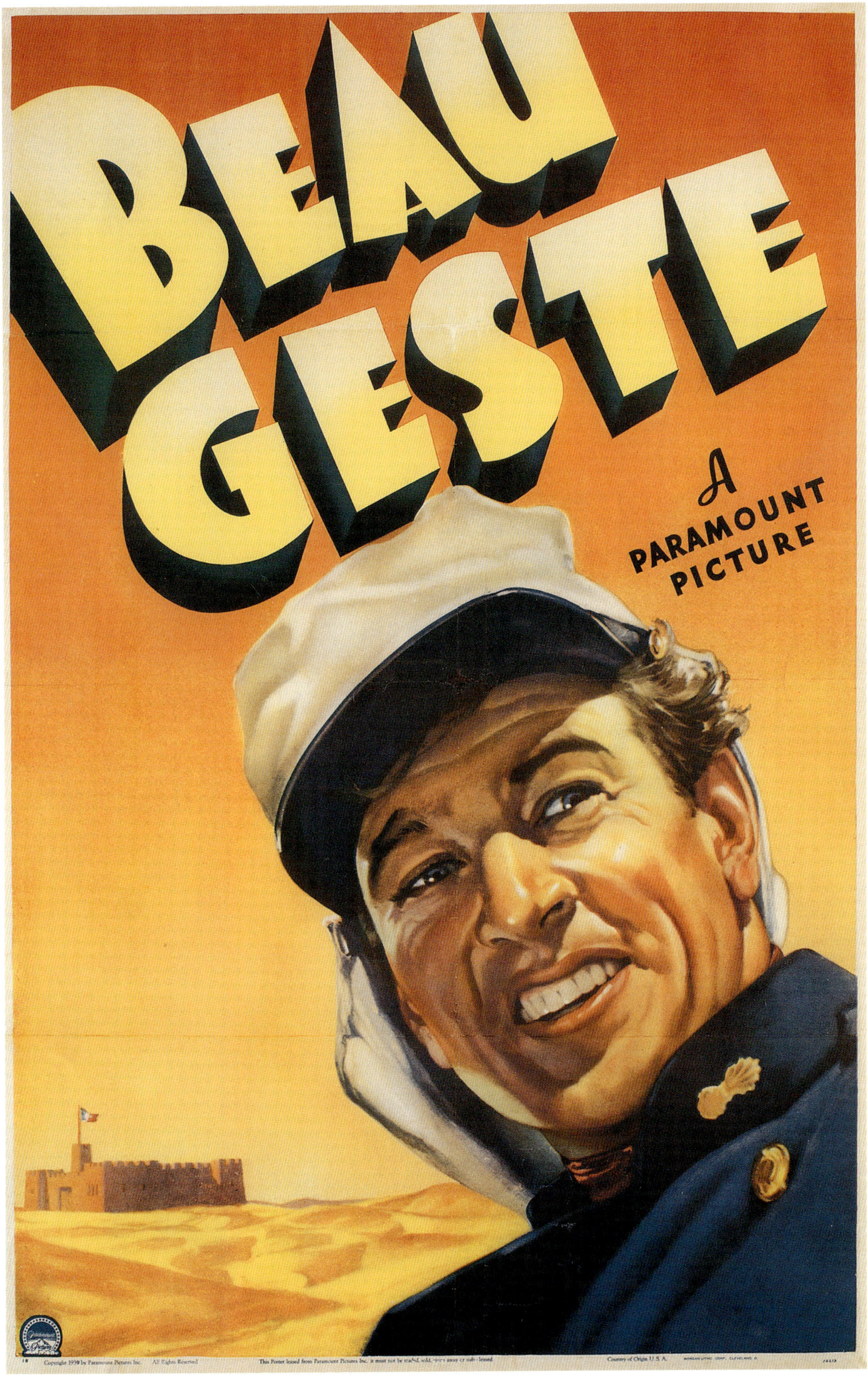

Beau Geste. 1939. One-sheet, style B. $5,000-7,000.

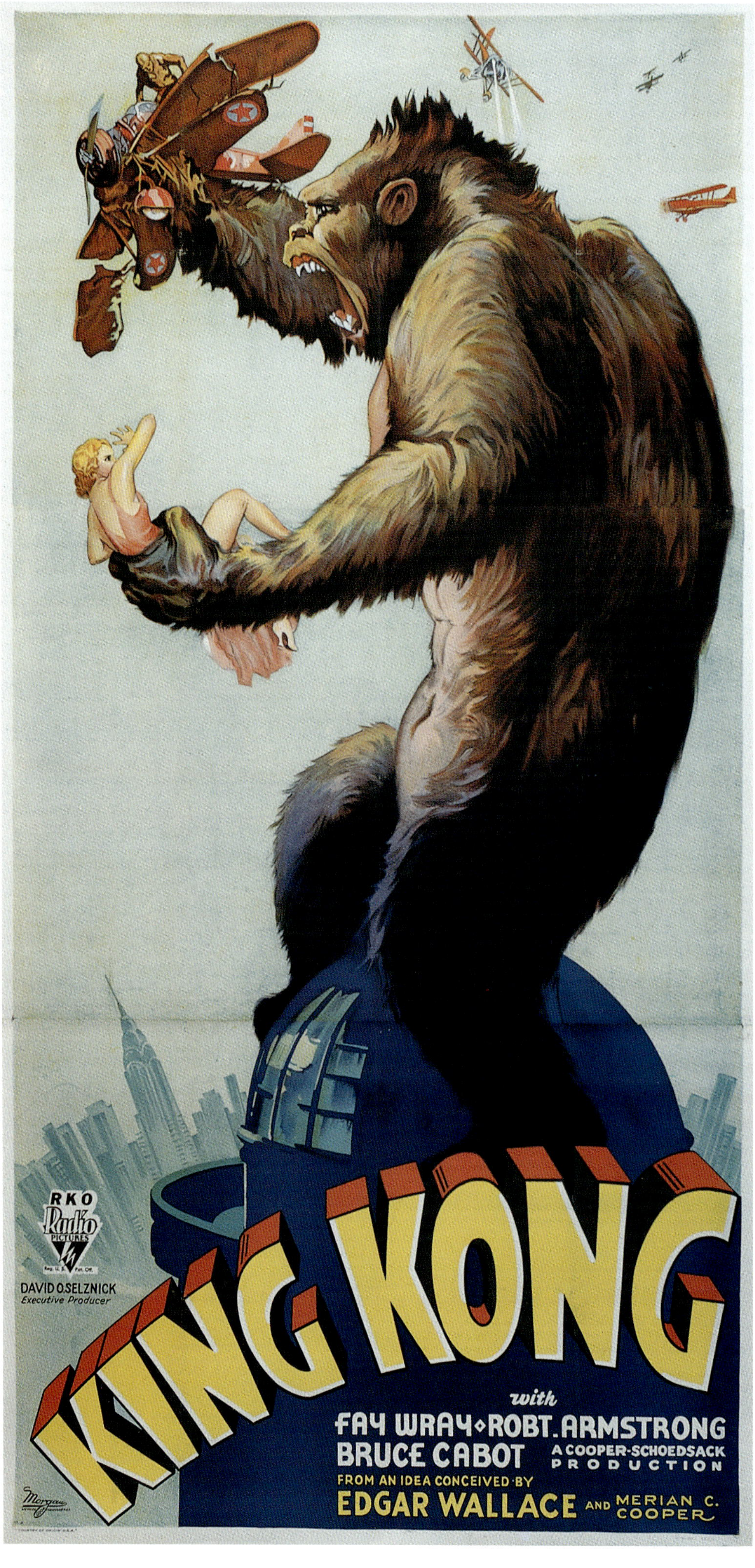

King Kong. 1933. Three-sheet, style A, art by S. Barret McCormick and Bob Sisk. $100,000-150,000.

Competition between rival studios chasing the audience's hard-earned buck became intense. Some gravitated towards continually producing similarly themed pictures after initial success within the genre. Nowhere was this more evident than at Universal, which developed its lucrative horror movie formula with *Dracula* in 1931. The film famously starred Bela Lugosi as the vampire and was hotly followed by director James Whale's gothic movie *Frankenstein* (1931) with an unbilled Boris Karloff as the Monster. Karloff was next to take top billing as the Egyptian corpse in *The Mummy* (1932) and as if to make the point that you can't have too much of a good thing, Universal then decided to team up their horror star duo Lugosi and Karloff in *The Black Cat* (1934). This, the first of eight horror films to feature the pair, was conceived as a winning combination for both studio and stars. Unfortunately as a sequence of movies they do little more than publicly catalog the sad demise of Lugosi's career. The public, however, reveled in the terror of these early horror flicks and, with R.K.O. releasing the sensational *King Kong* in 1933, Universal continued at a pace. Crowd pleasers they may have been, but the studio was undoubtedly creating masterpieces of the genre, arguably reaching the pinnacle with James Whale's *The Bride of Frankenstein* (1935), a brilliantly directed sequel to his earlier masterpiece. These Hollywood horror greats certainly owed a debt of gratitude to the European silents in the genre.

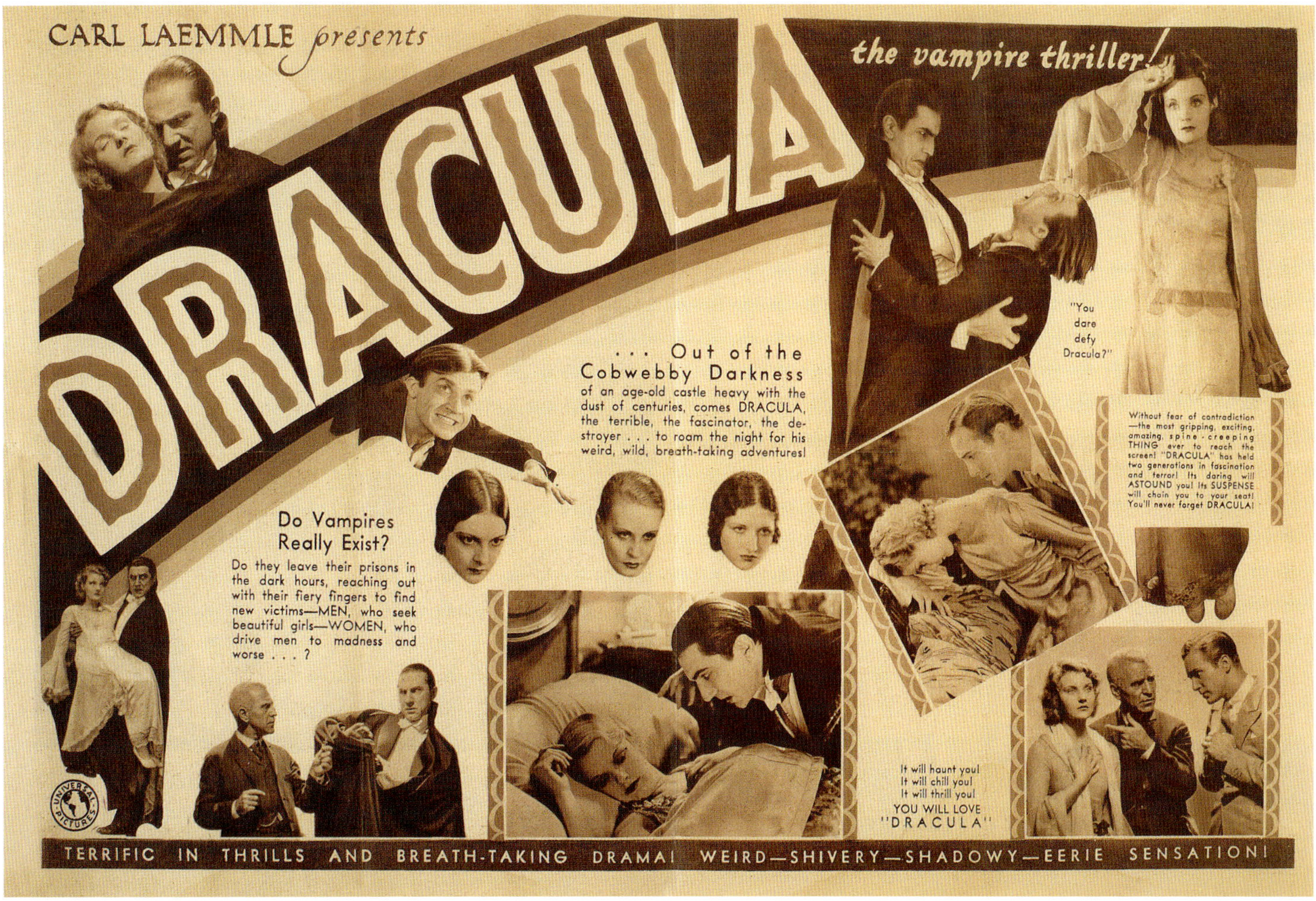

Dracula. 1931. Herald. $2,000-3,000.

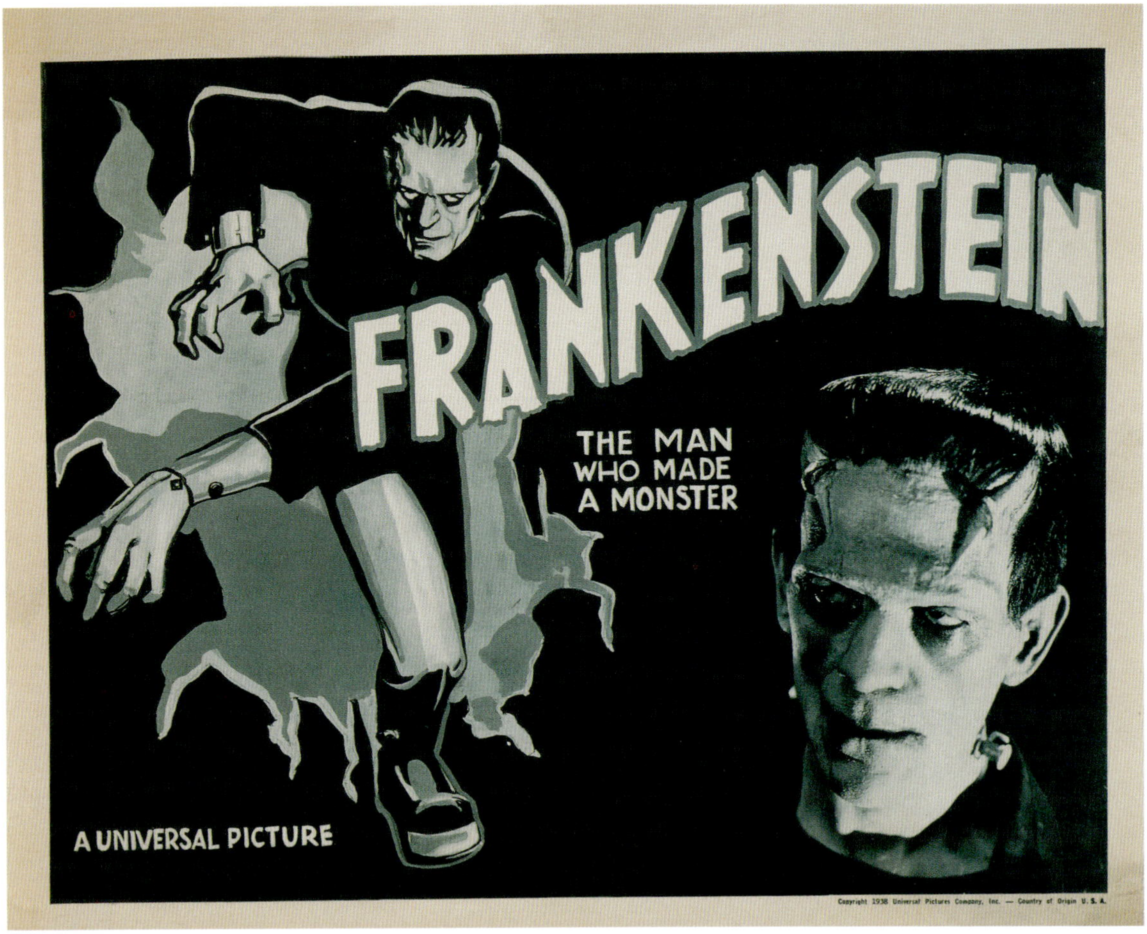

Frankenstein. 1938. Re-release, title lobby card. $1,500-2,000.

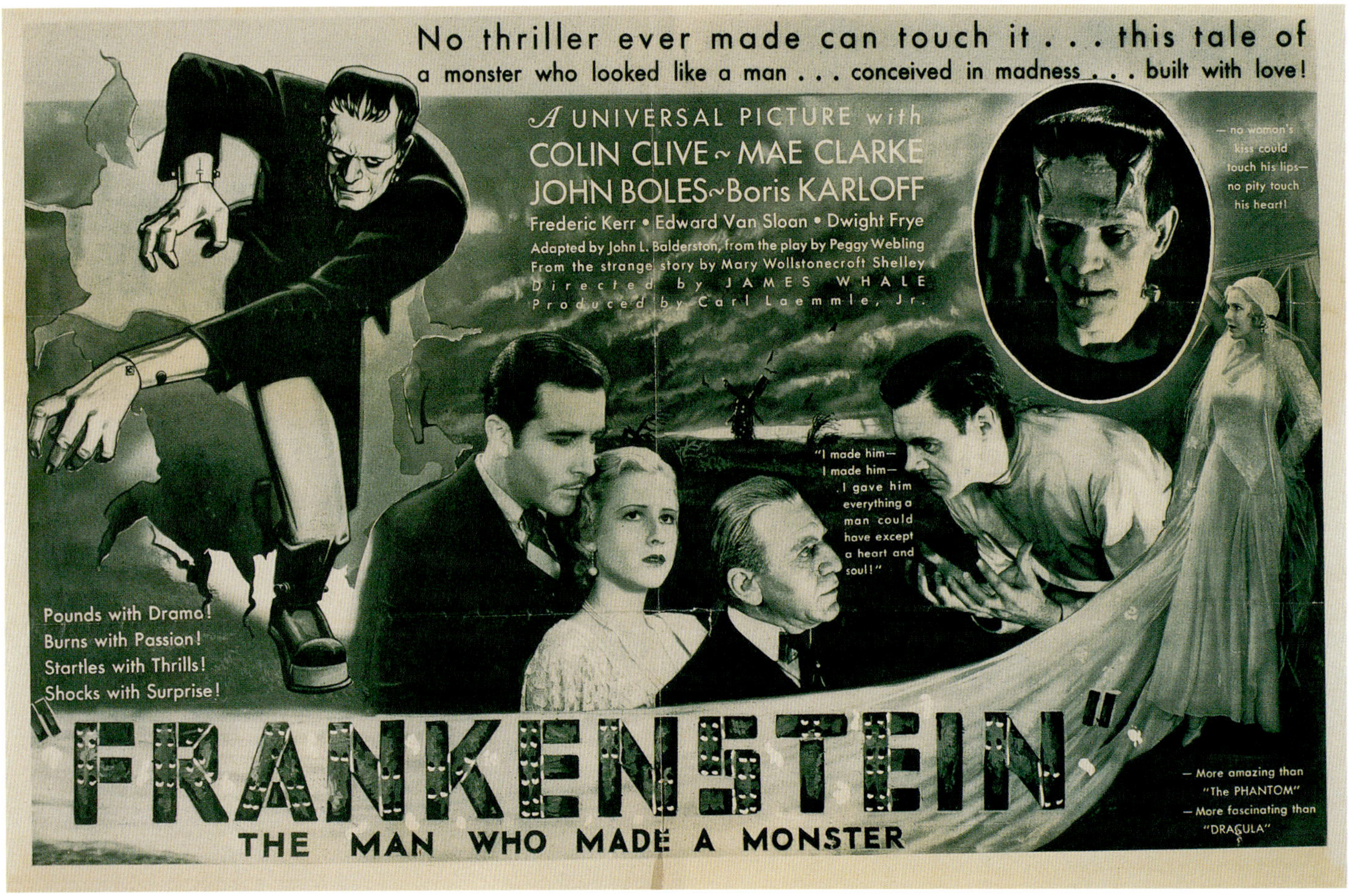

Frankenstein. 1931. Herald. $2,500-3,500.

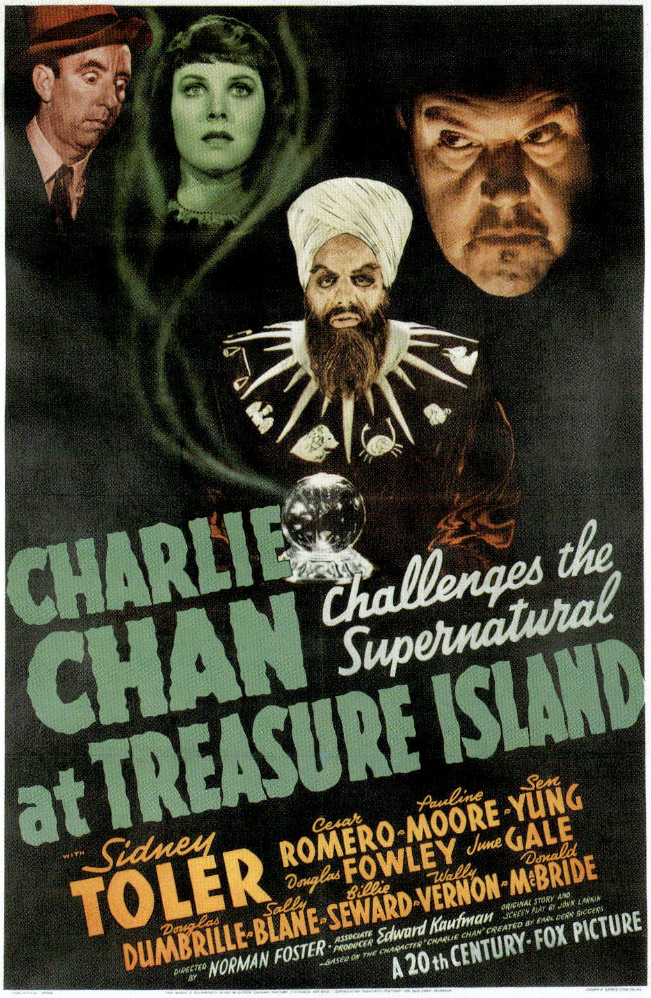

Charlie Chan at Treasure Island. 1939. One-sheet. $1,200-1,800.

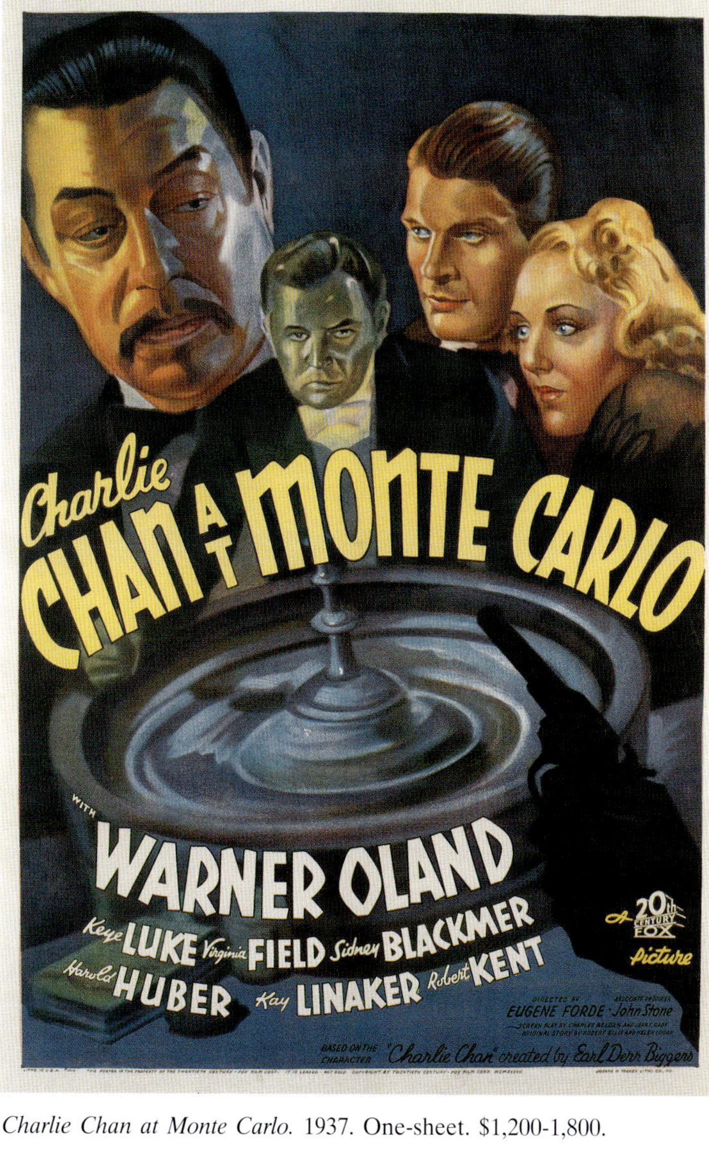

Charlie Chan at Monte Carlo. 1937. One-sheet. $1,200-1,800.

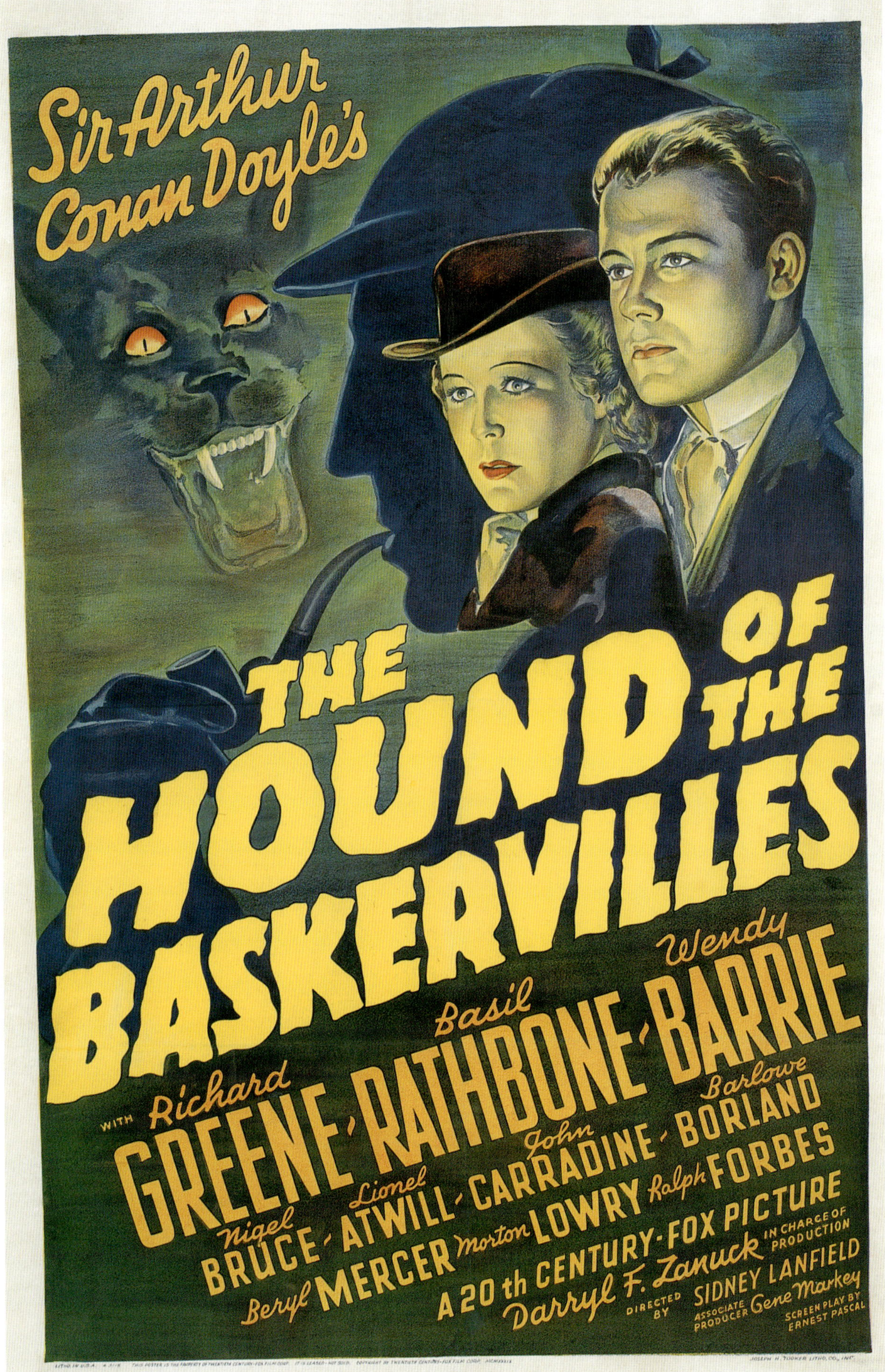

The Hound of the Baskervilles. 1939. One-sheet. $7,000-10,000.

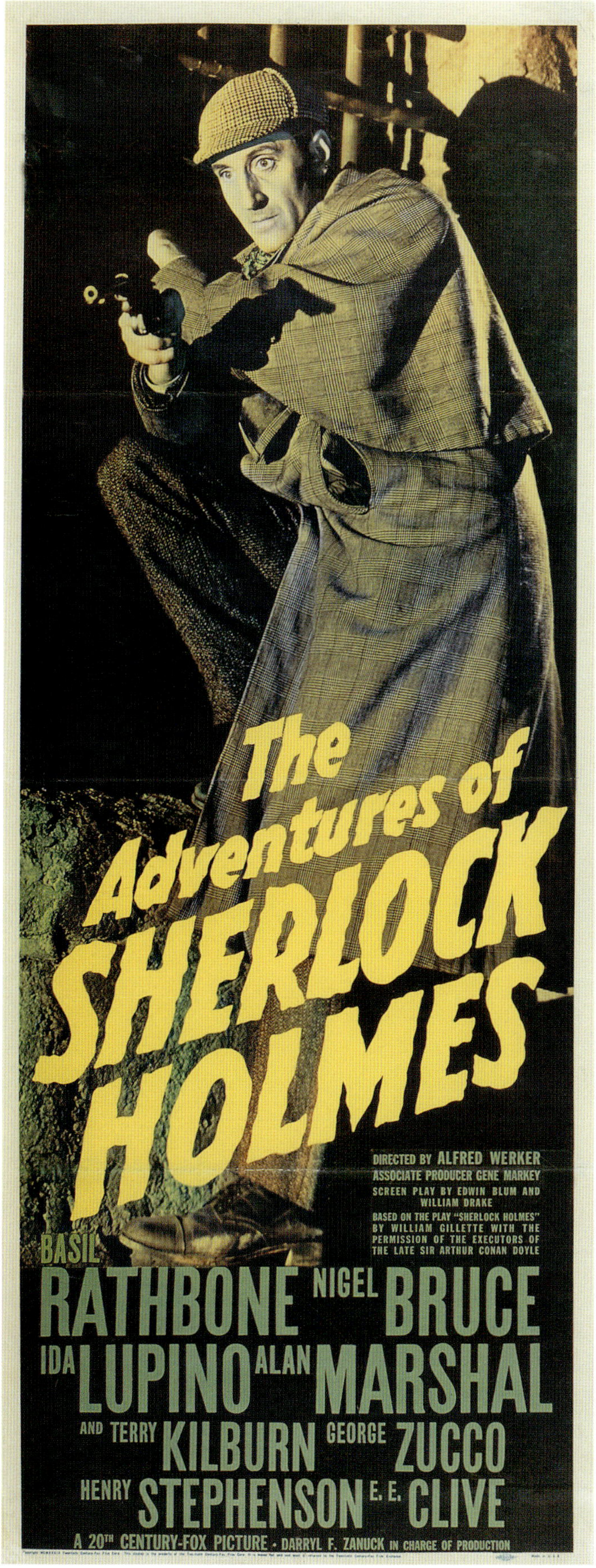

The Adventures of Sherlock Holmes. 1939. Insert. $2,000-2,500.

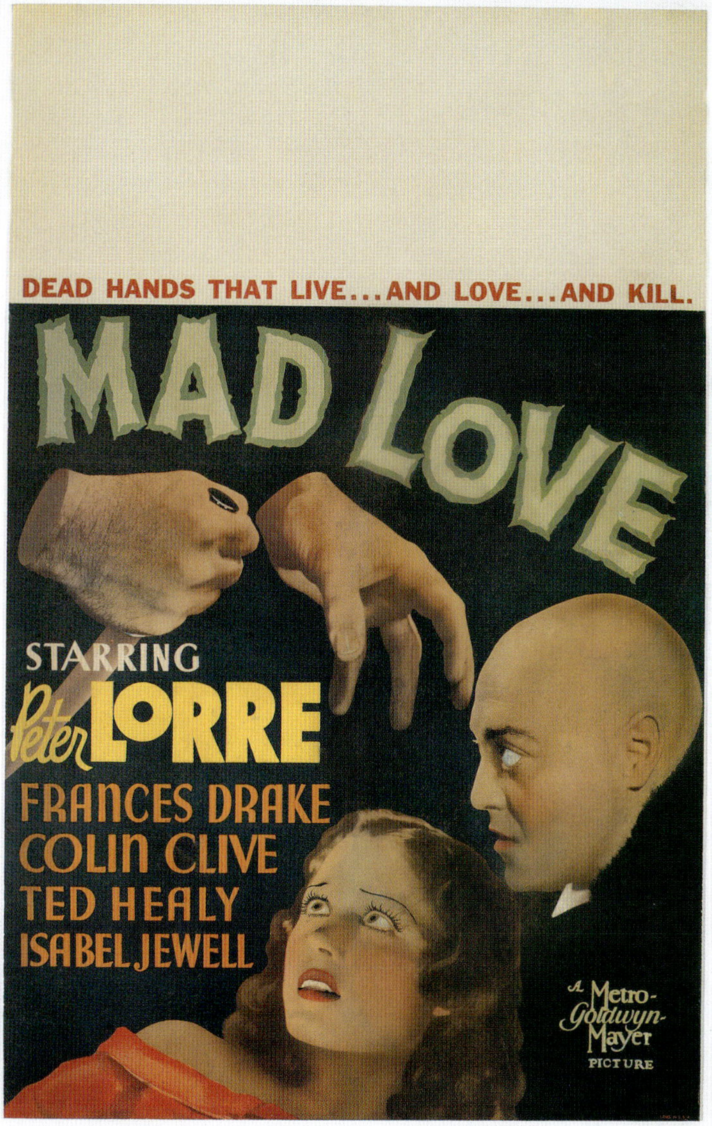

Mad Love. 1935. Window card. $5,000-7,000.

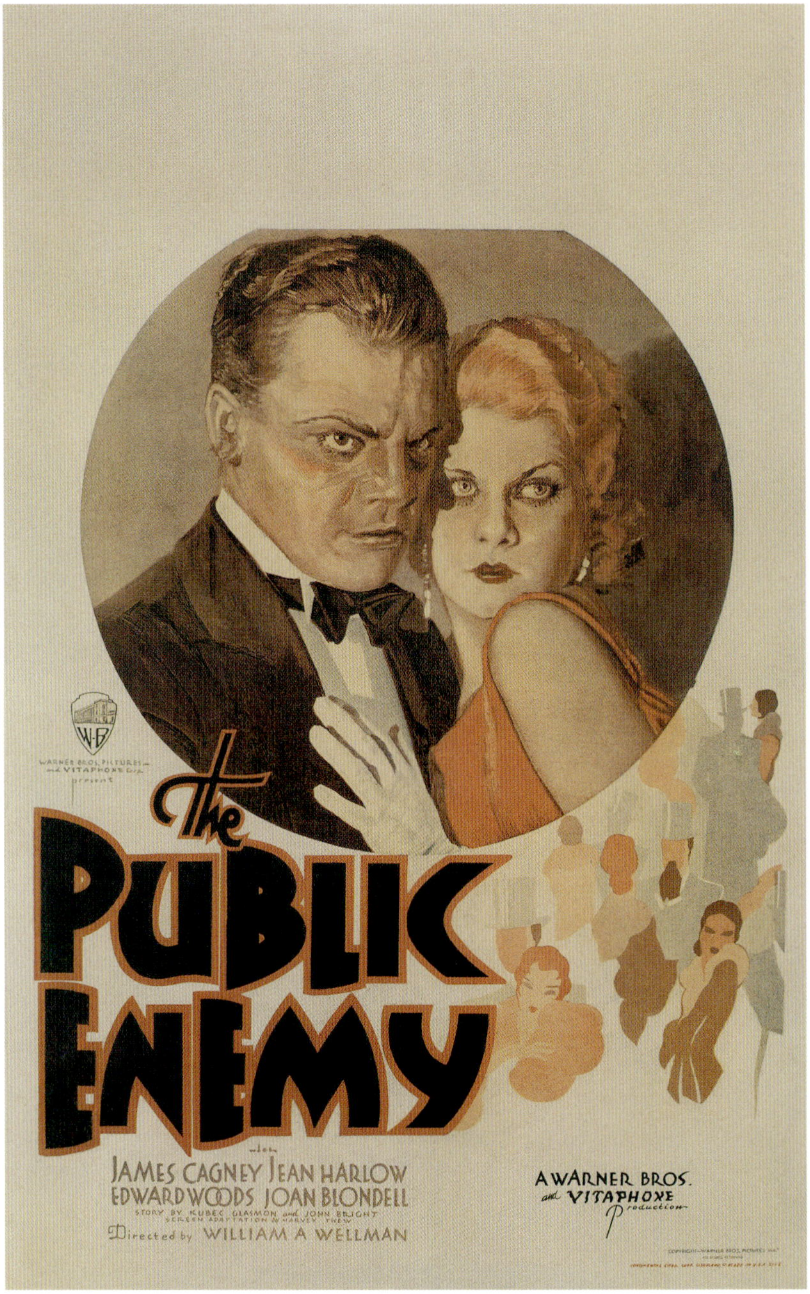

The Public Enemy. 1931. Window card. $8,000-12,000.

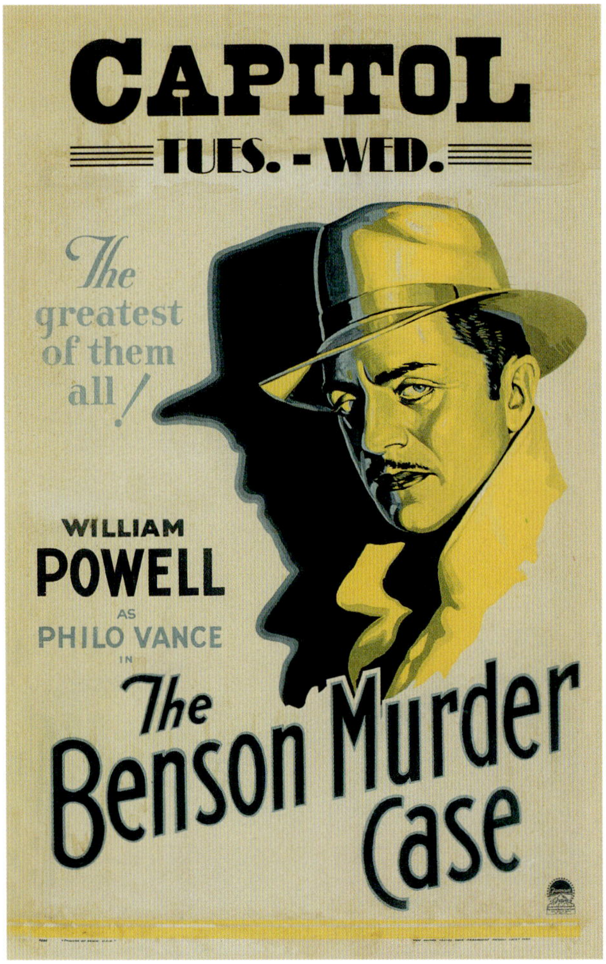

The Benson Murder Case. 1930. Window card. $1,200-1,800.

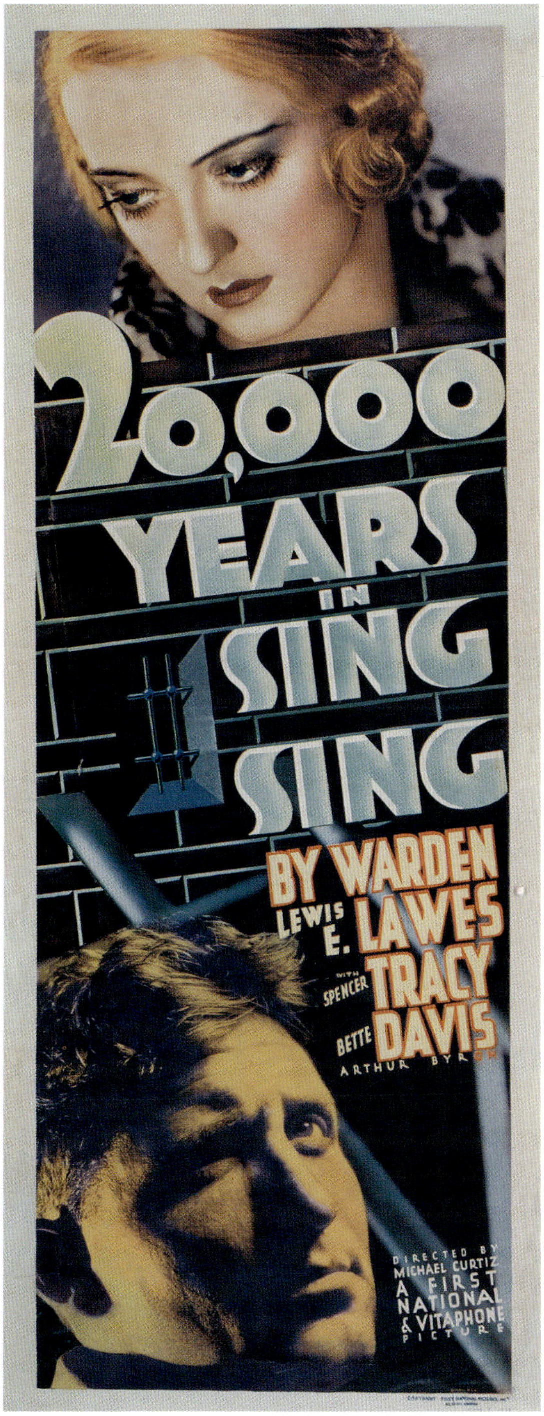

20,000 Years in Sing Sing. 1932. Insert. $1,200-1,800.

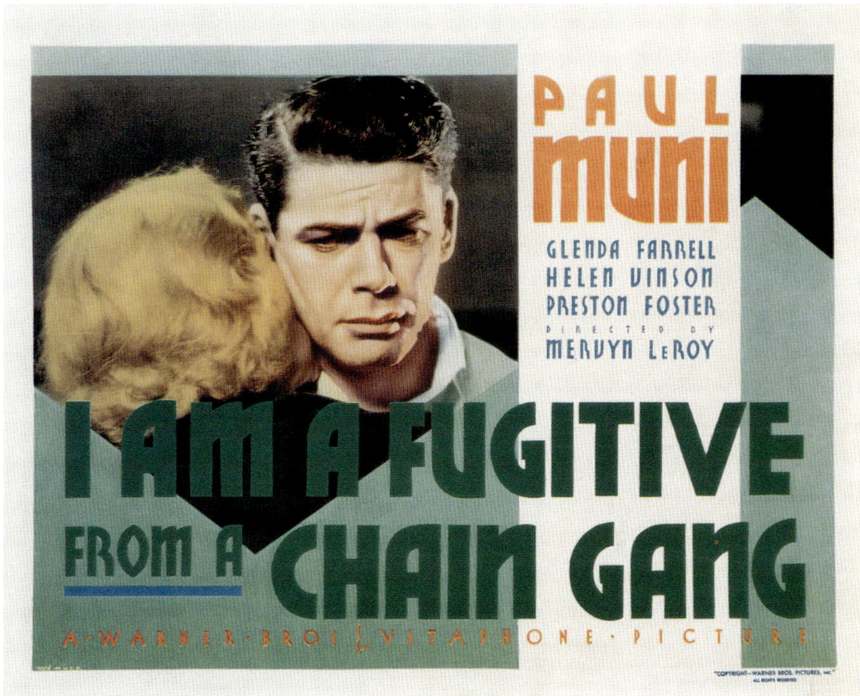

I Am a Fugitive from a Chain Gang. 1932. Title lobby card. $1,000-2,000.

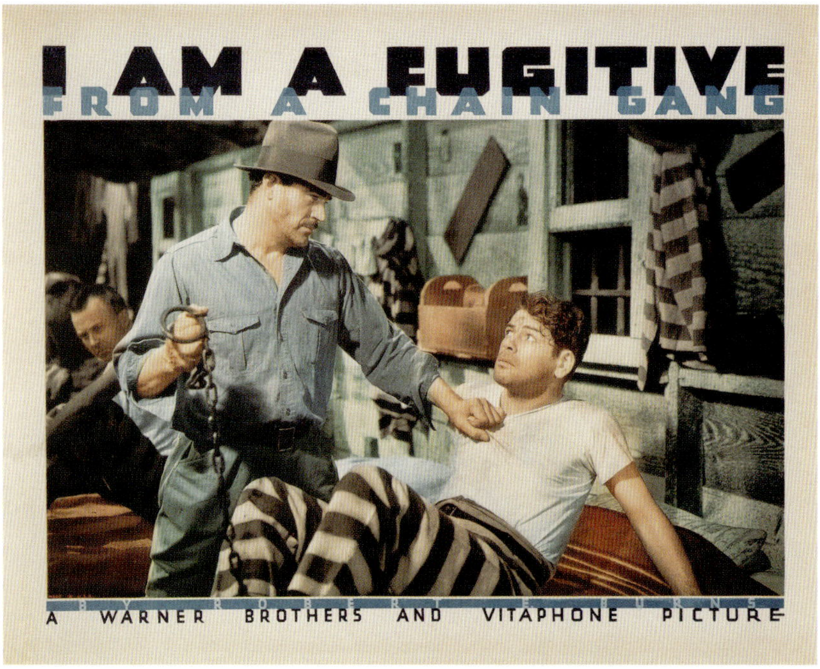

I Am a Fugitive from a Chain Gang. 1932. Lobby card. $800-1,200.

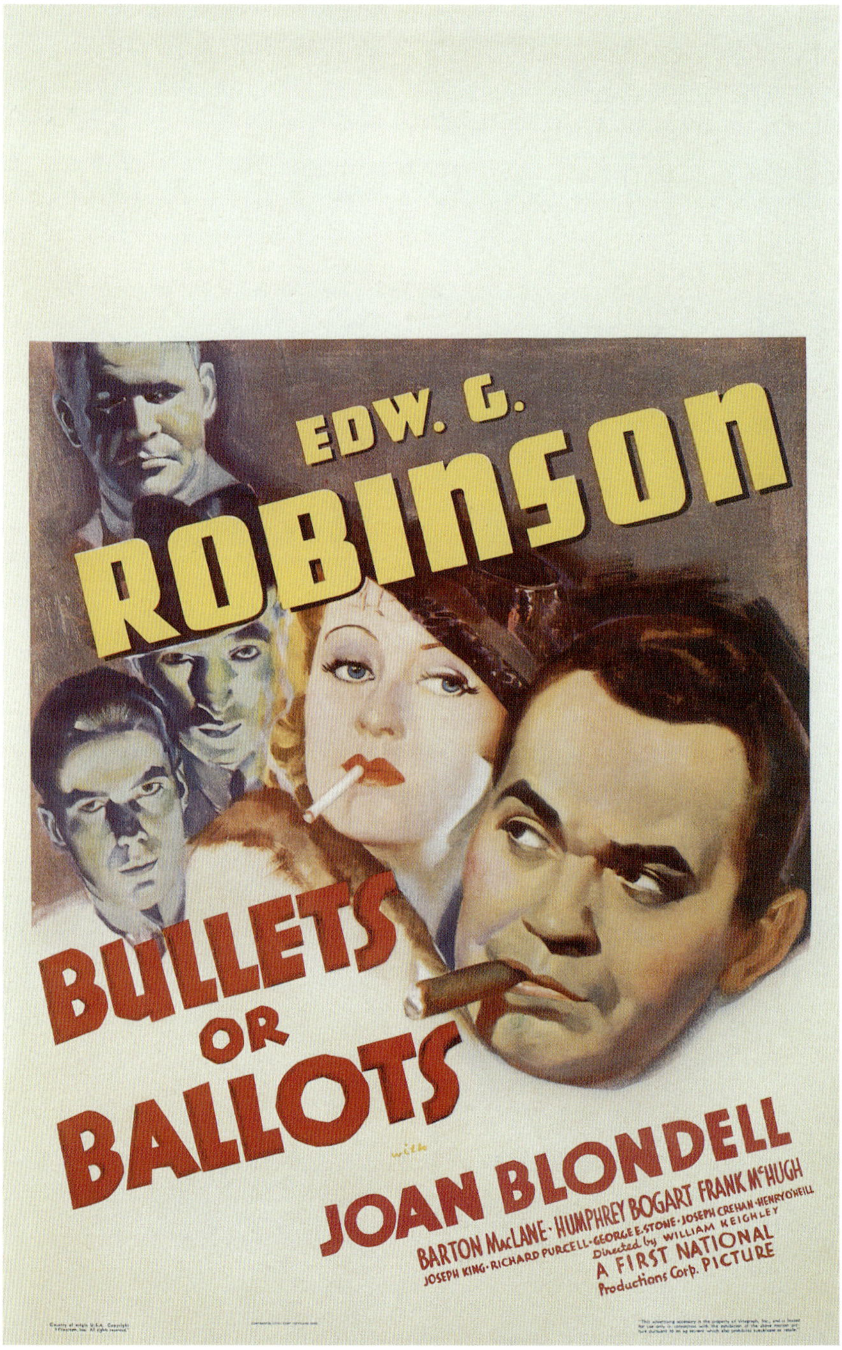

Bullets or Ballots. 1936. Window card. $1,200-1,800.

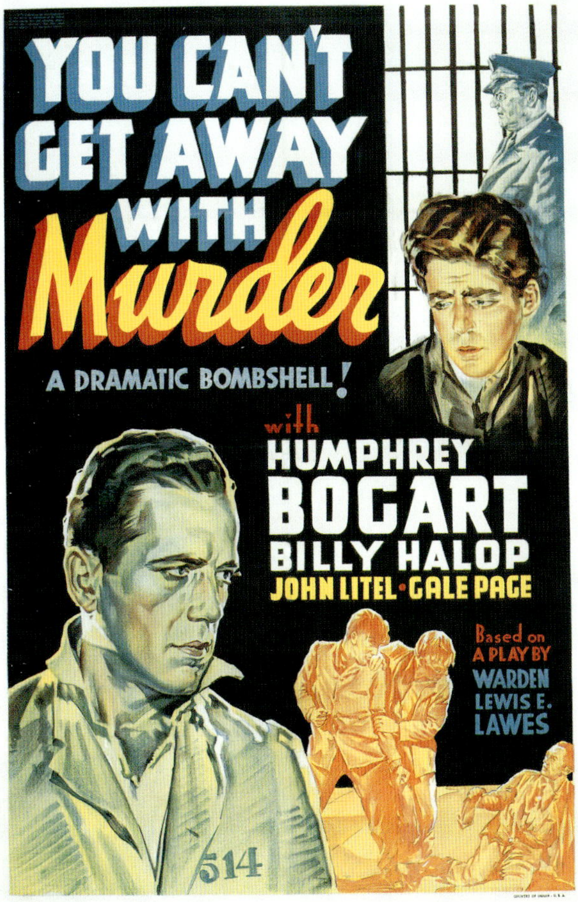

You Can't Get Away with Murder. 1937. One-sheet. $1,500-2,000.

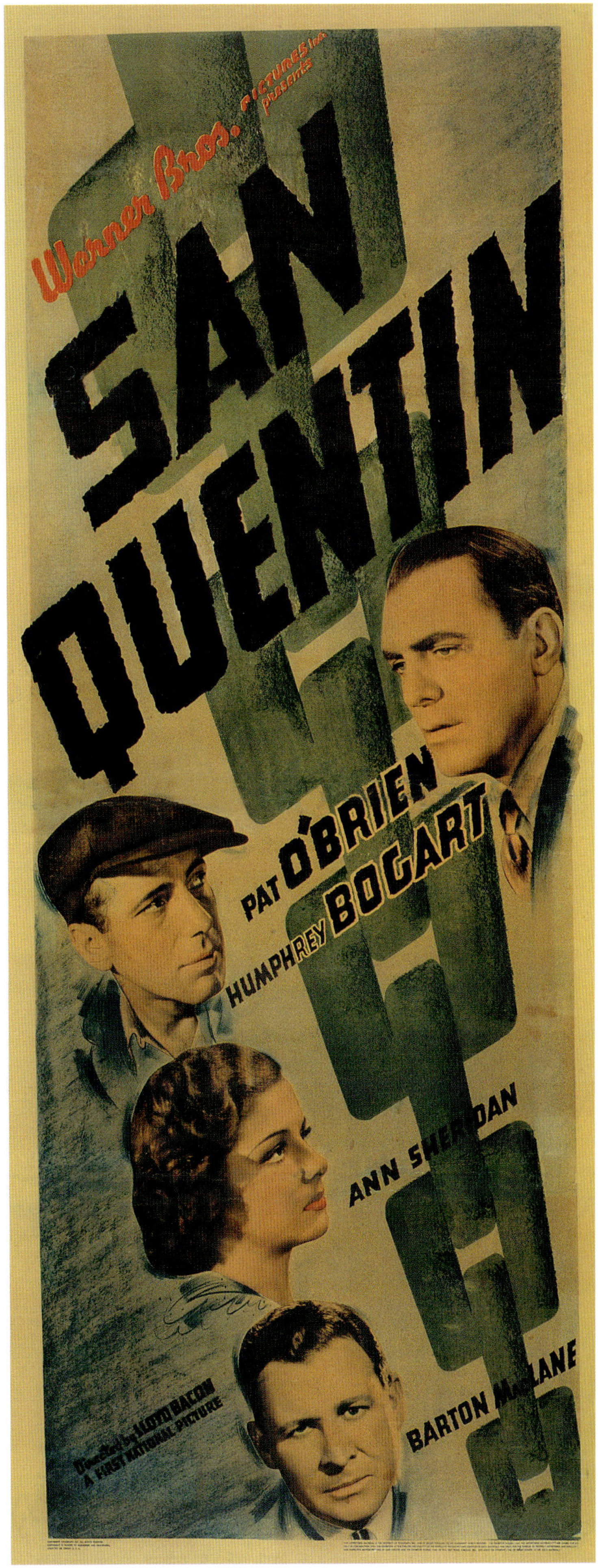

San Quentin. 1937. Insert. $2,500-3,500.

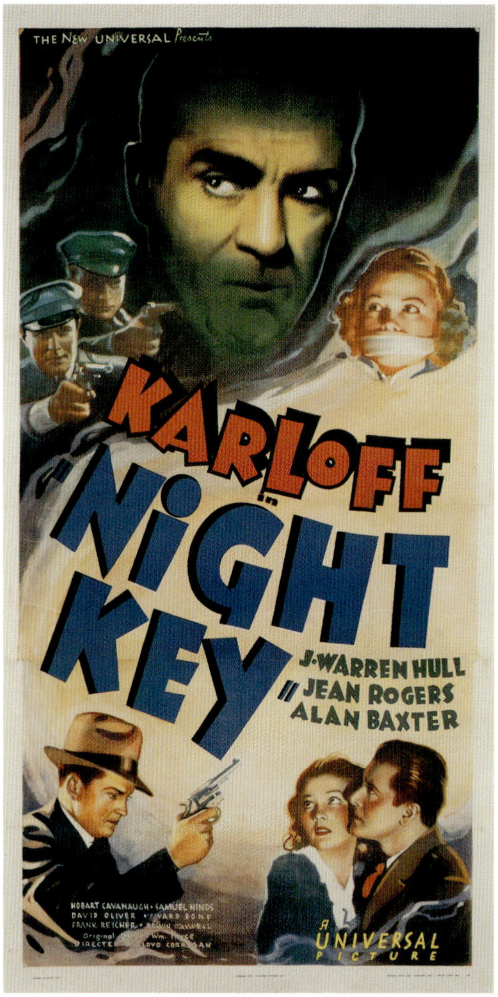

Night Key. 1937. Three-sheet. $1,500-2,000.

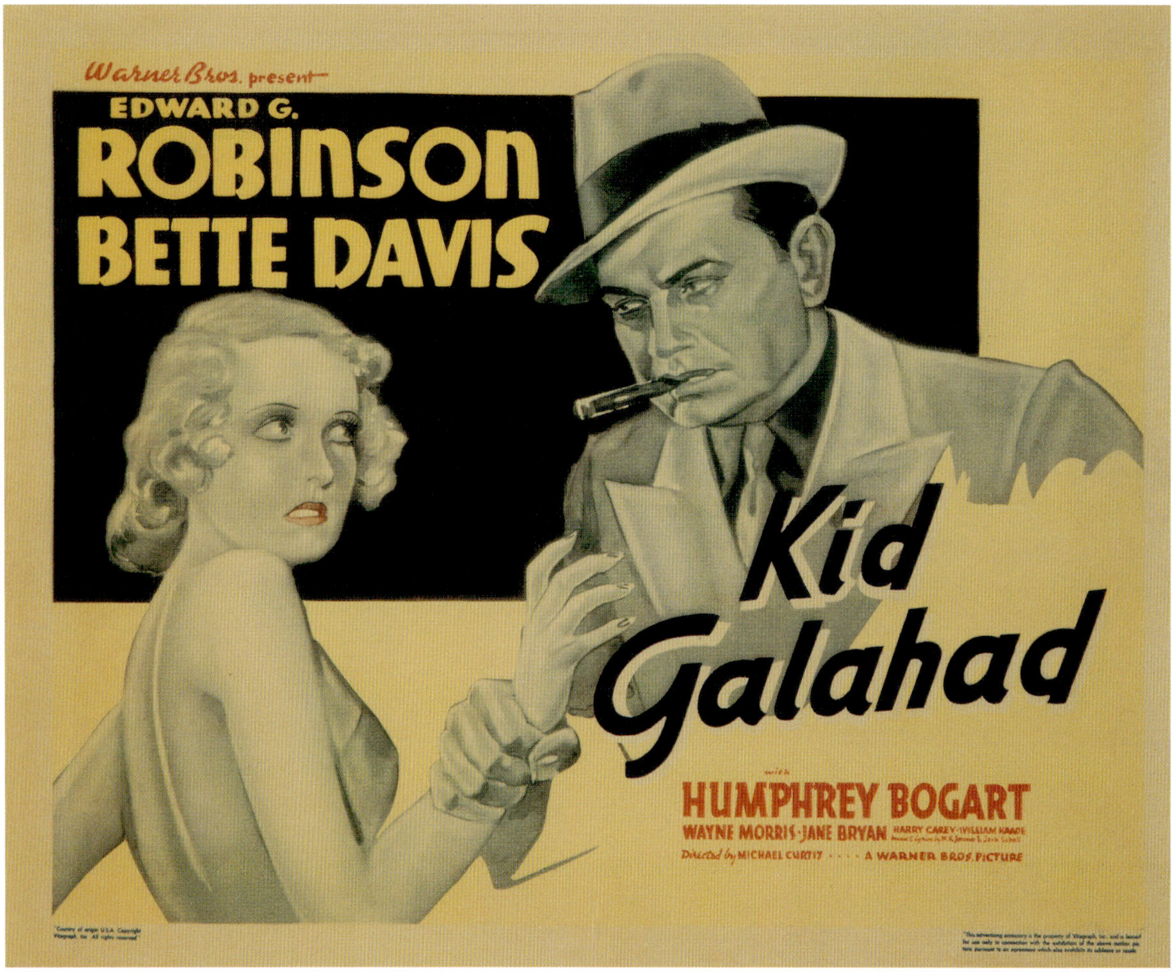

Kid Galahad. 1937. Title lobby card. $1,000-1,500.

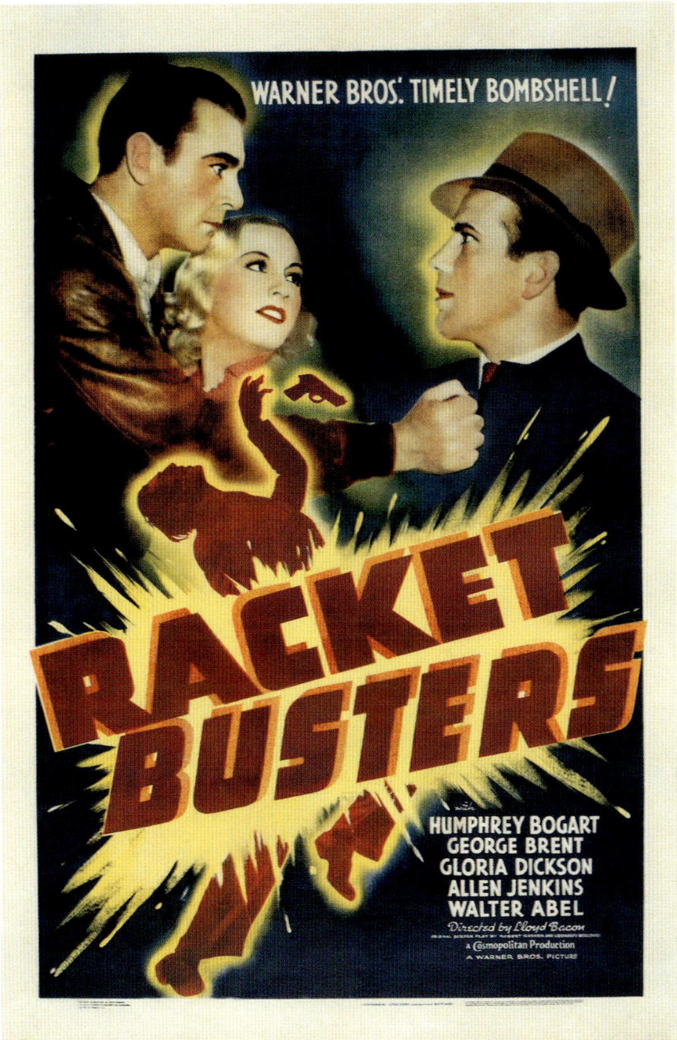

Racket Busters. 1938.
One-sheet. $1,200-1,800.

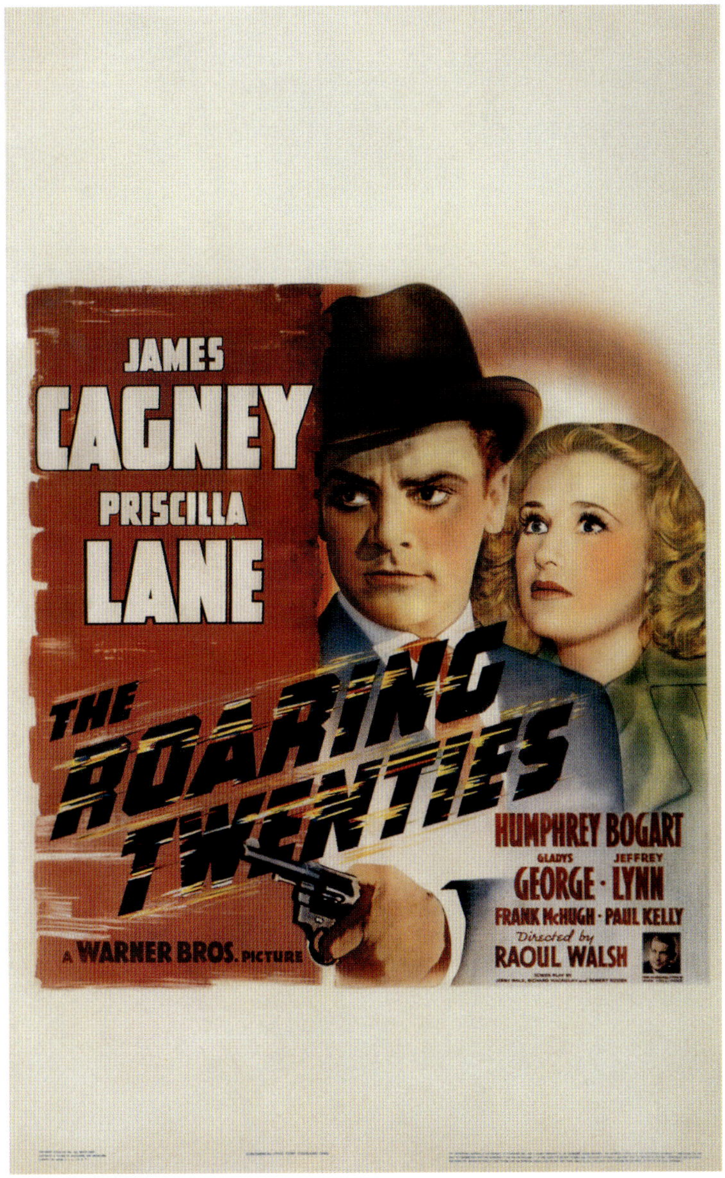

The Roaring Twenties. 1939.
Window card. $1,000-1,500.

M.G.M. famously promised "more stars than are in heaven" and, with a spectacular galaxy that included Joan Crawford, Clark Gable, Greta Garbo, Jean Harlow, Myrna Loy, William Powell, and Norma Shearer, they perhaps had every right to do so. Together with Paramount they produced a broad range of contemporary and historical movies that were often stylistically innovative and are now recognized as some of the all time greats in cinematic history. The posters produced during this period are perhaps some of the best designed, most loved and prized by collectors the world over. The art work was more sophisticated and accomplished with some of the best lithographic printing techniques being deployed to do justice to the brushwork of often unknown, but hugely talented, studio artists.

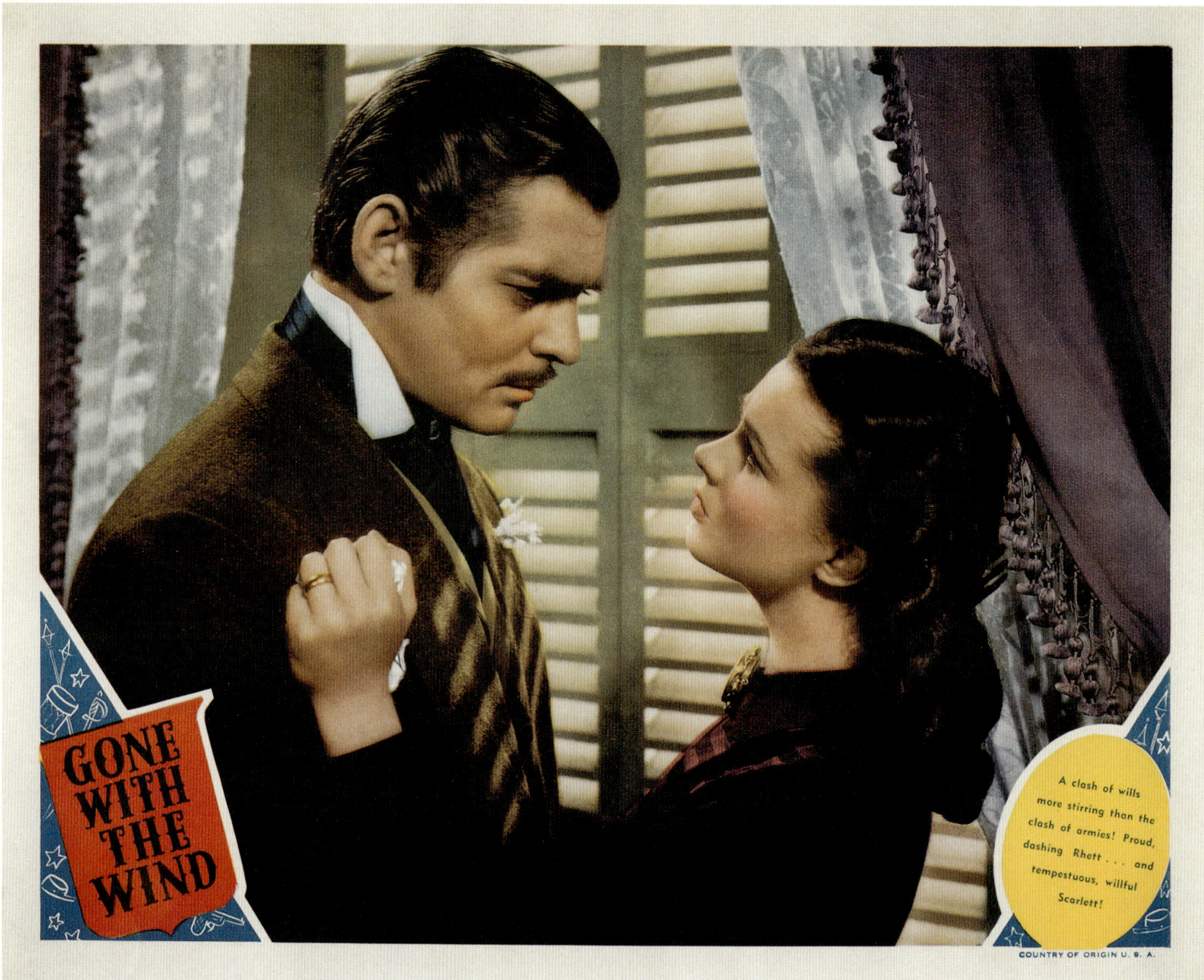

Gone with the Wind. 1939. Lobby card. $2,000-3,000.

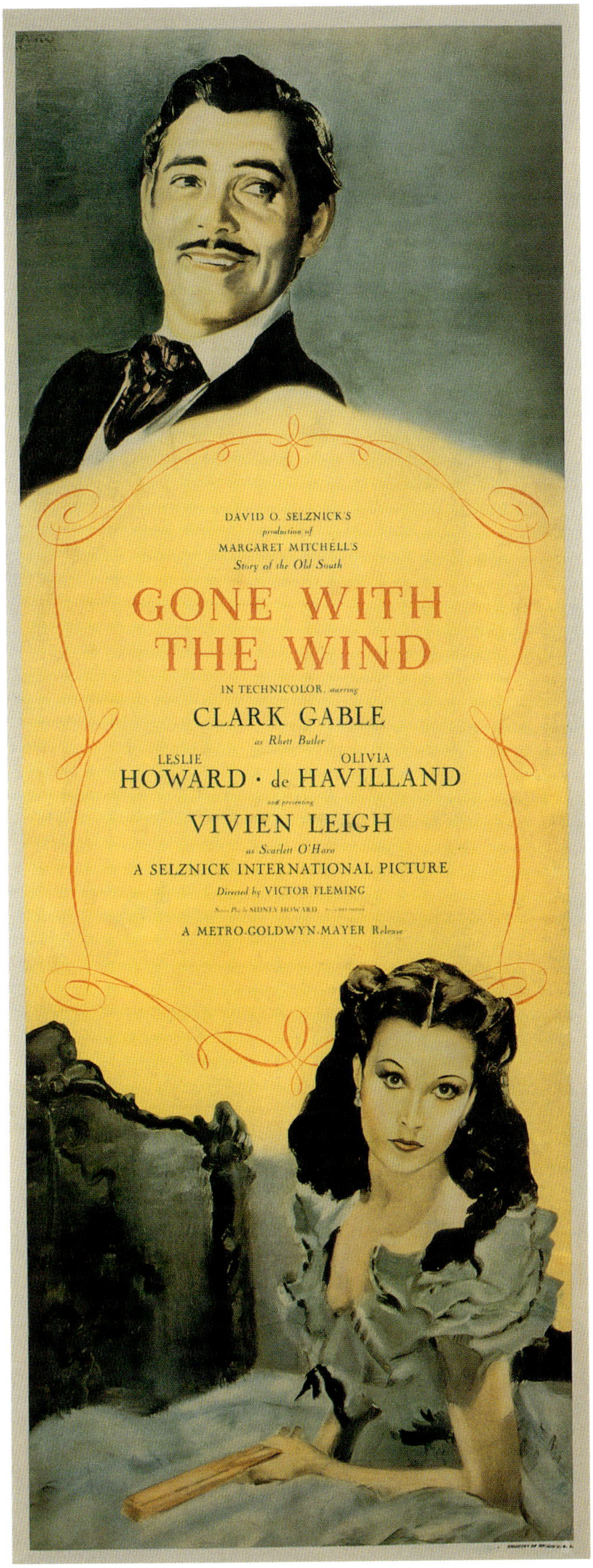

Gone with the Wind. 1939. Insert, art by Armando Seguso. $10,000-15,000.

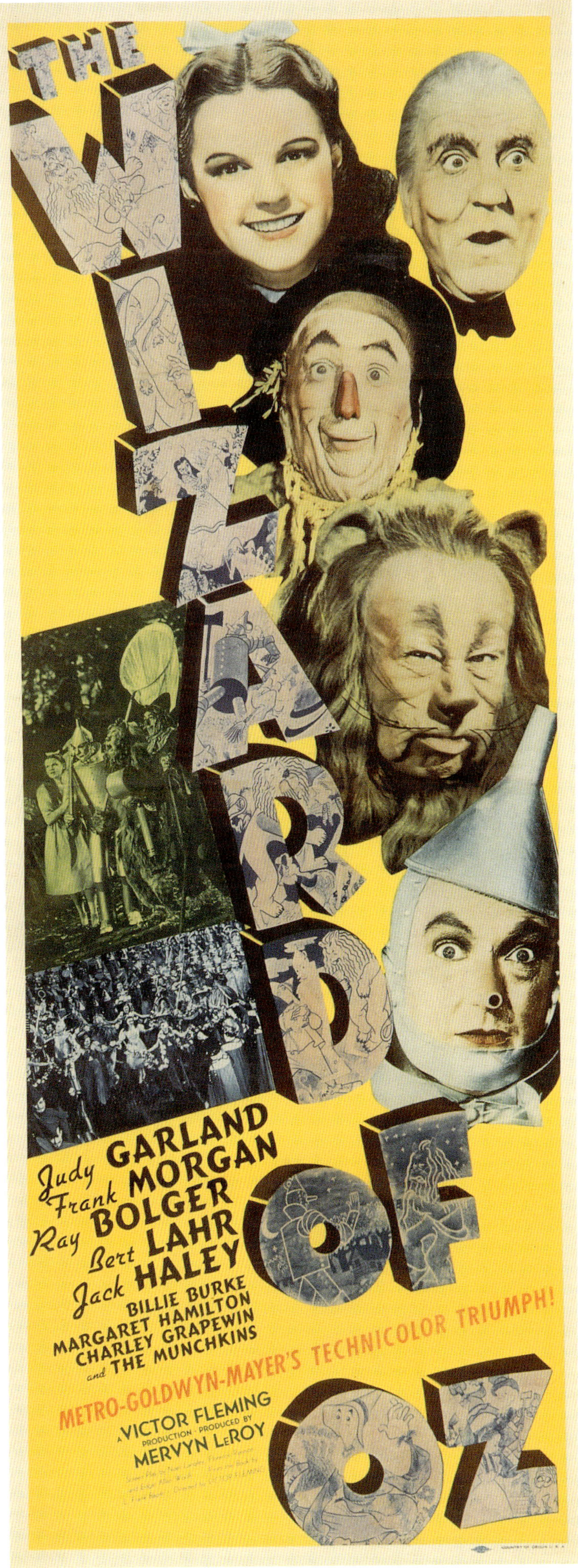

The Wizard of Oz. 1939. Insert. $9,000-12,000.

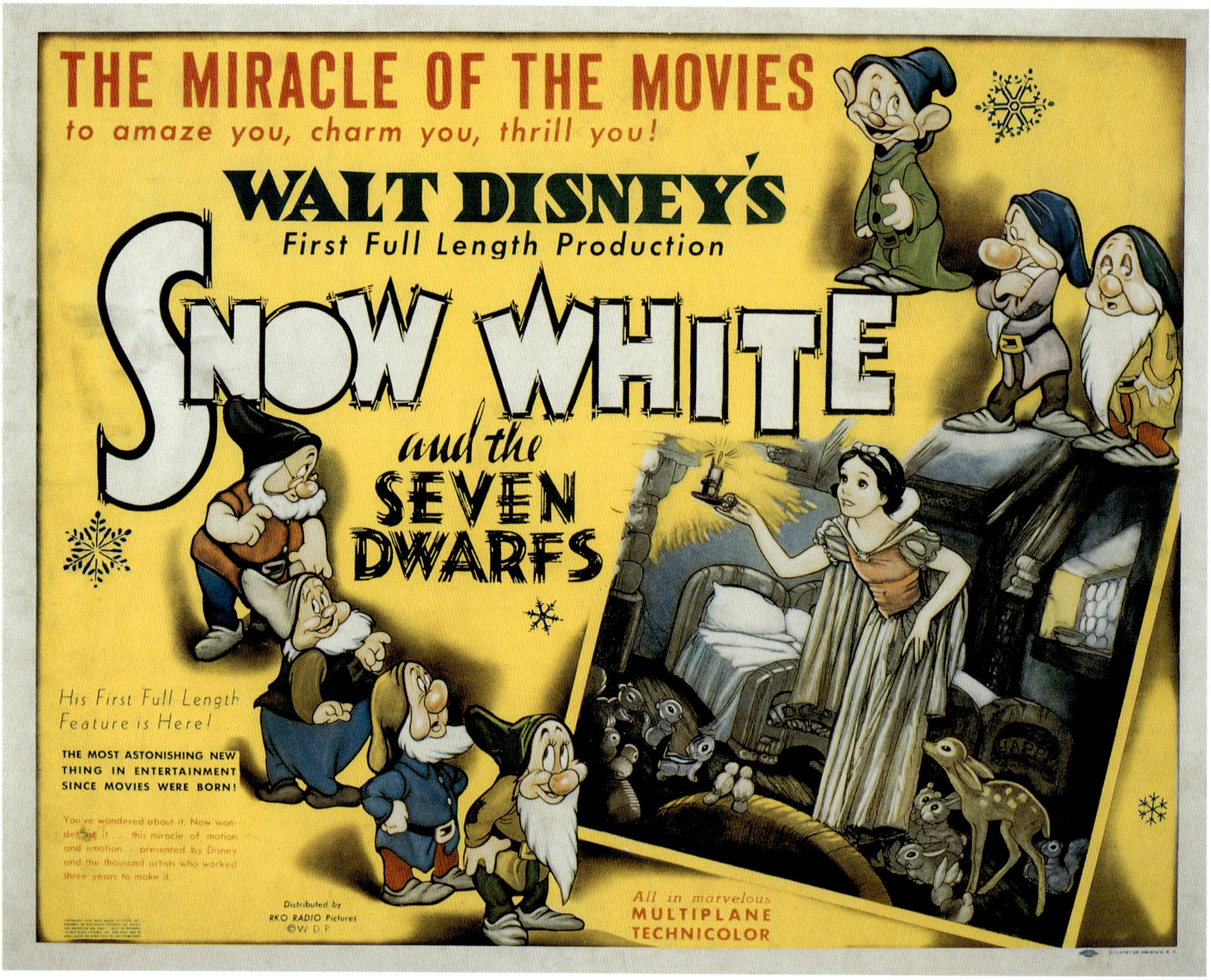

Snow White and the Seven Dwarfs. 1937. Half-sheet. $5,000-8,000.

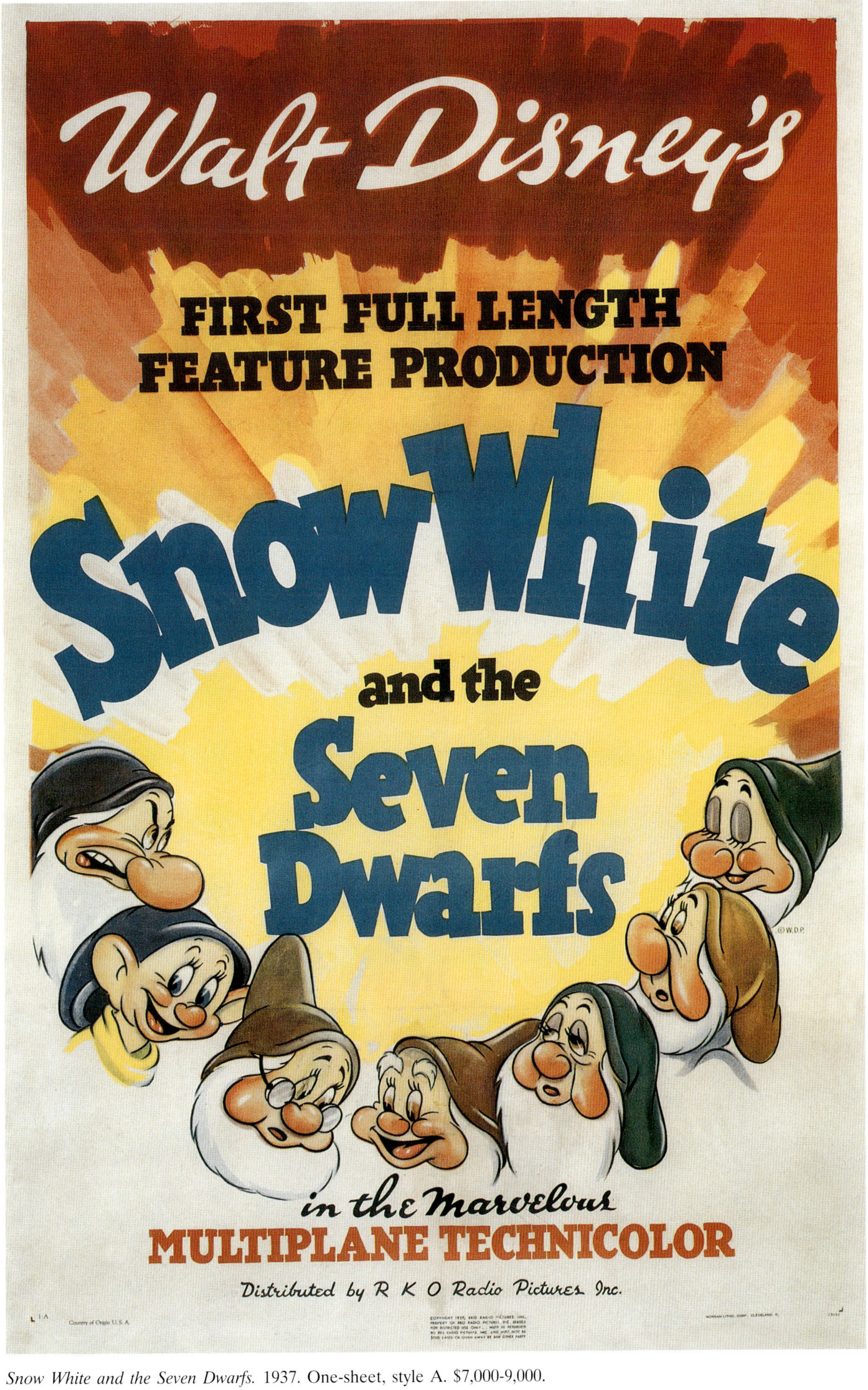

Snow White and the Seven Dwarfs. 1937. One-sheet, style A. $7,000-9,000.

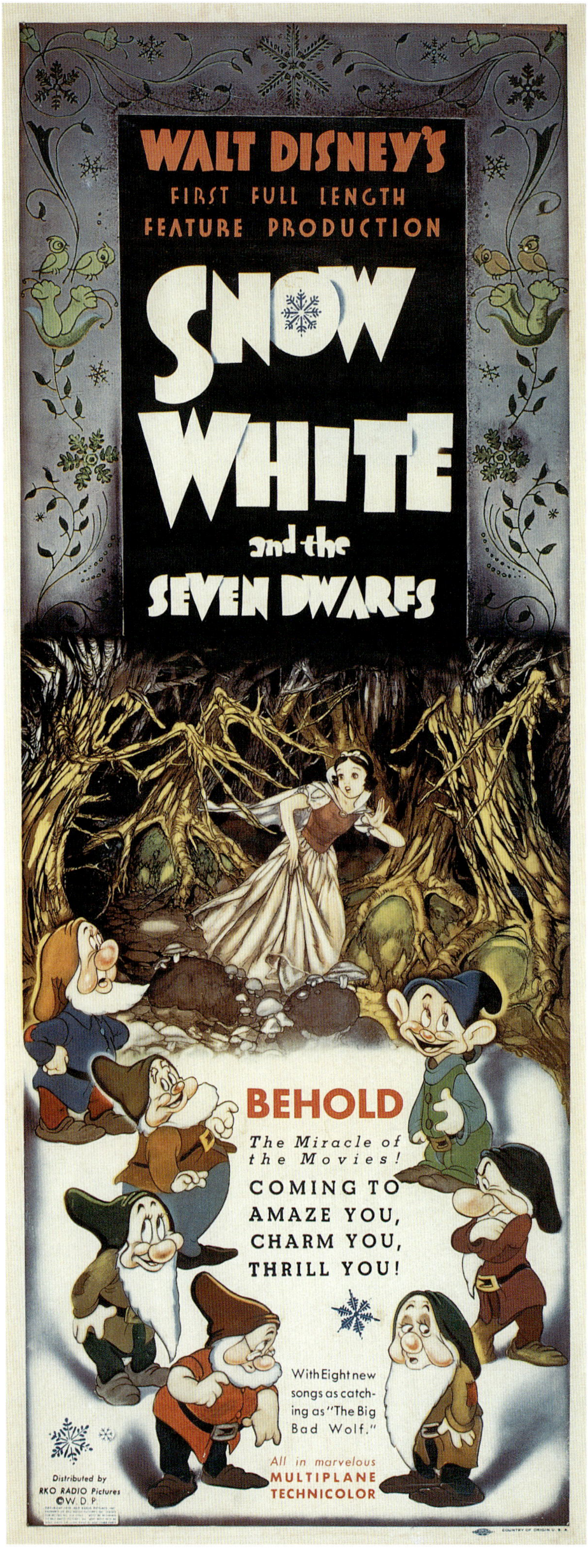

Snow White and the Seven Dwarfs. 1937. Insert. $10,000-15,000.

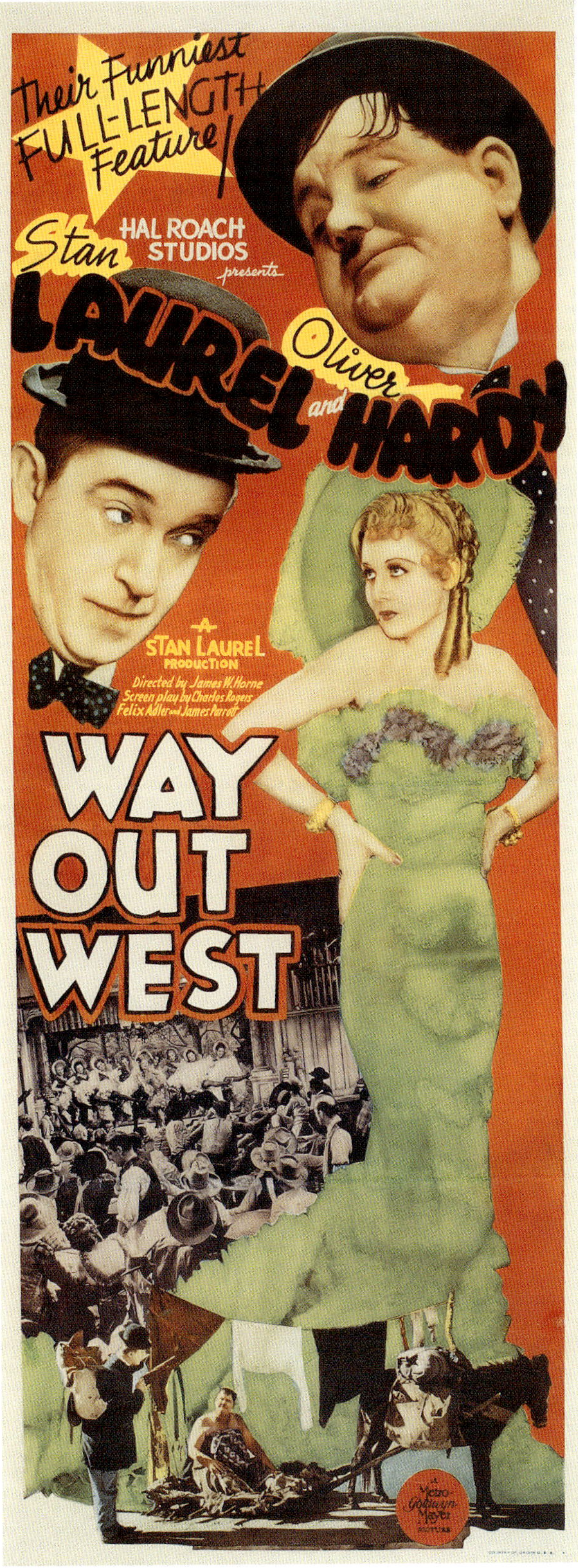

Way Out West. 1937. Insert. $2,500-3,500.

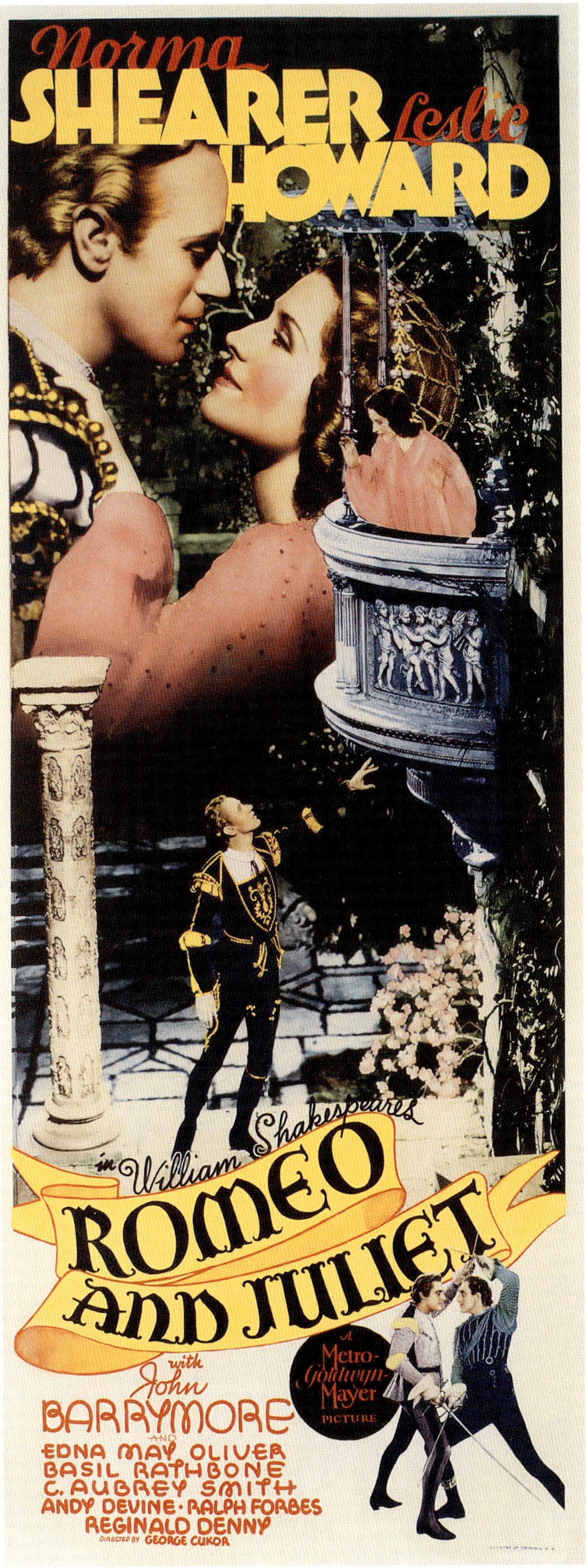

Romeo and Juliet. 1936. Insert. $1,000-1,500.

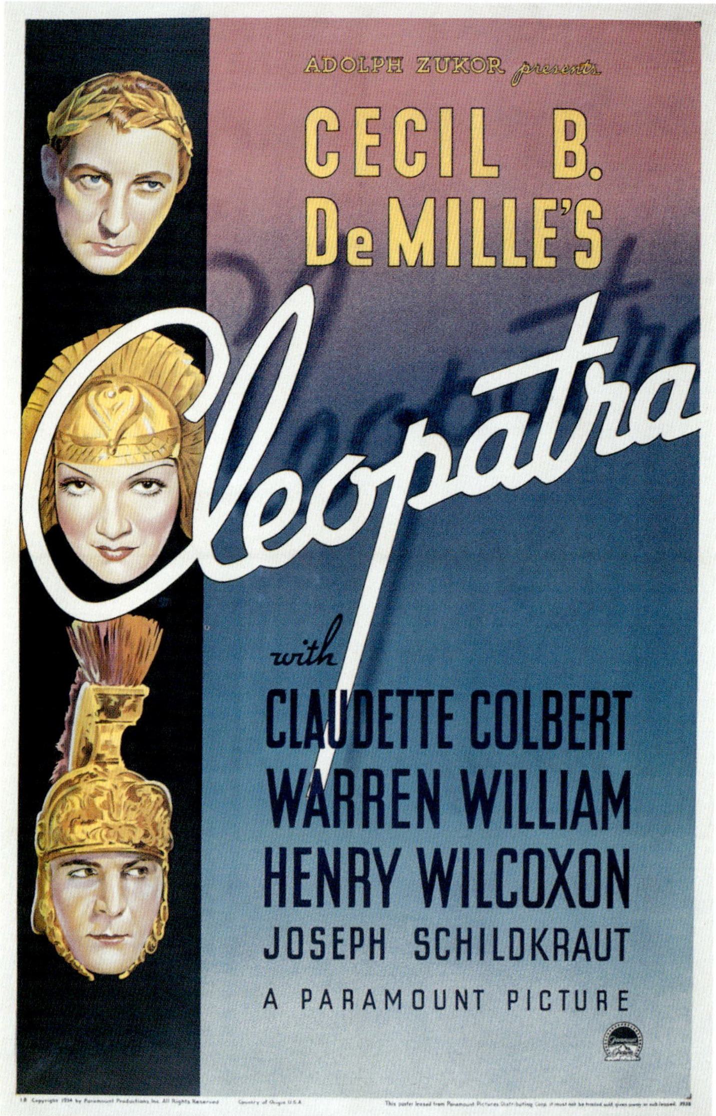

Cleopatra. 1934. One-sheet, style B. $2,000-3,000.

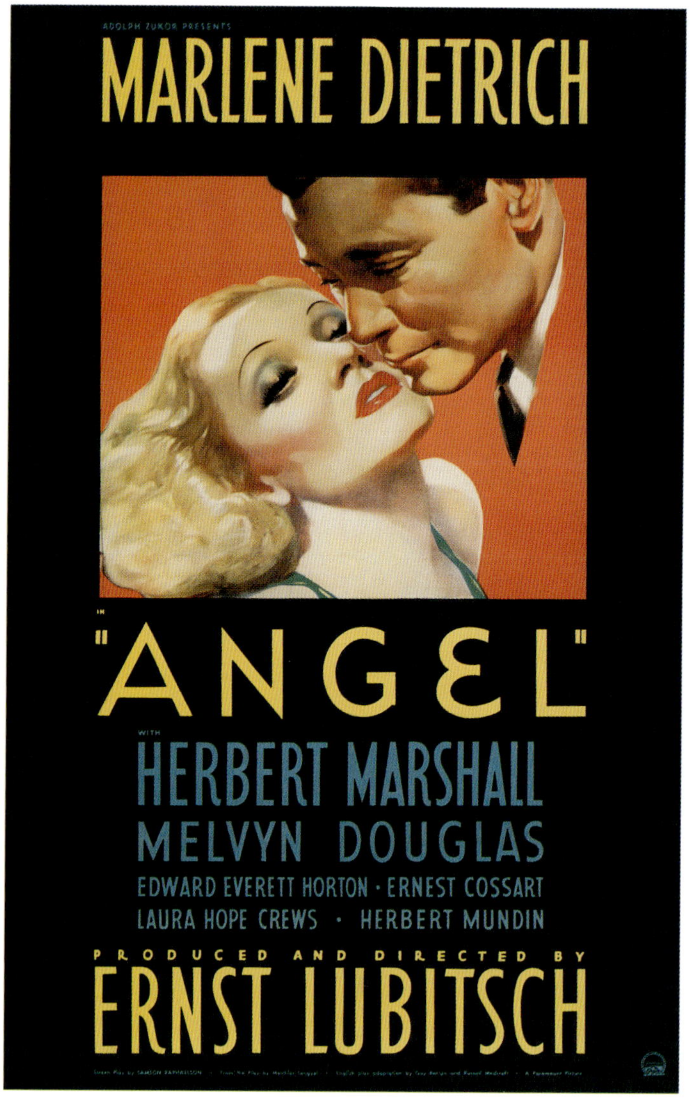

Angel. 1937. One-sheet. $4,000-6,000.

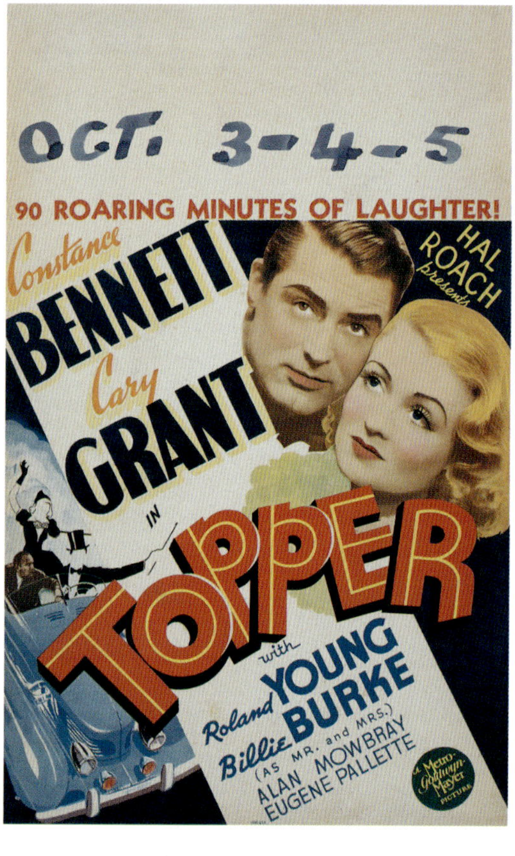

Topper. 1937. Window card. $1,200-1,800.

Stage Door. 1937. One-sheet.
$2,500-3,000.

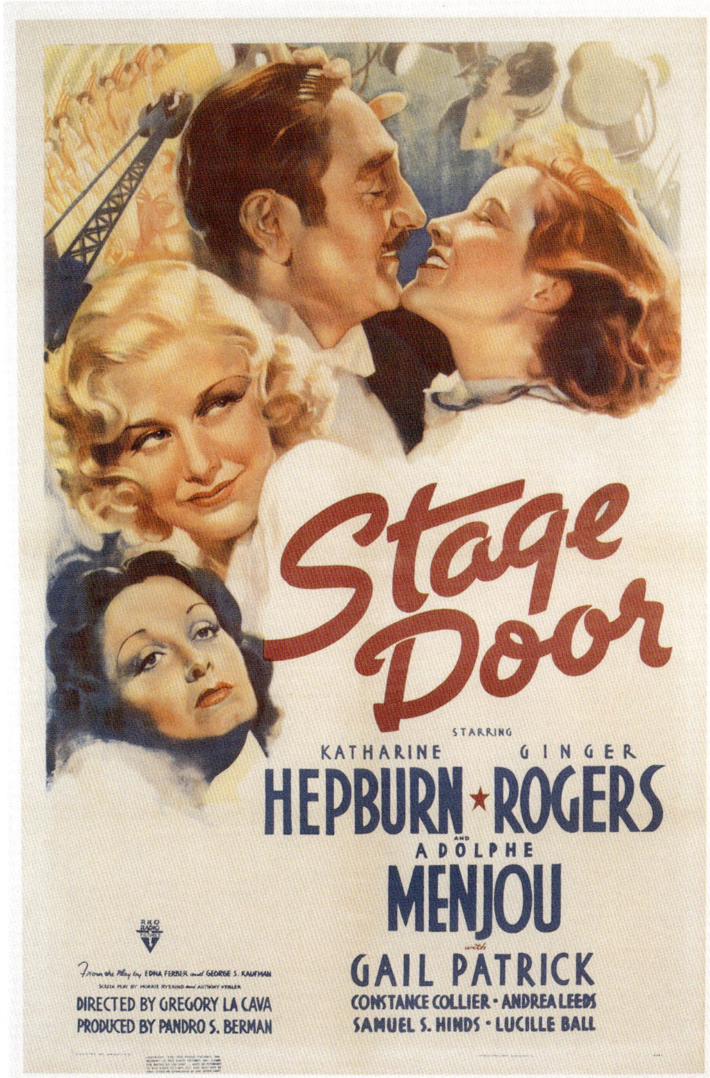

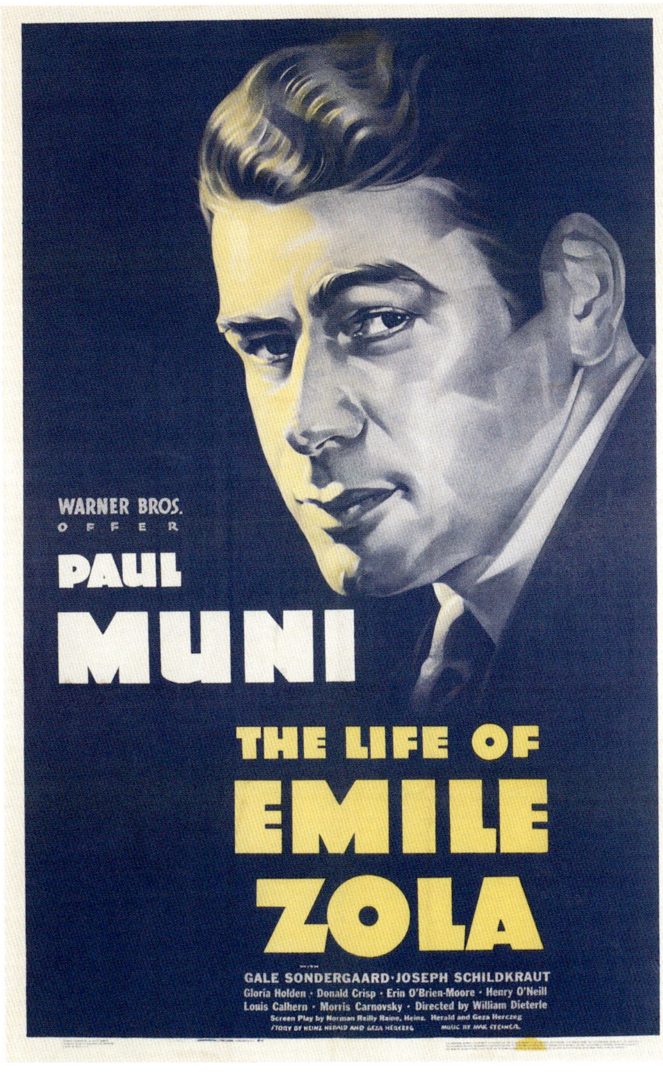

The Life of Emile Zola. 1937.
One-sheet. $3,000-5,000.

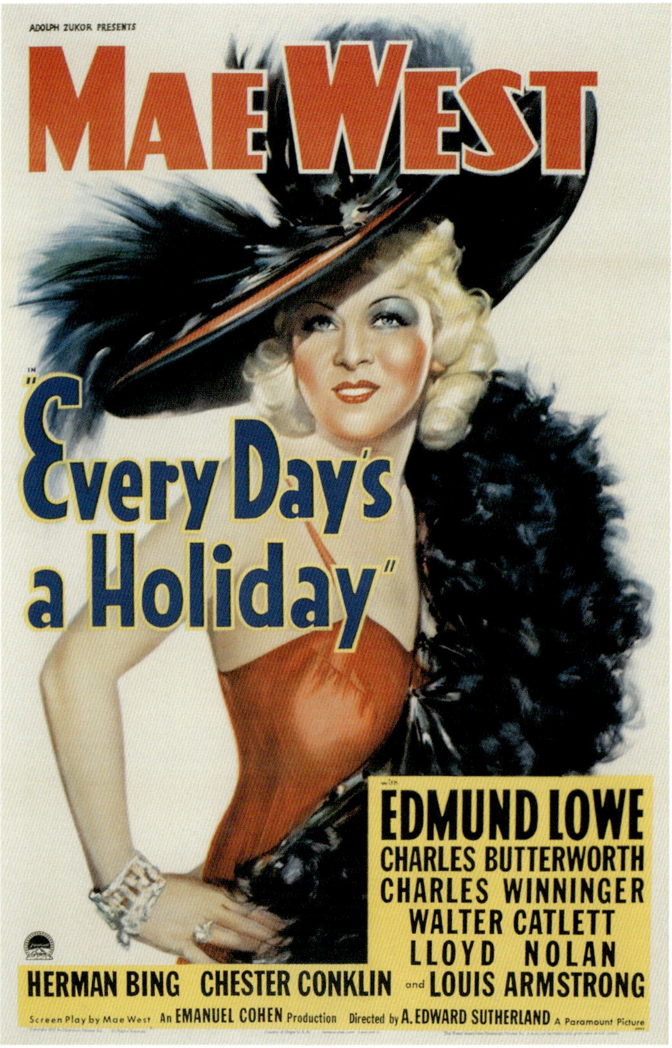

Every Day's a Holiday. 1938. One-sheet. $2,500-3,500.

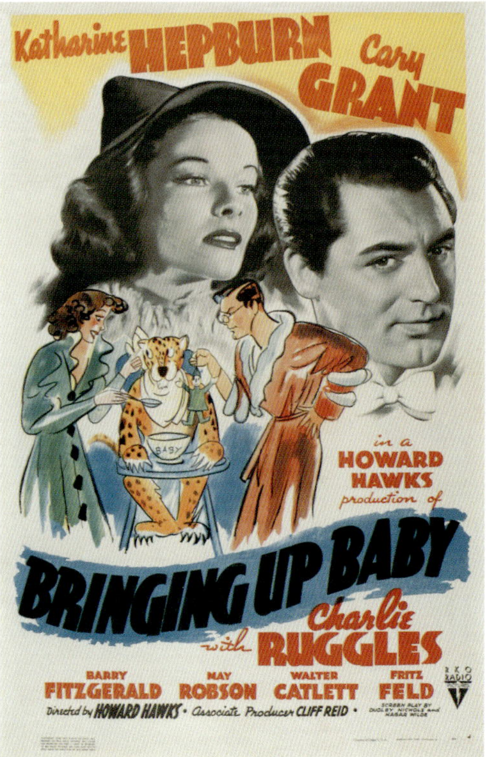

Bringing Up Baby. 1938. One-sheet. $1,500-2,000.

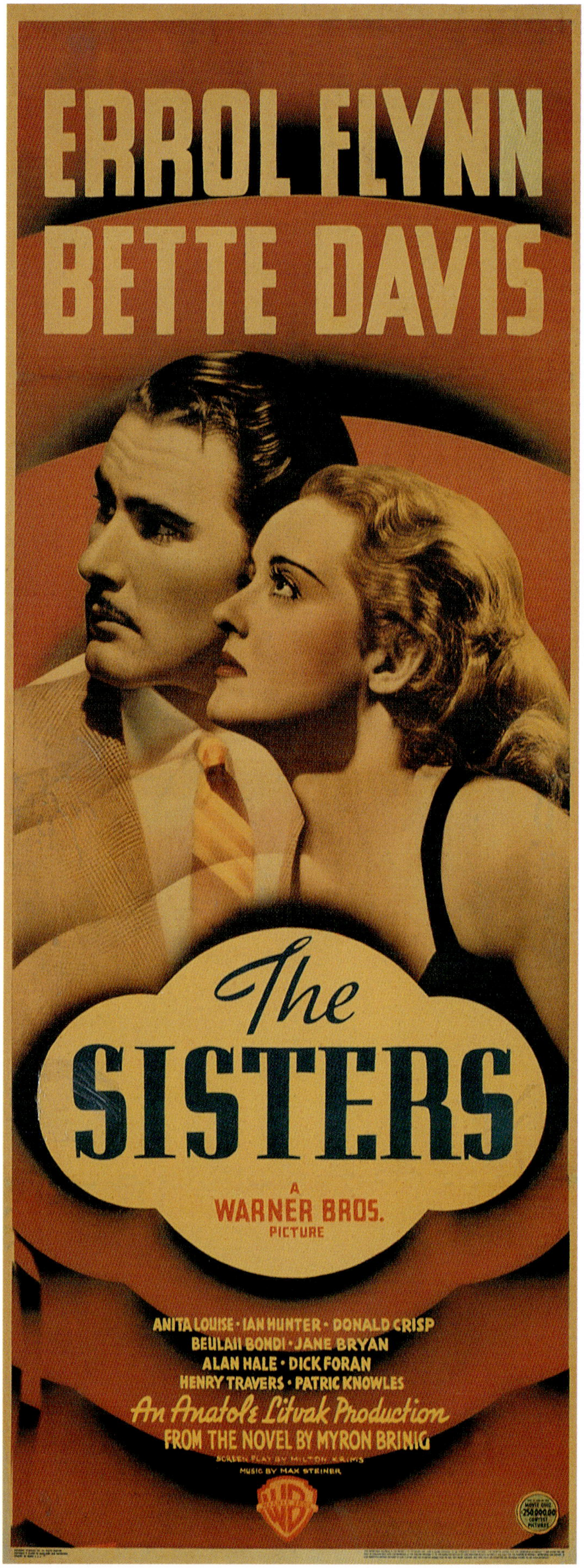

The Sisters. 1938. Insert. $1,500-2,000.

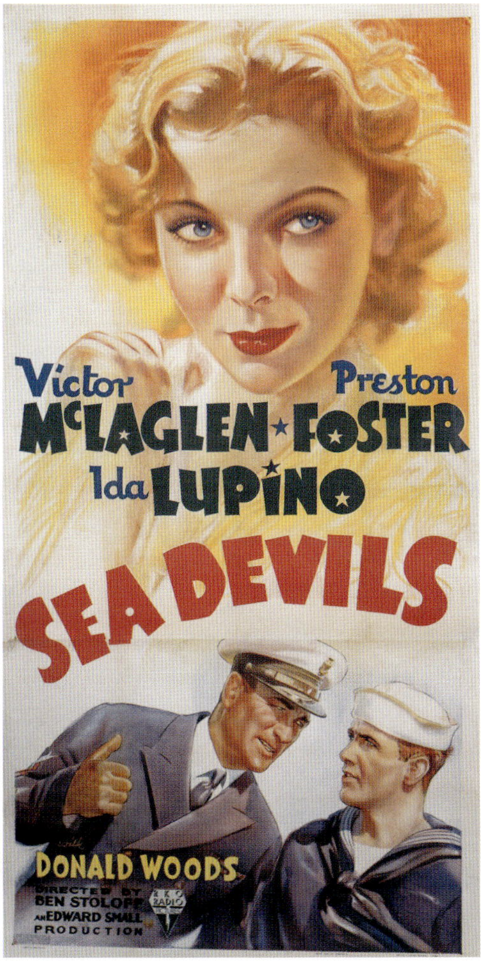

Sea Devils. 1938. Three-sheet. $1,200-1,800.

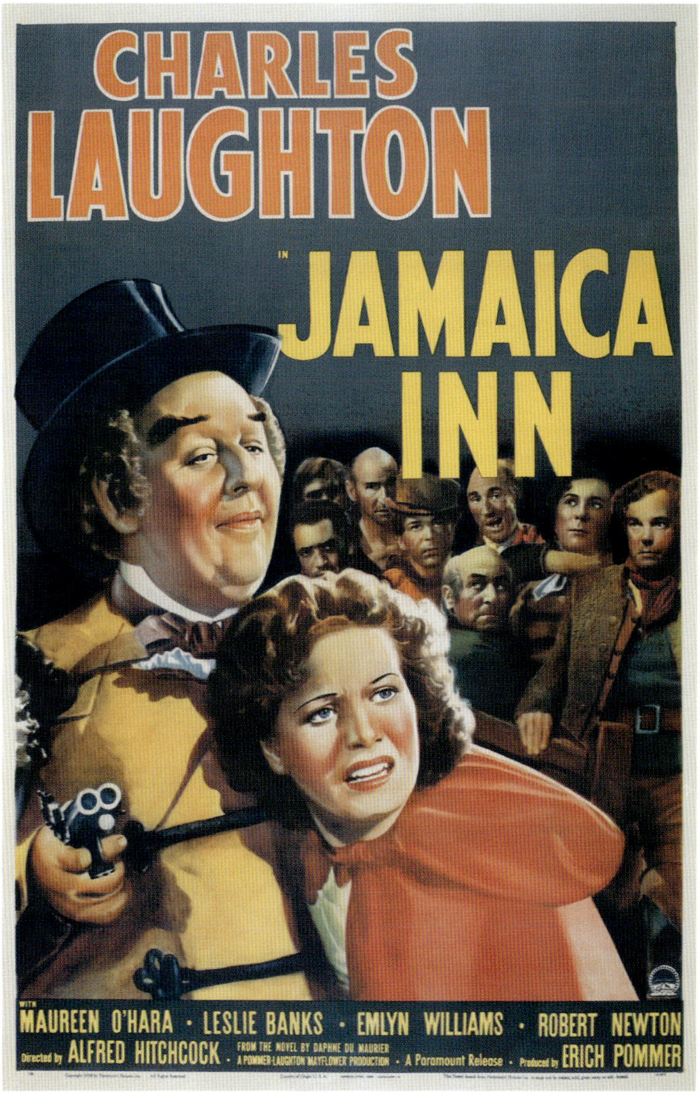

Jamaica Inn. 1939. One-sheet. $3,000-4,000.

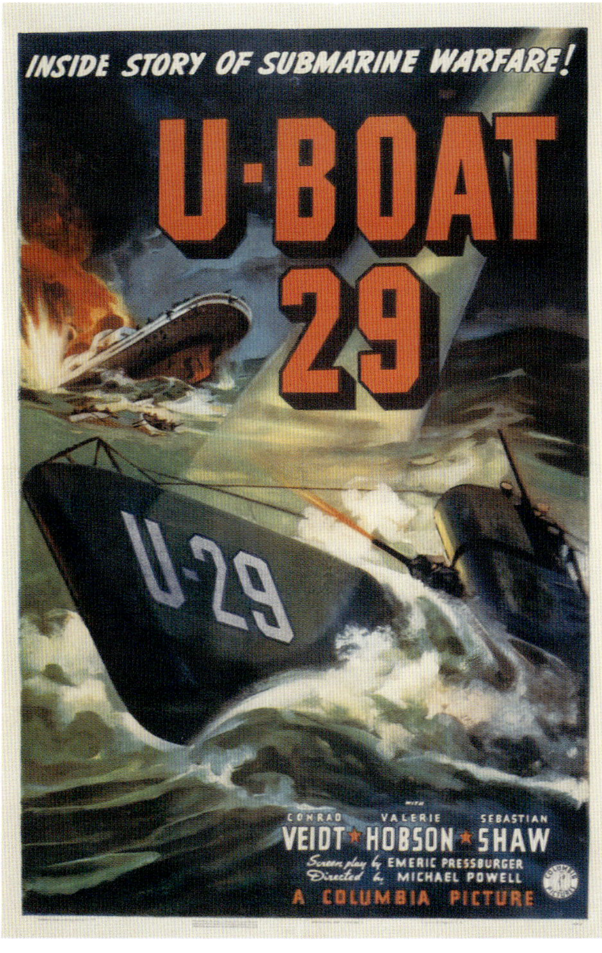

U-Boat 29. 1939. One-sheet. $1,000-1,500.

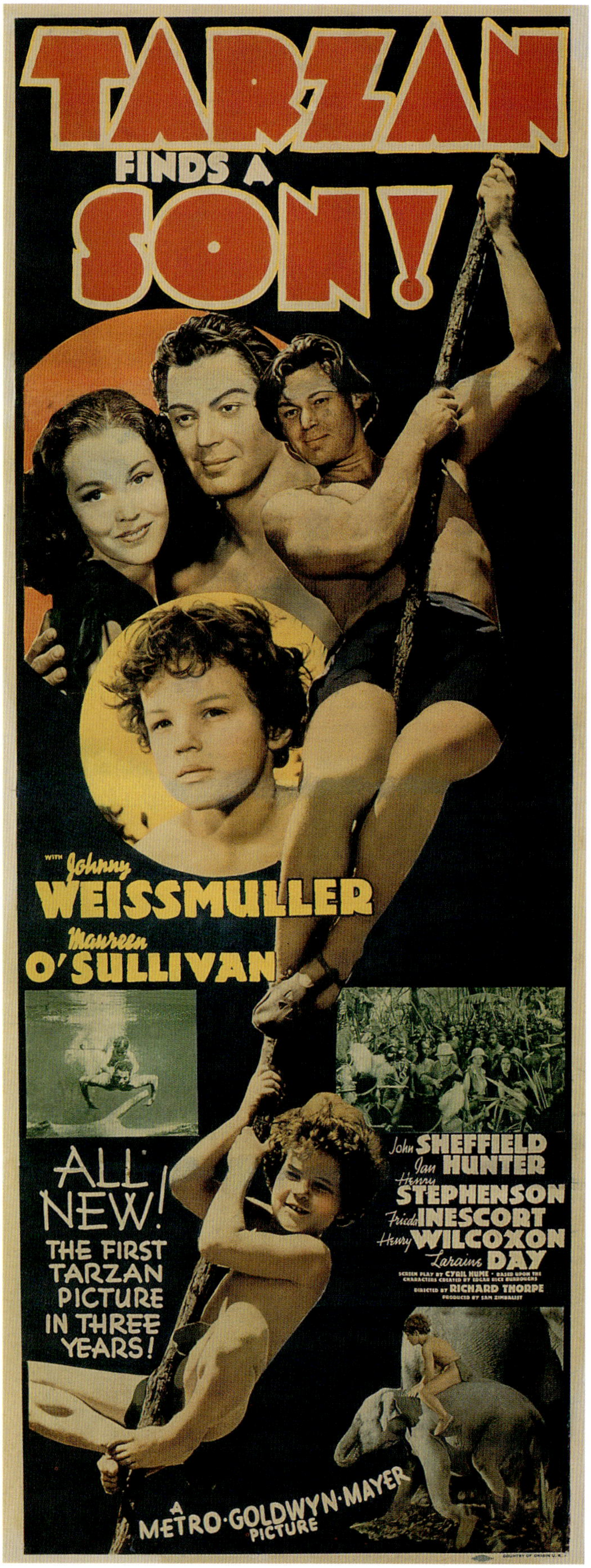

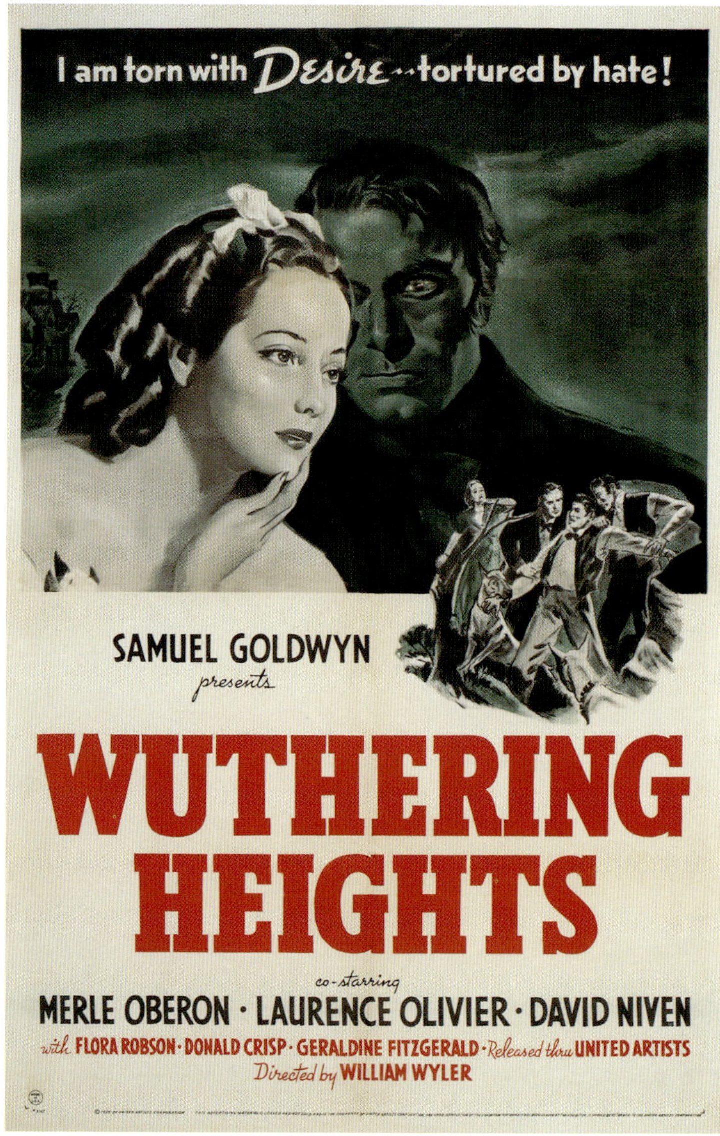

Wuthering Heights. 1939. One-sheet. $1,500-2,000.

Tarzan Finds a Son. 1939.
Insert. $1,000-1,500.

Chapter Three

War Torn Hollywood: The Forties

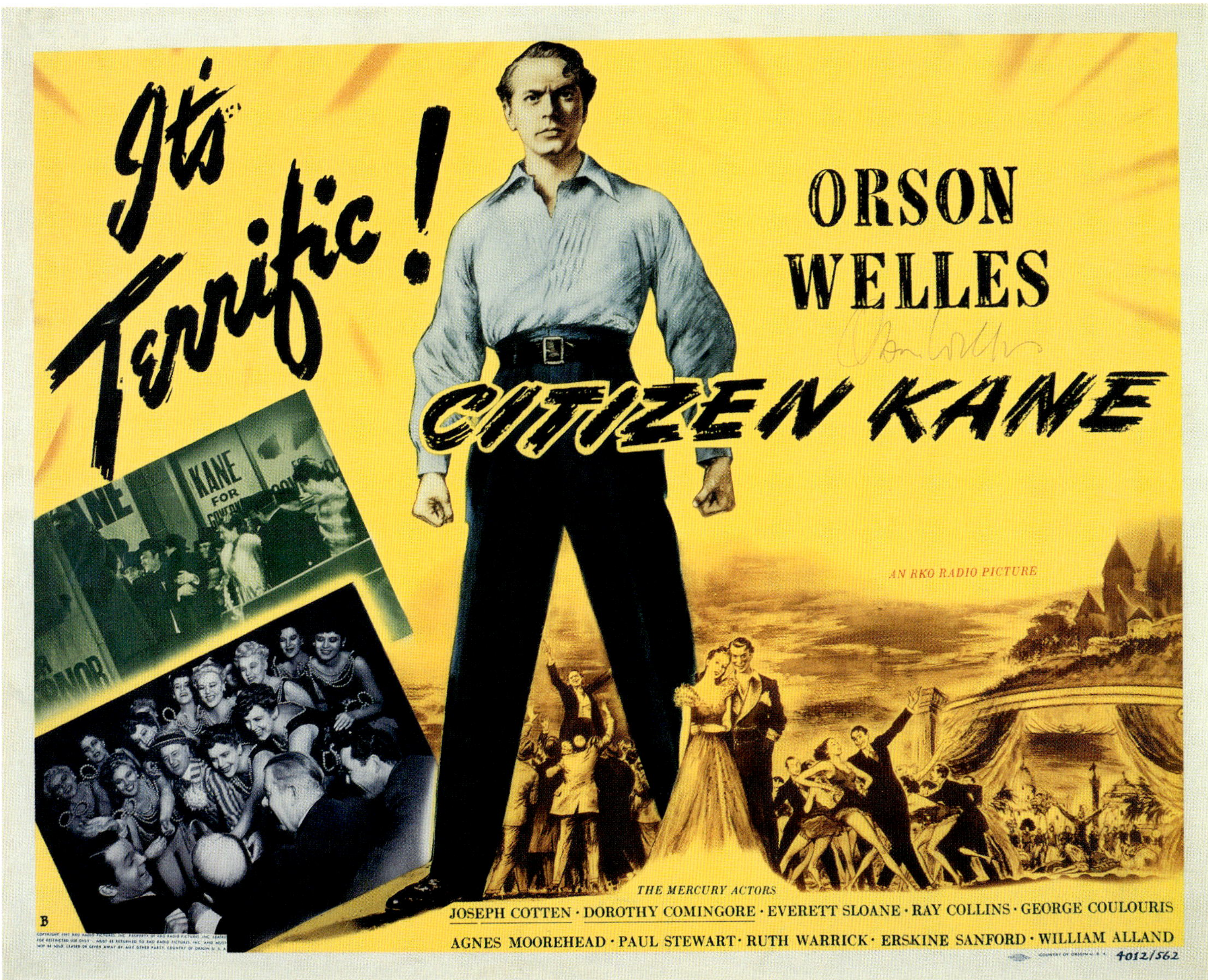

Citizen Kane. 1941. Half-sheet. $5,000-7,000.

This decade, perhaps more than any other, brought considerable change to Hollywood, with the optimism felt by the dwindling effects of the Depression superceded by the anxiety of another impending world war. The powerful studios, however, still remained extremely affluent and productive, with film output reaching its peak during 1943 to 1946. After 1945 it became clear, though, that the "golden age" would never be able to shine so brightly.

In the first instance, however, the studios responded to the onset of war with many patriotic, morale boosting life enhancers. Like the decade before, they endeavored to reflect the tough times that people faced, and through their struggle to inspire. Many leading lights in Hollywood themselves joined the armed forces including Clark Gable, James Stewart, and British expatriates such as David Niven and Stewart Granger.

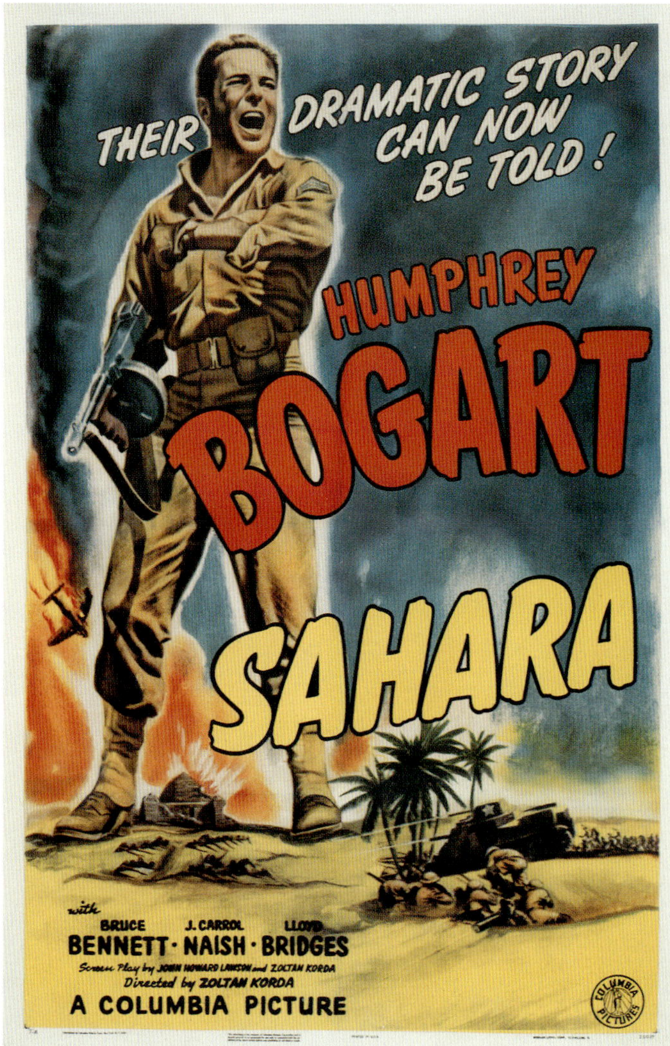

Sahara. 1943. One-sheet, style A. $800-1,200

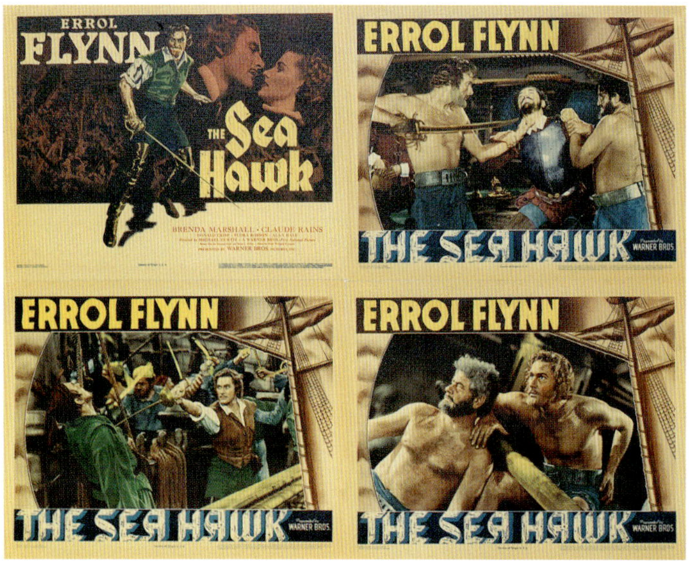

The Sea Hawk. 1940. Set of lobby cards. $2,500-3,500.

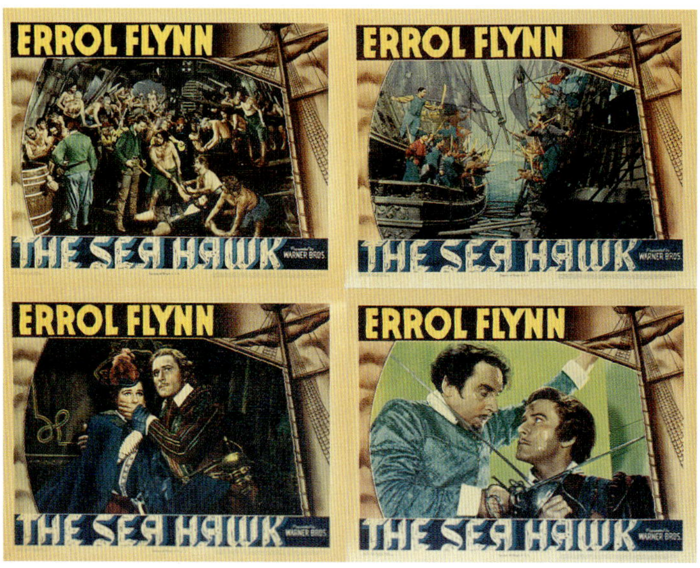

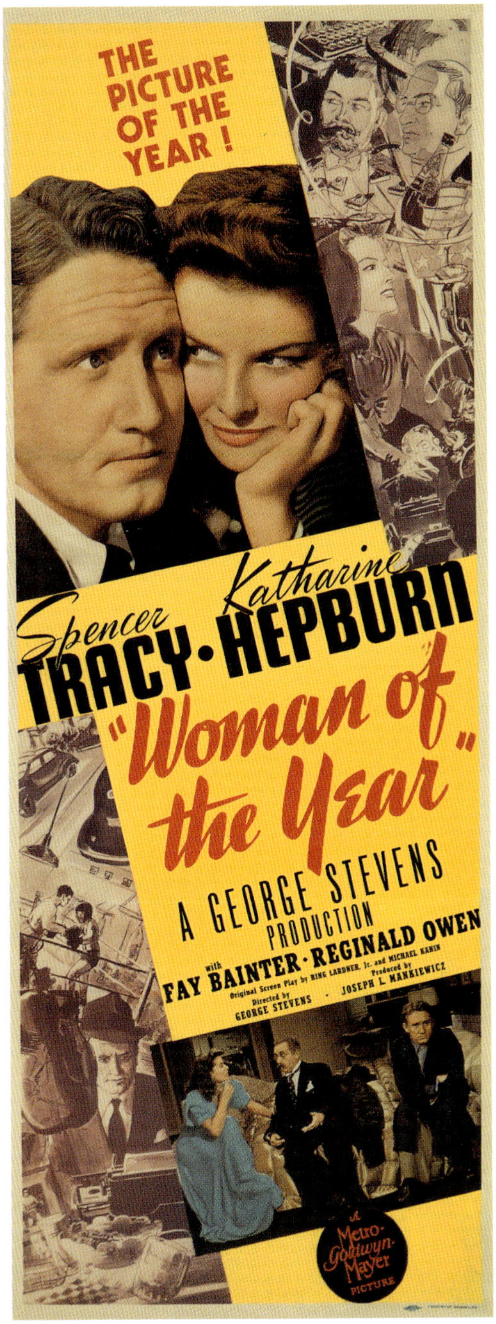

Woman of the Year. 1942.
Insert. $800-1,200.

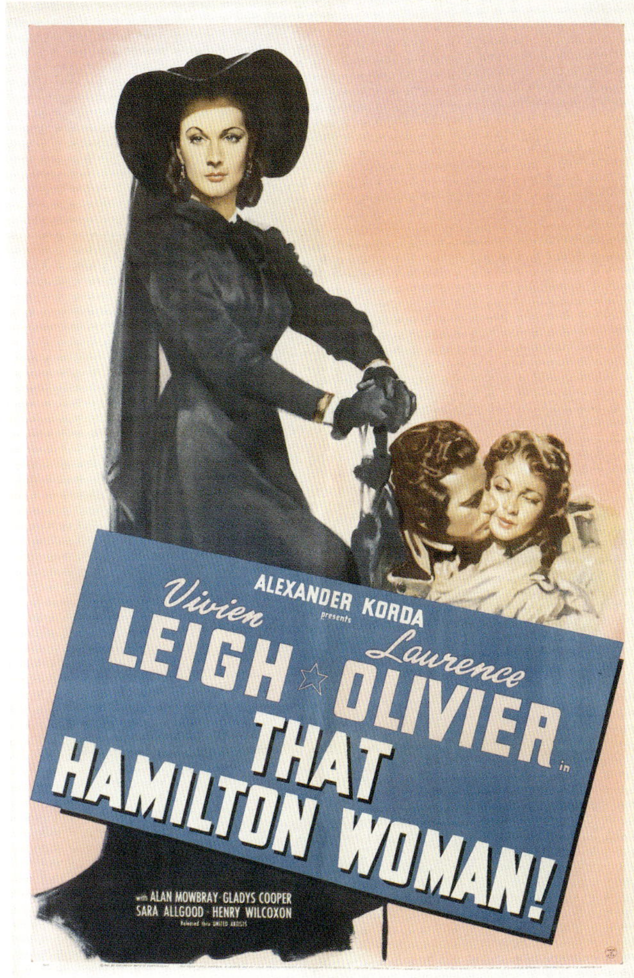

That Hamilton Woman! 1941. One-sheet. $1,500-2,000.

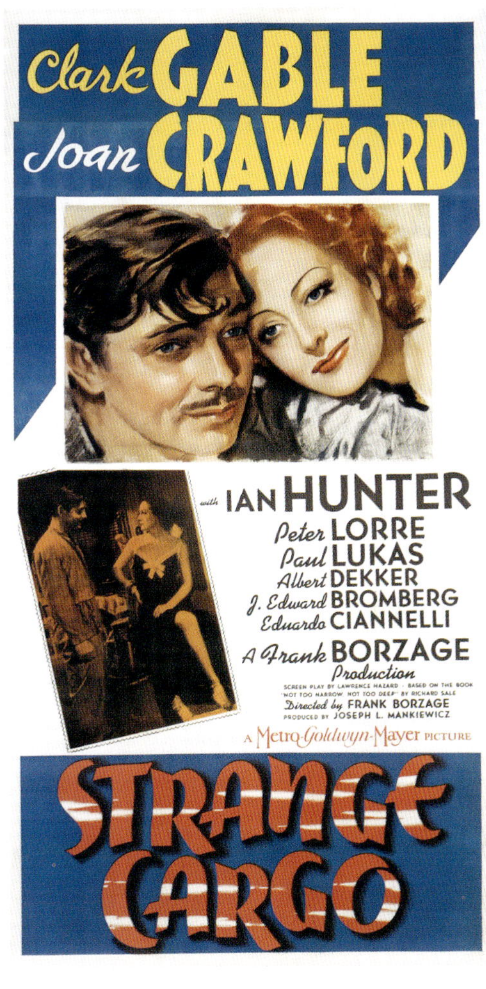

Strange Cargo. 1940. Three-sheet. $2,500-3,500.

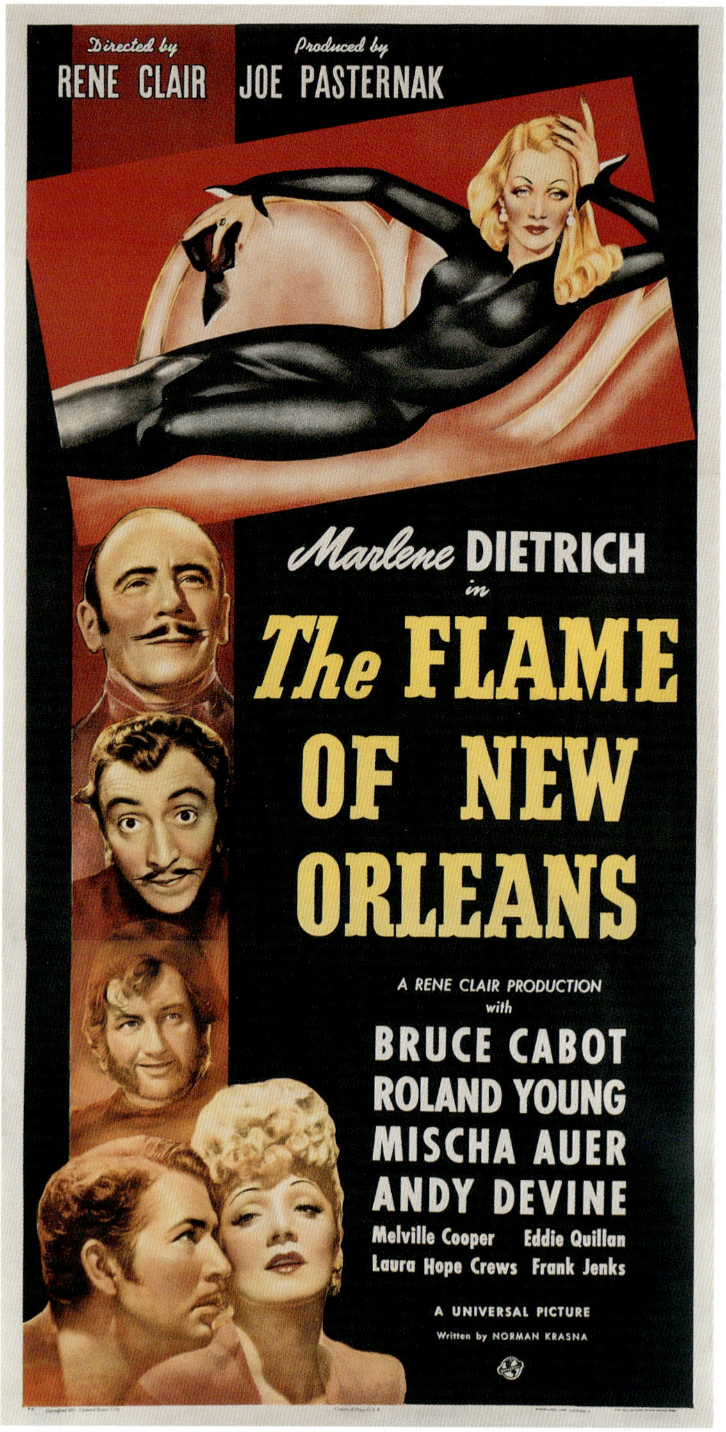

The Flame of New Orleans. 1941. Three-sheet. $2,000-3,000.

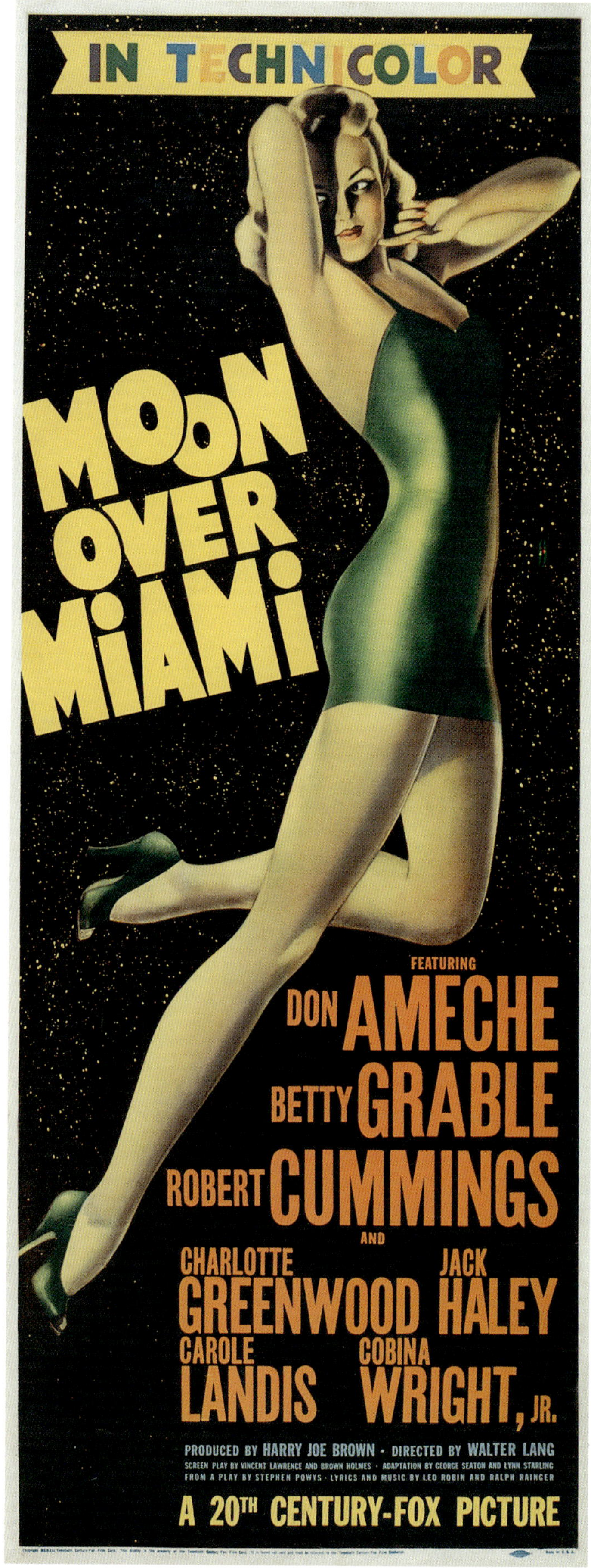

Moon Over Miami. 1941.
Insert. $3,000-4,000.

Amid the swaggering heroics, subtler productions aided the propaganda war on the home front. These included the classic *Casablanca* (1942) that made a star of its hero Humphrey Bogart and featured expatriate German Conrad Veidt as the excellently menacing Nazi officer Strasser; *The Great Dictator* (1940), Chaplin's memorable satire on Hitler and the Third Reich; and the thought provoking *Lifeboat* (1944) directed by the fairly new Hollywood recruit Alfred Hitchcock. Directed by William Wyler *The Best Years of Our Lives* (1946) was a provocative postwar Academy Award® winner that dealt with the plight of returning soldiers. Interestingly, one of the many awards that were bestowed on this film was to nonprofessional actor and disabled G.I. veteran Harold Russell who won the Best Supporting Actor that year.

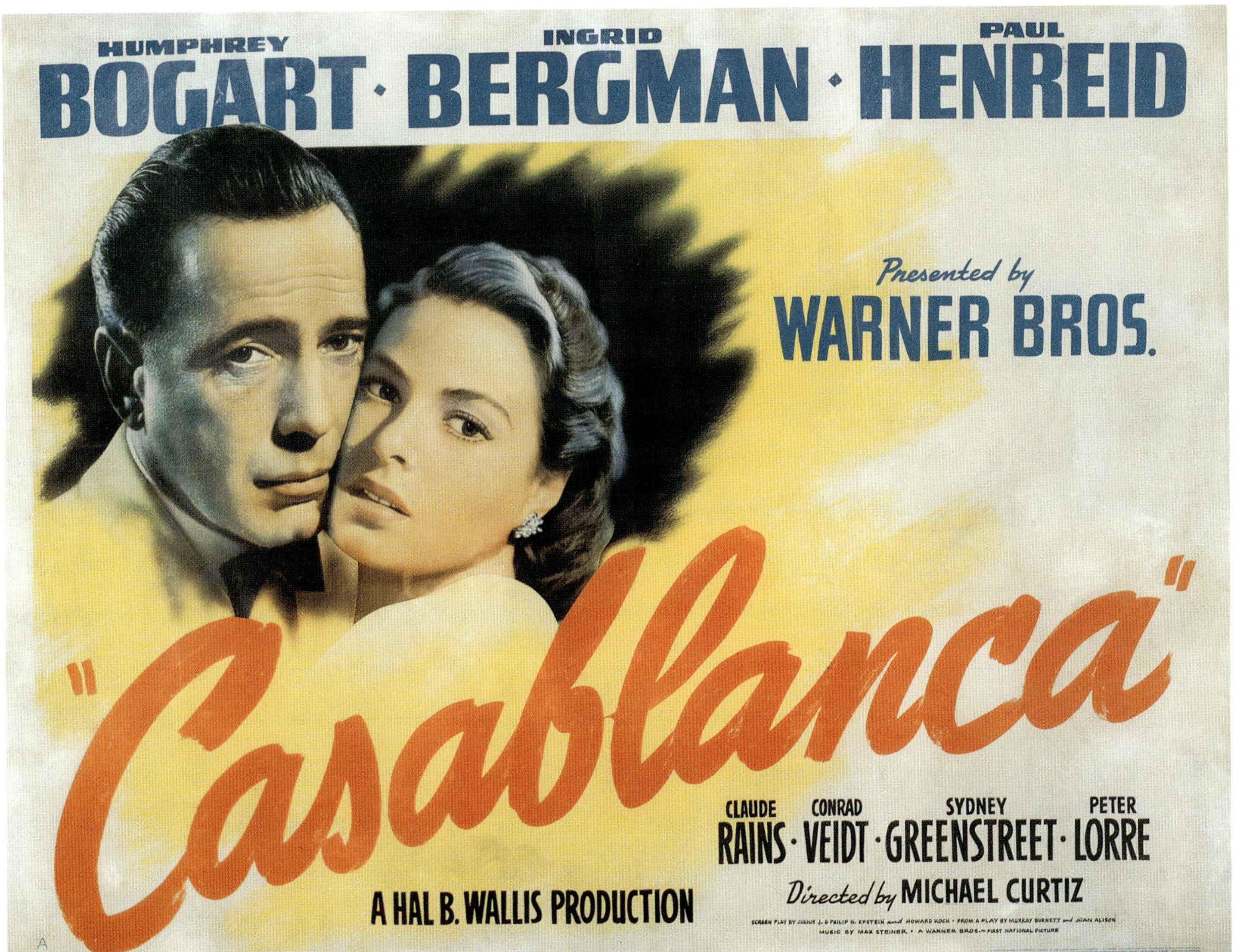

Casablanca. 1942. Half-sheet. $10,000-15,000.

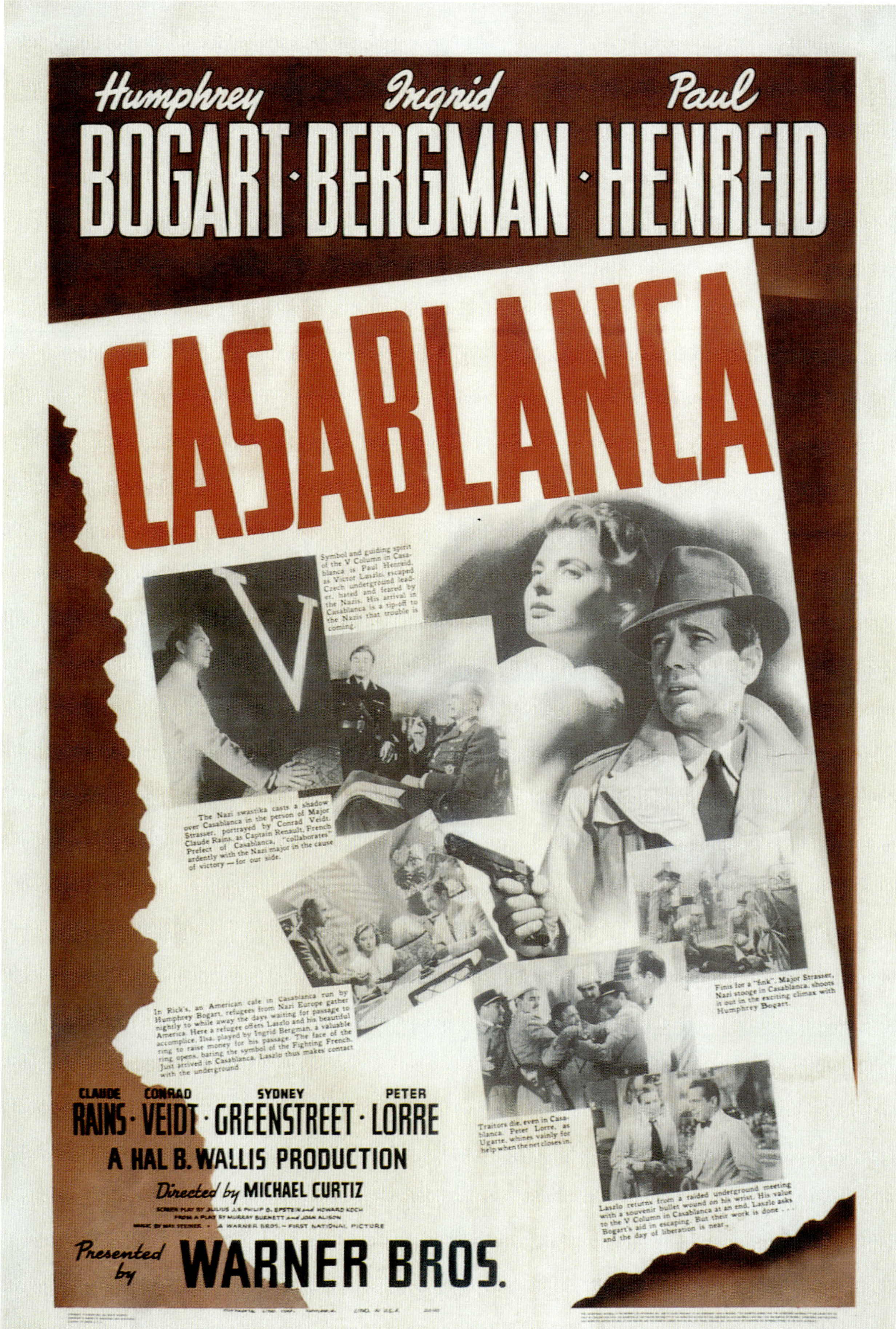

Casablanca. 1942. One-sheet. $15,000-18,000.

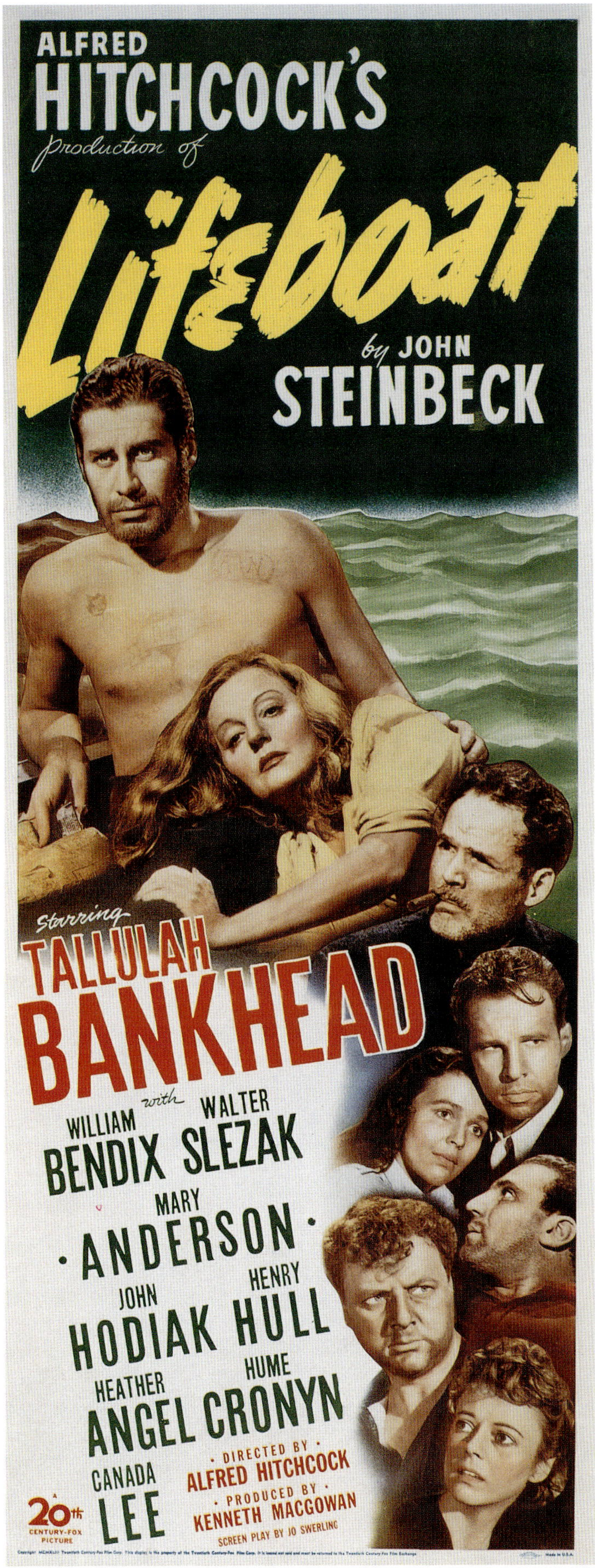

Lifeboat. 1944. Insert. $1,000-1,500.

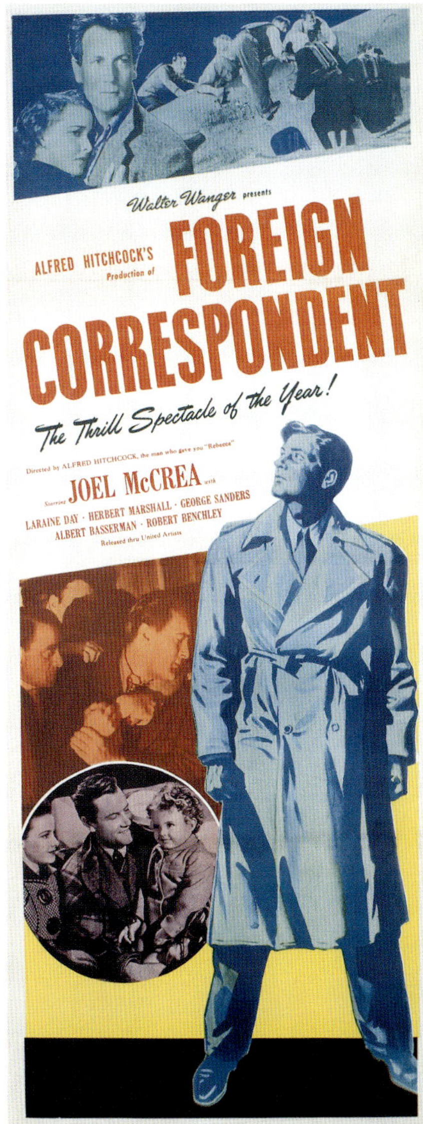

Foreign Correspondent. 1940. Insert. $1,000-1,500.

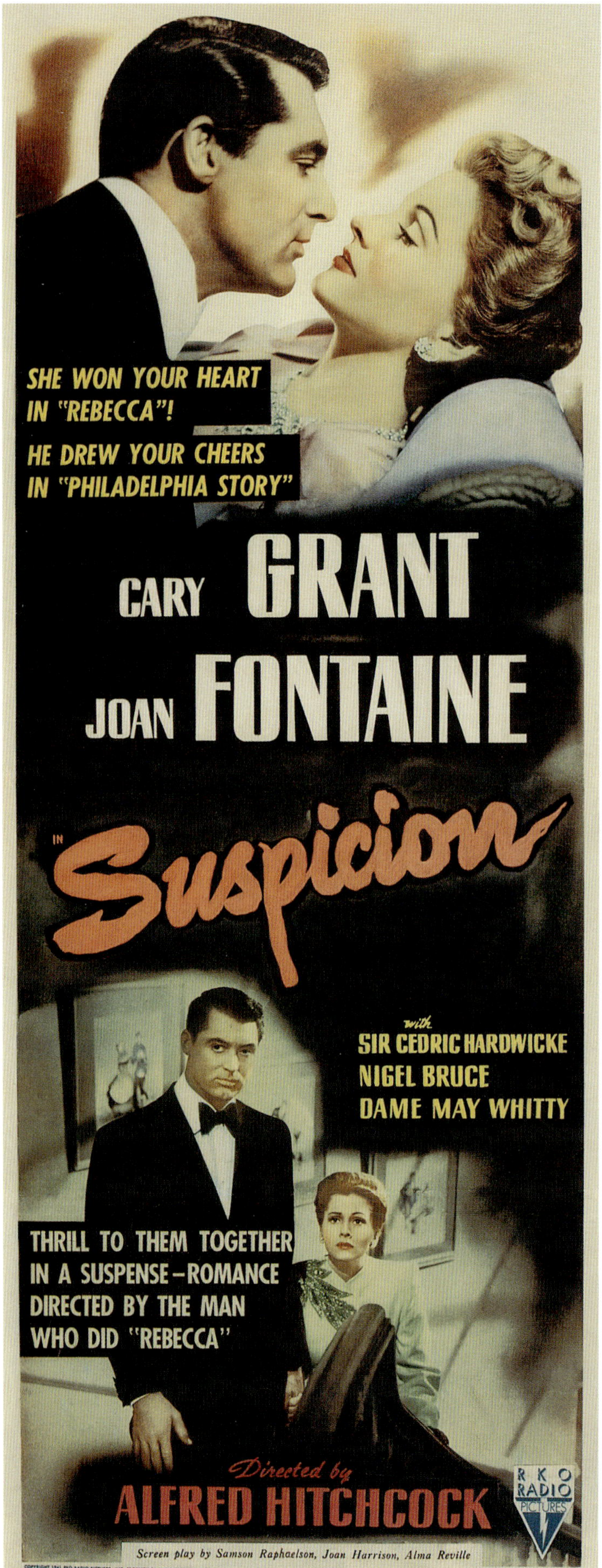

Suspicion. 1941. Insert. $1,200-1,800.

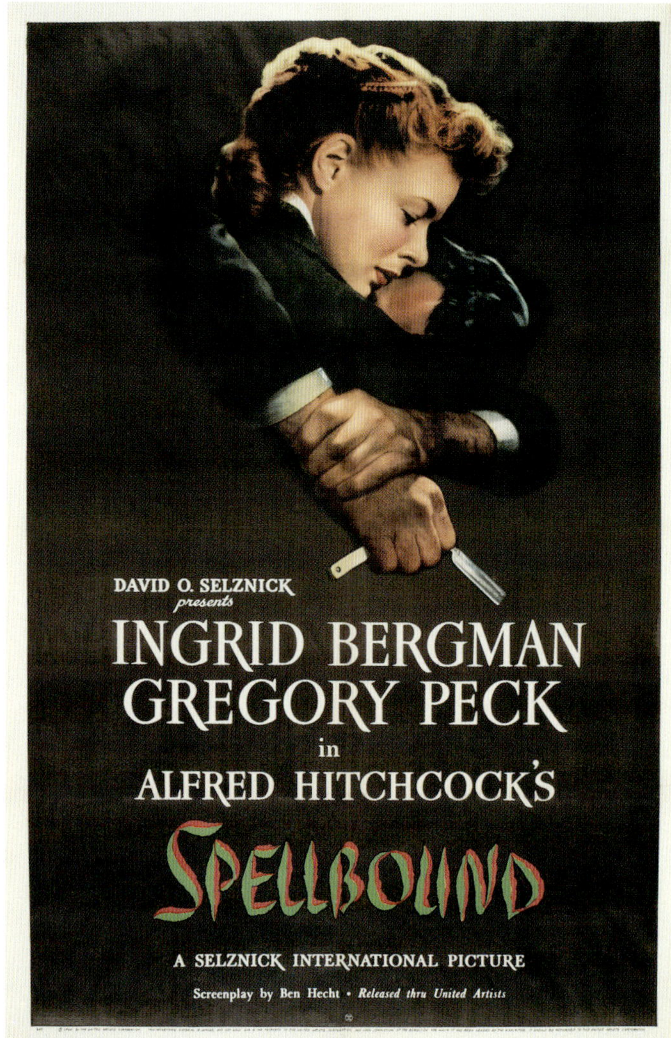

Spellbound. 1945. One-sheet. $2,500-3,500.

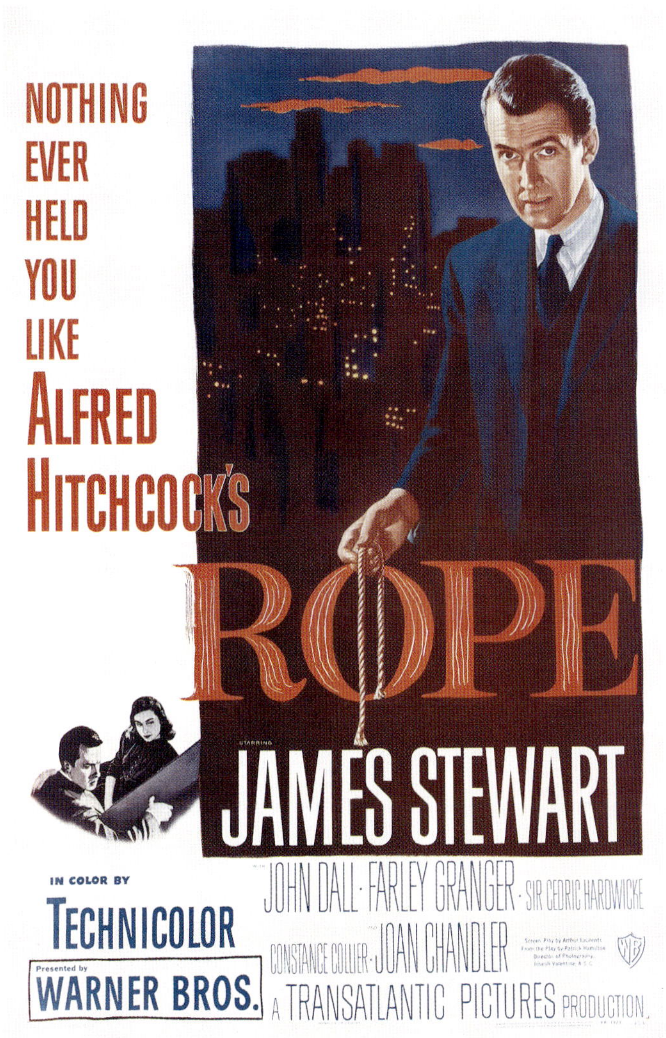

Rope. 1948. One-sheet. $3,000-4,000

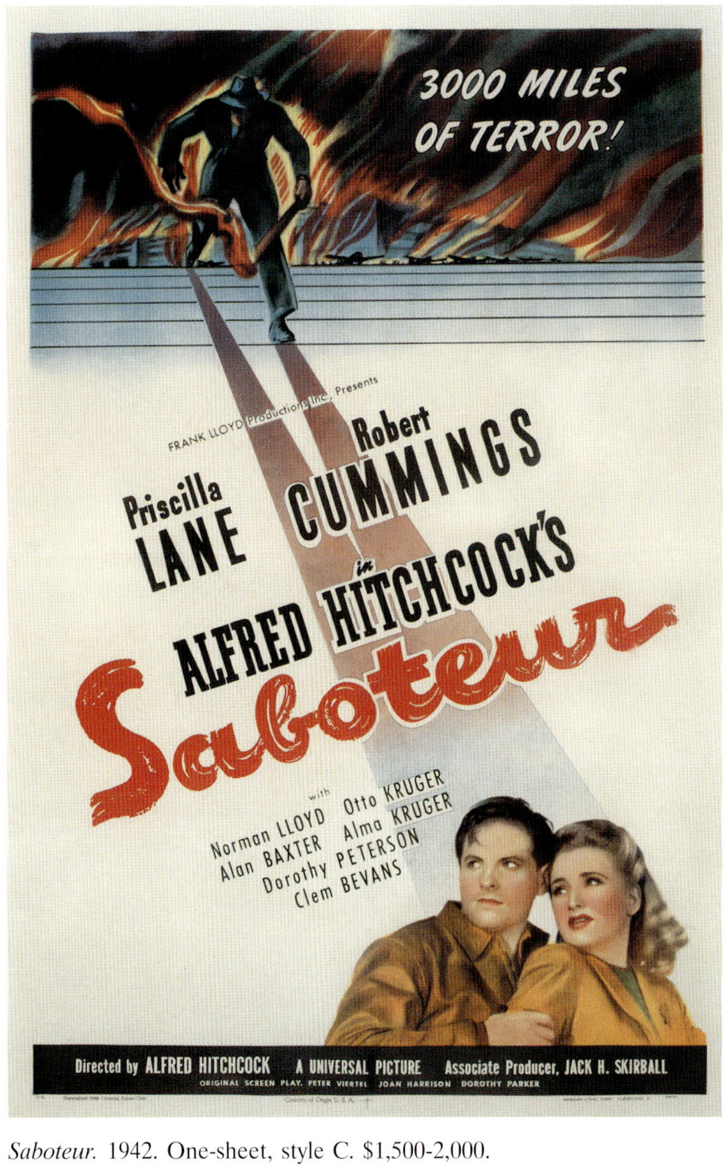

Saboteur. 1942. One-sheet, style C. $1,500-2,000.

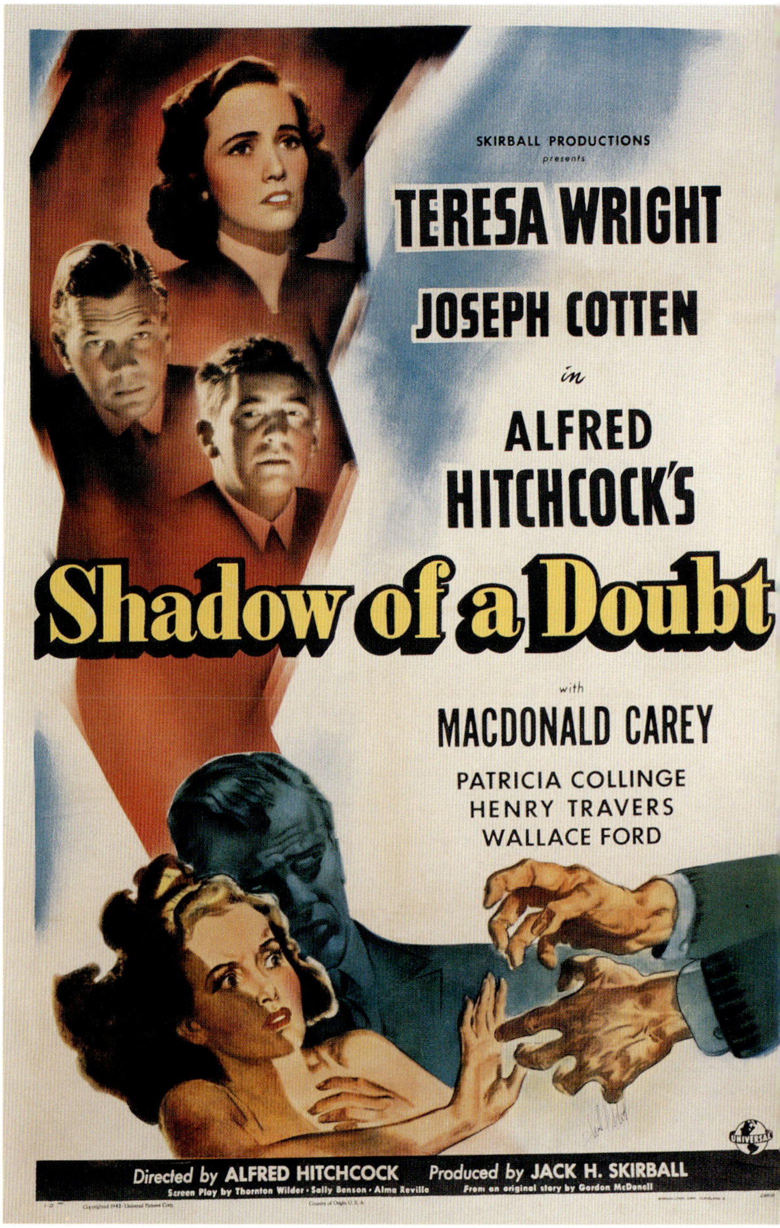

Shadow of a Doubt. 1943. One-sheet. $1,500-2,000.

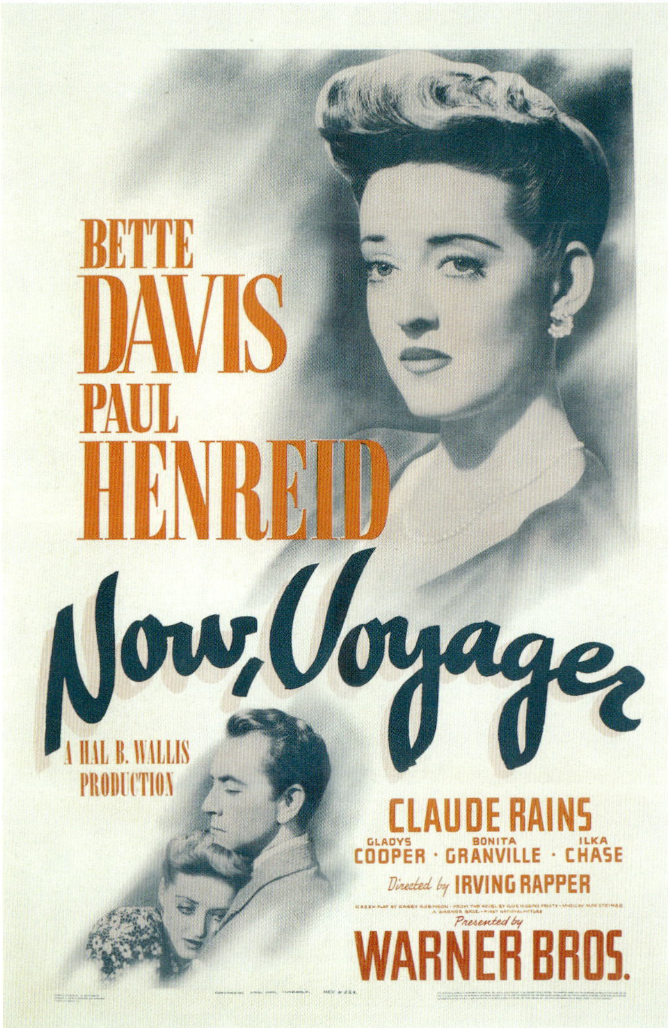

Now, Voyager. 1942. One-sheet. $1,500-2,000.

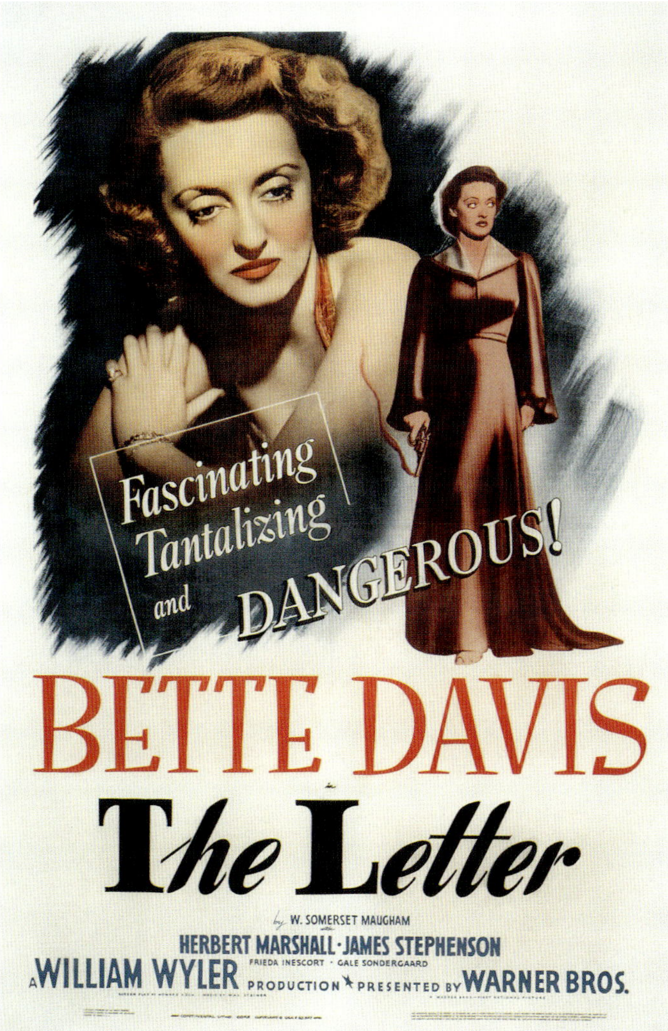

The Letter. 1940. One-sheet. $1,200-1,800.

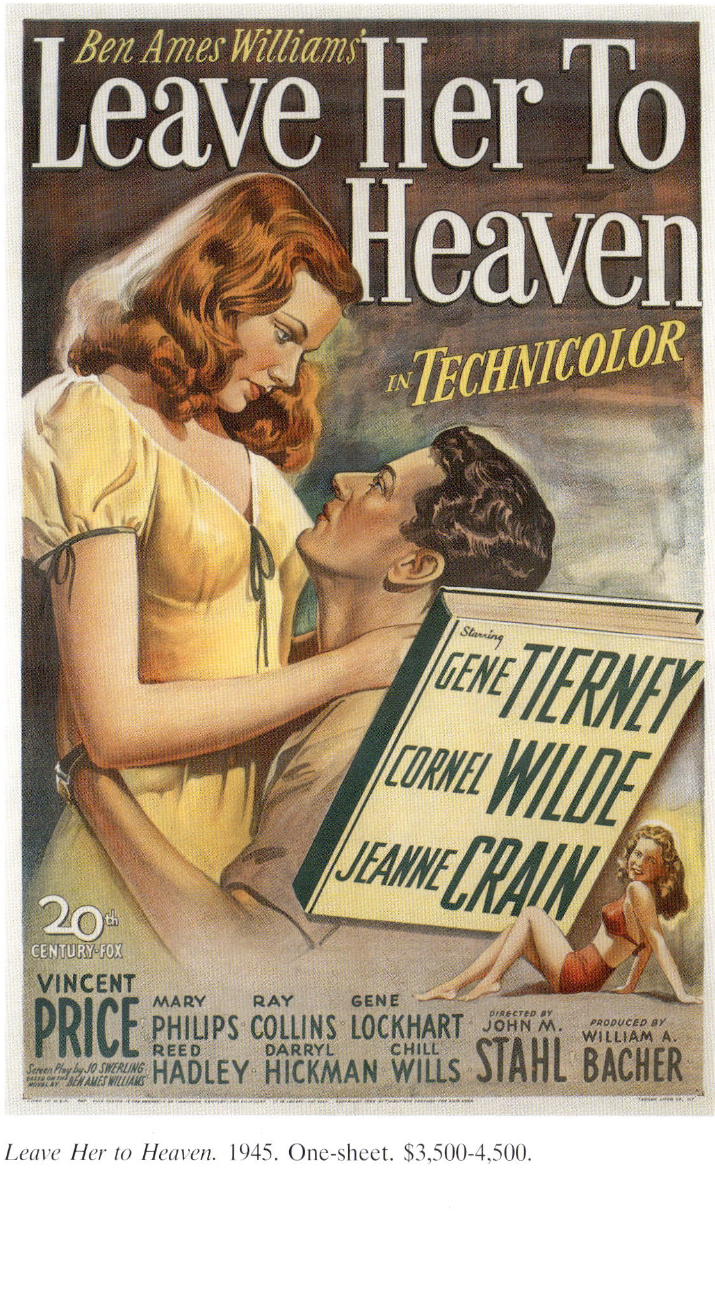

Leave Her to Heaven. 1945. One-sheet. $3,500-4,500.

The decade also saw, not surprisingly, the advent of the stylish "film noir" features that have become the hallmark of this period of Hollywood history. Through the dark years of war there evolved these somber, hard-hitting, often pessimistic movies that owed a debt to both the preceding gangster films of the 1930s and the earlier expressionistic European films of the 1920s. They tended to be socially gritty tales swathed in a world of sinisterly lit interiors that mirrored the feeling and intent of the characters. Tough, cynical, heroes and untrustworthy, double-crossing *femme fatales* all inhabited these quite unsavory worlds. Innovative camera angles, expressive sets, lighting, and costume all created the "noir" mood, with many a movie also indebted to the inspiring work of Orson Welles in his ground breaking classic *Citizen Kane* (1941). Noir it is not, but it paved the way for future directors of this genre to be more openly expressive in the medium of filmmaking.

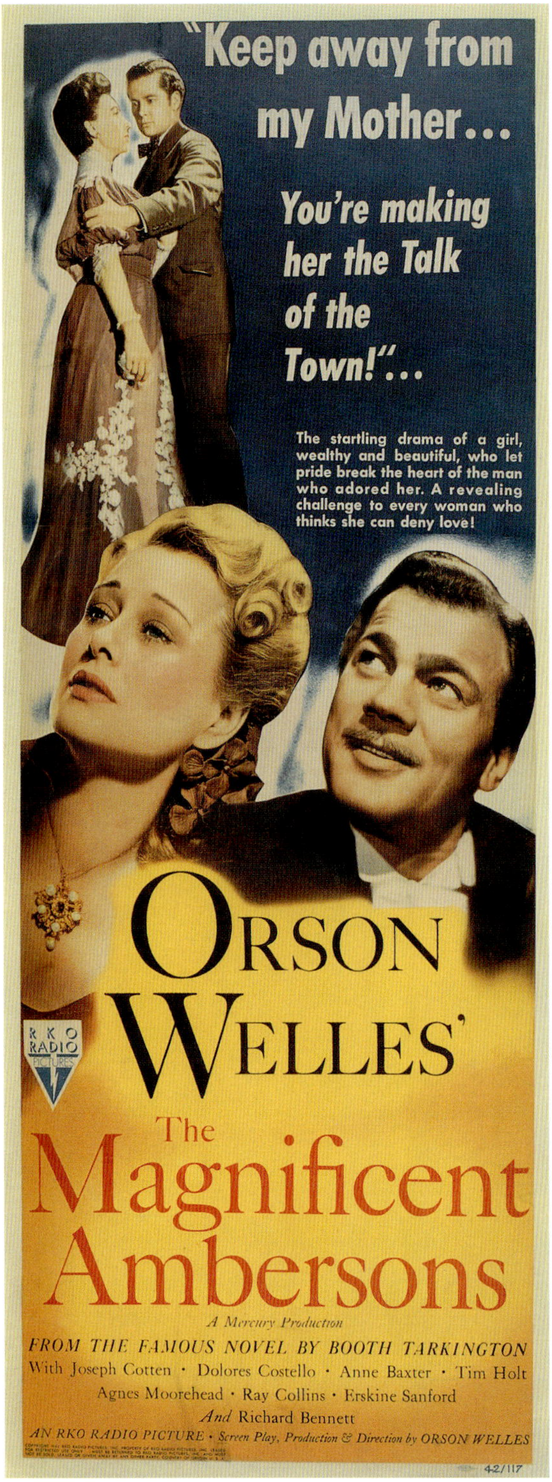

The Magnificent Ambersons. 1942. Insert. $1,200-1,800.

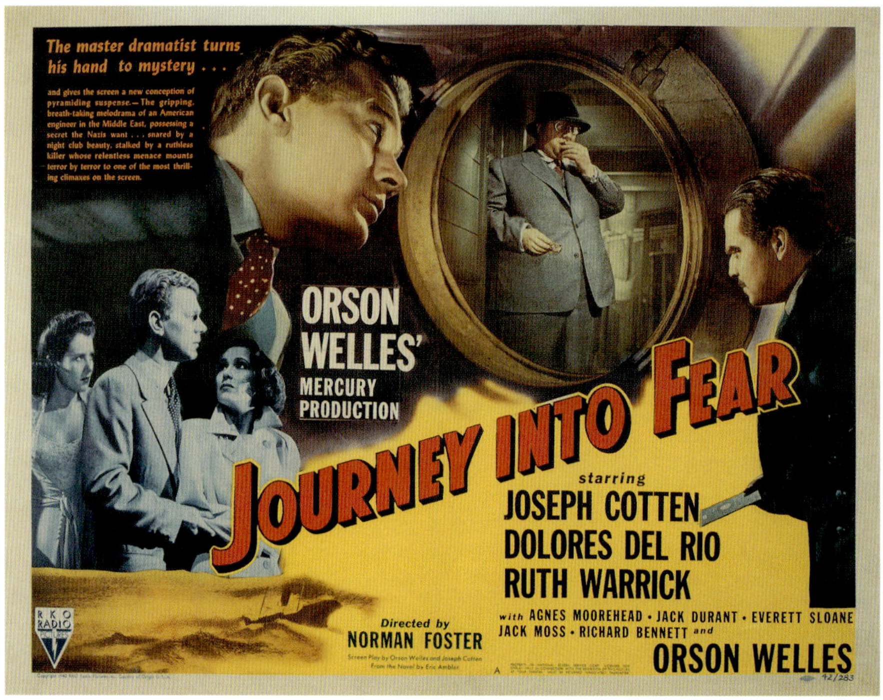

Journey into Fear. 1942. Half-sheet, style A. $1,000-1,500.

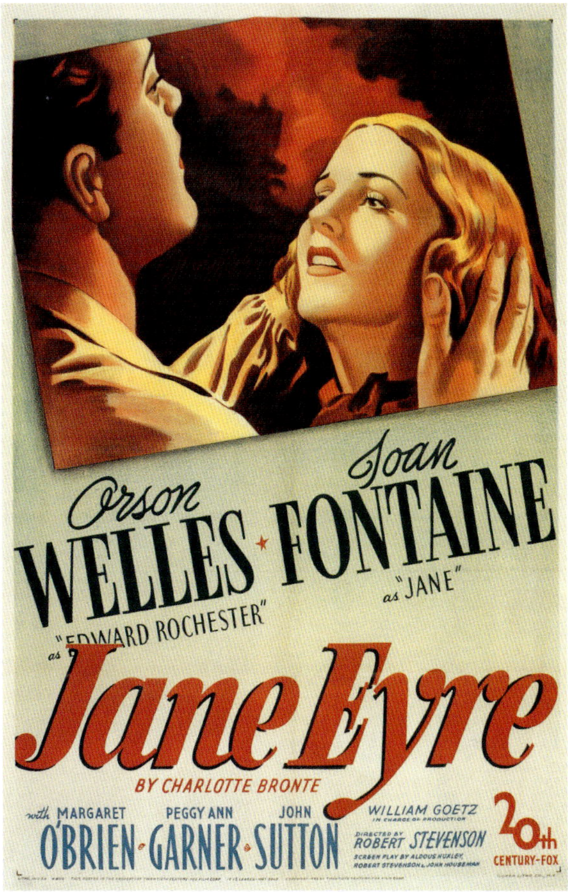

Jane Eyre. 1943. One-sheet. $1,000-1,500.

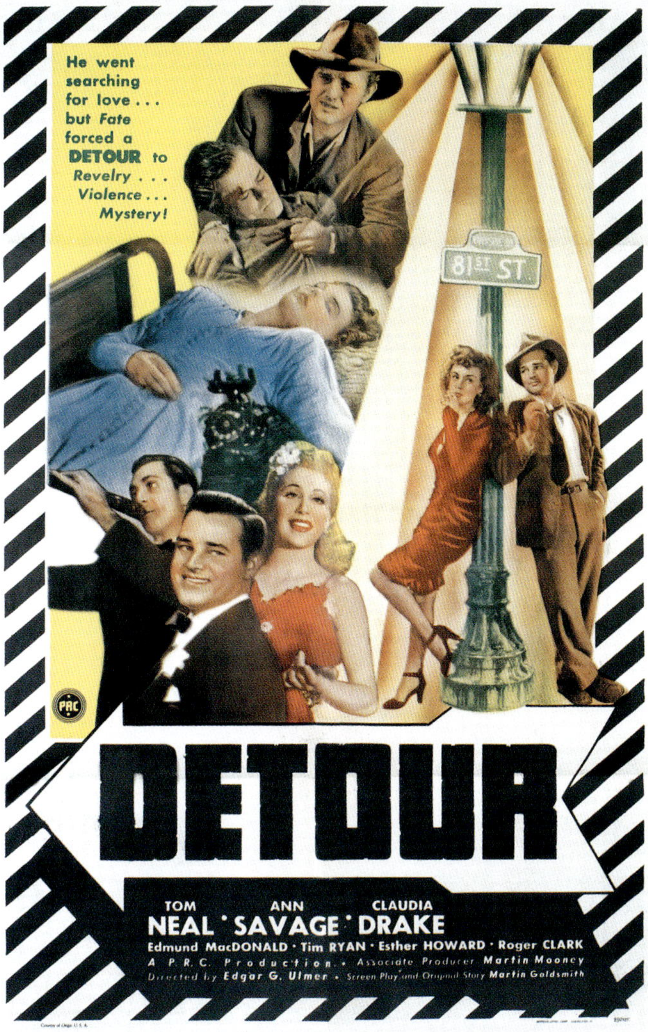

Detour. 1945. One-sheet. $2,000-2,500.

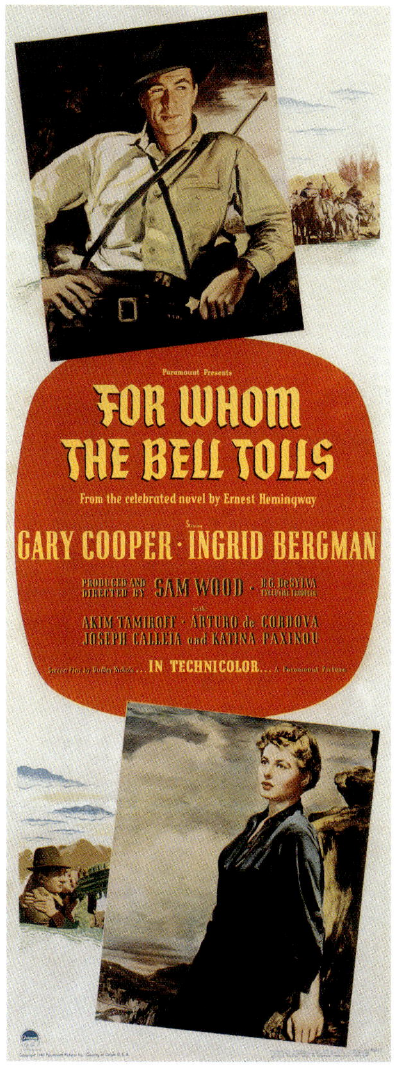

For Whom The Bell Tolls. 1943. Insert. $800-1,200.

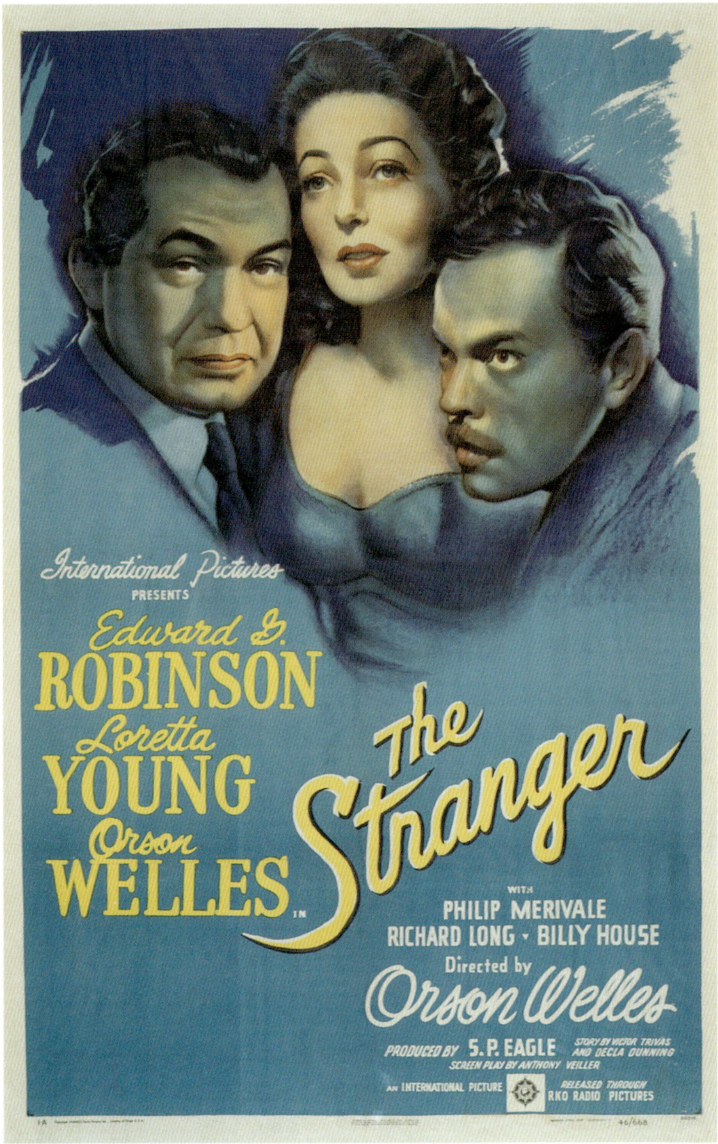

The Stranger. 1946. One-sheet. $1,500-2,000.

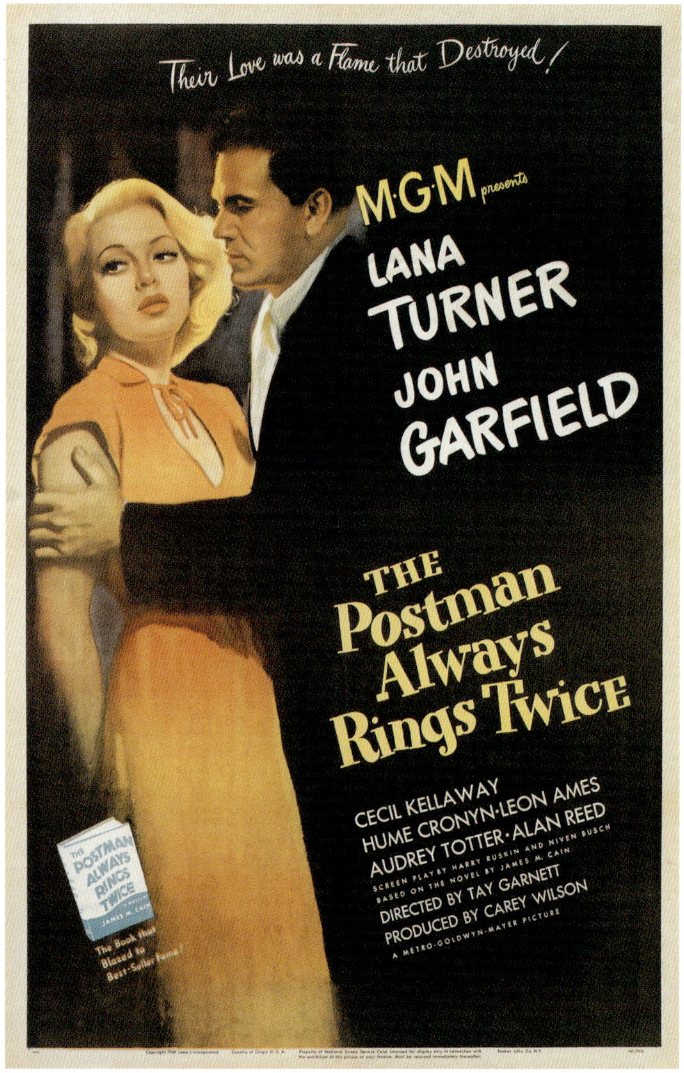

The Postman Always Rings Twice. 1946. One-sheet. $2,000-2,500.

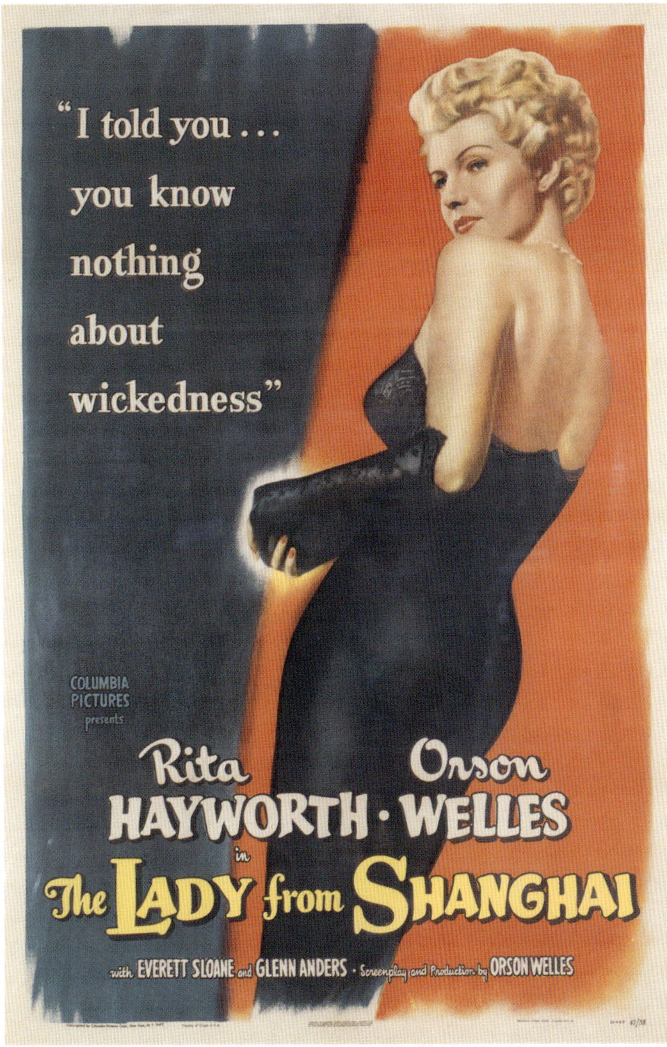

The Lady from Shanghai. 1947. One-sheet. $2,000-3,000.

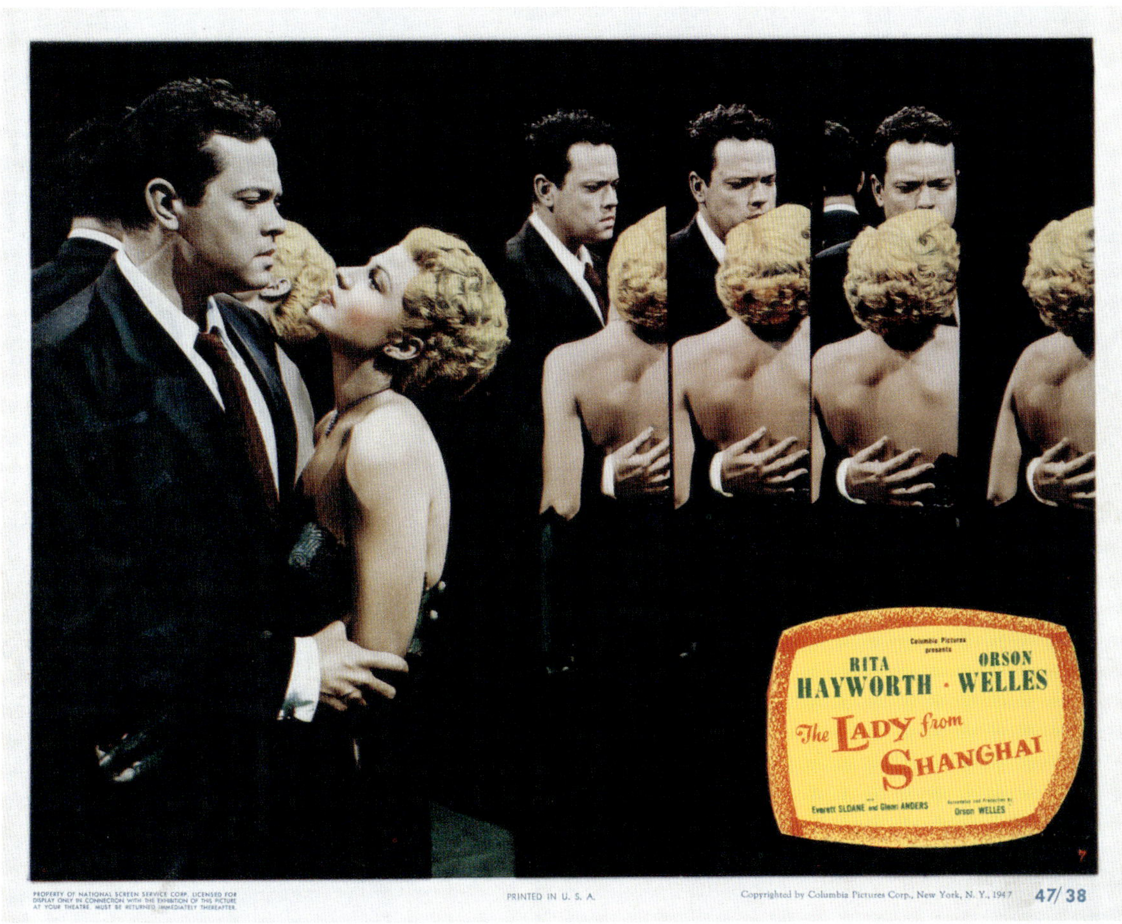

The Lady from Shanghai. 1947. Lobby card. $700-900.

The first definitive example of 1940s "film noir" was director John Huston's remarkable debut *The Maltese Falcon* (1941) with Bogart playing tough private eye Sam Spade. Alan Ladd was the star of *This Gun For Hire* (1942) a classic sinister revenge scenario co-staring sultry Veronica Lake who also starred in *The Glass Key* (1942). Both Barbara Stanwyck and Fred MacMurray starred in *Double Indemnity* (1944), a seedy tale of adulterous murder and corruption co-written for the screen by the director Billy Wilder and Raymond Chandler. Gene Tierney and Dana Andrews appeared in the Academy Award-winning murder mystery *Laura* (1944). *Murder My Sweet* (1945) and *Crossfire* (1947), saw Dick Powell as the tough detective Phillip Marlowe while the same character was played by Bogart in *The Big Sleep* (1946) with off-screen wife Lauren Bacall. Rita Hayworth seductively teased in *Gilda* (1946) while a year later Jane Greer was the romantic lead in the double-cross murder thriller *Out Of The Past* (1947). The style of these films extended to the publicity with some strikingly designed posters being made available to the distributors.

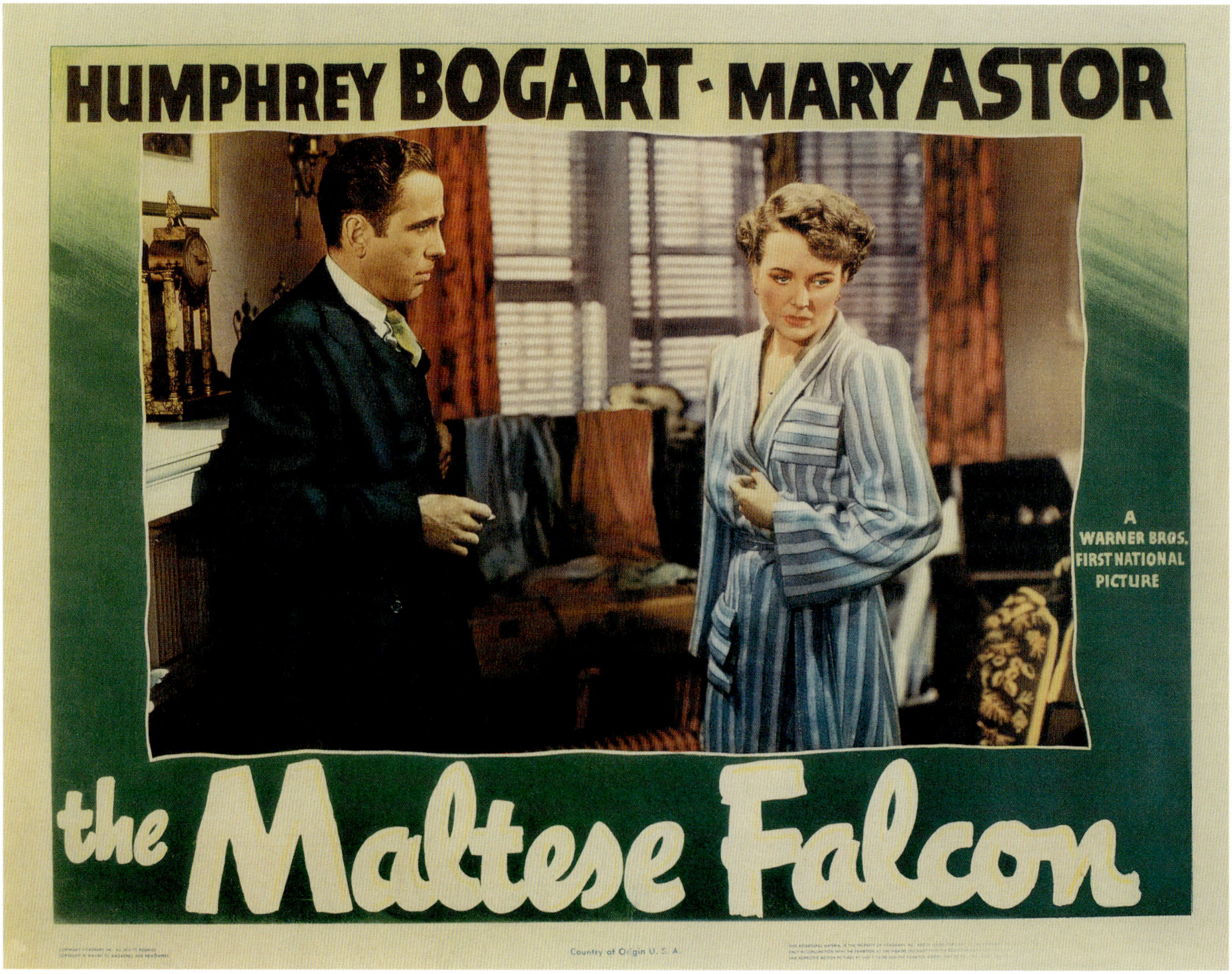

The Maltese Falcon. 1941. Lobby card. $1,000-1,500.

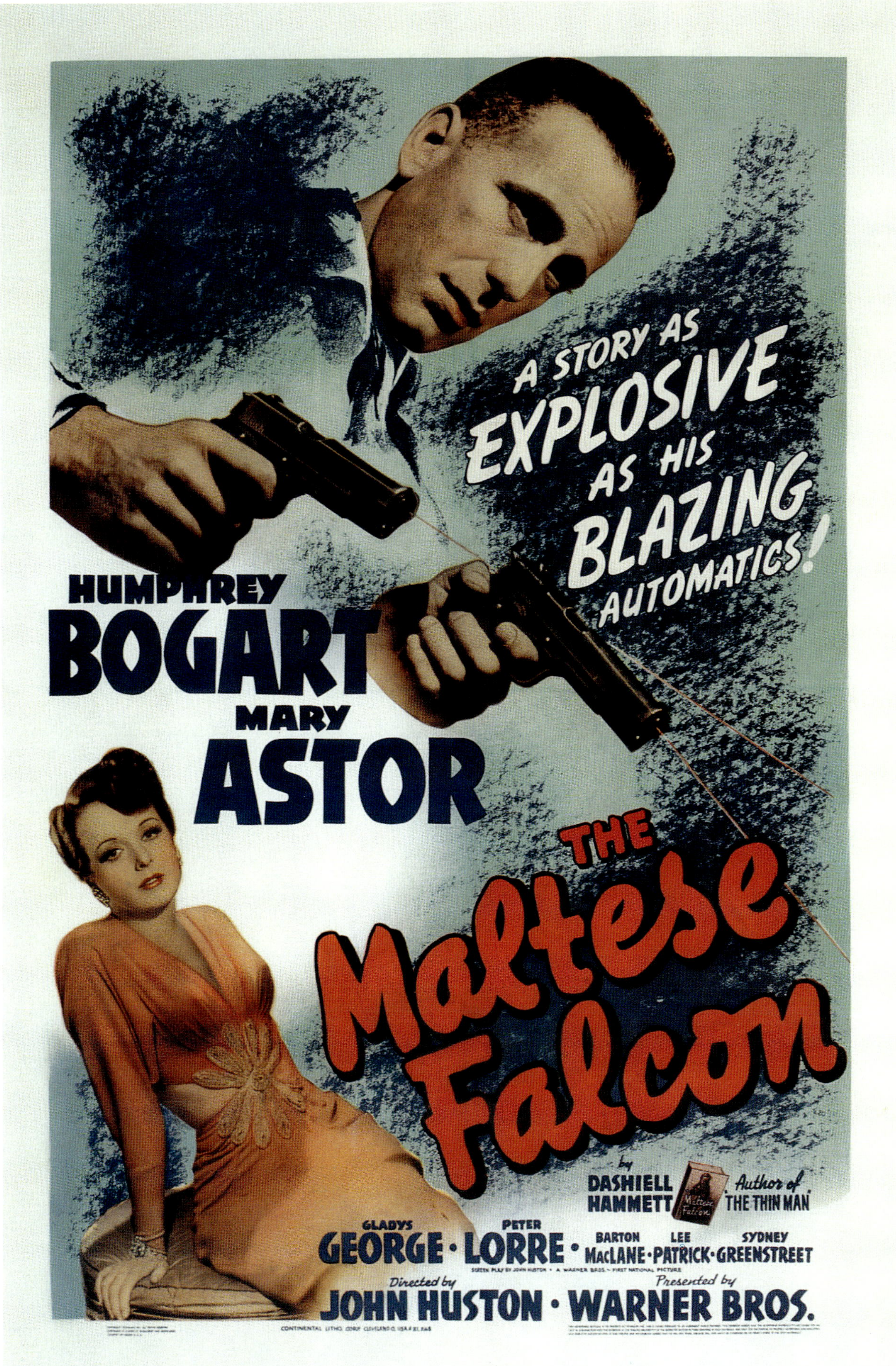

The Maltese Falcon. 1941. One-sheet. $6,000-8,000.

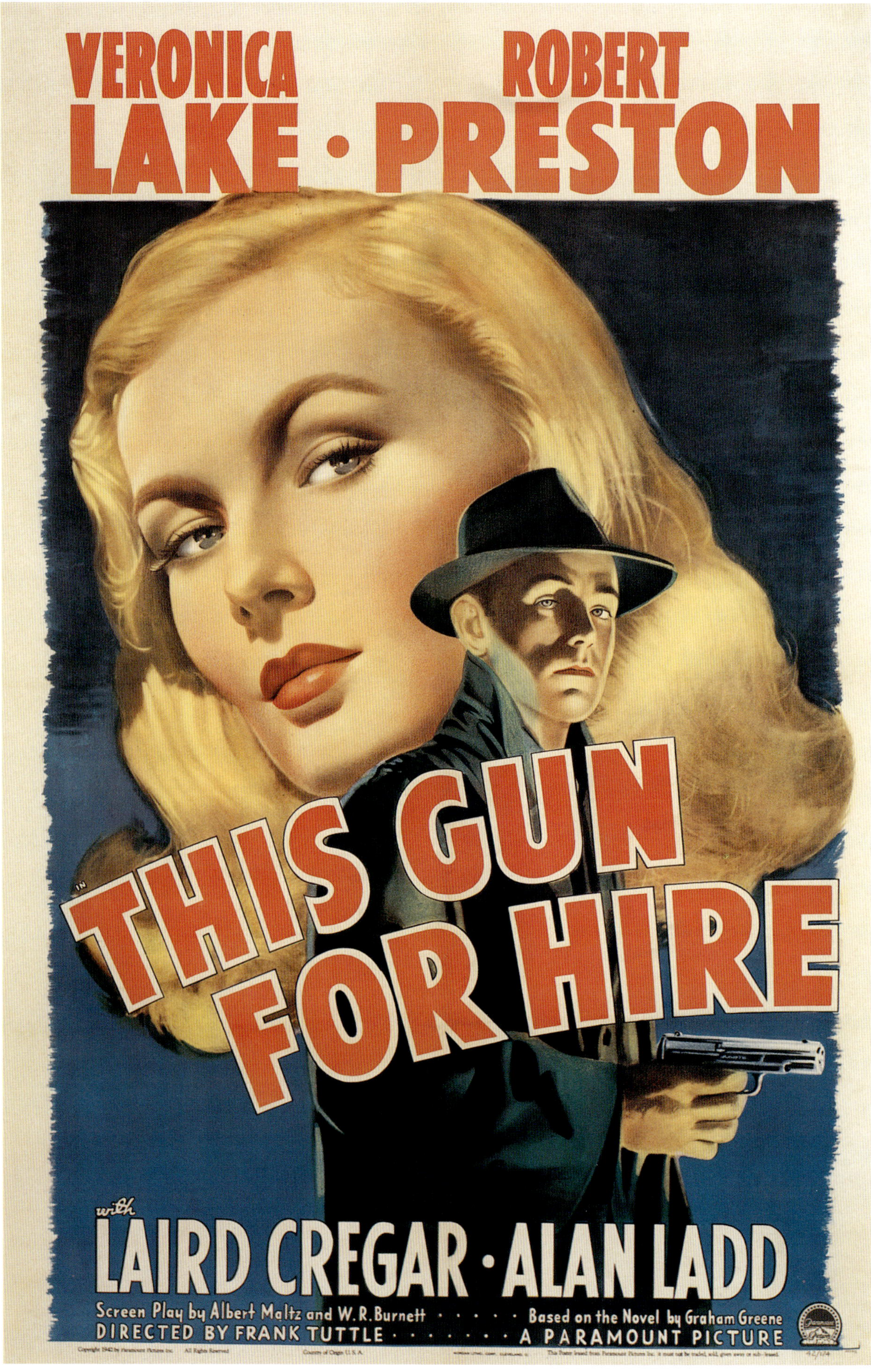

This Gun for Hire. 1942. One-sheet. $7,000-9,000.

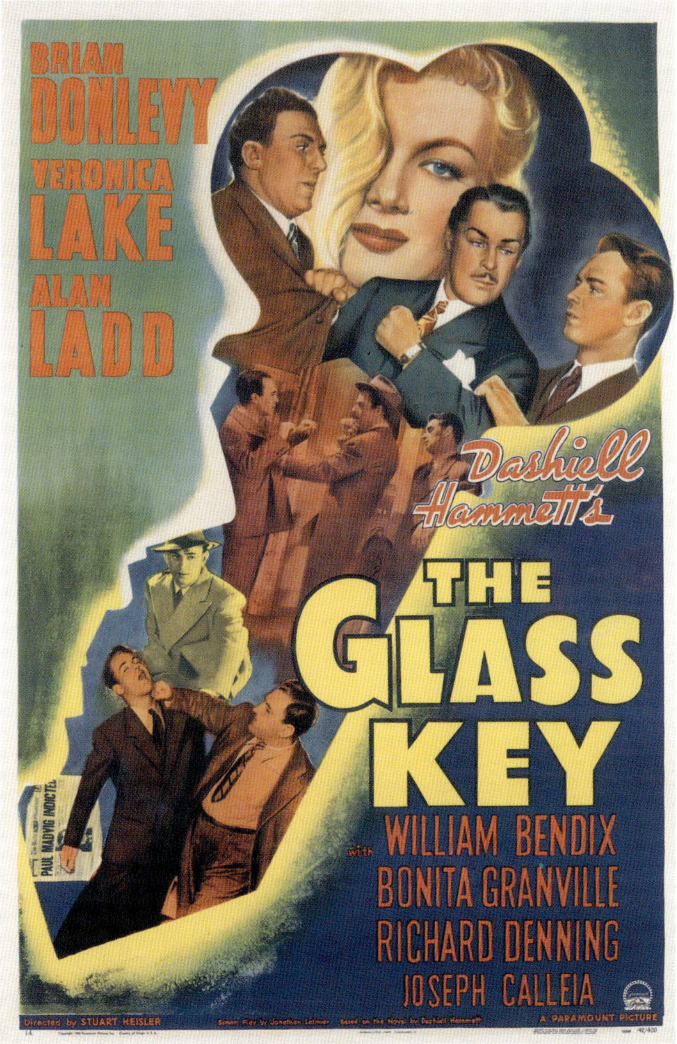

The Glass Key. 1942. One-sheet. $4,000-6000.

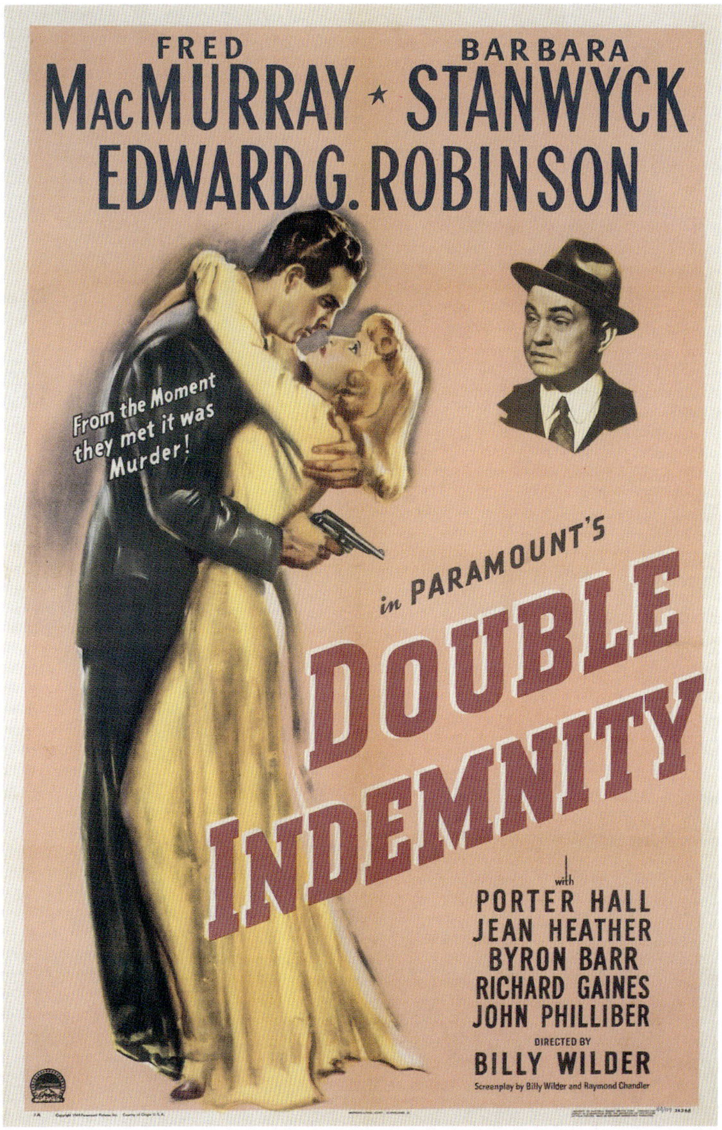

Double Indemnity. 1944. One-sheet. $2,000-3,000.

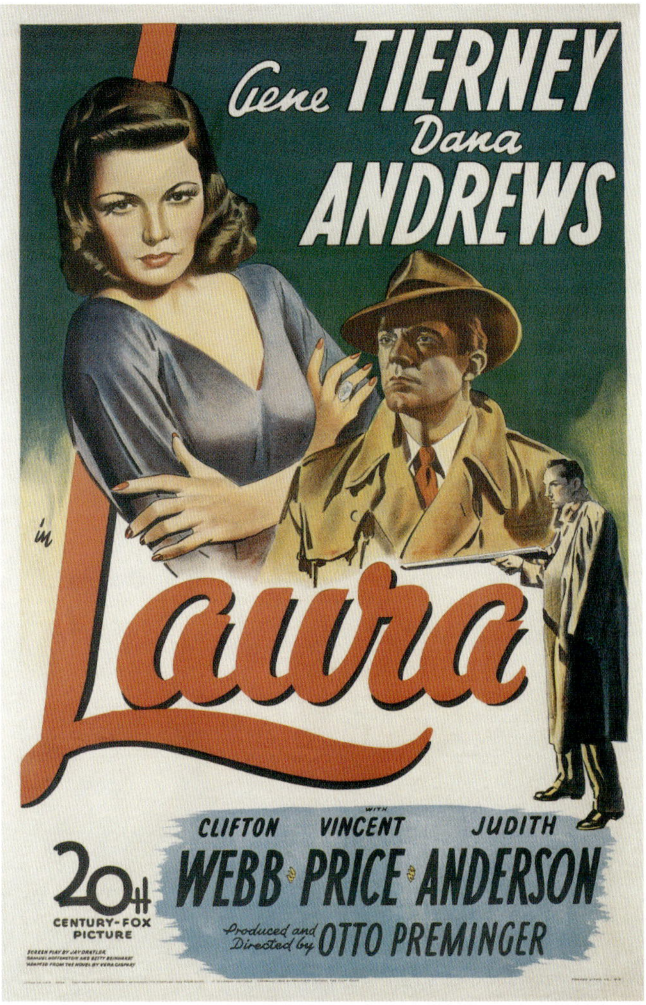

Laura. 1944. One-sheet. $3,000-4,000.

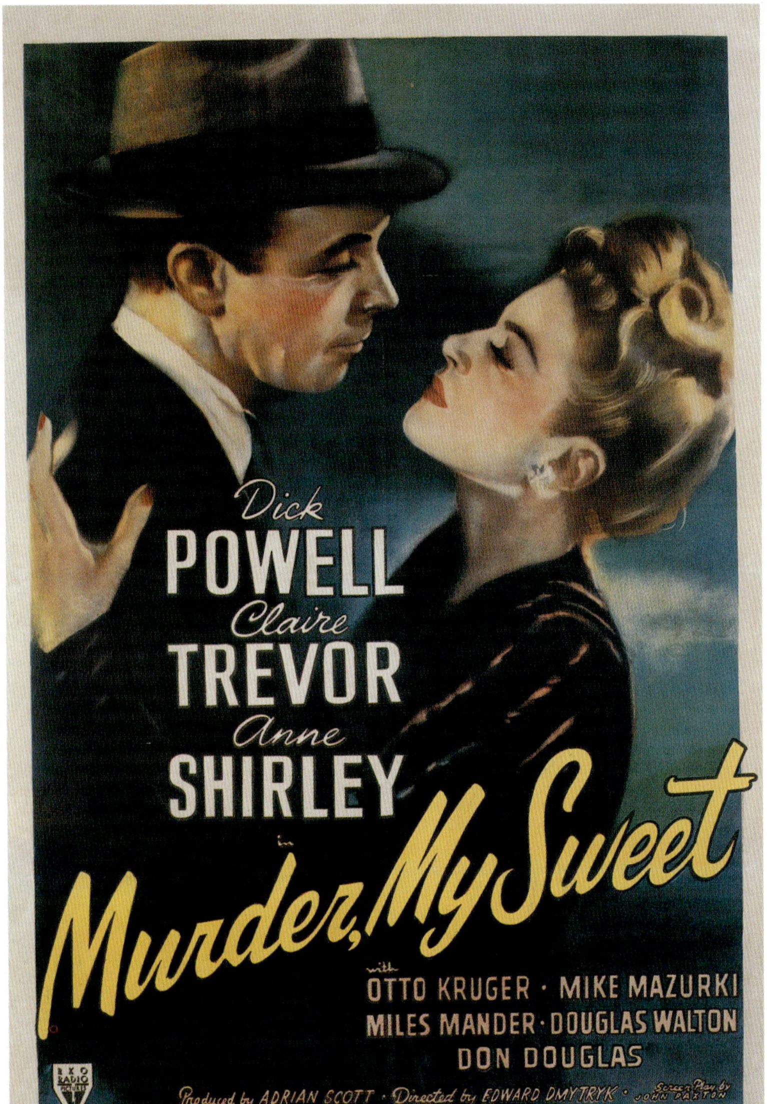

Murder, My Sweet. 1944. One-sheet. $2,000-3,000.

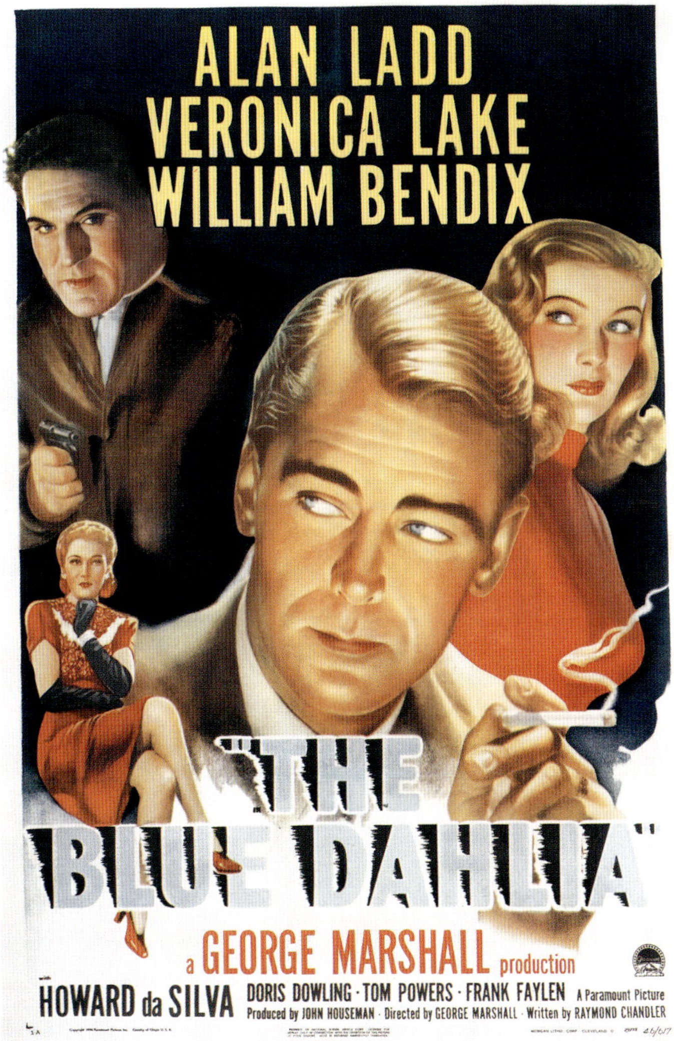

The Blue Dahlia. 1946. One-sheet. $3,000-5,000.

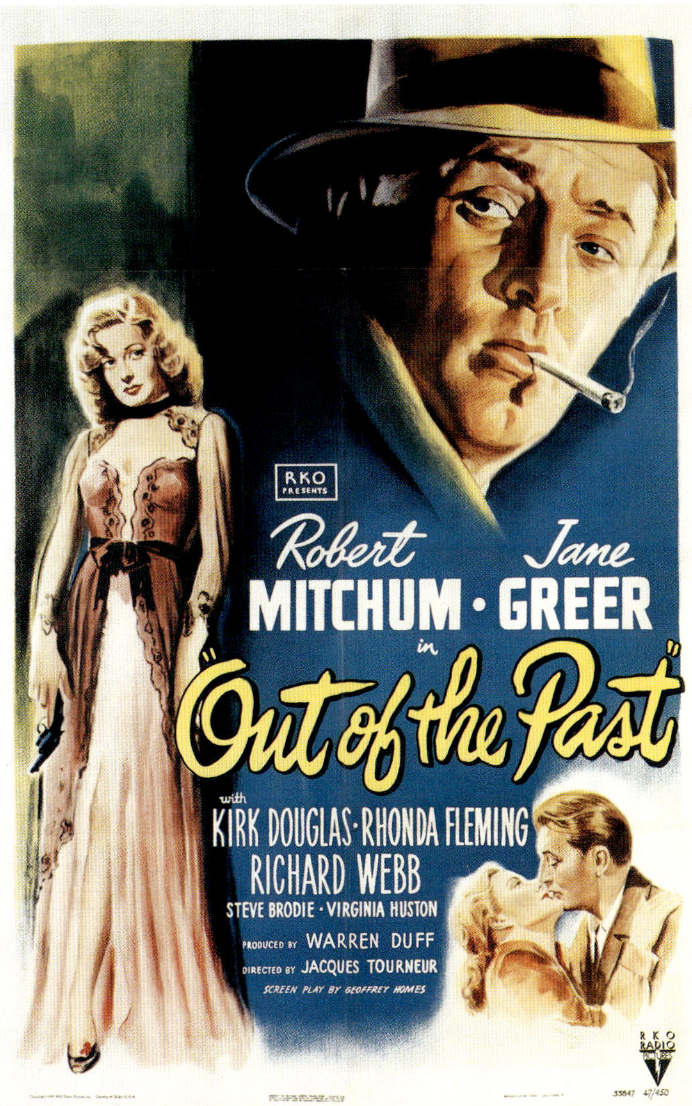

Out of the Past. 1947. One-sheet. $3,000-5,000.

The very nature of "film noir" plots meant that there was a lot of enthusiasm amongst the studios to continue producing the gangster formula that had proved such a success the previous decade. Stars such as Edward G. Robinson, James Cagney, and of course the consistently busy Humphrey Bogart provided the necessary gritty leads.

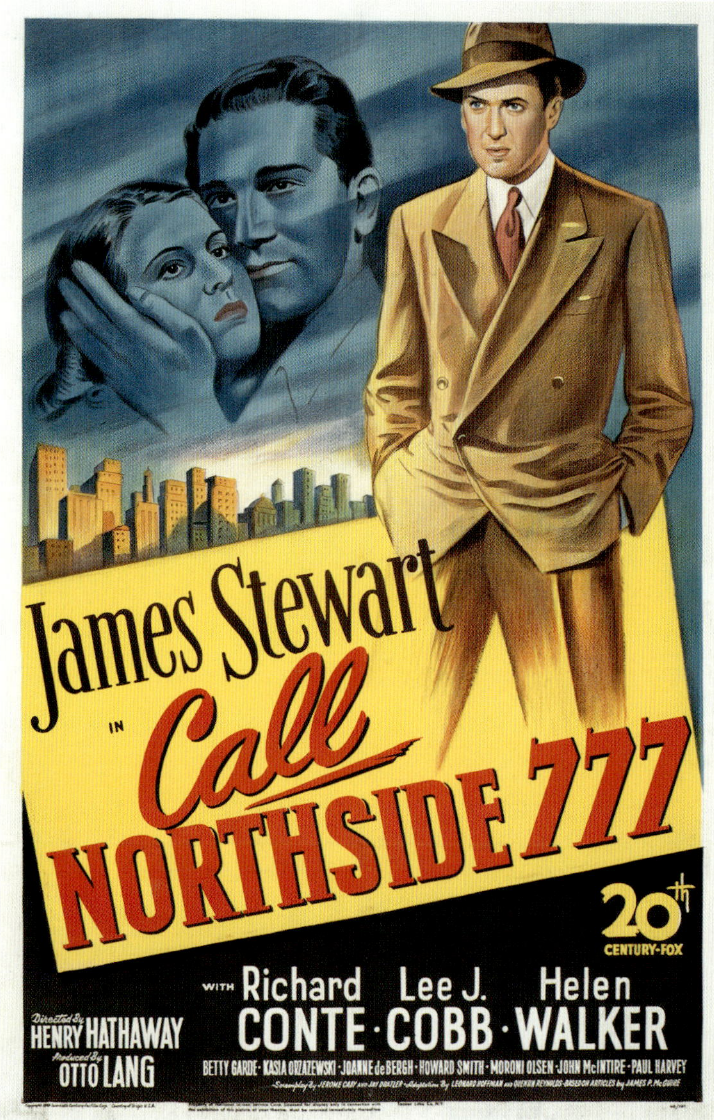

Call Northside 777. 1948. One-sheet. $1,200-1,800.

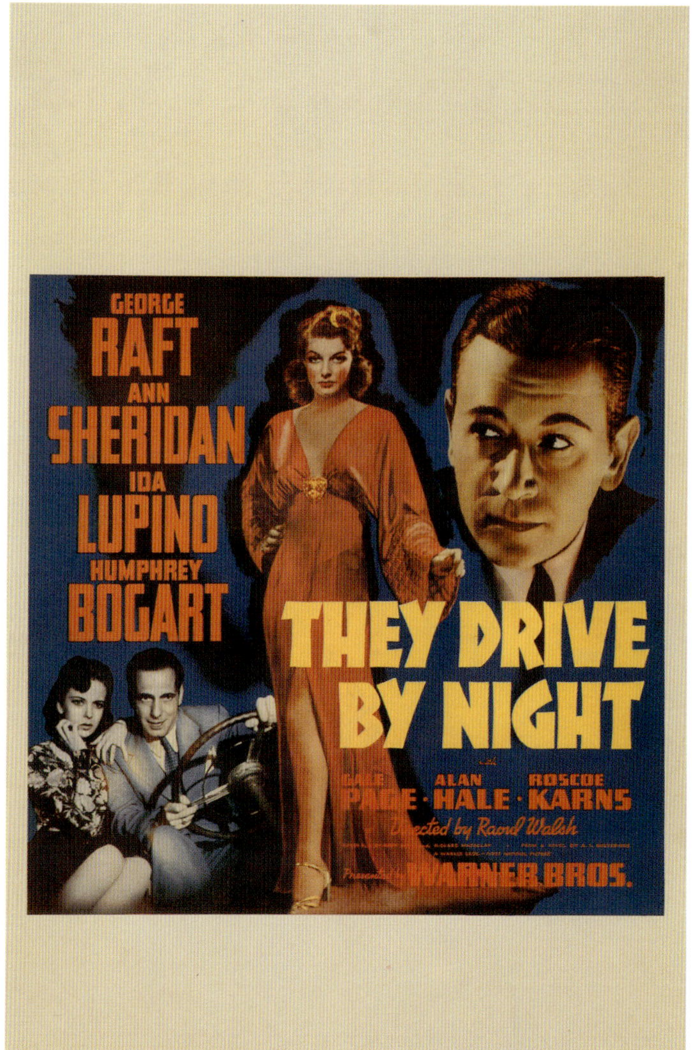

They Drive by Night. 1940. Window card. $800-1,200.

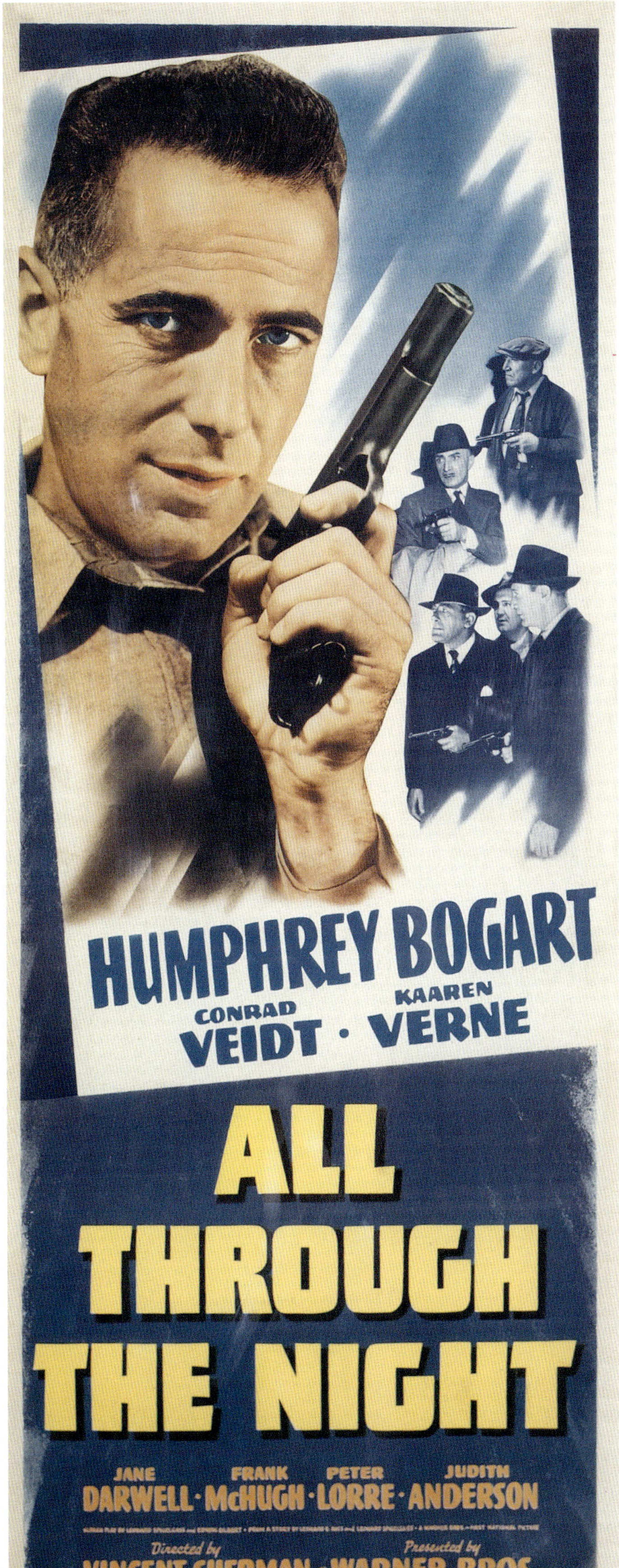

All Through the Night. 1942. Insert. $800-1,200.

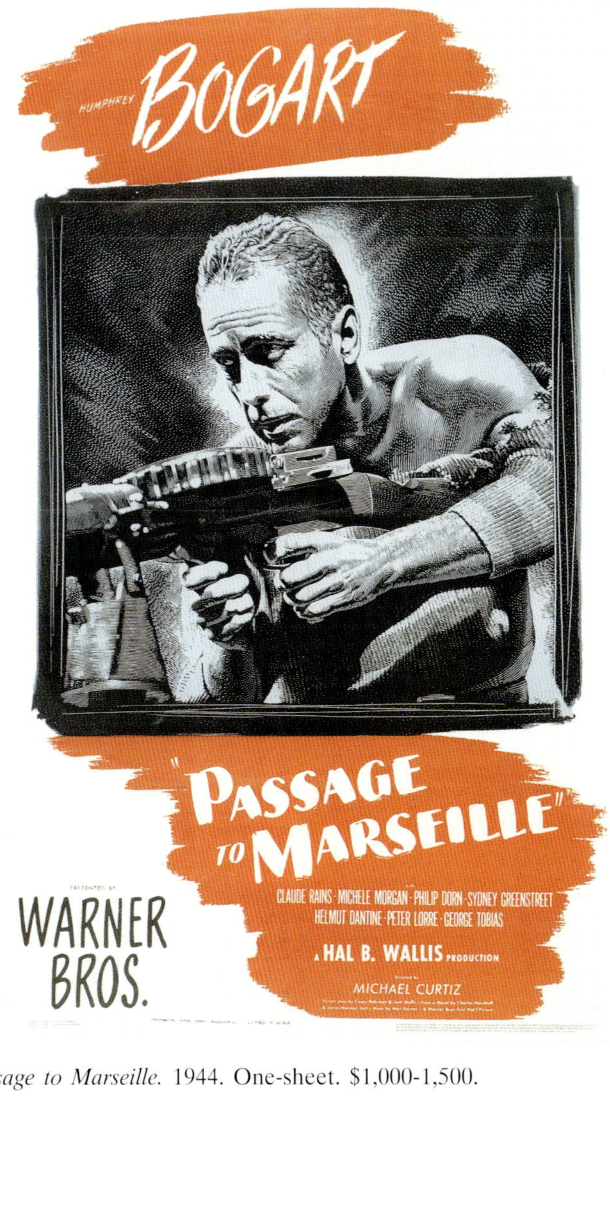

Passage to Marseille. 1944. One-sheet. $1,000-1,500.

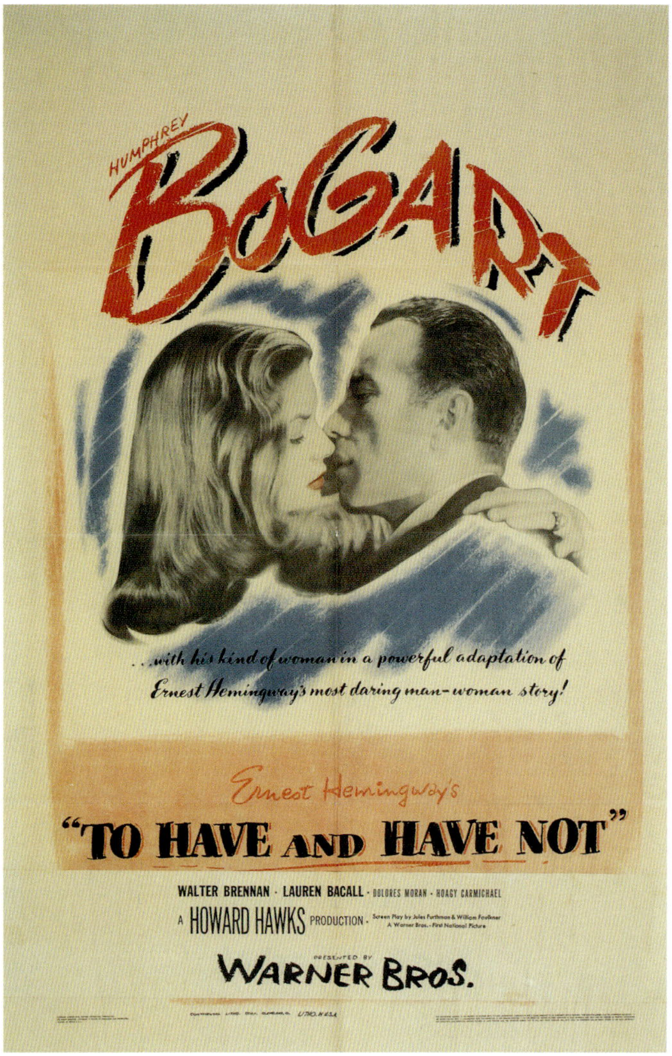

To Have and Have Not. 1944.
One-sheet. $2,000-2,500.

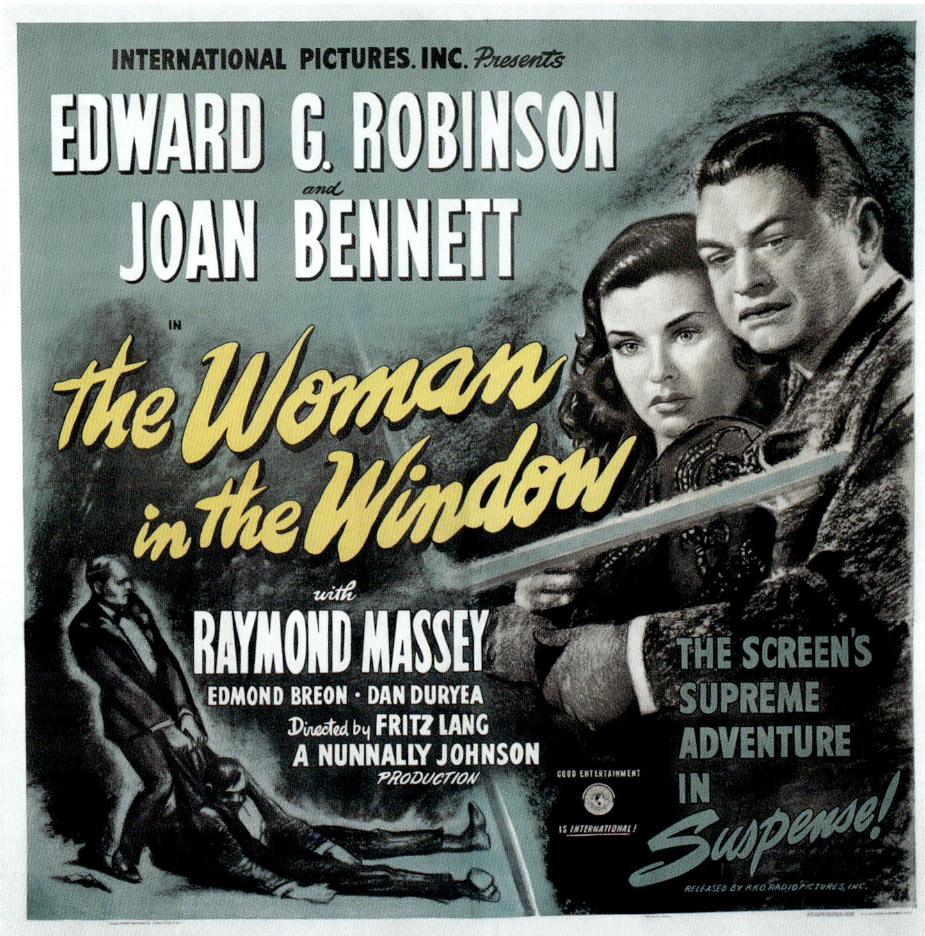

The Woman in the Window.
1944. Six-sheet. $2,000-2,500.

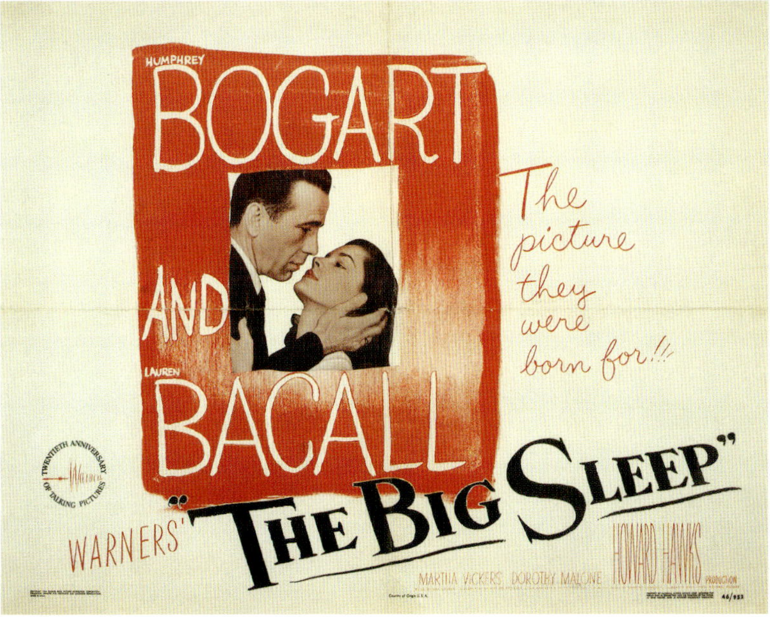

The Big Sleep. 1946. Half-sheet. $1,000-1,500.

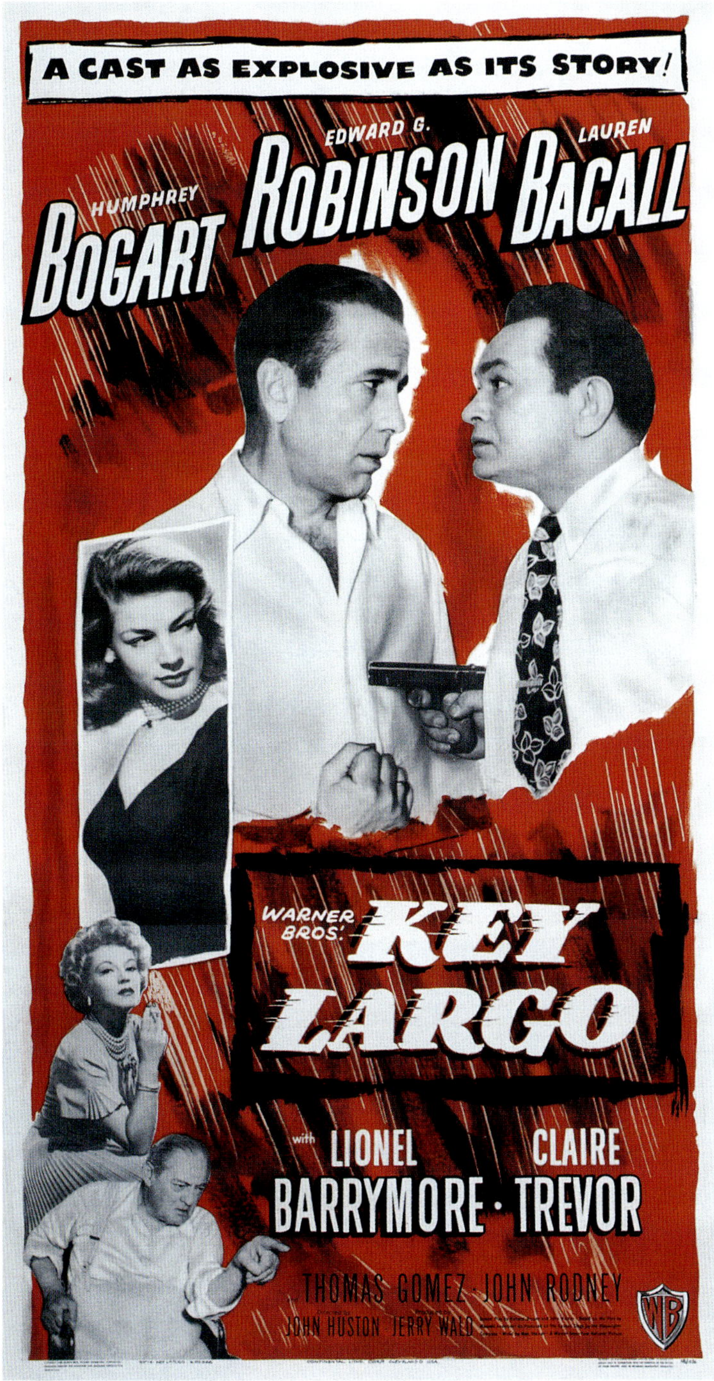

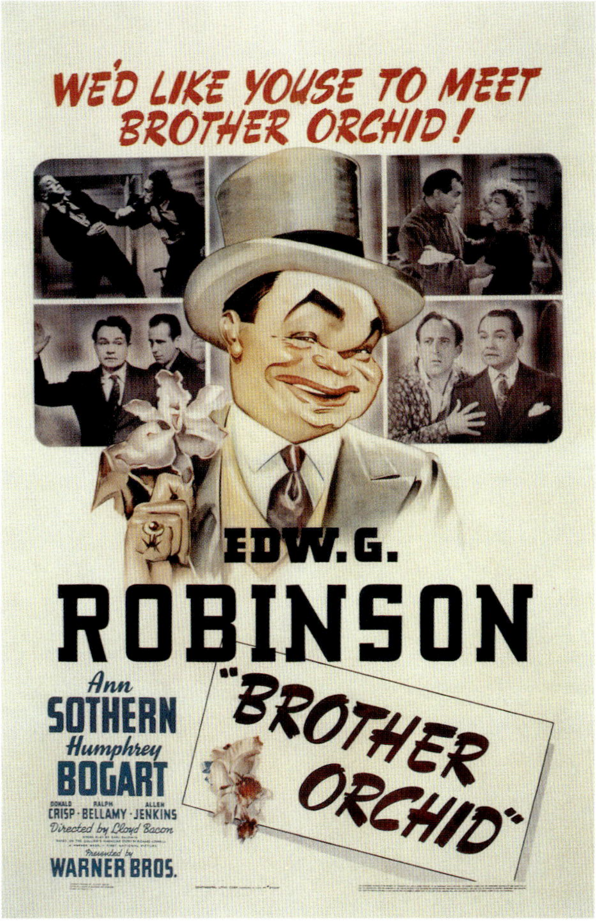

Brother Orchid. 1940. One-sheet. $1,000-1,500.

Key Largo. 1948. Three-sheet. $1,500-2,500.

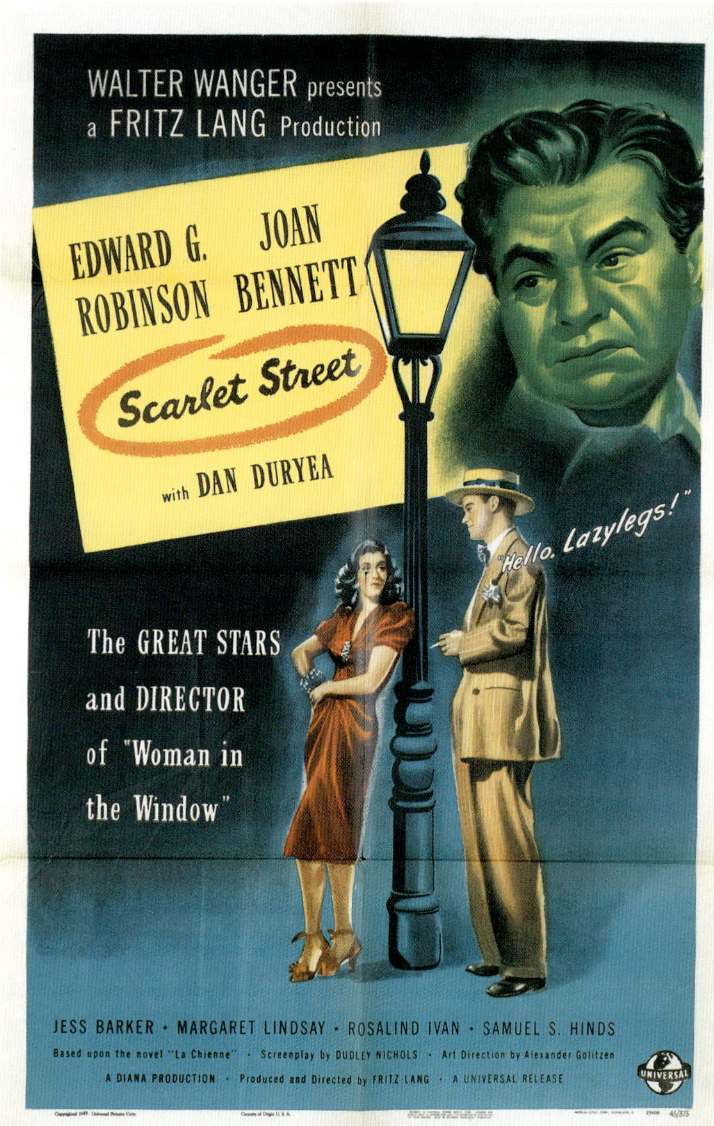

Scarlet Street. 1945. One-sheet. $1,500-2,000.

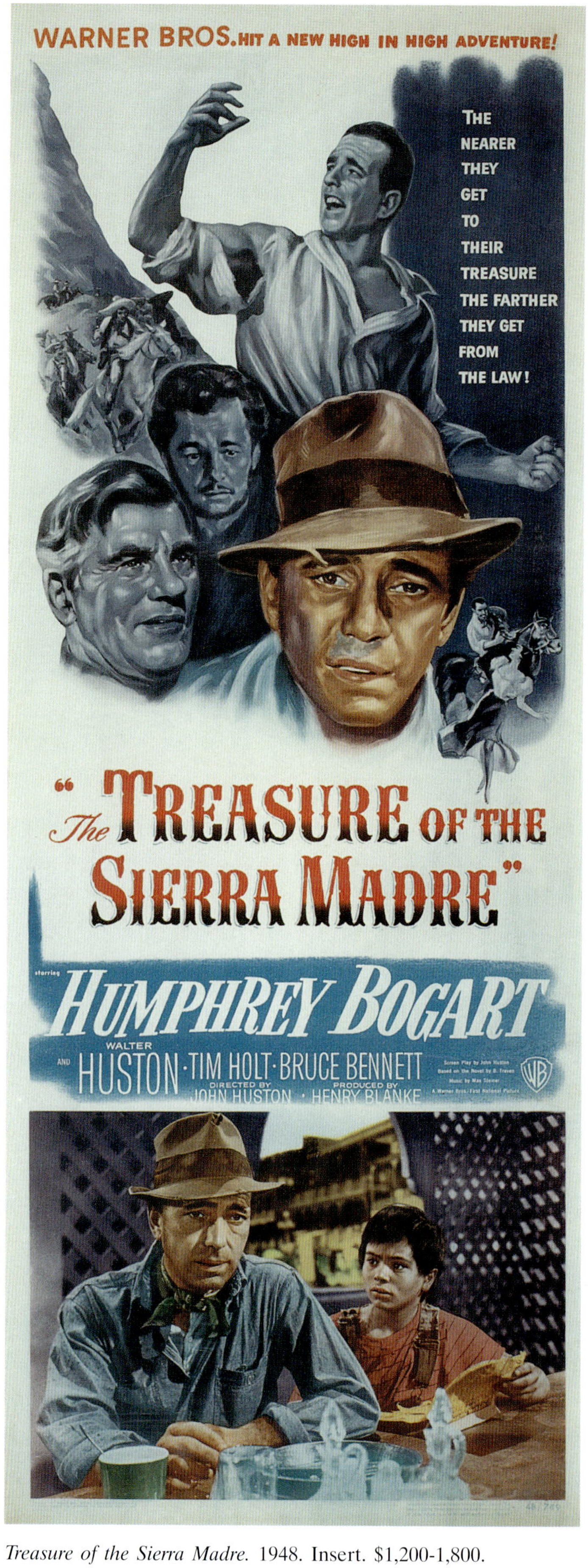

Treasure of the Sierra Madre. 1948. Insert. $1,200-1,800.

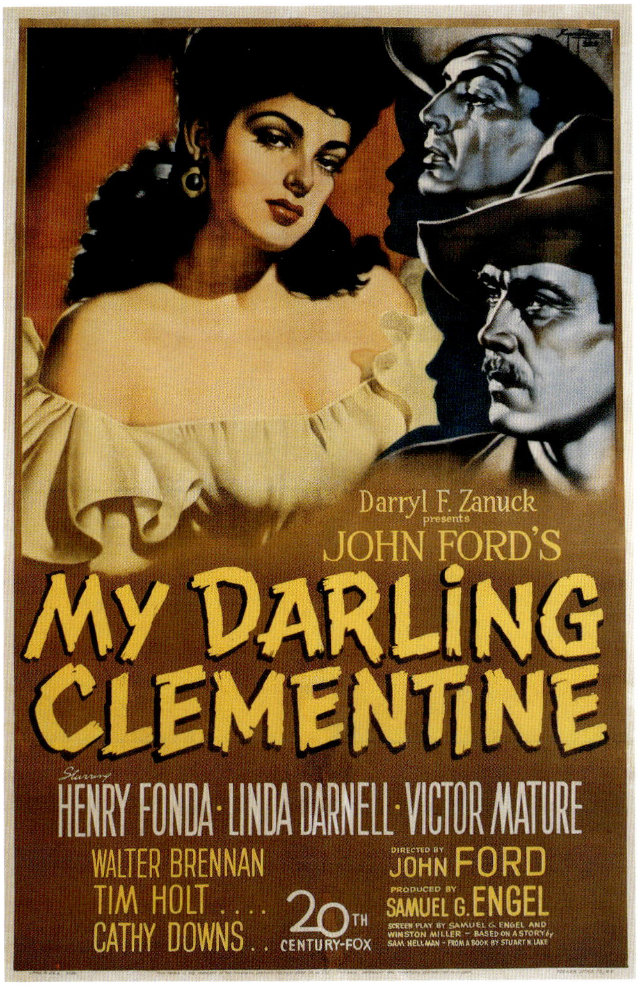

My Darling Clementine. 1946. One-sheet, art by Sergio Gargiulo. $3,000-4,000.

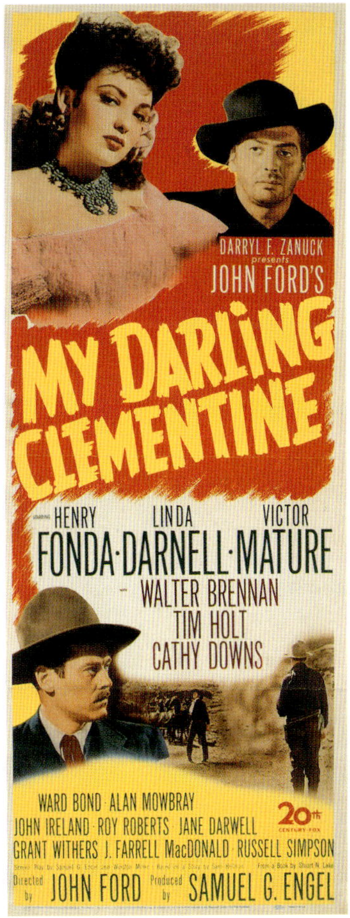

My Darling Clementine. 1946. Insert. $1,000-1,500.

Tales of revenge and heroics struck a chord and increasingly tough westerns were produced during this time, notably director John Ford's *My Darling Clementine* (1946) and his cavalry trio starring John Wayne *Fort Apache* (1948), *She Wore a Yellow Ribbon* (1949) and *Rio Grande* (1950). Meanwhile Errol Flynn reenacted General Custer's last stand in the historically liberal *They Died With Their Boots On* (1942).

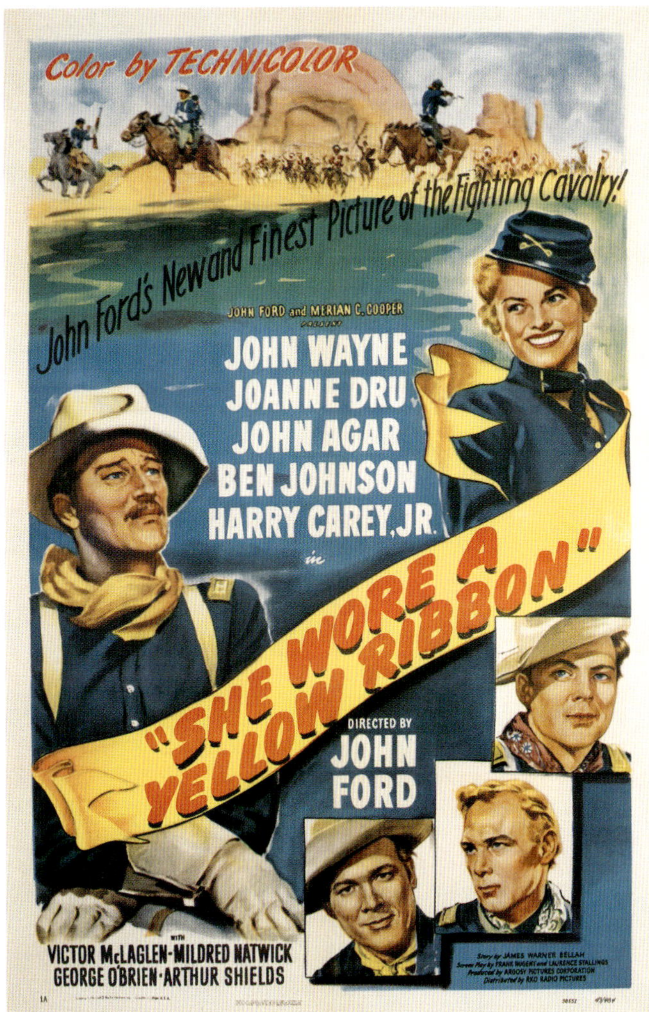

She Wore a Yellow Ribbon. 1949. One-sheet. $1,500-2,500.

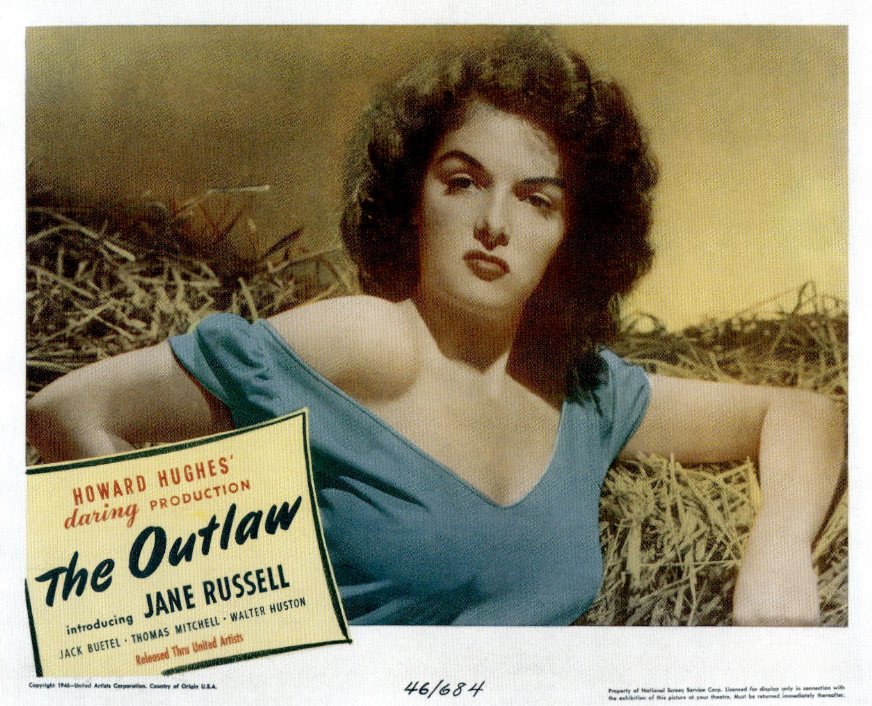

The Outlaw. 1941. Lobby card. $800-1,200.

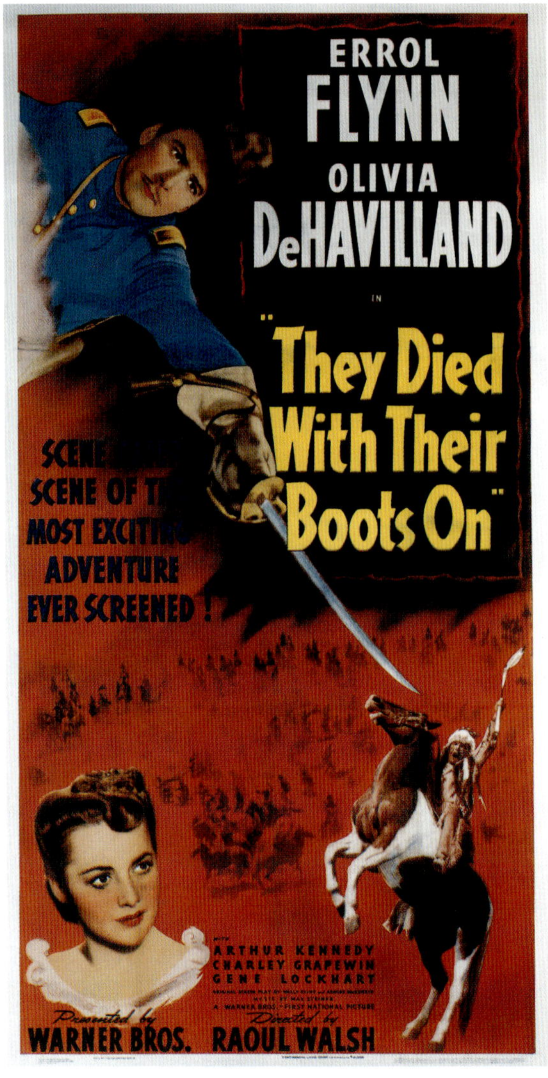

They Died with their Boots On. 1941. Three-sheet. $2,500-3,500.

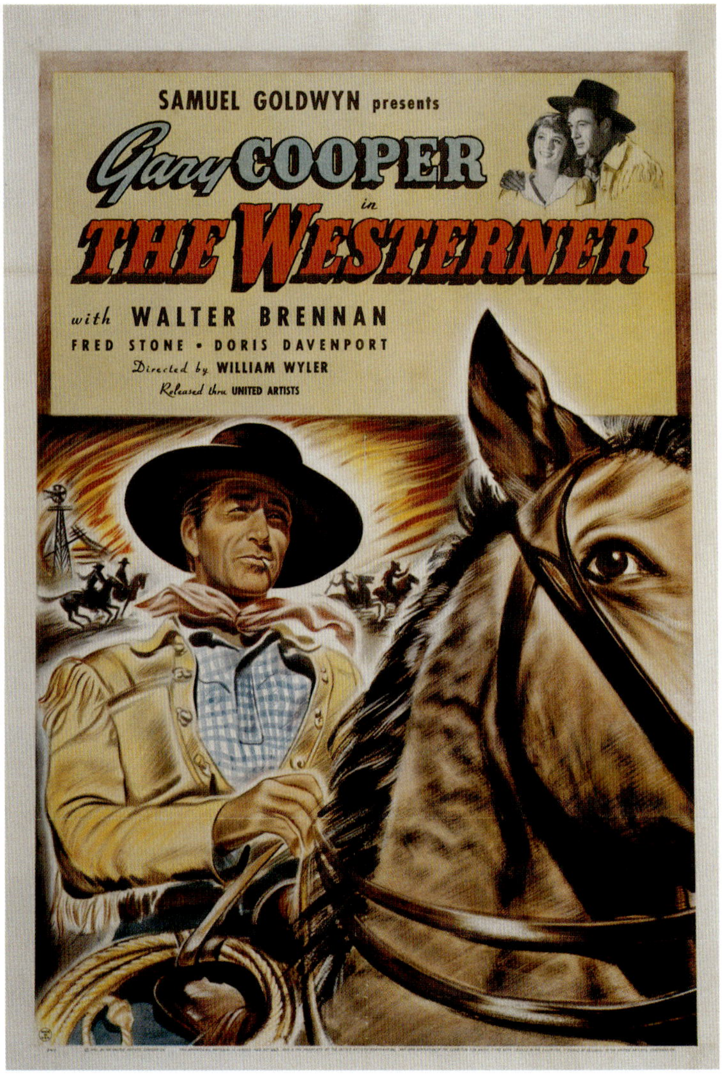

The Westerner. 1940. One-sheet. $2,500-3,500.

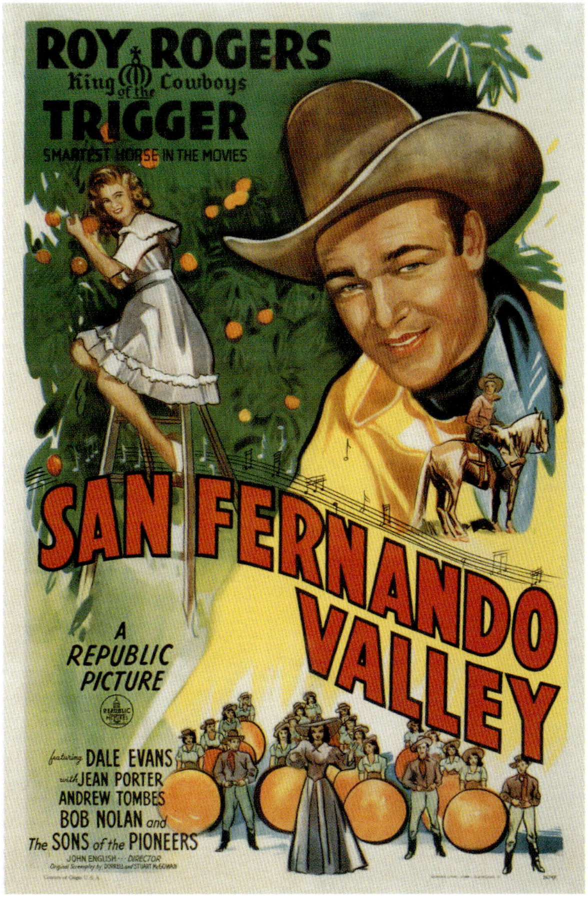

San Fernando Valley. 1944. One-sheet. $700-1,000.

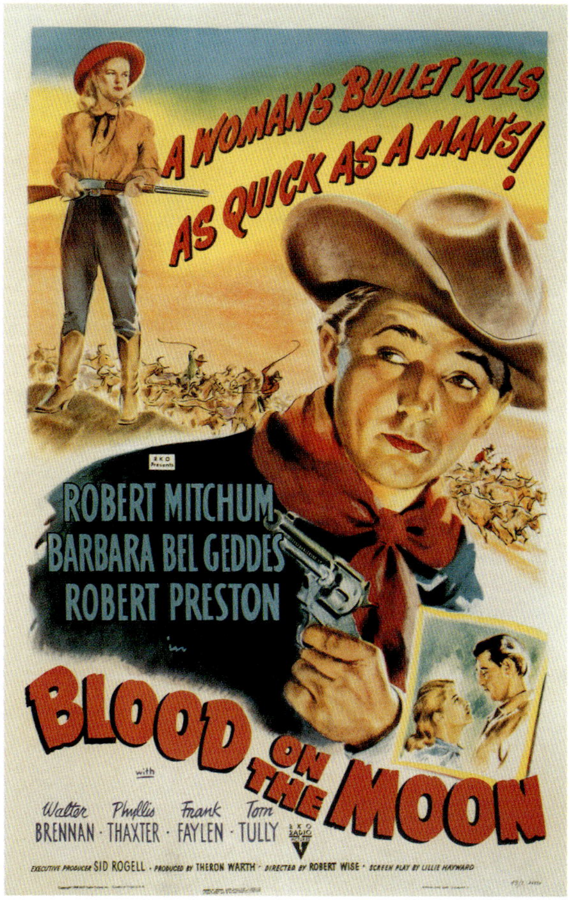

Blood on the Moon. 1948. One-sheet. $700-1,000.

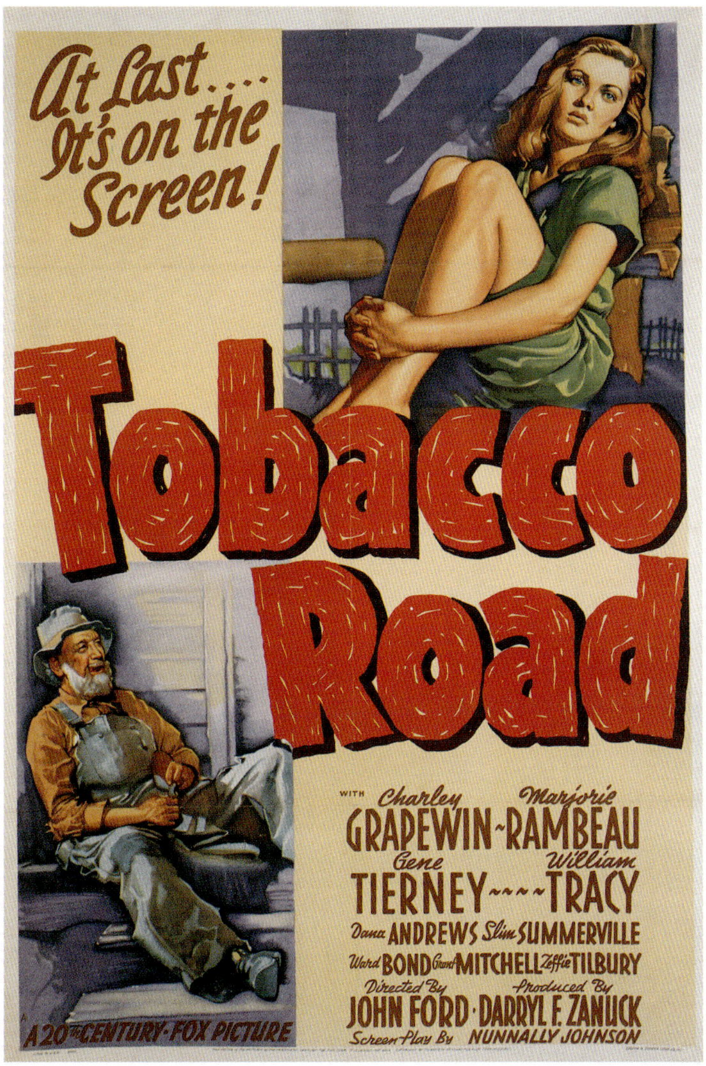

Tobacco Road. 1941. One-sheet, style A. $1,200-1,800.

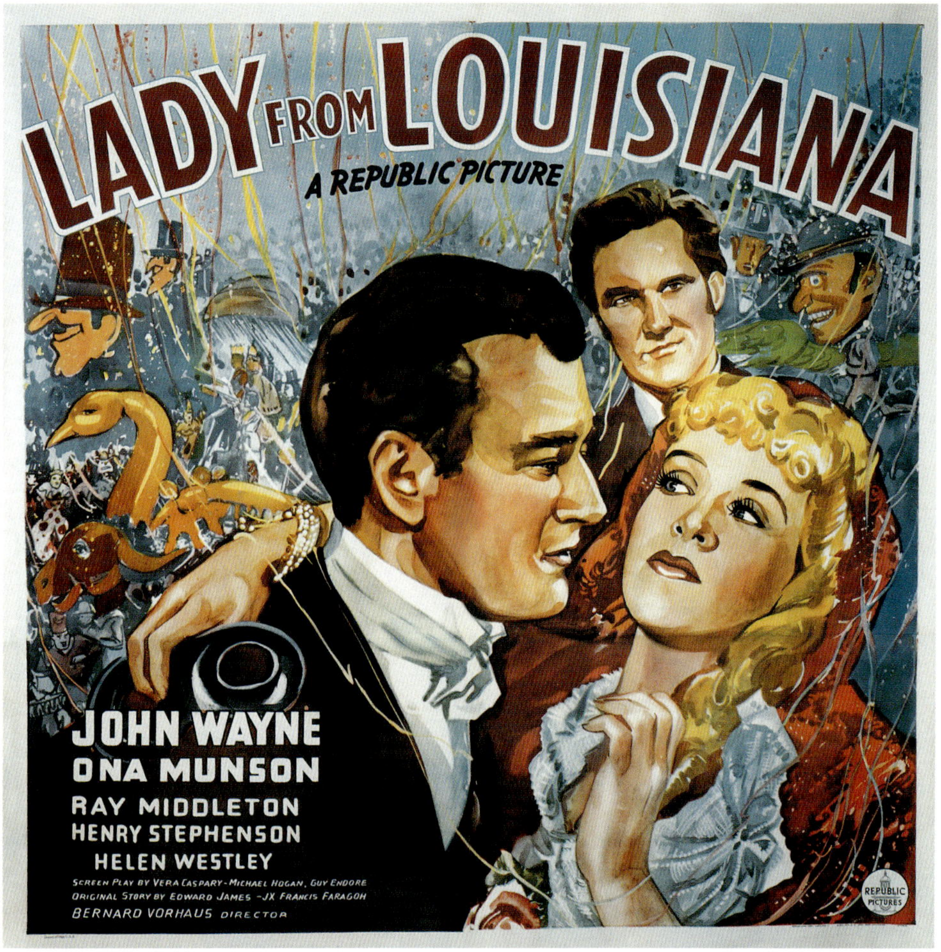

Lady from Louisiana. 1941. Six-sheet. $1,500-2,500.

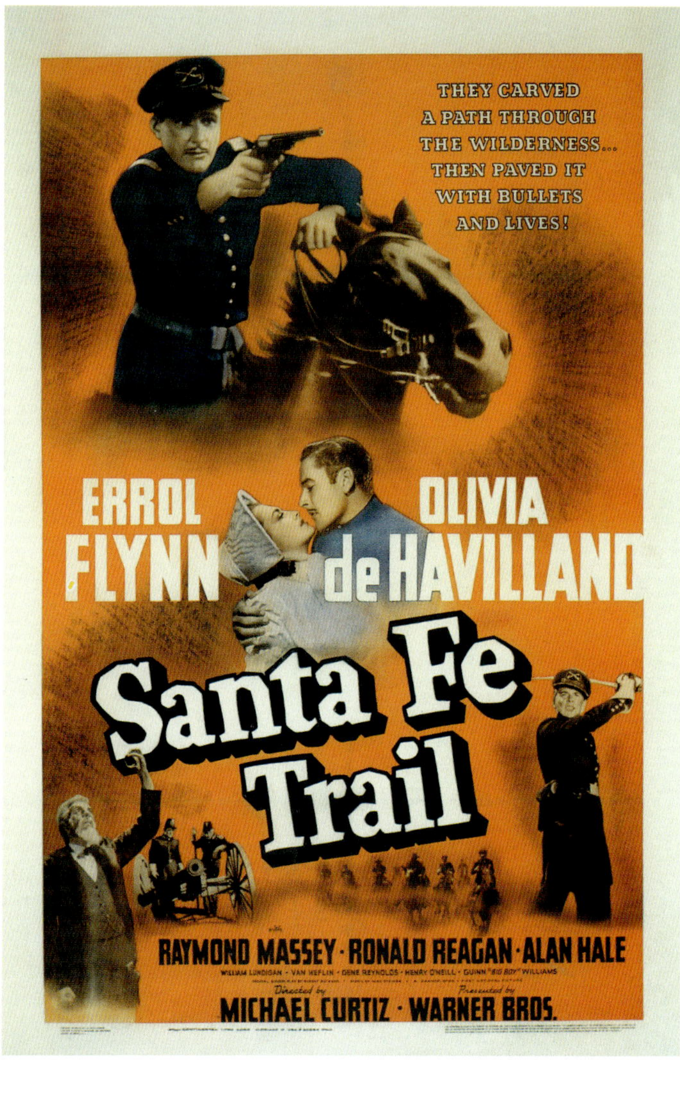

Sante Fe Trail. 1940. One-sheet. $800-1,200.

Though times could have been better Hollywood was able to laugh in the face of adversity. Many comedies and feel-good movies poured from the studios during this period in time honored escapist fashion. The likes of Bob Hope, Bing Crosby, Cary Grant, and Spencer Tracy all sang and joked their way across the screens. Musicals such as *Holiday Inn* (1942), *Cabin in the Sky* (1943), and *Meet Me In St. Louis* (1944) with Judy Garland, all spoke of happy times, some past, and some, hopefully, that were yet to come. Even ruthless gangster type James Cagney stepped in to the all-singing and dancing role of vaudevillian George M. Cohan in the madly patriotic *Yankee Doodle Dandy* (1942). Nothing could raise a smile like the antics of colorful cartoon characters. Some of the most memorable came courtesy of Walt Disney with *Pinocchio* (1940), *Dumbo* (1941), *Bambi* (1942) and *Fantasia* (1940).

Frank Capra, with his flair for escapism seen in some of his earlier films from the 1930s, directed one of the most successful sentimental tear-jerkers of all time with *It's A Wonderful Life* (1946). Emphasizing that out of hopelessness a bright future is possible, the suicidal James Stewart is reunited with his loving family only after being shown the ghastly bleakness of his hometown had he not lived and contributed his life to theirs.

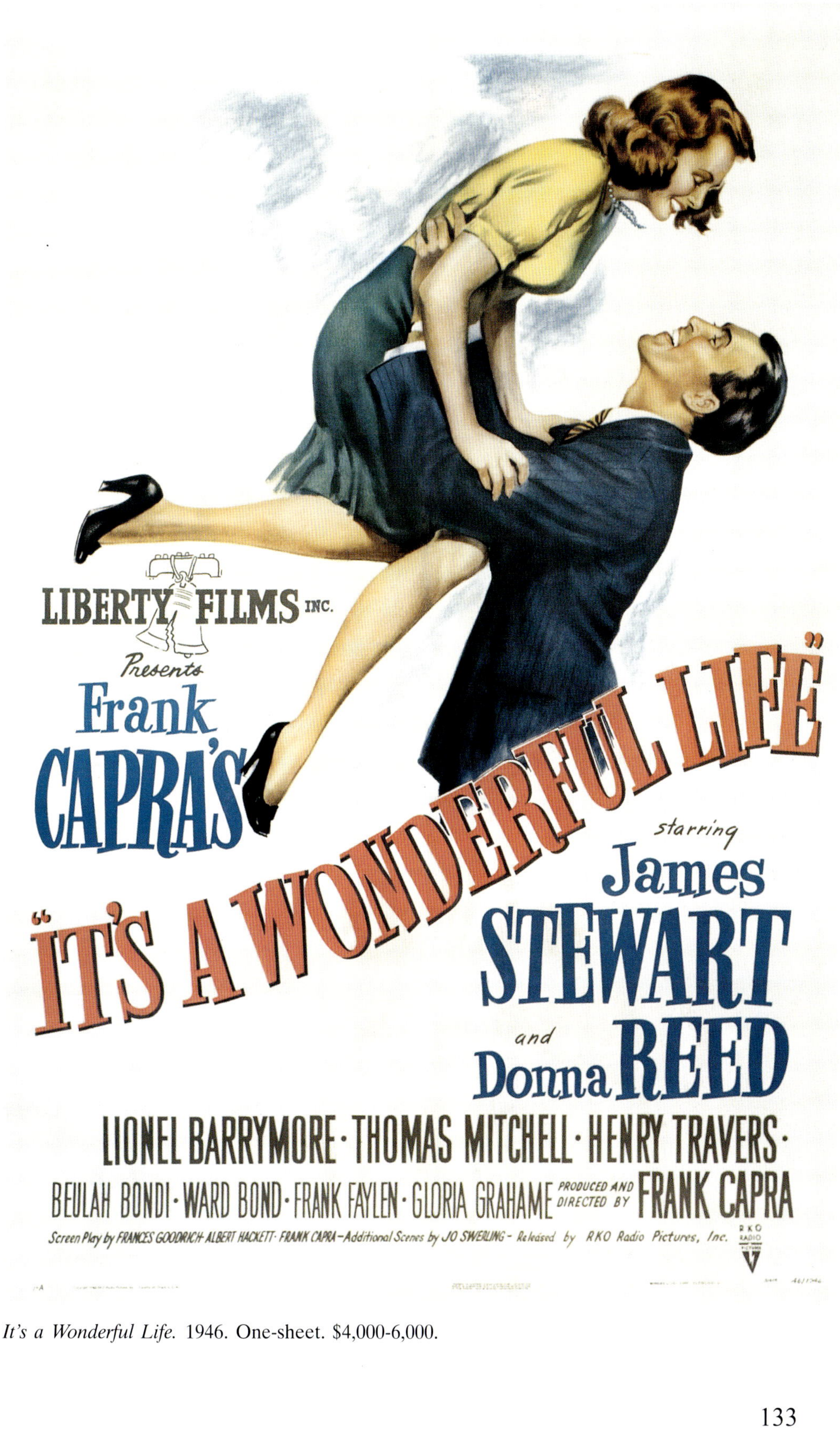

It's a Wonderful Life. 1946. One-sheet. $4,000-6,000.

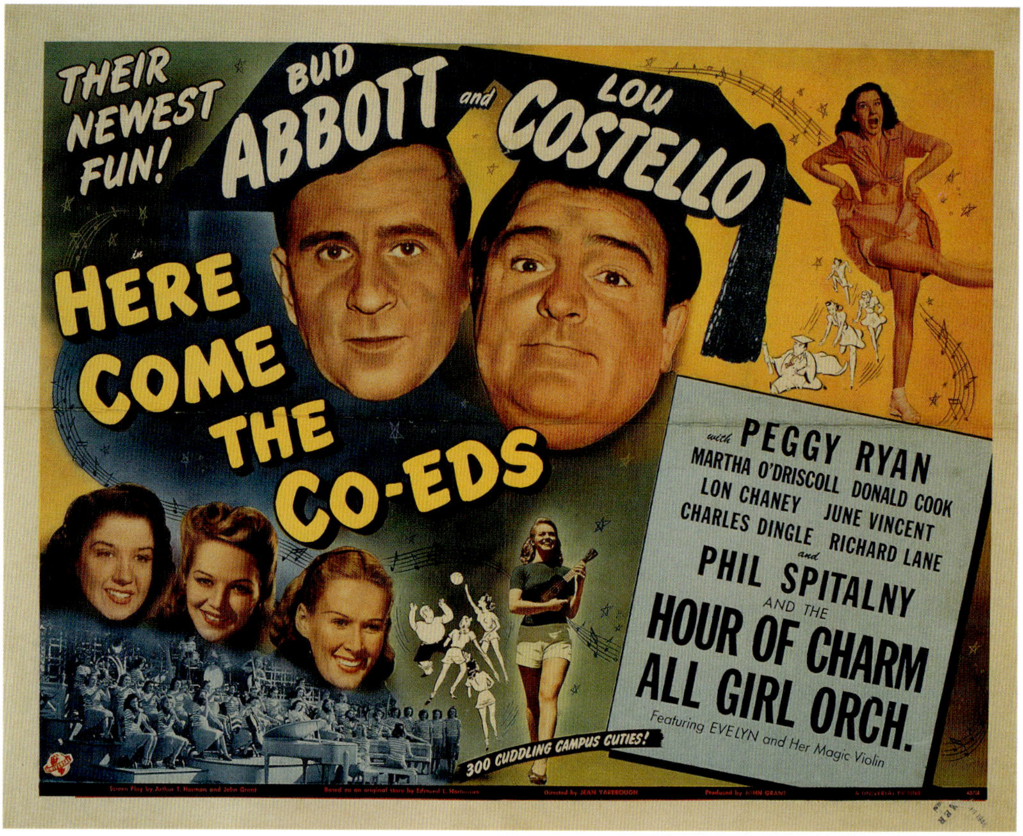

Here Come the Co-Eds. 1945. Half-sheet. $1,000-1,500.

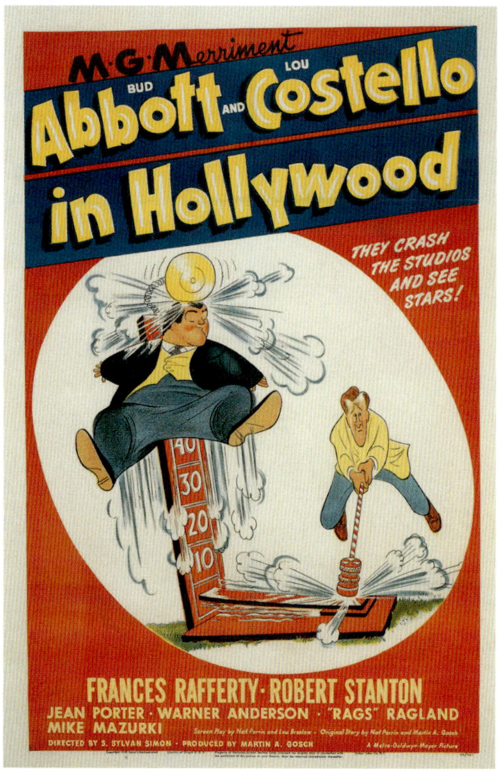

Abbott and Costello in Hollywood. 1945. One-sheet, art by Albert Hirschfield. $800-1,200.

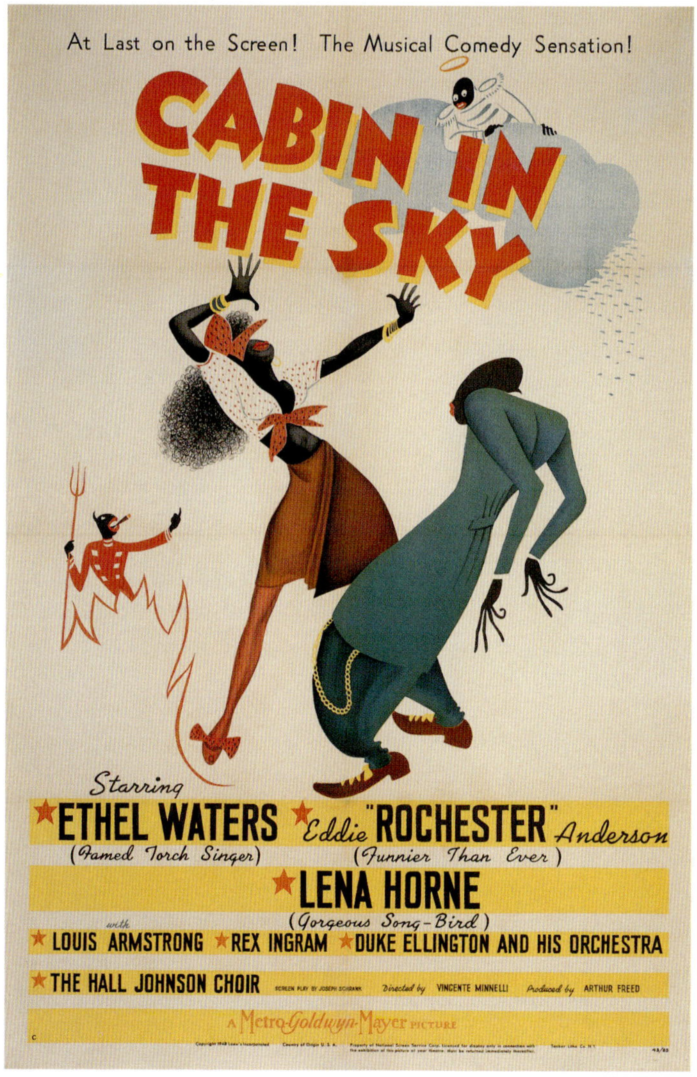

Cabin in the Sky. 1943. One-sheet, art by Albert Hirschfield. $5,000-8,000.

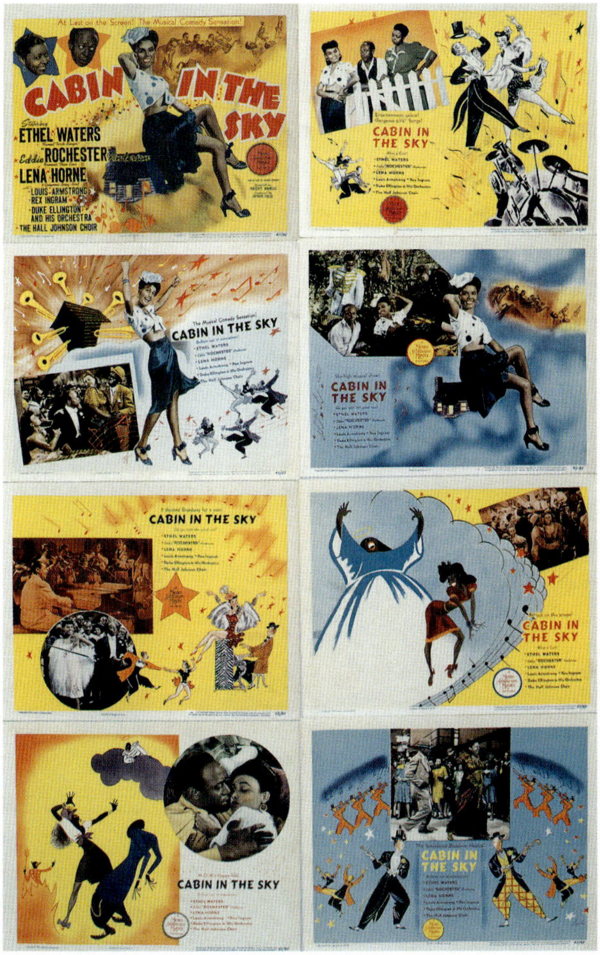

Cabin in the Sky. 1943. Set of lobby cards. $2,500-3,500.

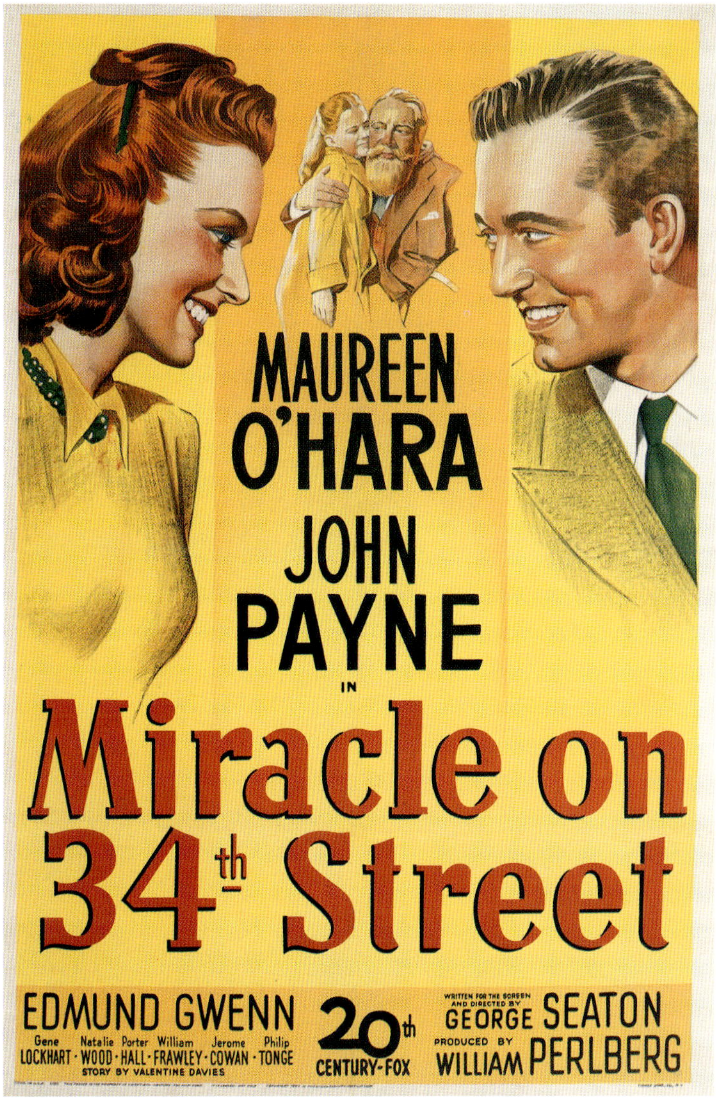

Miracle on 34th Street. 1947. One-sheet. $1,000-1,500.

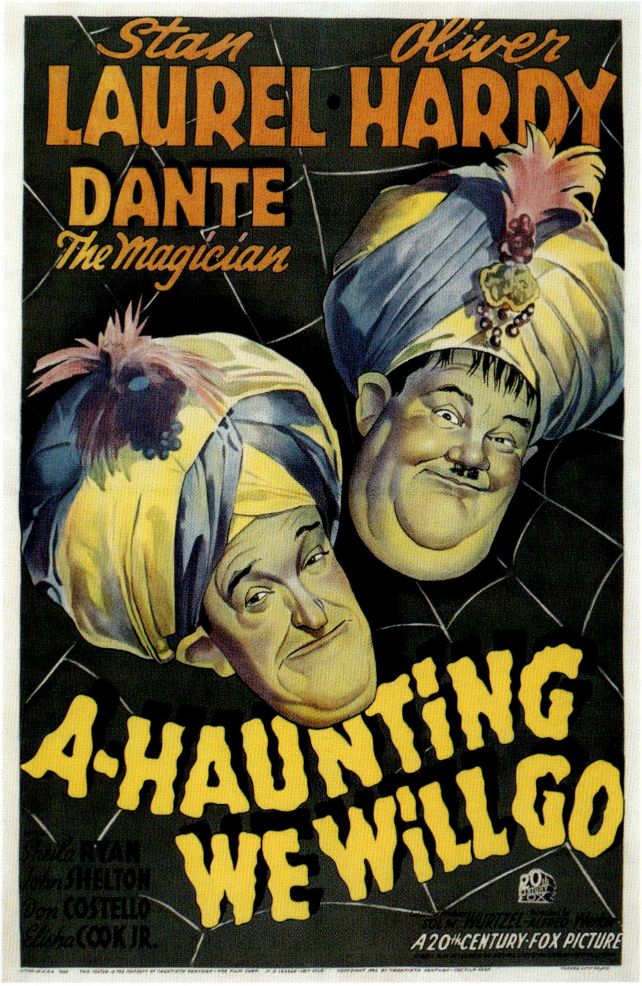

A-Haunting We Will Go. 1942.
One-sheet. $1,200-1,800.

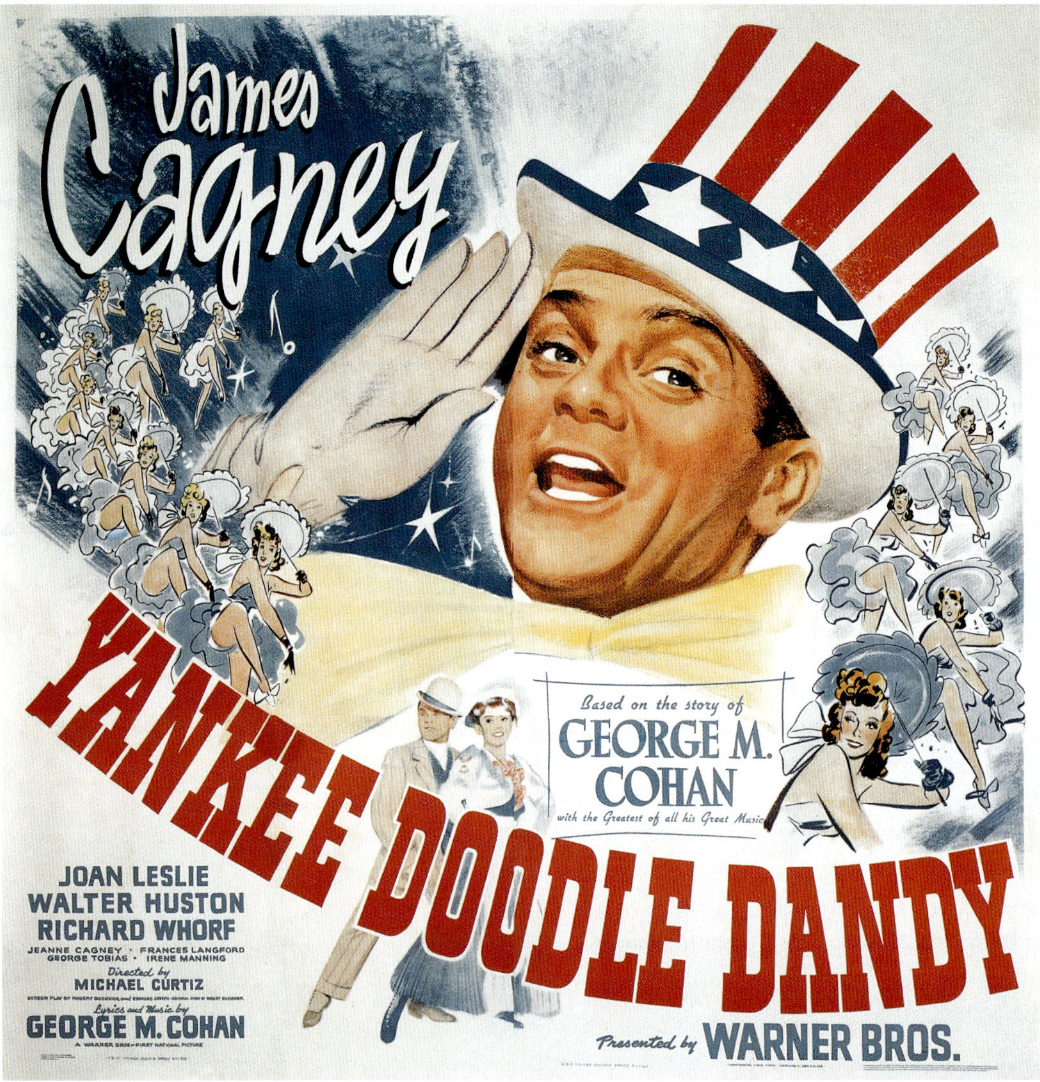

Yankee Doodle Dandy. 1942. Six-sheet. $3,000-5,000.

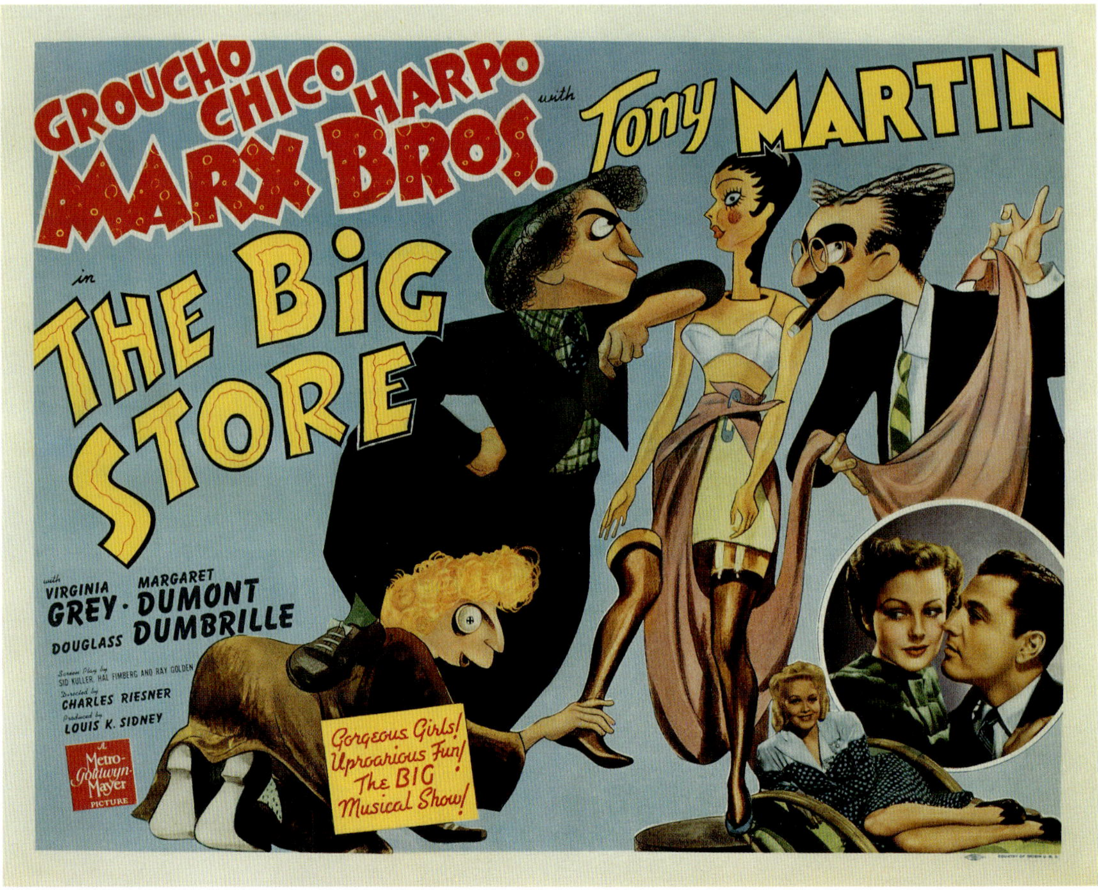

The Big Store. 1941. Half-sheet, style B, art by Albert Hirschfield. $1,200-1,800.

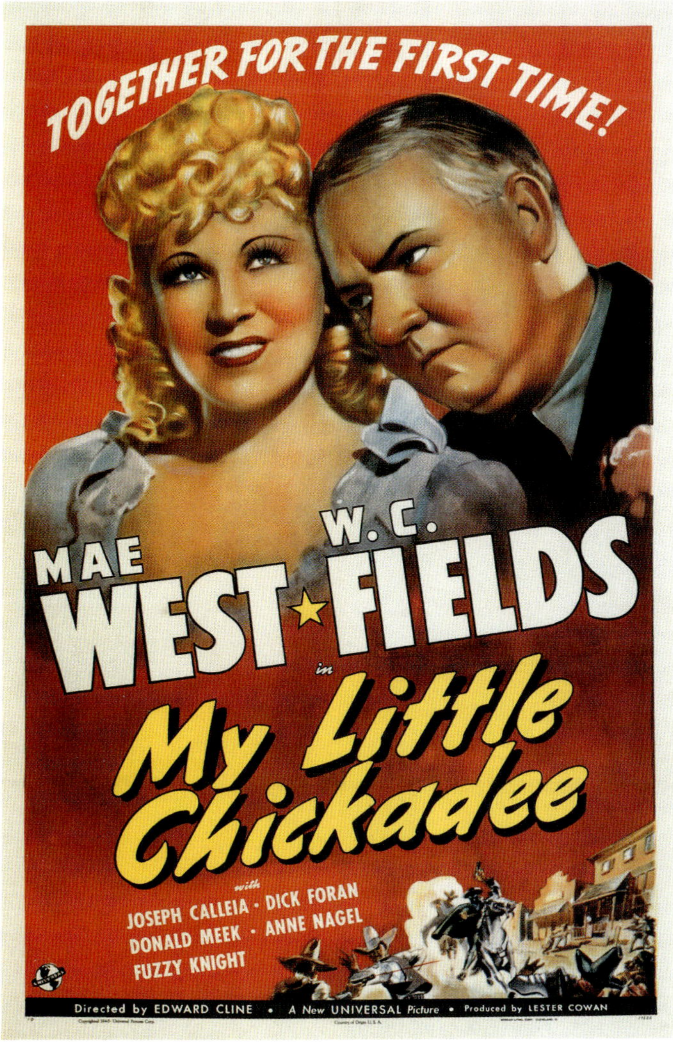

My Little Chickadee. 1940. One-sheet. $2,500-3,500.

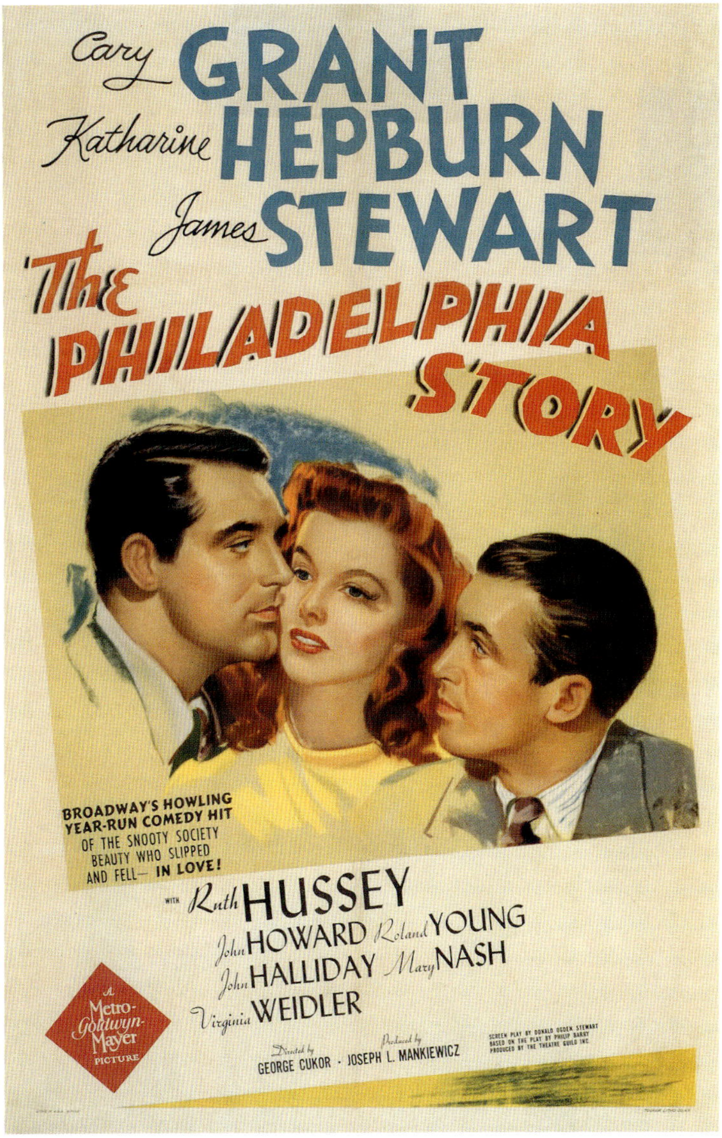

The Philadelphia Story. 1940. One-sheet, style D. $2,000-3,000.

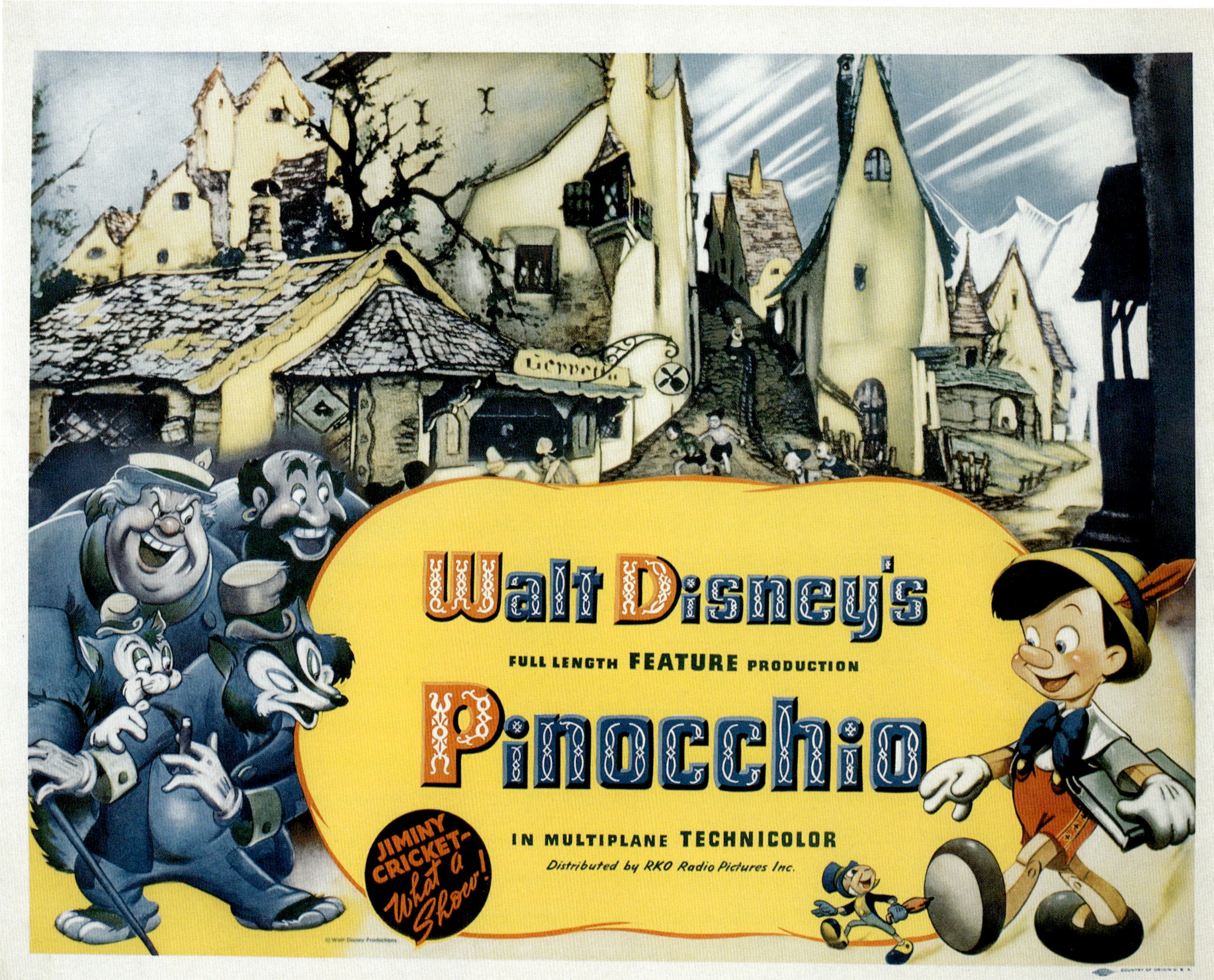

Pinocchio. 1940. Half-sheet. $7,000-10,000.

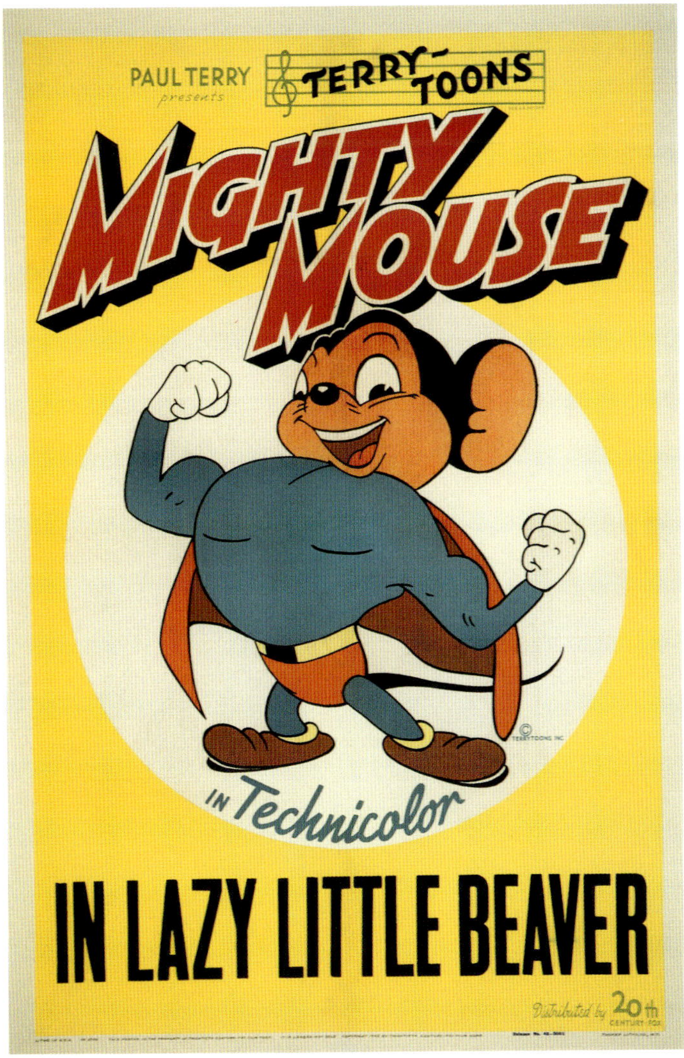

Lazy Little Beaver. 1943. One-sheet. $1,200-1,800.

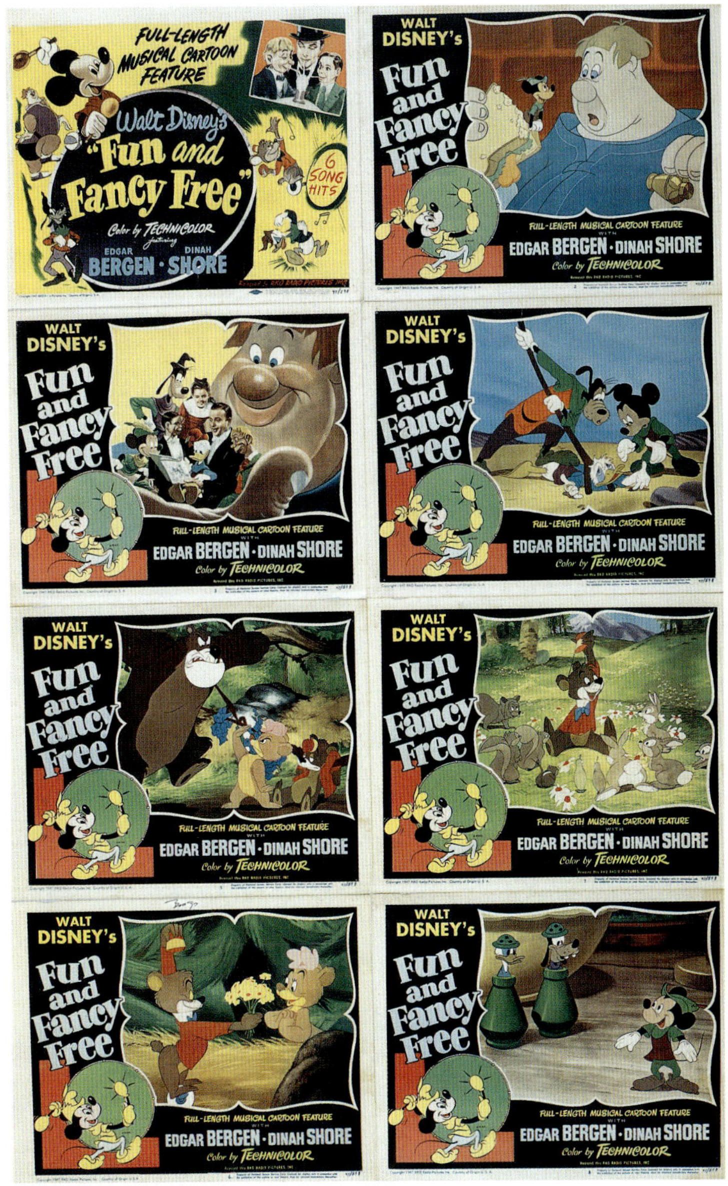

Fun and Fancy Free. 1947. Set of lobby cards. $1,000-1,500.

Towards the end of the decade the film community found itself under its worst onslaught to date and perhaps its darkest period. Hollywood had been under fire before, usually for reasons of morality (such as the "Fatty" Arbuckle affair of the 1920s), but nobody prepared themselves for the House of Representatives' Un-American Activities Committee. It charged leading members of the Hollywood community with being, at best, socialist sympathizers, and, at worst, members of a clandestine Hollywood Communist fifth column. Many well-known stars were unjustly accused including Orson Welles, Gregory Peck, Katharine Hepburn, Gene Kelly, Danny Kaye, Frank Sinatra, and Edward G. Robinson. Actors, writers, and directors, who were "blacklisted" as a result of dubious testimonies, were banned from the film studios, resulting in many working under assumed names. Between 1947 and 1952 over 200 movie industry figures and "blacklisted" stars had their careers ruined, with individuals to this day still remembering those within the film community who collaborated in this political charade.

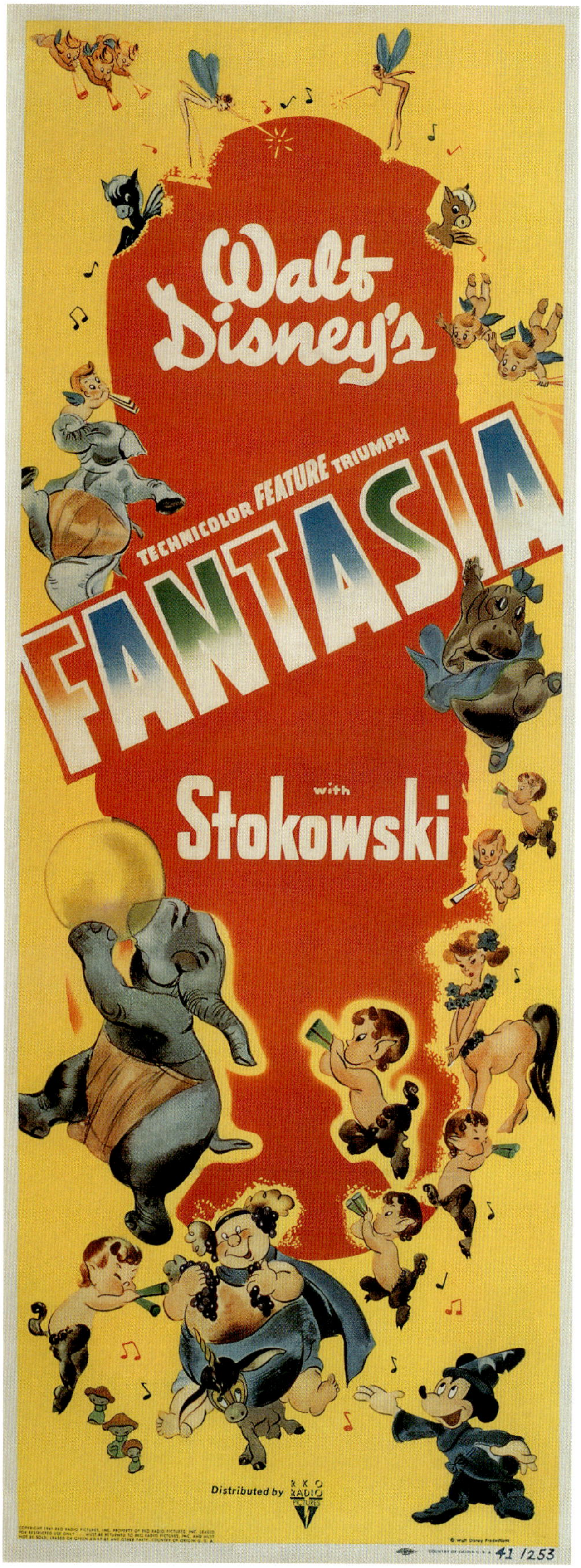

Fantasia. 1940. Insert. $2,000-3,000.

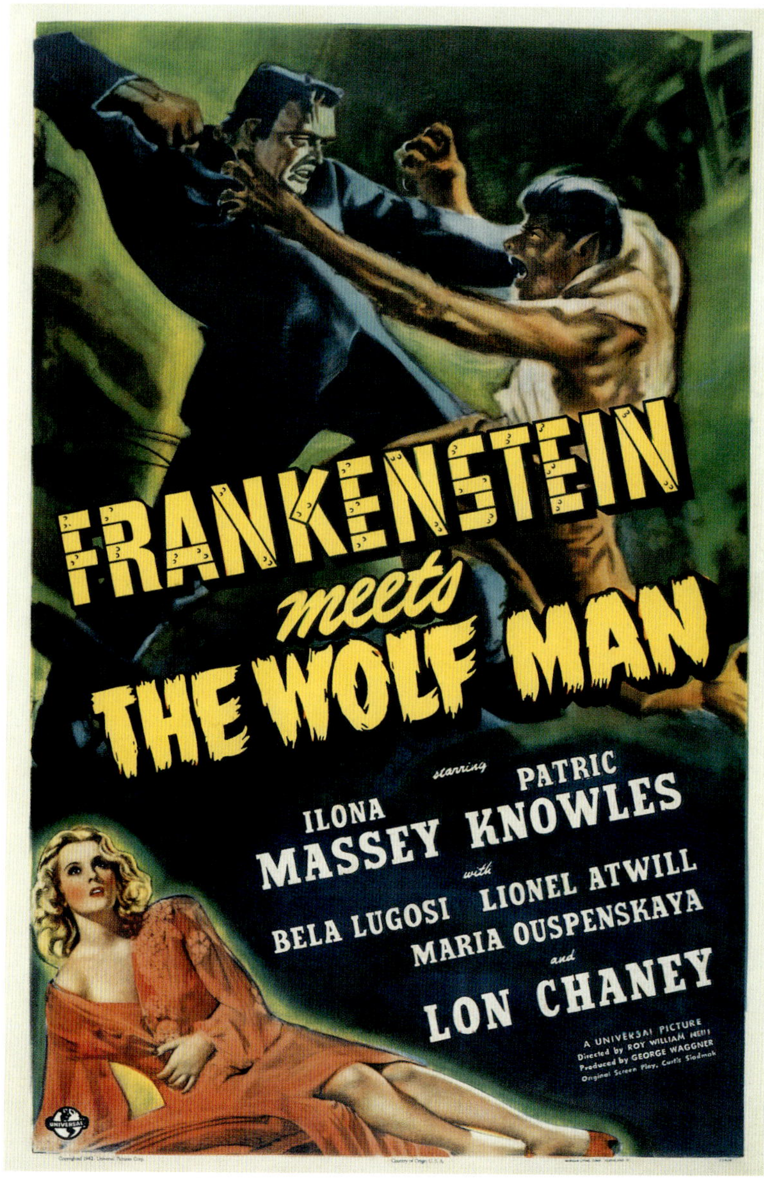

Frankenstein Meets the Wolf Man. 1943. One-sheet. $4,000-6,000.

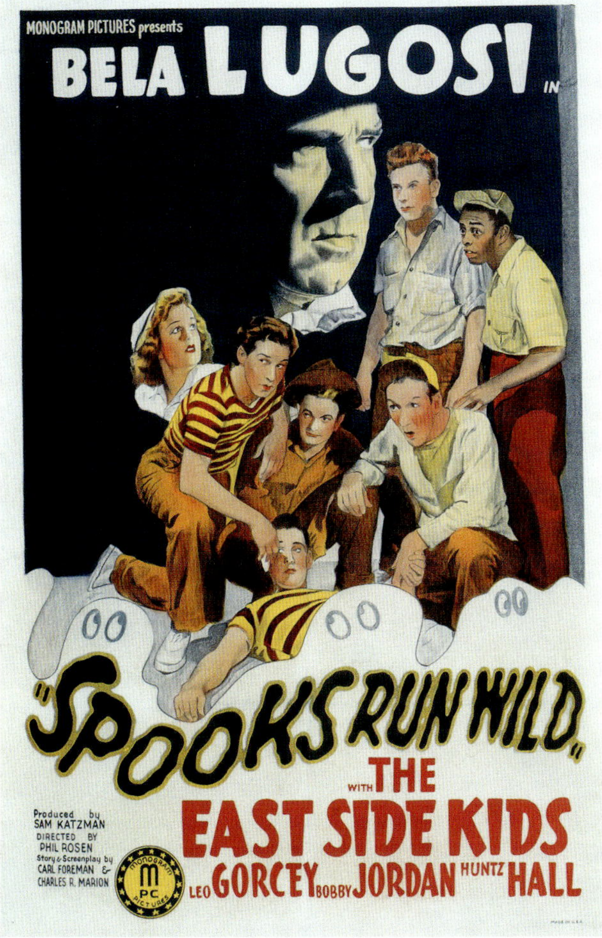

Spooks Run Wild. 1941. One-sheet. $1,000-1,500.

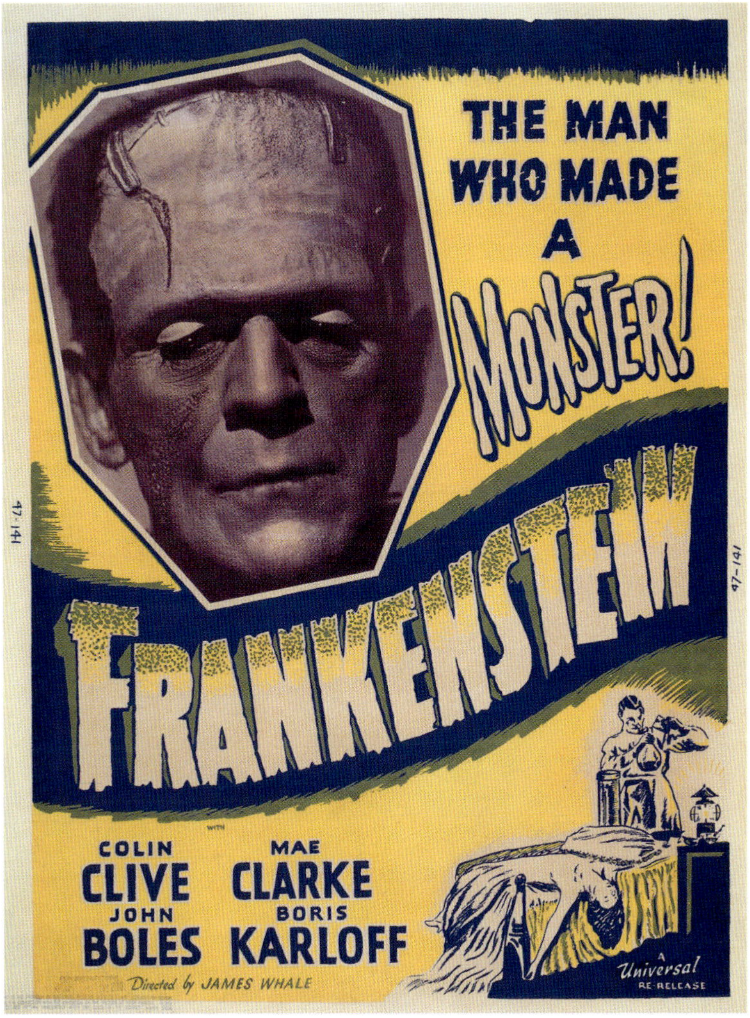

Frankenstein. 1947. Re-release. Special size 40" x 30". $4,000-6,000

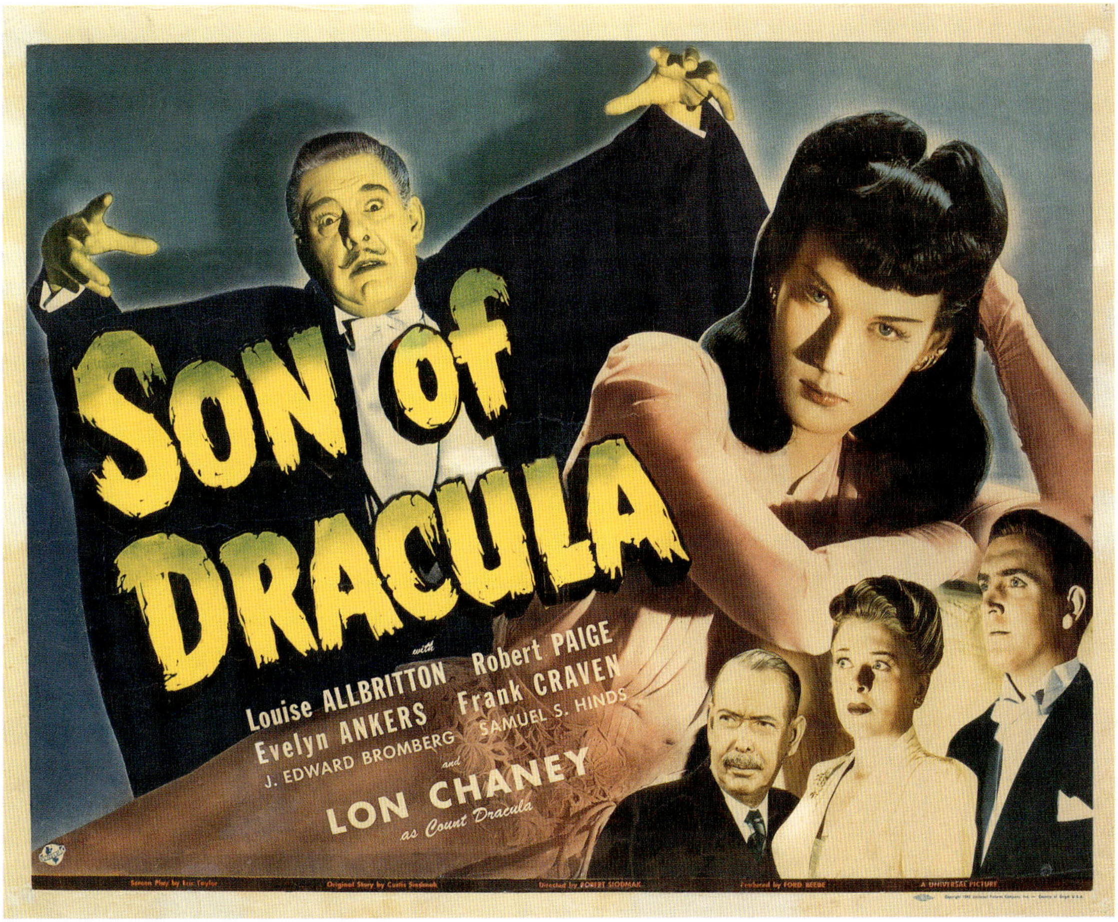

Son of Dracula. 1943. Half-sheet. $2,000-3,000.

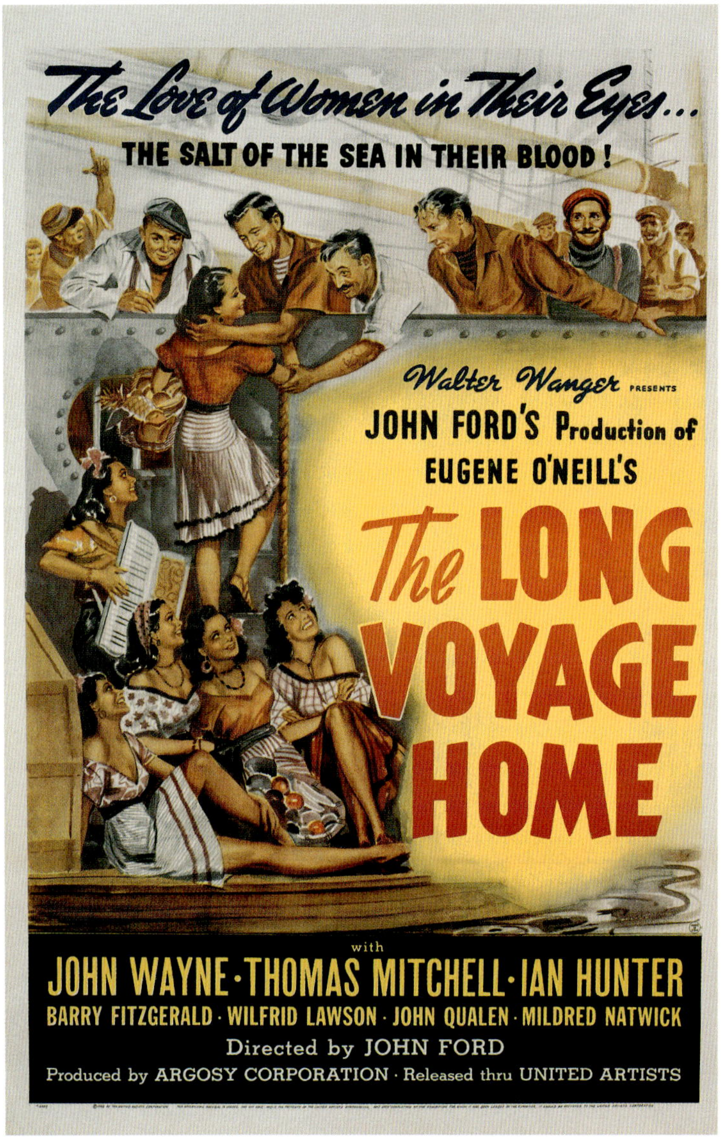

The Long Voyage Home. 1940. One-sheet. $400-600.

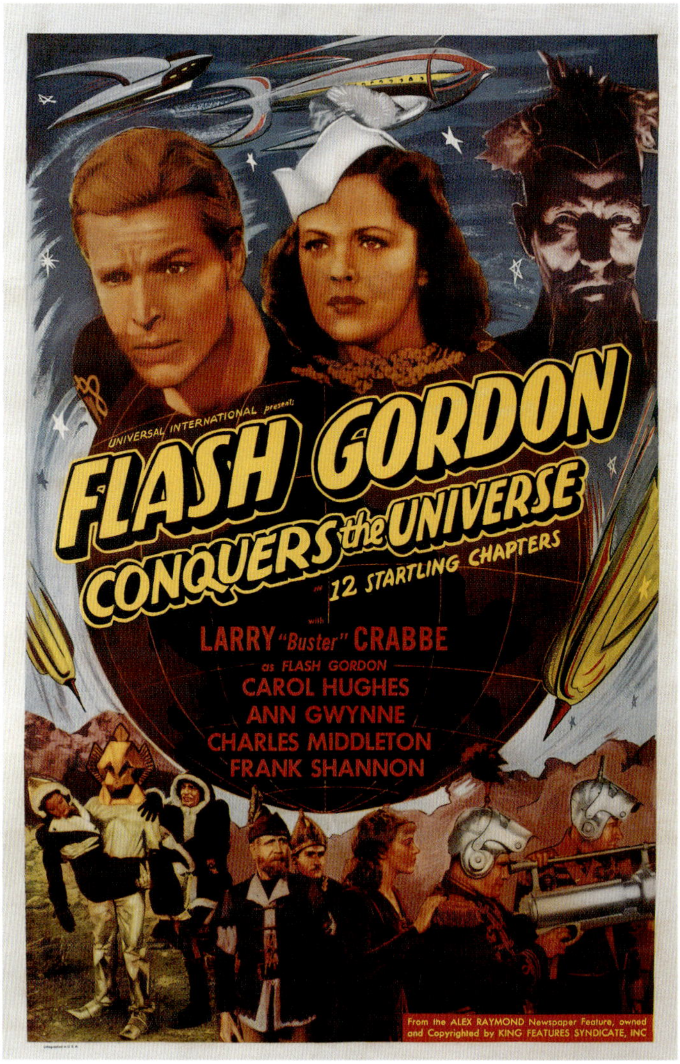

Flash Gordon Conquers the Universe. 1947. Re-release. One-sheet. $2,000-3,000.

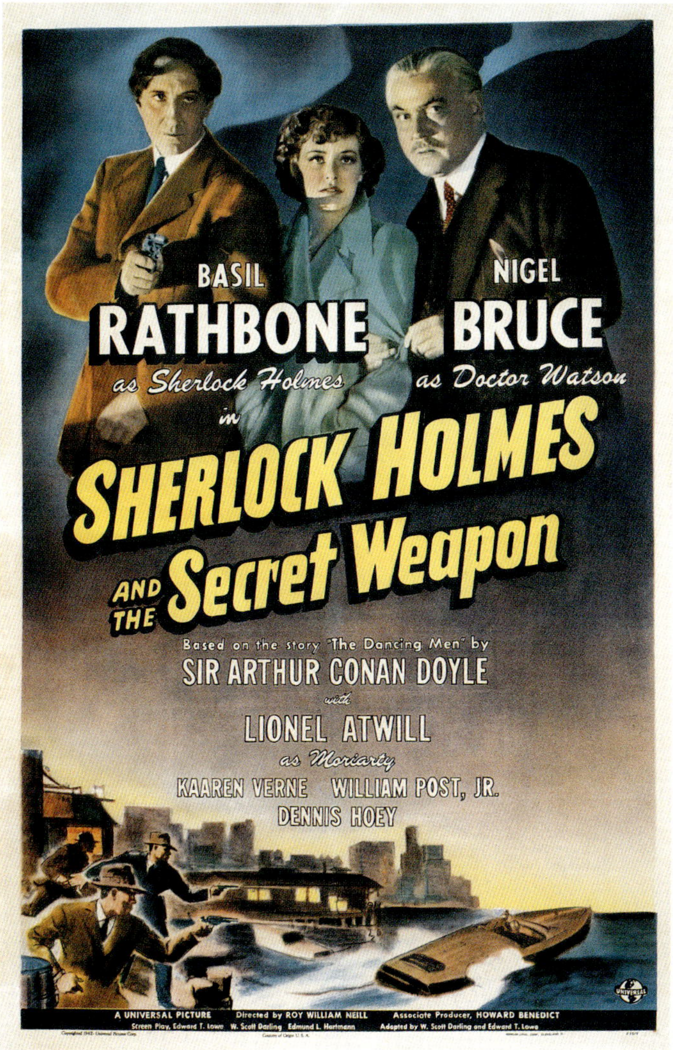

Sherlock Holmes and the Secret Weapon. 1942.
One-sheet. $1,200-1,800.

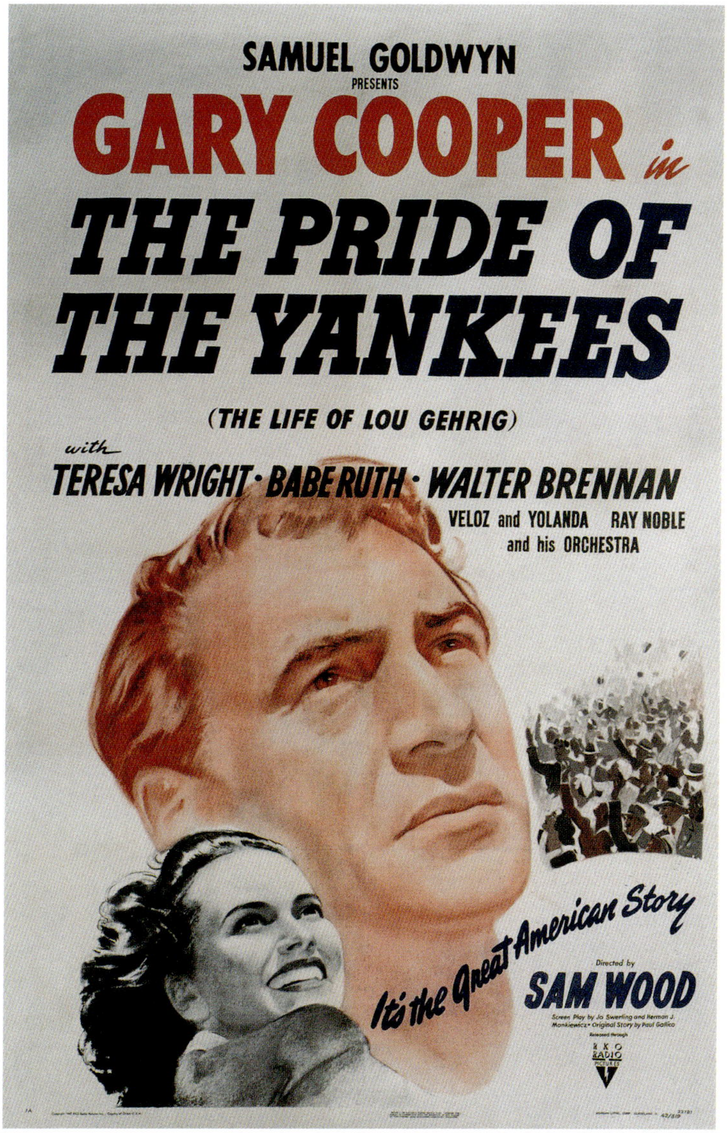

The Pride Of The Yankees. 1942. One-sheet. $2,000-3,000.

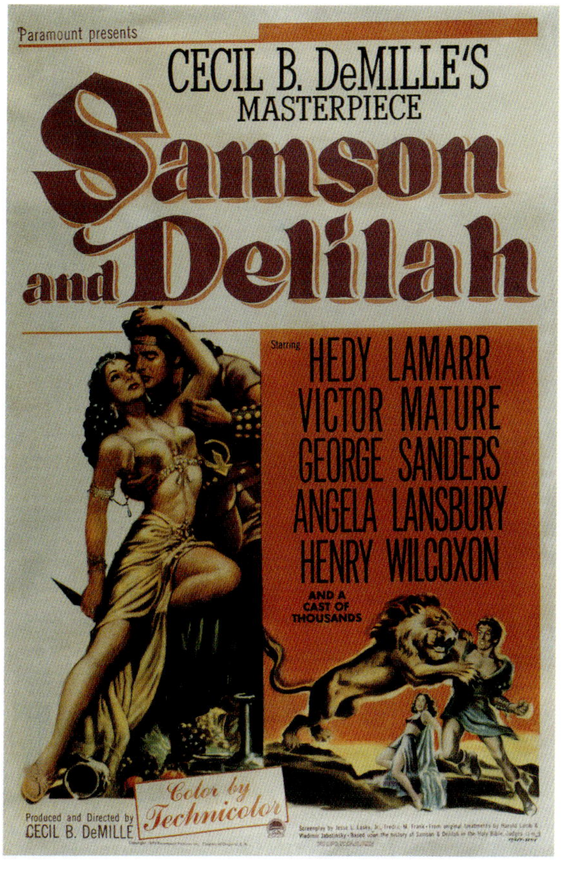

Samson and Delilah. 1949.
One-sheet. $700-900.

Chapter Four

Hollywood vs. Television: The Fifties

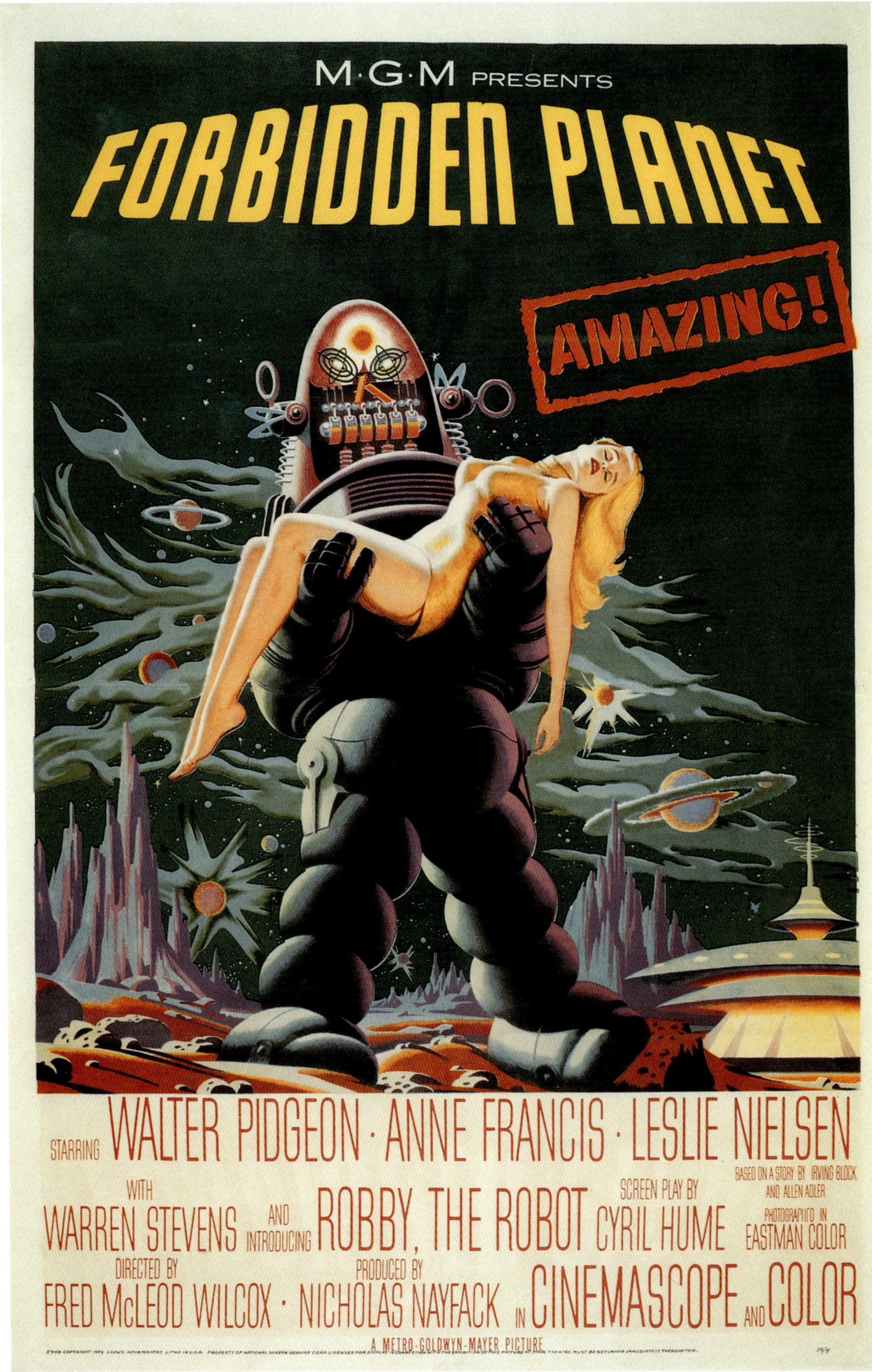

Forbidden Planet. 1956. One-sheet. $7,000-10,000.

On the face of it much was good in postwar American society. In time-honored fashion Hollywood did its best to reflect this. Beneath the façade, however, things were not good. The once omnipotent film industry started reeling as events beyond their control dictated a period of upheaval and decline for most of the major studios. Many factors contributed towards this, particularly the passing of many of the studio moguls who had kept the movie industry together, the communist witch-hunt, and the dawn of television with the consequent decline in theater audiences.

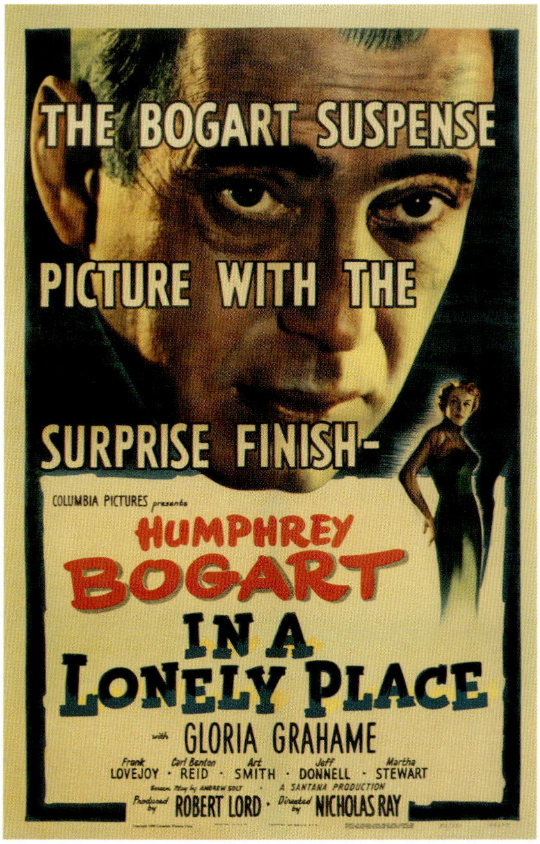

In a Lonely Place. 1950. One-sheet. $1,500-2,000.

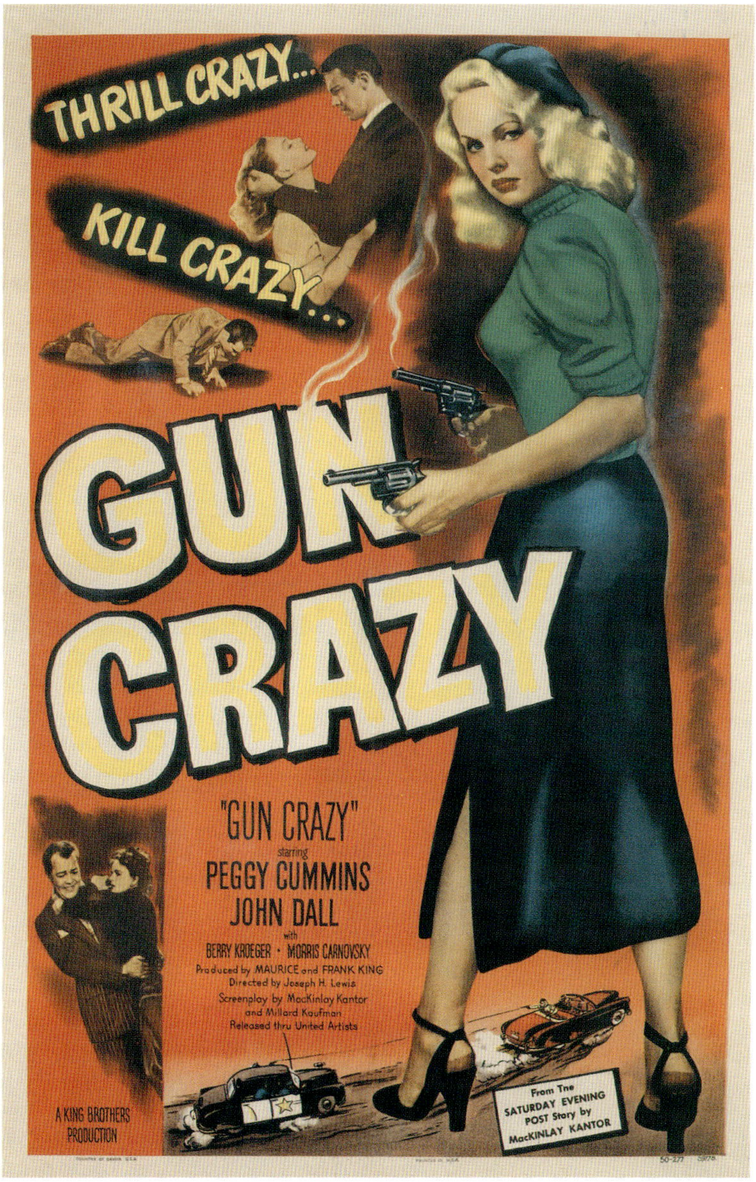

Gun Crazy. 1950. One-sheet. $3,000-4,000.

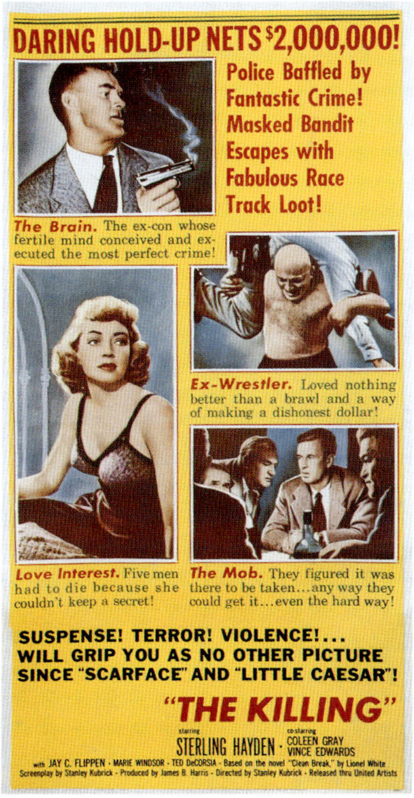

The Killing. 1956. Three-sheet. $1,200-1,800.

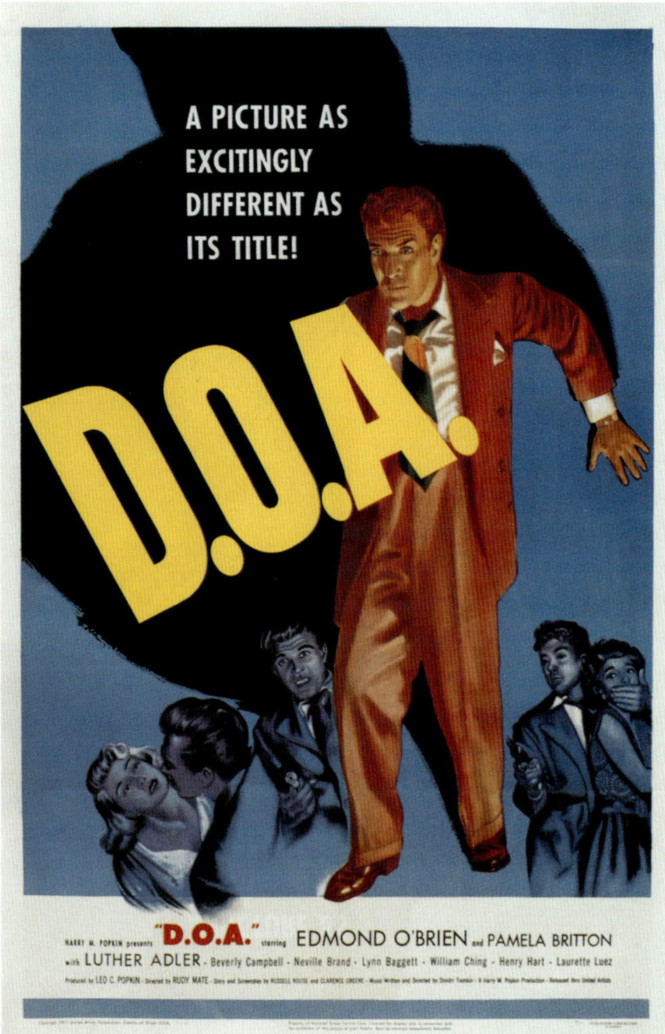

D.O.A. 1950. One-sheet. $1,200-1,800.

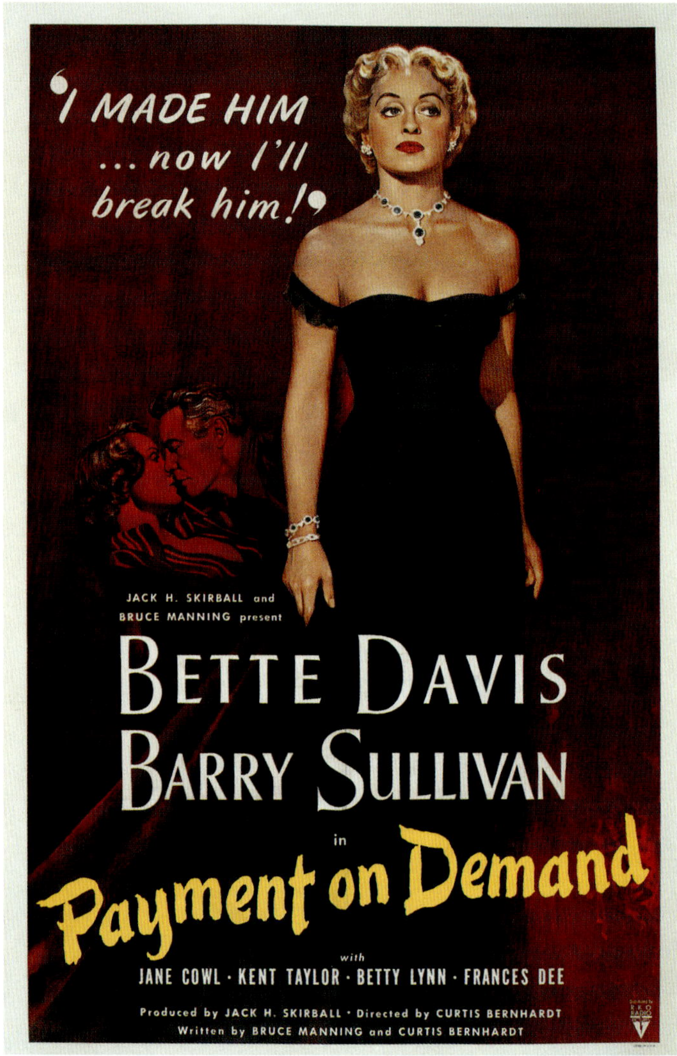

Payment On Demand. 1951. One-sheet. $1,500-2,000.

Antimonopoly federal laws were brought into force against the major studios in 1948, breaking their total control of production, distribution, and exhibition. No longer allowed to own cinema theatre chains, studios were forced to sell their movies separately to individual theaters based on the quality of the product. This had serious implications, as they could no longer be assured of box-office success through marketplace strength.

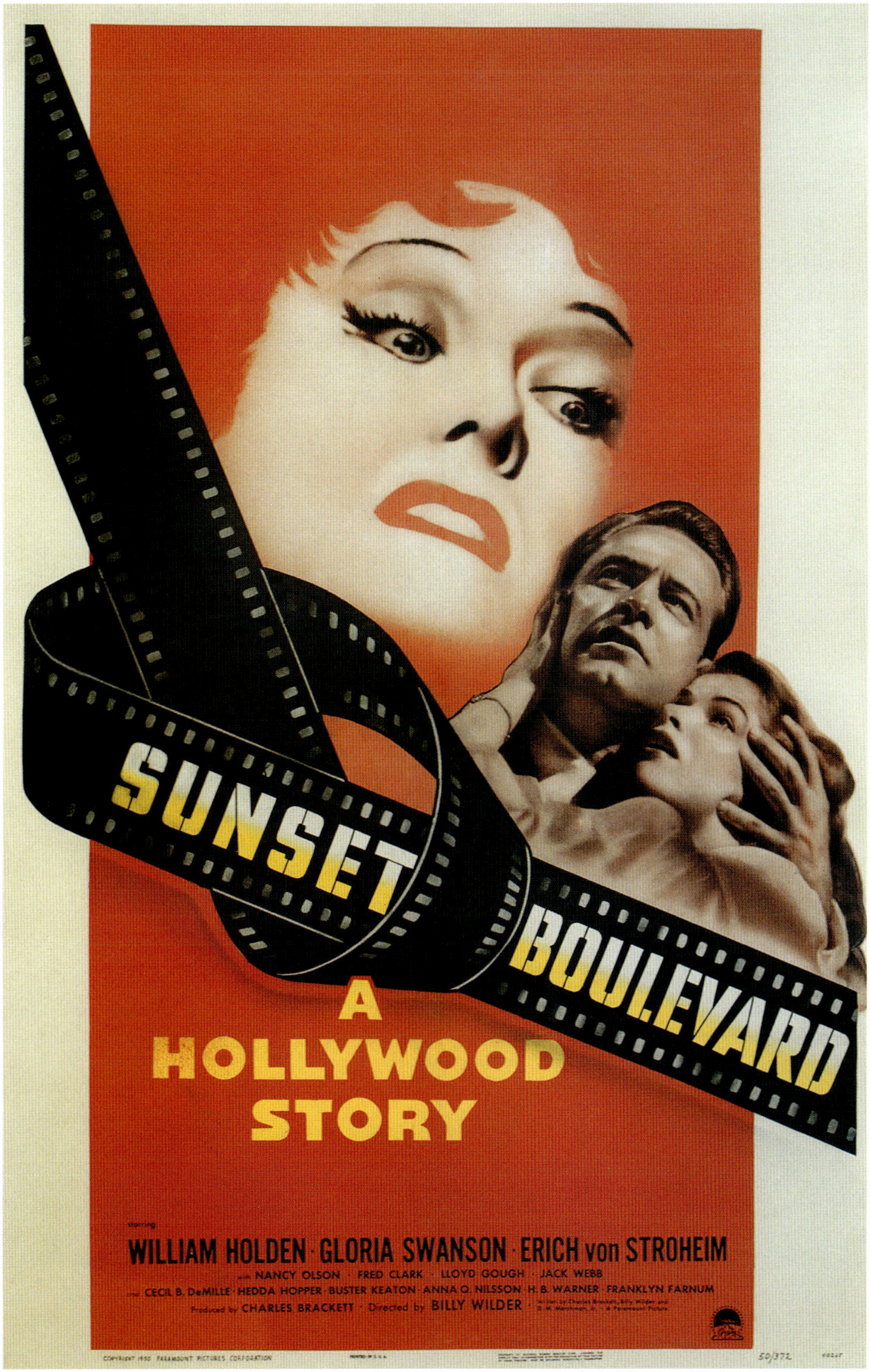

Sunset Boulevard. 1950. One-sheet, style A. $5,000-8,000.

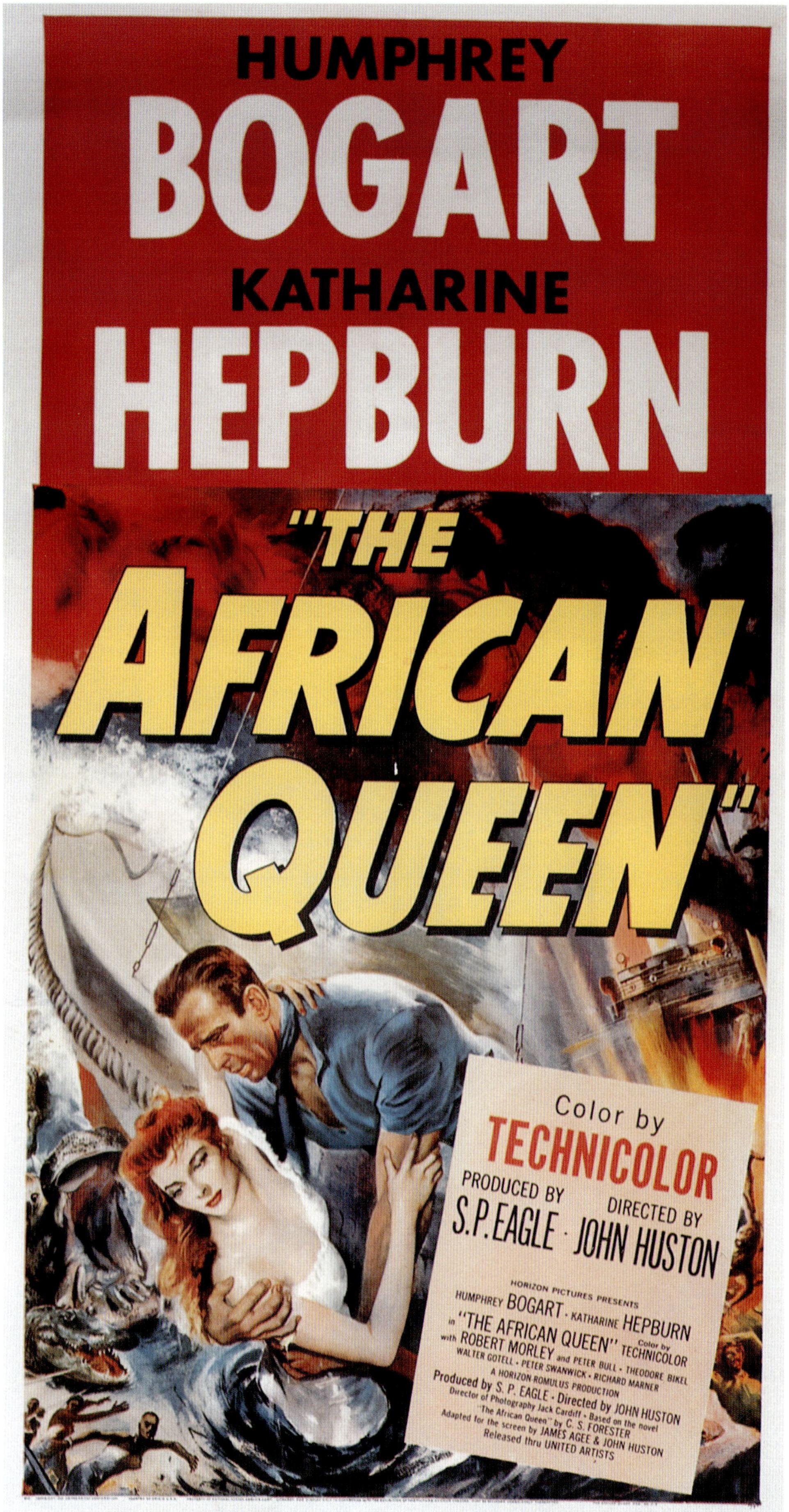

The African Queen. 1952. Three-sheet. $3,000-4,000.

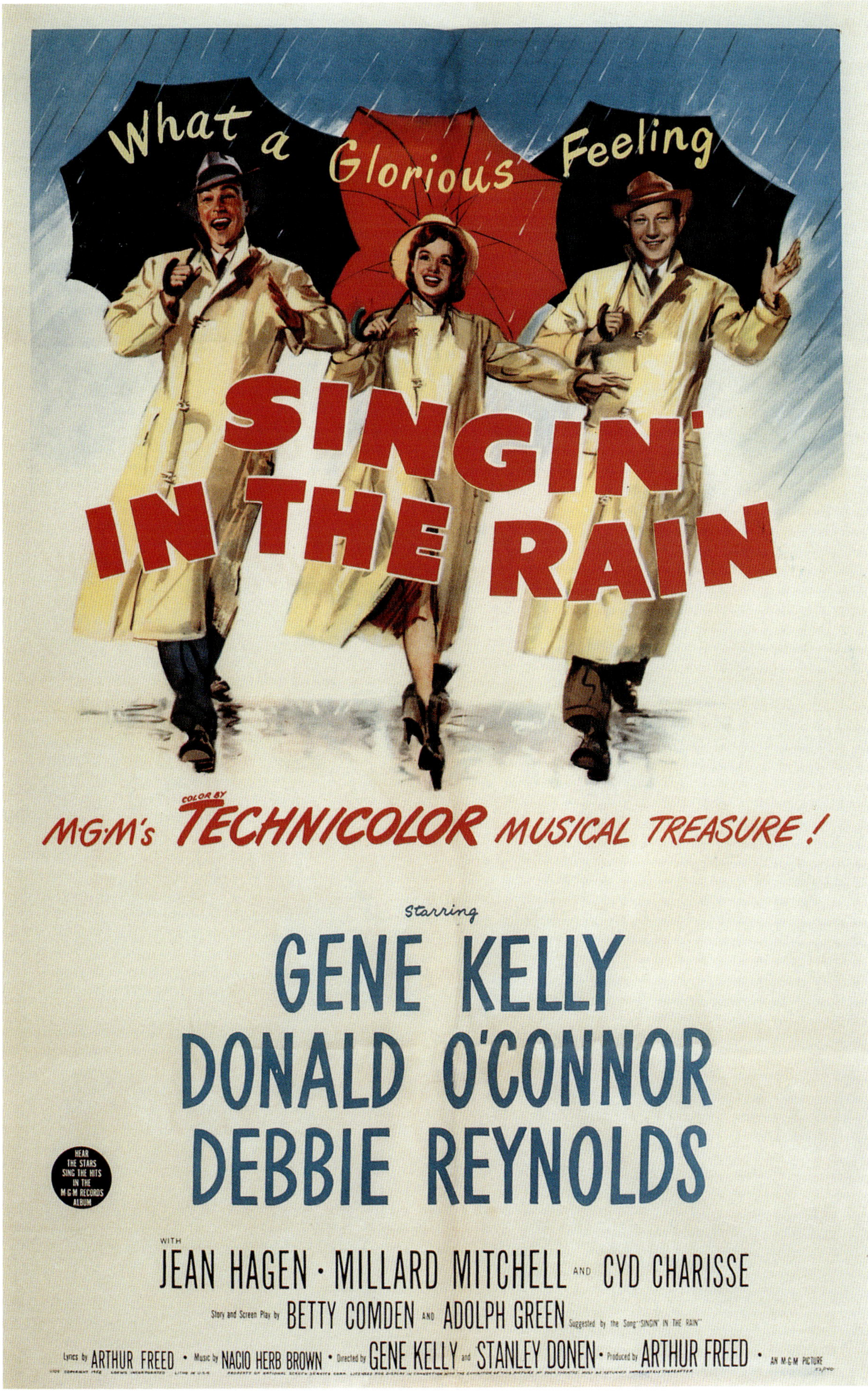

Singin' in the Rain. 1952. One-sheet. $3,500-4,500.

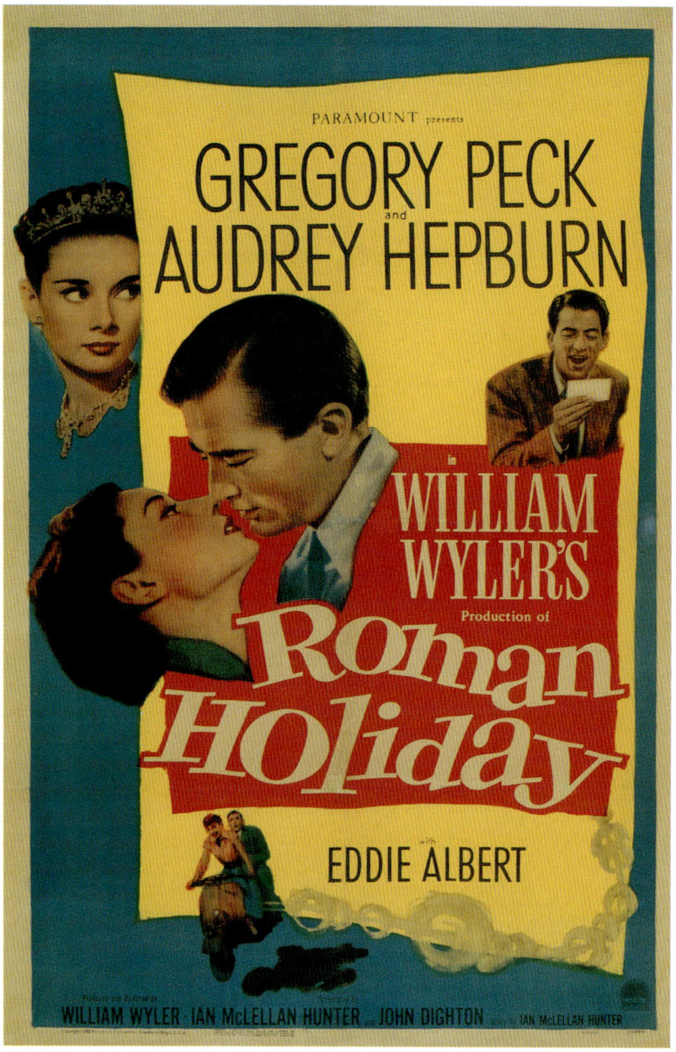

Roman Holiday. 1953. One-sheet. $1,500-2,000.

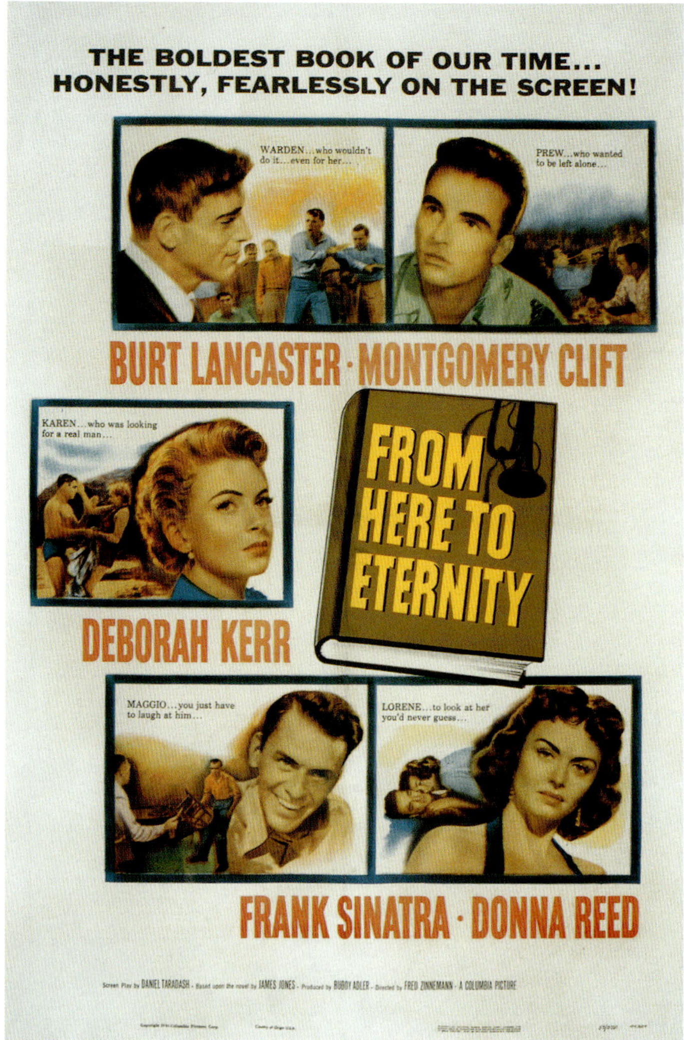

From Here to Eternity. 1953. One-sheet. $1,200-1,800.

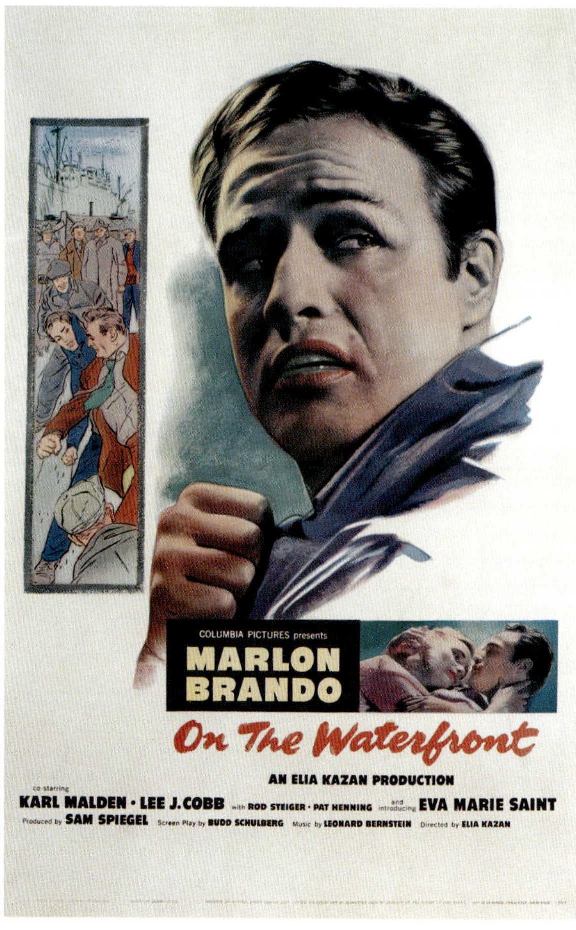

On the Waterfront. 1954. One-sheet. $1,200-1,800.

Notable as well was the gradual decline of the old studio contract star system with many major actors and, later, directors starting to operate independently for the first time. No longer feeling that the studios had total control, some stars took the free-lance route, capitalizing on the benefits of brokering their own deals via agents for a percentage of the overall profits of a movie. This shift of emphasis in power was to lay the foundations for the industry that we know today, with stars commanding massive salaries from single movie deals, making it a star-led industry rather than the studio dominated enterprise of old.

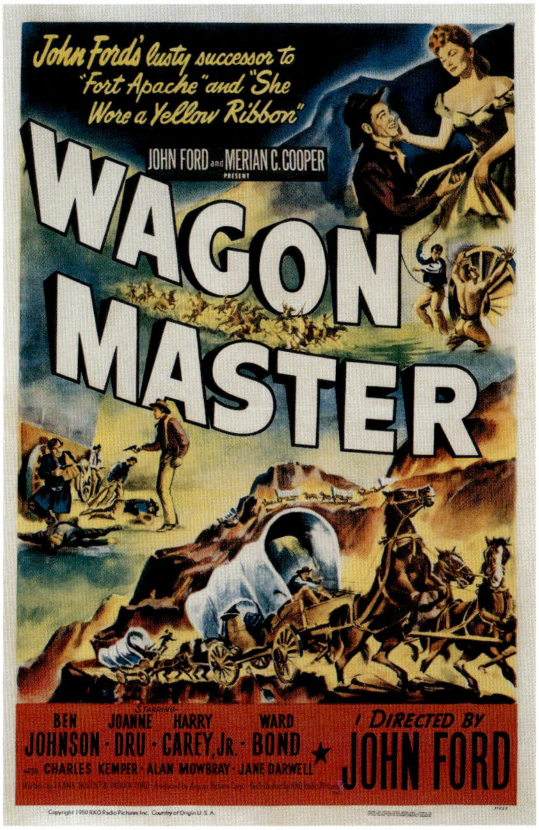

Wagon Master. 1950. One-sheet. $500-800.

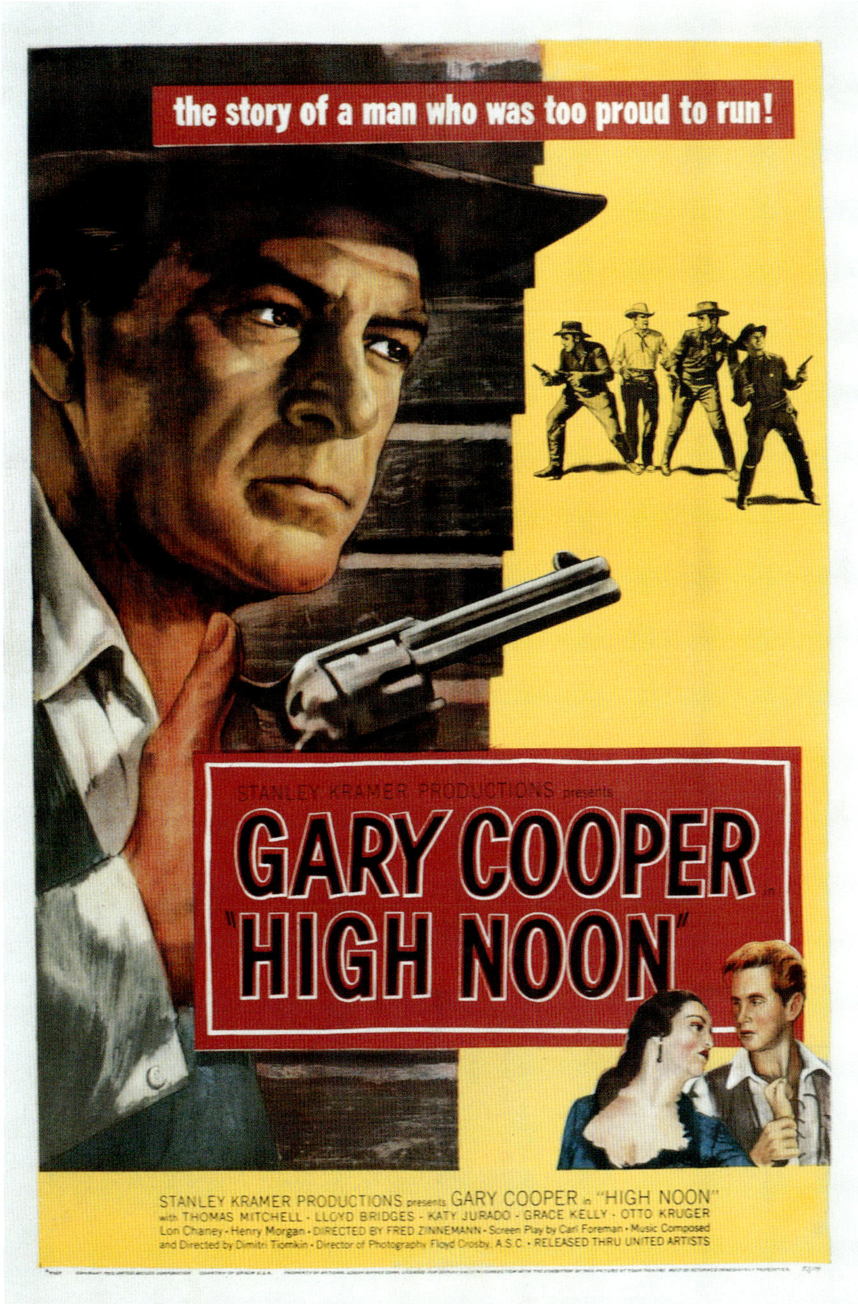

High Noon. 1952. One-sheet. $3,000-4,000.

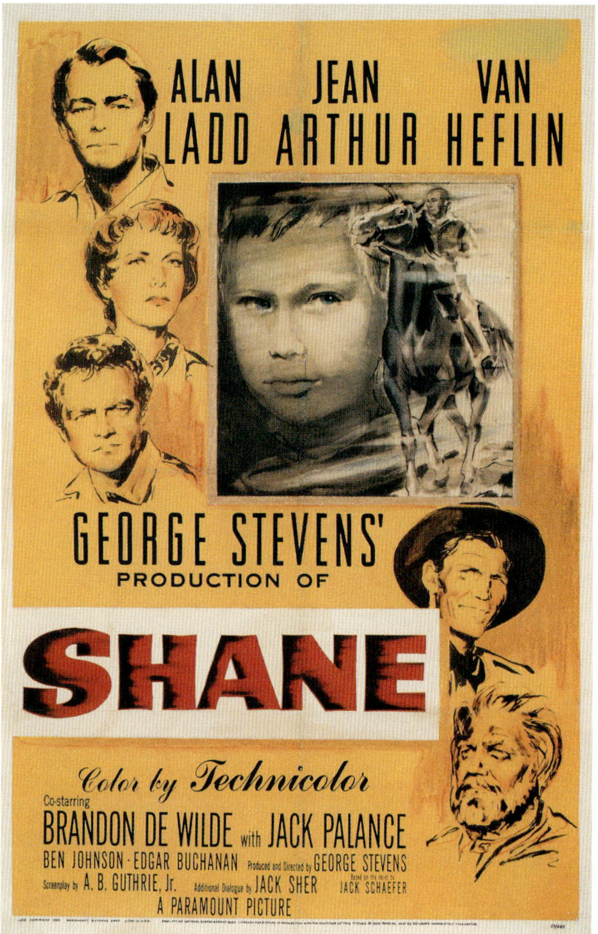

Shane. 1953. One-sheet. $1,500-2,000.

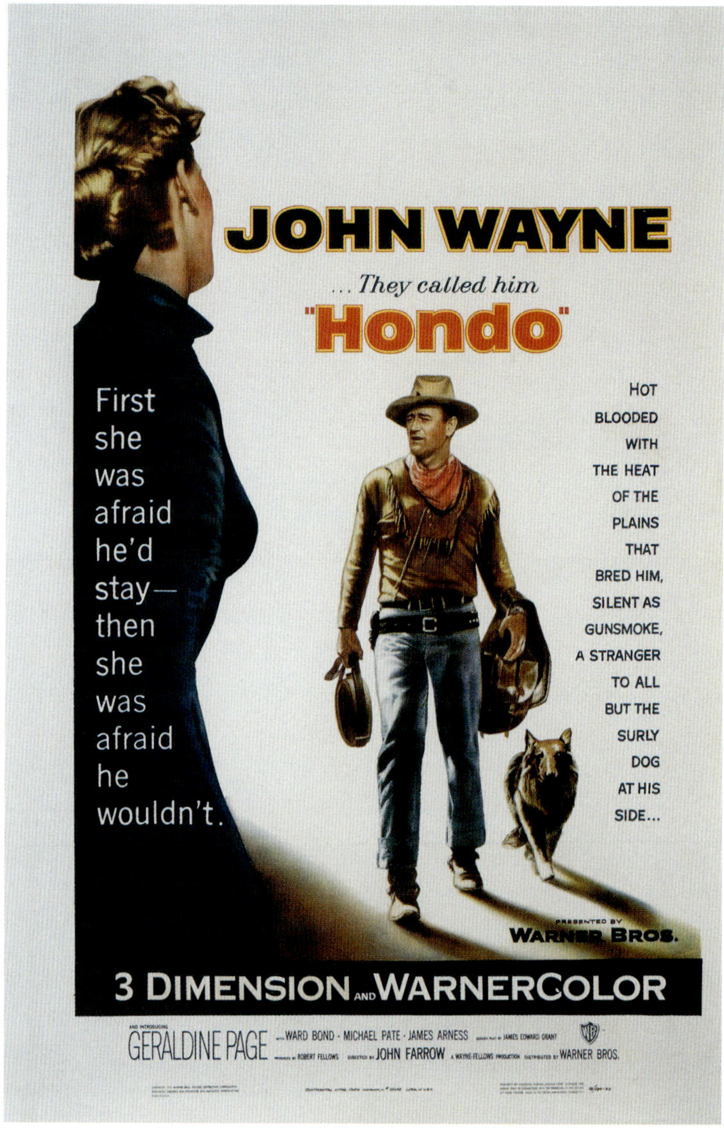

Hondo. 1953. One-sheet, 3D-type. $1,500-2,000.

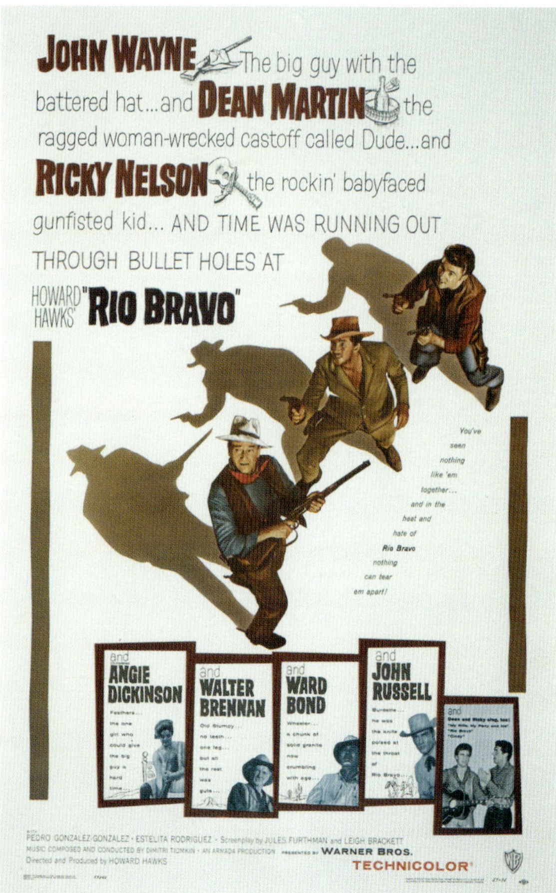

Rio Bravo. 1959. One-sheet. $1,500-2,000.

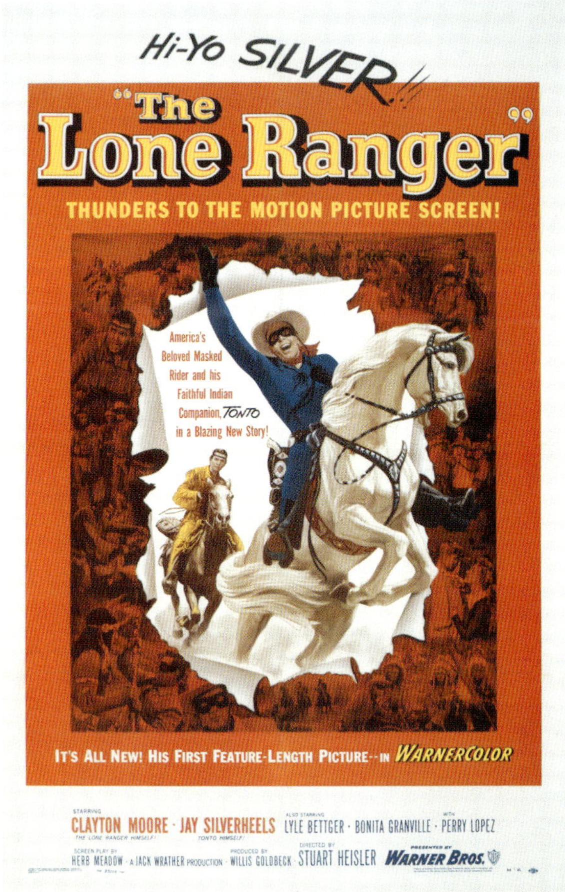

The Lone Ranger. 1956. One-sheet. $700-1,000.

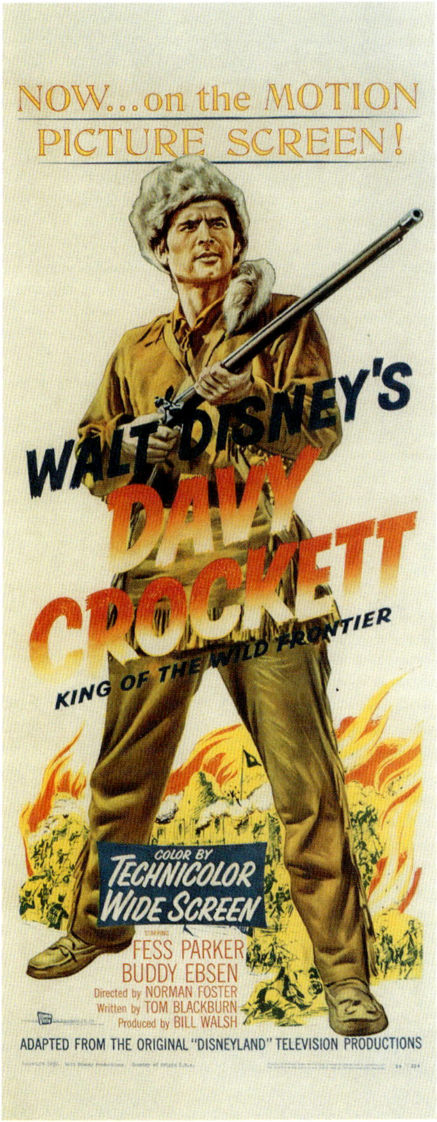

Davy Crockett. 1955. Insert. $700-900

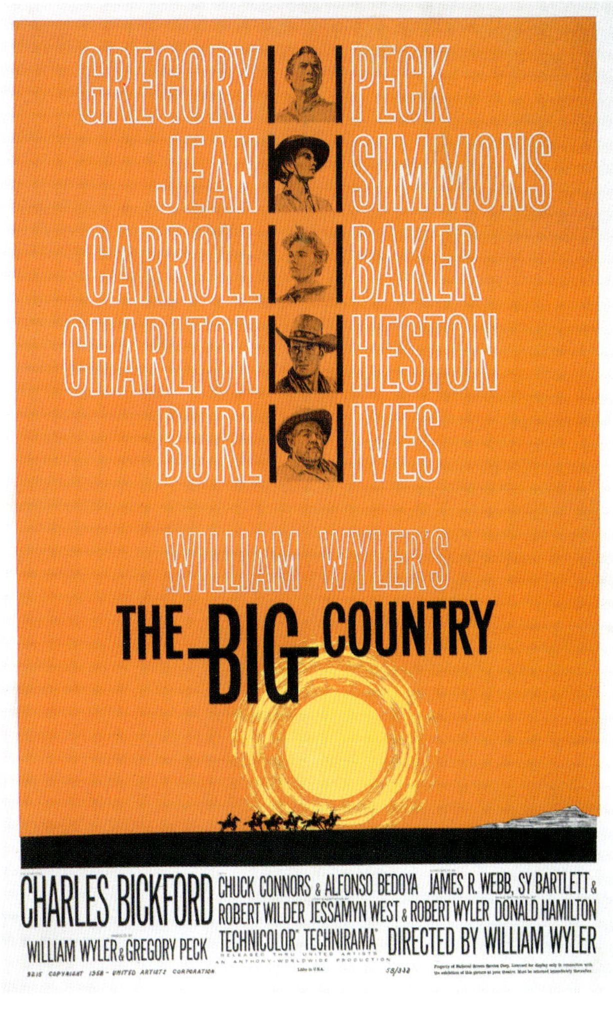

The Big Country. 1958. One-sheet. $700-900.

Other restrictions from the past were also challenged by those who had grown tired of unnecessary hindrances to their film making. Director Otto Preminger released the sex comedy *The Moon is Blue* (1953) without the necessary seal of approval from the Motion Picture Production Code that had been demanded since 1934. This code forced filmmakers to edit their movies to meet the moral standards deemed suitable for release. Preminger and others openly violated this and released films with provocative subject matter such as drugs (*The Man With The Golden Arm*, 1955) and rape (*Anatomy of a Murder*, 1959). Under so much pressure amendments were eventually made to the code allowing movies to contain story lines that were appropriate to, and reflected the concerns of, a changed and more modern society than the one that had originally created the puritanical code. Hollywood could now move away from satisfying the parochial and deal with more socially challenging and taboo subjects. To this end they unashamedly made the effort to embrace the angst of postwar teenagers and gain fresh audiences with such films as *East Of Eden* (1955) and *Rebel Without A Cause* (1955) both starring a youthful James Dean.

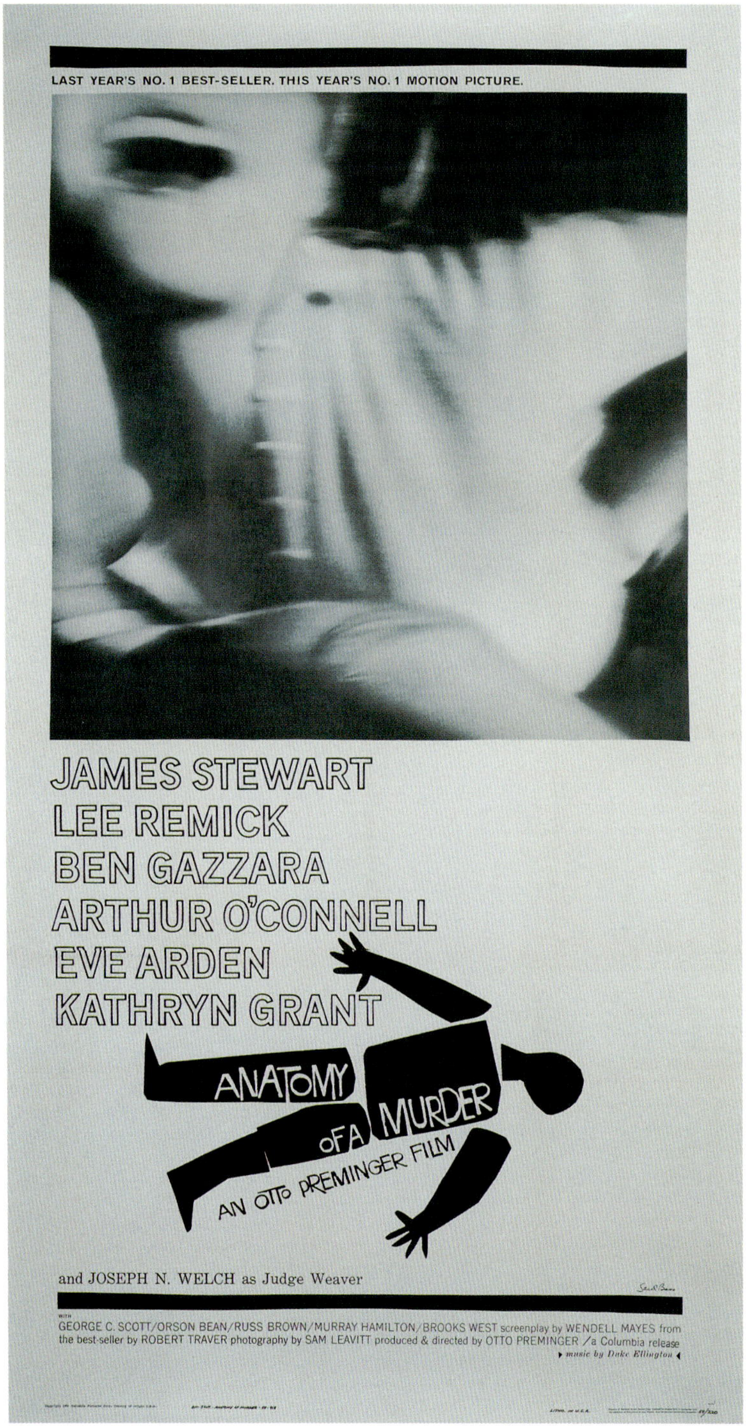

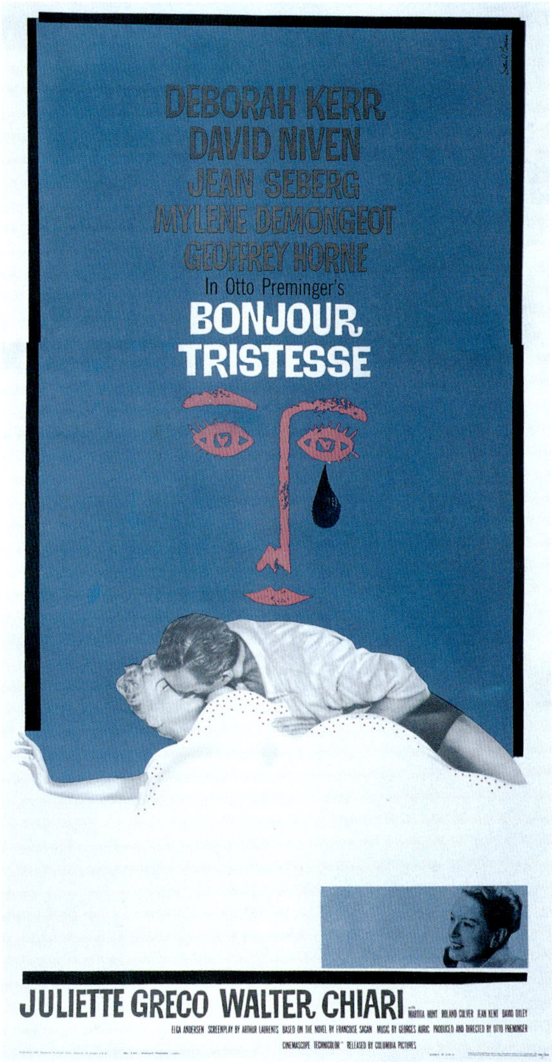

Bonjour Tristesse. 1958. Three-sheet, art by Saul Bass. $1,200-1,800.

Anatomy of a Murder. 1959. Three-sheet, style B, art by Saul Bass. $1,200-1,800.

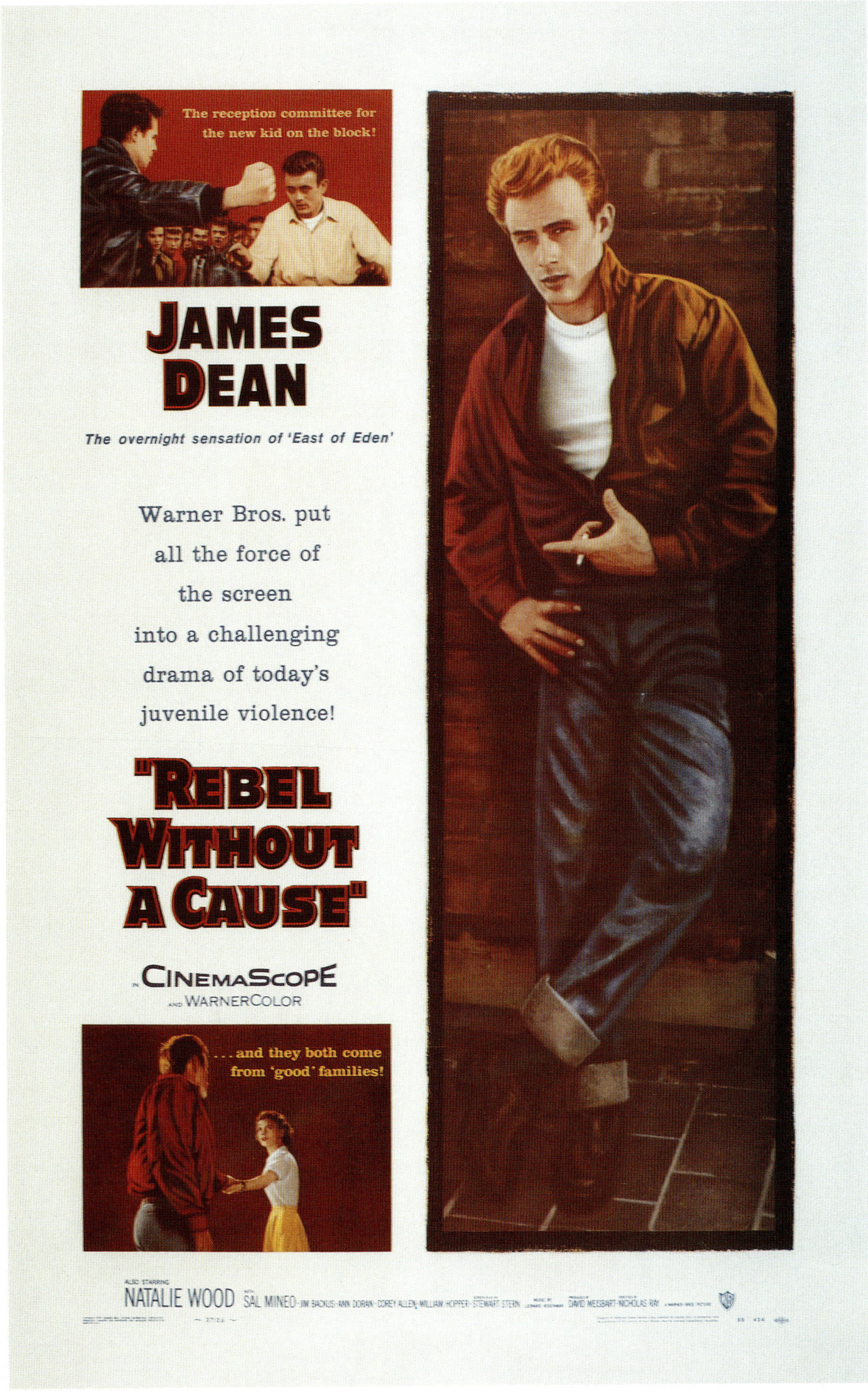

Rebel Without a Cause. 1955. One-sheet. $3,000-5,000

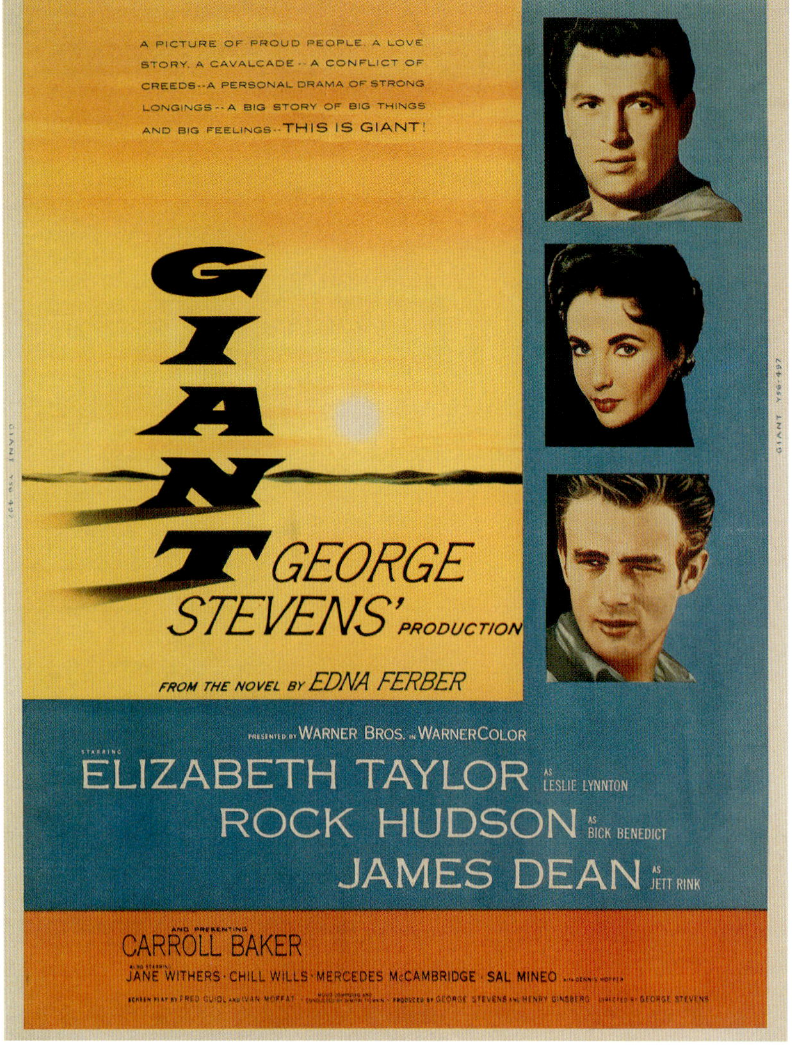

Giant. 1956. One-sheet. $1,500-2,500

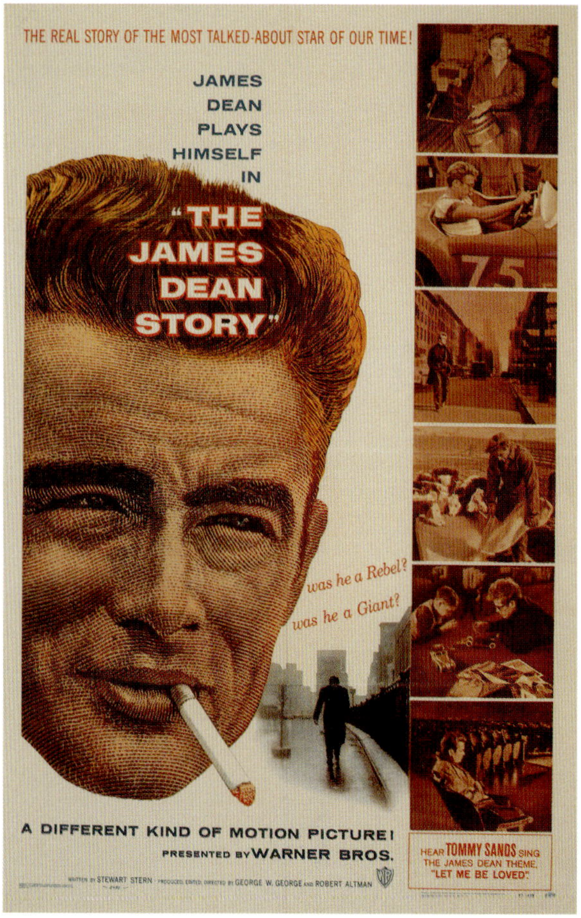

The James Dean Story. 1957. One-sheet. $1,000-1,500

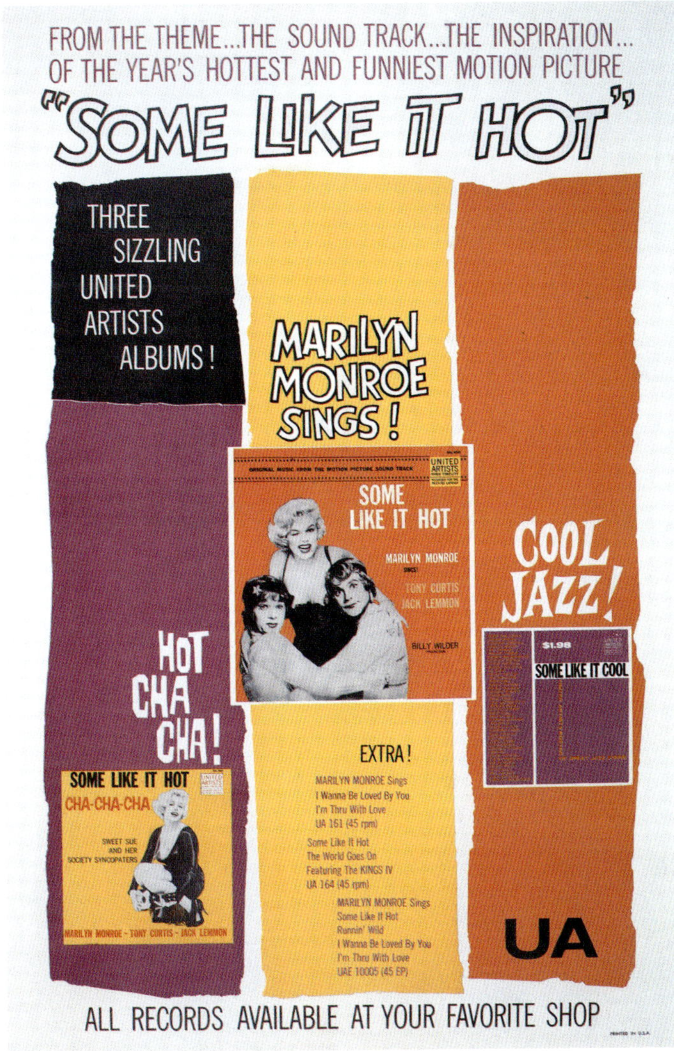

Some Like It Hot. 1959. Special one-sheet. $1,500-2,500

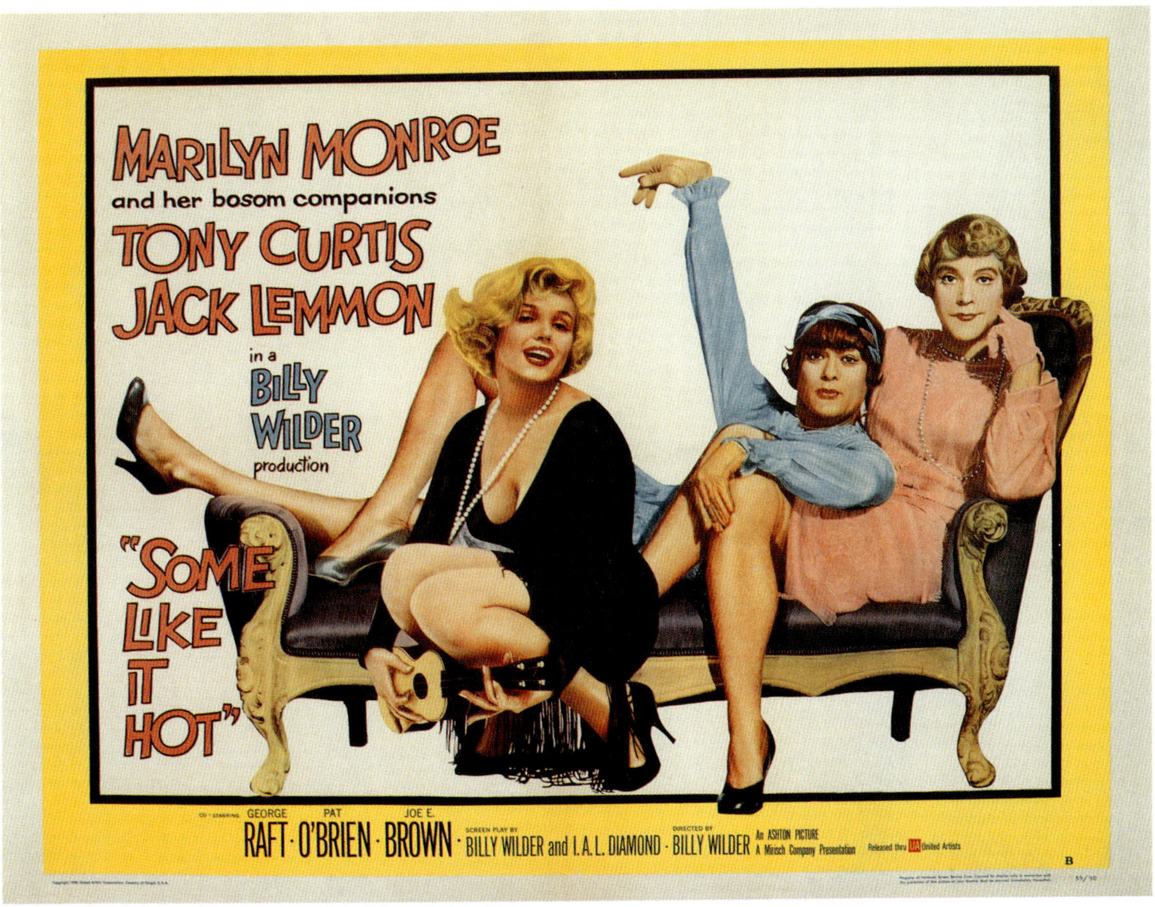

Some Like It Hot. 1959. Half-sheet, style B. $1,200-1,800

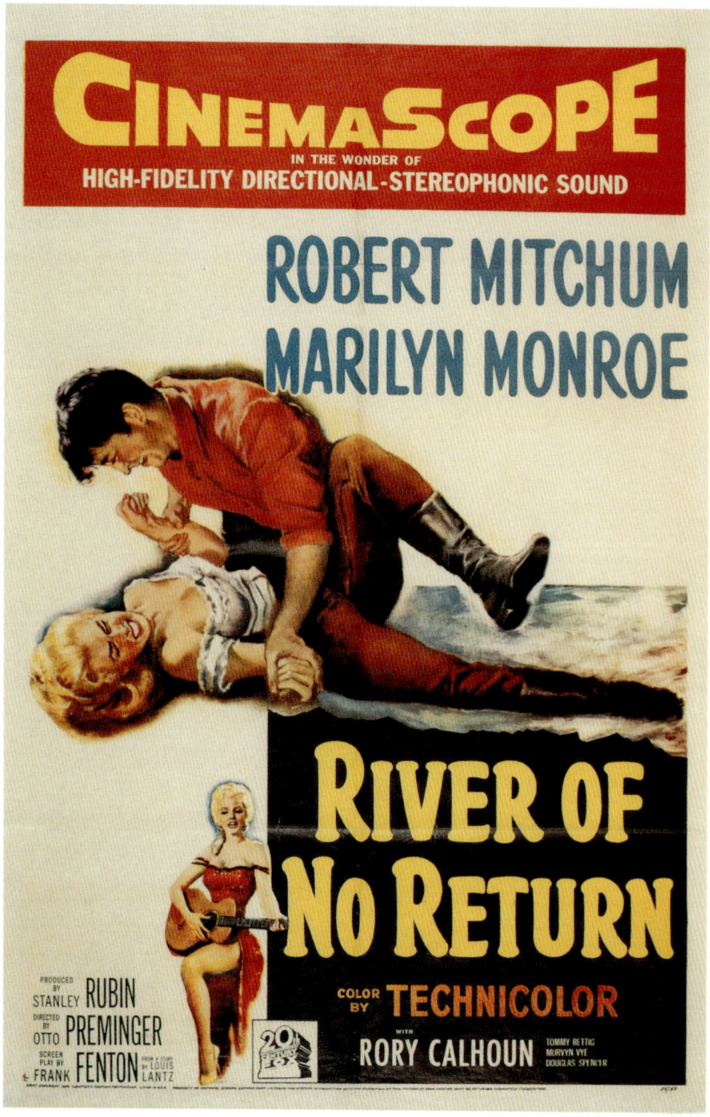

River Of No Return. 1954.
One-sheet. $800-1,200

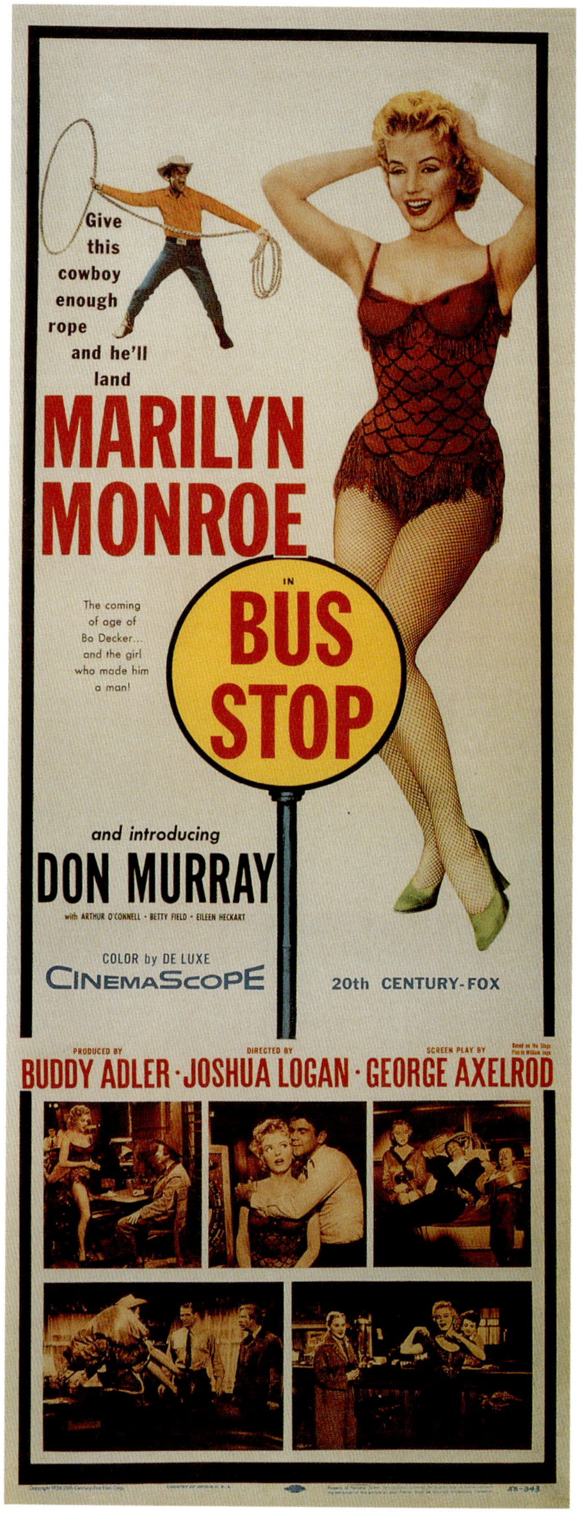

Bus Stop. 1956. Insert. $800-1,200

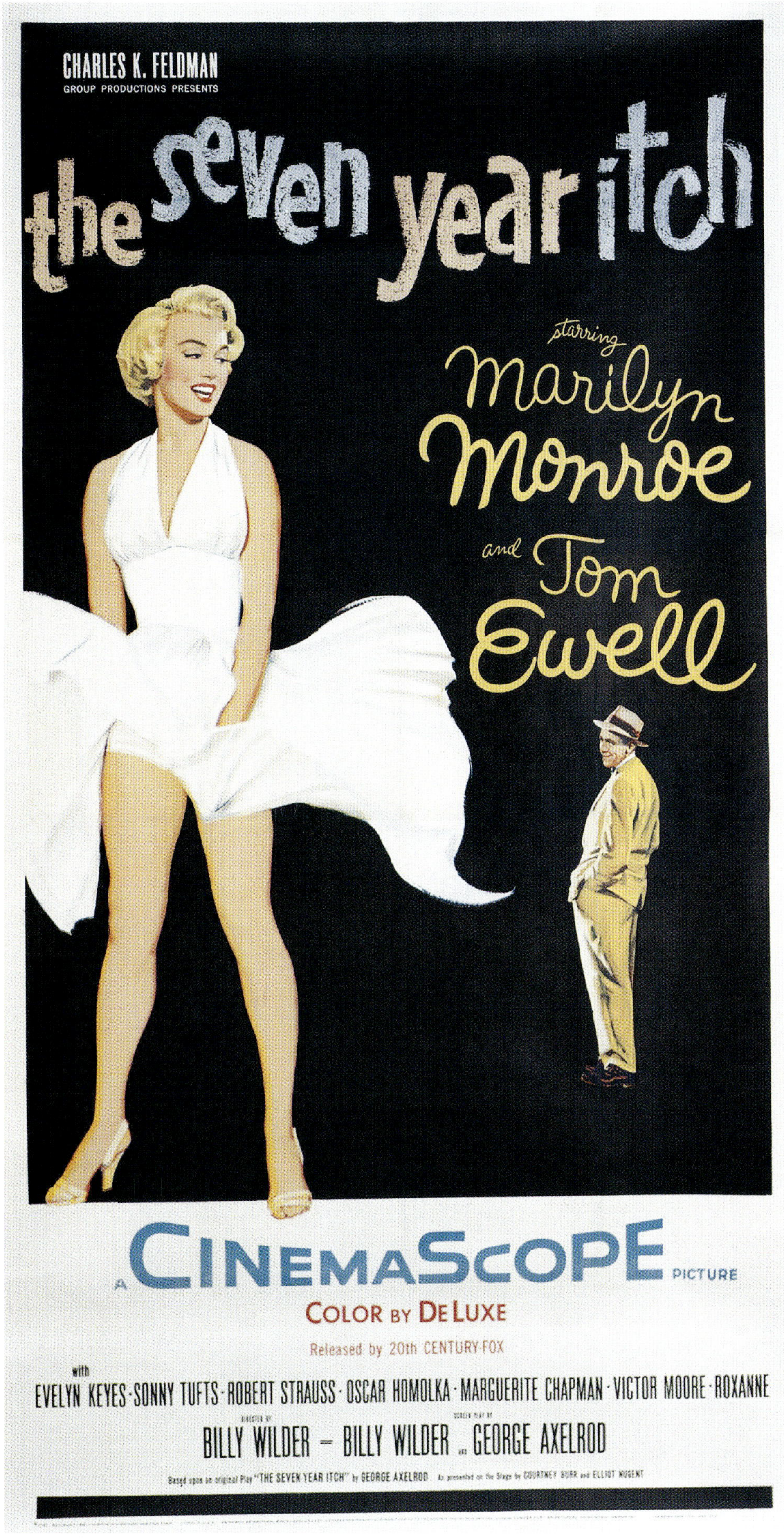

The Seven Year Itch. 1955. Three-sheet. $4,000-6,000

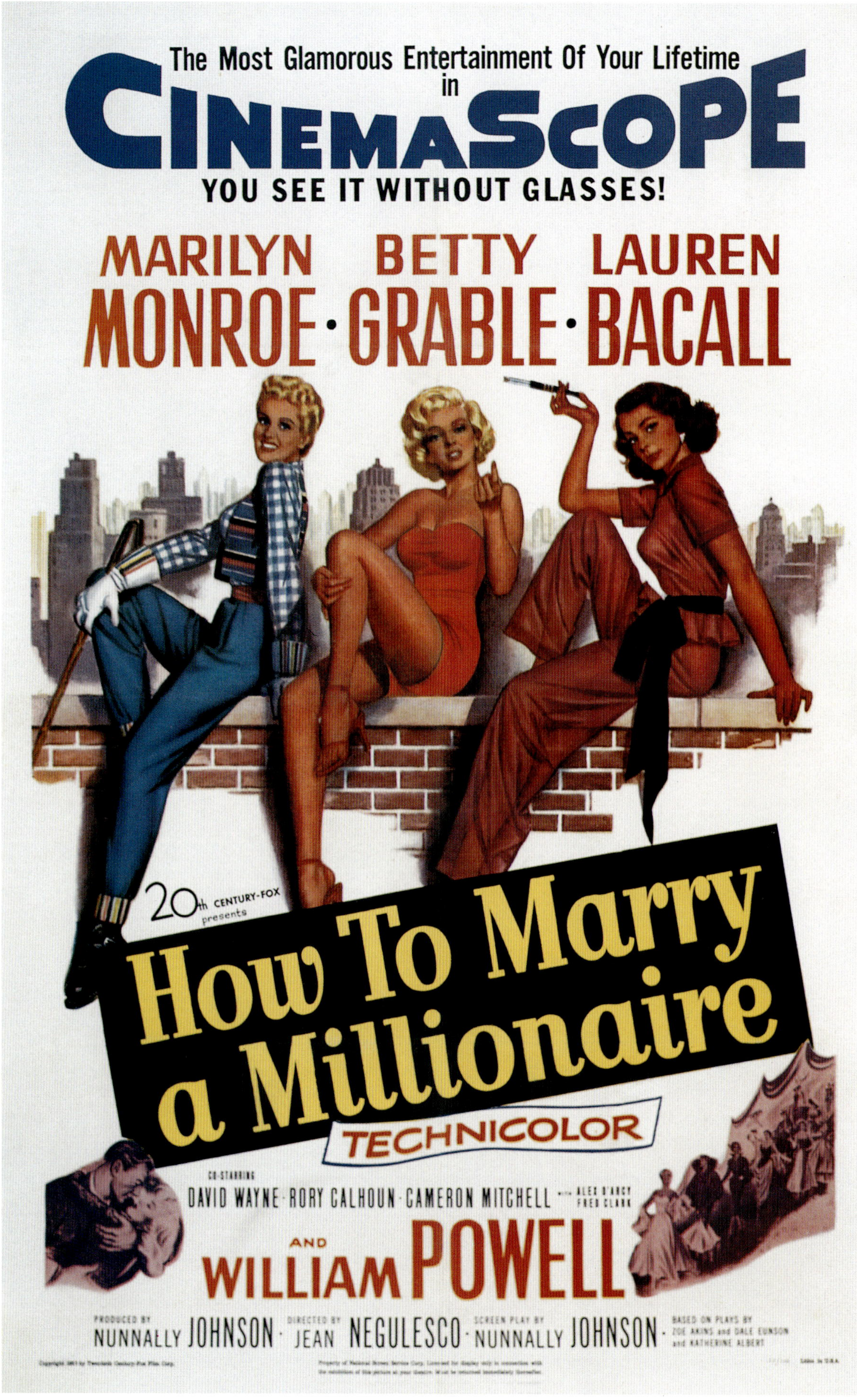

How To Marry a Millionaire. 1953. One-sheet. $1,500-2,500

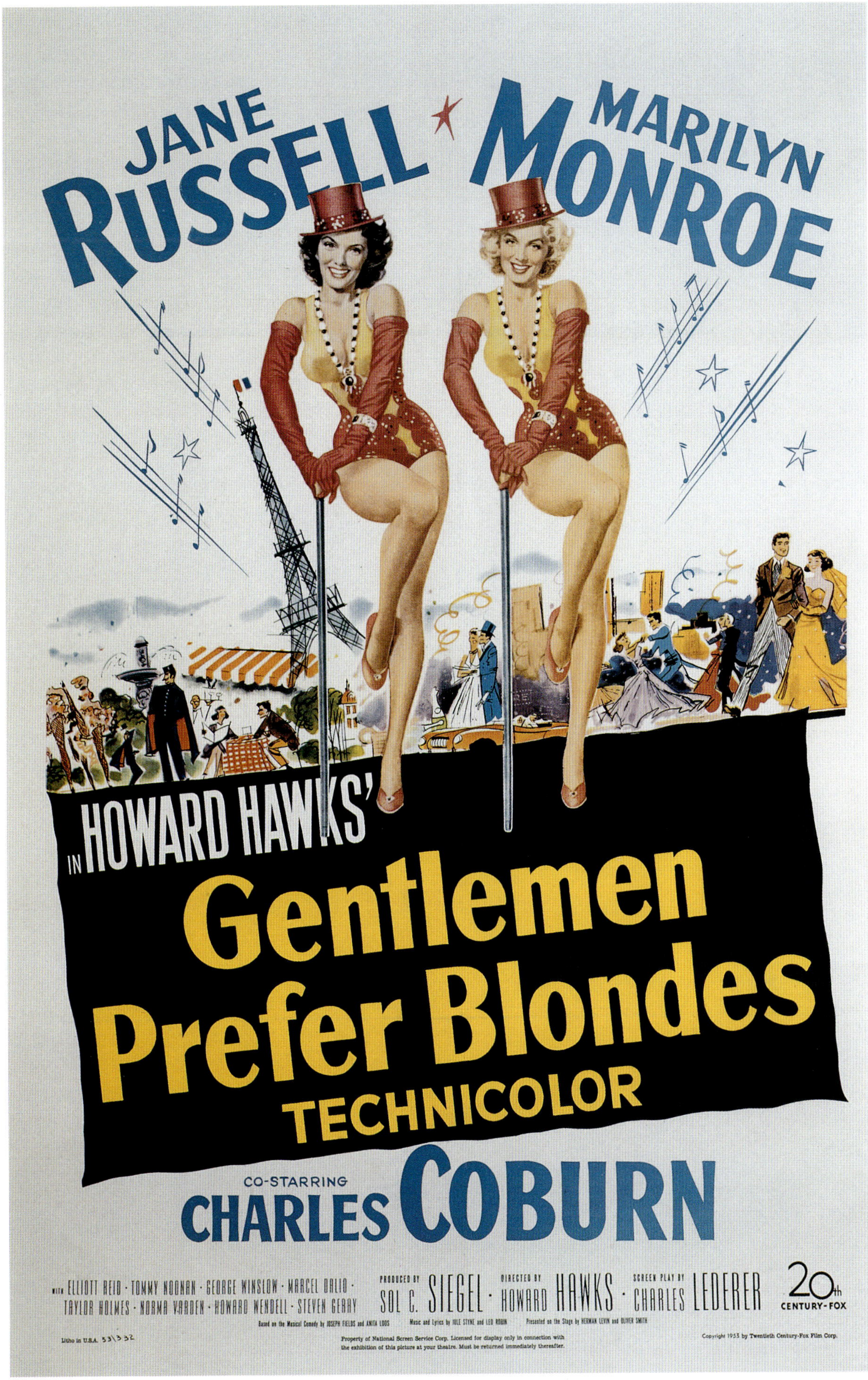

Gentleman Prefer Blondes. 1953. One-sheet. $2,000-3,000

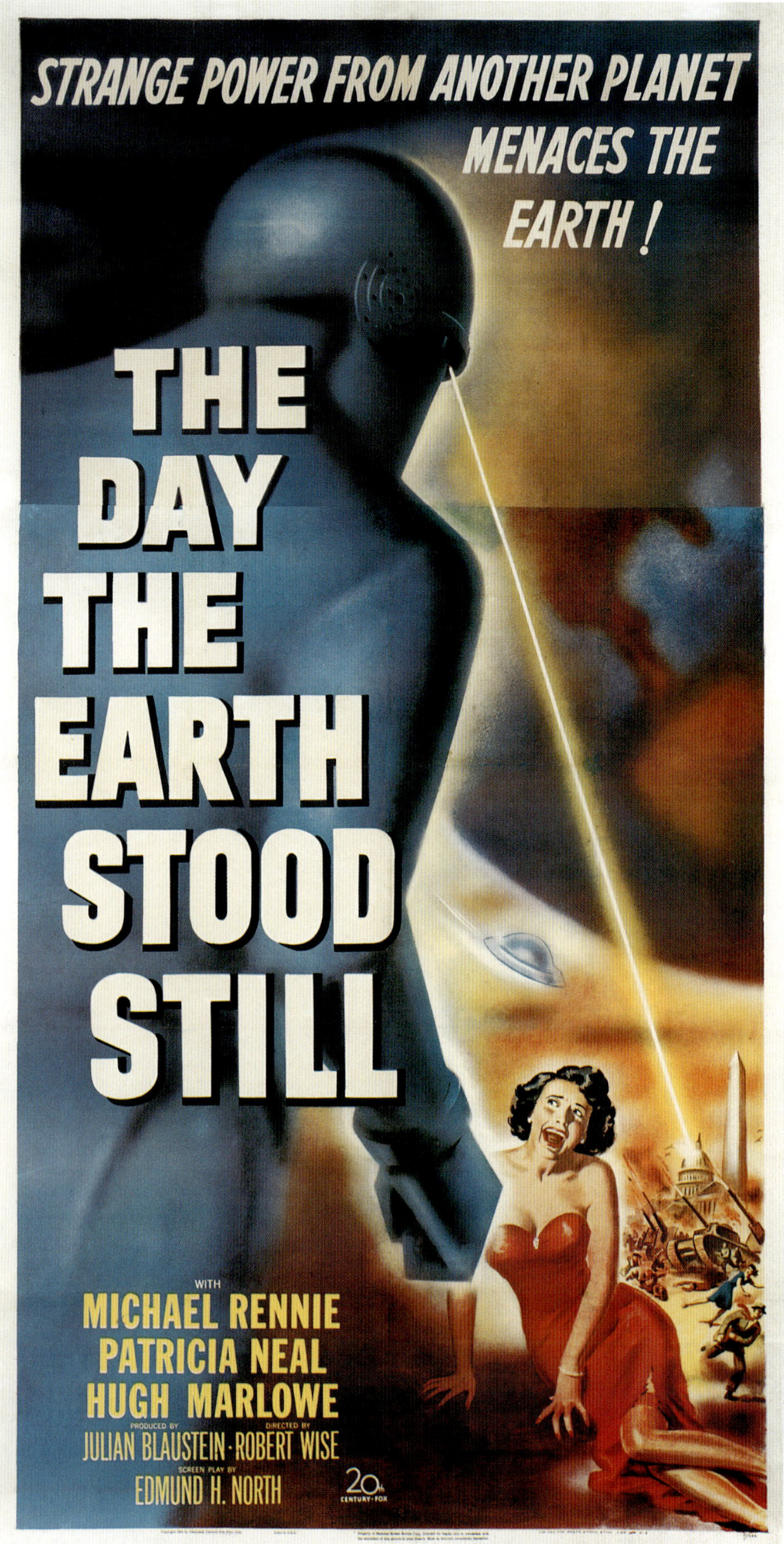

The Day the Earth Stood Still. 1951. Three-sheet. $5,000-8,000

Undoubtedly the one factor that reshaped Hollywood more than any other at this time was the birth of television. Movie theater audiences had trailed off fairly swiftly as the novelty of sitting in your own home to watch entertainment for free became very popular. At first resentful and suspicious of this upstart opposition, the studios soon realized they were going to have to come up with shrewd ways to turn the tide that was now clearly against them. Some chose to embrace the new medium with old film studios being turned to television use and film stars being allowed to feature in new television programs. However, it became clear more was going to be necessary if the movies were going to survive and reign supreme, and for that reason Hollywood decided to capitalize on the major asset they had over television at this time, color and size. Rather than be dictated to by the new small medium, now was the time to emphasize, or rather overemphasize, the greatness of the big screen and thereby win back the depleted audiences. And awestruck they must have been when these first efforts by the Hollywood studios reached the theater chains.

The most outrageous were the 3-D movies. Introduced in 1952 these required the audiences to wear cheap spectacles to enable the film to spring to life and leap from the screen at strategic moments. These were particularly good for the emerging shlock-horrors and sci-fi movies such as *House Of Wax* (1953), *It Came from Outer Space* (1953) and *The Creature From The Black Lagoon* (1954). Despite even master directors, such as Alfred Hitchcock, utilizing this format (*Dial M for Murder*, 1954), it failed to impress the majority of audiences who found the spectacles awkward to use and ranked the technology as mere gimmickry.

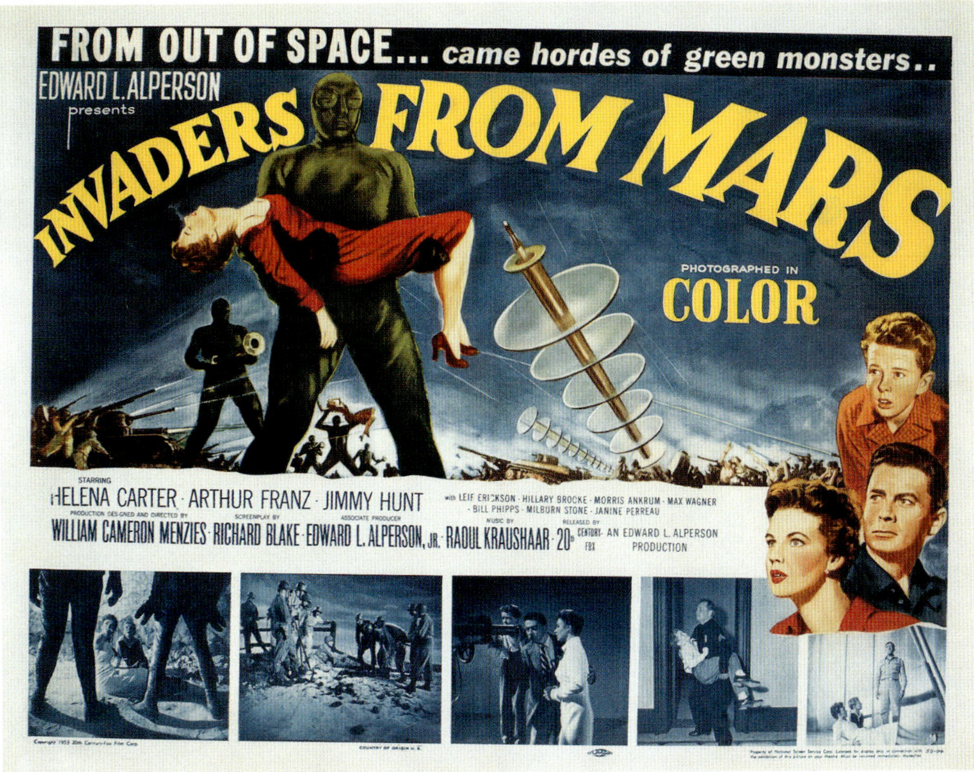

Invaders from Mars.
1953. Half-sheet.
$1,000-1,500

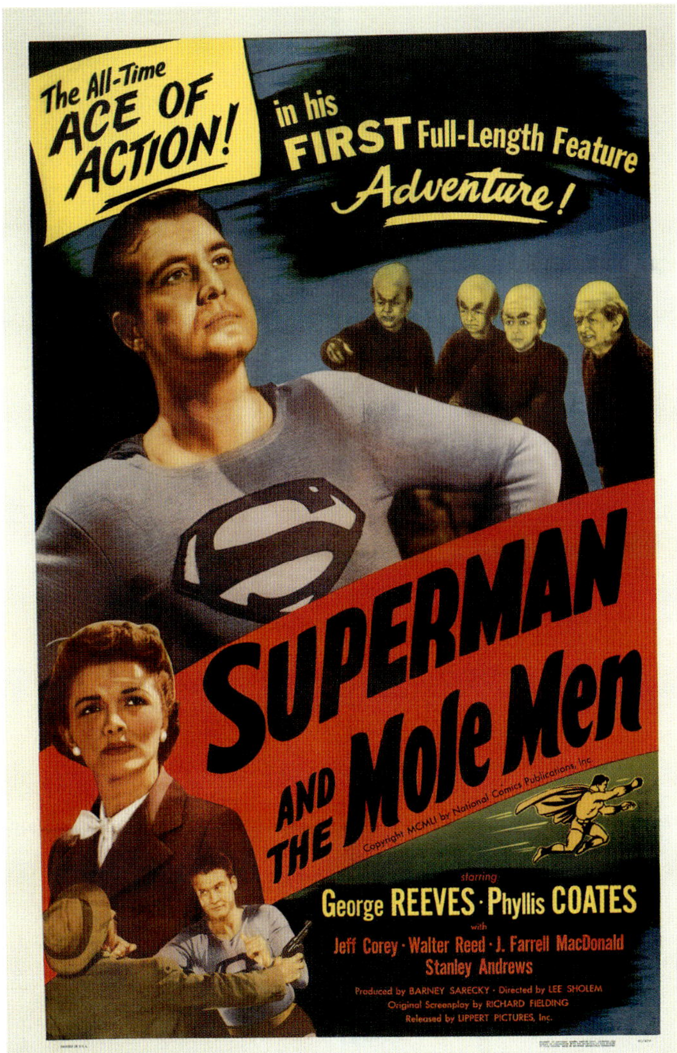

Superman and the Mole Men. 1951. One-sheet. $2,500-3,500

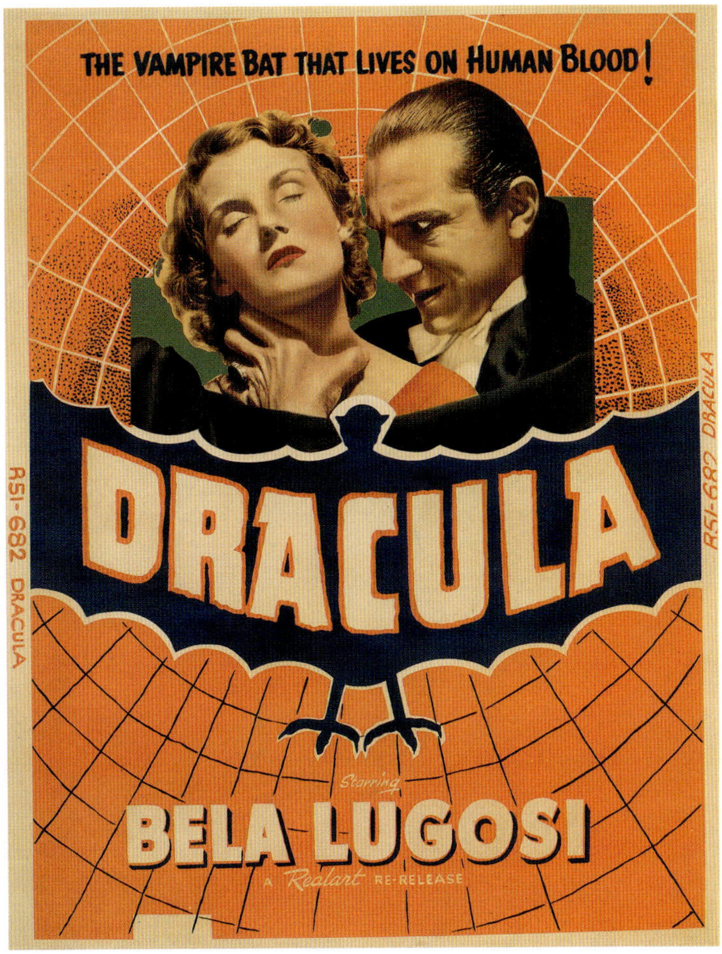

Dracula. 1951. Re-release. Two-sheet. $1,000-1,800

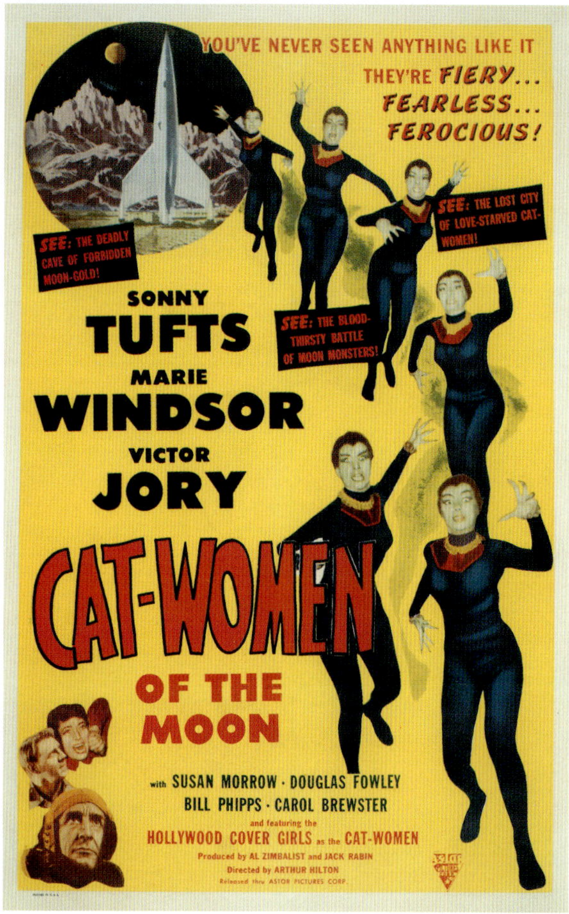

Cat-Women of the Moon. 1954. One-sheet. $600-800

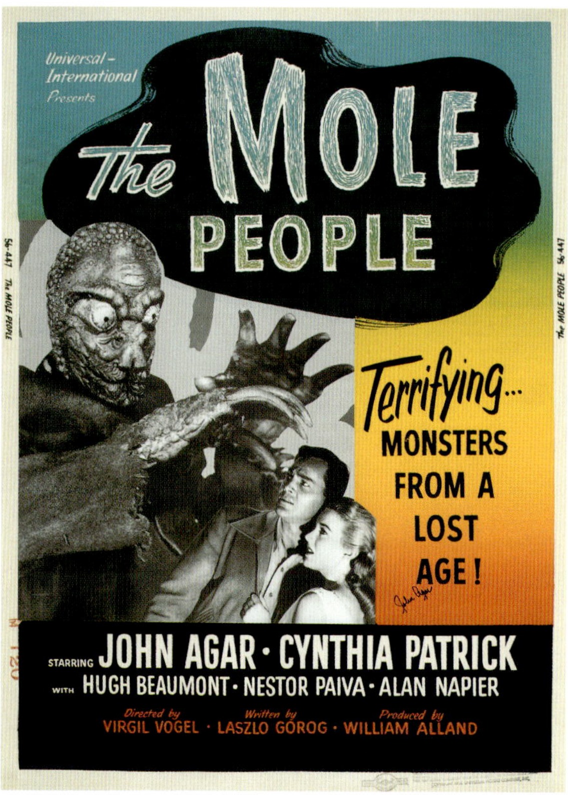

The Mole People. 1956. Two-sheet, signed by John Agar. $1,000-1,500

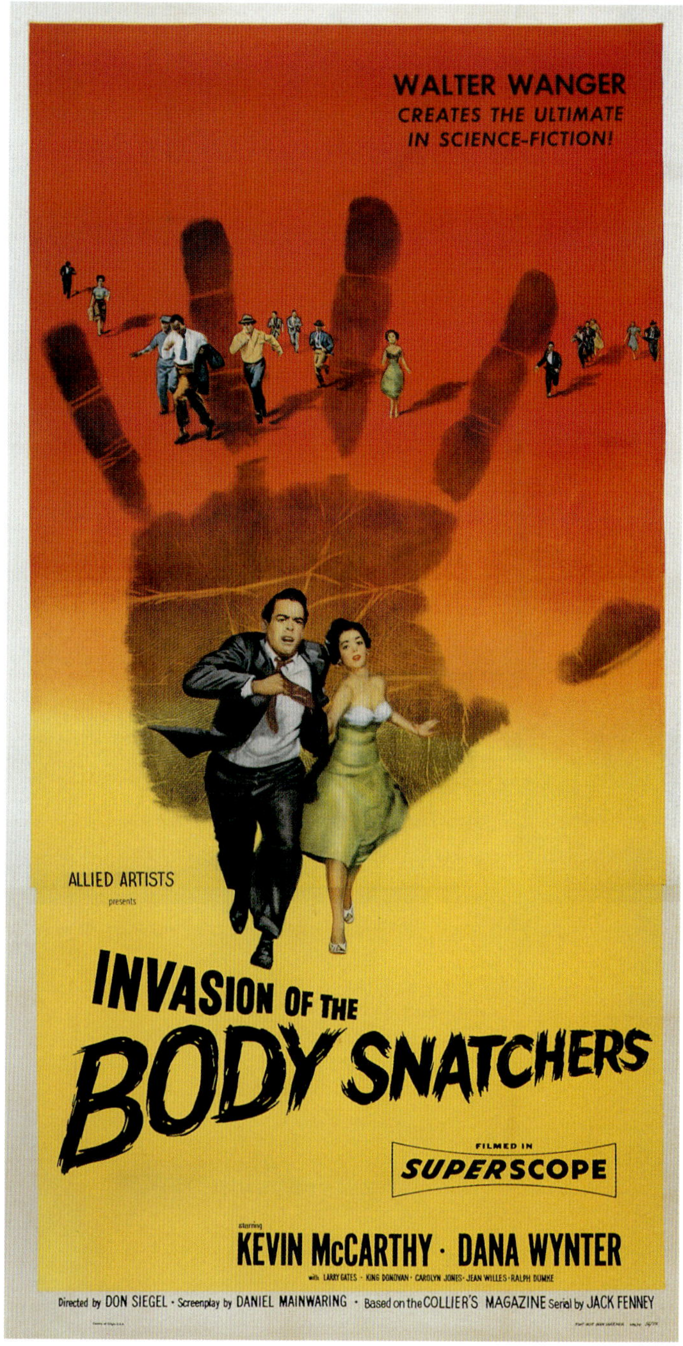

Invasion of the Body Snatchers. 1956. Three-sheet. $1,200-1,800

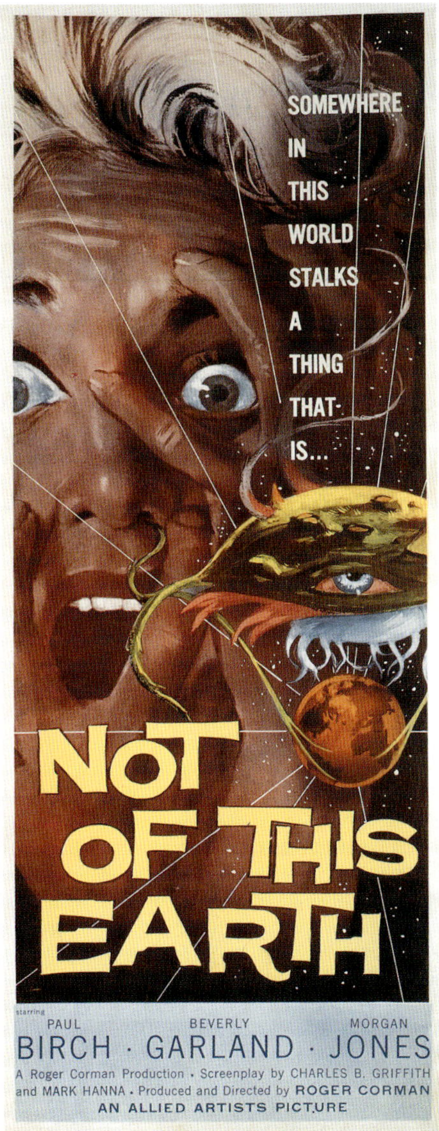

Not of this Earth. 1957. Insert. $700-1,000

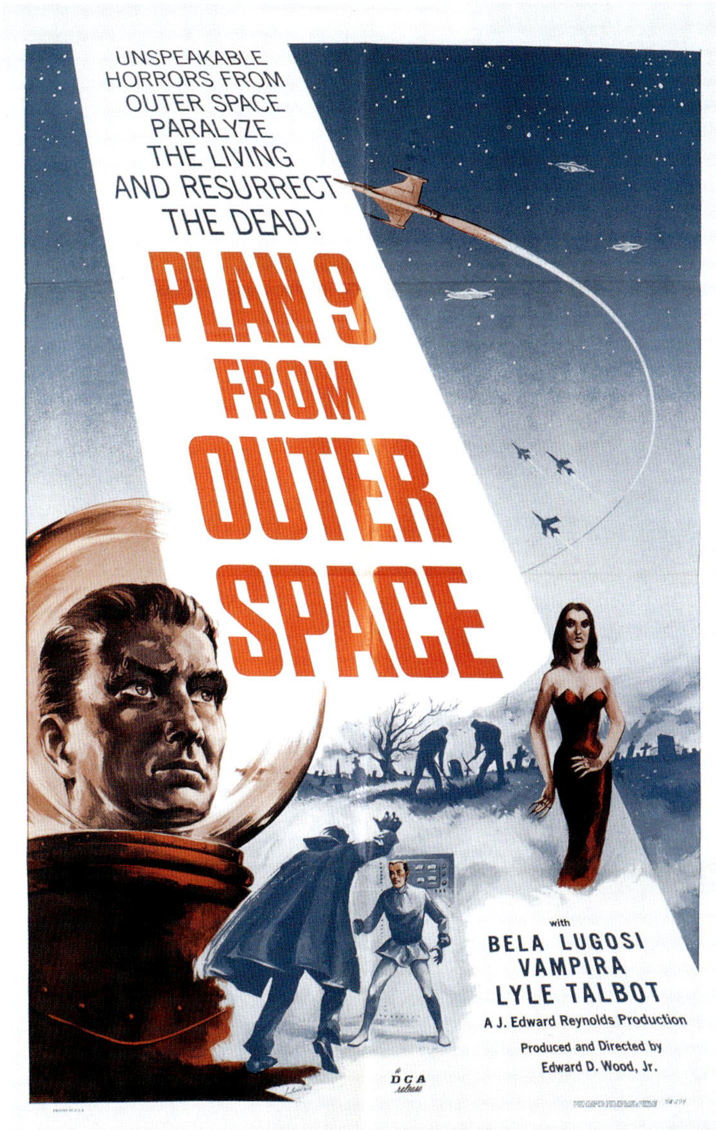

Plan 9 from Outer Space. 1956. One-sheet. $2,000-2,500

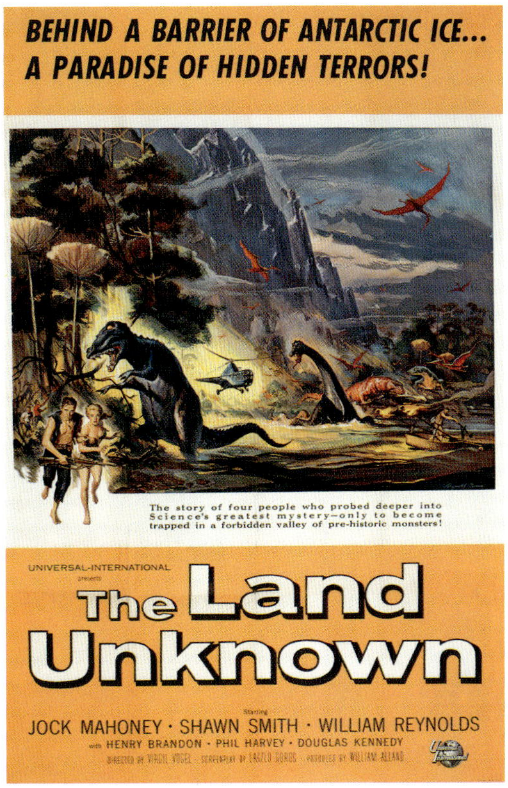

The Land Unknown. 1957. Special one-sheet. $600-800

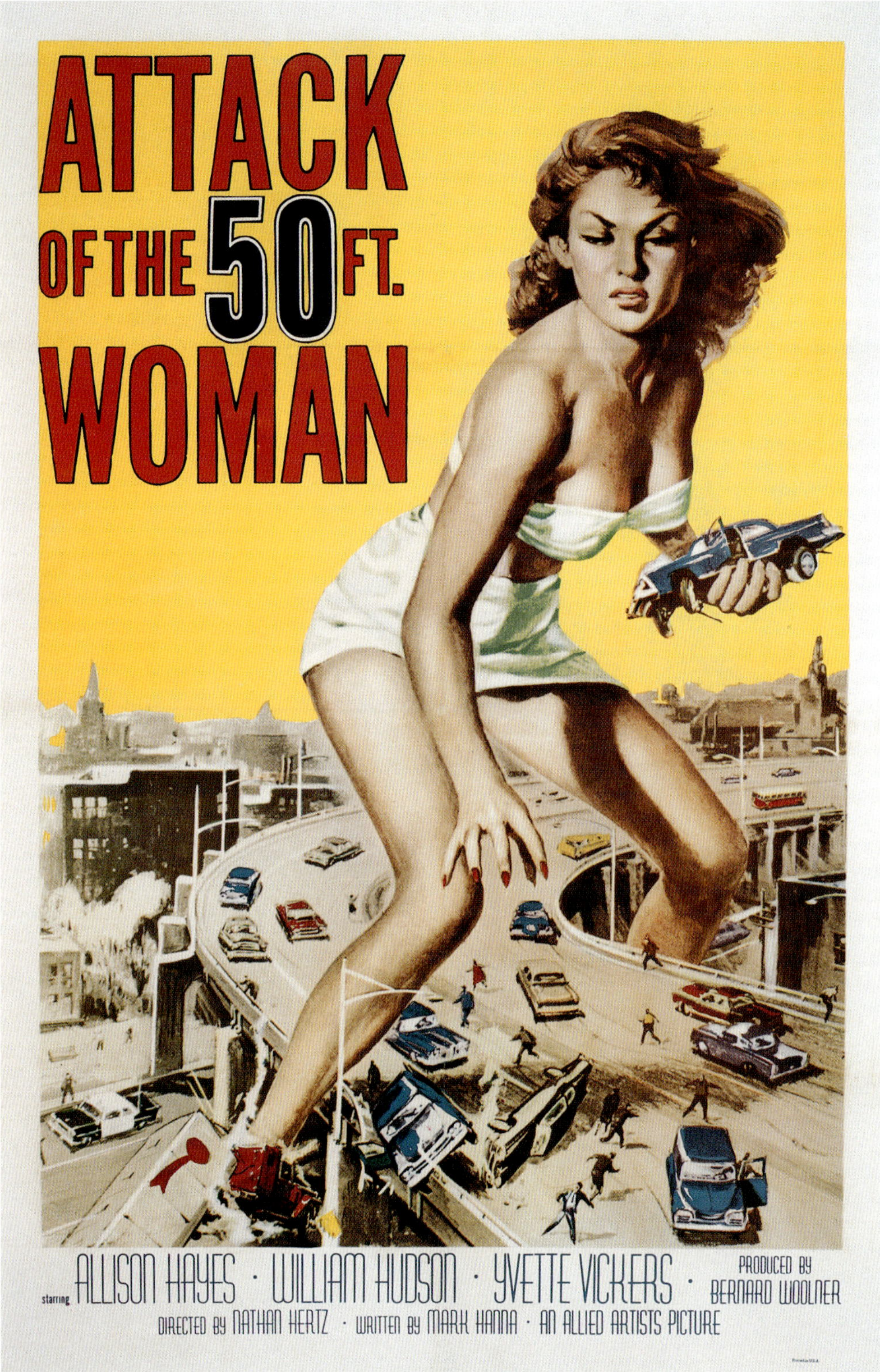

Attack of the 50ft. Woman. 1958. One-sheet. $4,000-6,000

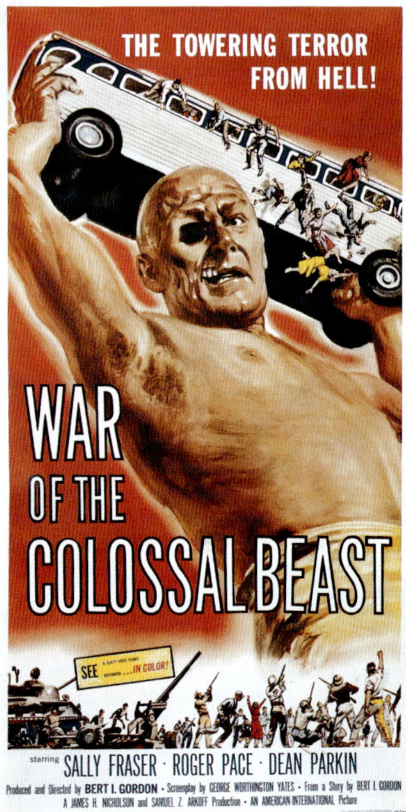

War of the Colossal Beast. 1958.
Three-sheet. $800-1200

Unperturbed by this, Hollywood launched their next offensive in the form of big screen formats, the first being Cinerama®. This process required huge curved screens, several cameras, projectors and much construction work! The idea was to draw audiences into the actual movie as it happened around them. Not enough people came to cover the costs, and cheaper concepts of size were developed instead. 20th Century-Fox's Cinemascope® created a widescreen effect by the use of an anamorphic lens to shoot the film. The first film released using this method was the Biblical epic *The Robe* (1953). Similar processes were adopted by other studios including Superscope® by R.K.O. and Vistavision® by Paramount. After his brief foray into 3-D, Hitchcock persisted with experimental new developments and released the famous thrillers *To Catch A Thief* (1955), *Vertigo* (1958), and *North By Northwest* (1959) all using Vistavision®.

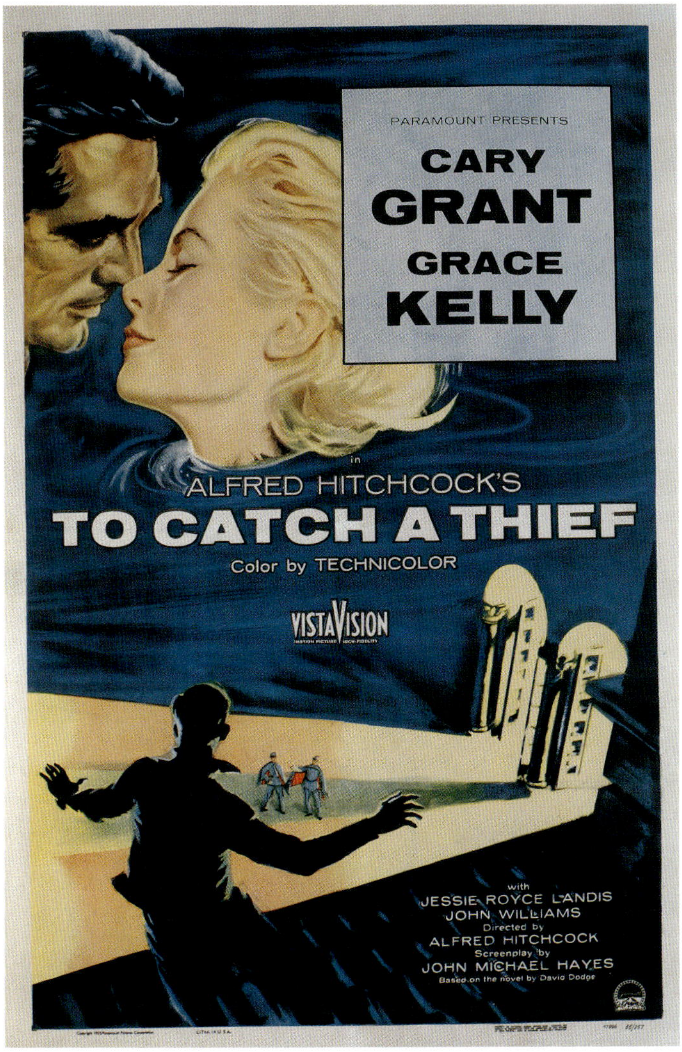

To Catch a Thief. 1955. One-sheet. $1,500-2,000

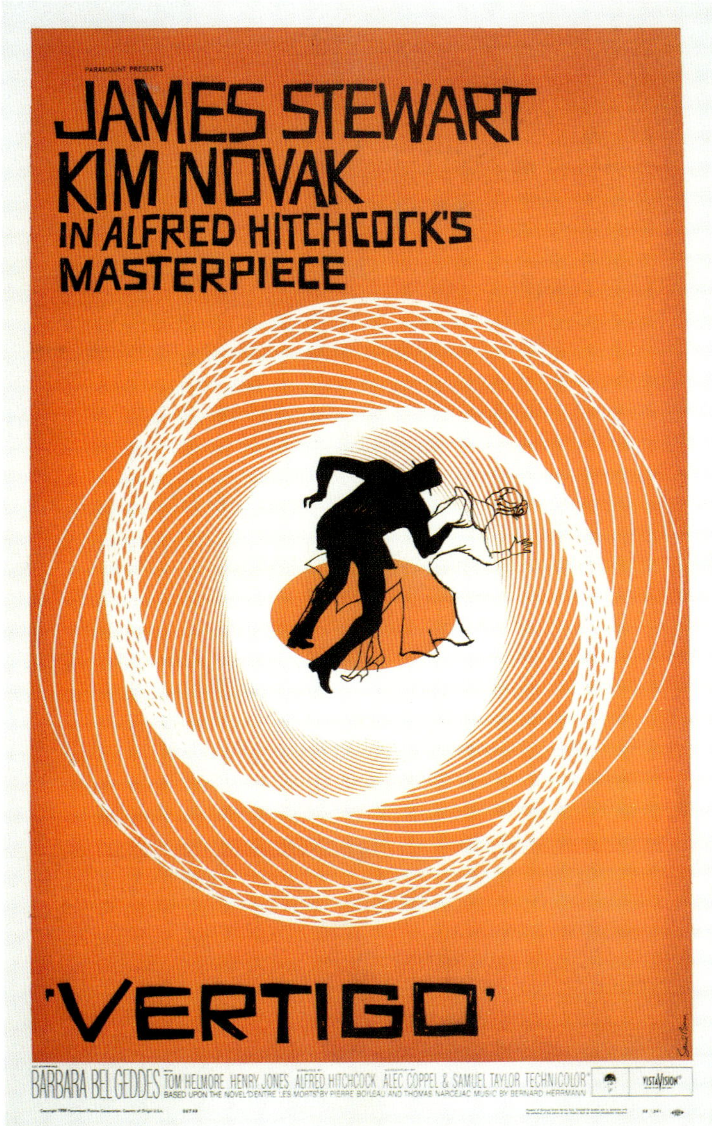

Vertigo. 1958. One-sheet, art by Saul Bass. $2,000-3,000

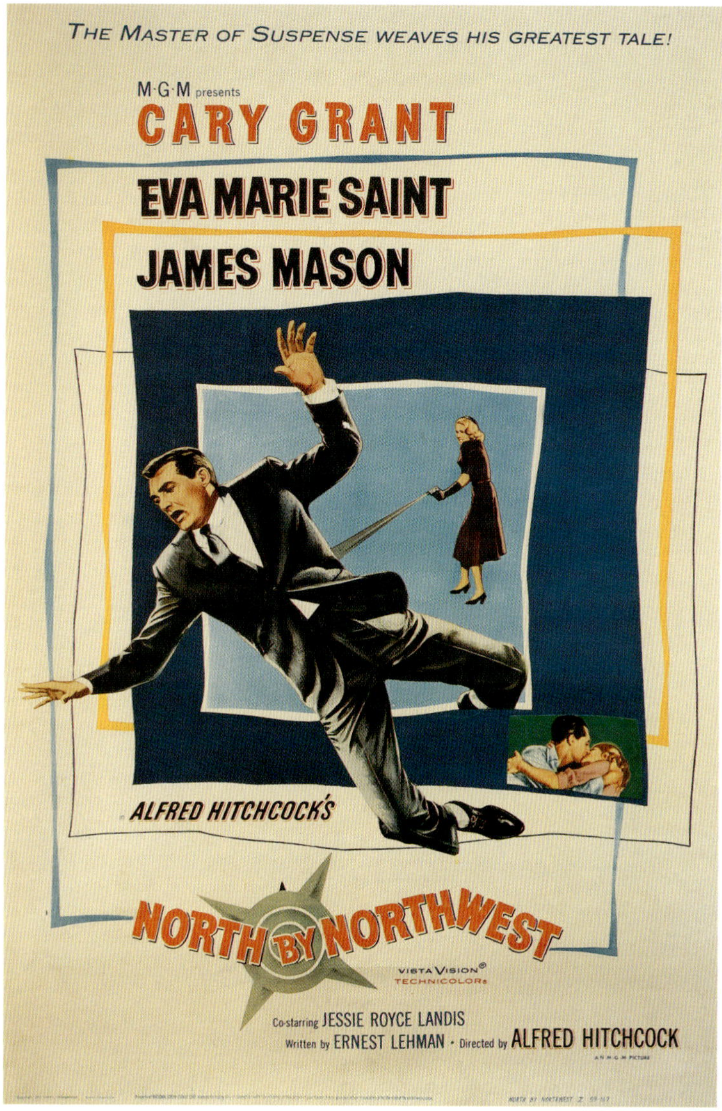

North by Northwest. 1959. Two-sheet. $1,200-1,800

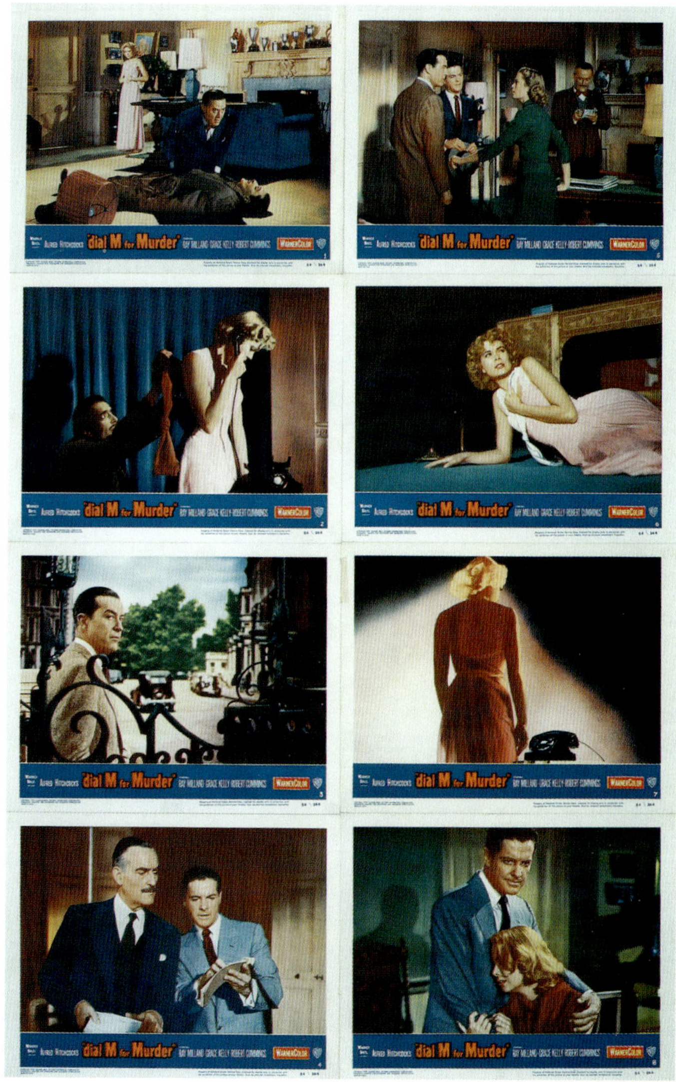

Dial M for Murder. 1954. Set of lobby cards. $1,200-1,800

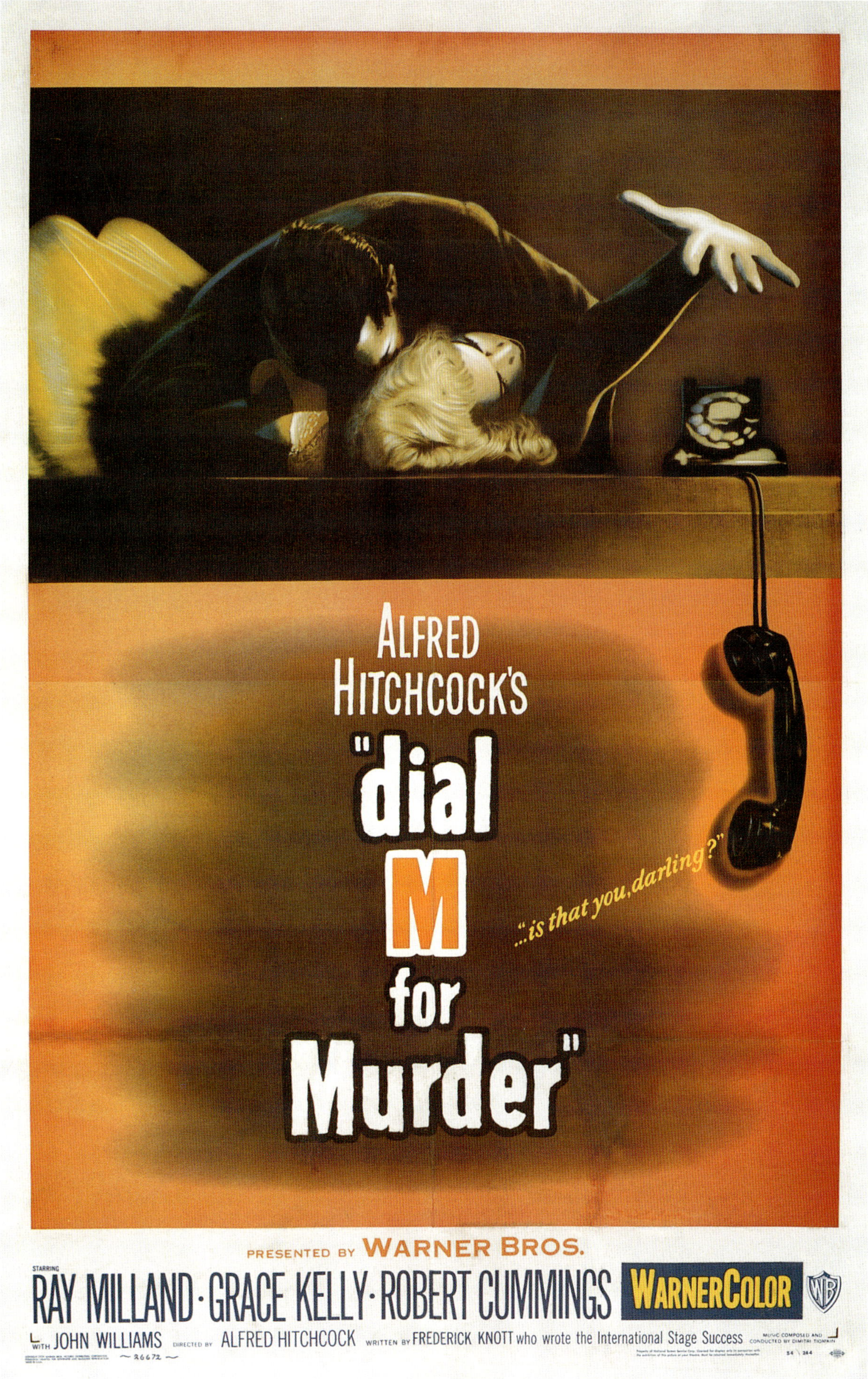

Dial M for Murder. 1954. One-sheet. $2,500-3,500

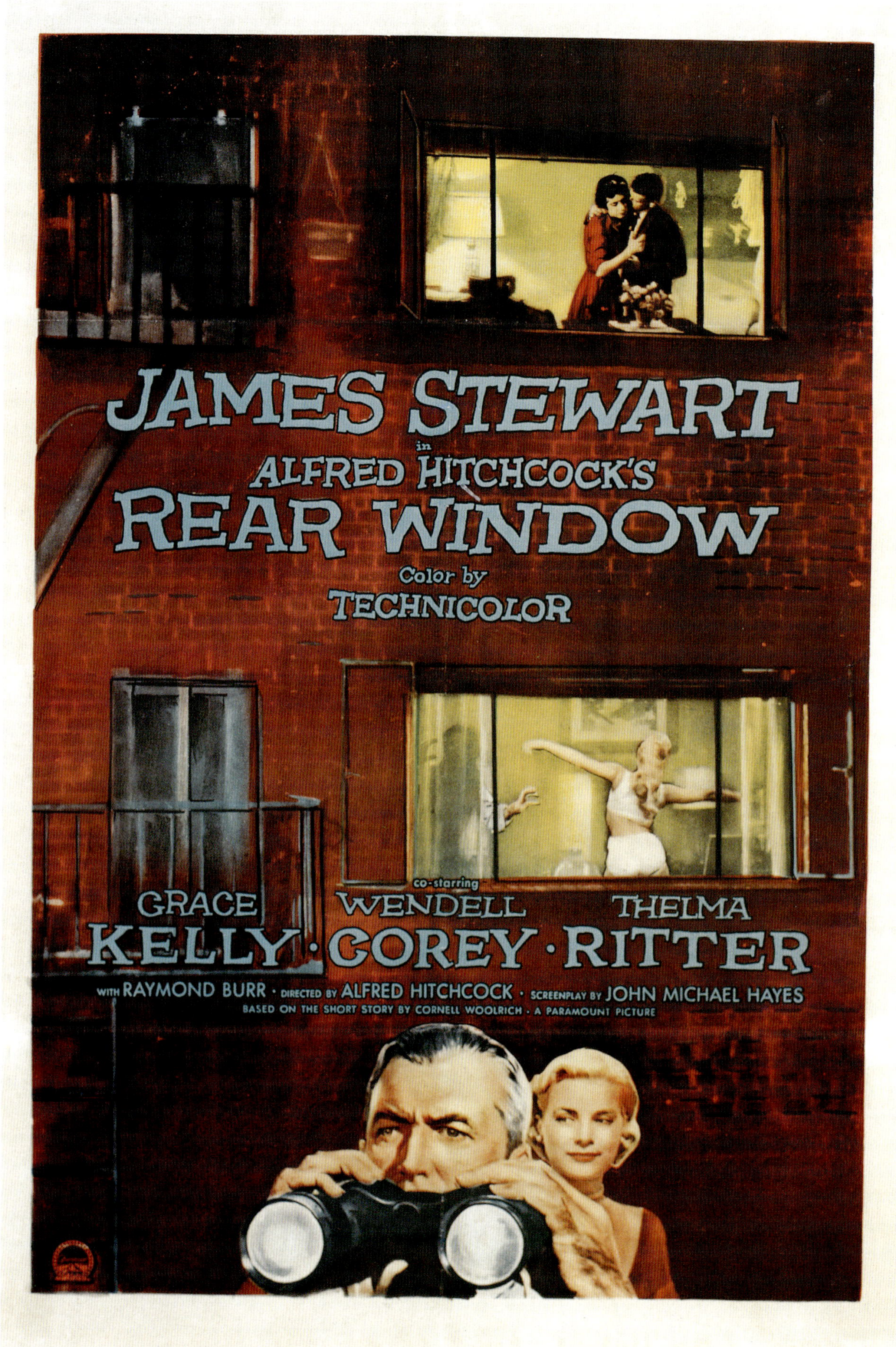

Rear Window. 1954. One-sheet. $5,000-7,000

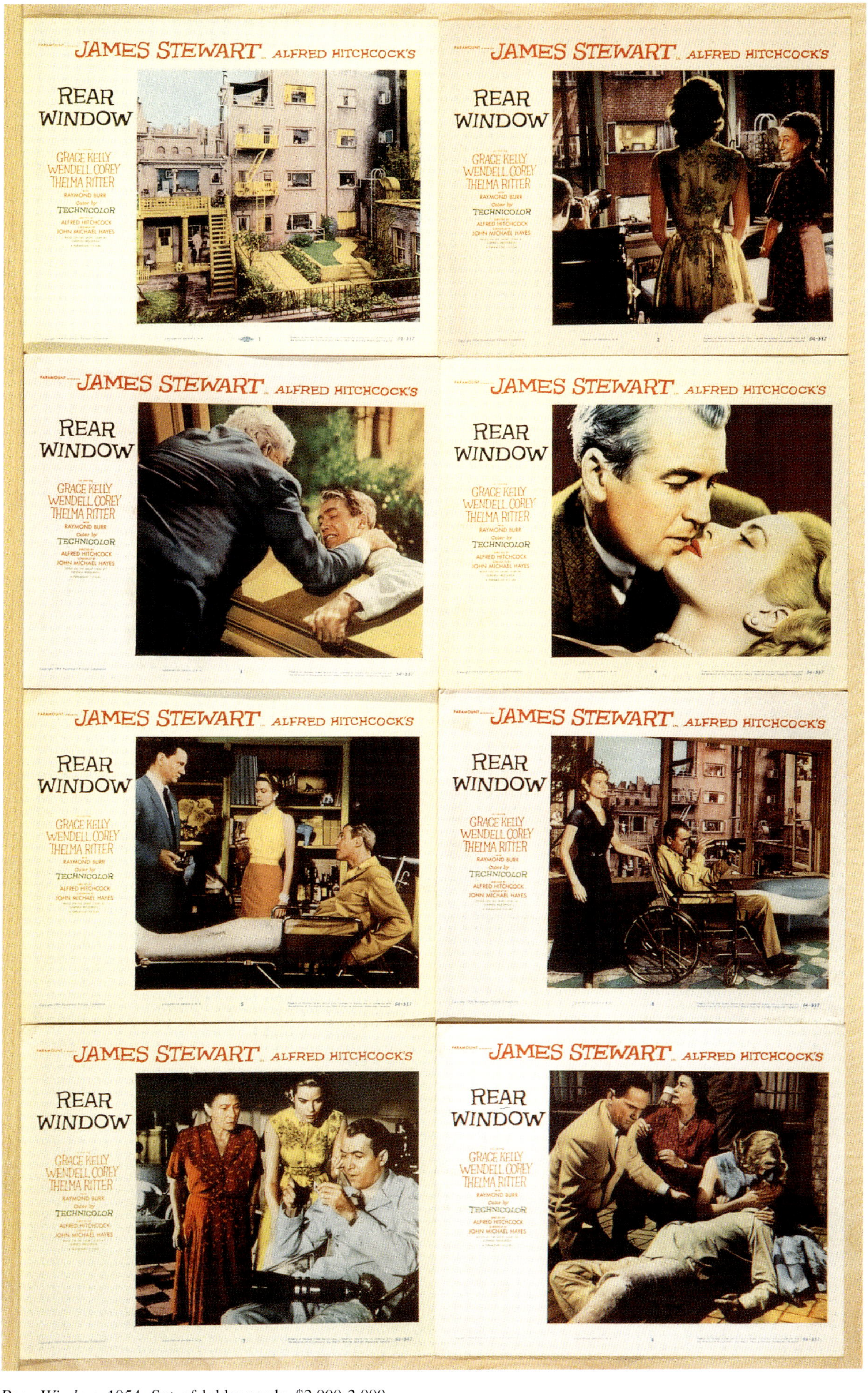

Rear Window. 1954. Set of lobby cards. $2,000-3,000

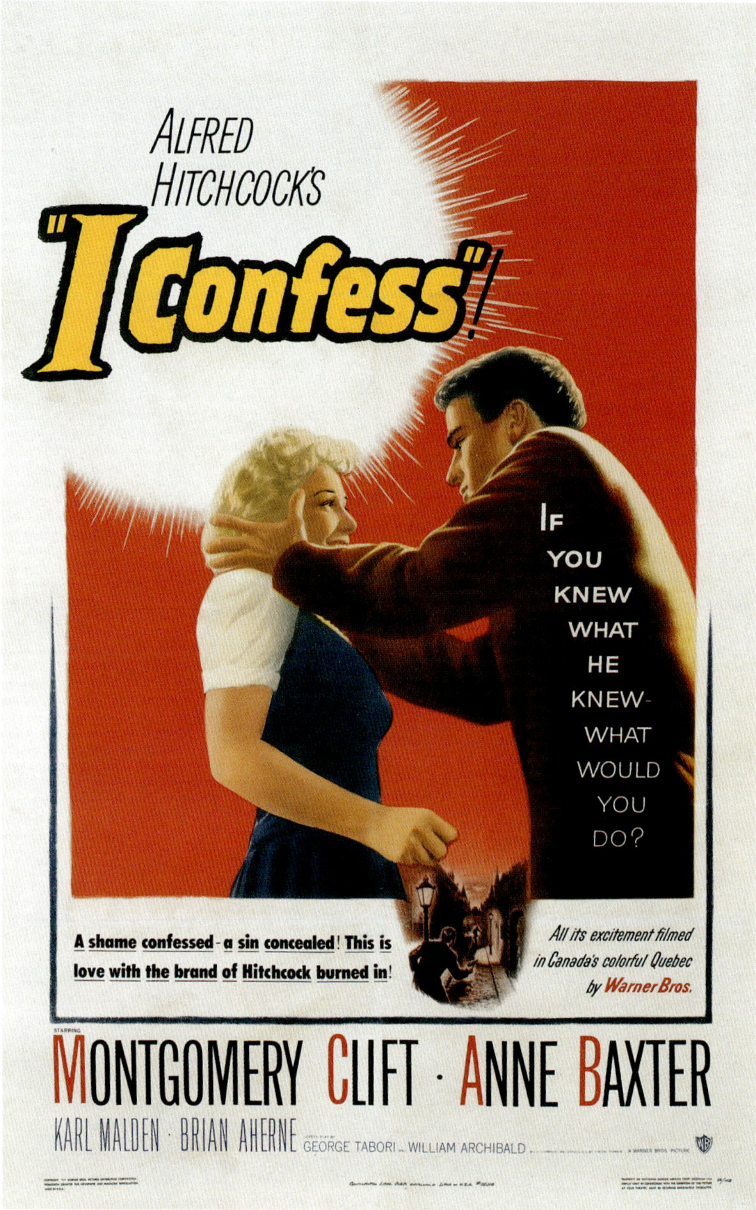

I Confess. 1953. One-sheet. $2,000-2,500

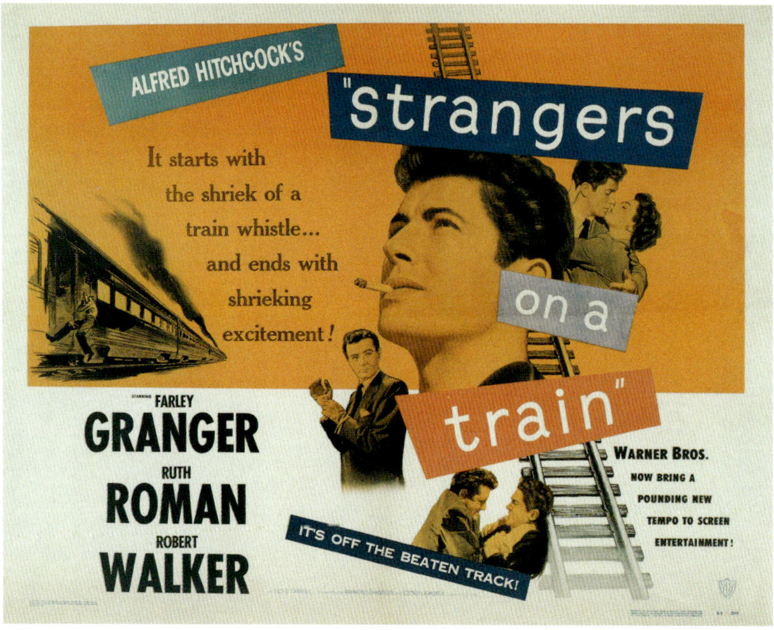

Strangers on a Train. 1951. Half-sheet. $900-1,200

Hollywood was not content just to dabble with fancy devices. In addition to physically enlarging the picture on screen they also decided to enlarge the movie in other ways and so began the era of "epics." These films were purposely longer than other films (the average length of a movie at this time being 90 minutes) and dealt with giant, often historic, subjects. During the war there had been a noticeable lack of color films because of the costs involved. Now these epic, visual spectaculars once more splashed it back with a vengeance, no doubt also because television could only manage black and white at this stage. The old master director of the epic, Cecil B. DeMille, contributed (among others) a remake of his earlier 1923 silent, *The Ten Commandments* (1956). William Wyler continued the winning formula by directing the smash hit *Ben-Hur* (1959). Previous to this audiences had been treated to the monumental delights of Tolstoy's *War & Peace* (1956), the Napoleonic *Désirée* (1954), *The Egyptian* (1954), *Land of the Pharaohs* (1955), *Helen of Troy* (1956), *The Vikings* (1958) and many more.

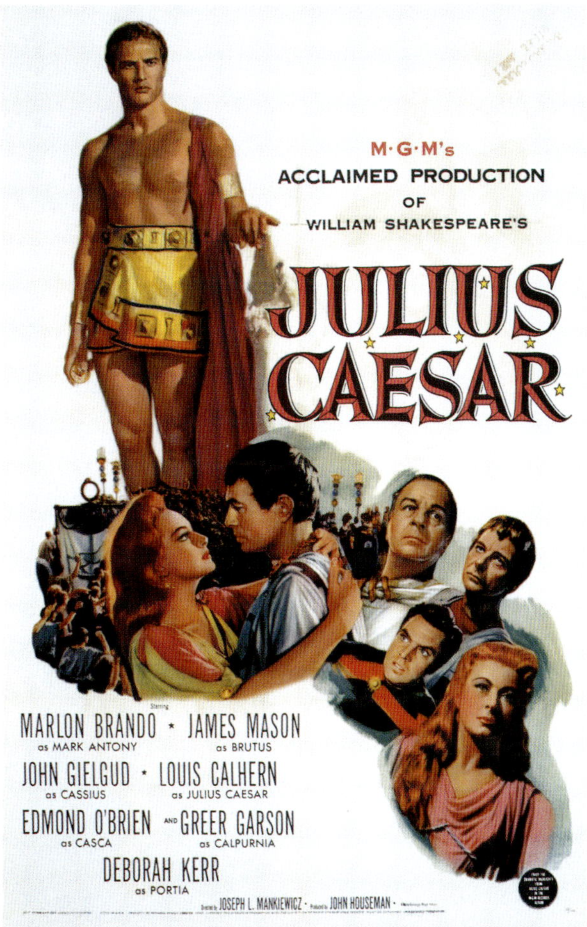

Julius Caesar. 1953. One-sheet. $600-900

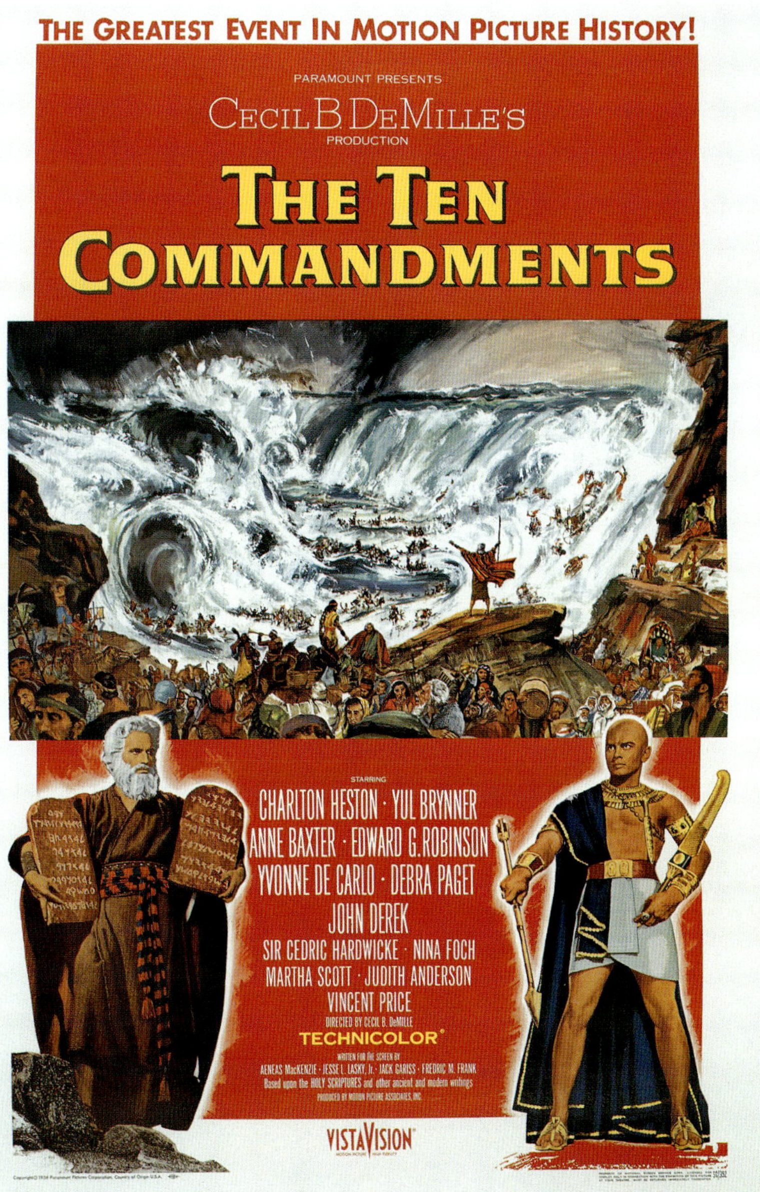

The Ten Commandments. 1956. One-sheet, style A. $1,000-1,500

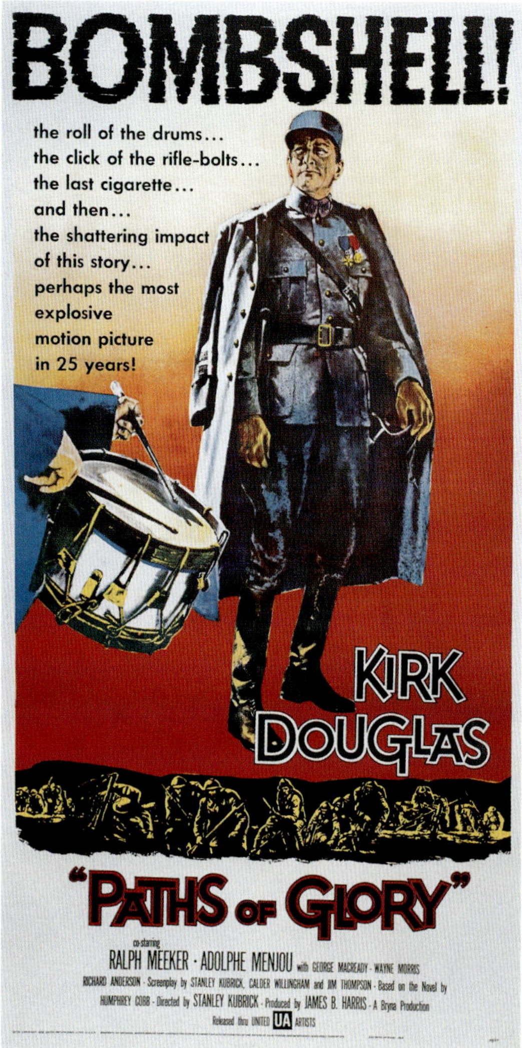

Paths of Glory. 1957. Three-sheet. $800-1,200

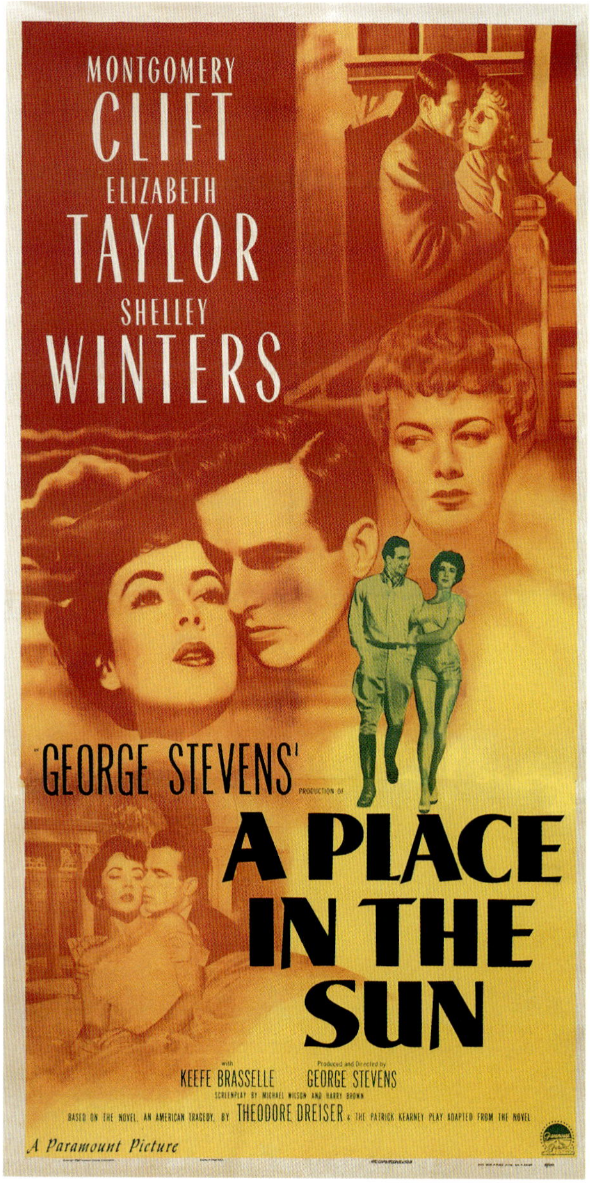

A Place in the Sun. 1951. Three-sheet. $1,200-1,800

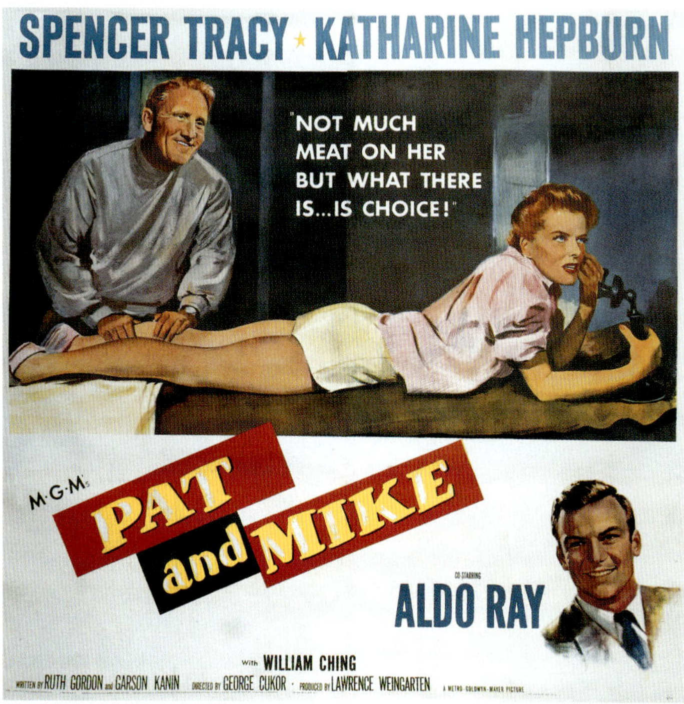

Pat and Mike. 1952. Six-sheet. $600-900

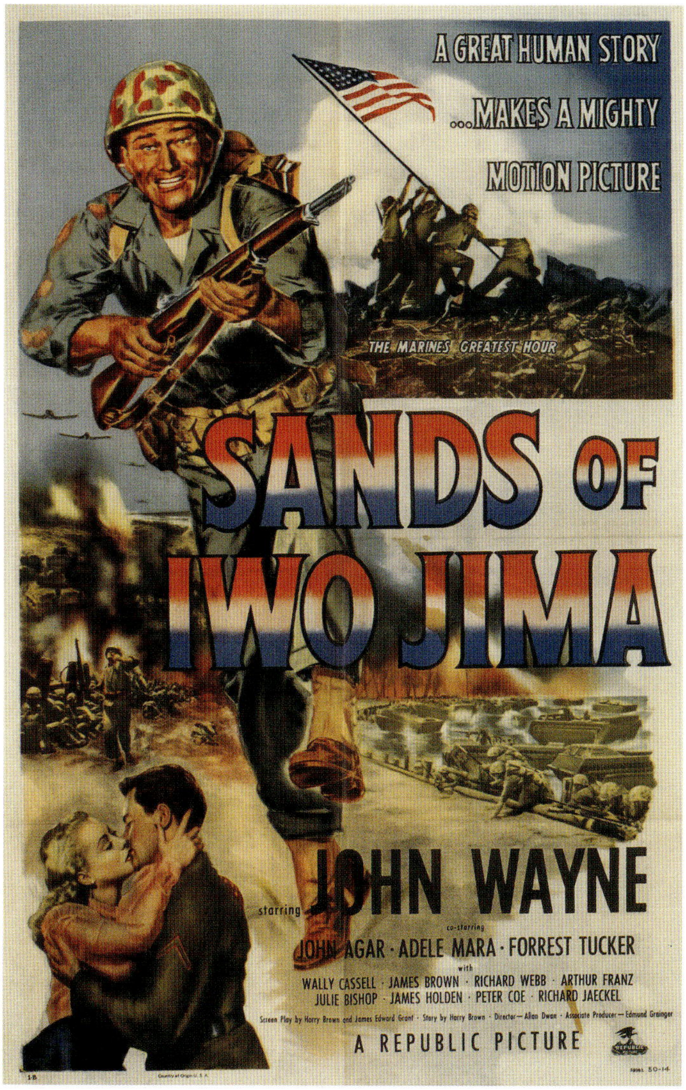

Sands of Iwo Jima. 1950. One-sheet. $1,000-1,500

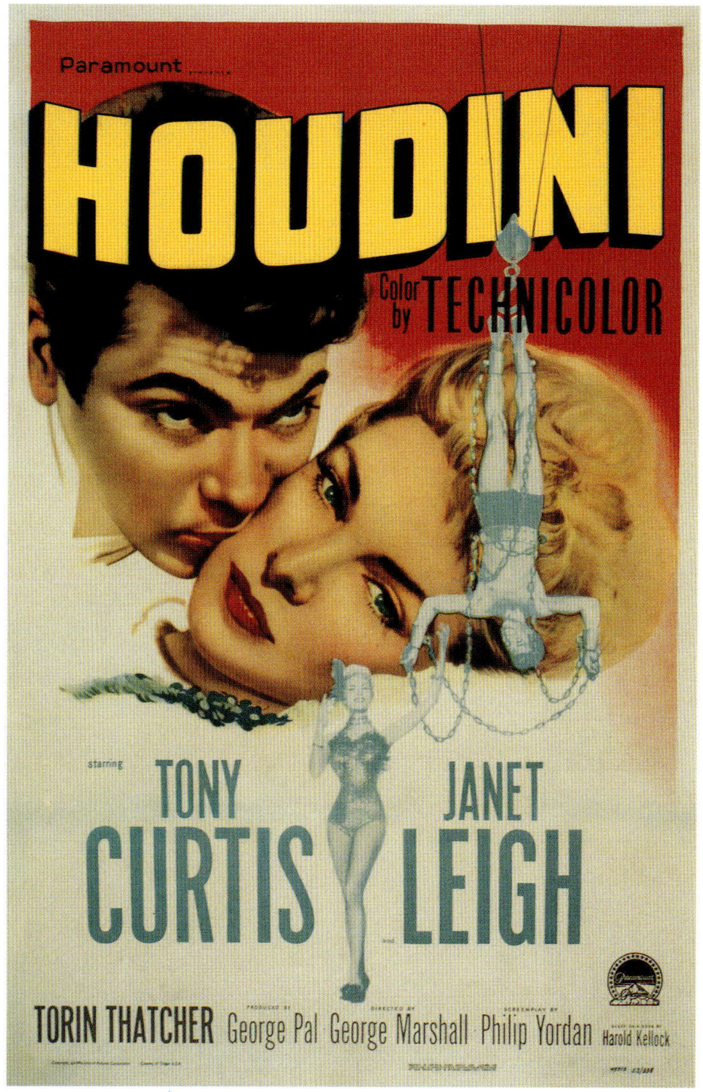

Houdini. 1953. One-sheet. $700-1,000

No one can doubt the sheer volume of creativity, invention, and diversity in this decade but despite all efforts the studios were still failing to get new audiences. The quantity of films released was seriously declining as the long-term effects of television began to penetrate the old Hollywood structure. Every major studio suffered with changes occurring at the board level involving many sell-offs and sell-outs by original owners. Corporate takeovers and asset stripping hit Hollywood big time.

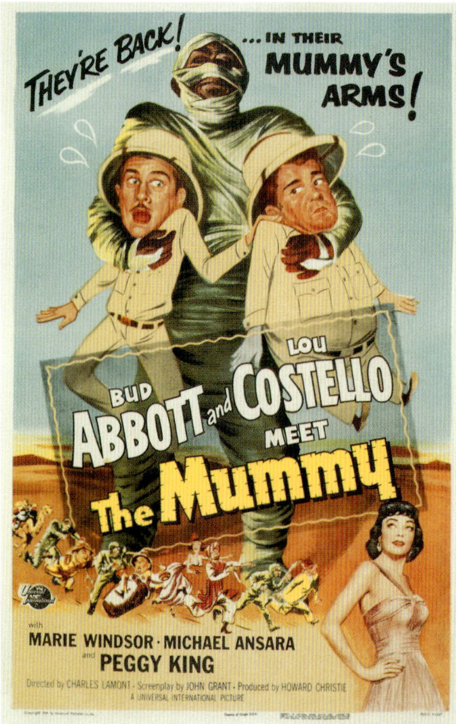

Abbott and Costello Meet the Mummy. 1955. One-sheet. $600-800

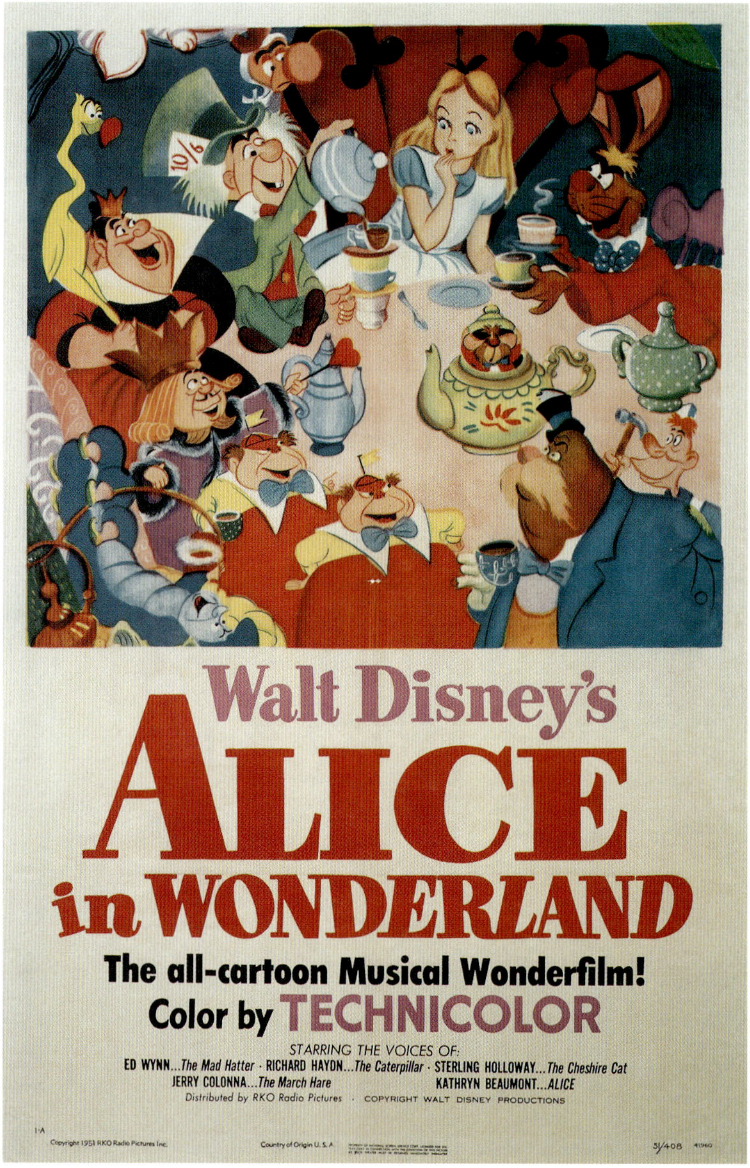

Alice in Wonderland. 1951. One-sheet. $1,000-1,500

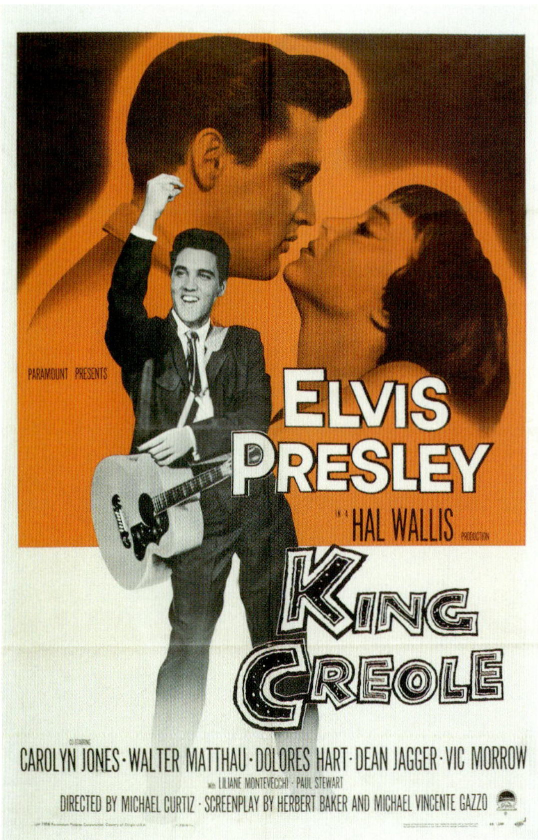

King Creole. 1958. One-sheet. $600-800

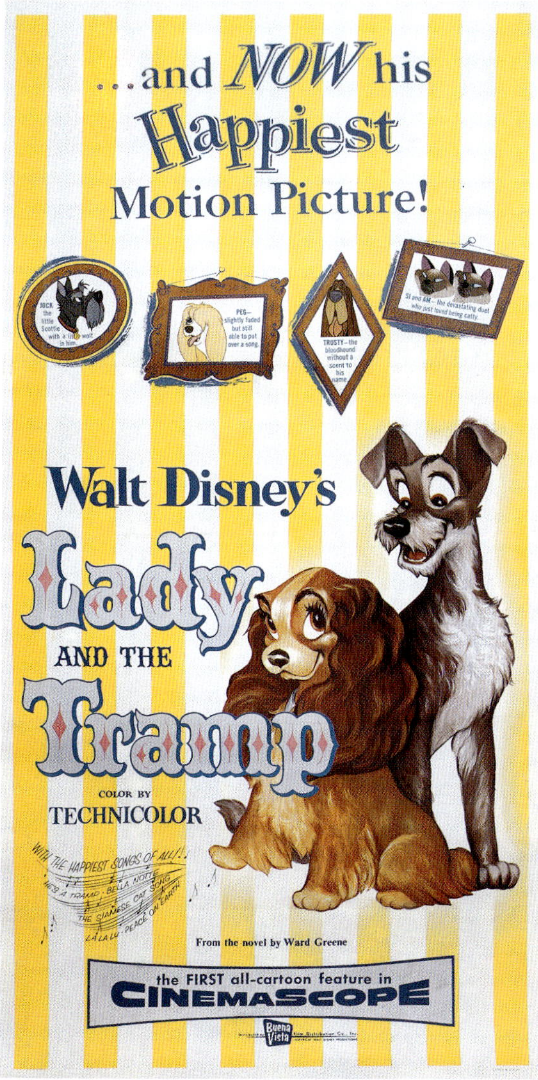

Lady and the Tramp. 1955. Three-sheet. $1,200-1,800

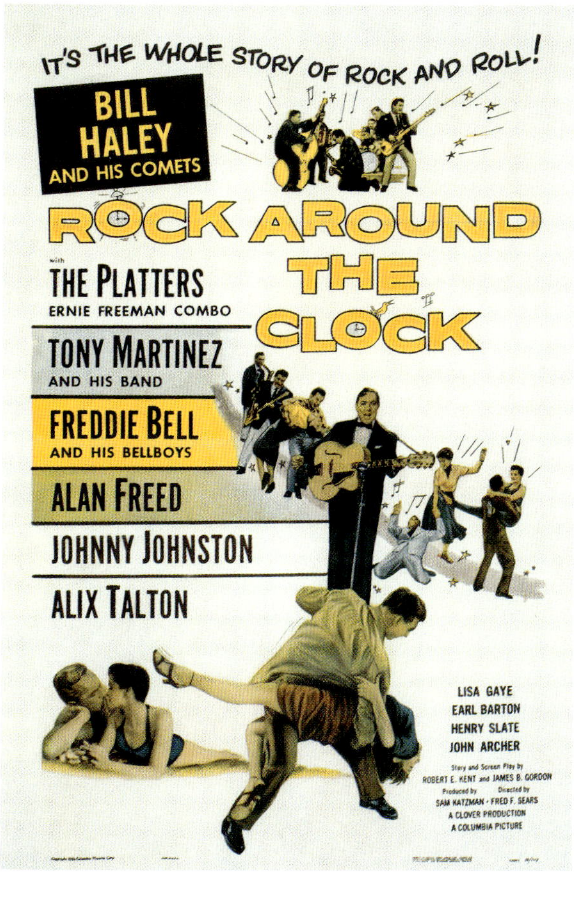

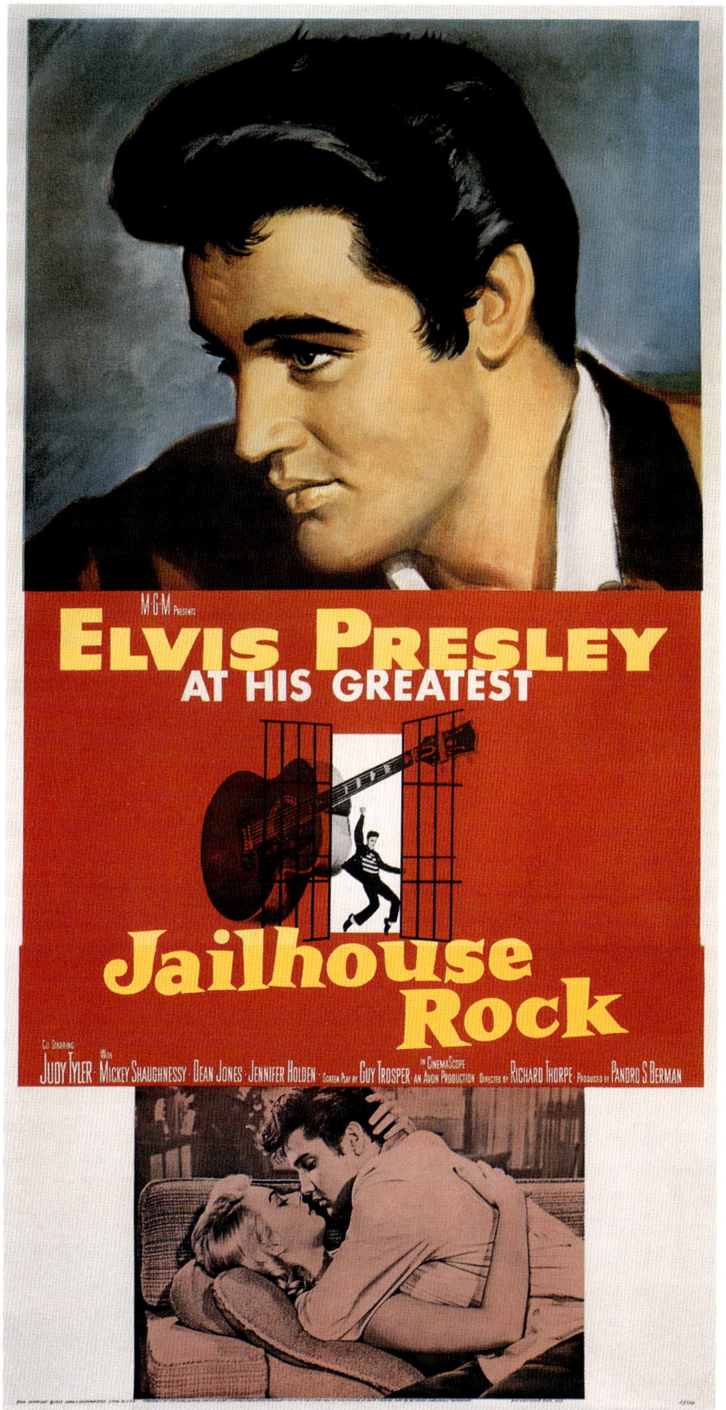

Jailhouse Rock. 1951. Three-sheet. $1,500-2,000

Rock Around the Clock. 1956.
One-sheet. $700-1000

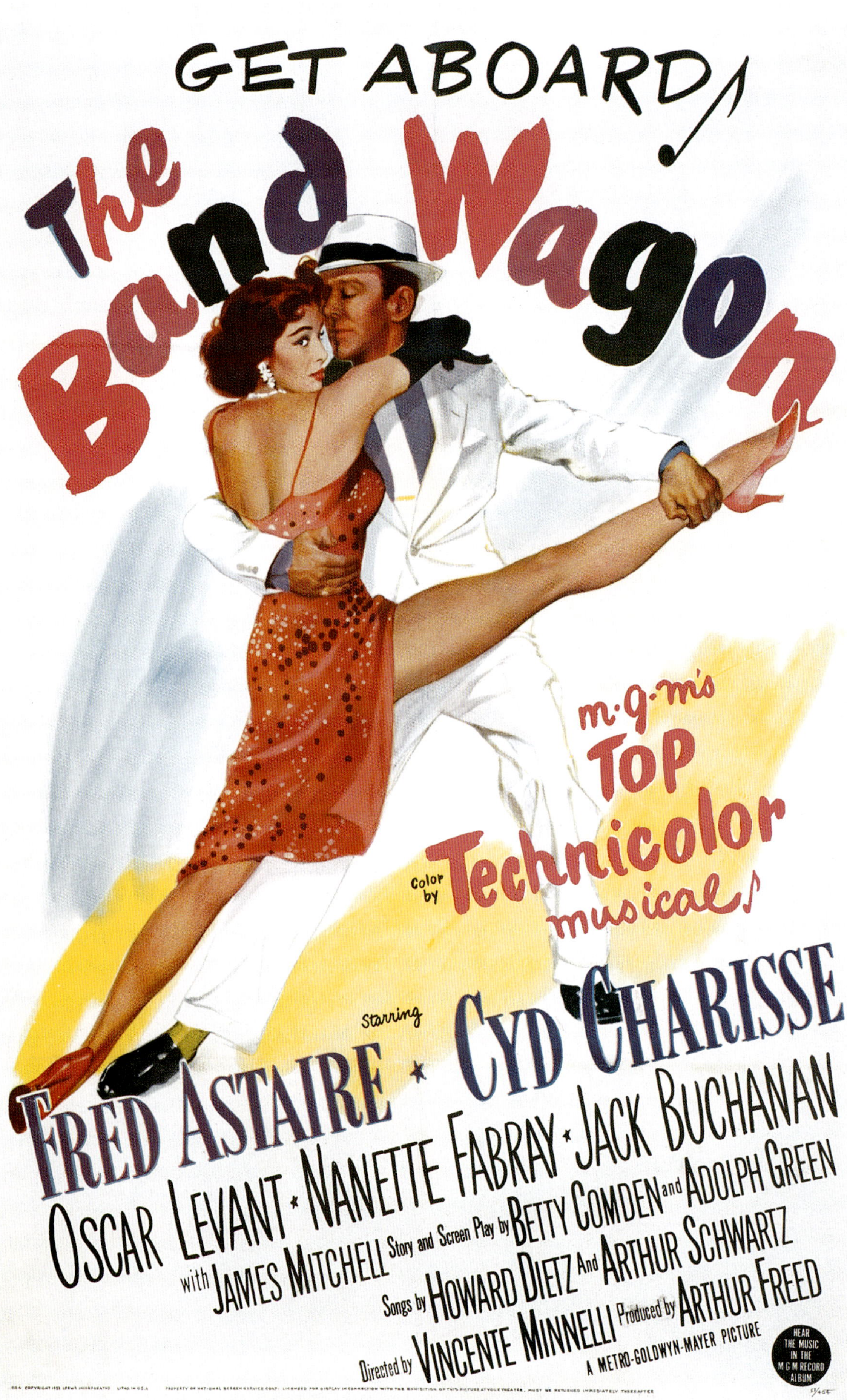

The Band Wagon. 1953. One-sheet,. $1,000-1,500

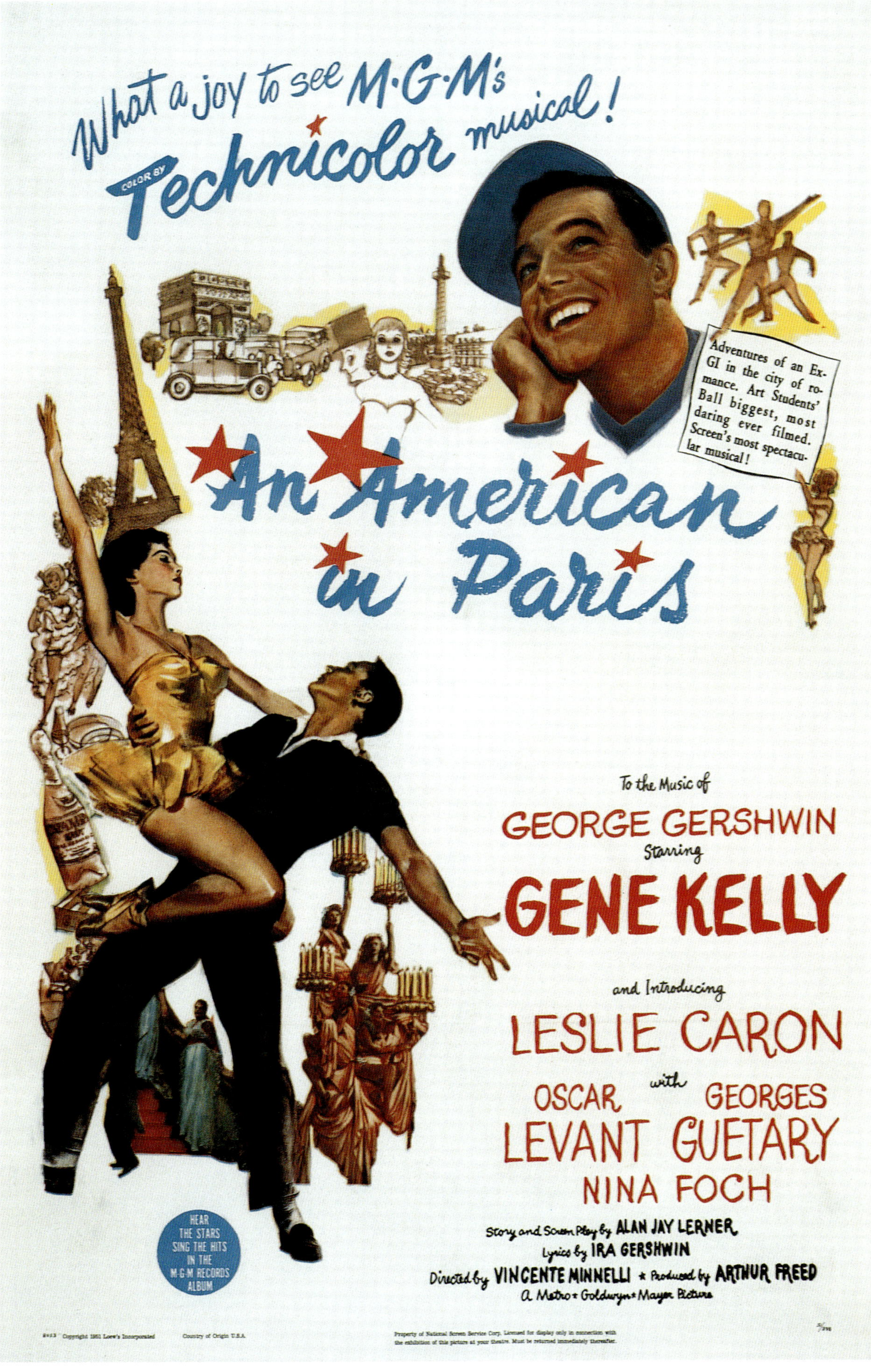

An American in Paris. 1951. One-sheet. $1,200-1,800

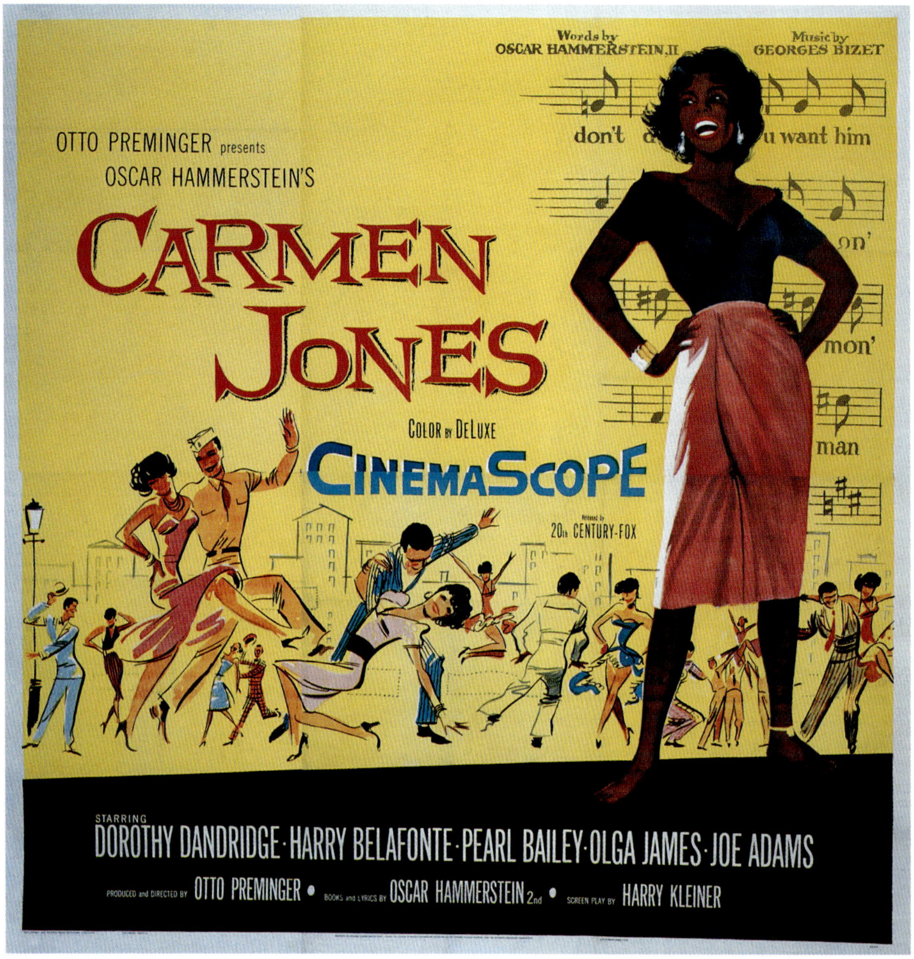

Carmen Jones. 1954. Six-sheet. $2,000-3,000

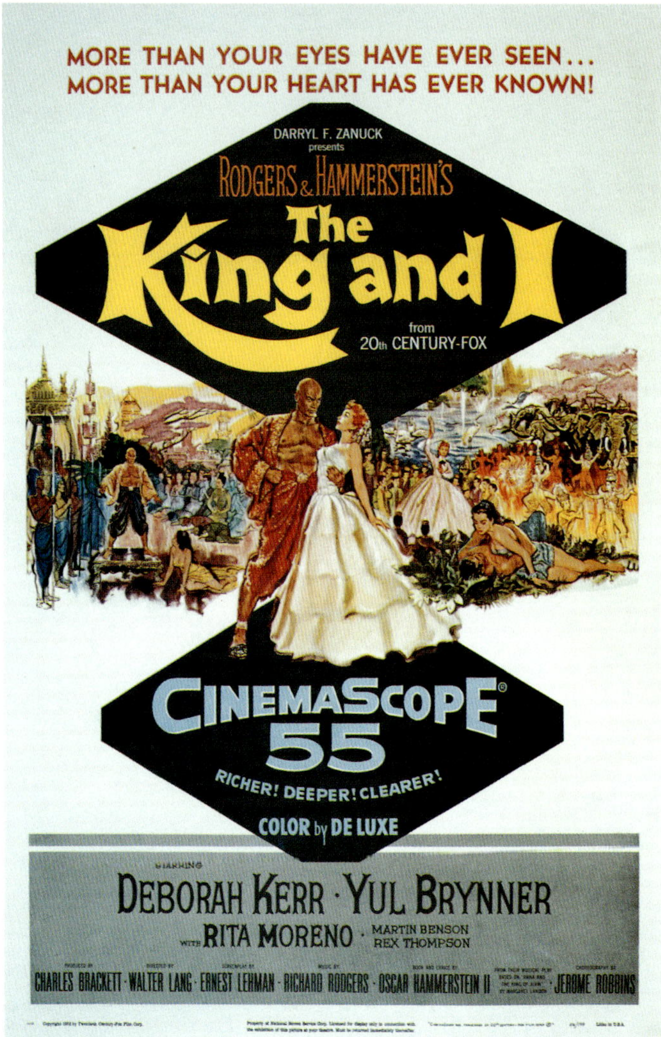

The King and I. 1956. One-sheet. $1,000-1,500

Chapter Five

Hollywood Evolves: The Sixties and Beyond

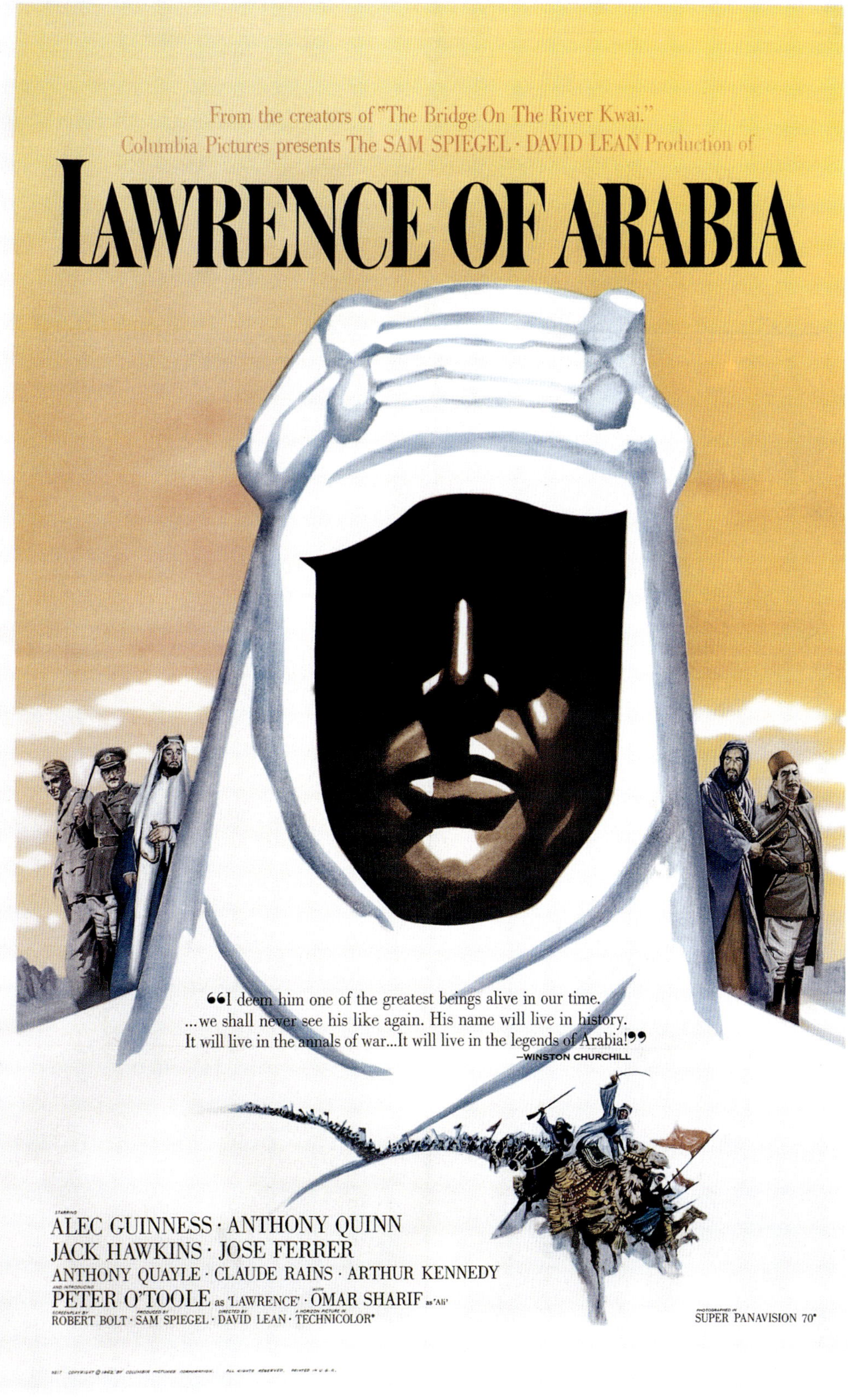

Lawrence of Arabia. 1962. One-sheet, road show version. $8,000-12,000

Hollywood movies and their posters reflected the changing times and attitudes perhaps more poignantly than ever during this period, as the very label "Hollywood" was starting to mean something quite different. More and more studios saw the benefits in increasing movie production abroad, given the costs involved at home, and turned to Europe and particularly England, whose film technicians were praised as being the best in the world. Increasingly the Hollywood studios reduced production in their back yards and became chiefly financiers and distributors, causing the boundaries of what is and what is not a Hollywood film to become very hazy indeed!

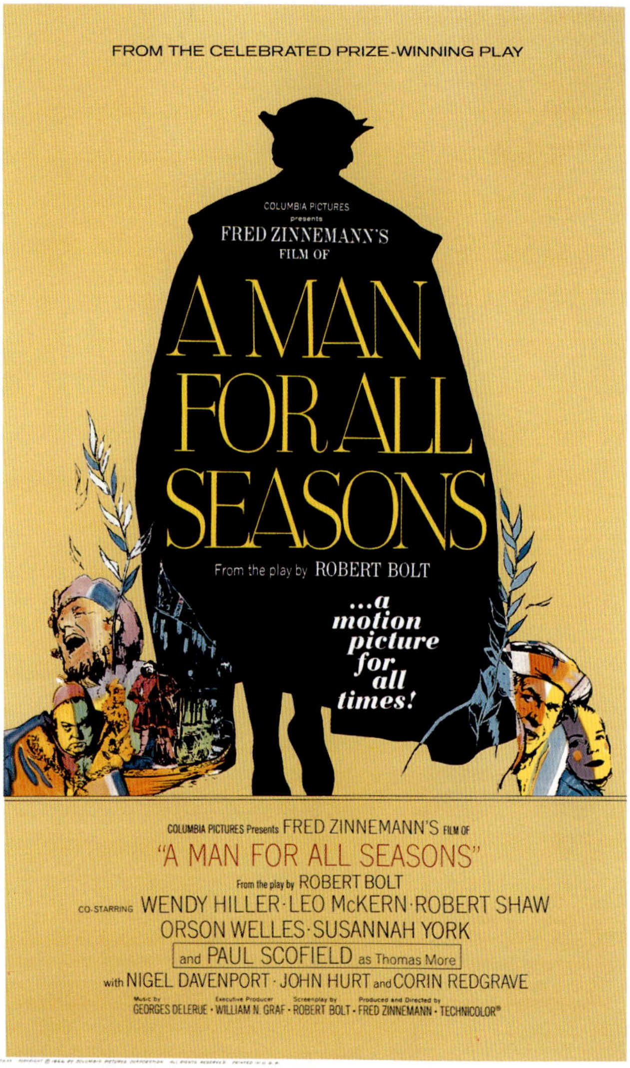

A Man for All Seasons. 1966. One-sheet, road show pre-awards version. $1,500-2,000

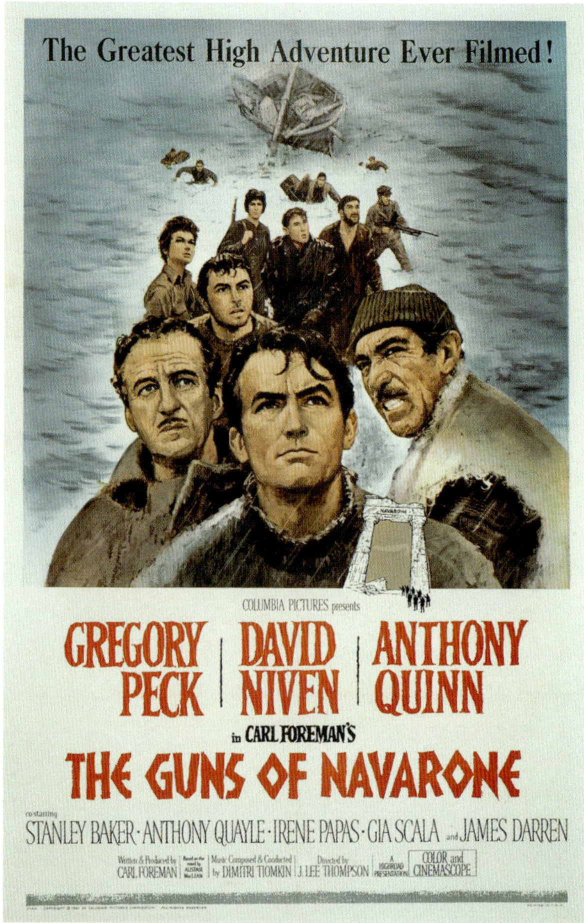

The Guns of Navarone. 1961. One-sheet. $700-1,200

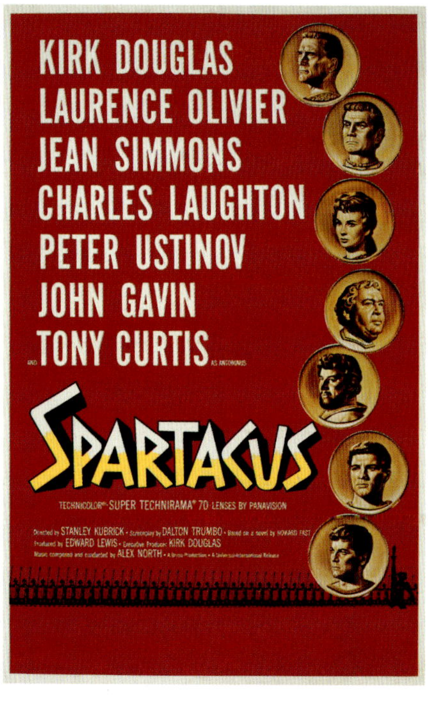

Spartacus. 1960. One-sheet, road show version. $800-1,200

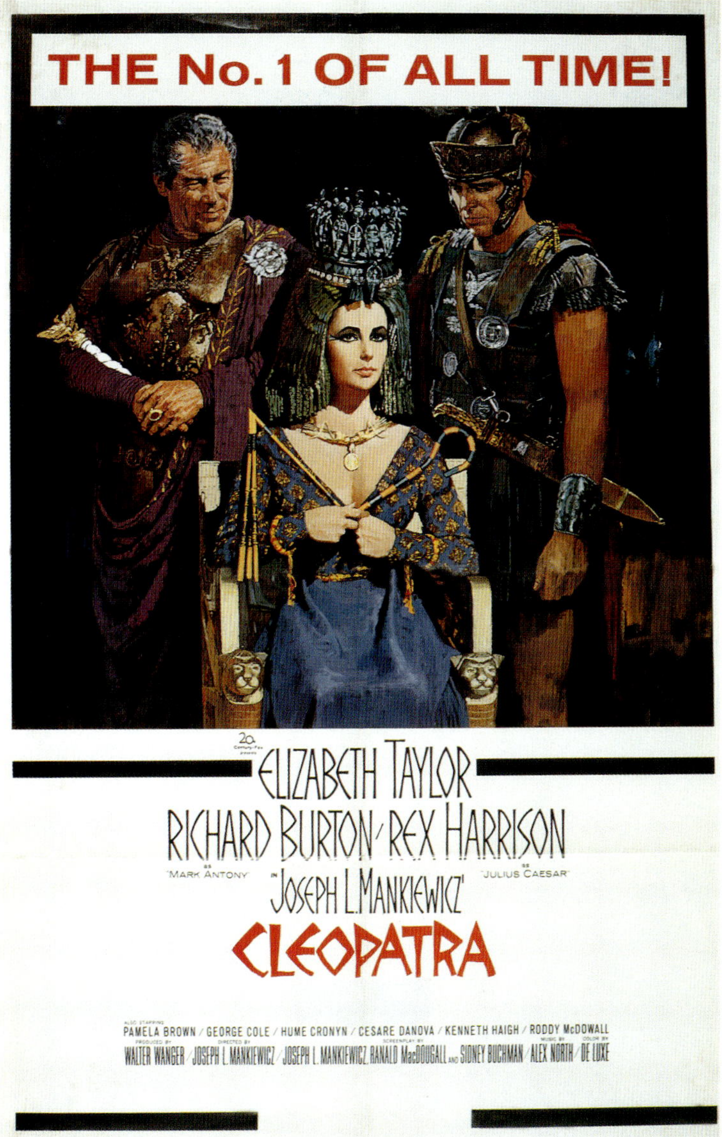

Cleopatra. 1963. One-sheet, road show version. $600-900

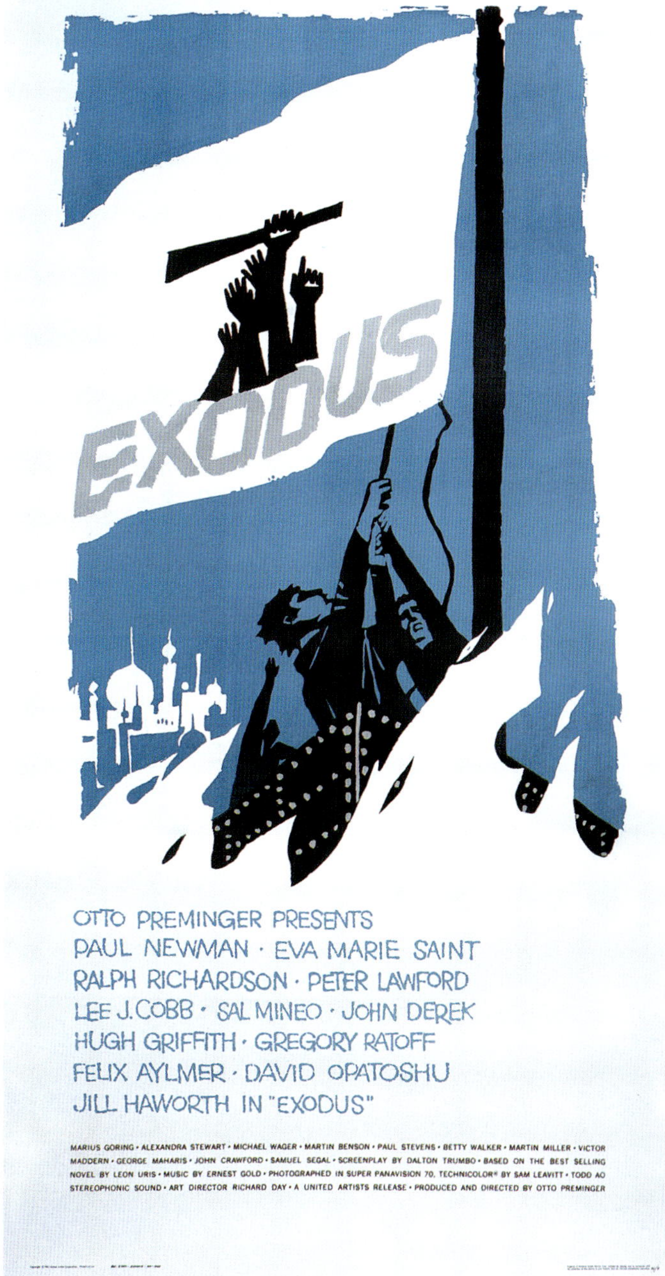

Exodus. 1961. Three-sheet, art by Saul Bass. $800-1,200

Dinosaurus! 1960. Three-sheet. $600-900

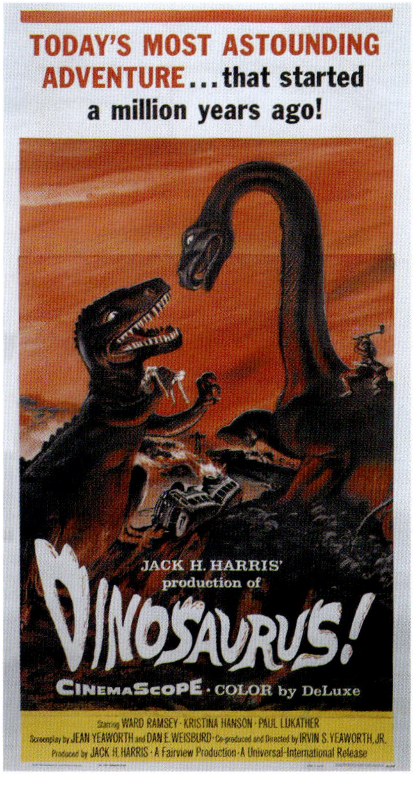

This change was down to a number of factors. As we have seen, throughout the 1950s the studios fought hard to maintain their power base, but reluctantly had to accept that those days were over. With the contract system gone (arguably the basis of their supreme power) and the rise of television, they diversified by backing independent movies, and making television programs. Some even sold valuable assets such as back lots, stages, and land to real estate developers. Other changes occurred as the weakened studios found themselves open to further corporate takeovers. The new owners, keen to exploit the most economically viable formula, favored less studio-bound and more location-based movie production.

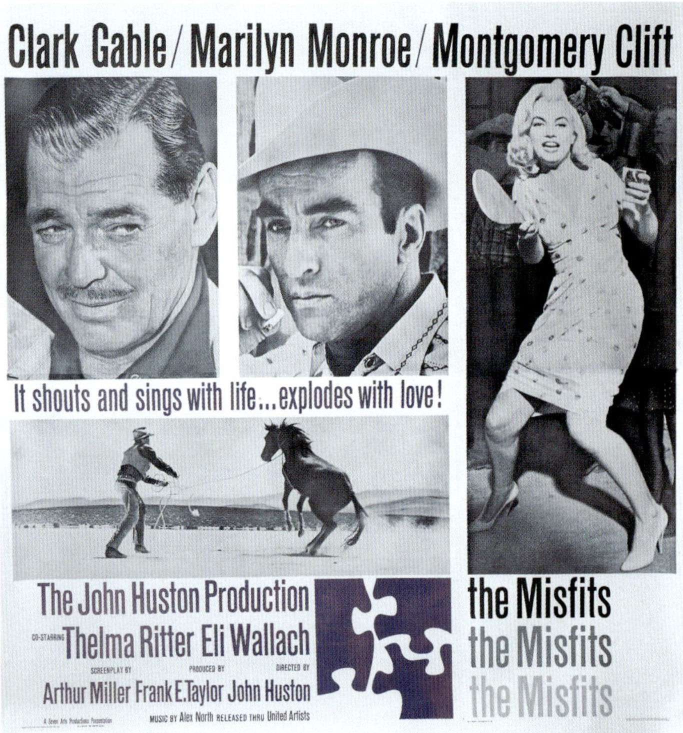

The Misfits. 1961. Six-sheet. $1,000-1,500

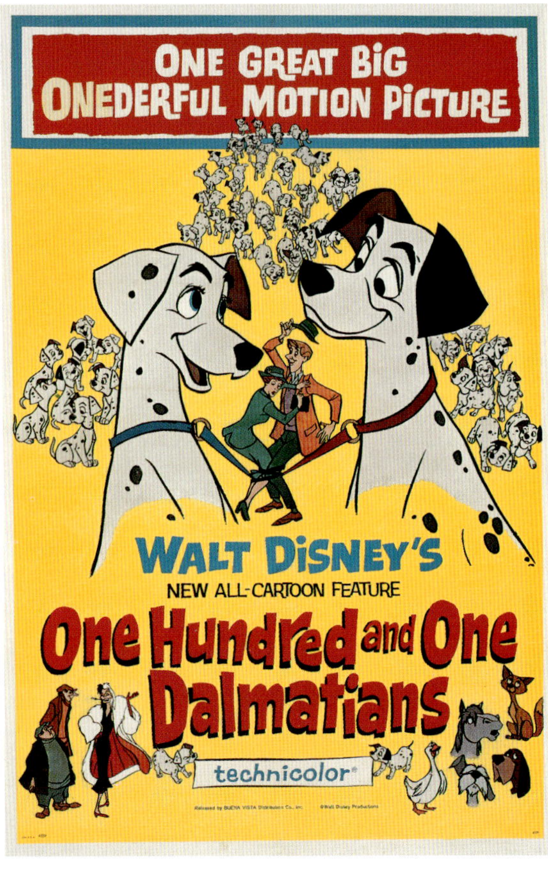

101 Dalmatians. 1961. One-sheet. $700-1,000

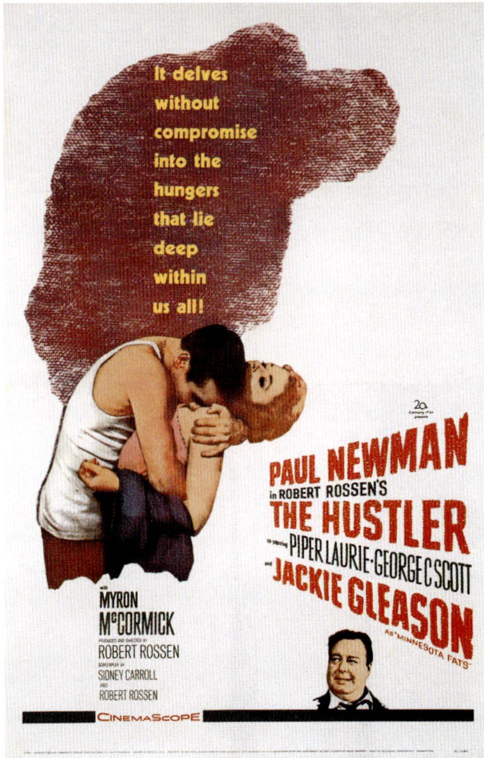

The Hustler. 1961. $500-800

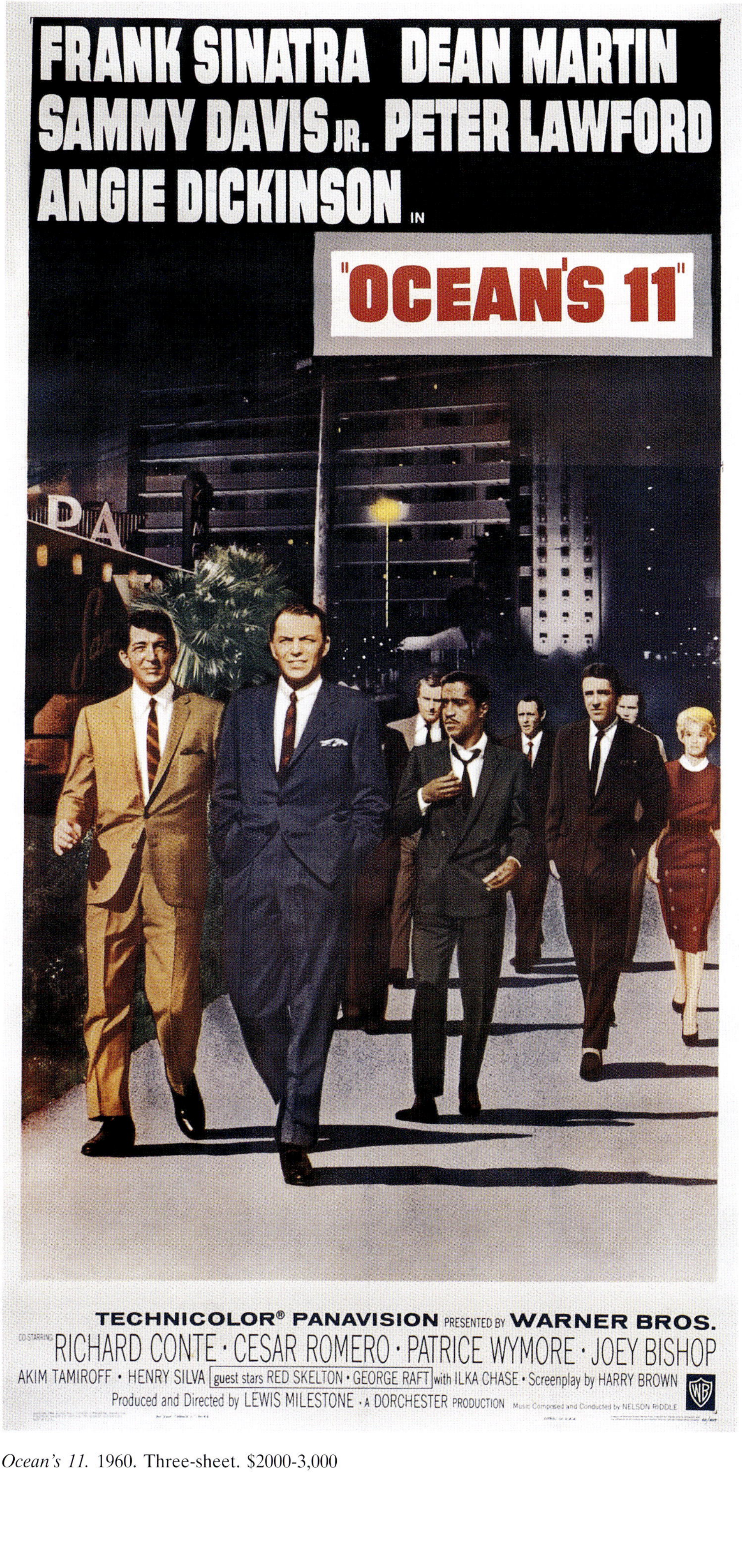

Ocean's 11. 1960. Three-sheet. $2000-3,000

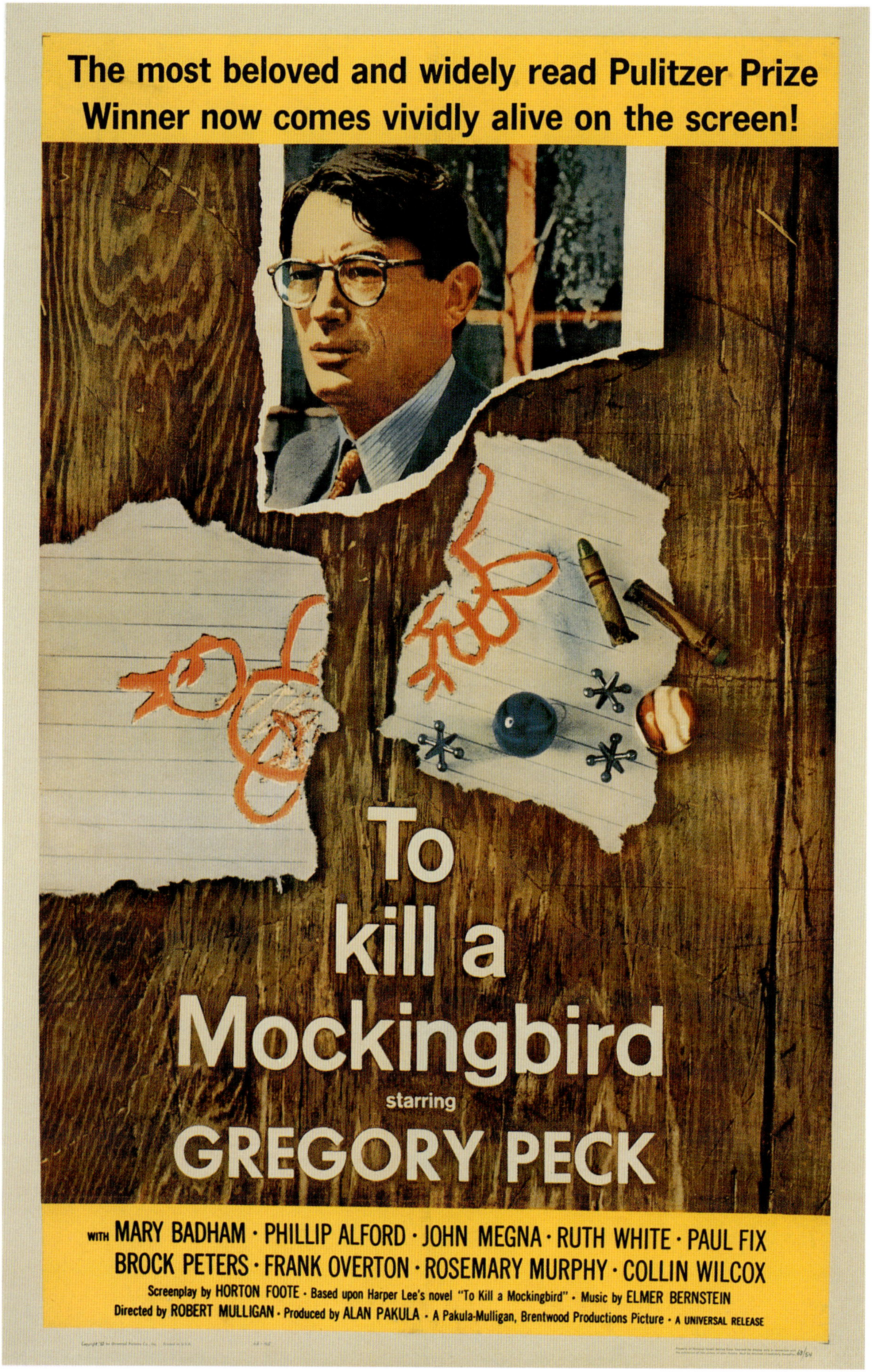

To Kill a Mockingbird. 1963. One-sheet. $1,500-2,000

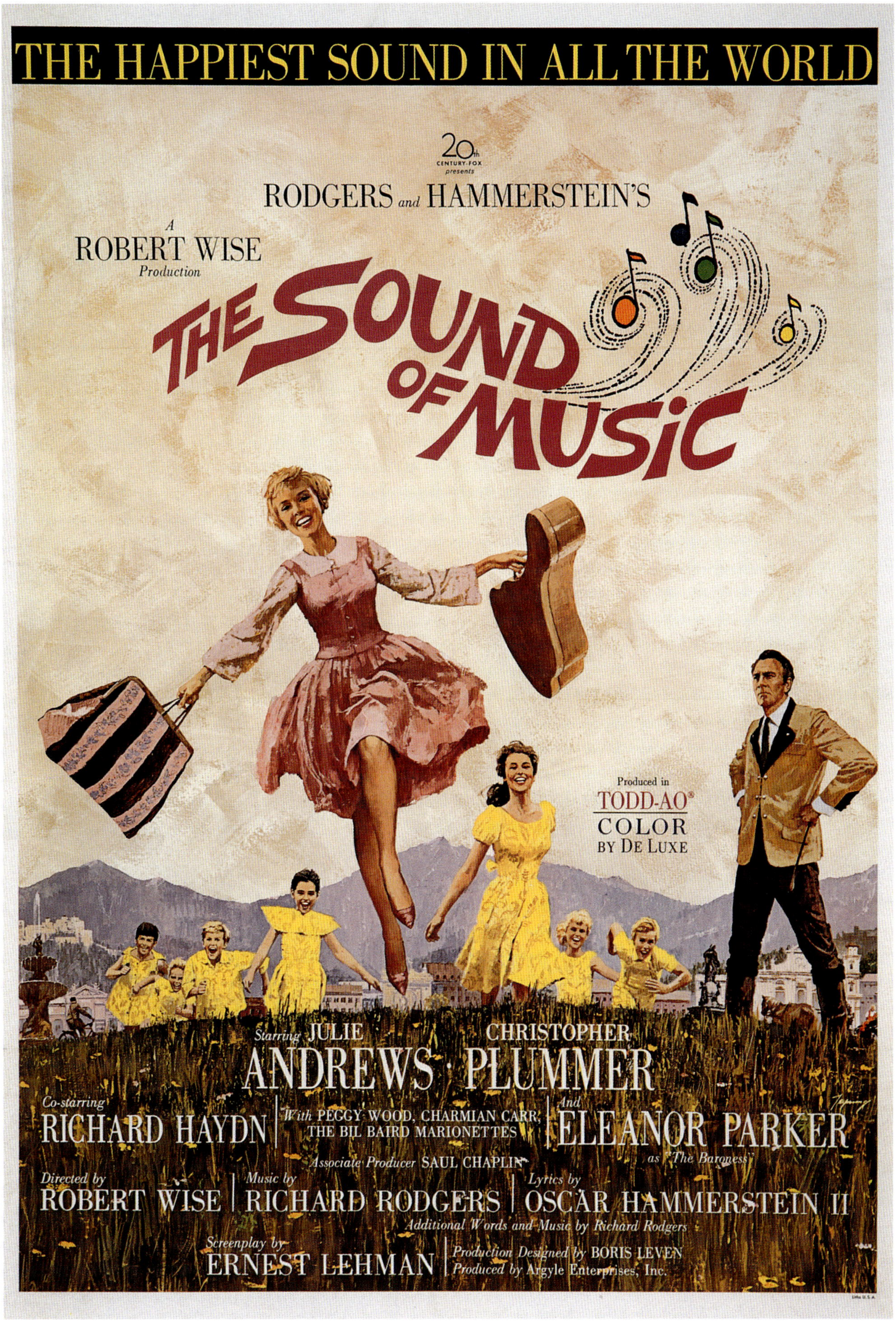

The Sound Of Music. 1965. One-sheet. $800-1,500

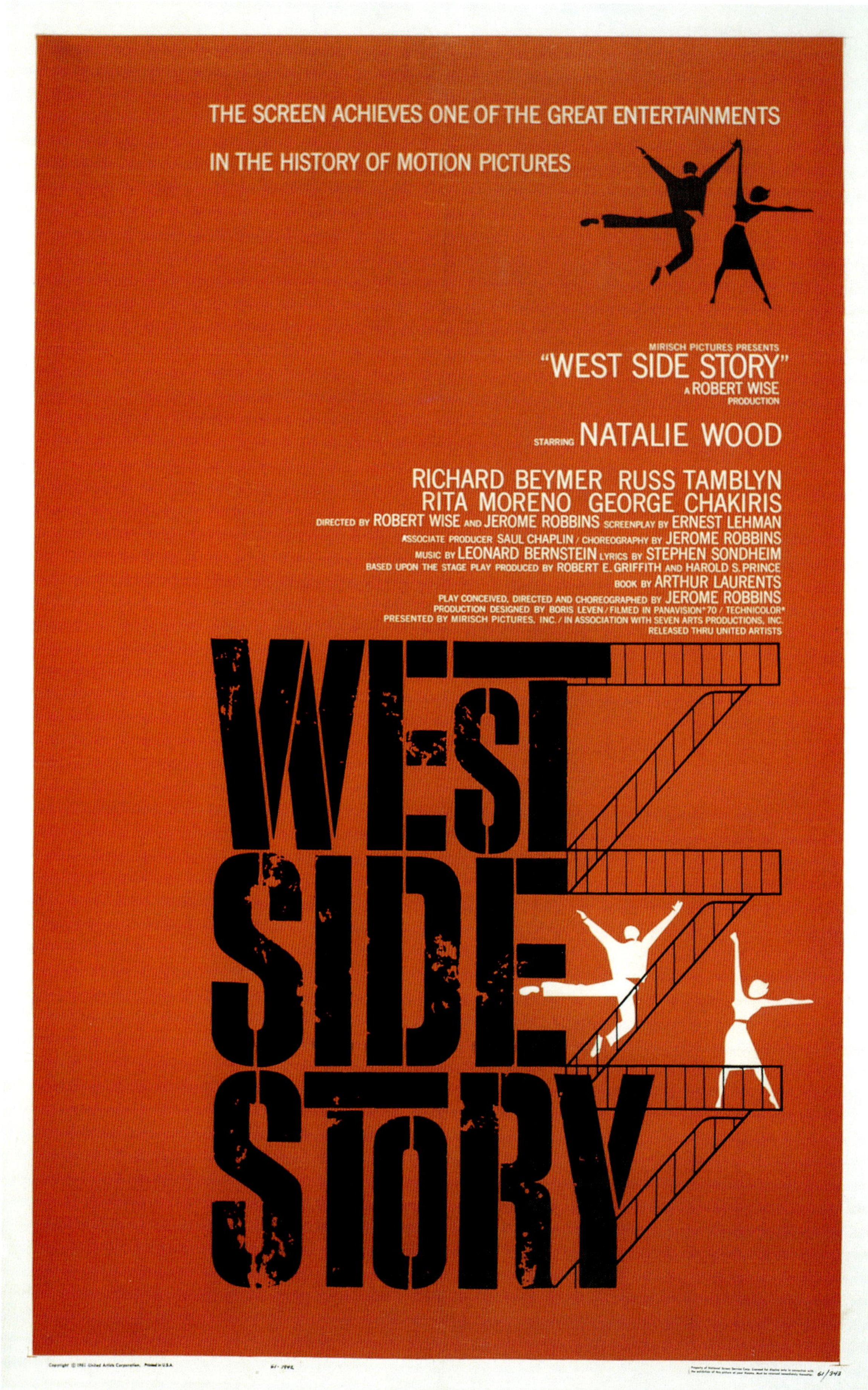

Westside Story. 1961. One-sheet, art by Saul Bass. $1,500-2,000

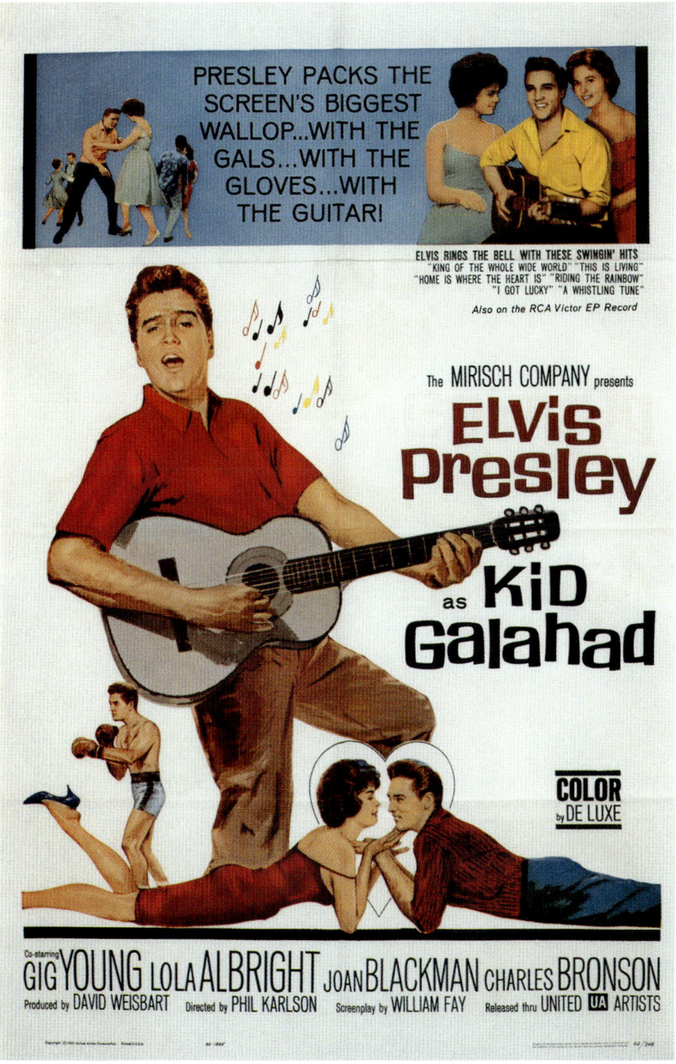

Kid Galahad. 1962. One-sheet. $800-1,200

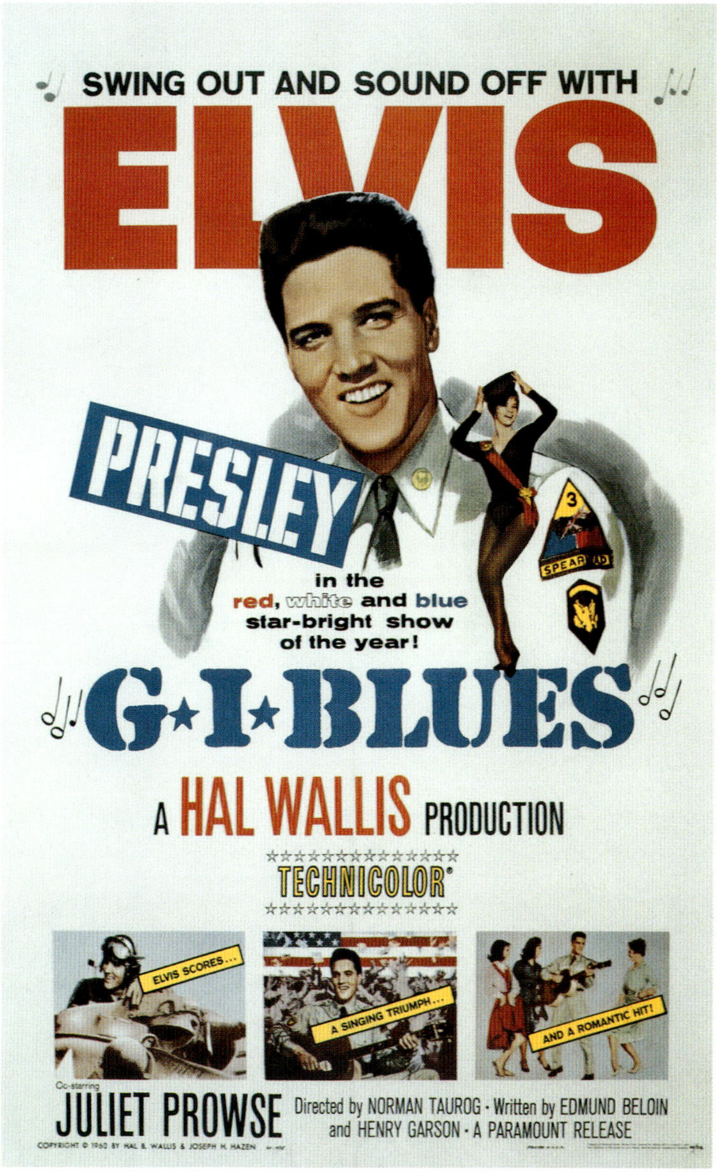

G.I. Blues. 1960. One-sheet. $700-1,000

The James Bond films, the most famous movie series of all time, benefitted greatly from this new attitude to filmmaking in the 1960s. Never before had audiences been treated to such a powerful cocktail of ingredients in one sitting. There were fantastic stories, exotic locations, spies, sex, and style. The early Bond films seemed to capture the essence of the exciting 1960s with Sean Connery perfect as the suave Martini-drinking, yet ruthless, British spy. United Artists financed these films with production being based in England at Pinewood Studios and on location.

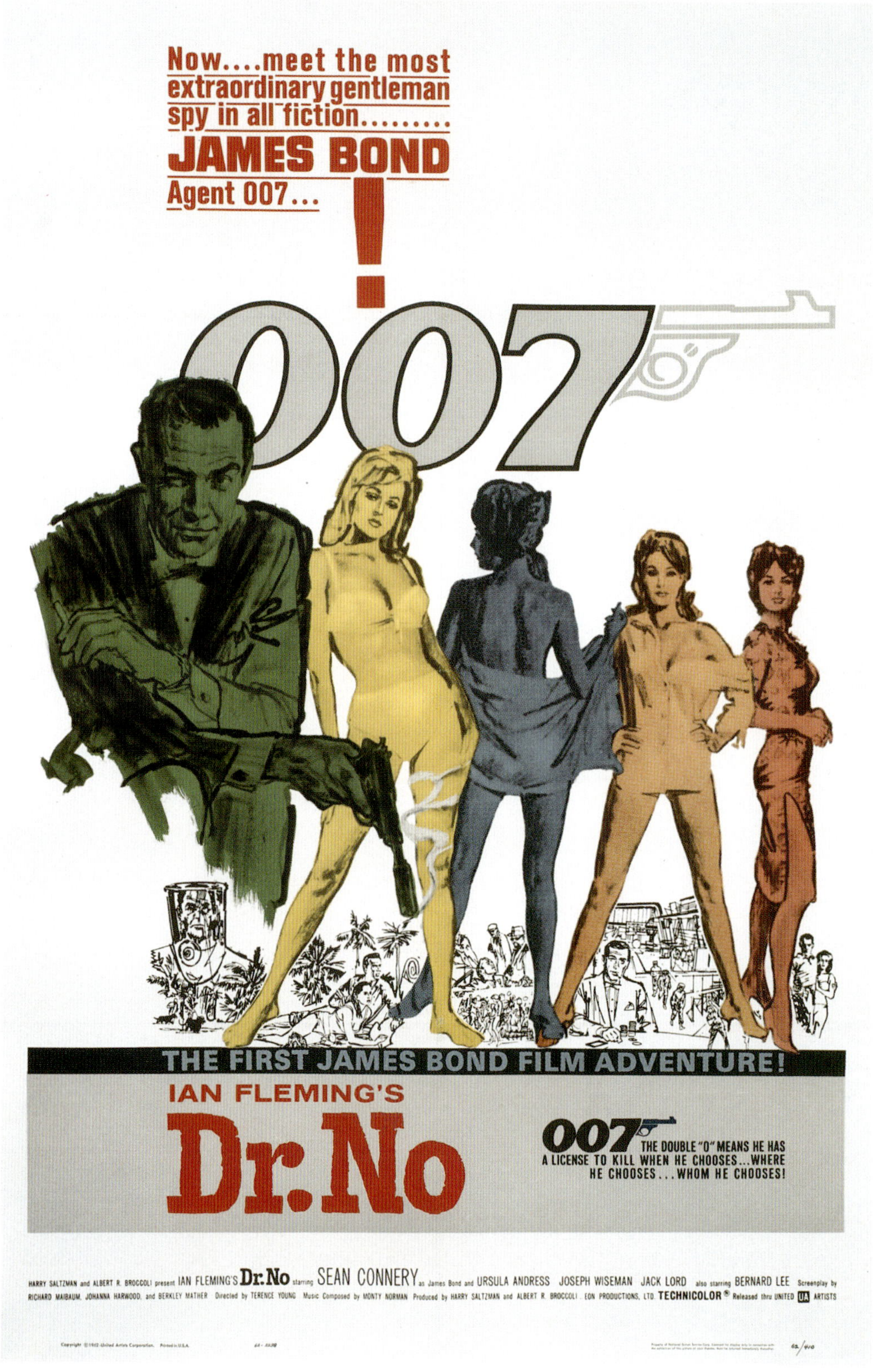

Dr. No. 1962. One-sheet. $1,500-2,500

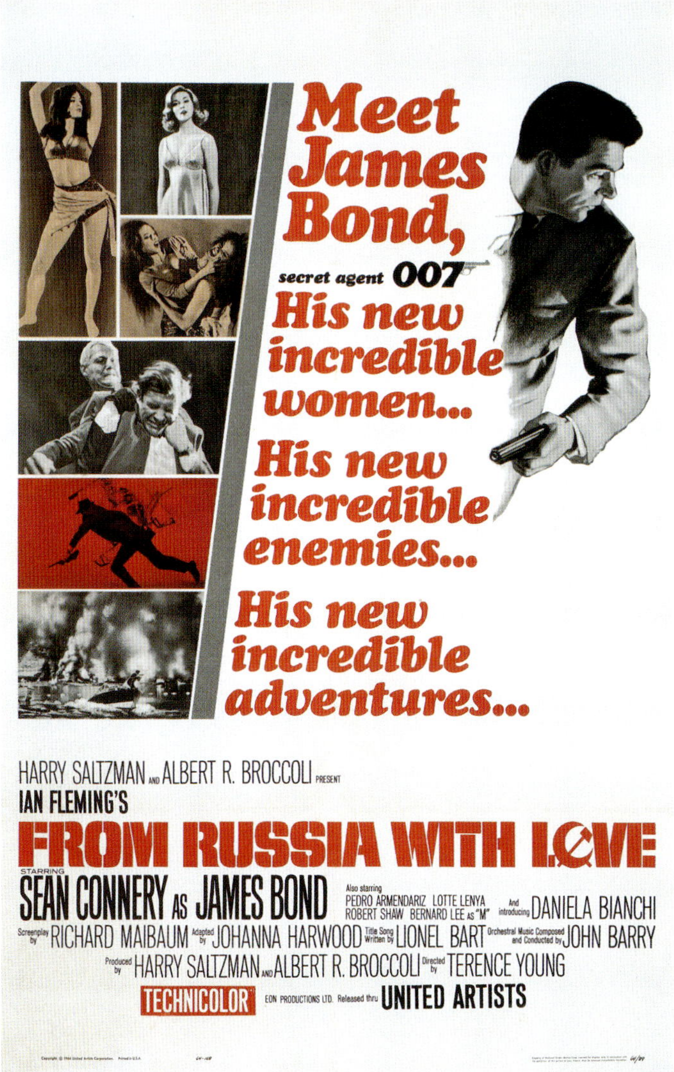

From Russia with Love. 1963. One-sheet, style A. $1,200-1,800

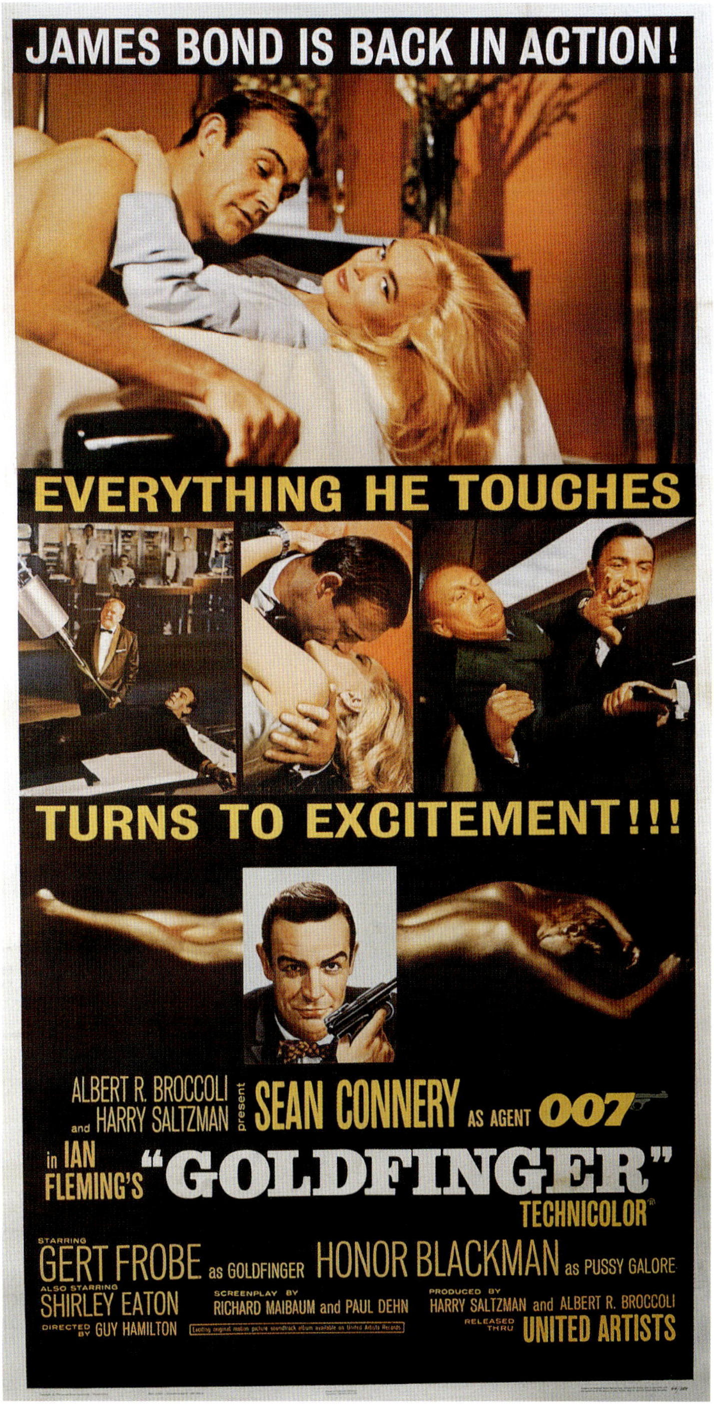

Goldfinger. 1964. Three-sheet. $1,500-2,000

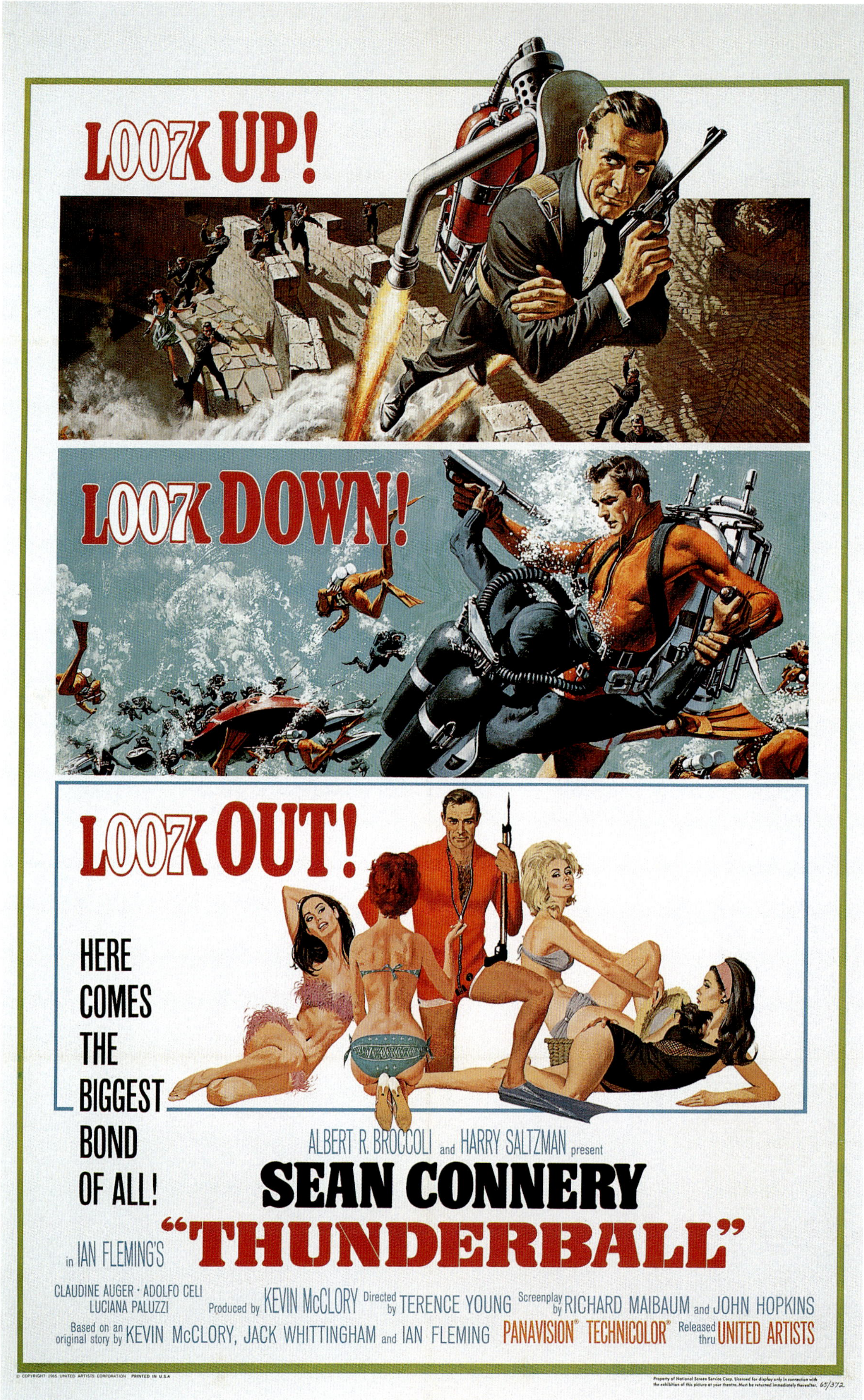

Thunderball. 1965. One-sheet. $1,000-1,500

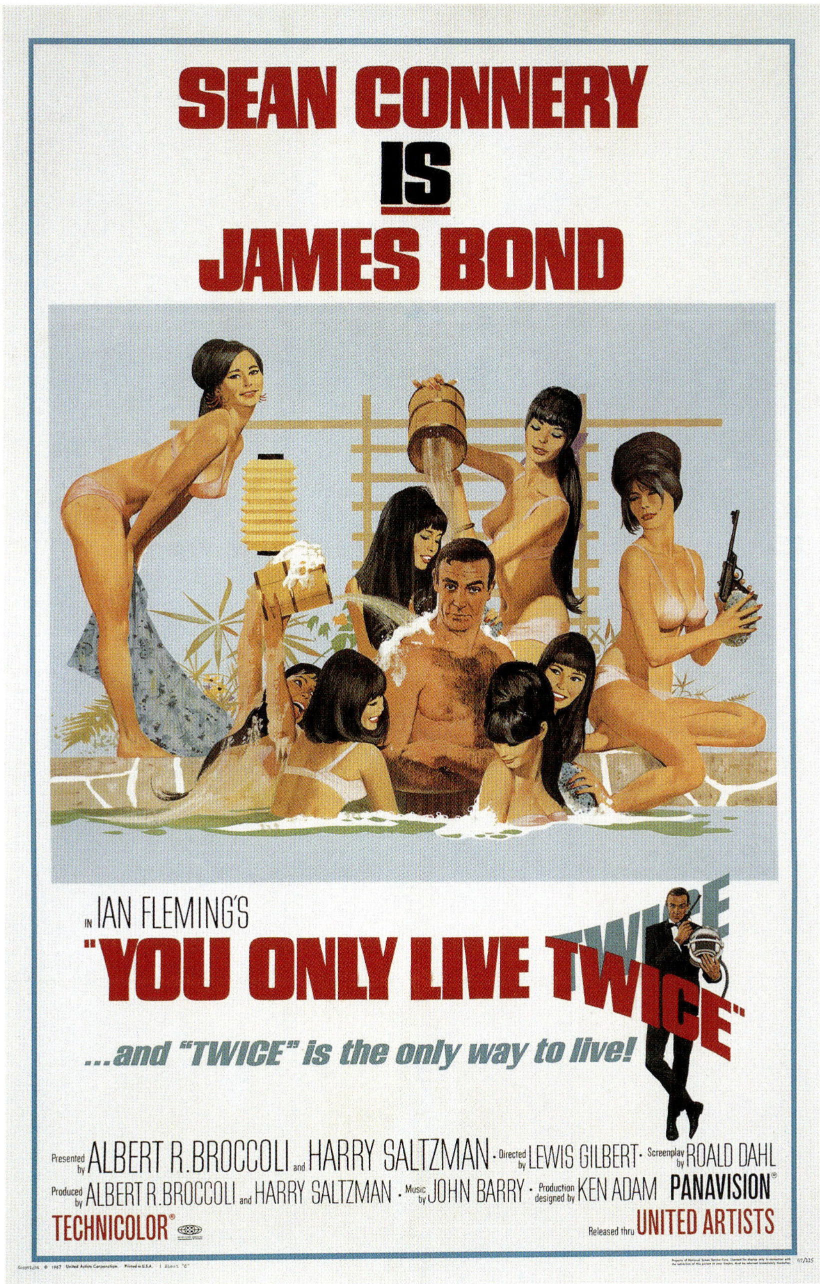

You Only Live Twice. 1967. One-sheet, style C. $1,000-1,500

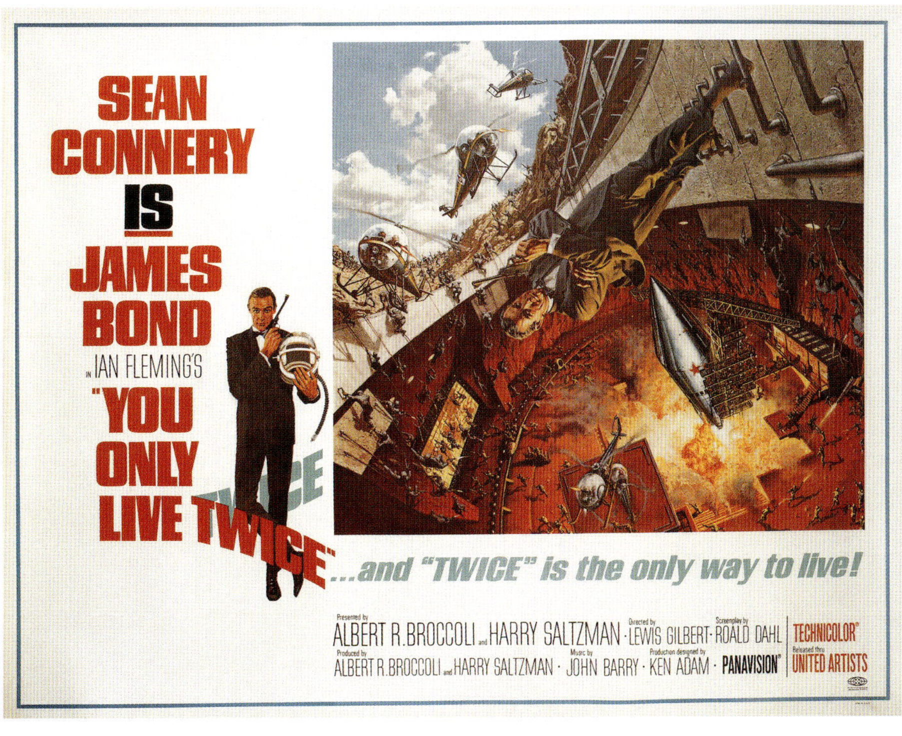

You Only Live Twice. 1967. Subway poster. $1,200-1,800

The cold war was to reach its height during this decade and audiences seemed enthralled by the antics of espionage. James Bond was the first in a long line of spying action heroes, a concept to which we are now so accustomed that we fail to see the novelty value, but then was decidedly in vogue. Other celluloid spies appeared on the scene in the form of James Coburn in the tongue-in-cheek Flint films; Dean Martin as Matt Helm; and Robert Vaughan and David McCallum in the *Man from Uncle* films. The direct antithesis to James Bond was intelligent, rebellious, working-class, British spy, Harry Palmer, played by Michael Caine. Produced by Harry Saltzman and made by other James Bond stalwarts, the three Palmer films display a grittier edge to the spy game but in some ways no less fantastical than Bond, particularly with the final film *The Billion Dollar Brain* (1967). It was the likes of Richard Burton, in the grimly realistic *The Spy Who Came In From The Cold,* (1965) who brought the seedy truthfulness of it all to the audience in no uncertain terms.

Using England for extensive filmmaking also brought English actors wholesale to American audiences for the first time. The trek to Hollywood for recognition no longer seemed necessary with Hollywood venturing to leafy English country studios. Consequently, some actors were catapulted to the top long before they took one step along Hollywood Boulevard, notably Peter O'Toole, Richard Burton, Albert Finney, Michael Caine, and Richard Harris.

The desire to create historical narratives continued unabated, the genre perhaps culminating with David Lean's grand *Lawrence Of Arabia* (1962). U.S. producer Sam Spiegel first collaborated with Lean on the award winning *The Bridge On the River Kwai* (1958). This successful partnership, backed by Columbia, moved to the epic exploits in the Middle East of the British academic and eccentric soldier T. E. Lawrence. The film became a multi Academy Award winner and made its unknown central lead, Peter O'Toole, an instant international star.

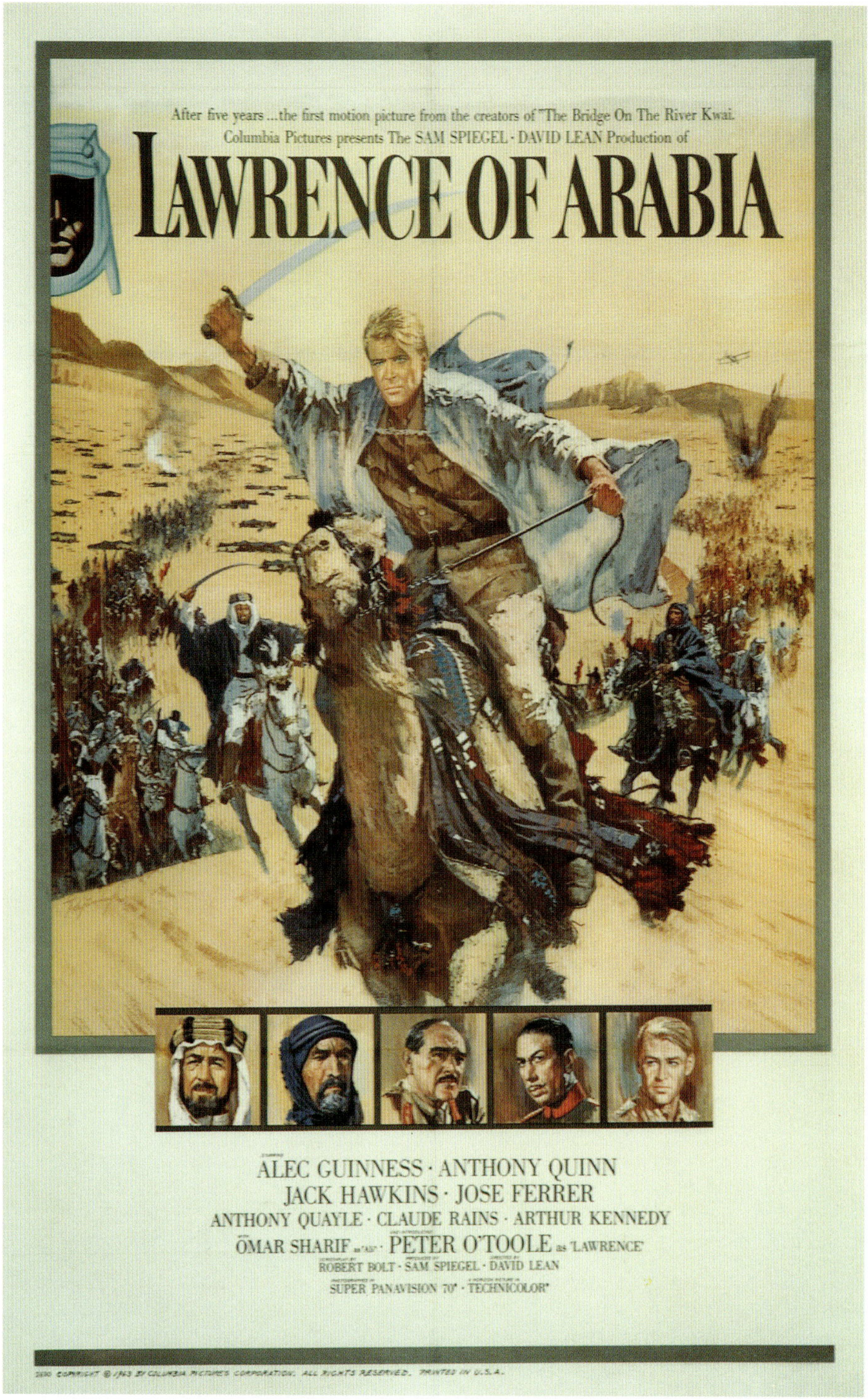

Lawrence of Arabia. 1962. One-sheet, style A. $5,000-8,000

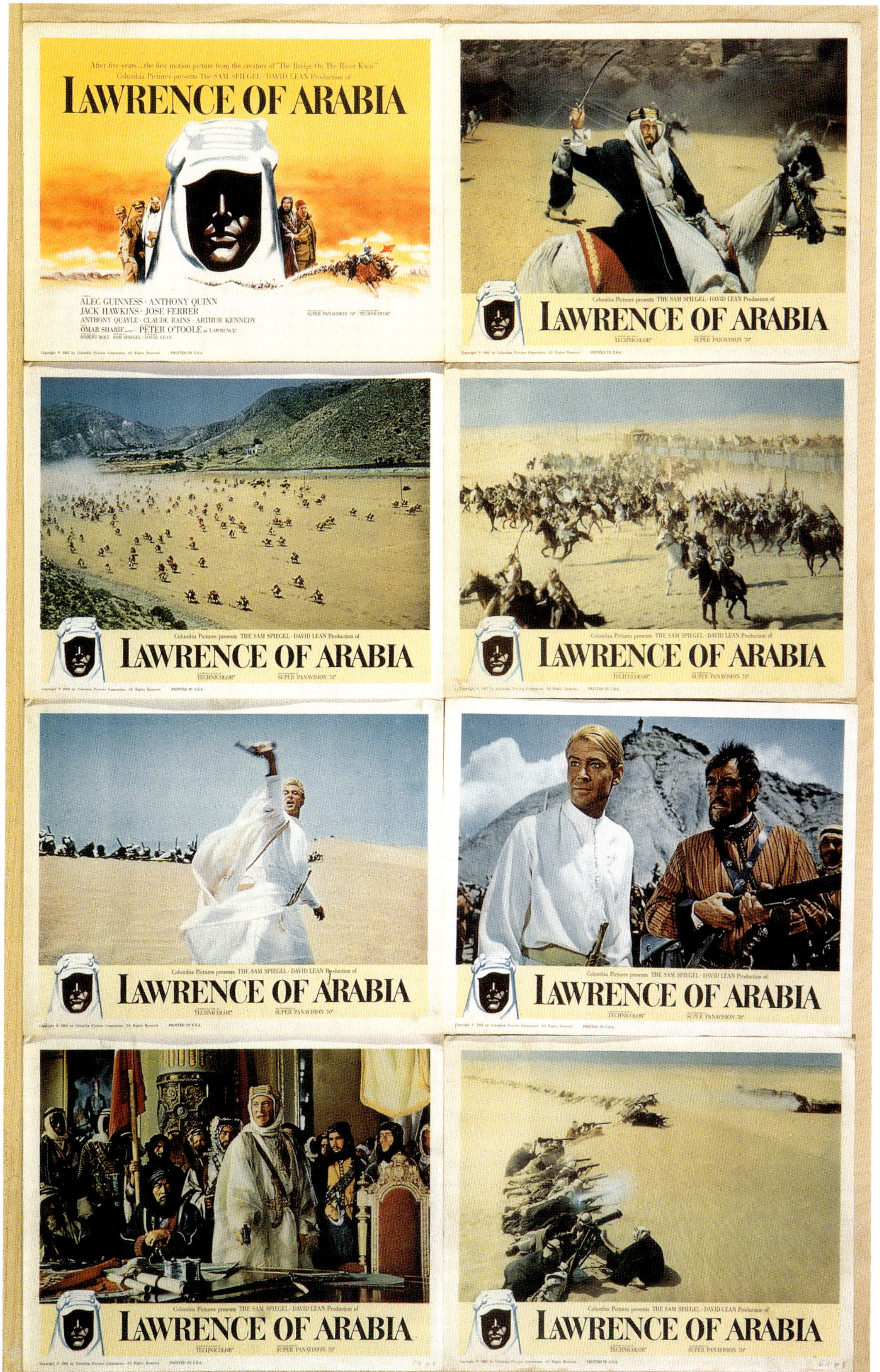

Lawrence of Arabia. 1962. Set of lobby cards. $3,000-5,000

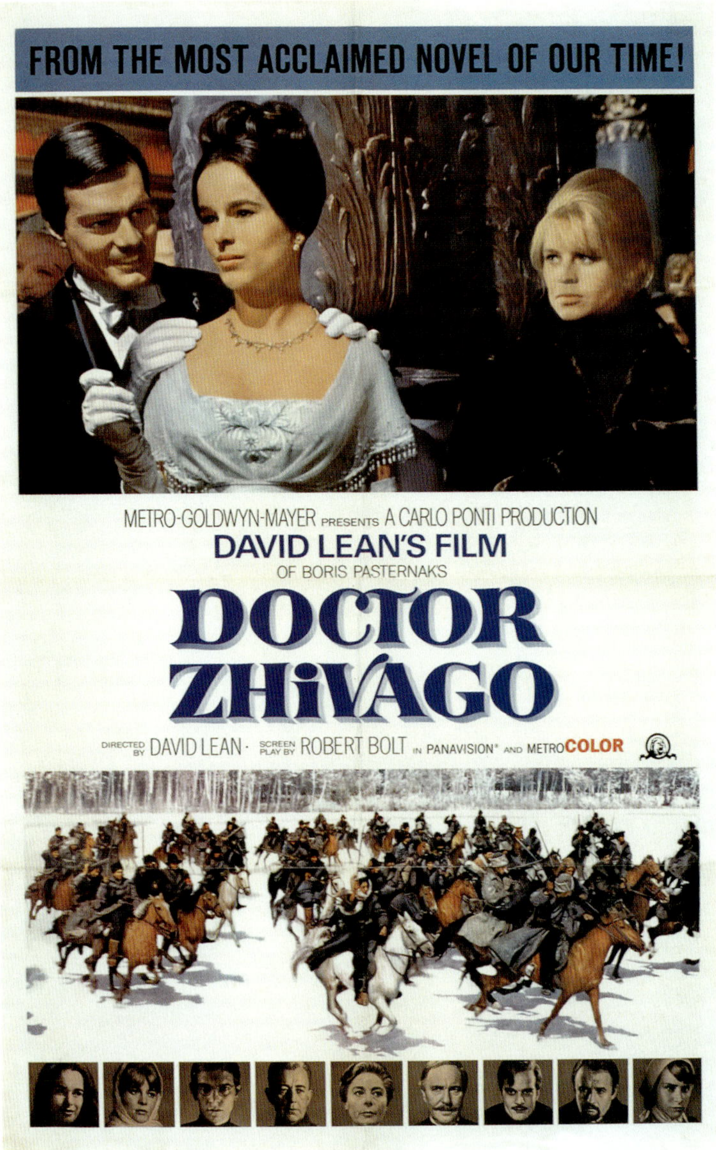

Doctor Zhivago. 1965. One-sheet, style B. $1,000-1,500

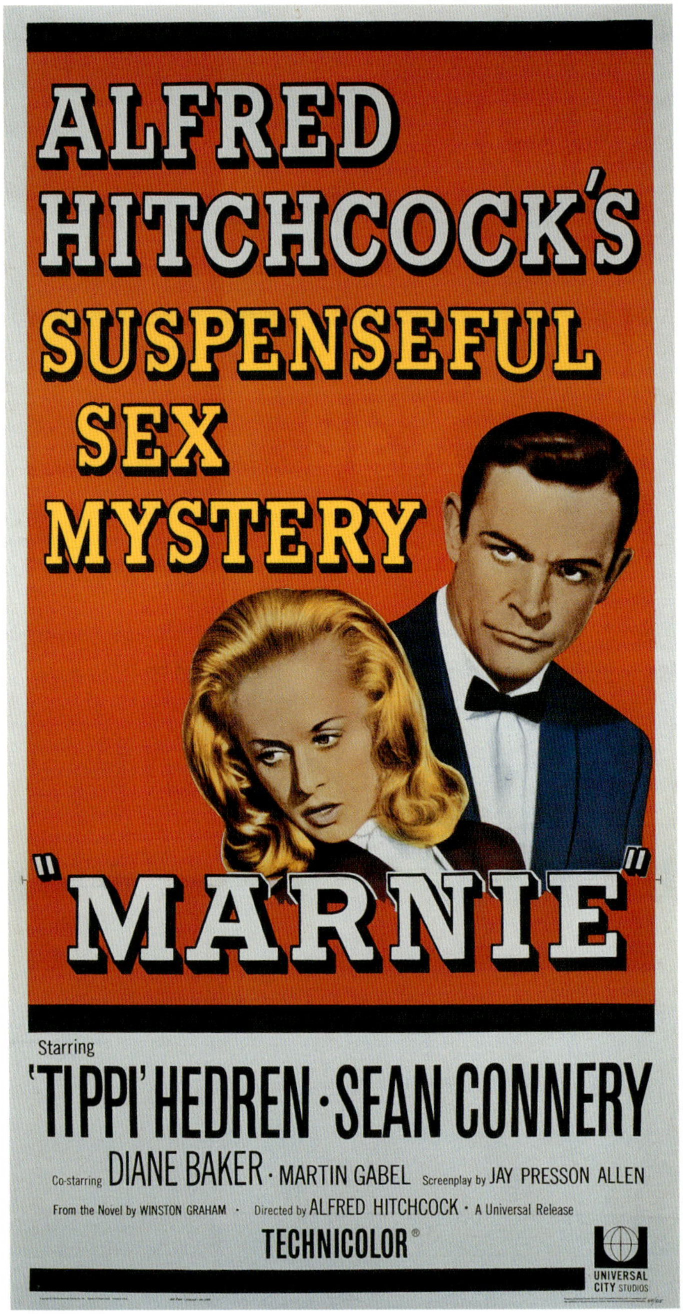

Marnie. 1964. Three-sheet. $800-1,200

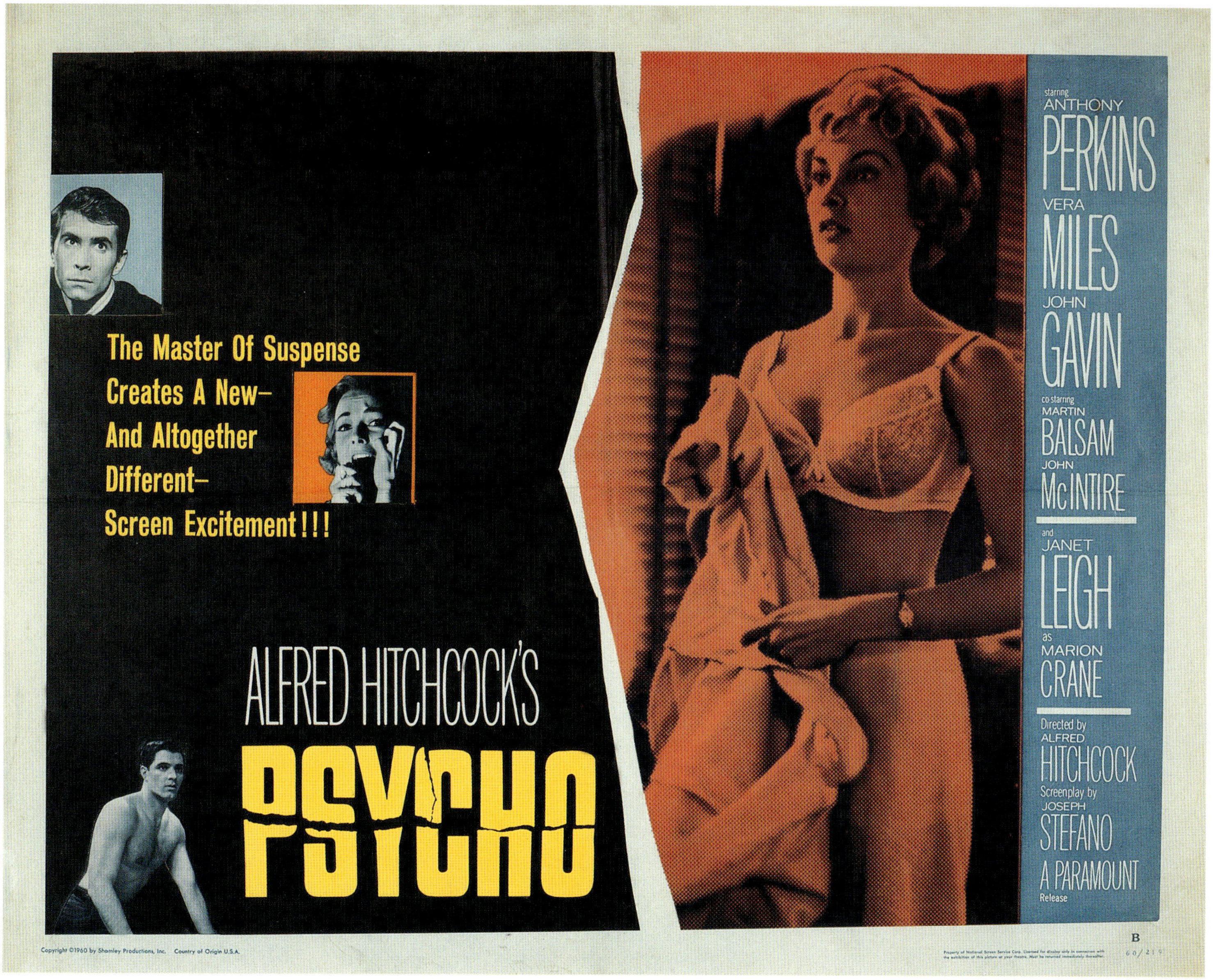

Psycho. 1960. Half-sheet, style B. $1,500-2,000

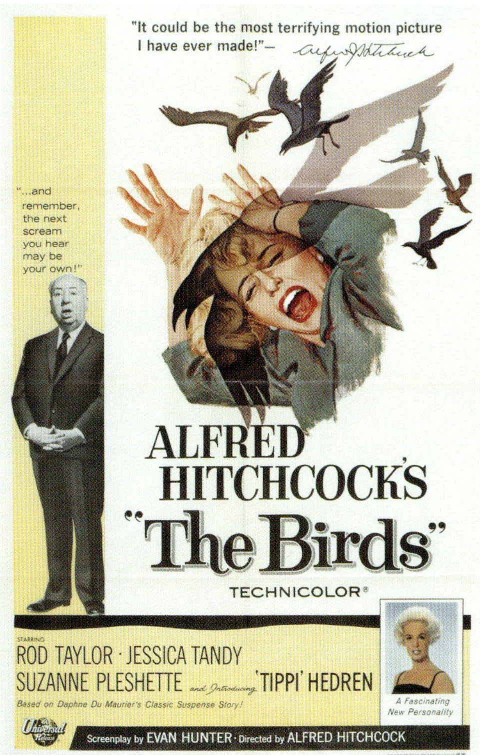

The Birds. 1963. One-sheet. $900-1,200

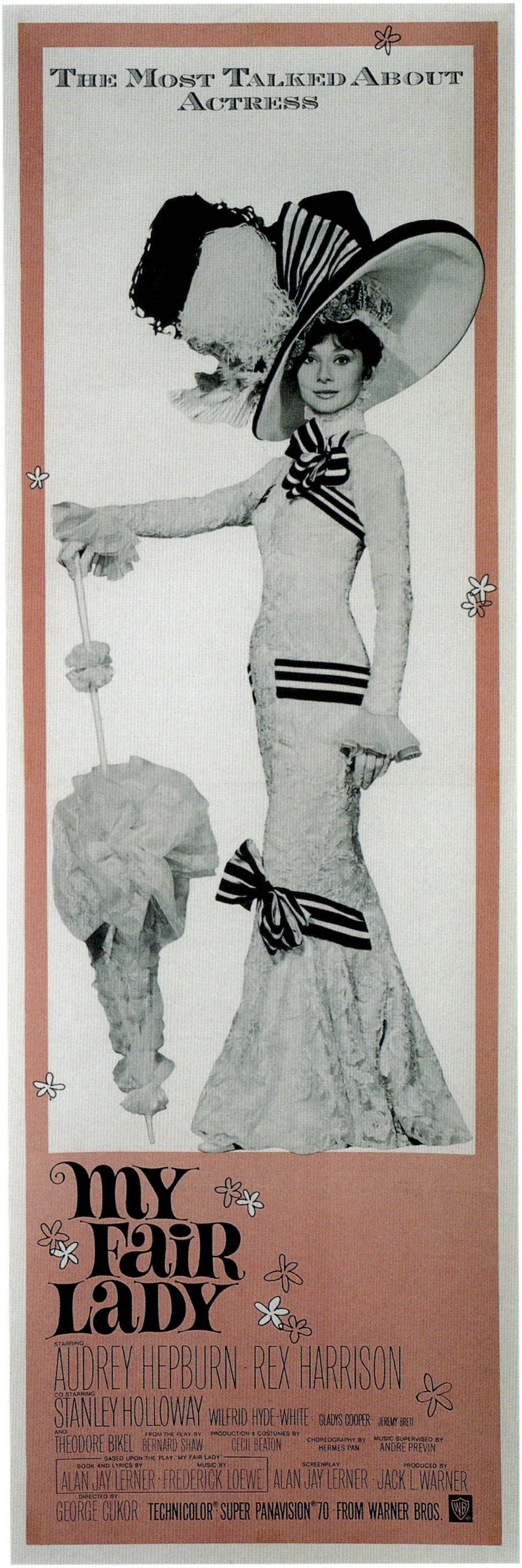

My Fair Lady. 1965. Door panel, photograph by Cecil Beaton. $9,00-1,200

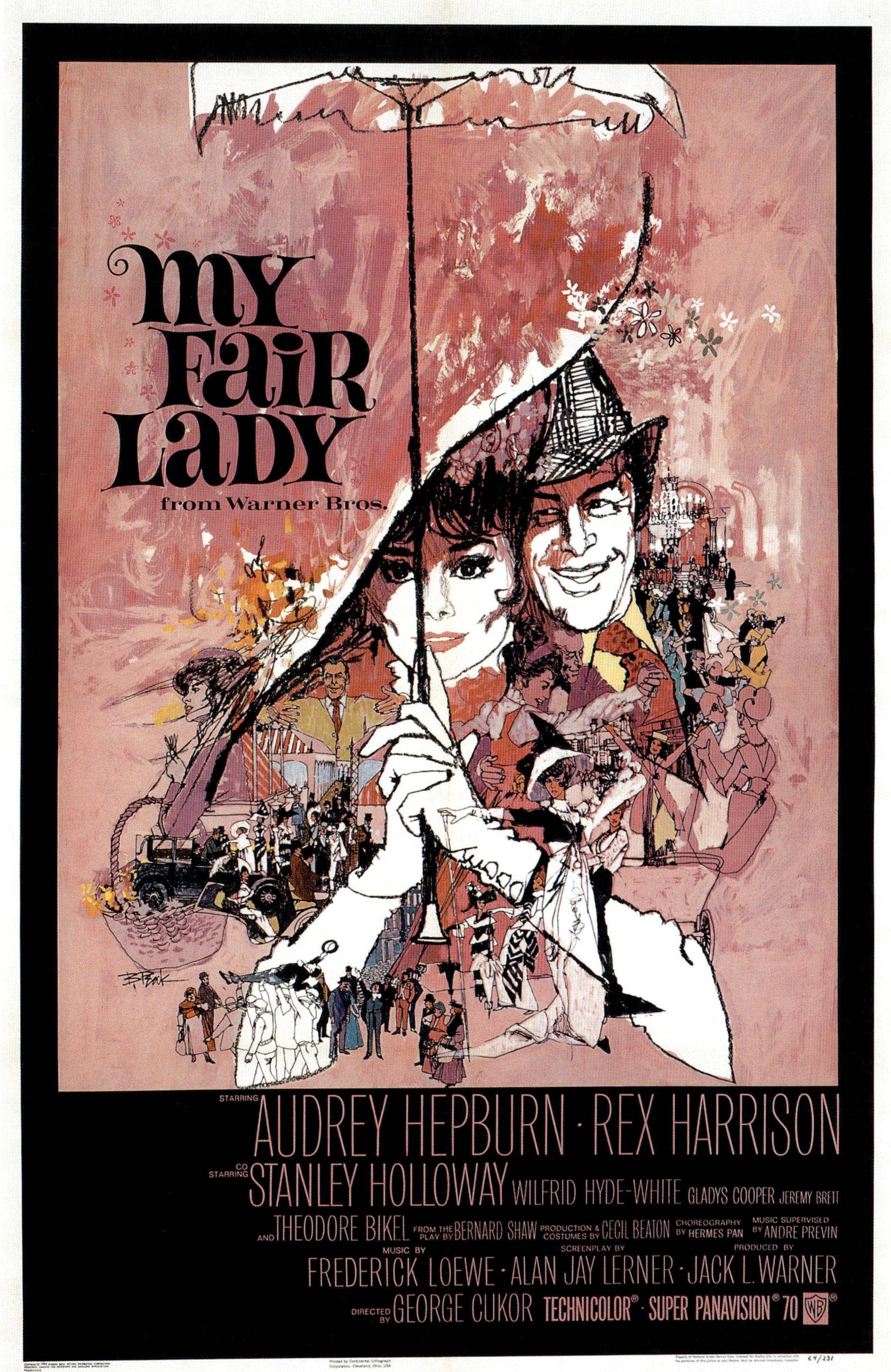

My Fair Lady. 1965. One-sheet, art by Bob Peak. $1,000-1,500

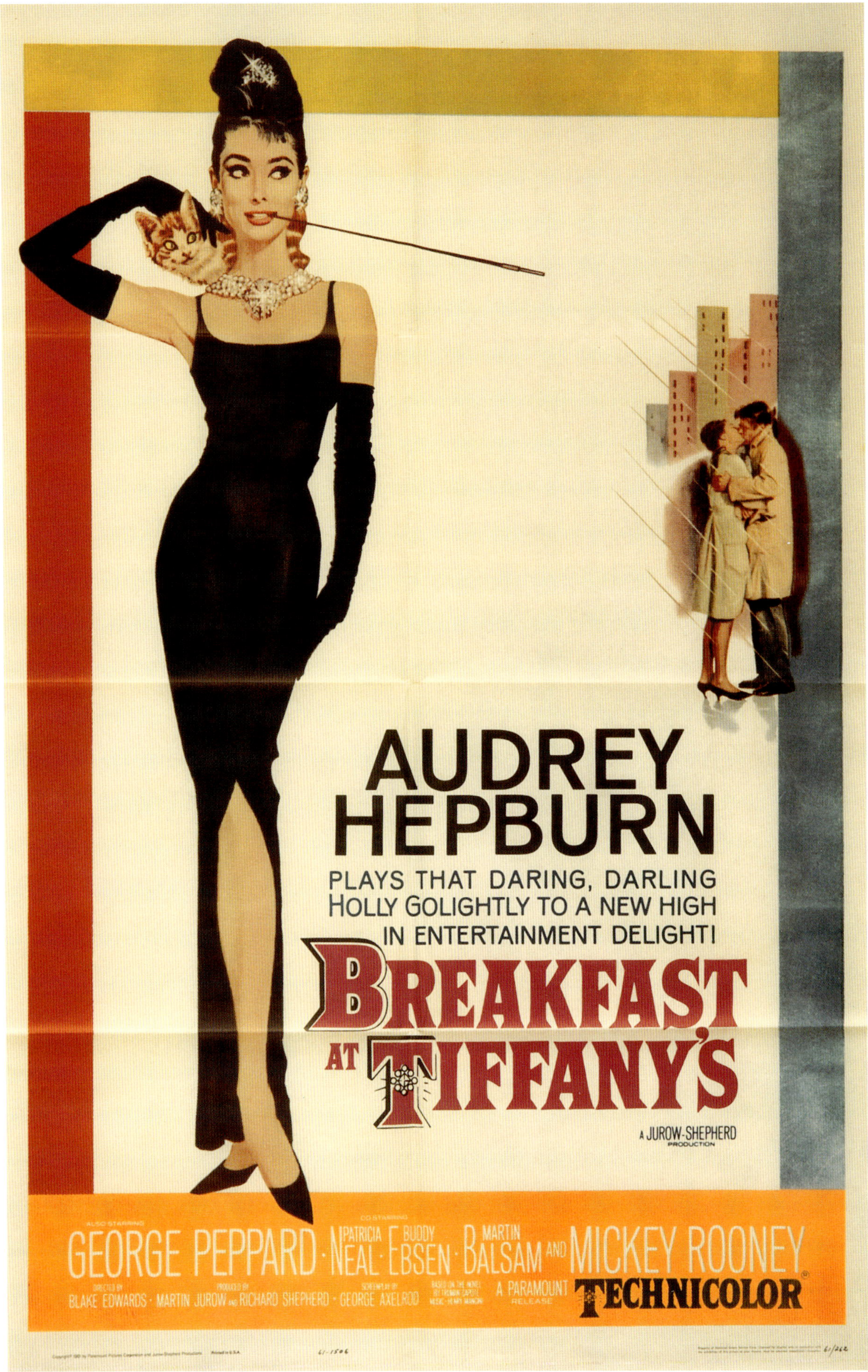

Breakfast at Tiffany's. 1964. One-sheet. $5,000-8,000

As the 1960s progressed, though, Hollywood was mindful of changing attitudes and tended to shift emphasis to more controversial subjects than empire-building in the desert. Both *Bonnie and Clyde* and *The Graduate* released in 1967 reflected the increasing size and influence of the youth audience; a growing market to be taken more seriously than ever before. Both movies were criticized for their antiestablishment stance; not only were gangsters glamorous, young, and socially rebellious but college graduates were rejecting their adoring parents and promising careers to find salvation in love.

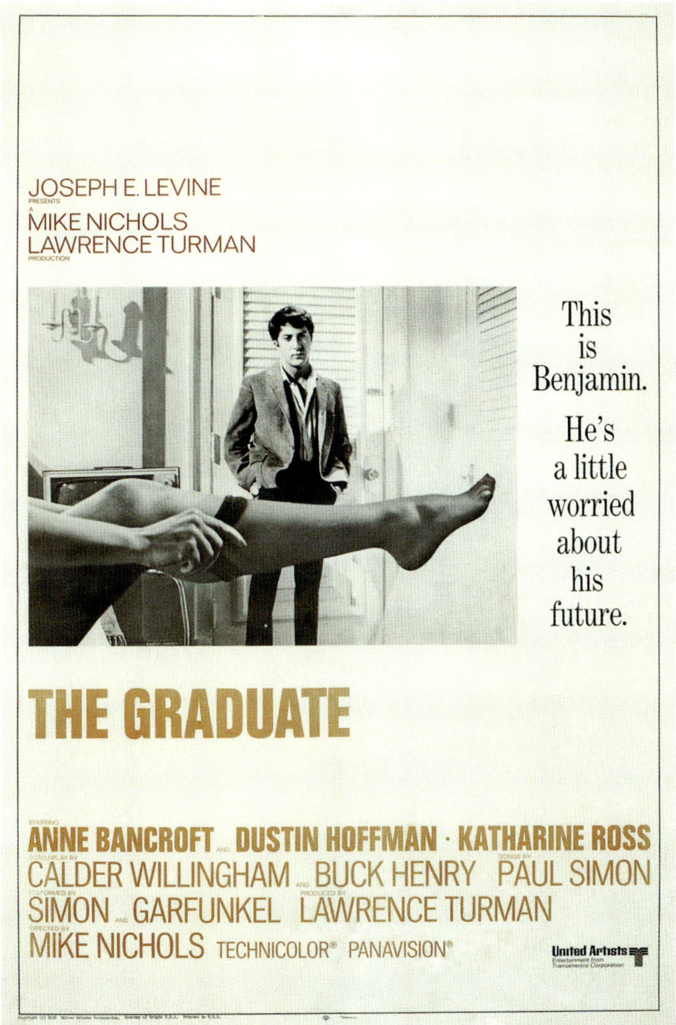

The Graduate. 1968. One-sheet. 1,500-2,500

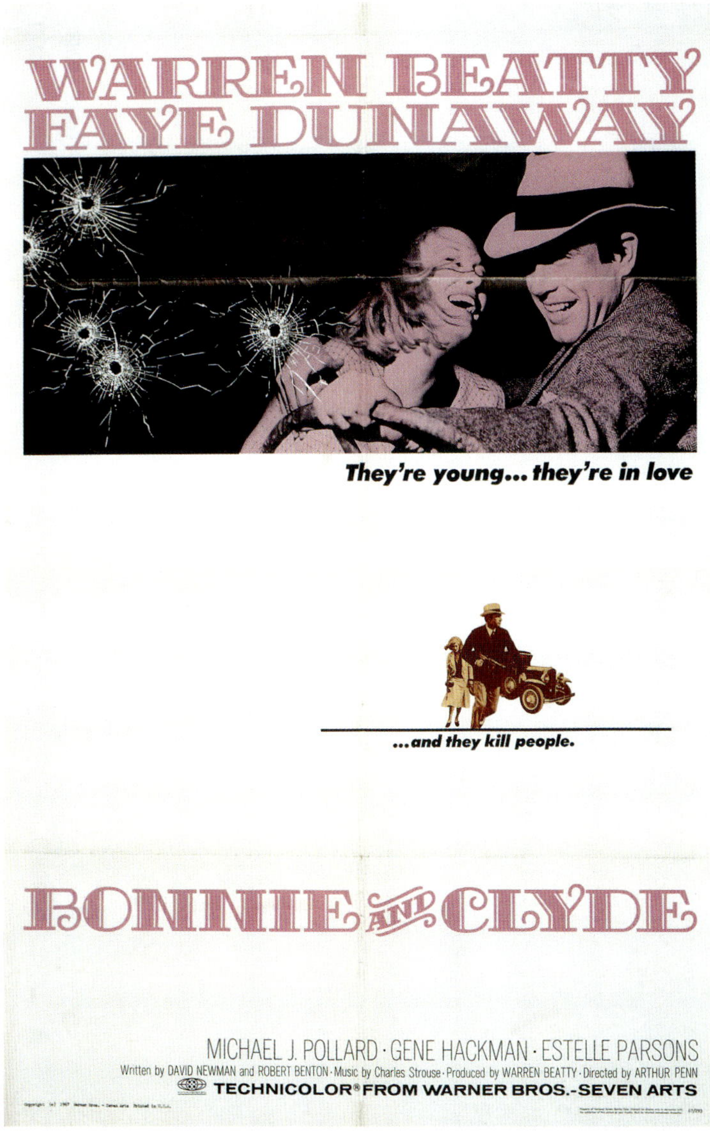

Bonnie and Clyde. 1967. One-sheet. $1,200-1,800

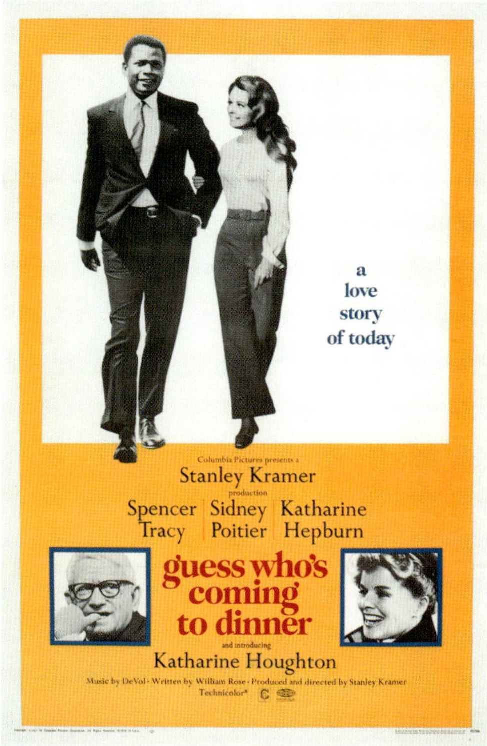

Guess Who's Coming to Dinner. 1967. One-sheet. $800-1200

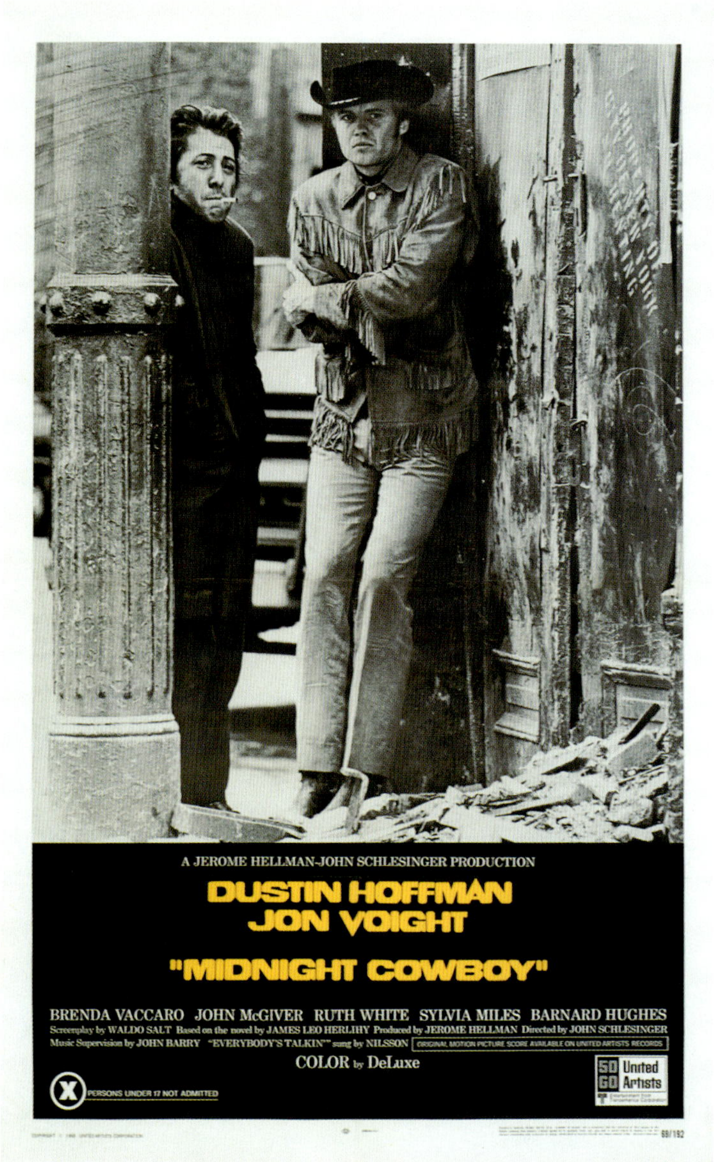

Midnight Cowboy. 1969. One-sheet. $1,200-1,800

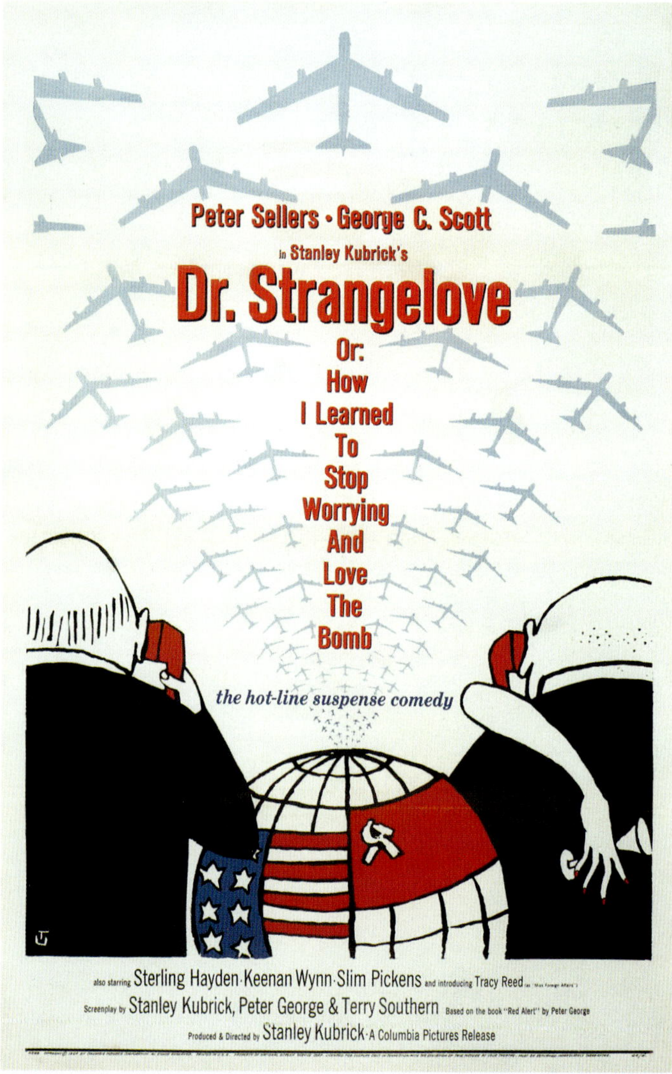

Dr. Strangelove. 1964. One-sheet. $1,000-1,500

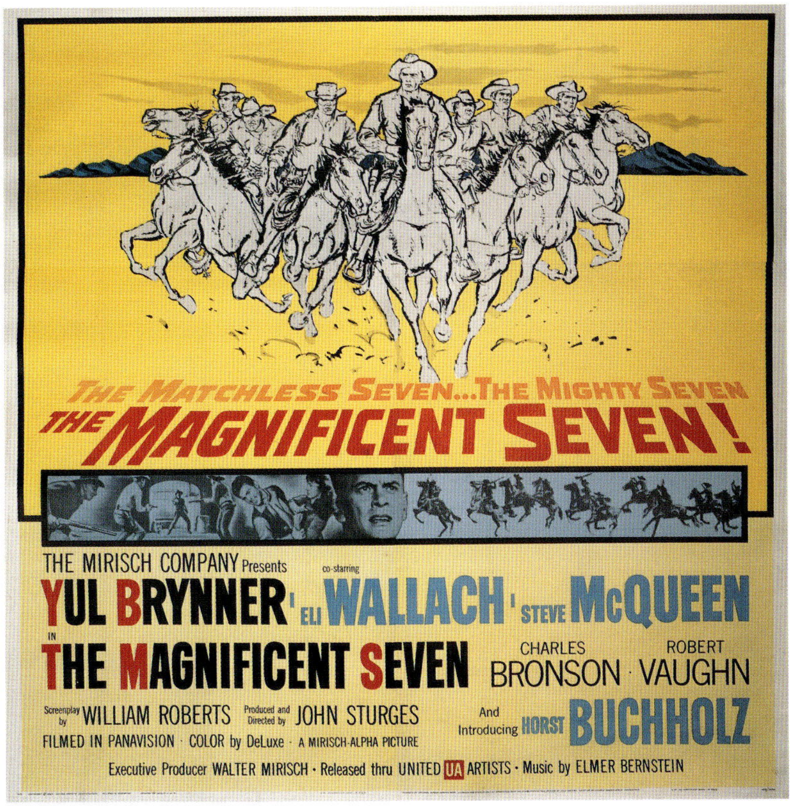

The Magnificent Seven. 1964.
Six-sheet. $1,200-1,800

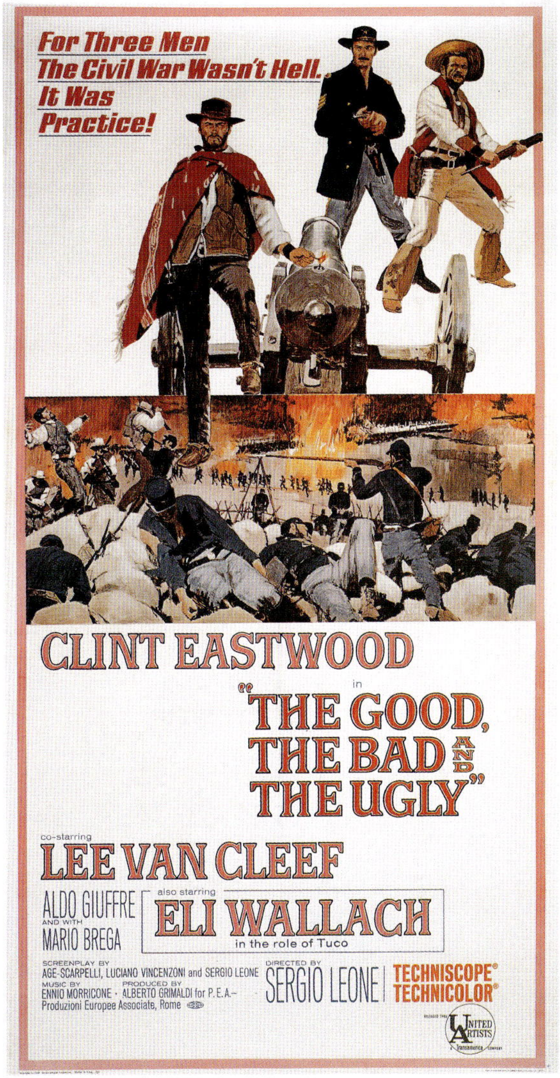

The Good, the Bad, and the Ugly.
1966. Three-sheet. $1,500-2,000

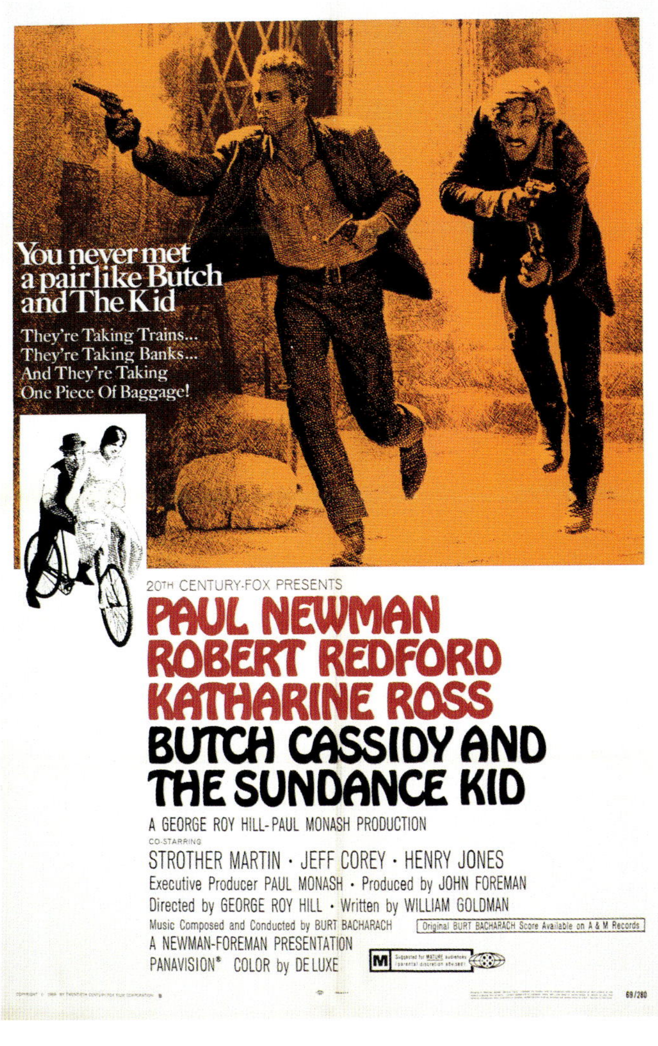

Butch Cassidy and the Sundance Kid. 1969.
One-sheet, style B. $800-1,200

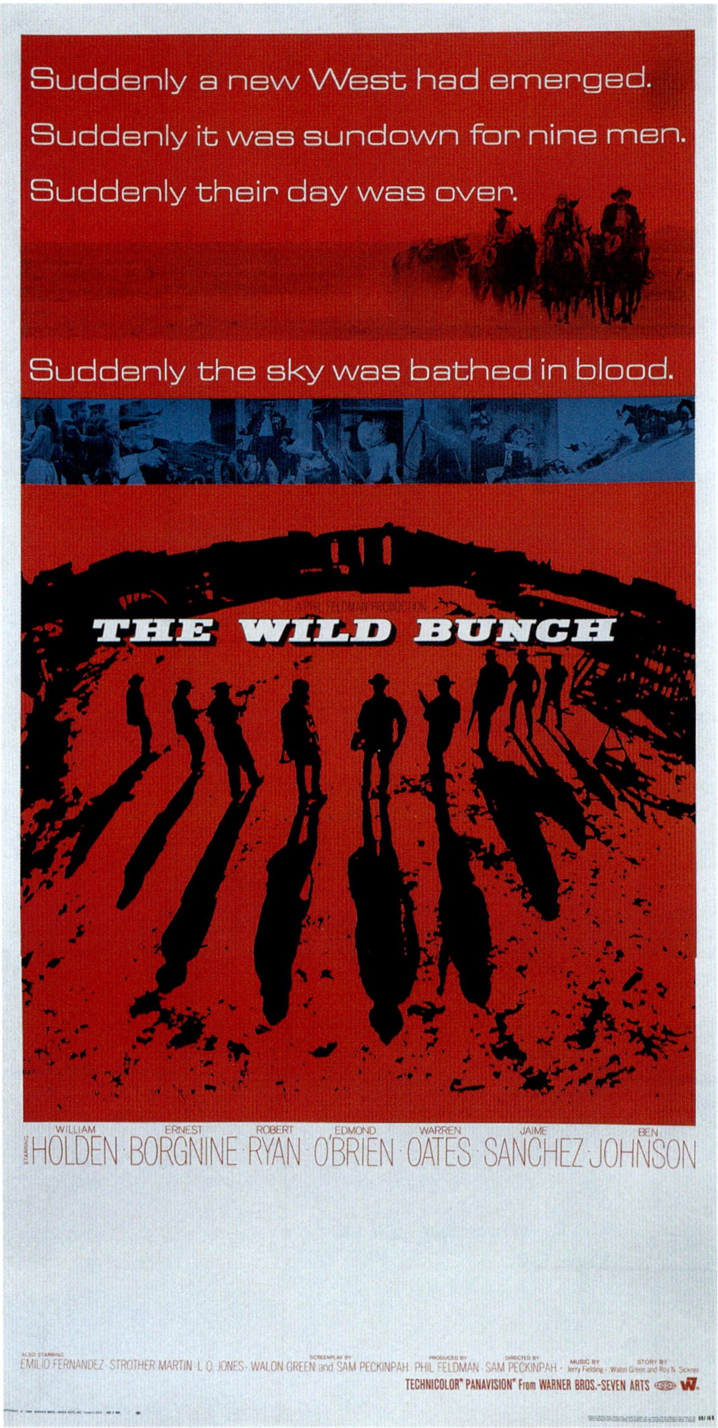

The Wild Bunch. 1969. Three-sheet. $1,500-2,000

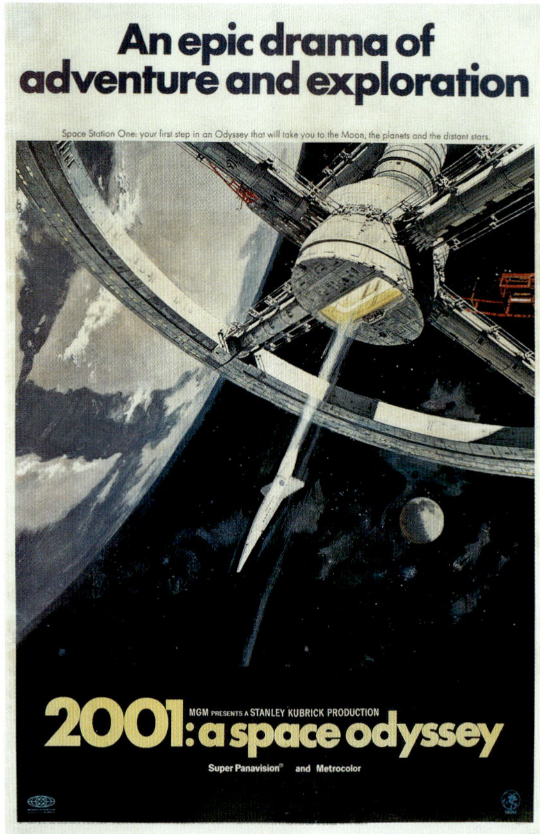

2001: A Space Odyssey. 1968. One-sheet, style A, art by Robert McCall. $1,000-1,500

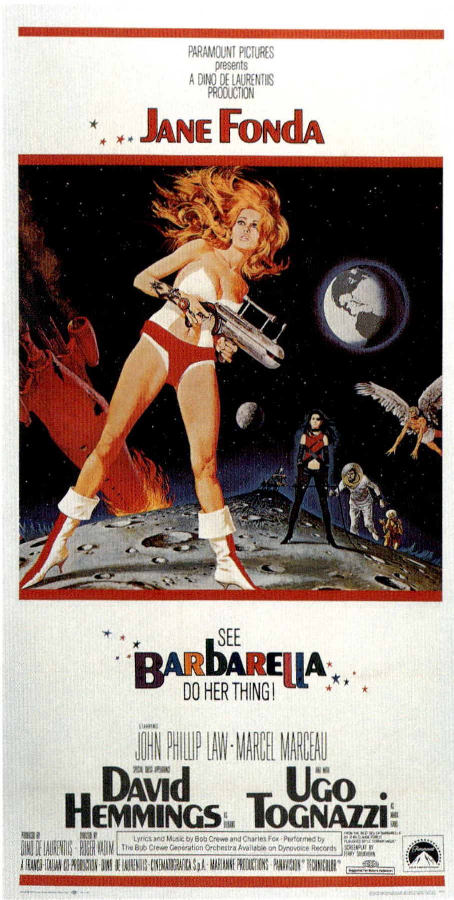

Barbarella. 1968. Three-sheet. $1,500-2,000

This era in Hollywood was principally about opportunity and making a distinct break from the past. The big stars and directors of old found themselves entering the twilight of their careers while all around them new talents were in the ascendancy. The hippie idealism of the previous decade gave way to cynicism and uncertainty in the wake of Watergate and the end of the Vietnam War. This fuelled a young generation of movie makers in Hollywood, spurring them to create pictures more socially reflective and relevant than ever before, especially as the Production Code had been finally scraped in 1968. Liberated by the decline of an old world studio system, the taboo-busting pictures of the 1960s and a diet of European art house pictures the youthful Spielberg, Lucas, and Coppola, among others, rewrote the rules on Hollywood movie making. In the 1970s the artistic, weird, and wonderful embraced the mainstream in a way that Hollywood had never experienced before and has not witnessed since.

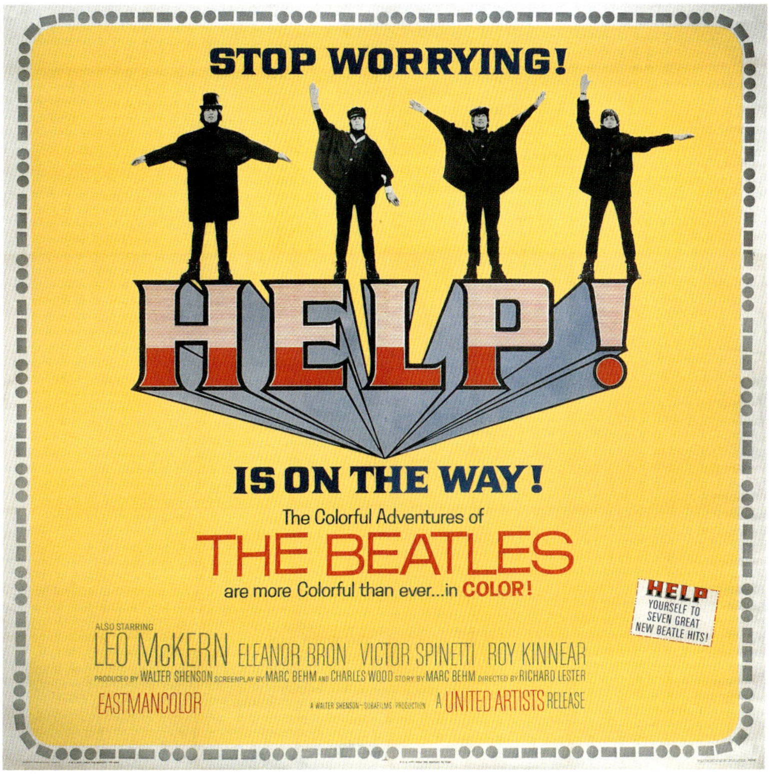

Help! 1965. Six-sheet. $1,200-1,800

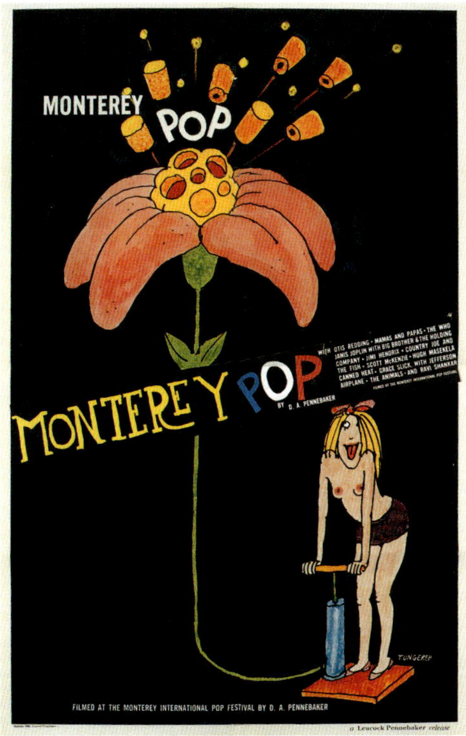

Monterey Pop. 1968. One-sheet. $500-800

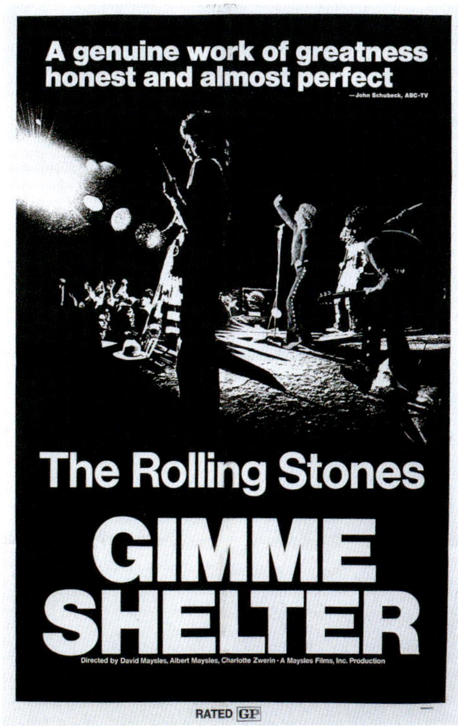

Gimme Shelter. 1969. One-sheet. $700-900

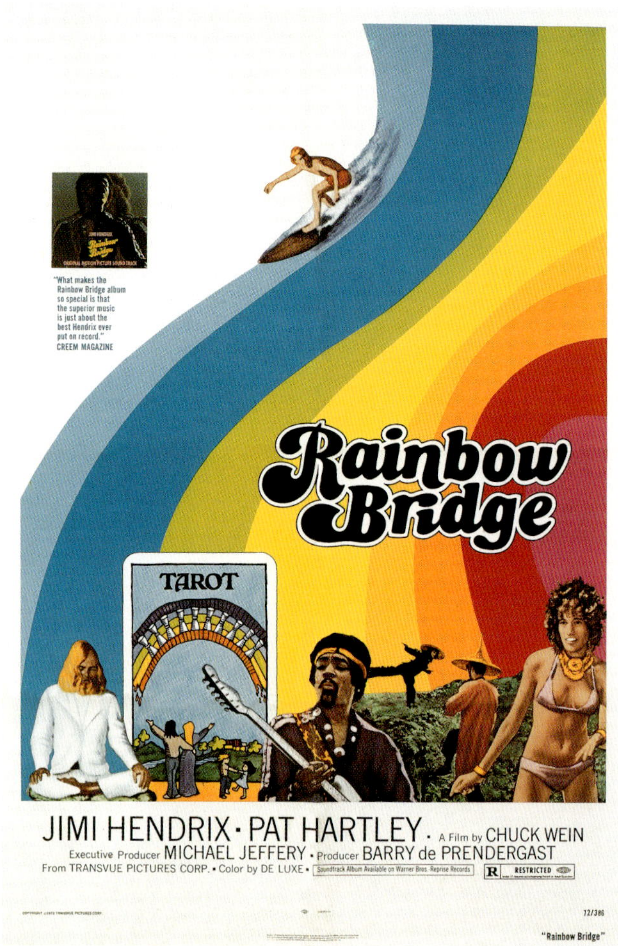

Rainbow Bridge. 1972. One-sheet. $400-600

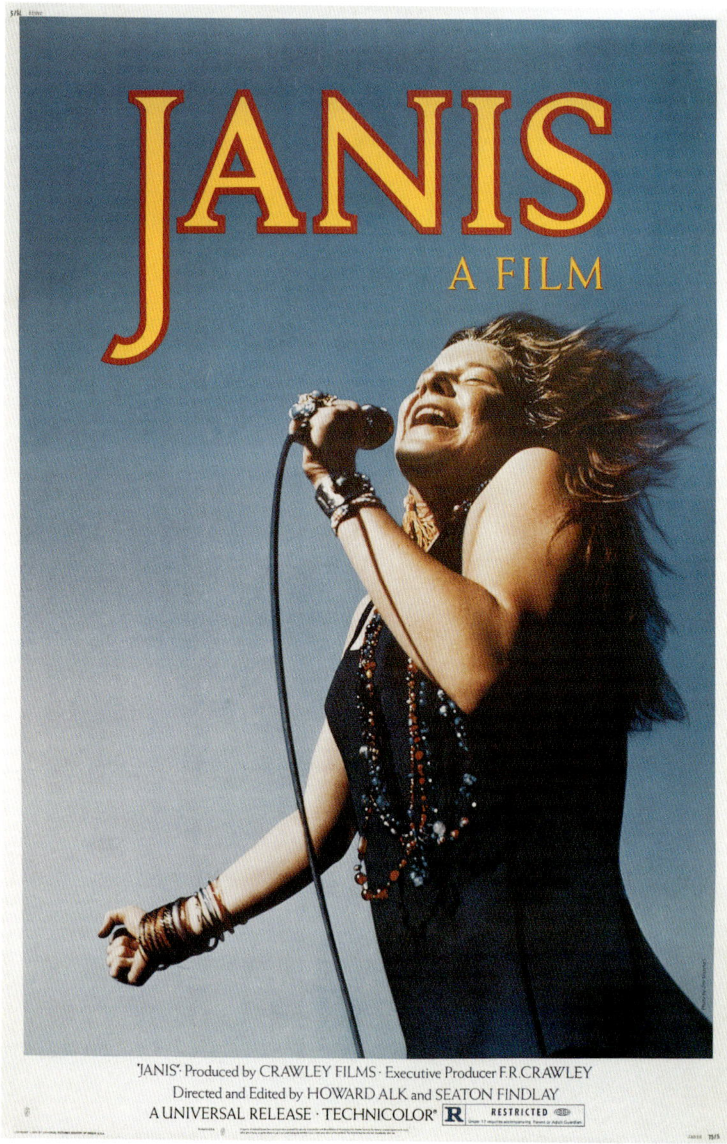

Janis. 1975. Two-sheet. $500-800

Old themes were given a shot in the arm. During the 1970s and 1980s movies no longer glorified war with the swaggering heroics of such Hollywood legends as John Wayne, but rather magnified the terrifying effects it can have on human nature. The returning Vietnam War veteran was portrayed as a dangerous killer always on the brink, such as Robert De Niro in *Taxi Driver* (1976) or Sylvester Stallone in *First Blood* (1982). Marlon Brando famously portrays a soldier driven mad by the madness of war itself in the acclaimed *Apocalypse Now* (1979). In Francis Ford Coppola's seminal work *The Godfather* (1972) the gangster genre is revised and enhanced by transforming it into a critical commentary on an immigrant family's pursuit of the American dream. This violent and bloody take on integral aspects of American society struck a chord and was a huge success spawning the famous sequels.

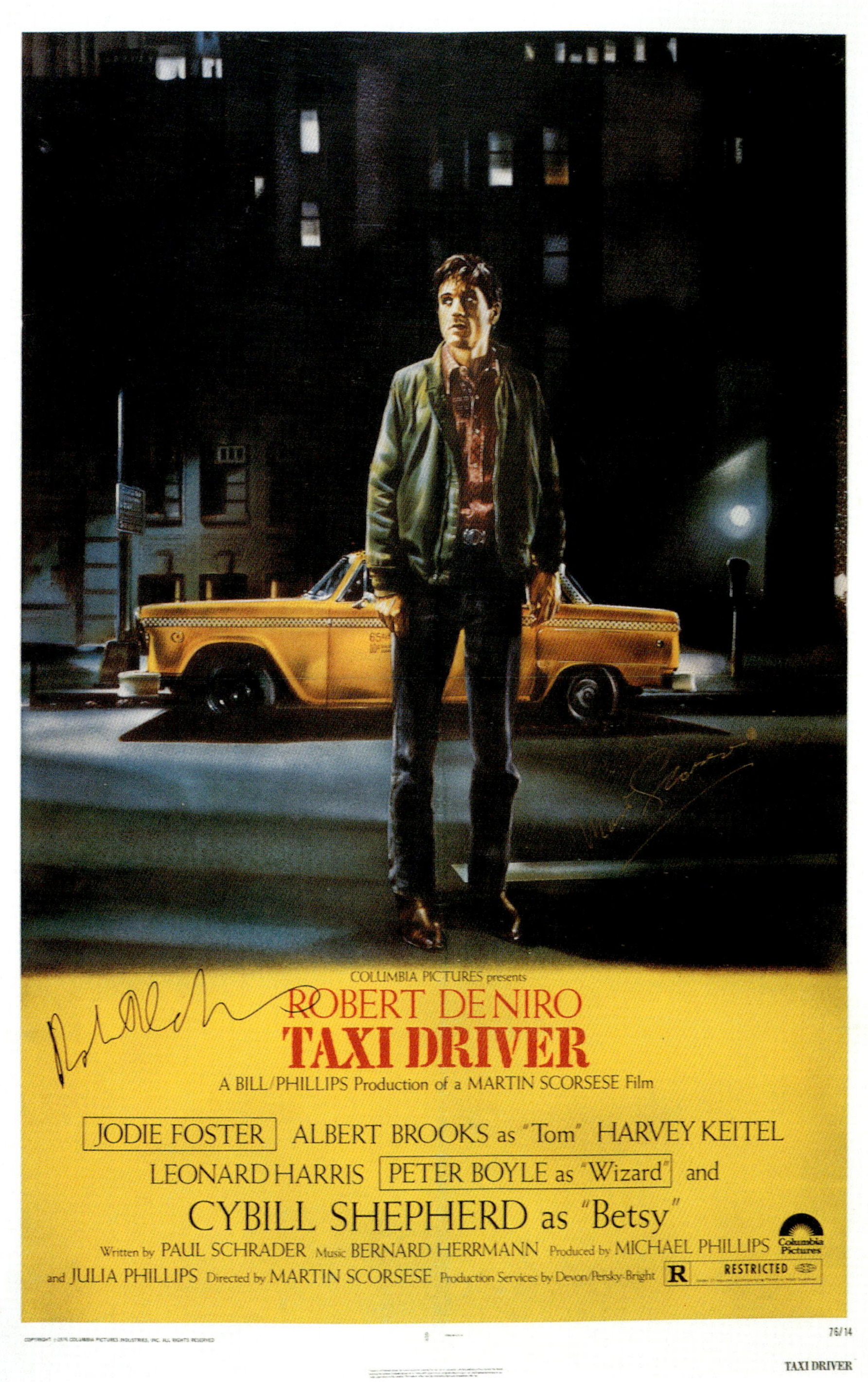

Taxi Driver. 1976. One-sheet, signed by Robert DeNiro and Martin Scorsese. $1,500-2,000

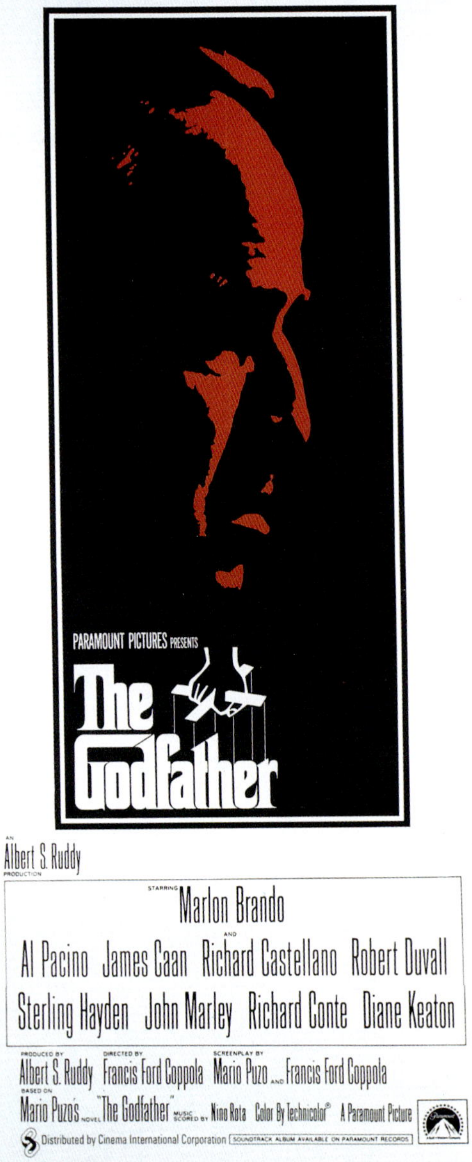

The Godfather. 1972. Three-sheet. $1,200-1,800

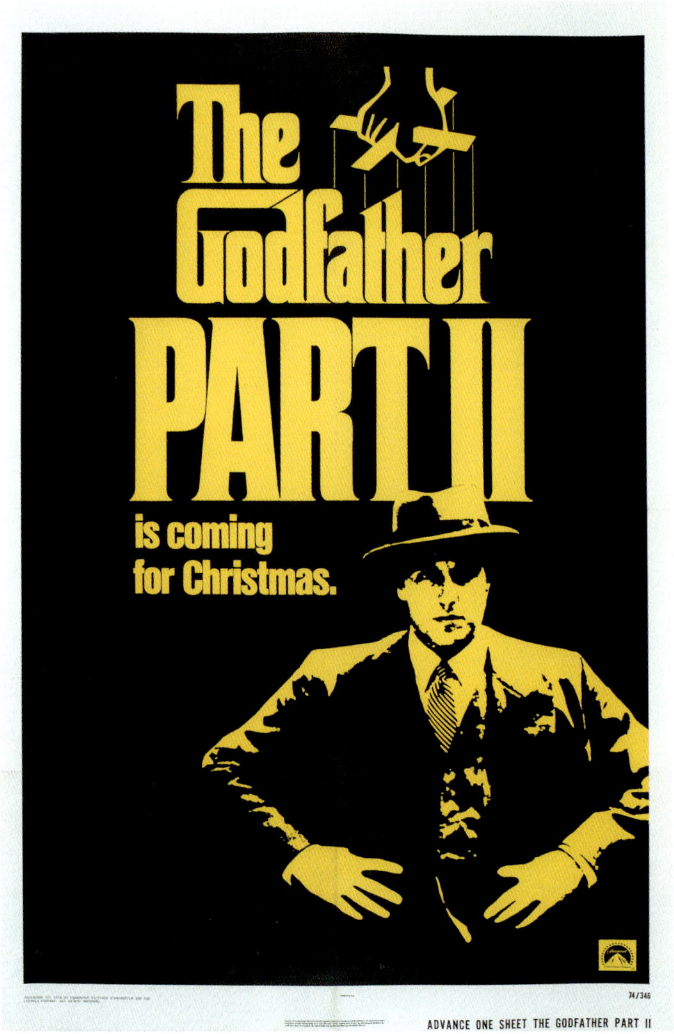

The Godfather Part II. 1974. Advance one-sheet. $1,000-1,500

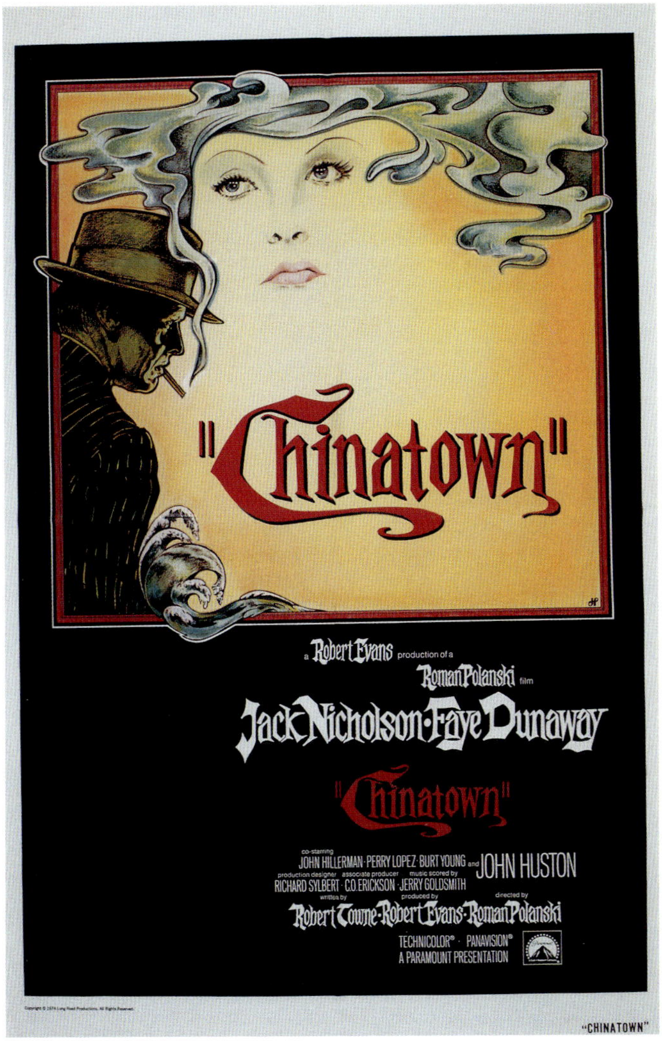

Chinatown. 1974. One-sheet, art by Jim Pearsall. $1,000-1,500

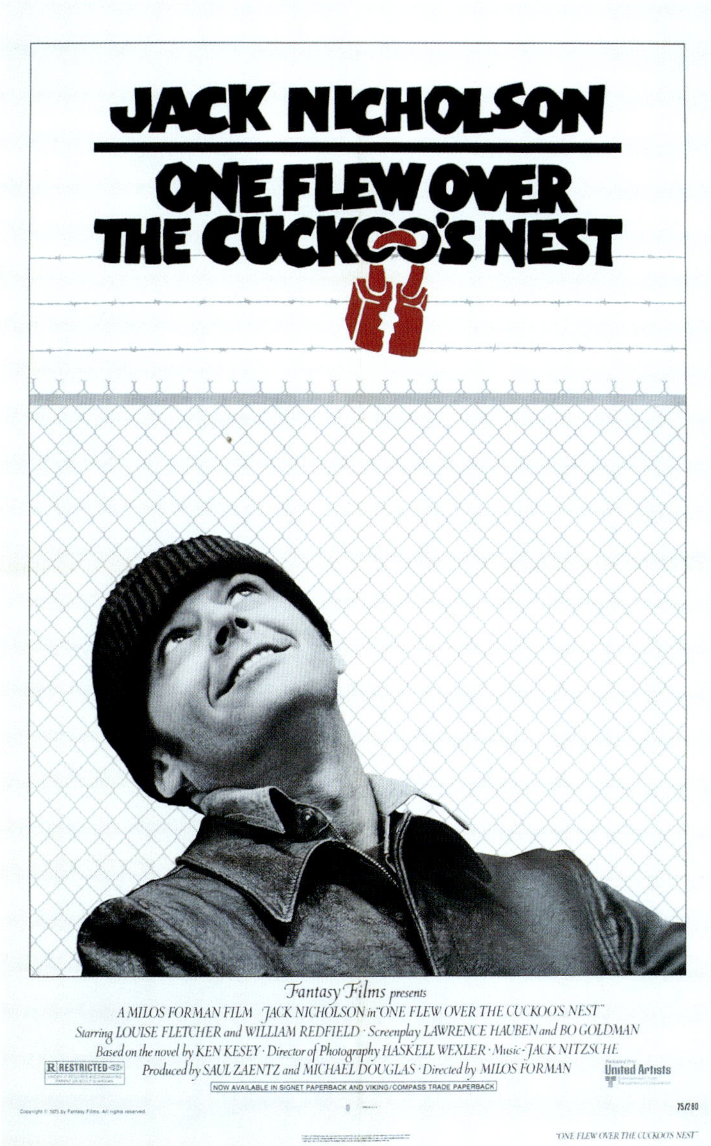

One Flew Over the Cuckoo's Nest. 1975. One-sheet. $1,200-1,800

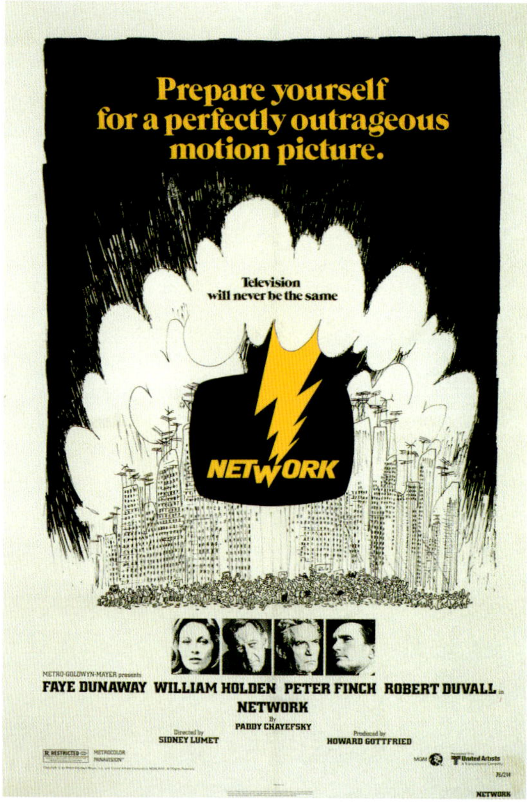

Network. 1976. One-sheet. $200-300

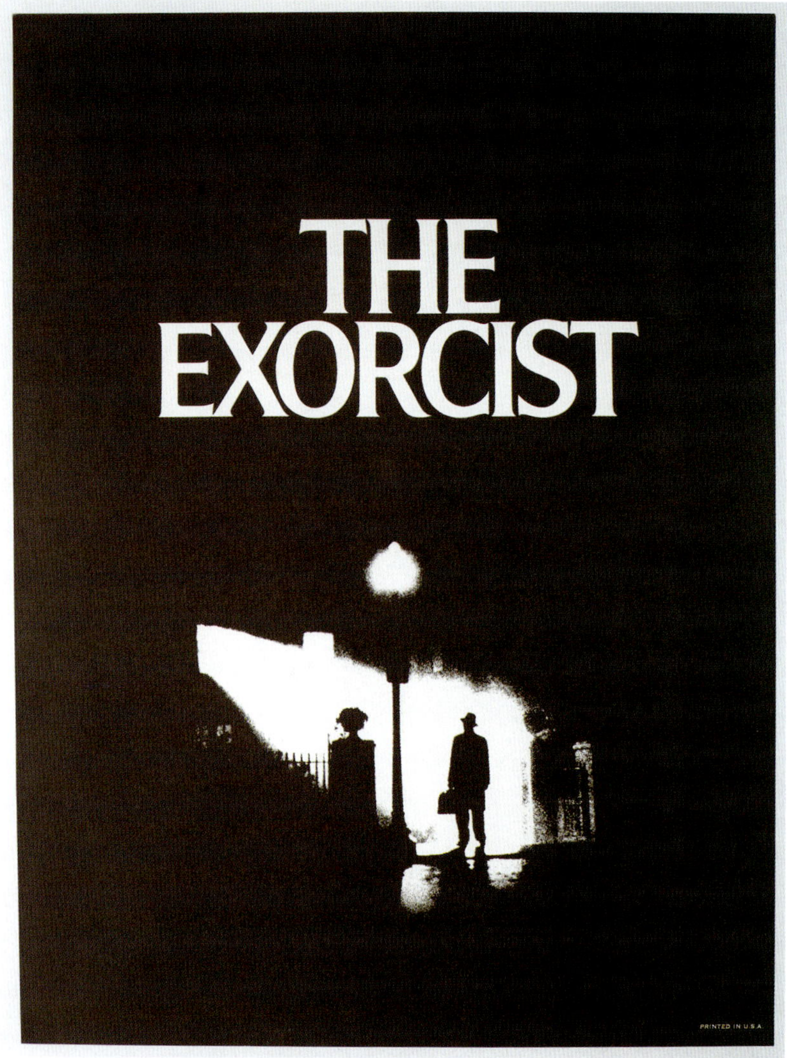

The Exorcist. 1974. Special poster. $1,000-1,500

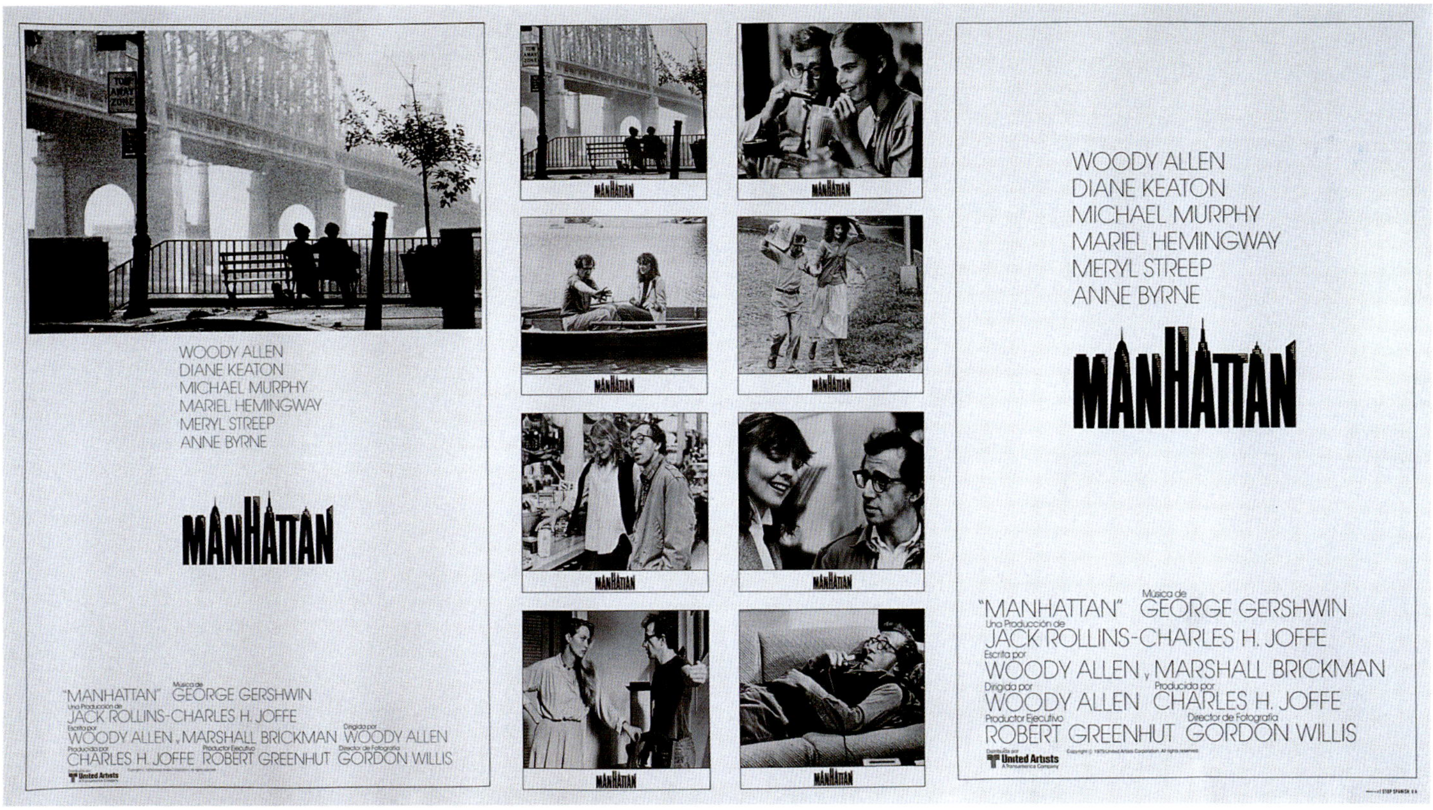

Manhattan. 1979. Subway poster. $1,000-1200

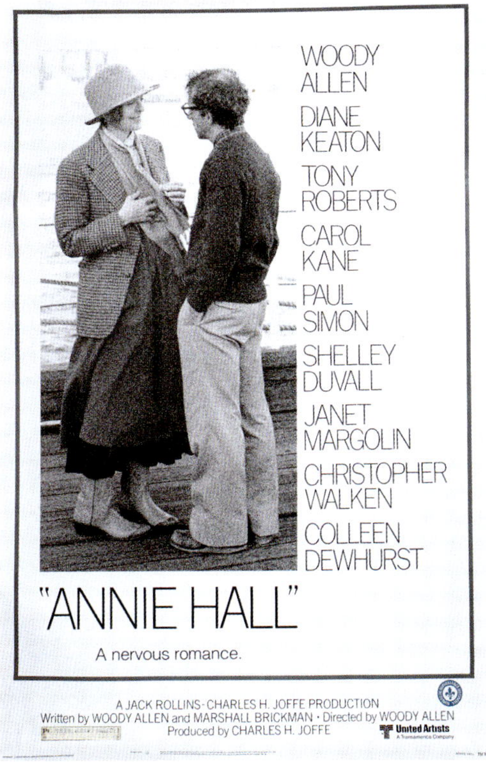

Annie Hall. 1977. One-sheet. $800-1,200

From the latter 1970s into the 1980s production shifted away from social-political pictures and embraced the escapist blockbuster. *Jaws* (1975) released with unprecedented promotional hype during the summer coined nearly $130 million within its first year. *Star Wars* (1977) took things one-step further with mass merchandising working in conjunction with the release. As a result the movie made over $190 million within the first year. These staggering totals for individual productions meant that a studio could survive on the success of just one film. Consequently the average cost of making a movie rose sharply to a level that can now ruin a studio unless success is guaranteed. It is this quest for success that has arguably led to Hollywood producing many upbeat, undemanding movies in more recent years rather than the more subversive and enlightening perspectives on American society that were made during the early 1970s.

A Hollywood, though, that at the same time can produce the thought provoking *Far From Heaven* (2003) and the heavily merchandised, special-effect driven *Matrix Reloaded* (2003) and *Hulk* (2003) has got to be a good thing. Hollywood continues to offer variety and entertainment, something it has always done since the silent days. This, in turn, is reflected in the plethora of image-based material now used to market movies above and beyond the confines of the standard film poster conceived almost a lifetime ago.

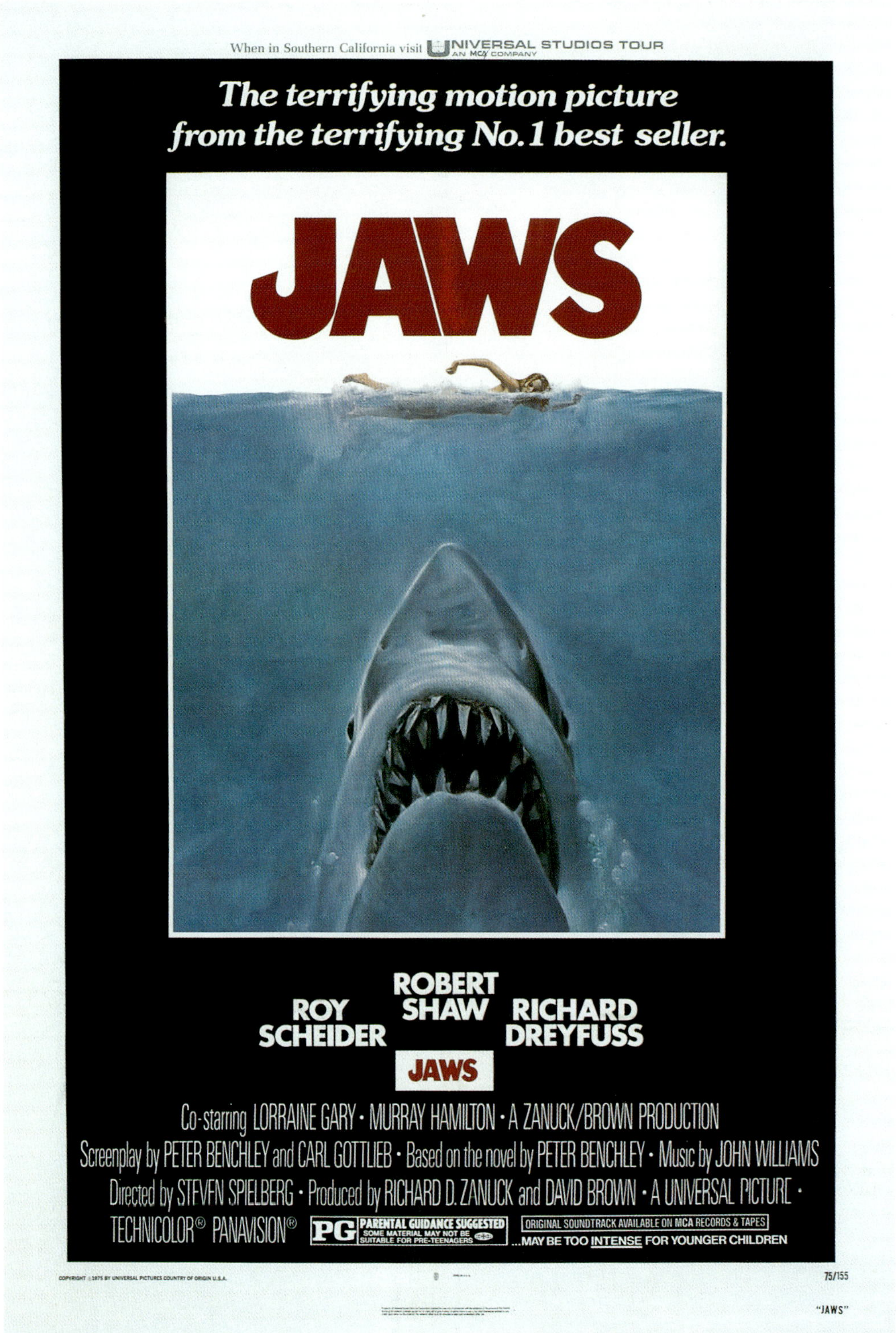

Jaws. 1975. One-sheet.
$800-1,200

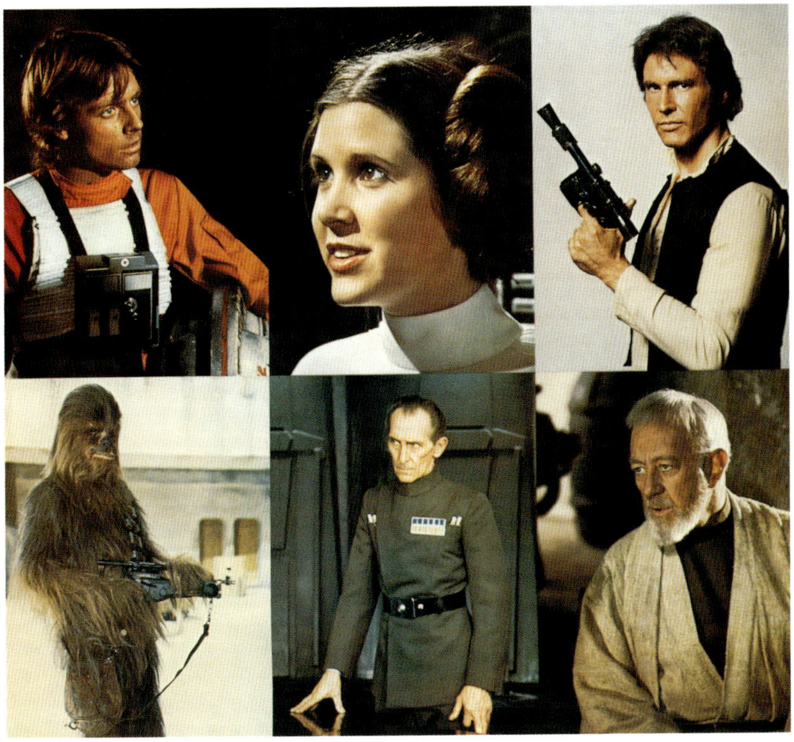

Star Wars. 1977. Special poster. $1,000-1,500

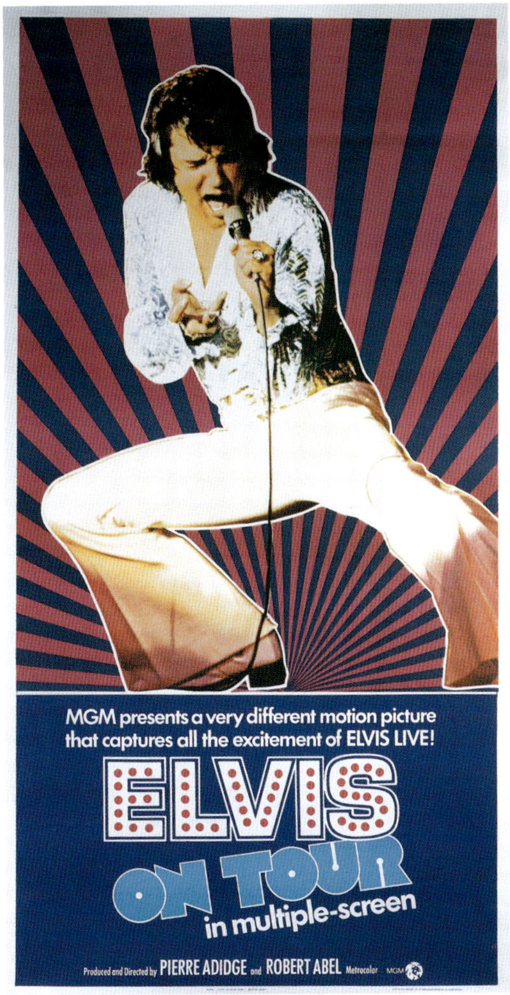

Elvis on Tour. 1972. Three-sheet. $700-1,000

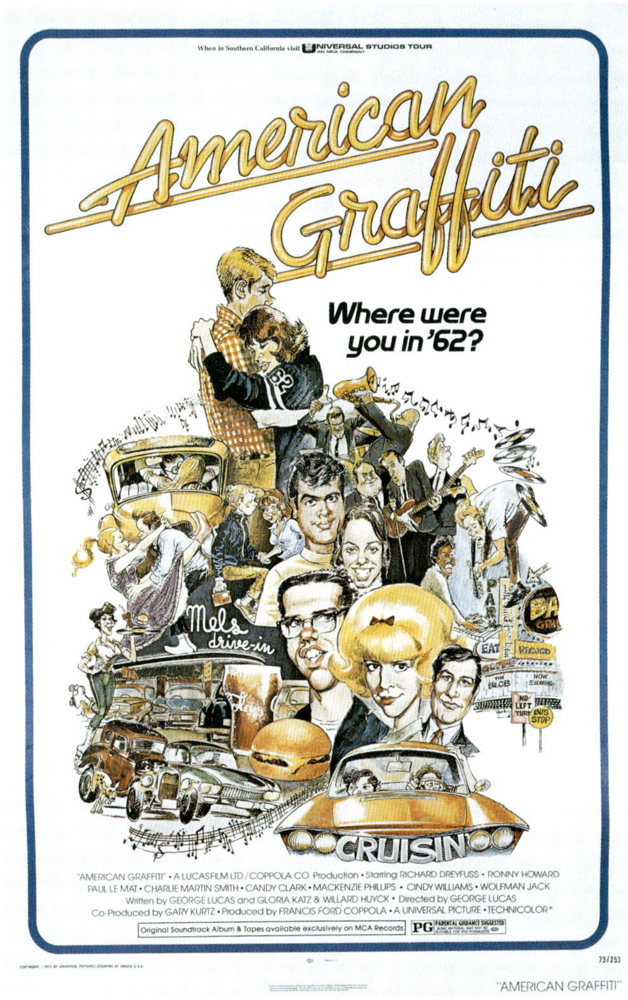

American Graffiti. 1973. One-sheet. $800-1,200

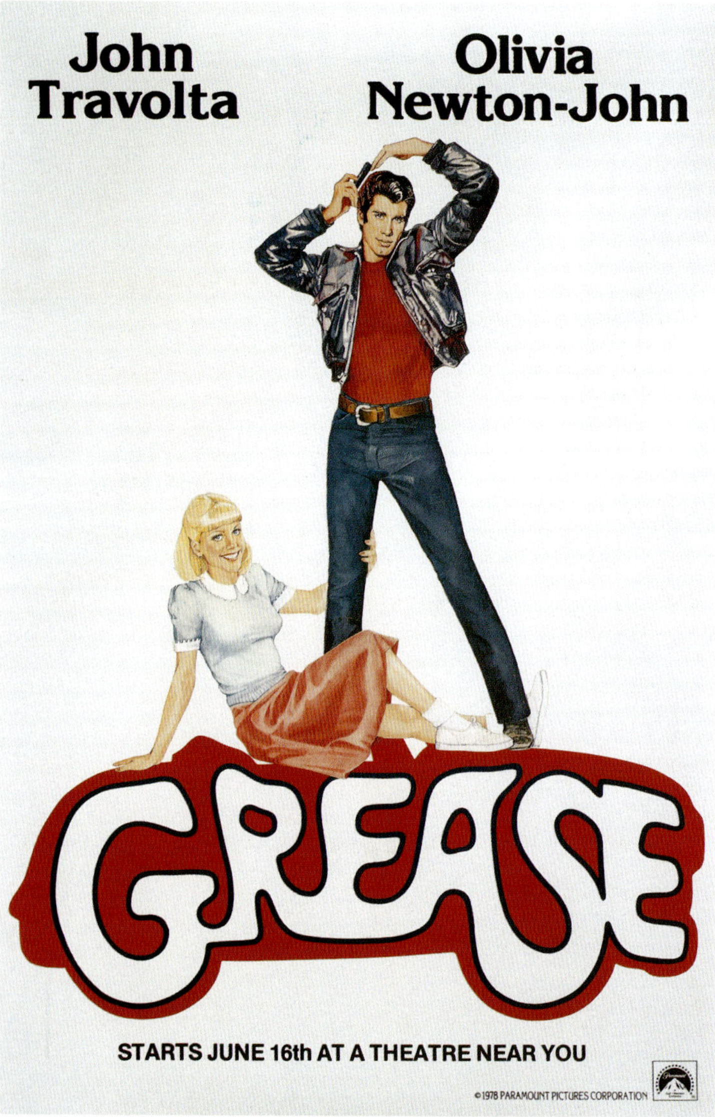

Grease. 1978. Advance one-sheet. $800-1,200

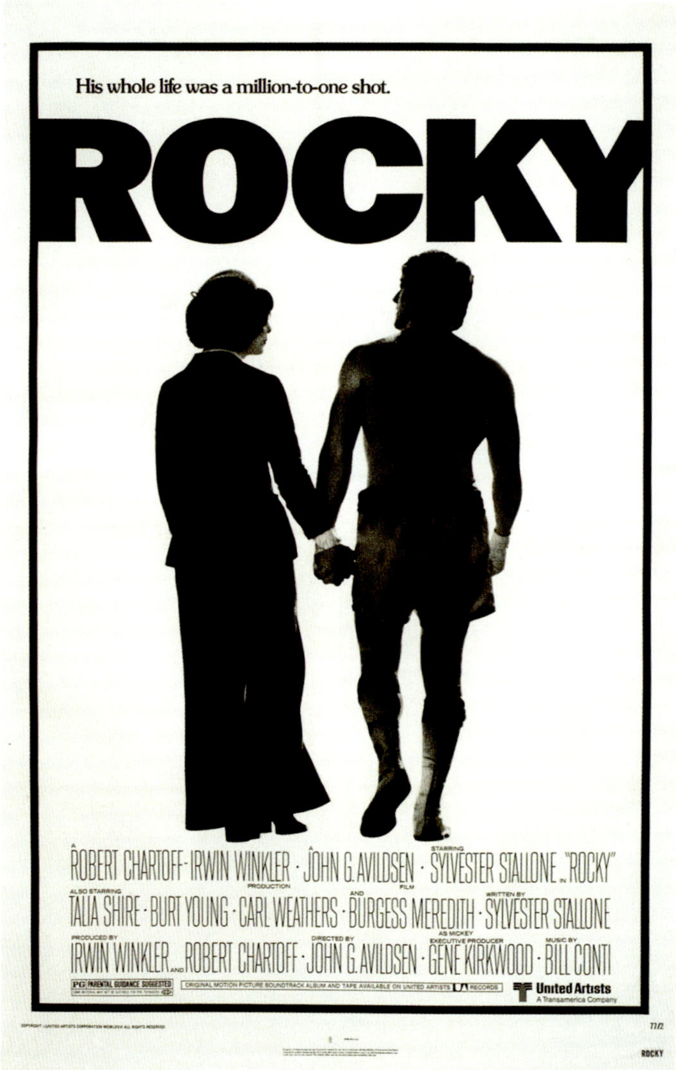

Rocky. 1977. One-sheet. $800-1,200

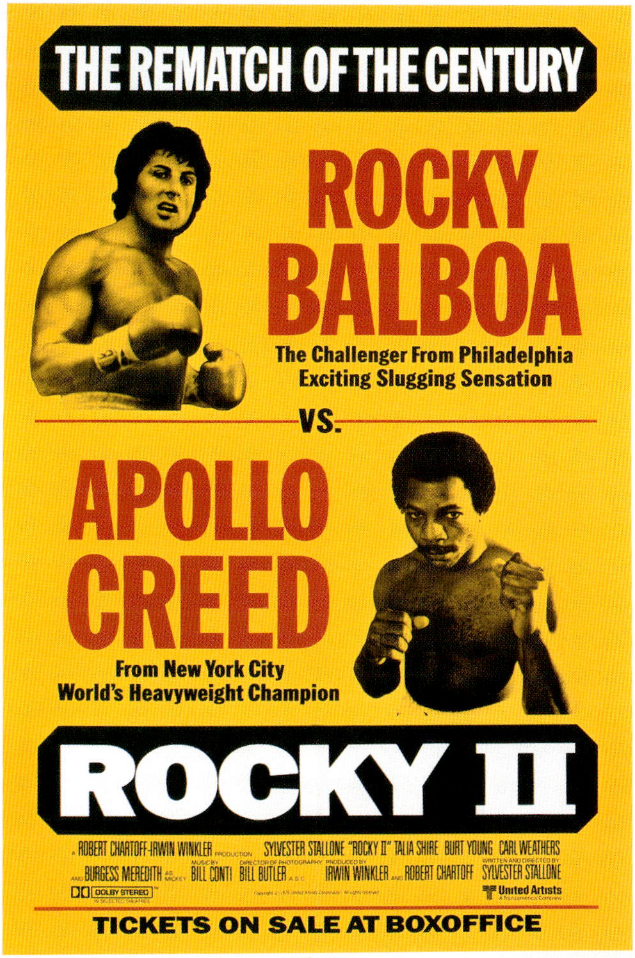

Rocky II. 1979. Special one-sheet. $800-1,200

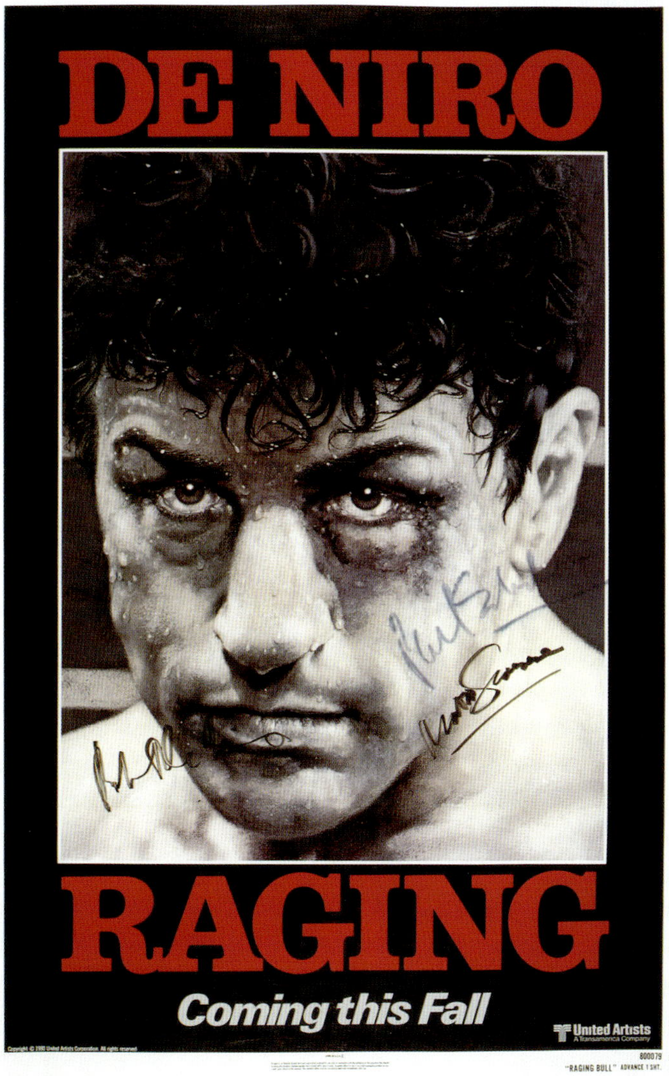

Raging Bull. 1980. Advance one-sheet, signed by Robert DeNiro, Martin Scorsese, and Paul Schrander. $1,000-1,500

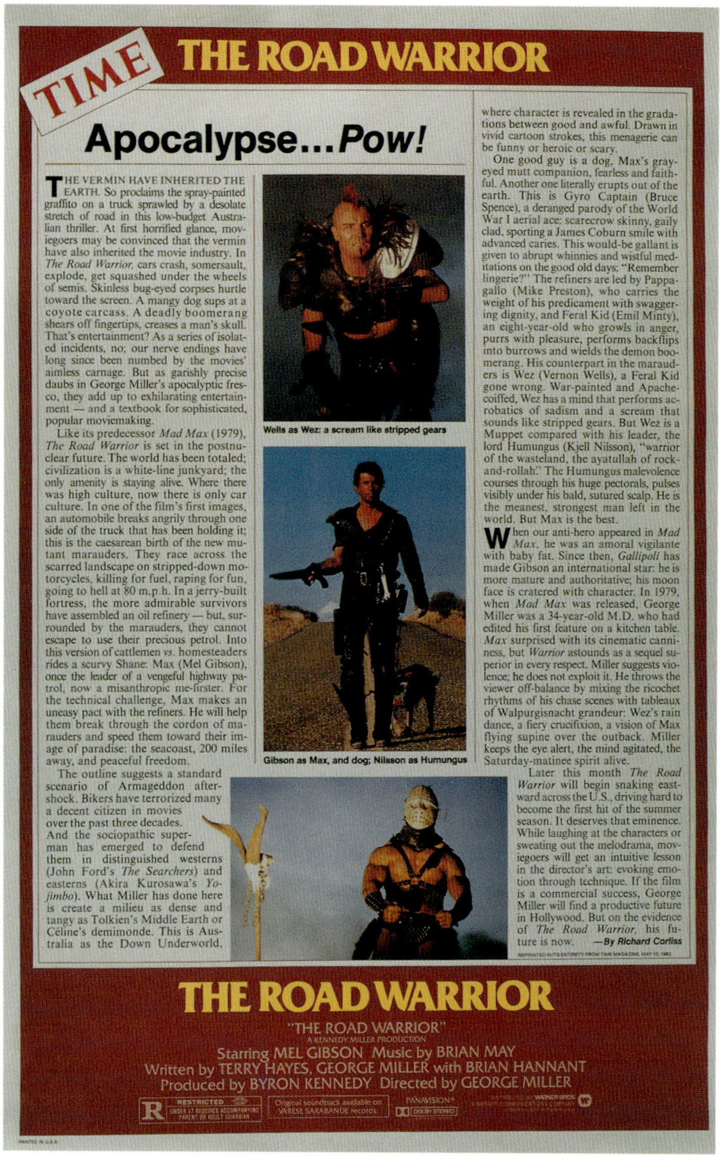

The Road Warrior (Mad Max II). 1982.
Special one-sheet. $800-1,200

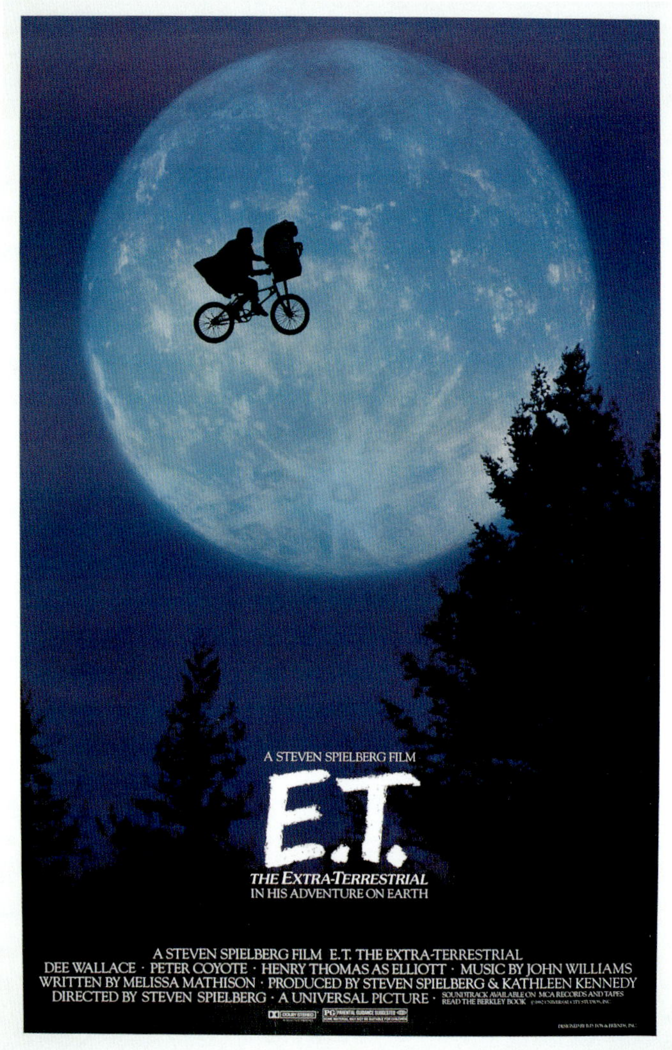

E.T. The Extra-Terrestrial. 1982. Special one-sheet $800-1,200

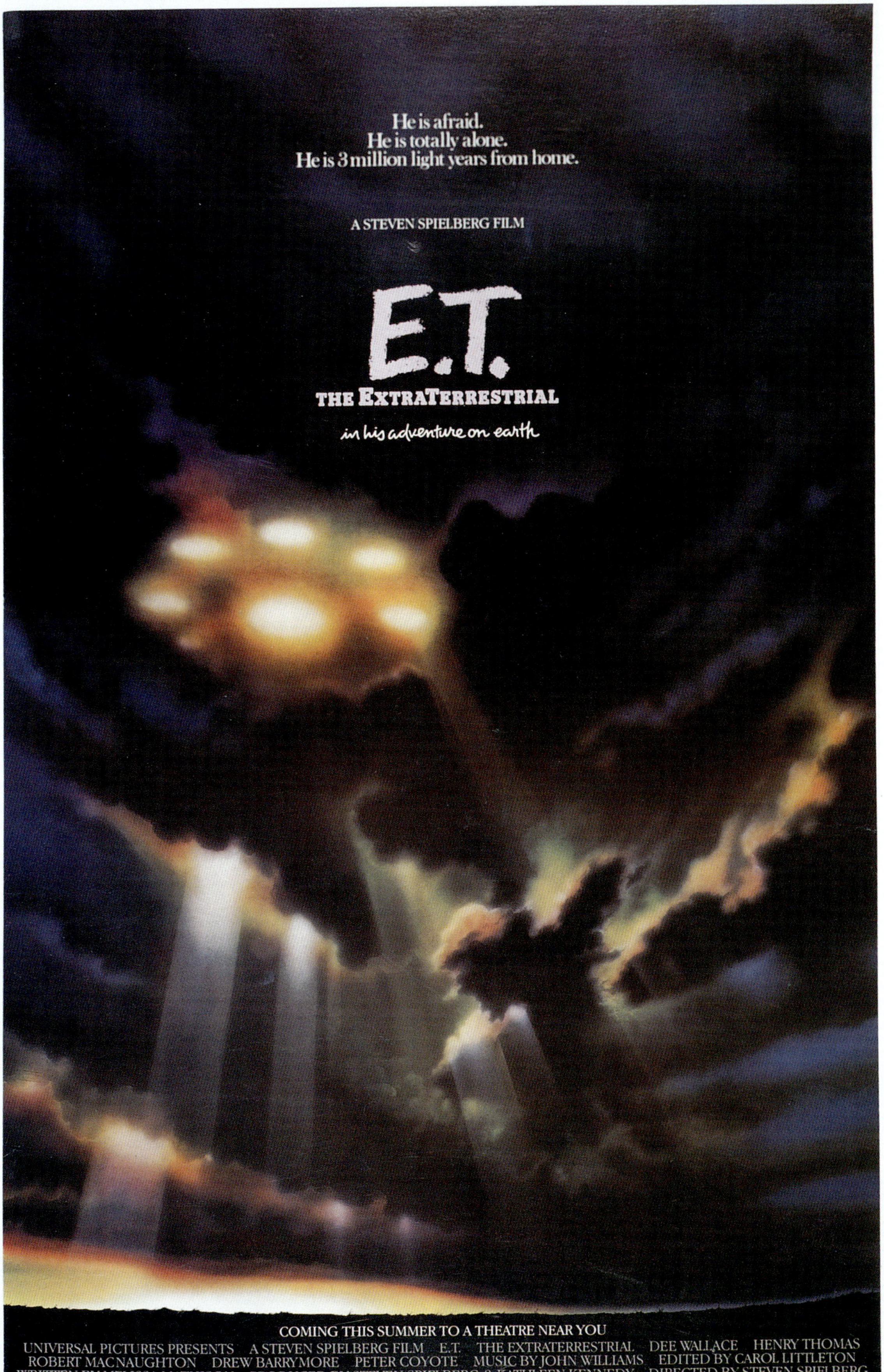

E.T. The Extra-Terrestrial. 1982. Advance one-sheet. $800-1,200

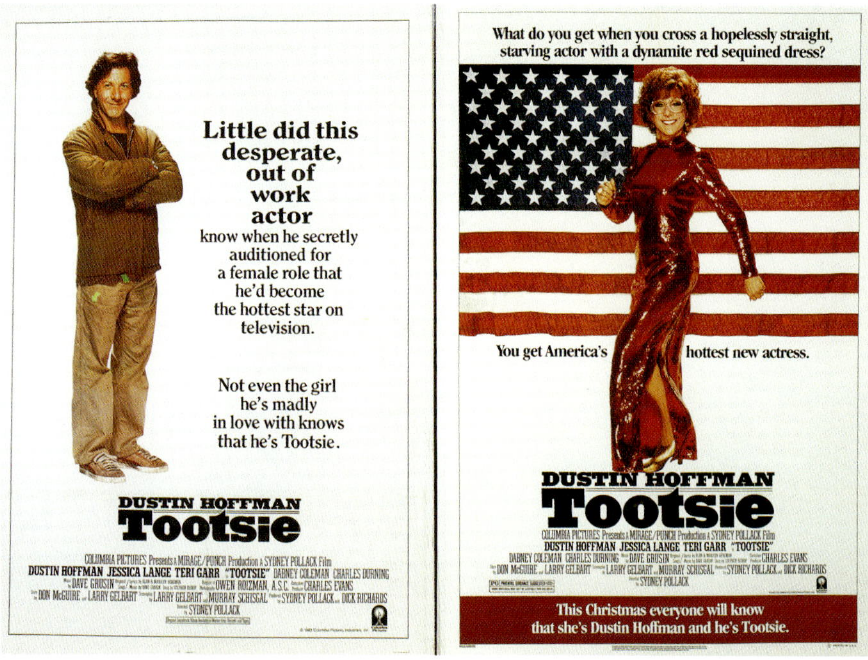

Tootsie. 1982. Advance and regular one-sheets, each $200-300

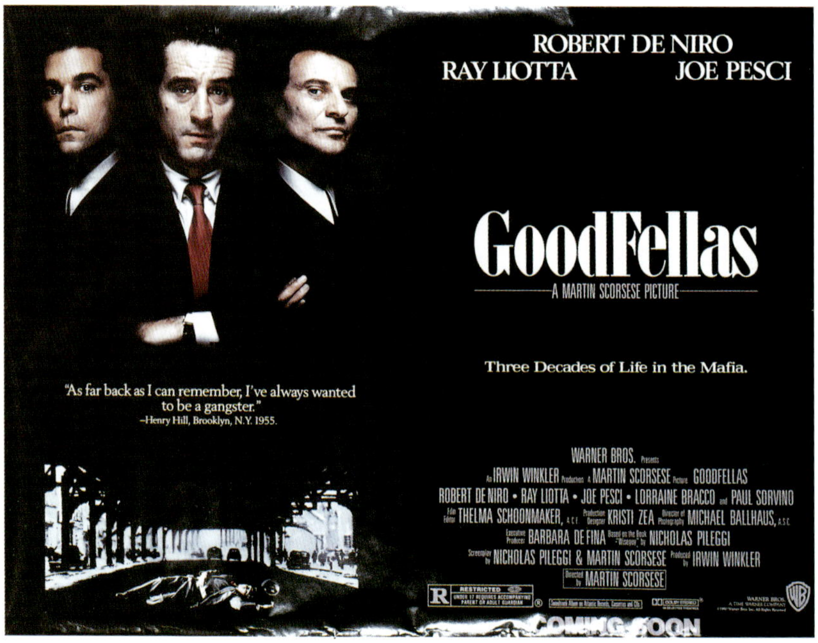

The Goodfellas. 1990. Subway poster. $500-800

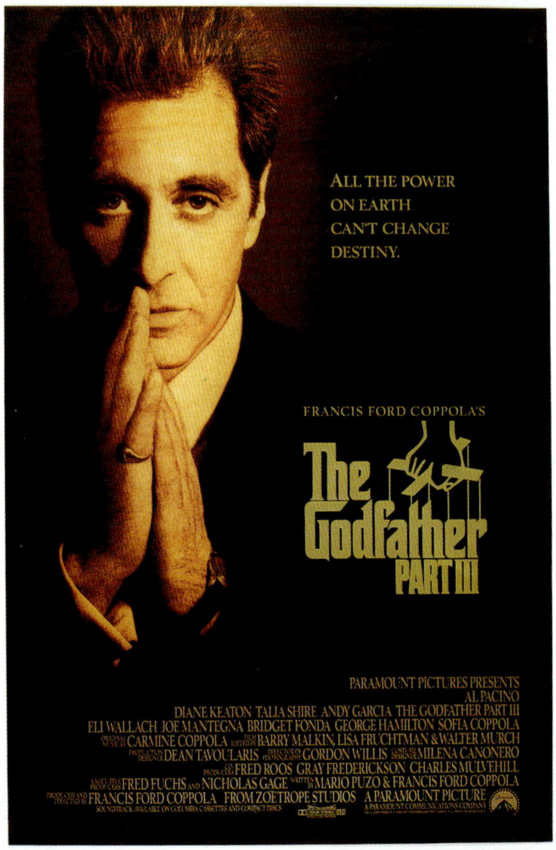

The Godfather Part III. 1990.
One-sheet. $500-800

Chapter Six

Collector's Guide

This book contains illustrations of some strikingly designed posters. This section explains some of the basic terminology used throughout the book to describe them, and other general advice useful to collectors.

Poster Sizes

Different ways of advertising a movie demanded different types of poster size. From the early days of Hollywood a fairly formulaic approach was adopted. Listed here are the more frequently found or discussed by collectors. There are some variations to this list as certain studios adopted gigantic images for some productions, but what is discussed here will help clarify what is found in this book.

Six-sheet (81 by 81 inches). Extremely large style often used on billboards and at the main city movie theatres. Folded and issued in four separate parts.

Three-sheet (41 by 81 inches). Large, taller style used in movie theaters often around the outside entrances. Folded and issued usually in two separate parts.

Two-sheet (40 by 60 inches). Not necessarily recognized by this name by some collectors, it is nevertheless larger than the one sheet and differs by being printed on card stock. It is commonly found rolled rather than folded and was delivered to the movie theaters in this way.

One-sheet (27 by 41 inches). The most popular standard issue used in movie theaters and therefore more plentifully printed and certainly the most keenly sought size by collectors. Until more recent times, these were always folded for distribution and as such it is virtually impossible to find any pre-1950s poster without such folds.

Half-sheet (22 by 28 inches). Approximately half the size of the popular one-sheet. These were printed on heavier stock paper and used for a range of publicity reasons within the movie theater. Found both with and without folding.

Insert (14 by 36 inches). Heavier stock paper of a narrow design. Used for similar reasons as the half-sheet. Usually found folded.

Window Card (22 by 14 inches). These are printed on card stock and were used to publicize the film in various commercial premises such as drug stores. They were designed with a blank top space that would display the screening details and movie theater. This has resulted in some being trimmed either by shop owners at the time reusing them for different movie theaters or by collectors who have disliked this feature. This damage is fairly expected with window cards. They were also issued in jumbo sizes and similar cards were used on trolley buses.

Lobby Card (11 by 14 inches). Usually printed on card stock, they were issued in sets of eight including a title card that would normally duplicate the poster art and have the credits. The other cards would feature photographic scenes from the movie, early versions often being hand tinted. As the name implies these were used throughout the theater lobby, often in conjunction with photographic stills, which were smaller and on lighter stock paper. Jumbo-sized versions are, as the name implies, larger in format and generally more glossy.

Herald (10 by 16 inches). Magazine type advertisement, often using similar artwork to the original poster, together with multiple photographic stills. Often valuable for earlier rare titles. Folded due to method of publication.

Advance. Often produced in one-sheet sizes, these were used well ahead of the mainstream publicity to herald the release of a film. These posters may be of a different design than the later poster artwork.

Styles. Some posters are mentioned as being of a particular style code. This is due to the different studios often releasing alternative designs to advertise the same movie in the same poster format. Some styles are more collectible than others and where significant this is mentioned in the poster caption.

Re-release. Some posters could be just as good for the subsequent cinematic releases as they were for the original. Major popular movies tended to be re-released for distribution many years after the original screening date and each time different graphics and images were often adopted. This is the case with such classics as *King Kong, Gone With The Wind, Frankenstein* and *Dracula* to name but a few.

Condition

For many years the grading of posters was wide open to misrepresentation and to a certain extent it still is. However, in the last ten years, with the increased involvement of major international auctioneers and dealers, the grading and terminology has been simplified. After extensive searching and observation of posters the eye will become honed and the different terms adopted will become second nature. The following is a record of basically understood definitions for terms used when describing condition in catalogs and other journals. However this is not written in stone and other collectors will no doubt argue to the contrary.

A point to bear in mind when considering condition is that often, as you can see from the grading, restoration is an integral part. In an ideal world it would be great to avoid restoration altogether but necessity dictates that some posters are treated in this manner. In some cases you will know only too well if something needs restoration! Some fully restored posters might look great when the work is done, in some cases better than when they left the printers all those years ago, but be careful about embarking on unnecessary work that will neither benefit the look nor increase the value of your prized possession.

Mint. A superb example with strong colors, no defects or faults other than that associated with its original distribution, such as folding.

Near Mint. An example that perhaps shows more faults than the last, such as border pin holes and wear at the folding creases, but still retains strong colors. May have some delicate restoration.

Fine. An example demonstrating more wear than the last with perhaps minor tears at the folds and even minor paper loss at edges. Possible evidence of minor restoration.

Very Good. An example showing similar wear to the previous but slightly more pronounced with the possibility of more restoration work.

Good. An okay example that probably shows its age. Folds will be pronounced, stains and paper discoloration expected, along with evidence of possible paper loss, but all over not too badly presentable.

Fair. An example with sure signs of damage with the possibility of paper loss from the image; tape, writing and stains all in the image area. A poster in need of restoration.

Poor. A hideous example! Usually extensive paper loss, staining, and tears, damage basically extensive all over and restoration desperately needed if a rare item.

Some major auctioneers have adopted the following definitions that are more simplified but broader in approach and are important to be familiar with.

Condition A . Very fine to near mint. Large posters with rich strong colors. If backed with conservation paper or linen, there maybe nominal touch-up at the folds or in the immediate fold area. Lobby cards inserts and half-sheets almost untouched but may have corner pinholes or negligible tears at the margin.

Condition B. Very good to fine. Larger posters above average. If backed there may be some minor restorations past the fold area. Smaller posters and lobby cards may have slightly more noticeable pinholes and tiny tears and look less pristine.

Condition C. Fair to good. Larger posters, average use, with more restoration in the artwork but otherwise okay. Lobby cards may have more apparent border damage and look slightly more used. Smaller posters may have more pronounced border and/or fold damage.

Preservation

Most movie posters nowadays are preserved by the methods of backing, a process universally used and liked by many collectors. Linen-backing enables the poster to be mounted with archival paste on to a paper that is attached to a thick linen support. This has the benefit of pasting up the poster very much as was the original intention. Often some of the cruelest creases will fade into obscurity and the poster is supported and protected for life. A large percentage of posters that find themselves for sale through the world's auction houses have been treated in this way and are protected for handling and hanging.

Paper-backing is also favored by many. A heavy-duty archival stock paper is used to paste the poster onto and it generally achieves just the same effect as with linen, but some believe it to be a favorable archival support for paper.

Storage

A lot to be said on storage really just comes down to common sense. Any paper with age is subjected to a battery of possible harming effects the most obvious being extremes of temperature, light and handling. Unfortunately for most of us it is impossible to have all our posters displayed on the wall where they were meant to be seen. Therefore storing them by other means is an important aspect to be considered when collecting.

Ideally lying posters flat in plan chests or stacks is a good idea, always making sure that there is suitable archival protection between the sheets such as an acid free board. Rolled posters can be placed in tubes but again you need to make sure that suitable protection is considered as the cardboard tube will over time discolor the poster. For helpful free practical advice a professional art and design supplier should be able to guide you, as should reputable poster dealers, museums, and auction houses.

Buying

Purchasing some of the wonderful posters illustrated in this book is not as difficult as you might think. Some of these gems come up for sale fairly regularly through experienced dealers and auctioneers. If you are wanting something particular you might have to wait a while, but for those who are generally more broad in their collecting tastes then there has never been a better time to get out there and take a look around whether on foot or on-line.

So where is best? Well it always helps to start locally and then look farther a field. As I said, a good way of locating dealers is to look on-line. Some of the rarer items find their way in to the auction houses where people believe the best prices can be achieved. A lot of the major worldwide auctioneers include poster sales in their schedules and it would be worthwhile getting annual details and attending the auction even if its just to look. Many seasoned dealers travel extensively to find what they desire and in many ways it is worthwhile doing the same when getting started. Fairs and flea markets in Europe can still reward the diligent seeker.

As with any market, trends vary over a period of time. Movie posters have certainly been susceptible to this volatility. In more recent years we have seen the increased interest in movie posters from the 1960s onwards with prices spiraling upwards. This in turn appears to have affected the earlier material with prices for some silent and early sound posters remaining remarkably affordable. Certain genres will always remain strong, though, and early horror posters top the list of all time high sellers. Activity in the auction houses, particularly Sotheby's and Christie's, seems to have highlighted the collecting habits of many and as such distinct trends of popularity can be observed. As a guide for the beginner the hottest areas of the market include horror and science fiction, musicals, westerns, James Bond, Alfred Hitchcock, Clint Eastwood, Audrey Hepburn, Marilyn Monroe, and animation.

Bibliography

Borst, Ronald V. *Graven Images*. New York, NY: Grove Press. 1982

Brownlow, Kevin. *Hollywood: The Pioneers*. London: Collins. 1979

Brownlow, Kevin. *The Parade's Gone By...* London: Seker & Warburg. 1968

Dirks, Tim. *Greatest Films (www.filmsite.org)*, 2001

Edwards, Gregory J. *The Book of International Posters*. London: Tiger Books. 1985

Karney, Robyn. *The Movie Stars Story*. London: Octopus Books Ltd. 1984

Katz, Ephraim. *The Macmillan International Film Encyclopedia*. London: Pan Macmillan Ltd. 1994

Rebello, Stephen and Allen, Richard. *Reel Art: Great Posters from the Golden Age of the Silver Screen*. New York, NY: Abbeville Press. 1988

Wallace, David. *Lost Hollywood*. New York, NY: LA Weekly Books. 2001

Index

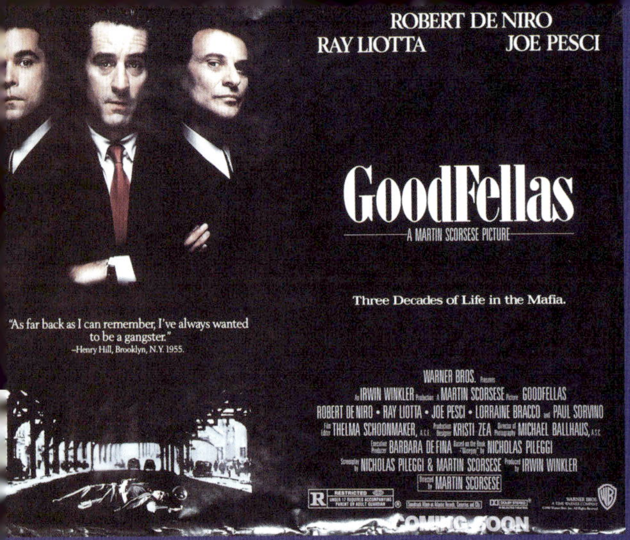
ROBERT DE NIRO
RAY LIOTTA
JOE PESCI
GoodFellas
A MARTIN SCORSESE PICTURE
Three Decades of Life in the Mafia.
"As far back as I can remember, I've always wanted to be a gangster."
–Henry Hill, Brooklyn, N.Y. 1955.
WARNER BROS. Presents
COMING SOON

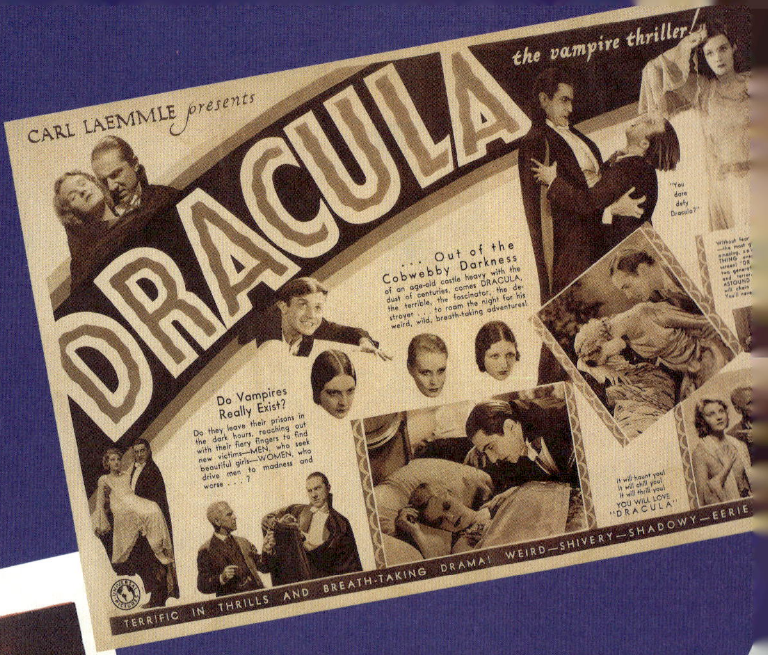
CARL LAEMMLE presents
the vampire thriller!
DRACULA
. . . Out of the Cobwebby Darkness of an age-old castle heavy with the dust of centuries, comes DRACULA, the terrible, the fascinator, the destroyer . . . to roam the night for his weird, wild, breath-taking adventures!
Do Vampires Really Exist?
Do they leave their prisons in the dark hours, reaching out with their fiery fingers to find new victims—MEN, who seek beautiful girls—WOMEN, who drive men to madness and worse . . . ?
It will haunt you! It will chill you! It will thrill you! YOU WILL LOVE "DRACULA"
TERRIFIC IN THRILLS AND BREATH-TAKING DRAMA! WEIRD—SHIVERY—SHADOWY—EERIE

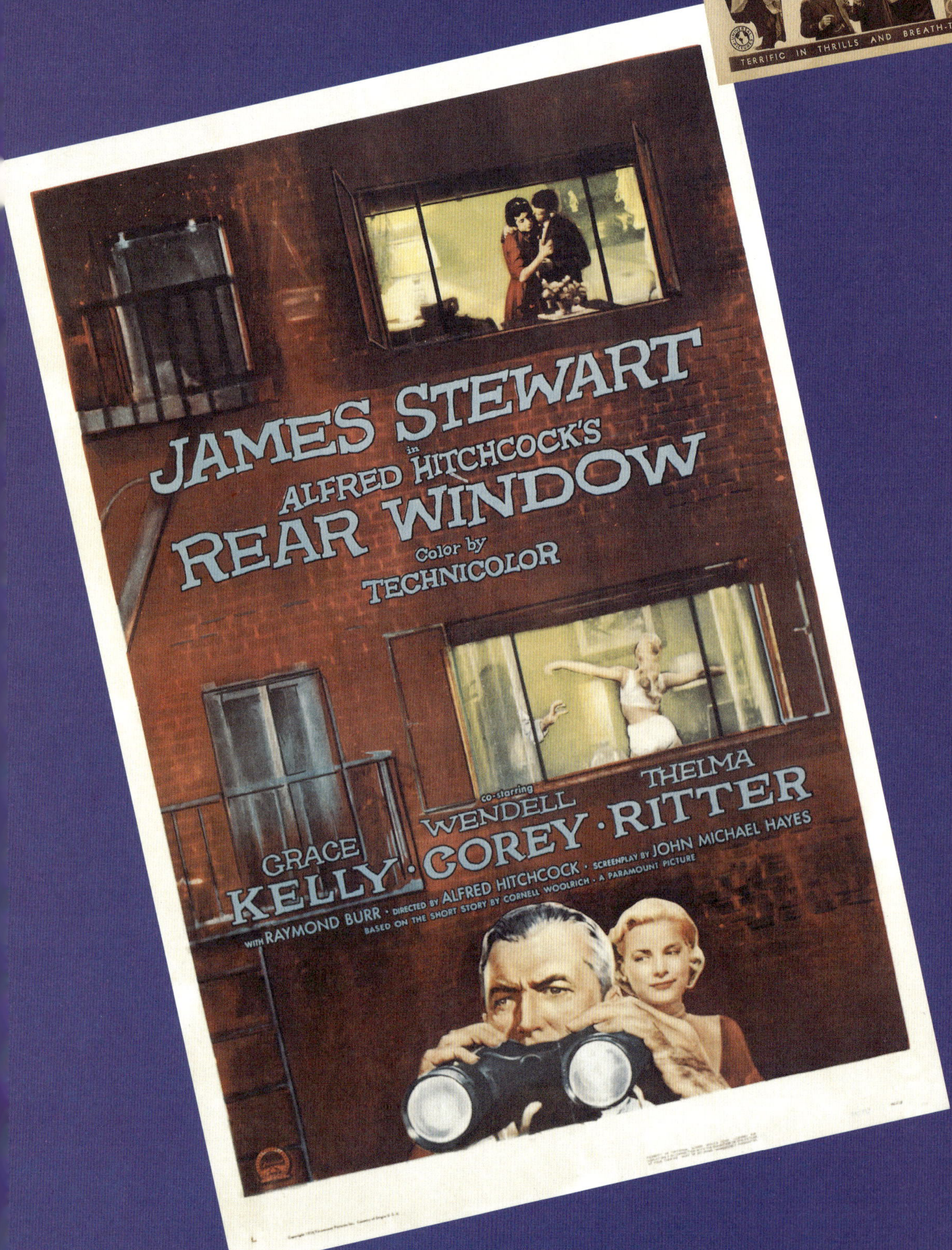
JAMES STEWART
in
ALFRED HITCHCOCK'S
REAR WINDOW
Color by
TECHNICOLOR
co-starring
GRACE KELLY · WENDELL COREY · THELMA RITTER
with RAYMOND BURR · DIRECTED BY ALFRED HITCHCOCK · SCREENPLAY BY JOHN MICHAEL HAYES
BASED ON THE SHORT STORY BY CORNELL WOOLRICH · A PARAMOUNT PICTURE

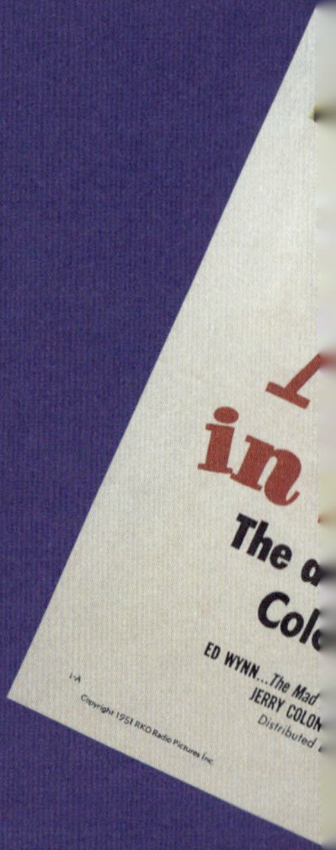

THEIR
STAN
LAUREL
OLIVER
IN